HEBREW UNION COLLEGE ANNUAL

VOLUME LXXVI

HEBREW UNION COLLEGE ANNUAL

Volume LXXVI

Cincinnati

2005

Library of Congress Catalogue Card Number 25-12620
ISSN 360-9049

Design and composition by Kelby and Teresa Bowers
Printed in the United States of America

The publication of this volume
of the Hebrew Union College Annual
was subventioned by

The Henry Englander-Eli Mayer Publication Fund
established in their honor by
Mrs. Esther Straus Englander and Mrs. Jessie Straus Mayer

Submissions

We welcome for consideration scholarly essays in Jewish and Cognate Studies, Ancient and Modern: Bible, Rabbinics, Language and Literature, History, Philosophy, Religion. Please address your submission inquiries to The Editor at *annual@huc.edu.*

Authors submitting manuscripts for publication are asked to do the following:

1 For manuscript formatting, follow *The University of Chicago Manual of Style* in general and *The SBL Handbook of Style* specifically.
2 All manuscripts, including notes, should be continuously paginated, double-spaced and employ generous margins all around.
3 Every manuscript must be accompanied by an English abstract of 200 words maximum.

Previous Volumes

The *Annual* office can supply vols. XLV–LXXV excluding vols. LV, LXIII, and LXVI (out of stock): vols. XLV–LII at $15.00, vols. LIII–LVIII at $20.00, vols. LIX–LXXII at $30.00, and vols. LXXIII–LXXV at $40.00. Printed copies of individual articles are available for a fee of $5.00. For more information email the *Annual* office at: *annual@huc.edu.* The American Jewish Periodicals Center at HUC-JIR, 3101 Clifton Avenue, Cincinnati, Ohio 45220 can supply microfilm copies of vols. XXXVIII–XLIV. ProQuest Company, 300 North Zeeb Road, Ann Arbor, Michigan 48106 can supply 16 mm, 35 mm, 105 mm microfiche, as well as photocopies.

Supplements

Yosef Hayim Yerushalmi. *The Lisbon Massacre of 1506 and the Royal Image in the Shebet Yehudah.* 1976.

Mark E. Cohen. *Sumerian Hymnology: the* Eršemma. 1981.

William C. Gwaltney, Jr. *The Pennsylvania Old Assyrian Texts.* 1982.

Kenneth R. Stow. *"The 1007 Anonymous" and Papal Sovereignty. Jewish Perceptions of the Papacy and Papal Policy in the High Middle Ages.* 1985.

Martin A. Cohen. *The Canonization of a Myth: Portugal's "Jewish Problem" and the Assembly of Tomar 1629.* 2002.

Hebrew Union College Annual
3101 Clifton Avenue, Cincinnati, Ohio 45220

Contents

Ezekiel as the Voice of the Exiles and Constructor of Exilic Ideology

Dalit Rom-Shiloni
Hebrew Union College-Jewish Institute of Religion

As a member of the Jehoiachin Exile (597 B.C.E.), Ezekiel's identification with the community of deportees is clearly apparent. The present paper suggests that Ezekiel's sympathy with his brethren audience leads him to build a separatist ideology, by which he constructs the Jehoiachin Exiles' exclusiveness over the community of Those Who Remained in the homeland prior to the destruction of Jerusalem (586 B.C.E.) and in its aftermath. I argue that Ezekiel's position in the conflict between Exiles and Those Who Remained in Judah governs his prophecies of judgment against Jerusalem, as much as it frames his perspectives in the prophecies of consolation kept only for the Exiles. To substantiate this argument, the study tracks down the interpretative devices by which Ezekiel rephrases the pentateuchal concepts of land and exile, and transforms (temporarily) the triangular relationship between God, People and Land. These theological paths that Ezekiel had paved, indeed, constituted the Diaspora ideology from the neo-Babylonian period and on as *the* national-religious community of God.

As a prophet of God, Ezekiel was ordained to speak for Yahweh, and never gained any official position as speaker for the Exiles.[1] The present paper focuses on Ezekiel's message (not on his persona), arguing that through his ideology of exile Ezekiel established the community of the Jehoiachin Exiles as the exclusive people of God. Thus in retrospect, Ezekiel should indeed be considered both as their voice and as the constructor of a new exilic ideology.

To set the stage, two introductory comments are in order. The first concerns the phenomenon of exile, and the second suggests the method employed in this study.

The Phenomenon of Exile

As a military punishment forced upon peoples, exile designates the last step in a war.[2] Subjugating peoples and territories led the neo-Assyrian, and later on,

1 D. I. Block, *Ezekiel 1–24*, NICOT (Grand Rapids, Mich.: Eerdmans, 1997) 11.

2 Exile had become an international imperial policy in the neo-Assyrian period, mainly under Tiglath-Pilesser III (745–27 B.C.E.) and his successors. B. Oded, *Mass Deportations and Deportees in the Neo-Assyrian Empire* (Wiesbaden: L. Reichert, 1979) 18–32, 41–74; F. M. Fales and J. N. Postage, *Imperial Administrative Records, Part II: Provincial and Military Administration*, SAA 11

the neo-Babylonian empires to rearrange daily life at both the center and the periphery of their domains in diverse ways.[3] In contrast to the propagandist formulae describing victory and exile, there are reasons to believe that exiles were always partial, dividing the subjugated peoples into exiles and those who remained in the homeland.[4]

Deportations from Israel and Judah, reported in the biblical literature as occurring in the course of the eighth to the sixth centuries B.C.E., appear to accord with this international policy and the overall experience of peoples in the Ancient Near East (see for example 2 Kings 15–17, 24–25).[5] This was certainly the case with regard to the Babylonian deportations.[6] 597 B.C.E. is a landmark in the history of Judah. In the month of Adar, the Babylonians led the first exile out of Jerusalem, the Jehoiachin exile (Babylonian Chronicle 5:11–13; 2 Kgs 24:8–17).[7] According to the biblical sources, this event divided the Judean peo-

---

(Helsinki: Helsinki Univ. Press, 1995) xxviii–xxx, 91–119. For studies of earlier exiles, see I. J. Gelb, "Prisoners of War in Early Mesopotamia," *JNES* 32 (1973) 70–98; J. M. Sasson, *The Military Establishments at Mari*, Studia Pohl 3 (Rome: Pontifical Biblical Institute, 1969) 48–49; S. Ahituv, "New Documents Pertaining to Deportation as a Political System in Ancient Egypt," *Beer Sheva* 1 (1973) 87–89.

3 For the neo-Assyrian two-ways exile and the organized Assyrian bureaucracy in the periphery, see Oded, *Mass Deportations*, 33–40. D. S. Vanderhooft discussed the neo-Babylonian policy of exile, highlighting differences of interests and administrative organization (*The Neo-Babylonian Empire and Babylon in the Latter Prophets*, HSMM 59 [Atlanta, Ga.: Scholars Press, 1999] 81–114).

4 In contrast to the "stereotyped scribal exaggeration" (Oded, *Mass Deportations*, 22), the partial character of the neo-Assyrian deportations can be gathered from both literary and archaeological evidence (see for instance A. C. Piepkorn, *Historical Prism Inscription of Ashurbanipal*, AS 5 [1933] 70:37–38; and Oded, *Mass Deportations*, 21–25).

5 I. Eph'al, "Assyrian Dominion in Palestine," in A. Malamat, ed., *The Age of the Monarchies: Political History*, in Benjamin Mazar, ed., *The World History of the Jewish People* (8 vols.; Tel Aviv: Massadah, 1979) 4.I:276–89; M. Cogan, "Judah under Assyrian Hegemony: A Re-examination of Imperialism and Religion," *JBL* 112 (1993) 406–8; N. Na'aman and R. Zadok, "Sargon II's Deportations to Israel and Philistia (716–708 B.C.)," *JCS* 40 (1988) 36–46; P. Machinist, "Palestine, Administration of (Assyro-Babylonian)," *ABD* (6 vols.; Garden City: Doubleday, 1992) 5:69–81.

6 For studies of the Israelite and Judean existence in exile, see I. Eph'al, "'The Samarian(s)' in the Assyrian Sources," in M. Cogan and I. Eph'al, eds., *Ah, Assyriah . . . Studies in Assyrian History and Ancient Near Eastern Historiography Presented to Hayim Tadmor* (Jerusalem: Magnes Press, 1992) 36–45; Cogan and Eph'al, "The Western Minorities in Babylonia in the 6th–5th Centuries: Maintenance and Cohesion," *Orientalia* 47 (1978) 74–90; B. Oded, "Observations on the Israelite / Judaen Exiles in Mesopotamia During the Eighth–Sixth Centuries BCE," in K. Van Lerberghe and A. Schoors, eds., *Immigration and Emigration within the Ancient Near East: Festchrift E. Lipinski*, OLA 65 (Leuven: Peeters, 1995) 205–12; R. Zadok, *The Jews in Babylonia During the Chaledean and Achamenian Periods* (Haifa: Univ. of Haifa, 1979); Zadok, *The Earliest Diaspora: Israelites and Judeans in Pre-Hellenistic Mesopotamia* (Tel Aviv: Tel Aviv Univ., 2002).

7 A. K. Grayson, *Assyrian and Babylonian Chronicles* (2nd ed.; Winona Lake, Ind.: Eisenbrauns, 1975, 2000) 102. B. Oded, "Judah and the Exile," *Israelite and Judean History*, OTL (Philadelphia: Westminster, 1977) 469–88.

ple into two communities, the Exiles with King Jehoiachin in Babylon on the one hand, and "The People Who Remained in the Land" under King Zedekiah on the other (see העם הנשארים בארץ, Jeremiah 40:6). This division is our starting point.[8]

These historical circumstances of the last eleven years of Jerusalem and Judah (597–586 B.C.E.) challenged major institutions and established concepts in Israel.[9] The ongoing existence of the Temple, the royal court, and the daily life in Jerusalem stood in contrast to Priestly and the Deuteronomic concepts of exile, which do not recognize partial deportation, and follow the linear sequence of 1. iniquity, 2. destruction/death in the land, and finally 3. dispersion of all survivors from the land of Israel to suffer further calamity (Deuteronomy 4:25–28; 8:19–20; Leviticus 18:24–30; 20:22–24; and the lists of curses in Lev 26:14 ff.; Deut 28:15 ff.).[10] For the Jehoiachin Exiles in Babylon, partial exile preceded destruction. For "the People who Remained," the ongoing existence of Judahite Exiles as the people of God does not accord with the concept that expulsion is a final national exclusion (as in Deut 28:36; 1 Samuel 26:19). Moreover, perceived as punishment for religious and moral sins, the early and partial exile from Judah raised questions with regard to the two communities' responsibilities for their respective fortune, and their future existence. Finally, understood as expulsion from God's land in retribution for violating His covenant, this partial exile presented the fundamental questions of religious-national identity: Should exile actually entail the exclusion of the deportees from the people of God, and should Those Who Remained be considered *the* Remnant, or vice versa? Such questions had major implications for the two communities' hopes for restoration.

The following discussion aims to illuminate the viewpoints of Ezekiel and his contemporaries on these ideological issues raised by the partial exile of 597 B.C.E.

8 Theoretically, we should see evidence of conflict between homeland and exile initially within Israel (733 B.C.E.); after 722–20 B.C.E. between Israel and Judah, etc. Remarkably, however, even the Judean exile of 701 B.C.E., reported only in Assyrian inscriptions, does not supply explicit biblical evidence for such a conflict. Compare S. Stohlmann, "The Judean Exile after 701 B.C.E.," in W. W. Hallo, J. C. Moyer and L. G. Perdue, eds., *Scripture in Context II* (Winnona Lake, Ind.: Eisenbrauns, 1983) 147–76. Rather, biblical sources focus on the Babylonian exiles, and hence scholars have concentrated on the different ideological reactions in that era, that is, P. R. Ackroyd, *Exile and Restoration: A Study of Hebrew Thought of the Sixth Century B.C.*, OTL (Philadelphia: Westminster, 1975); R. Klein, *Israel in Exile: A Theological Interpretation*, OBT (Philadelphia: Fortress, 1979).

9 The partial deportations have, furthermore, brought scholars to deny the very existence of exile per se, compare P. R. Davies, "Exile! What Exile? Whose Exile?" in L. L. Grabbe, ed., *Leading Captivity Captive: 'The Exile' as History and Ideology*, JSOTSup 278 (Sheffield: Sheffield Academic Press, 1998) 128–38; and carefully reconsidered by D. L. Smith-Christopher, *A Biblical Theology of Exile*, OBT (Minneapolis: Augsburg Fortress, 2002) 27–73.

10 Restoration to the land from a place of exile (as in Lev 26:39–45; Deut 4:29–31 and 30:1–10) is a

METHODOLOGICAL CONSIDERATIONS

Research of the biblical literature reflecting the decline of Judah, the destruction and the exiles, has turned to various disciplines, in addition to philological study of the texts. Among the fairly recent and intriguing ones, are sociological, anthropological, and psychological perspectives which look at the personal and/or the national reactions to the disastrous events.

Daniel Smith-Christopher has presented the crisis of exile as motivating the Exiles' social re-organization, and as the primary factor in the formation of their national identity as a minority facing foreign groups.[11] In his recent book, *A Biblical Theology of Exile*, Smith-Christopher has combined refugee studies and trauma studies to illuminate the biblical literature written in the exilic arena. In this conceptual framework, Ezekiel's prophecies demonstrate the post-traumatic reactions of an exile, a refugee.[12]

As Smith-Christopher, Kenton Sparks, and Reiner Albertz (among others) have shown, social anthropology and social psychology research, within the specific fields of ethnicity, group identity, as well as inter-group relations, indeed contribute to the study of different aspects of the Judahite communities' life during the neo-Babylonian era.[13] Yet, in contrast to the emphasis on inter-group relations of the Exiles as a minority among foreigners, the present study focuses on the ideological process of self-identification within each of the two Judahite communities, and on the inner disputes raised between them in the

---

second, exilic, level added to the pre-exilic concept of exile in both the Deuteronomic and the Priestly traditions; see commentaries.

11 D. L. Smith-Christopher, *The Religion of the Landless: The Social Context of the Babylonian Exile* (Bloomington, Ind.: Meyer Stone, 1989) 49–92.

12 Smith-Christopher, *A Biblical Theology of Exile*. Among other treatments of Ezekiel's personal trauma, compare D. J. Halperin, *Seeking Ezekiel: Text and Psychology* (University Park: Pennsylvania State Univ. Press, 1993); and T. S. Kamionkowski who has pointed out a psychological crisis over genderic self-identity in Ezekiel 16 (*Gender Reversal and Cosmic Chaos: A Study on the Book of Ezekiel*, JSOTSup 358 [Sheffield: Sheffield Academic Press, 2003]). Compare to C. L. Patton's emphasis on the function of the gender metaphors (in Ezekiel 23) on the rhetoric of defeat, arising from the prophet's experience as a member of the Exiles' community ("'Should Our Sister Be Treated Like a Whore?': A Response to Feminist Critiques of Ezekiel 23," in M. S. Odell and J. T. Strong, eds., *The Book of Ezekiel: Theological and Anthropological Perspectives*, SBLSymS 9 [Atlanta: SBL, 2000] 221–38).

13 Smith-Christopher, *Religion of the Landless*, 56–63. Methodological comments on ethnic identity research of biblical texts were presented by M. G. Brett, "Interpreting Ethnicity," in M. G. Brett, ed., *Ethnicity and the Bible*, BibInt Series 19 (Leiden: Brill, 1996) 3–22; and recently K. L. Sparks, *Ethnicity and Identity in Ancient Israel: Prolegomena to the Study of Ethnic Sentiments and Their Expressions in the Hebrew Bible* (Winona Lake, Ind.: Eisenbrauns, 1998) 1–22; see also R. Albertz, *Israel in Exile: The History and Literature of the Sixth Century* BCE, trans. David Green, Studies in Biblical Literature 3 (Atlanta: SBL, 2003) 1:231–42; 2:370–75.

wake of coping with the crisis of partial exiles from Judah.[14]

Employing five major principles that serve in definitions of identity, I suggest that the conflict between the Exiles and the People Who Remained rests on self-definitions of identity adopted by each group, definitions which were initially divisive.[15]

1. The ethnic identities of peoples or of groups within a people are well-rooted in their history and heritage, but tend to change under threat or distress.[16] The Babylonian waves of exile were the historical events that awakened within the separate Judahite communities the vital need for self-re-identification.[17]

2. Ethnic identity is built by using relative categories of distinction, in which boundaries of "otherness" are set. Jonathan Smith suggested the following definition of "otherness":[18]

> "Otherness". . . is a matter of relative rather than absolute difference. Difference is not a matter of comparison between entities judged to be equivalent, rather difference most frequently entails a hierarchy of prestige and ranking. Such distinctions are found to be drawn most sharply between "near neighbors," with respect to what has been termed the "proximate other." This is the case because "otherness" is a relativistic category inasmuch as it is, necessarily, a term of interaction.

According to social-psychological definitions used in studies of inter-group relations, proximity resides in geographical-physical contiguity.[19] With reference to the two Judahite communities, although physically detached, their

14 My study differs from that of Smith-Christopher in three major points: 1. Smith-Christopher chose not to challenge theology and ideology in his earlier study (*Religion of the Landless*, 53); 2. in both works he has focused on the Exiles' points of view; 3. Smith-Christopher mentions the possibility of inner-conflict between exiles and "those left in Palestine," but he considers such conflict to belong to the restoration period (*Religion of the Landless*, 65).

15 Compare R. A. Markus, "The Problem of Self-Definition: From Sect to Church," in E. P. Sanders, ed., *Jewish and Christian Self-Definition* (3 vols.; London: SCM, 1980) vol. 1: *The Shaping of Christianity in the Second and Third Centuries*, 1–15.

16 F. Barth, "Introduction," in F. Barth, ed., *Ethnic Groups and Boundaries: The Social Organization of Culture Difference* (Bergen-Oslo: Univ. of Bergen, 1969) 1–38, esp. 32–37; Sparks, *Ethnicity and Identity*, 18.

17 Compare Smith-Christopher, *Religion of the Landless*, 49–68.

18 J. Z. Smith, "What a Difference a Difference Makes," in J. Neusner and E. S. Frerichs, eds., "*To See Ourselves as Others See Us*"*: Christians, Jews, "Others" in Late Antiquity* (Chico, Cal.: Scholars Press, 1985) 3–48, citation from p. 15. Setting "ethnic boundaries" has been emphasized in social anthropology research, through the major contribution of Barth's studies, and the collection he edited (*Ethnic Groups*); binary division was stressed also by Brett (*Interpreting Ethnicity*, 10–15).

19 Compare H. Tajfel and J. Turner, "The Social Identity Theory of Intergroup Behavior," *Psychology of Intergroup Relations* (Chicago: Nelson-Hall, 1986) 7–24.

proximity is based on their common ethnic and religious origin, and on the ongoing contacts between them (Ezekiel 33:21; Jeremiah 28, 29 etc).[20] The urgent need to re-define their national identities sustains the relevance of the above definition of "otherness." Hence, attention is called here to "inner-ethnic identity," to communal distinctions arising in the relations between homeland and exile/diaspora within the people of Judah in the early sixth century B.C.E.

3. William S. Green says:[21]

> A society does not simply discover its others, it fabricates them by selecting, isolating, and emphasizing an aspect of another people's life and making it symbolize their difference.

In addition, Green points out the caricatural nature of definition by "otherness," which concentrates on the life of the collective, and stigmatizes (or stereotypes) the group according to one major characteristic.[22] Defining "us" and "them" is thus founded on selection, isolation and emphasis of one major divisive difference. In the conflict between the Exiles and Those Who Remained, geographic location – residence in the Land of Yahweh versus foreign lands – has come to "symbolize the difference," and the theological consequences of this division are examined in relation to the concept of God-People-Land.

4. "Otherness" as a relative category often involves re-identification of all parties. Indeed, this redefinition of identity was not restricted to the Exiles, whose interestedness seems vital. The discussion below shows that Those Who Remained had just as much at stake as the Exiles in building an exclusive identity.

5. "Otherness" as a term of interaction leads groups to improvise strategies in order to effect the self-affirmation and boundary building of one community vis-a-vis the other. Two major contradictory strategies govern re-definition of identity: *assimilation* and *dissimilation*.[23] Within the framework of *dissimilation* we find *division* (A yields B + C) to be the primary strategy utilized by both communities in the early sixth century B.C.E. *Division* results from the physi-

20 W. Scott Green writes: "The most critical feature of otherness thus presupposes familiarity and reciprocity, and perhaps resemblance, between and among groups." ("Otherness Within: Towards a Theory of Difference in Rabbinic Judaism," in Neusner and Frerichs, eds., "*To See Ourselves as Others See Us*," 49–69.

21 Green, "Otherness Within," 50.

22 On stereotyping as a result of *ingroup* and *outgroup* definitions, see W. G. Stephan and C. W. Stephan, *Intergroup Relations*, Social Psychology Series (Boulder, Colo.: Westview, 1996) 1–33, 89–114.

23 D. L. Horowitz suggested four patterns of identity changes within groups ("Ethnic Identity," in N. Glazer and D. P. Moynihan, eds., *Ethnicity: Theory and Experience* [Cambridge, Mass.: Harvard Univ. Press, 1975] 111–40). In choosing the *Assimilation* strategy the group adopts either *amalgamation* (A + B = C) or *incorporation* (A + B = A); while a group choosing the *dissimilation* strategy opts for *division* (A yields B + C) and *proliferation* (A yields A + B).

cal separation, which was forced on the people of Judah, and is articulated by announcements of superiority that present a hierarchy of prestige and rank.[24] Consequently, a binary opposition between the communities develops with each of them de-legitimating the "other" group's existence.

This study investigates Ezekiel's prophecies together with or in comparison to other literary sources of the period (Jeremiah, 2 Kings), from the perspective of group identity, in order to concentrate on the strategies and the constructs of division. Self-legitimation, on the one hand, and de-legitimation of the opposing group, on the other constitute the main strategies of division used to argue for superiority and even exclusivity of one community over the other. This strategy is employed on the axis of time, referring to the past, the present and the future:

Past. Each community relies on past national traditions and on cherished concepts, which through inner-biblical interpretation gain new relevance. Observing the past helps, furthermore, to de-legitimate the other community.

Present. Each community identifies itself as the present people of God, and gains the support of a prophet, a mediating person who contributes theological and ideological arguments to preserve the status of his community, and to denigrate the other.[25]

Future. Legitimation and its opposite de-legitimation, have important roles in each community's future projections of its fate. Forecast through prophecy, either in God's words of consolation (as well as the people's words that refer to God's promises) or in prophecies of judgment, clearly differentiate between the communities, and declare the priority of one community over against the other.

Hence, looking to the past, struggling with the present, and hoping for the future, motivate the rhetoric of division. These constructs of division will guide the discussion of the conflict's specific contents in Ezekiel's prophecies. I will

24 Smith, "A Difference," 15; Green, "Otherness Within," 49.

25 Since this study concentrates on Ezekiel, I will restrict myself to saying that Jeremiah is the prophet who supports the ongoing existence of Those Who Remained in Judah after Jehoiachin's Exile. This can be gathered from Jeremiah's biography (Jer 40:1–6); from his steady message regarding the necessity to remain in Judah under Babylonian subjugation (Jeremiah 27; 37–38; 40–42); and from his concept of exile as a calamitous punishment with no return (22:9–10, 24–30; also 29:4–7). However, the book of Jeremiah has gone through an exilic redaction which added a second line of thought similar to the exilic perspective of Ezekiel (as in Jeremiah 24). For ideological similarities between Jeremiah and Those Who Remained, and for the oppositions between Jeremiah and Ezekiel, see my paper "Exiles and Those Who Remained: Strategies of Exclusiveness in the Early Sixth Century BCE," M. Bar-Asher, et al., eds., *Shay: Studies in the Bible, Its Exegesis and language Presented to Sara Japhet* (Heb.).(Jerusalem: Bialik Institute, 2006) 119–38

first establish Ezekiel's position as the prophet of the Jehoiachin Exiles, that is their present support; and then, proceed to discuss his observations of the past, the present and the future with regard to both communities and to their status as the people of God.

Ezekiel as the Prophet of the "Jehoiachin Exiles"

Although the book of Ezekiel includes only scanty biographical details, the outstanding fact is that Ezekiel was a member of the Jehoiachin Exiles. The priest Ezekiel son of Buzi was called to his mission while "in the community of exiles" (בתוך הגולה, Ezek 1:1–3) by the Chebar Canal in Babylon, in the fifth year (592 B.C.E.) of the exile of King Jehoiachin, his court, and the Jerusalem elite to Babylon (597 B.C.E., 2 Kgs 24:8–17). The Exiles (הגולה) are his people, "Go to your people, the exile community" (בא אל הגולה אל בני עמך, Ezek 3:11; as also 11:24, 25); and Ezekiel's concept of time is directed by that event, as he counts the years "to our exile" (לגלותנו, 33:21; 40:1). The first plural pronoun clarifies that he is part and parcel of that community.[26]

The prophet's ideological orientation clearly favors his community. I will demonstrate this observation throughout the study, but first let me illustrate it by two examples.

1. Among the primary sources for studying ideological debates in the biblical literature of the sixth century B.C.E. are disputation-speeches.[27] In their two-part pattern, citation of the opponents' position and the prophet's counter-speech, this prophetic genre reflects some of the internal controversies between prophets and their contemporaries.[28]

Throughout the nine disputations in Ezekiel, the prophet differentiates be-

26 Contrary to the scholarly path which sets Ezekiel in the land of Israel, that is, C. C. Torrey (*Pseudo-Ezekiel and the Original Prophecy, and Critical Articles* [New York: KTAV Publishing House, 1930. 2nd ed., 1970]) and V. Hentrich (*Ezekielstudein*, BZAW 61 [Giessen: Töpelmann, 1933]); and see W. Zimmerli's commentary for solid refutations of these arguments (*Ezekiel 1 and 2*, trans. J. D. Martin, Hermeneia [Philadelphia: Fortress, 1979, 1983]). W. H. Brownlee unconvincingly tried to set Ezekiel in Gilgal (*Ezekiel 1–19*, WBC 28 (Waco, Tex.: Word Books, 1986] xxiii–xxxii). He therefore considered the disputations in Ezek 11:14–21 and 33:23–29 "the controversy over property rights which broke out among those left behind" ("The Aftermath of the Fall of Judah according to Ezekiel," *JBL* 89 [1970] 393–404, citation 394–95).

27 H. Gunkel, "Einleitungen," in D. H. Schmidt, trans., *Die grossen Propheten* (Göttingen: Vandenhöck & Ruprecht, 1923) xi–lxxii; C. Westermann, *Sprache und Struktur der Prophetie Deuterojesajas: Mit einer Literaturübersicht "Hauptlinien der Deuterojesaja-Forschung von 1964–1979," zusammengestellt und kommentiert von A. Richter*, Calwer Theologische Monographien 11 (Stuttgart: Calwer, 1981) 41–51, see esp. 42–43; A. Graffy, *A Prophet Confronts His People*, AnBib 104 (Rome: Biblical Institute Press, 1984); D. F. Murray, "The Rhetoric of Disputation: Re-examination of a Prophetic Genre," JSOT 38 (1987) 95–121.

28 Graffy, *A Prophet*, 105–29.

tween quotations of "the inhabitants of Jerusalem" (ישבי ירושלים, 11:15), or pronouncements made "upon the soil of Israel" (על אדמת ישראל, 12:21; 18:2),[29] and the assertions of his fellow Exiles, "your fellow countrymen" (בני עמך, 33:30), or "the House of Israel" (בית ישראל, 33:10; 37:11).[30] Categorized according to the speakers of the quotations, the nine disputation speeches in Ezekiel fall into two groups: Refutations of Jerusalemite quotations (11:1–13; 11:14–21; 12:21–25; 18:1–20; 33:23–29); and Refutations of Exiles' pronouncements (12:26–28; 20:1–38; 33:10–20; 37:1–14).[31] Ezekiel presents the quotations said על אדמת ישראל either as sinful speeches (11:3; 11:15; 12:22; 33:24), or as bitter protest (18:2), whereas he quotes the Exiles using terms of embarrassment and desperation (12:27; 18:19; 18:25, 29; 20:32; 33:10; 33:17, 20; 37:11).[32] The paramount importance of this difference in treatment is further shown in the prophetic refutations. Ezekiel answers sinful pronouncements with prophecies of judgment, which fall mainly upon the people remaining in Judah (as for instance, Ezek 11:1–13); but he speaks with consolation to the Exiles who are in a desperate mood (as in 37:1–11, and also in 11:14–21).

This distinction reveals, firstly, Ezekiel's inclination towards the Exiles and against the People Who Remained. Secondly, in observing Ezekiel's general tendencies, we can establish the existence of a lively and vital conflict between the Judahite communities in Jerusalem and in Babylon already by the early years of the sixth century B.C.E.[33] Finally, these disputation speeches cast Ezekiel in

29 For discussion of על אדמת ישראל, see Graffy, *A Prophet*, 53.

30 The use of בית ישראל to address the Exiles' community is in itself a marker of exclusion, see P. M. Joyce, "Dislocation and Adaptation in the Exilic Age and After," in J. Barton and D. J. Reimer, eds., *After the Exile: Essays in Honor of Rex Mason* (Macon, Ga.: Mercer Univ. Press, 1996) 45–58, esp. 51; and compare to W. Zimmerli, *Ezekiel 2*, trans. J. D. Martin, Hermeneia (Philadelphia: Fortress, 1983) 563–65.

31 This socio-geographic categorization differentiates Ezekiel from the other prophets who use the disputation speech to refute their audiences. Graffy pointed out Ezekiel's exilic orientation (*A Prophet*, 123–24 etc.), but did not distinguish Ezekiel as making special ideological use of this genre.

32 The status of the quotation in 12:26–28 attributed to "the House of Israel" is uncertain. Graffy suggests that, in contrast to the previous passage, which referred to words spoken "in the land of Israel" (12:21–25), the quotation in 12:26 was said in "a less aggressive tone," and thus refuted in an encouraging way (Graffy, *A Prophet*, 57–58). Following Zimmerli (*Ezekiel 1*, 414), I understand Ezek 20:32 as a desperate saying and not as a rebuke; see D. Rom-Shiloni, "Facing Destruction and Exile: Inner-Biblical Exegesis in Jeremiah and Ezekiel" *ZAW* 117 / 2 (2005) 189–205. In addition, Ezekiel refutes other sinful quotations pronounced in Jerusalem, such as 8:12; 9:9, but they are not cast in the disputation pattern. Sinful sayings attributed to the Exiles are rare in Ezekiel, and appear as the words of false prophets (13:6, 7).

33 The chronological headings of some of the prophecies specify the time period as extending from the sixth year after Jehoiachin's exile (8:1, 592 / 1 B.C.E.) to the fall of Jerusalem (33:21, 23–29, 586 B.C.E.), and probably to the following years as well (33:10–20; 37:1–14). Compare Ch. R. Seitz, "The Crisis of Interpretation over the Meaning and Purpose of the Exile," *VT* 35 / 1 (1985) 78–97; Seitz, *Theology in Conflict: Reactions to the Exile in the Book of Jeremiah*, BZAW 176 (Berlin-New York: De Gruyter, 1989) 201–2.

an important role as he supplies present ideological support to the community of the Jehoiachin Exiles.

2. Reference to the present leadership provide another angle through which Ezekiel's pro-exilic orientation is apparent. The allegory of the two eagles, the (lofty) top of the cedar, and the vine (Ezekiel 17) denotes a clear difference between Jehoiachin, the exiled king, who is symbolized by the cedar, and thus has royal legitimacy and respect (vv. 3b–4, 12–13), and Zedekiah, who is symbolized as the low vine. Although the latter could have achieved great political success, he failed because of his rebellion against the Babylonian king and against God (vv. 5–8, 9–10; 15–21). In contrast to the total judgment projected upon Zedekiah and the Jerusalemites (vv. 16–21), hope rests with "the lofty top of the cedar," who it is promised will be brought back to the land of Israel, and be replanted and prosper as "a noble cedar" (vv. 22–24).[34]

This allegory, and the allegory of the lioness and her two cubs, referring to Jehoahaz and Zedekiah (Ezek 19:1–14), as well as other straightforward prophecies against Zedekiah (12:8–16; 21:23–32), show Ezekiel's clear support for Jehoiachin in Exile, and his blunt condemnation of Zedekiah of Jerusalem.[35]

Ezekiel's membership in the community of the Jehoiachin Exiles is, then, not just a biographical datum reflecting his geographical setting. The prophet's empathy with the Exiles has brought him to more than a mere interest in their "mental and spiritual transformation."[36] In what follows, I want to illustrate the proposition that as a member of the Jehoiachin Exiles, the prophet was motivated to evaluate the status of both communities as the people of God and to supply the divisive ideological arguments for the one and against the other.[37]

34 M. Greenberg, *Ezekiel 1–20*, AB (Garden City, N.Y.: Doubleday, 1983) 317–24. The "topmost bough" of the cedar refers clearly to Jehoiachin in 17:3–4 as the object taken away and replanted afar (ויקח את צמרת הארץ: את ראש יניקותיו קטף ויביאהו), but the future leader's identity remains vague in the phrase ולקחתי אני מצמרת הארז הרמה ונתתי, מראש ינקותיו רך אקטף ושתלתי אני in v. 22. Hence, the phrase might refer to other, later scions of the Davidic line (so Greenberg, *Ezekiel 1–20*, 317). In any case, and in contrast to Jeremiah (22:24–30), the future belongs to an exilic leader, a descendent of Jehoiachin.

35 Ezekiel's attitude towards the two leaders has been interpreted as the prophet's political point-of-view by B. Lang, *Kein Aufstand in Jerusalem: Die Politik des Propheten Ezechiel* (Stuttgart: Verlag Katolisches Bibelwerk, 1978) 135–86. I suggest looking at the broader ideological context of this contention.

36 So Block, *Ezekiel 1–24*, 15–17, 222.

37 With these methodological framework and goals set, the present study differs greatly from K. F. Pohlmann's approach to Ezekiel and to the discussed polemic (*Ezechielstudien: Zur Redaktionsgeschichted des Buches und zur Frage nach den ältesten Texten*, BZAW 202 [Berlin: de Gruyter, 1992]; Pohlmann, *Das Buch des Propheten Hesekiel: Kapitel 1–19*, DAT 22/1 [Göttingen: Vandenhoeck & Ruprecht, 1996]). From a redactional-criticism point of view, Pohlmann has argued for multi-layers in Ezekiel; none of them has he connected to the prophet or to the early period of the sixth century B.C.E. (see *Hesekiel*, 40–41). In fact Pohlmann suggested that the "golaorien-

Ezekiel as Constructor of Exilic Ideology

Proceeding from the explicit to the implicit cases, the discussion below is built in three steps. First, I will present the two opposing ideologies and the dividing arguments, which are explicitly established in two disputation-speeches, Ezek 11:14–21 and 33:23–29. Then I will argue that in 16:1–43 and 20:1–38 Ezekiel implicitly supplies different retrospective histories for each of the two communities, thus differentiating their futures, contrasting calamity with continuity. Third, I will illustrate how Ezekiel's attitude towards the homeland community throughout chapters 1–24 consistently expresses his denigration of Jerusalem, and implicitly strengthens the binary distinction he makes between these communities. In these prophecies of Judgment, the prophet (and at times his disciples) struggles with the linear sequence of iniquity-destruction-exile-restoration, adapting it to the reality of the two separate Judahite communities.

Explicit Disputations between Exiles and Those Who Remained

Two of the nine disputation speeches in Ezekiel, Ezek 11:14–21 and 33:23–29, are critical for our discussion because they present the two sides of the argument. Ezekiel quotes the position of Those Who Remained in order to refute it from an Exile's point of view. Both parties use the above-mentioned strategies of division.

The disputation in 11:14–21 is in fact the second disputation speech in chapter 11. The chapter closes an amalgamation of prophecies in chapters 8–11 given to the prophet "in visions of God" (במראות אלהים, 8:3).[38] Led through the Temple

---

tierte Redaktion" is a second layer in the book which reworks original pro-royal/Judahite lament passages over the 587 destruction (Ezek 19:1–9, 10–14; 23:31). By announcing the exclusivity of the first exile, the 597 Exiles, this redaction denigrates the population that remained in Jerusalem as doomed to annihilation (Ezek 14:21–23; 15:4b–8; 17:19–21, 22–23; 24:2, 21b, 25b–26; 33:21–29). A third layer in the literary evolution of the book gives presidence to several diasporic voices, which do not present antagonistic perpectives against the population which remained in Judah after 597 (Ezekiel 20; 36:15–28; 38–39). Pohlmann thus understands this whole contention as late exilic and mainly postexilic reflections on early Jerusalemite laments. In contrast, the present study follows Greenberg's historical point of view and largely accepts his holistic approach to Ezekiel (*Ezekiel 1–20*, 12–27). I argue that the book of Ezekiel maintains an early sixth century dichotomy brought also in Jeremiah 24, which reflects the social division as of 597 B.C.E. and on. Furthermore, I henceforth claim that pro-597 exilic perspectives govern Ezekiel's general attitude against Jerusalem and for the Jehoiachin Exiles throughout, not only in the few passages suggested by Pohlmann. For further criticism on Pohlmann, see Alberts, *Israel in Exile*, 349–50, especially in reference to Ezek 11:14–21 and 33:21–33, which will be discussed below.

38 The literary structure of Ezekiel 8–11 is presented in M. Greenberg, *Ezekiel 1–20*, AB (Garden City, N.Y.: Doubleday, 1983) 192–205.

courts, the prophet sees Jerusalem's abominations (chapter 8). In retaliation for the idolatry and lawlessness (חמס, v. 17; and 9:9), Ezekiel describes Jerusalem's punishment (chapter 9), which brings him to fling himself on his face and cry aloud, "Ah, Lord God! Are you going to annihilate all that is left of Israel, Pouring out Your fury upon Jerusalem?" (אהה אדני ה׳ המשחית אתה את כל שארית ישראל בשפכך את חמתך על ירושלים, 9:8). God answers in the affirmative. Indeed, the iniquity in Jerusalem brings Him to act with no pity or compassion (vv. 9–10), and so it is executed (v. 11). The two disputations of chapter 11 continue this line of thought. The first refutes words of officials in Jerusalem (11:3), and prophesies total calamity to its inhabitants (11:1–13). This prophecy gains additional strength with the sudden death of the official Pelatiah son of Benaiah (פלטיהו בן בניה, v. 13).[39] In a dramatic reaction, the prophet again throws himself upon his face and cries out for the second time, "Ah, Lord God! You are wiping out the remnant of Israel!" (אהה אדני אלהים כלה אתה עשה את שארית ישראל, v. 13). The juxtaposition of the two disputations one after the other places the second, vv. 14–21, as a reply to the prophet's repetitive cry. Prior to the destruction, Ezekiel identifies the (new) "remnant of Israel" as the Exiles.[40] Ezekiel 33:23–29 brings us to the months after the fall of Judah (v. 21). The inhabitants of Jerusalem are now the inhabitants of the ruins of that city (ישבי החרבות האלה על אדמת ישראל, v. 24). Both disputations reflect an acute interest in the question of who continues to be the people of God, and their generic characteristics enable us to trace the ideological conflict.

THE PEOPLE WHO REMAINED

The two quotations that Ezekiel refutes in these disputations share the same final clause:

רחקו מעל ה׳, לנו היא נתנה הארץ למורשה 11:15

אחד היה אברהם ויירש את הארץ ואנחנו רבים, לנו נתנה הארץ למורשה 33:24

39 The name of the official פלטיהו is in itself significant, as the name means "Yahweh has delivered," see Block, *Ezekiel 1–24*, 338.

40 So Greenberg, *Ezekiel 1–20*, 193. The proximity of the two passages does not exclude the initial independence of each passage (11:1–13, and 14–21). Yet, this proximity should also not preclude Ezekiel from joining those units in keeping with the suggested theme. Both disputations serve as integral components in the whole prophetic unit of 8–11, and thus are prior to the destruction of Jerusalem. So Zimmerli who related the editorial work to either Ezekiel or his disciples (*Ezekiel 1*, 256, 260, 264); and Joyce, "Dislocation and Adaptation," 46–50. W. Eichrodt, on the other hand, based on Ezek 33:23–29 and on the consolation words in 11:16–21, has argued that the conflict in 11:14–21 is post-587 (*Ezekiel*, OTL [Philadelphia: Westminster, 1970] 142–43). D. I. Block took a kind of a middle way, suggesting a pre-586 prophecy which was placed by a pro-exilic redactor, though he does not exclude the possibility that the prophet himself was responsible for the juxtaposition (*Ezekiel 1–24*, 342–46).

"The land has been given as a heritage to us" (לנו [היא] נתנה הארץ למורשה) states the exclusive rights of those left in Jerusalem and Judah to possess the land, in contrast to those exiled from it. Tracing the traditional background of this argument brings us to Pentateuchal concepts of the land.

The concept that God gave the land to His people to inherit/to possess, לרשתה, is a major theme in Deuteronomy.[41] Yet this phrase נתן (ארץ) למורשה in Ezek 11:15 and 33:24 most closely resembles Exodus 6:8.[42] Exodus 6:2–8 builds the bridge between the patriarchs and the Exodus generation; the land that was promised to Abraham, Isaac and Jacob (vv. 3–4) will now be given to the Sons of Jacob, who were saved from servitude in Egypt.[43] This priestly unit emphasizes the pattern of promise and fulfillment.

Alluding to this tradition in the two quotations, the Jerusalemites give a new interpretation to the theme of promise and fulfillment.[44] They claim to hold a divine certificate over the land, announcing (implicit in the passive נִתְּנָה) that God has given them the rights to the land. It is the inhabitants of Jerusalem (and only they) who continue to fulfill that ancient promise to Abraham; they are the true descendents of those Sons of Jacob, the true people of God. Thus, the inhabitants of Jerusalem rely on past traditions concerning the promise of the Land (whether embedded in the patriarch stories and the Exodus traditions or in its amalgamated form in Exod 6:2–8). Based on this interpretation, they present a theological argument of divine legitimation for their continuing existence.

The two opening clauses of the quotations each suggest a different construct of division. The saying in Ezek 33:24 adds a positive argument based on past traditions in favor of Those Who Remained; while Ezek 11:15, in using the theological concept of exile, de-legitimates the existence of the Exiles.

Ezekiel 33:24: "Abraham was but one man, yet he was granted possession of

41 Compare Deut 4:5, 14; 5:28; 6:1; 7:1; 11:31; 12:1; 23:21; 25:19; 28:21, 63; 30:16, 18; 32:47. Yet, several priestly passages use לרשת as well, such as Gen 28:4; Lev 20:24; 25:46; Num 33:53.

42 The noun מורשה appears nine times in the Bible, once in both Exod 6:8 and Deut 33:4, and seven times in Ezekiel. In addition to the two citations under discussion, the term occurs in prophecies to the nations (25:4, 10), and in the prophecy of consolation to the mountains of Israel (36:2, 3, 5).

43 For the central position of Exod 6:2–8 in the Priestly redaction of the Pentateuch, see M. Noth, *Exodus*, OTL (Philadelphia: Westminster, 1962) 56–62; L. Eslinger, "Knowing Yahweh; Exod 6:3 in the Context of Genesis 1–Exodus 15," in L. D. de Regt, J. de Waard and J. P. Fokkelman, eds., *Literary Structure and Rhetorical Strategies in the Hebrew Bible* (Assen: Van Gorcum, 1996) 188–98. Its literary context as the introduction to the afflictions was discussed by M. Greenberg, *Understanding Exodus* (New York: Behrman House, 1968) 146–48.

44 The priestly unit of Exod 6:2–8 was probably known both to the people in Jerusalem and to Ezekiel, and not vice versa. See R. Levitt Kohn, *A New Heart and a New Soul: Ezekiel, the Exile and the Torah*, JSOTSup 358 (Sheffield: Sheffield Academic Press, 2002) 38, 43–44, 66–67, 98–104; in contrast to J. Lust, "Exodus 6,2–8 and Ezekiel," *Studies in the Book of Exodus* (Leuven: Leuven Univ. Press, 1996) 209–24.

the land. We are many (אחד היה אברהם ויירש את הארץ ואנחנו רבים); [surely, the land has been given as a possession to us]." To find Abraham mentioned in the words of the inhabitants of Jerusalem is in itself quite a surprise, since outside the book of Genesis, Abraham is mentioned only rarely, and this is the only occurrence of his name in Ezekiel.[45] What is of even more interest is to trace the exact features taken by the Jerusalemites from the Abraham stories. In this argument "from the minor to the major" (קל וחומר) – אחד היה אברהם ואנחנו רבים – the promise of the land is only implicitly hinted at. Weight is given to Abraham's actual inheritance of the land (ויירש את הארץ). The reference to Abraham's possession of the land recalls Exod 6:4 and Genesis 17:8, but even more so Gen 15:7. After the destruction of Jerusalem, God's covenant with Abraham had gained new relevance. By analogy, Those Who Remained counted themselves direct descendents of Abraham, and being many, they undoubtedly have been permitted to remain in order to continue to inhabit / inherit the land.[46]

This line of reasoning accords with the religious-national argument of "the merit of the forefathers" (זכות אבות), which characterizes the closing clause of this quotation as well. It commemorates the past constitutive connection between God and the patriarch Abraham. Emphasizing the ongoing genealogical bond between Abraham and the present community in Jerusalem, Those Who Remained claim the continuity of their own residence in and thus their rightful possession of the land. This, then, constitutes a central argument of divine legitimation presented by Those Who Remained.

The call "Keep far from the Lord" (רחקו מעל ה׳, Ezek 11:15), which according to MT is an imperative, commands the Exiles to distance/separate themselves from God.[47] The use of the imperative to a community that had already

45 Other occurrences outside of Genesis: in the repeated patriarchal formula, together with Isaac and Jacob (as in Exod 3:6, 15; 1 Kgs 18:36); Pss 47:10; 105:6, 42; and only seven times in all the prophetic literature (Jer 33:26 as part of the triple patriarchal formula; Micah 7:20; three [to four] times in Deutero [and Trito]-Isaiah, Isa 41:8; 51:2; 63:16; and once in Isa 29:22).

46 Compare to Isa 51:1–2, where Abraham appears to be central to the Exilic community of the second half of the sixth century B.C.E. In both passages (Ezek 33:24 and Isa 51:1–2) emphasis is given to the change in number from the individual patriarch to the multitudes of his descendents. But in opposition to the emphasis on the inheritance of the land of Those Who Remained, Deutero-Isaiah alludes to the call, the blessing, and the progeny, the three central elements of the promises to Abraham (Gen 12:2–3) as a reaffirmation to be fulfilled in the future restoration of the Exiles. On the allusion to Gen 12:1–4, see J. L. McKenzie, *Second Isaiah*, AB (New York: Doubleday, 1968) 123, 125; and M. Fishbane, *Biblical Interpretation in Ancient Israel* (Oxford: Clarendon, 1985) 375.

47 Interpreting the imperative, Greenberg suggests the close connections between the cult and the concept of the land as God's land, as clearly appearing in Josh 22:24–27 (*Ezekiel 1–20*, 189). Compare to the BHS suggestion to read the verb in the Perfect: רָחקו; and so Zimmerli, *Ezekiel 1*, 229; Brownlee, *Ezekiel*, 163; Joyce, "Dislocation and Adaptation," 51; Block, *Ezekiel 1–25*, 341, 347–48. Although the perfect form suits the causative perfect הרחקתים in the reply (v. 16), it presents a weaker, less polemical, statement. Commentators (such as Block, *Ezekiel 1–25*, 348–49) followed

been physically distanced suggests the demand that the exiles "let go" of God theologically and emotionally. The inhabitants of Jerusalem use the traditional concept of exile to establish their argument. There is an analogical connection between residence in God's land and worship of God that contrasts with residence in foreign lands and the worship of other gods (as in Deut 4:25–28; 28:36, 64; 1 Sam 26:19; and on this basis Jer 5:19; 16:10–13). Being away from God's land means that the Deportees are out of God's domain. This implies practical effects in worship – the Exiles should in consequence worship other gods; furthermore, according to Those Who Remained, the Exiles have been deprived of their religious-national identity as the people of God. This argument demonstrates the use of a well-known concept of exile, in order to de-legitimate the existence of the community of Exiles.[48]

To conclude, the anonymous quotations in Ezekiel suggest that Those Who Remained constituted their national re-identification using ideological strategies of division. They applied past traditions and established concepts to their community and thus built their present legitimate status as the people of God;[49] and they designated their exclusive status through de-legitimation of their sister community of the Jehoiachin Exiles. Although not exiled abroad, even if temporarily estranged from its lands (Jer 42:12), the community of Those Who Remained had an interest similar to that of the Exiles in re-building an exclusive identity.[50] They were, furthermore, anxious to bar those who had left the land of Judah from belonging to the people of God.

THE EXILES

Ezekiel's empathy to the Exiles is clearly marked by the three terms presenting his fellow community, the Jehoiachin Exiles: "your brothers, your brothers, men of your kindred, all of that very house of Israel" (אחיך אחיך אנשי גאלתך וכל בית ישראל כלה, Ezek 11:14).[51]

The refutation in Ezek 11:16–21 is structured according to the two statements

this path to explain the economic interest of Those Who Remained in taking over the Exiles' property. But, beyond its conjectural character, this suggestion reduces the importance of the ideological arguments, which Zimmerli had already pointed (*Ezekiel 1–25*, 261).

48 D. Rom-Shiloni, "Deuteronomic Concepts of Exile Interpreted in Jeremiah and Ezekiel," in *Prof. Shalom M. Paul Jubilee Volume* (Winona Lake, Ind.: Eisenbrauns, forthcoming).

49 The position of Those who Remained is further elaborated by Jeremiah (as in Jer 32:6–15; 42:9–17), but this will have to await a separate discussion.

50 O. Lipschits, "Demographic Changes in Judah between the Seventh and the Fifth Centuries B.C.E.," in O. Lipschits and J. Blenkinsopp, eds., *Judah and the Judeans in the Neo-Babylonian Period* (Winona Lake, Ind.: Eisenbrauns, 2003) 323–76.

51 For the MT and the Septuagint version: οἱ ἄνδρες τῆς αἰχμαλωσίας σου (אנשי גלותך), see Block, *Ezekiel 1–24*, 341, 346. See also בני עמך in Ezek 3:11 and 33:30.

of the quotation. First, Ezekiel answers the imperative "Keep far from the Lord" (רחקו מעל ה׳, v. 15), admitting that God Himself had distanced the exiles "I have indeed removed them far" (כי הרחקתים, v. 16). Then, in reply to the Jerusalemites' claim "the land has been given as a heritage to us" (לנו היא נתנה הארץ למורשה, v. 15), Ezekiel promises that God will give the land to the Exiles "and I will give you the Land of Israel" (ונתתי לכם את אדמת ישראל, v. 17).[52] In its general content, the refutation contradicts the implicit message of doom in the quotation with a prophecy of consolation that defines the *Exiles* as the Remnant and hopes for *their* restoration (vv. 17–21).

In v. 16 God declares "Indeed it was I who distanced them and dispersed them" (כי הרחקתים בגוים וכי הפיצותים בארצות). In accordance with the Deuteronomic concept of exile, Ezekiel ascribes the deportation to God (compare Deut 28:36: "The *Lord* will drive you, and the king you have set over you, to a nation," יולך ה׳ אתך ואת מלכך אל גוי). However, in contrast to Deut 4:25–28; 28:36, 64, Ezekiel redefines the relationship between God and His people in exile, and thus focuses his refutation on the divine legitimation of the Exiles' community. Although they were exiled to foreign lands, the Exiles were not destined to serve foreign gods, they were not expelled from the presence of God.[53] On the contrary, those expelled are themselves the objects of restoration. They will be gathered from among the peoples to be given the land (v. 17). Upon return they will purify the land from its detestable things and abominations (v. 18), and God will transform their hearts (v. 19) in order to renew the covenant relationship exclusively with *this* community of His people (v. 20). In contrast, annihilation is going to be the fortune of those holding to abominations (v. 21).

Verse 21 poses a difficulty with regard to its implicit subject "But as for them whose heart is set upon their detestable things and their abominations" (ואל לב שקוציהם ותועבותיהם לבם הלך).[54] Designating the "others" as "those holding to" שקוצים and תועבות sets v. 21 in opposition to v. 18. Since upon return, the Repatriates are expected to "do away" with those illegitimate cults in the land, it seems likely that "those holding to them" (v. 21) are Those Who Remained. If so, this prophecy marks a cultic differentiation between the Exiles (the future Repatriates) and Those Who Remained.[55] This distinction is among the first signs to

52 This relationship was suggested already by Eliezer of Beaugency, *Kommentar zu Ezechiel und den XII kleinen Propheten von Eliezer aus Beaugency*, hrsg. S. Poznanski (Warschau: Mekize Nirdamim, 1909) on Ezek 11:17. Such literal, structural, and thematic accordance between quotation and counter-speech often appear in the disputation speeches; see Graffy, *A Prophet*, 105–19.

53 So Eliezer of Beaugency, *Kommentar zu Ezechiel*, on Ezek 11:16.

54 Greenberg (*Ezekiel 1–20*, 191) identifies the oppositional community in Ezek 11:14–21 according to the contradictory phrases הלך בחקותי (v. 20) and לב (v. 19); and see Eliezer of Beaugency on Ezek 11:18.

55 A similar dichotomy is implicitly suggested also in Jer 29:16–20 in the contrast between the disobedient king and people in Jerusalem: תחת אשר לא שמעו (v. 16–19), and the demand presented to

a hierarchal differentiation between Exiles and Those Who Remained, in which the latter are accused of worshipping other gods in God's land.[56]

Ezekiel's innovative perception gains further strength in the words ואהי להם למקדש מעט בארצות אשר באו שם (v. 16) which has garnered many interpretations. Two major paths have been taken in interpreting היה להם למקדש מעט. According to the first, מקדש serves in its usual meaning, "a sanctuary," and מעט, already by the early translations (and continuously by traditional commentators), was interpreted as an adjective that signifies diminution.[57] According to a second path of interpretation, which most of the critical commentaries suggest, מקדש is taken as a metonymy for the presence of God, and מעט is interpreted as an adverb that minimizes His presence with the Exiles.[58] Although מקדש in this metonymical sense is a *hapax*, Ezekiel coins this phrase to proclaim that exile does not bring separation from God.[59] God continues to be present in the life of the Exiles, though in reduced fashion compared to His previous presence in His temple. Ezekiel advocates here that in exilic circumstances God has a dynamic presence, adjusting His appearances to His people's different dwelling places.[60]

---

the Exile community to change its ways: ואתם שמעו (v. 20). Ezekiel 20 suggests yet another interpretation in which evaluative categorization (or selection) is done among the Exiles (vv. 35–38).

56 This categorization plays a major role in the Persian period contest between the Repatriates, designated as זרע הקדש and the עמי הארצות or בני הנכר, the residences of Judah, who are presented as foreigners (as in Ezra 4:2–3; 9:1–2; Neh 9:2–3; 10:29). See S. Japhet, "Law and 'The Law' in Ezra-Nehemiah," *Proceedings of the Ninth World Congress of Jewish Studies, Panel Sessions* (Jerusalem: Magnes Press, 1988) 99–115.

57 Linguistically, although מעט comes after the noun it describes, it can be an adjective, as in other rare instances, all occurring in late books: Eccl 9:14; Dan 11:34; Ezr 9:8; Neh 2:12. See the Septuagint (and the Vulgate), the Peshitta, and the Targum, which suggest a concrete reference for this small temple as the synagogue of its time. The Targum thus presents a double translation of מעט. First referring back to the Temple, and second, to the people in exile.

58 According to this interpretation, מעט is an adverb of measure (and not of time), as in 2 Kgs 10:18; Zech 1:15. So G. A. Cooke: "and I became to them a sanctuary in small measure (*Ezekiel*, ICC [Edinburgh: T&T Clark, 1936, 1985] 125); Zimmerli: "and I have been to them (only) a little for a sanctuary" (*Ezekiel 1*, 126); so also Greenberg who translated it as "reduced presence" (*Ezekiel 1–20*, 190); and compare Joyce's suggestion that the figurative use of מקדש מעט presents "the motif of Yahweh himself becoming a 'sanctuary'" ("Dislocation and Adaptation," 54).

59 מקדש occurs seventy three times in the Bible, none of them in this abstract sense. It is either the Temple itself, so twenty nine times in Ezekiel (12 in 1–39, and 17 in 40–48); the designation of a holy artifact (like the tithe, Num 18:29); the tabernacle vessels (Num 3:38); and finally, the holy zone of the tabernacle (Exod 25:8) or the house of God (Lam 1:10; as also the plural: מקדשים, Ezek 21:7; Jer 51:51).

60 This concept of God's presence in v. 16 accords with Ezekiel's perception throughout (compare Joyce, "Dislocation and Adaptation," 56–58). God is immanently present in the Temple on the one hand (Ezekiel 9–10, and 43:1–7), just as he has dynamic and transcendent presence in the lands of dispersion (as in Ezek 1–3:15, 11:16–21). See J. F. Kutsko, *Between Heaven and Earth: Divine Presence and Absence in the Book of Ezekiel* (Winona Lake, Ind.: Eisenbrauns, 2000) 77–100, esp. 96–99.

In his refutation Ezekiel crafts a new concept of exile. In contrast to the exilic layer of Deuteronomy (Deut 4:29–31; 30:1–10) and the Holiness Code (Lev 26:39–45), Ezekiel's innovation establishes God as the initiator of the restored relationship with the Exiles (Ezek 11:16–21; 36:22–32).[61] In this polemical context, the accent on the divine initiative illustrates further Ezekiel's inclination towards the community in exile.[62] This ideology constituted the new exclusive status of the Exiles as away from the land of Israel, but not distanced from God, and in separation from Those Who Remained in Judah. Hence, Ezekiel's consolation prophecy exemplifies the prophet's vital contribution to the evolution of an exilic ideology during the first years of exile.

In Ezek 33:23–29 the prophet confronts the declaration of rights of Those Who Remained in ruined Jerusalem: "the land has been given as a possession to us" (לנו נתנה הארץ למורשה, v. 24). In contrast to the disputation in Ezek 11:14–21, in these verses the prophet does not explicitly set his prophecy of doom against a consoling fate of the Exiles.[63] This silence about the Exiles is spurred by the quotation itself, which does not mention them (contra 11:15). This could, therefore, be simply explained as another sign of the formal and thematic accord maintained between the quotation and the refutation.[64] Yet, the lack of reply or comment on the central argument of Those Who Remained, relying on the Abraham tradition, seems significant.[65] To confront Jerusalemite reasoning, Ezekiel chooses a different ideological argument altogether, based on the law. In two rhetorical questions (vv. 25–26), Ezekiel mentions cultic, social and sexual sins committed in the land of Judah, as an introduction to the rhetorical cry: "yet you expect to possess the land?!" (והארץ תירשו?!).[66]

61 The importance of the divine transformation of the heart in Ezekiel's prophecies of consolation was presented by Greenberg, *Ezekiel 1–20*, 341; *Ezekiel 21–37*, 735–38; and thoroughly discussed by T. M. Raitt, *A Theology of Exile: Judgment / Deliverance in Jeremiah and Ezekiel* (Philadelphia: Fortress, 1977) 132–34, 147–50, 175–84. Ezek 6:8–10; 20:43–44; 36:31 (as also 16:59–63) present the people's regret and repentance only as a reaction to God's initial salvific actions.

62 Compare to Greenberg's explanation of this idea as resting on a pessimistic perspective concerning the people's repentance (*Ezekiel 1–20*).

63 R. Kasher suggests that the juxtaposition of 33:30–33 to our passage (vv. 23–29) designates favoring the Exiles called בני עמך and even עמי (v. 31), and is in itself a comforting proclamation (*Ezekiel 25–48*, Mikra LeYisra'el [Jerusalem and Tel Aviv: Magnes Press and Am Oved, 2004] 641).

64 Graffy, *A Prophet*, 105–29. Compare to Greenberg (*Ezekiel 21–37*, 688), who argues that the disputation in Ezek 33:23–29 confronts a perspective held by Edom (Ezek 36:2). I would rather focus on the inner-conflict.

65 M. Fishbane (*Biblical Interpretation*, 375) and Greenberg (*Ezekiel 21–37*, 689–90) explain the concentration on the people's sins as the prophet's furious reaction, recalling traditions of Abraham's righteousness. But, there is no trace of any such tradition in Ezekiel's refutation. It rather seems that, lacking an adequate response based on the Abraham traditions, Ezekiel shifts the entire question into the realm of legal obligation.

66 In contrast to the commentators who understand והארץ תירשו as a rhetorical question, the NJPS translates this phrase as an indicative sentence, perceiving it then as a clear mocking or sarcasm.

The three capital crimes of which Ezekiel accuses Those Who Remained and the question והארץ תירשו allude to the Holiness Code's concept of land and exile. According to Leviticus 18 and 20 idolatry, bloodshed and sexual offenses defile the land to the point that it vomits its inhabitants (Lev 18:24–30; 20:22), and brings God to drive out its inhabitants and to total abhorrence (Lev 20:23).[67] Ezekiel's cry והארץ תירשו (Ezek 33:25, 26) echoes the promise of the land: ואמר לכם אתם תירשו את אדמתם ("You shall possess their land," Lev 20:24). Yet, by posing it as a rhetorical question directed against those in Jerusalem, the prophet abolishes the promise for "those who live in these ruins in the land of Israel" (Ezek 33:24).

Moreover, Ezekiel applies to the community left in Judah the threats of removal from the land in Lev 18:24–30. This passage from the Holiness Code catalogues the fates of "the people who were in the land" (אנשי הארץ, v. 27), or the Canaanite peoples (20:23, MT גוי, but pl. in the versions), in order to deter Israel from the calamitous results of following in their ways.[68] The Canaanite peoples of the land were expelled because of their "abhorrent practices" (חקות התועבות, 18:30), which were mainly of a sexual nature (Lev 18:6–23). But the prohibitive speech of 18:24–30 does not settle for the threat of expulsion of Israel from the land; it warns of further calamity: "All who do any of those abhorrent things – such persons shall be cut off from their people" (כי כל אשר יעשה מכל התועבות האלה, ונכרתו הנפשות העשות מקרב העם, v. 29).[69] Accordingly, in contrast to the argument for continuity in the possession of the land, Ezekiel does not even prophesy exile, but rather total annihilation of Those Who Remained, by sword, beast and pestilence (Ezek 33:27), and he further widens the prospect of his prophecy to include desolation of the land (vv. 28–29).[70] In drawing

G. Brin sees the line of sarcasm and condemnation already present with the demonstrative pronoun האלה (33:24), in "The Date and Meaning of the Prophecy against 'Those Who Live in These Ruins in the Land of Israel' (Ezekiel 33:23–29)," in M. V. Fox and others, eds., *Texts, Temples, and Traditions: A Tribute to Menahem Haran* (Winona Lake, Ind.: Eisenbrauns, 1996) 29–36 (Heb. sec.).

67 *B.Menaḥ.* 13.2; discussion of the sins and their relationship to the Holiness Code in Greenberg, *Ezekiel 21–37*, 684–85; see also J. Joosten, *People and Land in the Holiness Code: An Exegetical Study of the Ideational Framework of the Law in Leviticus 17–26*, SVT 67 (Leiden: Brill, 1996) 169–92.

68 B. J. Schwartz, *The Holiness Legislation: Studies in the Priestly Code* (Jerusalem: Magnes Press, 1999) 222–37; Milgrom, *Leviticus 17–22*, 1571–78.

69 Schwartz suggested a clear distinction between expulsion and calamity (*The Holiness Legislation*, 228–37). Yet, on the analogy of the fate of Israel (18:29), it seems rather that in three passages (Lev 18:24–30; 20:20–24 and in Num 33:50–59) expulsion does mean annihilation, even if there is no reference to the vehicle of execution. Thus, these passages differ from Leviticus 26's perspective on exile.

70 Total calamity and empty land characterize other judgment prophecies against Jerusalem, see p. 41 below. Milgrom argued that in the Holiness Code the land "automatically regurgitates its inhabitants in the process of cleansing itself," and thus in contrast to the Priestly perception, the land is not irrevocably impure (*Leviticus 17–22*, 1573–74). Ezekiel then takes the Priestly position prophesying that the sins require desolation of the land itself (as in Ezek 6:11–14).

these analogies to Lev 18:24–30, Ezekiel rejects the possibility that Those Who Remained might join the community of the Jehoiachin Exiles in Babylon.

Ezekiel, then, not only supplies divine de-legitimation for the continuous existence of Those Who Remained in Judah, he emphatically reflects the superior-exclusive tendency of the Jehoiachin Exiles that had developed from the very start, from 597 B.C.E. and on.[71]

To summarize, Ezekiel as an advocate of the Exiles formulates a concept of exile that enables continuity of Judahite existence *outside* the Land of Israel. He clearly knows and deviates from both the Deuteronomic and the Holiness Code's concepts of land and exile. Furthermore, in his prophecy of restoration (11:16–21), Ezekiel supplies divine legitimation to this community of Exiles seen as the Remnant of the people of God. In opposition, the prophet de-legitimates the community in Jerusalem, accusing them with various cultic sins (11:21; 33:25–26), that estrange them from the land.[72] These strategies of division create explicit differences of prestige between the groups.

IMPLICIT DISPUTATION
SEPARATE HISTORIES & FUTURES FOR THE TWO JUDEAN COMMUNITIES

In his social-anthropological studies, Fredrick Barth mentioned the importance given to questions of origin in the evolution of the group's present identity.[73] Having outlined the rival arguments in this conflict, we can now proceed to Ezekiel's observations on the history of the God-people relationship, and thus on the two communities' possibilities for present and future existence.

In two passages, Ezek 16:1–43 and 20:1–38, which were not connected through the editorial process of the book, I suggest that Ezekiel expresses his perspective on each of the two Judahite communities.

The two prophecies have several characteristics in common. First, they open with the call to the prophet to proclaim abominations, "O mortal, proclaim Jerusalem's abominations to her" (בן אדם הודע את ירושלים את תועבתיה, 16:2); "Arraign, arraign them, O mortal! – Declare to them the abhorrent deeds of

71 This separation is explicitly suggested in Jer 24:1–10; and appears implicitly also in the diverse descriptions of the Jehoiachin Exile in 2 Kgs 24:8–17, in comparison to the general reference to the 586 destruction and exile in 2 Kings 25. For the exilic perspective of 2 Kings 24–25 see Seitz, *Theology in Conflict*, 215–21.

72 Religious behavior as a de-legitimating device to determine hierarchal differentiation between groups is also implemented in the historiography; see the various denigrations of the Northern Kingdom accused for following "the ways of Jeroboam son of Nevat and the sins he caused Israel to commit" down to its destruction and exile (1 Kgs 12:25–33; 13:33–34; 1 Kgs 15:26, 34 and constantly through the Book of Kings; finally, 2 Kgs 17:21–22 which suggests a somewhat different yet still denigrating perspective).

73 Barth, *Ethnic Groups*, 29.

their fathers" (התשפט אתם התשפוט בן אדם, את תועבת אבותם הודיעם, 20:4).[74] The former aims at Jerusalem, while the latter is directed to the Exiles. A second common denominator is structural; both passages start with a retrospective which goes back to the initial constitution of the relationship between God and His people (16:1–14; 20:5–26),[75] proceed to the present generation in a chronological contraction (16:15–34; 20:30–33), and look to the future (16:35–43; 20:34–38). The third is thematic, in both prophecies the prophet lays out his agenda concerning the question "who is the people of God," recognizing that it could only be one of the two communities, the Jehoiachin Exiles or Those Who Remained in Judah. However, in other features the two passages differ.

The literary genre. Ezekiel 16:1–43, the metaphoric story of the abandoned baby, the beautiful bride, and the harlot-wife stands in the structural framework of a judgment prophecy. The first part presents a long description of the sinful wife's guilt and ingratitude (vv. 1–34), followed by a passage suggesting her punishment (vv. 35–43).[76]

In contrast, Ezek 20:1–38 is construed as a disputation speech, though with special structure.[77] As is typical of the genre, the core of the disputation is the refutation of the Elders' words of despair quoted in v. 32: "We will be like the nations, like the families of the lands, worshipping wood and stone" (נהיה כגוים כמשפחות הארצות לשרת עץ ואבן).[78] The Elders of Israel approach the prophet with a reflection in which they seek correlation between the traditional concept of

74 An even closer opening to Ezek 20:4 appears in Ezek 22:1: ואתה בן אדם התשפט התשפט את עיר הדמים והודעתה את כל תועבותיה ("Further, O mortal, arraign arraign the city of bloodshed; declare to her all her abhorrent deeds!"). Yet, the passages differ, first, in the grammatical person of the address; second, in content, Ezek 22:1–12 deals with Jerusalem's present iniquities and does not present a retrospective history of the God-people relationship; third, in style, explicit apodictic charges influence Ezekiel 22 in contrast to Ezekiel 20's reliance on historical traditions of the covenant (compare Zimmerli, *Ezekiel 1*, 454–55).

75 Ezek 20:27–29 (as also vv. 39–44) are secondary, see n. 85 below.

76 Ezek 16:1–43 is one of five different passages in Ezekiel 16 and 23 which use the family metaphors of adoption and marriage in diverse ways. For their self-contained initial character and their literary nature as metaphoric stories (not allegory), see J. Galambush, *Jerusalem in the Book of Ezekiel: The City as Yahweh's Wife*, SBLDS 130 (Atlanta, Ga.: Scholars Press, 1992) 10–11.

77 In a previous paper I have suggested a different division to chapter 20 than is commonly adduced (Rom-Shiloni, "Facing Destruction," 194–204). I hereby bring only the necessary points for the present argument. Most commentators have divided chapter 20 into two initially independent units: the historical speech (vv. 1–31), expanded by the disputation speech (vv. 32–44). So Eichrodt, *Ezekiel*, 276–84; Zimmerli, *Ezekiel 1*, 404, 413–14; L. C. Allen, *Ezekiel 20–48*, WBC 29 (Waco, Tex.: Word Books, 1990) 5; and also Graffy, *A Prophet*, 65–66. In contrast, Greenberg and Hoffman argued for the unity of the chapter (Greenberg, *Ezekiel 1–20*, 376–81; Y. Hoffman, "Ezekiel 20 – Its Structure and Meaning," *Beit Miqra* 20 [1975] 480–86).

78 So Zimmerli, *Ezekiel 1*, 414; further discussion of the saying and its traditional background, see Rom-Shiloni, "Facing Destruction," 194–98.

exile and their present existence in Babylon. The Deuteronomic concept, which they cite, indeed threatens that exile will be the place for worshipping wood and stone ("There you will serve man-made gods of wood and stone," ועבדתם שם אלהים מעשה ידי אדם עץ ואבן, Deut 4:28; and 28:36, 64). This analogy threatens the Exiles' continued existence as the people of God.

The furious rejection of the Elder's inquiry is accentuated in an *inclusio* repetition, which frames the whole retrospective speech as the disputation's introductory section.[79]

verse 3 הלדרש אתי אתם באים, חי אני אם אדרש לכם נאם אדני ה׳
Have you come to inquire of Me? As I live, I will not respond to your inquiry – declares the Lord God.

verse 31 ואני אדרש לכם בית ישראל, חי אני נאם אדני ה׳ אם אדרש לכם
shall I respond to your inquiry, O house of Israel? As I live – declares the Lord God – I will not respond to you.

Within his speech the prophet proclaims first the abhorrent deeds of "their fathers" (vv. 4–26). Returning to his contemporaries (vv. 30–32a), Ezekiel then quotes their words (v. 32b), and disproves them with a unique prophecy of deliverance, describing God as reigning over the people "with a strong hand, and with an outstretched arm, and with overflowing fury" (ביד חזקה ובזרוע נטויה ובחמה שפוכה, vv. 33–38). Ezekiel's special perspective on the relationship between God and His people is thus the focus of this disputation presented in both his *retrospective* account and in his *prospective* articulation of the ongoing relationship during the exile.[80]

Future prospect. The generic difference emphasizes the distinct opposing content of the two prophecies. Ezek 16:1–43 prophesies judgment and calamity to Jerusalem, while Ezek 20:1–38 forecasts consolation and hope for the Exiles.

Metaphors serving in the God-people covenant relationship. The contrast in content and particularly in the future prediction to Jerusalem versus that to the Exiles has brought Ezekiel to use different metaphors to designate contrasting perspectives on the God-people covenant relationship.

79 In addition, all the literary features of the introductory section of the disputation-speech are present: 1. The prophetic formula ויהי דבר ה׳ אלי לאמר (v. 2; as in Ezek 11:14). 2. The essential features preceding the quotation: the verb אמר, and the identification of its subject, אתם, v. 32; 3. Rejection of the quotation, which appears twice in Ezekiel 20, first, in the *inclusio* pattern, and second, in the immediate context of v. 32 and on. Compare Graffy, *A Prophet*, 105–29.

80 So Block, *Ezekiel 1–24*, 613. For other suggestions for the possible content of Ezekiel 20 see Hoffman, Ezekiel 20, 473; Greenberg, *Ezekiel 1–20*, 387–88; and Kasher, *Ezekiel 1–24*, 385.

The metaphor in Ezekiel 20 is the well known theological-political metaphor which designates God as king and the people as His vassals.[81] The retrospective speech (vv. 4–31) depicts four periods (covering three generations) in a graduated pattern of three and four: 1. The servitude in Egypt – the first generation of the fathers (vv. 5–10); 2. The Exodus through the desert of this first generation (vv. 11–17); 3. The second generation in the desert (vv. 18–26); 4. Ezekiel's contemporary generation in Babylon (vv. 30–31), where the historical retrospective reaches its climax.[82] In order to repeat God's rejection of the inquiry, the prophet straightforwardly reproves his contemporaries in exile: "Do you defile yourselves in the manner of your fathers" (הבדרך אבתיכם אתם נטמאים, v. 31).[83]

In order to characterize the God-People relationship, Ezekiel builds the first three periods with repetitive components. 1. God has benefited His people by choosing them and constituting a covenant relationship with them by oath (20:5–6), and has further committed them to his covenant through specific commands (vv. 7, 11–12, 18–20, 25–26).[84] Yet, 2. they have sinned against him in their disobedience (vv. 8, 13, 21, 24). 3. God should have punished them with a calamitous judgment "Then I resolved to pour out My fury upon them, to vent all My anger upon them there" (ואמר לשפך חמתי עליהם לכלות אפי בהם, vv. 8b, 13b, 21b, and למען אשמם "that I might render them desolate," v. 26). However, 4. "for the sake of His name, that it might not be profaned in the sight of the nations" He repeatedly refrained from that (ואעש למען שמי לבלתי החל לעיני הגוים, vv. 9, 14, 22), and 5. instead God reduced the judgment against them (vv. 10, 15–17, 22–26). Thus, following the political metaphor, covenant as initiated by God-the king, includes specific commitments and stipulations, and the vassals' disobedience brings the sovereign time and again to punish the rebels.

Ezekiel selected these four eras from the people's history to emphasize two

81 To mention only selected comparative studies on the vassal treaties and the biblical covenant concept, see D. R. Hillers, *Treaty Curses and the Old Testament Prophets*, BibOr 16 (2nd ed.; Rome: Pontifical Bibilical Institute, 1964); M. Weinfeld, "The Covenant of Grant in the Old Testament and in the Ancient Near East," *JAOS* 90 (1970) 184–203; Weinfeld, "Berit – Covenant vs. Obligation," *Biblica* 56 (1975) 120–28; B. K. Waltke, "The Phenomenon of Conditionality within Unconditional Covenants," in A. Gileadi, ed., *Israel's Apostasy and Restoration: Essays in Honor of R. K. Harrison* (Grand Rapids, Mich.: Baker Book House, 1988) 123–40.

82 Contra Greenberg, *Ezekiel 1–20*, 377–78.

83 Translated thus by Greenberg, *Ezekiel 1–20*, 362.

84 The divine initiative and hierarchy in setting the conditions of the covenant parallel the neo-Assyrian treaties, which usually refrain from pronouncing the Sovereign's obligations towards his vassal(s), see S. Parpola and K. Watanabe, *Neo-Assyrian Treaties and Loyalty Oaths*, SAA 11 (Helsinki: Helsinki, 1989) xiv–xv. The sovereign-vassal relationship differ in the neo-Hittite treaties, as presented by G. Mendenhall, "Covenant Forms in Israelite Tradition," *BA* 17 (1954) 50–76; and M. Weinfeld, *Deuteronomy and the Deuteronomic School* (Winona Lake, Ind.: Eisenbrauns, 1972. 2nd ed., 1992) 68, 70–74.

main points to his fellow Exiles. First, the geographical horizon: The common denominator of the depicted eras (with the exception of the secondary verses 27–29) is the existence outside the Land of Israel.[85] This special geographical point of view in Ezek 20:1–32 has been overlooked by scholars. In contradistinction to the traditional perception of the exile as a period of distance and separation from God, Ezekiel points out the fact that God had initially established the relationship with His people outside the land of Israel, in an exilic environment.[86]

Second, the commitment of God to the covenant: Within Ezekiel's accent on the fact that God initiated the covenant relationship with His people in Egypt (v. 5), the prophet suggests the exceptional claim that disobedience to God and to His ritual demands started at this very first stage (vv. 7–8), and has persisted ever since (vv. 13, 21, 30).[87] Time and again the people have deserved to be punished with total calamity (vv. 8b, 13b, 21b), but God decided unilaterally not to destroy them, for the sake of His prestige in the face of the foreign peoples (vv. 9, 14, 22).[88] Although the divine oath had changed as a consequence of the people's sins (vv. 6, 15, 23), God did not retract it, and the people's behavior did not abrogate the everlasting existence of His commitments.

In Ezekiel's prophecy of consolation (vv. 33–38) those two central lessons of the retrospective speech connect the present generation of the Exiles in Babylon to the first generations in Egypt and in the desert.[89]

Hence, the prophet vigilantly bypasses the inherited concept of exile with a different analogy based on Priestly (especially Exod 6:2–8) and Deuteronomic

85 For the secondary nature of vv. 27–29 (as also vv. 39–44), see Zimmerli, *Ezekiel 1*, 405, 412; and recently Rom-Shiloni, "Facing Destruction," 200–201; compare to Greenberg (*Ezekiel 1–20*, 378); Hoffman (*Ezekiel 20*, 482); Block (*Ezekiel 1–24*, 641–45); and Kasher (*Ezekiel 1–24*, 385–86), all still consider vv. 27–29 part of the original words.

86 Ezekiel 20 joins other covenant traditions which are set outside the Land of Israel (exceptional is only Joshua 24). See D. Sperling, "Joshua 24 Re-examined," *HUCA* 58 (1987) 119–36, esp. 133–36.

87 Idolatry practiced prior to the Settlement connects Ezekiel 20 to Psalm 106 (and to Josh 24:14). Compare G. W. Coats, *Rebellion in the Wilderness* (Nashville: Abingdon, 1968) 227–28, 233–34; Block, *Ezekiel 1–24*, 615–16.

88 Alluding to Exod 32:9–14, see Fishbane, *Biblical Interpretation*, 366.

89 Various allusions to the Exodus in vv. 33–38 prove this intention: והוצאתי אתכם מן- (v. 34), ביד חזקה ובזרוע נטויה (vv. 33, 34), והבאתי אתכם אל מדבר העמים (v. 35), מסרת הברית (v. 37), and the even more explicit allusion במדבר ארץ מצרים (v. 36). For allusions in vv. 33–38 (as also vv. 5–6 and others) to the Priestly tradition in Exod 6:2–8, see M. A. Fishbane, *Text and Texture: Close Reading of Selected Biblical Texts* (New York: Schocken, 1979) 131–32; Fishbane, *Biblical Interpretation*, 366–67. Nevertheless, Ezekiel's words differ considerably from that tradition: 1. He does not mention the fathers as the recipients of the promise to the land (Exod 6:2, 8; and see Greenberg, *Ezekiel 1–20*, 364). 2. Unparalleled in Exodus 6, Ezekiel suggests an immediate requirement to obey God's demands (Ezek 20:7). 3. Ezekiel describes the salvation using idioms of wrath aimed at the people. Compare *b.Roš Haš* 32b, and Greenberg's discussion of חמה שפוכה in Ezekiel (*Ezekiel 1–20*, 371–72).

Exodus traditions.[90] Accordingly, he perceives the Exiles as a direct continuation of the first generation in Egypt. Ezekiel illustrates an opposing picture – the Exiles do have hope. Although in exile, they are still God's people, and He is their King.

Ezekiel 16:1–43 integrates two metaphors from the family sphere, the adoption and the marital metaphors, in which God is father and then husband, and the city is first His daughter and then His wife.[91] This passage in Ezekiel has attracted vast scholarly attention; I will restrict myself to the covenant concept that it presents in three main points: initiation of the covenant relationship, its violation, and finally the wife's / the city's judgment.

1. Initiation of the covenant relationship in 16:1–14 appears as a two-stage process, designated by the repetition on "When I passed by you and saw you" (ואעבר עליך ואראך, vv. 6, 8). First, Jerusalem a baby-born in the land of Canaan (ומלדתיך מארץ הכנעני, v. 3) to an Amorite father and a Hittite mother, who was abandoned at birth, is adopted by God (vv. 4–7).[92] Second, when the young girl reaches maturity, God establishes the covenant relationship with her through marriage: "and I entered into a covenant with you by oath-declares the Lord God; thus you became Mine" (ואשבע לך ואבוא בברית אתך נאם אדני ה׳ ותהיי לי, vv. 8).[93] As in marital commitments, the hierarchy between the two parties in this covenant relationship is clear. God-the husband initiates the relationship, and the result is that He owns the bride-Jerusalem (ותהיי לי, v. 8).[94] Throughout vv. 8–14 ותהיי לי is the only phrase which hints at the bride's obligations of loyalty towards her husband. In contrast, the story focuses on an impressive list of the benefits God as husband has given her (vv. 9–13). The description reaches the point where the bride is prepared for the position she ought to

90 Compare Levitt Kohn, *A New Heart*, 98–103. For different evaluations of the wilderness traditions in Ezekiel's speech, see Eichrodt, *Ezekiel*, 279–80; and Coats, *Rebellion*, 240–41.

91 The marriage metaphor with the people or the city as God's wife, were thoroughly discussed by Galambush, *Jerusalem*. For the adoption metaphor in the God-people relationship, and the comparative use of adoption terminology in the diplomatic relationships, see S. M. Paul, "Adoption Formulae: A Study of Cuneiform and Biblical Legal Clauses," *Maarav* 2 / 2 (1979–80) 173–85. The two family metaphors are integrated in Jer 3:4 as well, and the common terminology was presented by Weinfeld, *Deuteronomistic School*, 80–81; Greenberg, *Ezekiel 1–20*, 254.

92 M. Malul, "Adoption of Foundlings in the Bible and Mesopotamian Documents: A Study of Some Legal Metaphors in Ezekiel 16.1–7," JSOT 46 (1990) 97–126.

93 An oath does not appear as a component in the marital ceremony (but see Ruth 3:13; and the appearance of "covenant" to designate marriage in Mal 2:14; Prov 2:17). Thus Greenberg considers ואשבע לך to be of the tenor (*Ezekiel 1–20*, 278). Yet, God taking an oath is also uncommon (Deut 4:31; 28:9), and thus Zimmerli designated this as a unique feature in Ezekiel's use of the metaphor (*Ezekiel 1*, 349).

94 The phrase היה ל(ו) ל designates the subject change of status in relation to the object (BDB, 226).

undertake, being God's wife: "and < you > became fit for royalty" (ותצלחי למלוכה, v. 13). Likewise her beauty results from her patron: "for it was perfected through the splendor which I set upon you" (כי כליל הוא בהדרי אשר שמתי עליך, v. 14). This description clarifies that the metaphors of the family sphere are sub-metaphors to that of God as King. Nevertheless, the family metaphors function independently in Ezekiel, and together with the political metaphor, the two even serve the prophet to present his counter-positions regarding the two Judahite communities.[95]

2. Violation of the covenant, 16:15–34: In complete opposition to the constitution of the marriage / the covenant, the wife / Jerusalem in total ingratitude has given to other gods what she had gotten as bride-price from God (vv. 15–22), and further betrayed Him with human "foreigners," "lovers" (vv. 23–34). The figurative sexual description reaches its apex as the adulteress is parodied for behavior unheard of even among prostitutes, "You were the opposite of other women: you solicited instead of being solicited; you paid fees instead of being paid fees. Thus you were just the opposite!" (ויהי בך הפך מן הנשים בתזנותיך ואחריך לא זונה ובתתך אתנן ואתנן לא נתן לך, ותהי להפך, v. 34).[96]

The adulterous nymphomaniacal behavior is construed in constant transitions between the vehicle of the metaphor and its implicit tenor.[97] The wife / Jerusalem is accused of adultery, formally separated into two paragraphs (vv. 16–22, 23–34), which stand for sins taken from two spheres. In the religious sphere, worshipping other gods include building cultic sites (vv. 16, 24–25), producing figurines (v. 17), serving them various offerings (vv. 18–19), and the most severe of all, sacrificing God's sons and daughters to them (vv. 20–21; as also 23:37).[98] In the political sphere, adultery means counting on foreigners from among the Egyptians (16:26), the Assyrians (v. 28), and the Babylonians (v. 29).[99] Both spheres add up to the general accusation of the wife / city for not remembering her youth, "you did not remember the days of your youth" (ולא זכרתי [ק: זכרת] את ימי נעוריך, vv. 22, 43).[100]

95 The two metaphorical systems operate interchangeably in Ezekiel and Jeremiah, yet they function independently according to the particular messages of these prophets. This polemical usage is specific to Ezekiel. For a fuller discussion, see D. Rom-Shiloni, "God in Times of Destruction and Exiles: Theology and Ideology in the Prophetical Literature and in the Poetry of the First Half of the Sixth Century B.C.E." (Ph.D. Diss.; Jerusalem: Hebrew Univ., 2001) 237–83.

96 Galambush, *Jerusalem*, 98.

97 So P. L. Day, "The Bitch Had It Coming to Her: Rhetoric and Interpretation in Ezekiel 16," *BibInt* VIII/3 (2000) 231–54.

98 במות טלאות (v. 16), as also גב and רמה (v. 24, 31) are all designators of cultic sites, see Greenberg, *Ezekiel 1–20*, 280–82, and his discussion of the unique language and style, 296–97.

99 The political sphere is the focus of attention in Ezek 23:1–35, 36–49; whereas the religious sphere in the first prophecy holds only minor position (vv. 7, 30 and 14). This is then one major difference between the metaphorical passages in Ezekiel. See Galambush, *Jerusalem*, 110.

100 זכר is an important component in the biblical political-covenant terminology throughout the bib-

Although the tenor appears explicit at times, the story remains faithful to the marital metaphor in perceiving the sins. Varied forms of the roots זנה and נאף dominate the terminology of sin.[101] Even the general term תועבות "abominations" (16:22, 36), which in Deuteronomic sources refers to cultic, moral and sexual offenses, appears as if through the lens of the Holiness Code's writer to concentrate on sexual misconduct.[102] The adulterous behavior illustrated so vividly through the marital metaphor demonstrates Jerusalem's sins of disloyalty as profound betrayal of the old covenant with God. Yet, in contrast to Ezekiel 20, and to the general usage of the political metaphor, there is no mention of disobedience to God's laws and rules (compare Ezek 20:11, 13).[103]

3. The judgment upon the wife / the city, 16:35–43, continues this line of metaphor. In contrast to her initial salvation from disgrace and helplessness, salvation which had brought her to prestigious status among the peoples (v. 14), and in retaliation to her sins (vv. 15–34), the wife is now accused of adultery and murder. Hence, she is doomed to return to shame and helplessness, to total destruction (vv. 39–41).[104]

Jerusalem is accused of two capital crimes and sentenced accordingly: "I will inflict upon you the punishment of women who commit adultery and murder" (ושפטתיך משפטי נאפות ושפכת דם, 16:38; 23:45; see also 23:37). The juxtaposition of the two crimes, adultery and sacrificial murder, alludes to Leviticus 20.

This Holiness Code passage is the second (in addition to Leviticus 18) to

lical literature (historiography, law, prophecy and poetry). The command to remember refers to God's salvation from the bondage in Egypt (Deut 16:3 and 7:18); to his leadership in the wilderness (8:2); and to his constant beneficial involvement (8:18; as also Isa 62:6; Neh 4:8). These objects of remembrance are all rooted in the Exodus traditions, and exemplify God's roles as warrior who has saved his people in times of distress (as in Exod 13:3). See H. Eising, זכר, *TDOT* IV.67–69. Since in Ezek 16:1–43 Ezekiel ignores the Exodus tradition, זכר in vv. 22, 43 must be understood as a further implicit tenor.

101 For זנה, זנות and תזנות (an Ezekelian hapax, which appears twenty times in Ezekiel 16 and 23), as other unique features of language and style of Ezekiel 16, see Greenberg, *Ezekiel 1–20*, 296.

102 תועבות (and the phrase חקות התועבת in v. 30) in Lev 18:24–30 according to B. Schwartz bear a general and abstract meaning in order to present the implications of this impurity and abominations for the national fate (*Holiness Legislation*, 222–23). For the difference between the use of תועבות in Deuteronomic versus Priestly sources, see Milgrom, *Leviticus 17–22*, 1581.

103 This is, then, another unique feature of Ezek 16:1–43, by comparison with the other occurrences of the marital metaphor stories in Ezekiel. Compare to the Ezek 16:59–63, which opens with a phrase resembling the vassal oath (אשר בזית אלה להפר ברית, v. 59); and the implicit tenor that appears in 23:38–39.

104 Block presented this "ironical twist" in Jerusalem's fortune (*Ezekiel 1–24*, 500–503). I accept Day's observation ("The Bitch," 237–54), that the lovers' participation in the harlot's execution is another example of the implicit tenor in this section as well (compare to the adultery laws, in Lev 20:10; Deut 22:22–24). Nevertheless, this intrusion of the tenor does not exclude the basic line of thought in this passage, which rests on the different judgments directed at sexual offenses in the Holiness Code (Leviticus 20).

connect the contrasting commands of God with the abominable laws of the foreign Canaanite peoples (20:22–23; and 18:1–5, 26). The (detestable) laws (חקות הגוי, 20:23,[105] or חקתיהם in 18:3, and כל התועבת האלה, vv. 26, 27) are specified in the cultic sphere by the sacrifice of sons to the Molech (20:2–6), and in the moral sphere by sexual offenses (20:9–21). Leviticus 20 names two sets of punishments one after the other. The first, in the third person singular (or plural) activated against individual sinners (20:1–21). The second, in the second person plural, extended to the whole people (vv. 22–24), presents clear conditional threat stating that disobedience to God's commands results in the land vomiting its inhabitants (v. 22).[106] Since the people of Israel inherited the land of those who had lost it because of their sins (v. 24), a constant threat hangs above the heads of those who live in God's land.

The allusive connections to the Holiness Code's concepts of land and exile are the keys to understanding Ezekiel's selection of this specific marital metaphor with regard to God-Jerusalem's relationship.[107] Leviticus 20 supplies the legal basis to completely de-legitimate Jerusalem as the people of God, and even to illustrate the prediction of that community's eventual physical calamity.

Just as Ezekiel refutes the words of the Jerusalemites in Ezek 33:24–29 with allusions to Leviticus 18 and 20,[108] so does the prophet adapt those central themes in his metaphoric judgment prophecy in Ezek 16:1–43. The analogy serves the prophet's views concerning the origin of Jerusalem, its sins, and its punishment. As for Jerusalem's origin, Ezekiel goes even further than what he expresses in 33:24–29, when he not only identifies Jerusalem and her conduct with the denigrated "practices of the nation that I am driving out before you" (חקות הגוי אשר אנכי משלח מפניכם, Lev 20:23); but furthermore, argues in 16:1–43 that Jerusalem is actually Canaanite in origin, the daughter of an Amorite and a Hittite from the land of Canaan (vv. 2–3). Her adoption and the tremendous benefits poured on her by God could not have erased this initial "biography."[109] With regard to her sins, they resemble further the parallel between the city and the Canaanite peoples. In analogy to Leviticus 20, Jeru-

105 חקות) הגוי) in 20:23 appears in the plural form in the versions, cohering with the plural forms at the end of the verse, עשו ואקץ בם; and in accordance with 18:24 (however, 18:28 uses the singular). See Milgrom, *Leviticus 17–22*, 1759.

106 Schwartz presented the independent position of the two chapters (*Holiness Legislation*, 135–44); and see Milgrom, *Leviticus 17–22*, 1577, 1765–68.

107 Compare to Galambush's suggestion that the key theme to this metaphoric passage, is Jerusalem's impurity and specifically the sanctuary's defilement, which prepares the ground for God's abandonment of His city (*Jerusalem*, 103–5).

108 See the discussion on pp. 18–20 above.

109 Block saw the polemical nature of Jerusalem's genealogy (*Ezekiel 1–24*, 475), but he did not complete Ezekiel's interests as an opponent.

salem follows the very same abominations.[110] Judged as harlot and as "cultic murderer," Jerusalem's sins are unforgivable and her punishment irrevocable. Finally, as to Jerusalem's judgment, Ezekiel deviates his message from Leviticus 20. According to the latter, God expelled the Canaanites from the land, an expulsion which ended in their extinction (Lev 20:23, and 18:28). In his words to Jerusalem Ezekiel does not foresee displacement from the land as part of Jerusalem's punishment. The prophet rather combines Leviticus 20's two sets of punishment.[111] The individual death penalty of the murderer and the adulteress becomes the only retaliation to Jerusalem's offenses, foreseeing total calamity within the land, no exile.[112]

Using the two metaphors to describe the God-people relationship, Ezekiel differentiates sociologically between the past and the future fates of the two communities in exile and in the land of Israel, as can be seen in the table on the following pages.

The political metaphor in Ezek 20:1–38, on the one hand, enables Ezekiel to emphasize the constitution of the covenant outside the land of Israel, in Egypt, with God as initiator and the preserver of the covenant despite the people's repeated disobedience. As proven before, God is committed to His people, and thus the continuous covenant relationship is guaranteed for the future as well: God is the Exiles' King.

The family metaphors in Ezek 16:1–43, on the other hand, enable Ezekiel to keep Jerusalem in an inland vicinity, in Canaan. From origin, through constant misconducts, to her punishment, Jerusalem resembles the Canaanite peoples, the previous peoples of the land, whom God had expelled. But, in Ezekiel's extreme position, Jerusalem is not even doomed to exile, only to death, to total calamity.

Through these lines of argumentation and the ideological strategies of division which Ezekiel uses in the two passages, the prophet recalls different

110 Condemnation of the Canaanite peoples with sexual misconduct has its roots in several stories in the book of Genesis, that is, the story of Ham, Canaan's forefather (Gen 9:22–27); Dinah's rape (Genesis 34); as also the story of Sodom and Gomorra (Genesis 19); and see Schwartz, *Holiness Legislation*, 157–62.

111 Milgrom considers verses 22–23 a separate unit appended to the list of chapter 20 under the influence of chapter 18 (*Leviticus 17–22*, 1759).

112 The similarities between Leviticus 20 and Ezek 16:35–43 with regard to the penalties are scant and doubtful, mainly because verses 39–43 present rapid changes from the metaphoric vehicle to its realistic tenor. Nevertheless, two of the death penalties appear in both: pelt in stone for the sacrifice of sons to the Molech (רגם באבן, Lev 20:2, as in Ezek 16:40), and flaming in fire for sexual offenses (שרף באש, Lev 20:14, as in Ezek 16:41). See Greenberg, *Ezekiel 1–20*, 287; Block mentions only Deut 22:23–24 as alluded in Ezek 16:40 (*Ezekiel 1–24*, 503); and P. L. Day, "Adulterous Jerusalem's Imagined Demise: Death of a Metaphor in Ezekiel xvi," *VT* 50/3 (2000) 285–309.

Legitimation – Ezekiel as the Jehoiachin Exiles' Advocator (20:1–38)	*De-legitimation – Those Who Remained in Jerusalem* (16:1–43)
את תועבת אבותם הודיעם "Declare to them the abhorrent deeds of their fathers" (v. 4)	הודע את ירושלים את תועבתיה "proclaim Jerusalem's abominations to her" (v. 2)
The God-People Relationship	
Illustrated by the political metaphor of God as Sovereign and the people as His vassals (v. 33).	Illustrated by the family metaphors (adoption and marriage).
Constitution of the Covenant Relationship	
God had chosen Israel in Egypt (vv. 5–6), and established the covenant on a divine oath and obligation of the people to obey His rules and to worship God exclusively.	God had adopted a deserted newborn baby of Canaanite origin. As she reached maturity God married her and brought her to be "worthy of kingship" (vv. 1–14).
Violation of the Covenant	
The people disobeyed God's commandments throughout the mentioned periods: 1. The servitude period in Egypt (vv. 5–10, esp. 8); 2. This first generation in the desert (vv. 11–17, esp. 13); 3. The second generation in the desert (vv. 18–26, esp. 21); 4. Ezekiel's contemporary generation of Exiles (vv. 30–31).	Jerusalem has turned to be an adulteress woman. Being unfaithful to God she committed adultery with other gods (on the religious-cultic sphere, vv. 15–22) and with human "foreigners" (on the political sphere, vv. 23–34).

historical and legal traditions from the Pentateuch, with which he establishes two distinctive histories of the God-people relationship. Relying on the Exodus traditions, Ezekiel legitimates the Exiles' ongoing existence as the people of God, with whom the covenant is expected to be restored in "the desert of peoples," and who will be led back to the land of Israel. In contrast, the prophet delegitimates the homeland community by referring back to the legal and historic traditions related to the Settlement, which demand clear separation from the Canaanite peoples. Construing a similarity between Those Who Remained and the Canaanite peoples is a strategy Ezra and Nehemiah will later use during the

Legitimation – Ezekiel as the Jehoiachin Exiles' Advocator	*De-legitimation – Those Who Remained in Jerusalem*
Retaliation	
Although God intended to annihilate His people time and again (vv. 8, 13, 21), He refrained from doing so for the sake of His prestige among the nations (vv. 9, 14, 22); and though judgment aggravated, it repeatedly lessened the calamitous verdict (vv. 10, 15–17, 23–26). In this context, God had destined the people to exile (v. 23). But in contrast to the Deuteronomic pre-exilic concept of exile (such as Deut 4:25–28; 28:36), which the Exiles paraphrase (v. 32), Ezekiel proclaims that the covenant relationship between God and the Jehoiachin Exiles continues. God is still their King, and they are His people (v. 33).	Jerusalem is judged according to her sins. Being of Canaanite origin, and following Canaanite practices, she is sentenced as adulteress and cultic-murderer: משפטי נאפות ושפכת דם "the punishment of women who commit adultery and murder" (v. 38) Echoing Leviticus 18 and 20, Jerusalem is doomed to total death within the land (vv. 35–43).
Restoration	
The covenant relationship will be reaffirmed in the wilderness of the peoples, the wilderness of the land of Egypt, before leading the entitled people of Exiles to the land of Israel (vv. 34–38).	No exile, No restoration.

Persian period (as in Ezra 9:1–2, 10–14; Nehemiah 10:29–31; 13:23–27). Ezekiel can thus be considered as the founding father of that ideological denigration.

EZEKIEL AGAINST JERUSALEM

On the basis of the de-legitimating arguments against Jerusalem already adduced, I can now widen the perspective on the whole first part of the book of Ezekiel, chapters 1–24; the spotlight is trained on the prophecies of judgment against Jerusalem with their two components: accusation and punishment. Since according to the historical circumstances the 597 B.C.E. partial exile preceded Jerusalem's destruction, what is and what should be the role of exile in determining the subsistence of the two separate Judahite communities by the first decades of the sixth century B.C.E.? The answer to this question can be found in Ezekiel's re-conception of the linear concept of exile, which essentially follows the three-step sequence of iniquity – death / destruction – exile, but adds selective prospects for restoration.

In Ezekiel's prophecies of judgment one often recognizes the prophet's distinction between the object of the prophecy and the audience to which his prophecy is addressed.[113] This distinction is of paramount importance with regard to the evaluation of the prophecies against Jerusalem.[114]

Indeed, the commissioning prophecy (1:1–3:15) names Ezekiel's audience, his fellow-Exiles, "a rebellious breed" (בית המרי, 2:5, 6, 8). The Exiles are descendents of generations of rebels against God, "They as well as their fathers have defied Me to this very day" (המה ואבותם פשעו בי עד עצם היום הזה, 2:3), and the circumstances of exile have not yet and are not expected to, change their "brazen of face and stubborn of heart" (קשי פנים וחזקי לב, 2:4). Traces of condemnation of the Exiles' ongoing disobedience are also found in Ezek 14:1–11; 20:1–32; 33:30–33. Nevertheless, throughout this first part of the book, judgment is not aimed against the Exiles.[115] Judgment in Ezekiel's prophecies focuses on Jerusalem, and to a lesser extent on the land of Israel (7:1–27), the mountains of Israel (6:1–10), and several peripheral areas in southern Judah (21:1–5, 6–10). The few prophecies of consolation which appear in the first section of the book (and throughout) focus on the community in exile (as in 17:22–24; 20:1–38, 39–44).[116]

This distinction complicates Ezekiel's message.[117] Jerusalem in Ezekiel's prophecies is the distant object of judgment, the fortunes of which the immediate

113 Another judgment prophecy outside chapters 1–24 is Ezek 33:23–29.

114 Commentators have of course discussed Ezekiel's harsh judgment over Jerusalem, but did not ascribe it to the prophet's pro-exilic polemical tendencies; see, for instance, Greenberg, *Ezekiel 1–20*, 15–7; Zimmerli, *Ezekiel 1*, 56–9.

115 Exceptions are the prophecies against the peace prophets (13:1–16); and the rebuke of the Elders of Israel in 14:1–11, which nonetheless calls them to repent (v. 6), and sets the future goal to be restoration of the covenant relationship with them (v. 11; see also 18:21–32).

116 Ezek 16:44–58 and 59–63, however, prophesy hope and restoration to Jerusalem. Though drawing on the language and literary style of vv. 1–43 (as Greenberg has shown, *Ezekiel 1–20*, 295–97), the two passages differ from the first in themes (Jerusalem's disgrace and shame in vv. 44–58; and restoration of the covenant in 59–63), in the use of metaphors for the God-people covenant (adding phraseology typical of the political-covenant metaphor to the family metaphors of 1–43, bridged over by the implicit tenor of זכר in vv. 22, 43), and even moreso in the hope expressed for Jerusalem, which contradicts vv. 1–43 and all other prophecies against Jerusalem. Therefore, chapter 16 indeed illustrates what Zimmerli called "the development of tradition in the book of Ezekiel" (*Ezekiel 1*, 334), and it further illustrates a difference between Ezekiel and later tradent generations with regards to attitudes towards Jerusalem.

117 The usual scholarly treatment of the main genres in Ezekiel has construed these distinctions

audience in exile is anxious to learn about (for instance see Ezekiel 8–11, with the *inclusio* of 8:1–3 and 11:22–24; 14:21–23; 33:21–22, 30–33). While it is reasonable to assume that during the first years in exile and certainly prior to Jerusalem's destruction, the Exiles still identify with the Jerusalemite community in the homeland, it seems that Ezekiel draws clear ideological lines to differentiate between the communities with respect to their misdeeds and thus to their fate.[118]

JERUSALEM'S GUILT

Ezekiel rebukes Jerusalem with both metaphoric and straightforward lists of sins. Disobedience to God, with idolatry as its major expression, occupies most of the prophet's attention (5:5–9; and chapter 8; as also 16, 23). Highly accentuated are moral misdeeds generalized as "lawlessness" (חמס, 7:11; 8:17), "crime" (מֻטֶּה, 9:9) and "bloodshed" (דמים, 9:9). Both spheres, the moral and the cultic, are joined in the lists of Ezek 18:1–20 and 22:1–16, and in the general term "abominations" (תועבות, 5:9; 7:3, 4, 8, 9; 9:4; 12:16; 16:2, 47, 50; 18:13, 24; 20:4; 22:2; 23:36; 33:26, 29; 36:31), which at times stands for particular transgressions committed in Jerusalem: sins of idolatry (5:11; 6:9, 11; 8:6[2x], 9, 13, 15, 17; 11:18, 21; 14:6; 16:36; 18:12; 43:8; or other cultic misconducts in 44:6–7, 13) and sexual offenses (16:22, 51, 58; 22:11). In addition, beyond the metaphoric stories of chapters 16 and 23, the emphasis on religious and moral misdeeds performed in Jerusalem and in the land of Judah / Israel is phrased with "an implied or latent personification" of the city (5:7–17; 22:1–6; 24:1–14).[119] This tendency governs the terminology of sin, which is taken from the sexual / marital spheres. Abominations are labeled with a term that designates sexual intention, "depravity" (זמה, 22:9, 11; 24:13),[120] and detested like menstrual blood, "unclean thing" (נדה, 7:19, 20; and טמאת הנדה "the impurity of a menstruous woman," 22:10; 36:17).[121] Blood occupies a major place in Jerusalem's transgressions and in the description of her state of defilement. In Ezek 16:1–43 the blood of birth appears first, then the menstrual blood, and at last the bloodshed of cultic murders in

chronologically; judgment is said to precede 586, consolation to post-date 586 B.C.E. Consequently, the few consolation prophecies within chapters 1–24 are suspected to be late and secondary. But see Joyce's criticism ("Dislocation and Adaptation," 47–49). The sociological framework I have suggested releases us from this invalid chronological categorization.

118 With this I disagree with Greenberg, *Ezekiel 1–20*, 16.

119 See Galambush, *Jerusalem*, 130–41.

120 Out of its twenty nine occurrences in the whole Bible, זמה appears thirteen times in Ezekiel, in chapters 16 and 23 and once in 22:9. Although זמה has the general meaning of "wicked plan, intention" (as in Isa 32:7; Job 31:11), its three occurrences in Leviticus refer to sexual offenses (18:17; 20:14). This legal usage is adopted by Ezekiel, and is also reflected in Jer 13:27 in parallel to נאופים, in a prophecy which uses the marital metaphor as well. S. Steingrimsson recognized Ezekiel's use of זמה to particularize Jerusalem and Judah's sins (*TDOT* IV.89–90).

121 Greenberg, *Ezekiel 1–20*, 152.

the sacrifice of sons. In Ezek 22:1–16, Jerusalem is even called "city of bloodshed" (עיר הדמים, 22:2), in reference to both cultic and social capital crimes, as well as sexual offenses (22:9–12). These diverse misdeeds provide the metaphor for the city's impurity, "defilement" (טמאה, 5:11; 22:15; 24:11, 13[2x]; 36:25, 29),[122] and all add up to her shame and disgrace (5:14, 15; 22:16),[123] Jerusalem is, then, constantly identified with the adulteress wife and the murderer of the metaphoric story of Ezek 16:1–43.

By way of comparison, neither the marital metaphor nor nearly any of these terms function in the restricted references to the Exiles' guilt or misconduct. תועבות as also the verb טמא occur in the context of idolatry (14:6, 11), and only general disobedience and materialistic profits (בצע) are specified as the offenses of Ezekiel's audience (33:31–32). Exceptions are the rhetorical questions in Ezekiel 20, which Ezekiel addresses to his generation of Exiles: "Do you *defile* yourselves as your fathers did and *go astray* after their detestable things" (הבדרך אבותיכם אתם נטמאים, ואחרי שקוציהם אתם זנים, vv. 30–31). It seems that Ezekiel purposely uses these extreme terms, which usually designate sinful Jerusalem, in order to shock his audience in exile and accentuate the absurdity of their thought (in v. 32). Nevertheless, the prophet sets a chronological distinction between the Exiles (אתם) and all earlier generations (אבותיכם). Ezekiel's generation has the opportunity and will be led by God to a change (vv. 33–38).

JERUSALEM'S PUNISHMENT

Jerusalem's capital crimes set the ground for her *talio* punishments, which together give the prophecies of judgment their primary importance in service of Theodicy. In addition, in his projections for retaliation against Jerusalem, Ezekiel presents different perspectives on the conceptual sequence of the concept of exile: iniquity-destruction-exile and restoration.

Iniquity-Destruction. In addition to the passages already discussed (16:1–43; 33:23–29), most of the prophecies of judgment against Jerusalem and Judah foresee total calamity within the land, or on its boarders (6:1–7, 11–14; 7:1–27; 11:1–13; 12:17–20; 21:1–5, 6–12, 13–22, 23–32; 22:17–22, 23–32; 23; 24:1–14). Hence, the three part sequence is fragmented, and includes only the first two. No men-

122 The verb טמא appears in reference to sexual offenses in Ezek 18:11; 22:11 and 33:26. Otherwise in Ezekiel it refers to idolatry, and has the metaphorical usage as cultic defilement (14:11; 20:7, 18, 30–31; 22:4; 36:17–18; 37:23); compare G. Andre, טמא, *TDOT* v.337–40.

123 In opposition to honor and prestige, shame and disgrace result from the woman's exposure and nakedness and thus are part of the harlot's punishment (16:37–41). This is further elaborated in the two appended passages which directly present this message using the noun כלמה (16:52, 54, 63) and the verb בוש (16:63). Curiously, the variety of nouns and verbs from the roots זנה and נאף, which dominate the language of Ezekiel 16 and 23, do not appear in other prophecies against Jerusalem. זנה, however, is addressed to the Exiles in 20:30 (see above); and 6:9.

tion is made of deportation or of the possibility of the Jerusalemites joining the Jehoiachin Exiles in Babylon. These prophecies exemplify Ezekiel's interpretation and adaptation of the Deuteronomic pre-exilic concept of exile, which understands dislocation as annihilation and does not perceive the possibility of existence outside the land of Israel (as in Deut 6:10–15; 8:19–20; 11:13–17).[124]

Iniquity-Destruction-Exile, and Death. The sign-acts in Ezek 4:1–5:4 present another variant to this concept of exile. The prophetic unit in chapters 4–5 brings together commands to symbolize the siege over Jerusalem (4:1–3, 4–8, 9–11, 16–17) and her destruction (5:1–4), intertwined with references to the existence in exile (4:12–15).[125] Struggling with what seems "heterogeneous" and thus secondary (even) to Greenberg,[126] or "a redactional conflation" of separate sign-acts according to Friebel and Block,[127] scholars have sought their ways tracking down the linear order of siege-destruction-exile in this passage, and accordingly have re-differentiated the sign-acts and their verbal interpretations from secondary expansions.[128]

Three basic sign-acts demonstrate different stages in the siege over Jerusalem: the first two commands, to incise a model of the besieged city and to set an iron griddle, resemble setting the siege and its prolongation (4:1–3); the order to eat rationed food illustrates the misery of famine in town (9–11, 16–17); and finally, shaving the hair and destroying it in three parts elucidate the city's fall and the total death of its inhabitants (5:1–4).

In Ezekiel's schematic style, the inhabitants of Jerusalem are to be divided in three groups (5:1–2). One third is to be burnt in fire within the city, the second

124 See Rom-Shiloni, "Deuteronomic Concepts" (forthcoming).

125 This division is based on the repetition of the imperative clauses ואתה (בן אדם) קח לך (4:1, 3, 9; 5:1). Accordingly, Ezek 4:4–8 as a whole is considered a secondary addition (or even amalgamation of interpretations), which according to Zimmerli may have been appended even in the prophet's life time (*Ezekiel 1*, 155, 163–65, 168). Greenberg argues for intertwining references to exile in 4:6, 12–15 (*Ezekiel 1–20*, 118; and Friebel, among others, add 5:2–4). Indeed, 4:4–8 raise tremendous interpretive difficulties which have not yet been solved (compare Greenberg, *Ezekiel 1–20*, 104–6; Zimmerli, *Ezekiel 1*, 163–64). To add another difficulty, these verses draw back to the iniquity, in contrast to the other sign-acts which all refer to the punishment. K.G. Friebel's discussion of Israel and Judah in this passage convincingly argues against Greenberg's differentiation between 390 years of iniquity, and 40 years of punishment-exile (*Jeremiah's and Ezekiel's Sign-Acts*, JSOTSup 283 [Sheffield: Sheffield Academic Press, 1999] 209–24, esp. 218–19). Unfortunately, I do not find traces of exilic circumstances in either 5:2–4 or 4:6, and thus will concentrate below only on 4:12–15 as addressed to Ezekiel's immediate audience in Babylon (contra Friebel, *Sign-Acts*, 247).

126 Greenberg, *Ezekiel 1–20*, 118; Zimmerli, *Ezekiel 1*, 154–55.

127 So Block, *Ezekiel 1–24*, 168–169; Following Friebel, *Sign-Acts*, 195–202.

128 Zimmerli (*Ezekiel 1*, 168) has argued that even the expansions could have been added by the prophet himself, and in any case the additions are not later than 547 B.C.E. (understanding the 40 days to designate 40 years of exile from 586 B.C.E. on).

will be stricken by sword all around it; the third will be scattered to the wind (והשלישית לכל רוח אזרה ;והשלשית תזרה לרוח, vv. 2, 12) and God will unsheathe a sword after them (וחרב אריק אחריהם, v. 2). Similarly, in the interpretative prophecy, 5:5–17, one third will die within the city from pestilence and famine, another shall fall by the sword around it, and the third will be scattered in every direction, and God will unsheathe the sword after them (v. 12). In both descriptions, the division into three illustrates the totality of this annihilation.[129]

The intriguing phrase is the one concerning the third part: "and scatter a third to the wind and I will unsheathe the sword after them" (והשלשית תזרה לרוח וחרב אריק אחריהם, v. 2, 10, 12; as also 12:14). זרה לרוח, which at face value describes dislocation, differs from the common agricultural imagery behind the phrase זרה בארצות (as in Ezek 6:8, 36:19). The latter, which Ezekiel uses regularly in the phraseology of exile, evokes the image of the scattering of seeds as part of sowing, and thus promises resettlement and continuity.[130] זרה לרוח, however, in Ezekiel 5 and 12 applies to the separation of the wheat from the chaff, scattering the latter to the wind as no further use or existence.[131]

Moreover, the scattered people are further doomed to be pursued to death by God, who will unsheathe the sword against them (וחרב אריק אחריהם).[132] The change into the first person with God as the agent is commonly interpreted as an intrusion of the tenor, which illustrates the clear influence on Ezekiel of Lev 26:33: "And you I will scatter among the nations, and I will unsheathe the sword against you" (ואתכם אזרה בגוים והריקתי אחריכם חרב).

Leviticus 26:27–39 describes the consequences of destruction, and includes famine (vv. 27–29, and already in v. 26), destruction of cultic places and cities (vv. 30–31), desolated land (vv. 30–32), and dispersion (v. 33). Verses 36–39 adds that even this dislocation does not bring peace to the deportees, but further fear and death:

> ולא תהיה לכם תקומה לפני איביכם. ואבדתם בגוים, ואכלה אתכם ארץ איביכם.
> והנשארים בכם ימקו בעונם בארצת איביכם[133]

129 Compare to Ezek 14:12–23 which divides the judgment into *four* terrible punishments (ארבעת שפטי הרעים): sword, famine, wild beast, and pestilence.

130 Although זרה does not occur in Isa 28:24–25, הפיץ and זרק, verbs in the semantic field of sowing, appear in the detailed description: "Does he not rather broadcast black cumin, and scatter cumin, or set wheat in a row, barley in a strip, and emmer in a patch?" (והפיץ קצח וכמון יזרק, ושם חטה שורה ושערה נסמן וכסמת גבלתו).

131 This agricultural imagery elucidates the calamity of Israel in Jer 15:7, or the fate of Israel's enemies (Isa 41:14–16; and see the realistic description in Ruth 3:2). See also Jer 13:24.

132 הריק חרב with God as agent appears also in Ezek 12:14; הריק חנית "spear" in Ps 35:3; with human agents in Ezek 28:7; 30:11; as also Exod 15:9. Compare ריק, KBL³, 1228. The sword as additional means to annihilate the deportees appears also in Jer 9:15 and Amos 9:4.

133 ימקו בעונם in Lev 26:39 according to Milgrom comes from מקק and means "rot" as in Isa 34:4; Zech 14:12; Ps 38:6; and in Rabbinic Hebrew. This negative prospect of suffering in exile occurs in Ezek 4:17; 24:23 (*Leviticus 24–27*, 2326–27).

> You shall not be able to stand your ground before your enemies, (38) but shall perish among the nations; and the land of your enemies shall consume you. (39) Those of you who survive shall rot over their iniquity in the land of your enemies.

The allusions to Leviticus 26 have led scholars to point further similarities between Ezek 5:3–4 and the remnant concept in Lev 26:40–45.[134] According to the Holiness Code's concept, a remnant of the deportees from their places in exile will repent and restore the relationship with God. Corresponding to this concept, Ezek 5:3–4 is said to foresee hope in the few who will survive the exile.[135] Yet, this interpretation cannot be accepted. The sign-act in Ezek 5:3 presents the preservation of a small amount of hair to be treasured in the prophet's skirt, and thus raises the expectation of salvation. But although hope was given to that remnant at first, v. 4 excludes every optimistic prospect. The prophet is commanded to throw some of them (the hair) to the fire, which will inflame the whole House of Israel. Hence, those few scattered survivors from Jerusalem will become dangerous to the whole House of Israel, that is, the already resettled Judean community in exile. This calamitous perspective gains further strength from its place in the context. First, in the sign-act itself, the three thirds constitute a whole and the consuming fire does not leave room for survivors. Second, the verbal interpretation in 5:5–17 follows the division into three and repeats the scattering to the wind and the unsheathed sword (v. 12), but never mentions any remnant of survivors from Jerusalem (vv. 13–17). Hence, 5:3–4 do not suggest an optimistic viewpoint on a Jerusalemite remnant in exile. On the contrary, these verses close the sign-acts with additional intensification of the forecast of Jerusalem's total annihilation.

These dramatic sign-acts describing Jerusalem from siege to fall, were expanded with a salient comment concerning the Exiles.[136] Passage 4:9–17 presents a sign-act focused on rationed food and drink under siege in Jerusalem (vv. 9–11), which is verbally interpreted in vv. 16–17.[137] In between the sign-act and its interpretation intrudes a passage which focuses on eating defiled bread among the nations (vv. 12–15).[138]

This expansion (vv. 12–15) does not accord the surrounding sign-acts. First,

134 For the clear allusions of Ezekiel 4–5 to Leviticus 26, see Greenberg, *Ezekiel 1–20*, 109; Block, *Ezekiel 1–24*, 194; and Milgrom, *Leviticus 23–27*, 2348–52.

135 So Friebel. *Sign-Acts*, 241–42; Block, *Ezekiel 1–24*, 194–95; and Greenberg, while accepting that the verses prophesy calamity, based on מהם still talks about preservation of a remnant which will continue to suffer persecution in Exiles (*Ezekiel 1–20*, 108–9 and 126).

136 See note 125 above.

137 4:9–11 continues the situation of siege, as they apply to circumstances where the prophet still lies on his side for three hundred and ninety days (v. 9b and see v. 5). Compare Friebel, *Sign-Acts*, 224–26.

138 See Friebel, *Sign-Acts*, 199–200.

it does not continue the line of rationed food supplies during siege, but rather introduces a different issue altogether. Second, it clearly has no relevance to Jerusalem, and does not contribute to the logical development in the sign-acts referring to its siege and calamity. Rather, the dialogue starts with a command to eat a "barley cake" (עגת שערים) baked over human excrement (בגללי צאת האדם, v. 12). This is explained as a symbol to the unclean (טמא) bread the Exiles will eat among the peoples (v. 13). The prophet arises to protest, claiming he has never been defiled (v. 14). Since Ezekiel has already been at least five years in exile, this comment is of particular interest. In addition, Ezekiel does not restrict himself to bread, and talks of eating meat.[139] In reply God changes the human excrement to cow's dung (צפיעי הבקר), over which the prophet is then allowed to prepare his bread (ועשית את לחמך עליהם, v. 15). The dialogue which starts with clear denigration of exilic circumstances, reaches through Ezekiel's protest a point of compromise.[140] This divine concession is of paramount importance for the ongoing daily life of the Exiles as the people of God, since it contrasts the accepted concept of exile known, for instance, from Hos 9:3, and replaces it with a divine approval.[141] Yet, in its present context, this message is almost implicit, as vv. 16–17 change the geographic setting again, and return to Jerusalem. The city is doomed to suffer famine – lack of bread and water, to continue to be reduced until the inhabitants suffer its total absence, and starve death, "they shall stare at each other, heartsick over their iniquity" (ונשמו איש ואחיו ונמקו בעונם, v. 17).[142]

To conclude, in a fairly pessimistic perspective, chapters 4–5 perceive both the siege over Jerusalem and the exile as long term punishments justified by the people's sins.[143] Jerusalem's misery is beyond encouragement, the siege will end in famine and in total death of its inhabitants in the city or on its surroundings. In the sequence iniquity-destruction-exile and restoration, Jerusalem

139 Friebel explains the jump from eating a barley cake baked on human excrement to eating unclean meat of נבלה וטרפה as an analogical expansion of "derived uncleaness" and not as inherent (*Sign-Acts*, 249).

140 Zimmerli raises the question whether v. 15 should be understood as part of the general declarations of the sign-acts or only as a personal concession, and indeed takes the former option (*Ezekiel 1*, 171). Amazingly, the positive compromise and the general comforting message it holds for the Exiles was overlooked by scholars, who in interpreting this sign-act did not refer to the significant point that Ezekiel, while being in exile, confesses for not ever eating defiled food. It seems that 4:12–15 should add to other examples of adaptation to living in exile (diaspora) which Joyce has pointed out ("Dislocation and Adaptation," 56–58).

141 The concept that the exilic arena includes eating defiled food is reflected also in Dan 1:8; in addition to general references to foreign lands as defiled in Josh 22:19; Amos 7:17.

142 Translation by Greenberg, *Ezekiel 1–20*, 99.

143 This general statement is not to cover over the interpretive difficulties in the phrase נשא עון and the years 390 and 40 for the House of Israel and that of Judah respectively. For נשא עון, see Zimmerli, *Ezekiel 1*, 164; and for differentiating the meaning of iniquity and punishment between Israel and Judah, see Greenberg, *Ezekiel 1–20*, 105; Block, *Ezekiel 1–24*, 176–79.

according to Ezekiel 4–5 is to suffer immensely through its destruction, and the minor survivors that will be dispersed to the wind will suffer further calamity. Exile, thus, still means annihilation to this community. In contrast, 4:12–15 establishes the prophet as mediator between God and the Exiles' community to which Ezekiel belongs, that is, the Jehoiachin Exiles, to find a solution that will normalize life for them away from God's land.

This differentiation of fates, shown through the juxtaposed and implicitly reversed sign-acts, suggests that Ezekiel (or his tradents) further interprets Leviticus 26. The prophet (or his tradents) seems to be aware of the juxtaposition of Lev 26:33–39 and vv. 40–45.[144] Despite the contextual proximity of the two different fortunes foreseen to the expelled, Ezekiel distinguishes them sociologically, and thus differentiates between two modes of existence in exile. The first declines to annihilation (vv. 33–39), which in the prophet's view concerns Those Who Remained in Jerusalem till its destruction in 586 B.C.E. The second promises resettlement and restoration of life in exile (vv. 40–45), accompanied by the necessary practical and ideological changes that the prophet helps to phrase. Hence, the traditional sequence iniquity-destruction-exile and finally restoration is not automatically applied. Just as exile can mean annihilation for Those Who Remained, it can signify continuation and restoration to the Jehoiachin Exiles.[145]

Looking at these chapters from the perspective of the internal conflict between the communities illuminates yet a further rhetorical technique that Ezekiel uses time and again in chapters 1–24 of intertwining and juxtaposing prophecies against Jerusalem with comments or complete passages of hope to the Exiles.[146]

Iniquity-Destruction-Exile, yet Exclusion. In contrast to Ezekiel's tendency to negate the existence, beyond 586 B.C.E., of Those Who Remained in Jerusalem,

144 Milgrom has shown that in parallel to the five units of blessings in 26:3–13, vv. 27–39 close a five unit pattern of curses ordered in increasing severity (*Leviticus 23–27*, 2287–90, 2304); This literary argument leads up to the thematic change in vv. 40–45, with the Exiles' confession of sins, and God's response in promises of restoration. Hence, form and content establish the secondary appendix nature of these verses of consolation (*Leviticus 23–27*, 2329–30). Furthermore, Milgrom has convincingly argued that Ezekiel knew MT Lev 26:3–39.

145 Ezek 22:13–16, which prophesies exile for the Jerusalemites, is considered a secondary addition by the prophet or his school (Zimmerli, *Ezekiel 1*, 455, 459). Another argument for its secondary character is the prospect of exile to Jerusalem, and not annihilation within, as in Ezek 5:1–17; 16:1–43. Yet, it still accords Ezekiel's perspective, which sees further calamity in exile, and certainly does not accept the 586 Exiles to the previous community.

146 Other examples are the editing of chapters 8–11, and specifically the two disputations in 11:1–13 versus 14–21; and also 6:1–7, 11–14 and the intertwining of vv. 8–10 referring to hope in a remnant in exile.

the prophet does present several prophecies in which survivors from Jerusalem reach the community in Babylon. Ezek 12:15–16 and 14:21–23 give a didactic mission to those survivors from Jerusalem, which are designated as a minor number of people (אנשי מספר, 12:6) or survivors of sons and daughters (פלטה המוצאים בנים ובנות, 14:22). In the first passage they are to tell their abominations in the nations (12:16). The second configures the refugees as object-lessons for the Exiles, such that the account of the survivors' ways and deeds will console them, showing them that the survivors have been properly and justifiably punished (14:22–23).[147]

Although in opposition to Ezekiel's prophecies for Jerusalem's total annihilation, these two prophecies uphold the Jehoiachin Exiles' superiority. Even after 586 B.C.E. and in the setting of exile, the Jerusalemite survivors are clearly marked and denigrated as the continuous reminder of Jerusalem's iniquities. These passages indicate the enduring hostility and certainly the patronistic view of the Exiles, accentuating the distinctions in prestige and rank between the Judean communities (as presented above in Ezek 11:14–21; 33:23–29 etc).

Contemplating this perspective to the sequence iniquity-destruction-exile and restoration, this line of thought recognizes the existence of survivors from Jerusalem in Babylon after 586, but does not legitimate their integration into the community of the Jehoiachin Exiles. This remarkable sectarian attitude exemplifies the severity of the conflict between the two Judean communities. In Ezekiel's evaluation of exile, the linear sequence applies only to Jerusalem. Being in exile prior to Jerusalem's destruction, the 597 B.C.E. Exiles are not counted among the community that will suffer destruction, expulsion and further death. Thus Ezekiel transfers the focus of his audience of fellow-Exiles from Jerusalem to their own community in exile. Restoration is confined to the Jehoiachin Exiles (as explicit in Ezek 11:14–21; 20:1–38).

THE DESOLATED LAND OF JUDAH

One repeated component in Ezekiel's prophecies of judgment against Jerusalem is the portrait of the damage executed on the ecological substance of the land, which adds to the fatal blows aimed at the population of Judah. Ezekiel prophesies that the land will become empty of man and beast (והכרתי ממנה אדם ובהמה, 14:13, 17, 19). The destruction of the urban and the agricultural life will bring wild beasts to occupy the ruins and thus hasten its desolation (והיתה שממה מבלי עובר מפני החיה "and it became a desolation with none passing through it because of the beasts," v. 15). Desertion and desolation in both rural and peripheral areas is the projection with which Ezekiel concludes several of his prophecies against Jerusalem and the land of Israel (Ezek 6:14; 12:19–20; 15:8; 21:1–5; 33:28–29; as also 38:8).

147 So Zimmerli, *Ezekiel 1*, 312–13; Block, *Ezekiel 1–24*, 451.

This description further influences Ezekiel in illustrating restoration in the land. The empty desolate mountains of Israel will revive in preparation for accepting the gathered Exiles, who are called "My people Israel" (עמי ישראל, 36:5–12). No mention at all is made to an existence of Those Who Remained in the land throughout the exile. The annihilation of man, beast and the land itself designates a definite and total end to one era, and prepares the ground for the restoration of the Exiles in the days to come.[148] These prophecies exemplify the extreme degree of Ezekiel's transfer of exclusive significance to the community in exile. The prophet not only excludes the Jerusalemite community, but further intensifies this exclusion through the emphasis on the uninhabited desolation of that land.

The theme of the empty land, which has its origin in descriptions of total destruction brought by God / the gods in biblical and Mesopotamian sources alike, is utilized in Ezekiel's message as a rhetorical argument in the disputation between the communities.[149] Without further delving into the scholarly debate over the theme of the empty land in the exilic and post-exilic literatures, suffice it to say that Ezekiel can be identified as one of the first advocates of this ideology, already by the very early years of the sixth century.[150]

JUXTAPOSITION OF THE CONTRASTING FATES

The socio-ideological transfer from Jerusalem to Babylon is implicitly illustrated also by using the literary technique of juxtaposition in several prophecies in chapters 1–24. As presented above, Ezekiel 11 (or even 8–11 as a whole) with its two disputations is one example, another is Ezekiel 24 which ends the first part of the book.[151] After the horrific judgment on "the city of blood" in 24:1–14, the

148 Transformation in the ecological state of the land from destruction to restoration appears also in Jer 32:42–44; 33:10–11, 12–13.

149 Desolation of the landscape functions as a common motif in biblical descriptions of destructions. See for instance Ezekiel's prophecies against the nations (Ezek 25:5, 13; 35:3–4, 7–9), and regularly in Jeremiah's prophecies of judgment against Israel and the nations (as in Jer 9:9–11; 51:26, 62); as well as in Lamentations (Lam 1:7; 2:15, 16; 5:18). This motif is well attested in the lists of curses in neo-Assyrian political treaties (compare Hillers, *Treaty Curses*), and in the Mesopotamian lament literature over the destruction of cities and temples, compare F.W. Dobbs-Allsopp, *Weep, O Daughter of Zion: A Study of the City-Lament Genre in the Hebrew Bible*, BibOr 44 (Rome: Editrica Pontificio Instituto Biblico, 1993) 66–72; P. Michalowski, *The Lamentation over the Destruction of Sumer and Ur* (Winona Lake, Ind.: Eisenbrauns, 1989) lines 300–330.

150 Ezekiel's polemical use of this motif in this conflict stands against R.P. Carroll's late date for the ideological contention he finds over the theme of the empty land, compare "The Myth of the Empty Land," *Semeia* 59 (1992) 79–93; and H.M. Barstad, *The Myth of the Empty Land: A Study in the History and Archaeology of Judah During the "Exilic" Period*, SO Fasc. Suppl. XXVIII (Oslo: Scandinavian Univ. Press, 1996).

151 Juxtapositions or intertwining of passages with the same intention occur further in 6:1–7, 11–14 and the intertwining of vv. 8–10 referring to hope in a remnant in exile; 4:12–15 in the sign-acts

prophet's clear differentiation between the communities reaches its apex, in the most painful sign-act the prophet is commanded to take, Ezek 24:15–27.[152] The prohibition to mourn his wife, the delight of his eyes, and Ezekiel's exact implementation of that command, establish Ezekiel as a portent for the Exiles (והיה יחזקאל לכם למופת, vv. 24 and 27). The delight of their eyes and the desire of their hearts is God's Temple in Jerusalem, their pride and glory (גאון עזכם, v. 21). The Exiles are not to mourn its physical destruction, nor the death of sons and daughters in Jerusalem (v. 25; compare 14:21–23). The prohibition against mourning the homeland community designates the Exiles' final separation of the Jerusalem community, as Margaret Odell says in characterizing mourning:[153]

> ... the act of mourning appears to have little to do with the expression of grief; rather, it is concerned with establishing and severing ties between the living and the dead. Prohibitions against mourning reflect an attempt to dissociate from the deceased.

Indeed, this passage completes the prophecies of judgment in Ezekiel with the clearest message regarding Jerusalem's death versus the ongoing life of the Exiles. They, the Jehoiachin Exiles, are the living remnant of the people of God, and none other.

Ezekiel's negative attitude towards Jerusalem is further accentuated by the disappearance of Jerusalem from the prophets' future message of consolation. Jerusalem is not mentioned in the second unit of the book, chapters 25 and on,[154] and restoration is restricted on the one hand to the scattered people (chapters 34; 36–37) and on the other to the desolated mountains of Israel which will revitalize with the return of the people of God (36:1–15).

Summary and Conclusion

To close this discussion, reference should be made to the factors that may have motivated Ezekiel to establish this binary relationship between the two

---

of chapters 4–5 which focus on Jerusalem from siege to fall, and not on exile. Kasher suggests this same juxtaposition in 33:23–29 and vv. 30–33 (*Ezekiel 25–48*, 641).

152 D. Block emphasized the anti-Jereusalemite perspective of 24:1–14, suggesting it is an "unannounced disputation address" in which Ezekiel refutes the Jerusalemites' sense of superiority based on the fact that they remained in the inviolable city ("Ezekiel's Boiling Cauldron: A Form-Critical Solution to Ezekiel XXIV 1–14," *VT* 41 (1991) 12–37; as also in his commentary: *Ezekiel 1–24*, 769–83, followed by a discussion of 24:15–27, there pp. 785–94).

153 M. S. Odell, "Genre and Persona in Ezekiel 24:15–24," *The Book of Ezekiel: Theological and Anthropological Perspectives*, eds. M. S. Odell and J. T. Strong, SBLSymS 9 (Atlanta: SBL, 2000) 195–220, quotation from 201. Compare to Block who suggested that the refrain from mourning designates the Exiles' recognition of "the dawn of a new age" (*Ezekiel 1–24*, 794).

154 One exception is Ezek 36:38 where the memory of Jerusalem's past is mentioned.

Judahite sister-communities, which were forcibly separated by the Babylonian policy of exile in 597 B.C.E.

Ezekiel's intensive reference to Jerusalem and its fate is, first of all, a response to his immediate audience in exile. During the first years of dislocation before the city's destruction, the Exiles express interest and concern regarding their homeland, the city of God, the Temple, and the fortunes of their fellow Judahites (as can be gathered for instance from Ezek 24:15–27; and see also Psalm 137). The prophet in reply builds the ideological separation between the communities.

In addition, the severe prophecies of judgment against Jerusalem hold a central position in Ezekiel's theology. The prophet justifies God in His measures against Jerusalem, declaring that the city's punishments accord her sins. Thus, theodicial arguments motivate Jerusalem's condemnation.

Beyond all that, I believe, Ezekiel understands the ideological demand to redefine the religious-national identity of the Exiles. The prophet had to reconcile well-known and cherished Pentateuchal conceptions of land and exile with the partial exile which took place eleven years prior to the destruction of Jerusalem. If Deuteronomic and Priestly traditional concepts had remained unaltered, the historical circumstances would have endangered the existence of the Jehoiachin Exiles. As the inhabitants of Jerusalem had claimed, the Exiles could have been doomed to annihilation (Ezek 11:15; 33:24 as also Jer 22:24–30).

From the disadvantageous situation of expulsion, Ezekiel arises with a competing agenda, through which he builds a distinct identity for the Jehoiachin Exiles as the exclusive community of the people of God. By establishing legitimating arguments in support of his fellow Exiles and de-legitimating arguments against Those Who Remained in Jerusalem, Ezekiel constitutes an exilic ideology which enables continuity of national existence in exile and promises restoration to the Exiles.

Ezekiel's main strategy of division is his reliance on past historical and legal traditions from the Pentateuch, which are presumably known to his fellow Exiles. Ezekiel sets his arguments on solid ground, as he presents innovative perspectives which are all rooted in Israel's past. This explains his immediate influence on his contemporaries, and his ongoing impact on the exilic community, as this may be seen in the prophecy and historiographic literature of the late sixth and fifth centuries B.C.E.

To summarize Ezekiel's major contribution for generations that followed, I will highlight the arguments that comprise Ezekiel's concept of exile and his observations on the exclusive status of the exilic community.

Past Traditions. Legitimation of the Exiles rests on the Exodus traditions concerning God's constitution of covenant relationship with His people in Egypt, away from the land of Israel. The exilic arena is in fact an advantageous context for future restoration of the covenant (Ezek 20:1–38). This in turn accounts for the centrality of the Exodus traditions in the exilic literature, for instance in Deutero-Isaiah.

De-legitimation of Those Who Remained is based upon equating them with the "People of the Land" alluded to in the Settlement traditions and invoking the general legal demands to keep away from the Canaanite peoples. Ezekiel dwells on Those Who Remained's supposed ongoing adherence to despised local abominations (Ezek 16:1–43), to suggest that their existence in the land of Israel will end in expulsion and annihilation, in accordance with the conception of the Holiness Code (Lev 18:24–30 and 20:22–24). This tactic of categorizing Those Who Remained as of foreign (Canaanite) origin appears in Ezra-Nehemiah's denigrations of the local community in Yehud.

Present status. Ezekiel differentiates between the communities with respect to their religious and moral qualities in various ways. The Jerusalem community trespasses capital offenses, both religious and moral, which determine their doom, total calamity, according to both Deuteronomic and Priestly/Holiness Code's legal traditions. At the same time, concentrating on Jerusalem's offenses alleviates the burden from the Exiles. Since Ezekiel does not consider the Exiles obedient or virtuous, Jerusalem's present sins serve as a warning for the Exiles (14:1–11 and implicitly, Ezek 18:1–20). By comparison with the community in Jerusalem, the Exiles enjoy higher prestige. As a community they are certainly not doomed to annihilation (14:11).

Future Prospects. Passages of hope within chapters 1–24, as well as the prophecies of consolation (chapters 34–37), express the legitimation of the Exiles as the future restored community. The God-people relationship will resume in exile (20:32–38). God's dynamic presence will constantly escort the Exiles (11:16). In the future restoration God will gather them again into the land of Israel, their land (11:17), and transform their hearts to promise eternal obedience (11:18; 36:26–27). The covenant formula which constituted the covenant relationship between God and the Sons of Israel (Lev 26:11; Deut 26:17), will apply to *this* community of Exiles (11:20; 36:28; and 34:30).

The prospects of the Exiles' restoration in the land correspond to several prophecies of judgment against Jerusalem and Judah, in the description of the desolation of cities and land (as in 6:11–14). Hence, the idea that the land lays barren and awaits the returnees is already part of Ezekiel's message to his community of Exiles (36:4–15).

In opposition, de-legitimation of Those Who Remained in Jerusalem brings Ezekiel to adapt the linear sequence of iniquity-destruction-exile and restoration in the concept of exile as presented in the Pentateuchal legal codices. But

Ezekiel either cuts the sequence, perceiving the Jerusalemites' catastrophe as involving neither exile, nor survivors (as in 5:1–17); or treats refugees from Jerusalem as further doomed to complete annihilation (5:1–4). In any case, survivors of the 586 destruction will not join the Exiles in Babylon (12:15–16; 14:21–23). Hence, Ezekiel holds to his separatist exclusive perspectives against Jerusalem both before its destruction and in the aftermath of the disaster. No reconciliation is offered to those few refugees of the past sister community.

Ezekiel's sociological identification with the Jehoiachin Exiles has brought the prophet to set clear ideological distinctions between the two Judahite communities. With his rhetorical skills and his innovative adaptations of Pentateuchal traditions to accommodate the complicated reality of his time, Ezekiel has established himself as the first major speaker for the Exiles in Babylon.

This study was written with the help of the "Dorot" Foundation and the Hebrew Union College – Jewish Institute of Religion, Jerusalem, who sponsored my post-doctoral fellowship over the years 2002–4. My mother, Yael Rom ז"ל, was the first to read this study and had raised insightful comments. This paper is dedicated to her with appreciation and love.

Siqoriqin
Forfeited Land

MOSHE GIL
Tel Aviv University

The article deals with the term *sīqorīqīn*, which was understood as derived from *sica*, a dagger, and describing those extremist zealots, the *sicarii*, who, in the words of Josephus, carried short daggers, with which they stabbed their enemies. This was the view of Grätz and others. Elbogen, in 1925, sought another explanation, and was followed by Feist and others, who sought to understand the term against the background of agrarian matters discussed in talmudic literature, mainly in the Mishnah and Tosefta, and in the Talmud of the Land of Israel, where this term appears.

After an overview of the talmudic sources, I looked into the background of the term (the correct pronunciation of which I discuss in note 36), in the framework of the legal status of land owned by absentees, both in Jewish and non-Jewish law. Comparing and contrasting the talmudic sources with sources from Roman law, as well as with epigraphic and papyrological evidence, inclusive of some documents from the Judaean Desert, I arrived at the conclusion that the term is derived from a Greek word describing the *cessio bonorum*, the transfer of property. This term and the legal procedures behind it were of tremendous significance in the days that followed the Bar Kokhba revolt; the *sīqorīqīn* meant an agreement signed by the absentee regarding a compromise enforced by the Jewish courts.

The political upheavals in the Land of Israel, the great revolt as well as the Bar Kokhba revolt, Roman oppression and the struggle against the occupier, greatly impacted the country's agrarian condition. Many land owners and tenants were killed or fled, and for generations afterwards problems arose regarding the new owners and tenants who had replaced their predecessors, especially: the ownership and right of possession that had to be defined so as to protect the new cultivators against legal suits. Thus was birthed the *sīqorīqīn* law. Information regarding the *sīqorīqīn* and attendant laws, may be found in a number of places in the talmudic sources.

From many places in the sources we get the impression that the *sīqorīqīn* were a type of people whose land ownership had no halakhic validity; they did not present the first fruits (*bikkurim*) at the Temple. We shall see, however, that the term under discussion was not the name of a group of people but of a legal matter.

The Tosefta says: Why do they not offer [the first fruits]? Because it is written: "The first of the first-fruits of thy land" (Exodus 23:19, 34:26) – meaning that all the crops are to be from *your* land. Neither do the land tenants, the share-croppers, the *sīqorīqīn*, nor the land-robbers, present [first fruits] for the same reason, for it is written: "The first of the first-fruits of *thy* land."[1] However, their *t'ruma* (one percent of the harvest – for the priests) is acknowledged as also their tithes and their consecration.[2]

There are three main fragments on the *sīqorīqīn*:

FRAGMENT A, THE MISHNAH

> There was no *sīqorīqīn* in Judaea regarding those killed in the war; after the matter of those killed in the war there was *sīqorīqīn*. How is that? He who bought from the *sīqorīqīn*, and then bought again, from the owner – his (first) purchase is void; if he bought from the owner and then bought again from the *sīqorīqīn* – his (first) purchase is valid; if he bought from the man and then bought again from the woman – his purchase is void; if he bought from the woman and then bought again from the man – his purchase is valid. This is the first Mishnah. The later court said: he who bought from the *sīqorīqīn* gives the owners a fourth. When is that? When they (the owners) are not able to purchase, but if they are able to purchase they have precedent over all others. Rabbi convened a court and they voted that if it (the land) was in a state of *sīqorīqīn* twelve months – whoever is the first to buy gets it (the land), but he gives the owners a fourth.

FRAGMENT B, THE TALMUD OF THE LAND OF ISRAEL

> There was no *sīqorīqīn* in Judaea, etc. At first a destruction was decreed on Judaea because they (the Romans) had a tradition from their forbears that Judah killed Esau as is stated "thy land shall be in the neck of thine enemies" (Genesis 49:8). And they kept enslaving them, expropriating their fields and selling them to others; then the owners would come and seize them, whereas the country was completely held under *sīqorīqīn*. Then people avoided buying (land), so they (the courts) disposed to abolish the *sīqorīqīn* in Judaea. Who was intended? Those killed before the war and during the war; but those killed after the war are under no *sīqorīqīn*. But is there any difference between people killed before the war and people killed after the war? The answer is that the *sīqorīqīn* was imposed, and there was robbery (of land) and lawlessness and there was no time to write legal deeds. Therefore the (law of) *sīqorīqīn* was imposed on every-

1 *M.Bik.* 1:2, 2:2. *Mekhīltā deR. Ishmael, Mishpaṭīm*, 20 (Horovitz and Rabin, 335); *Sifre debe rav, Ki tavo*, 297 (Ish Shalom, 127b; Finkelstein, 317). The transcript *sīqorīqīn* is used throughout this article; see pp. 14f. below, and n. 36.

2 *T.Ter.* 1:6.

body so that justice should be universal. In Galilee there has always been a law of *sīqorīqīn*. It was taught (by Sages of the Mishnah): whoever have been share-croppers for generations are not affected by *sīqorīqīn*; (also) whoever was displaced because of debts or because of taxes, is not eligible for *sīqorīqīn*.

FRAGMENT C, THE TOSEFTA

The land of Judaea did not have (the law of) *sīqorīqīn* (for) the repopulation of the country (*Yiššuv hamedina*); to what extent is it true? (only) concerning people killed before the war; but as concerns people killed during the war and thereafter it has (the law of) *sīqorīqīn*: if one buys from the *sīqorīqīn* and buys again from the owner, the purchase is valid; if one buys from the owner and buys again from the *sīqorīqīn*, the purchase is void. If the owner wrote him a deed his purchase is valid. This was the first rule of the Mishnah; (but) our Sages said: let him buy without impediment (only) let him give the owners one fourth in land (or) one fourth in money; the owners have precedence: if they are able to buy they should be before anybody. Rabbi has convoked a court, where it was voted that if (the land) has been under *sīqorīqīn* for twelve months, any first buyer will give the owners a quarter in land or a quarter in money, while the owners have precedence; if they are able to buy they are before anybody. The *sīqorīqīn* does not apply to share-croppers, tenants, nor movable goods. The *sīqorīqīn* does not apply when one was removed because of a debt, or taxes; as to taxes alone, one has to wait for the owners twelve months.[3]

Let us attempt to interpret these somewhat enigmatic texts. Fragment A of the Mishnah states a number of facts: the purchase, usually carried out from the owner, is now also possible from the *sīqorīqīn*; the owners have precedence over the *sīqorīqīn*, and – as a matter of course – have it over their wives. The rules refer to the period after the revolt, that is, that of Bar Kokhba. If the *sīqorīqīn* ownership of the land extends beyond one year, the purchase is to be done "with them"; be that as it may, if the original owners are known they are entitled, according to the ruling of the court of Rabbi, to a fourth of the payment.

Fragment B of the *Yerushalmi* adds some details: a process of land expropriation was perpetrated by the rulers. However (on the basis of the well-known imperial policy of seeing to it that every parcel of land be cultivated, produce a crop and be levied), the government would sell the expropriated land. This

3 *M.Giṭ.* 5:1–2. *y.Giṭ.* 5:47b (Jer. 1076f.; this abbreviation refers to the new Jerusalem edition of the Talmud of the Land of Israel); *b.Giṭ.* 44a, 45b; *t.Giṭ.* 5:1–2. *Yiššuv hamedina*; see a similar meaning in the words of R. Yoḥanan, *y.B.Bat.* 2:13c (Jer. 1242).

aroused opposition among the original owners. The phenomenon existed before the revolt as well, but was vastly expanded afterwards, when the regulation was made whereby the owners were entitled to a fourth of the payment, with the regulation applying to all expropriated land, whether ante- or post-revolt. This regulation existed in Galilee even before the revolt and was extended to the land of Judaea. The families of regular share-croppers ("from generations") were exempt from the quarter payment. However, the owners could not demand that compensation if they lost their land because of debt, including a tax debt.

Fragment C of the Tosefta emphasizes the priority of the owners, who "if they are able to buy they should be before anybody."

ABSENTEES AND THEIR LANDS

It seems to me that in order to understand the background of the *sīqorīqīn* issue one should see the way Roman and other legal sources deal with two problems: that of the absentees and that of uncultivated land. The regime was interested in all the land being worked. Contemporary research affords us an understanding of the empire's policy in this area. There are inscriptions, especially from the area of Tunisia, two of which are of particular interest. The first, of the time of Trajan, about A.D. 116–17, contains a permit granted by the governors to work derelict state land, according to principles of what was known as *lex Manciana*; the other is of a similar issue that is based on this law and also on another one, which is actually from the time of the matter we are dealing with, the *lex Hadriana de rudibus agris*. The inscriptions relate to a plan to expand agricultural production and the ensuing legal problems.

The main workforce employed in the agricultural units established in the area where the inscriptions were found, the Majarda valley, was composed of tenants, the *coloni*. Therein we find the duty of the tenant to hand over to the owner a third of the wheat or barley crop with different quotas for other crops. The tenants have the right of bequeathing to children born from legal marriages (*e legitimis matrimoniis*).[4]

Regarding the absentees, Roman law developed the view, "if more than ten years have passed the right (of the prior owners) is annulled"; however, if the

4 See details on the two inscriptions with similar contents and on the region in which they were placed, in: Dennis P. Kehoe, *The Economics of Agriculture in Roman Imperial Estates in North Africa* (Göttingen: Vandenhoek, 1988) 185; see Roth Clausing, *The Roman Colonate* (repr.; New York: Columbia Univ., 1925) 215; Michael I. Rostovtzev, *Studien zur Geschichte des römischen Kolonates* (Leipzig: Teubner, 1910) 313–41, in the fourth chapter, which deals with matters of Roman rule in Africa, has a thorough analysis of the inscription. See also: Michael I. Rostovtzev, *Geschichte der Staatspacht* (Leipzig: Teubner, 1902) 436–39, about the Manciana; it was named after T. Curtilius Mancia, who was consul in A.D. 55; see Kehoe, *Economics*, 48–51.

absentee and the receiver of his land "are each one in a different province, then it is a case of negotiations between *absentees*, and a special rule will apply, [that of] 20 years."[5]

A similar distinction concerning the right of possession of the absentee's property is also in the Jewish sources, with the difference we saw above between Judaea and Galilee, as is also found in the Mishnah: "if he was in Judaea and claimed possession in Galilee, or was in Galilee and claimed possession in Judaea, he has no right of possession, unless he was with the opponent in the [same] state."[6] We find it also in the statement of R. Eleazar: "Even in the case of two *euthēnias* such as Š'lomi and N'viro, which the Jordan divides from each other, and the man stands there and sees the man who took possession of his field, which is his property, he cannot claim his possession rights as long as they are not in the same city and the same state."[7]

LAWS OF THE RIGHT OF POSSESSION

In the rules regarding the *sīqorīqīn*, one should therefore be cognizant of the echoes of the emergency period right after the revolt, and the effort to arrange special, but uniform, conditions for Judaea and Galilee with regard to obtaining the right of possession; we have seen that the right of acquiring possession was reduced to a minimum, to twelve months; this is in contrast to the usually accepted time period of three years that we see in the statements of R. Ishmael and R. Akiva, and the Sages: "until there are three date harvests, three grape harvests and three olive harvests."[8]

It would appear that the term *sīqorīqīn* belongs to the time after the Bar Kokhba revolt, when the shortened period for the right of possession became entrenched. R. Judah bar Ilai, and also R. Ishmael ben Yossi adopted the opinion that the right of possession was acquired after one year, or that it was even immediate.[9] According to the *lex Hadriana* mentioned above, all areas not

5 See *Codex Justinianus*, 7.33.12.

6 *M.B.Bat.* 3:2; the text has *'vṭynyh*.

7 *Y.B.Bat.* 3.14a, (Jer. 1244); the meaning is: district, from εὐθηνία which in Latin is *annona*, and there seems to have been a division of the districts, named according to the collection centers of this tax. N'viro, perhaps Nimre or Nimrin, today Tall Nimrin, in Jordan, with Š'lomi on the opposite, western bank of the Jordan, probably in the vicinity of Jericho. See Samuel Klein, *Sefer ha-yishuv* (Jerusalem: Mosad Bialik, 1939) 108, 155, whose explanation for *'vṭynyh* is "autonomy."

8 *M.B.Meṣ.* 3:1; *t.B.Bat.* 2:7; *b.B.Bat.* 36b.

9 *B.B.Bat.* 41a, and see Rafael N. Rabbinovicz, *Diqduqei sof'rim* (Munich: Roesl, 1897) ad loc. In Hellenistic Egypt, a period of two to three years was required as proof of *possessio*; see Raphael Taubenschlag, *Law of Gr.-Rom. Egypt* (Warszawa: Panstwowe Wydown. Naukowe, 1955) 244. Compare also the chapter on *ḥezqat hašanim* in Asher Gulak, *L'ḥeqer hamišpaṭ haᶜivri bit'qufat hatalmud* (Jerusalem: Iunovich, 1928/29) 95–108; see Daniel Sperber, *Roman Palestine 200–400, the Land* (Ramat Gan: Bar-Ilan Univ., 1978) 100f.

cultivated or derelict for two years would be free to all comers, with the lessee benefiting from the full rights of the *possessio*.[10]

IN RESEARCH

Grätz's study, "das Sikarikongesetz," was published a year after his death.[11] The main idea was an etymological connection between *sīqorīqīn* and *sicarii*. A year later, 1893, Rosenthal's article[12] elaborating on that of Grätz appeared; according to him, the *sīqorīqīn* law was an ancient *halakhah* meant as protection against strong-arm operators. In 1925, Elbogen's article appeared,[13] which argued that the law had nothing do to with the *sicarii*, but with people who held lands granted them by the Roman regime, and that the law required them to reach a compromise with the previous owners. In 1927, Feist's article appeared[14] with the novel argument that the term was not Roman but Greek, and derived from συγκρίνω (to adjudicate a law), even though he noted that the transition from *synkrinon* to *synkrikon* was hard to explain, for why would the additional *k* appear?

Gulak[15] suggested solving the problem with the term κῆρυξ (a herald) speculating that there was an expression: σὺν κήρυκι (with a herald) as in μισθῶσαι ὑπὸ κήρυκα, or πρᾶσις ὑπὸ κήρυκι which may be found in Greek law, meaning to publicly announce, accompanied by a clarion call. The term usually used for the above action is: προκηρικεύομαι, προκηρύσσω.[16]

Safrai,[17] in his article סיקריקון, argued that the origin of the term was in the punishments meted out to Jews who circumcised their sons, who would be

10 Clausing, *Roman Colonate*, 181f., and see his discussion on the Hadriana, 149ff.

11 See the article of Heinrich Grätz, "Das Sikarikon-Gesetz," in *Jahresbericht des jüdisch-theologischen Seminars* (Breslau: Schlesische Buchdrukerei, 1892) 3–18; Grätz, *Geschichte der Juden* (11 vols.; Leipzig: Leiner, 1908) 4:390f.

12 Ferdinand Rosenthal, "Das Sikarikongesetz," *MGWJ* 37 (1893) 1–16, 56–63, 105–10.

13 Ismar Elbogen, "סיקריקון," *MGWJ* 69 (1925) 249–57.

14 Sigmund Feist, "Zur Etymologie von סיקריקון," *MGWJ* 71 (1927) 138–41; the etymology of non-Hebrew corresponding terms should be sought in Greek rather than in Latin, as Greek was the language used more often among Jews, inclusive of the rural population; regarding this see: Baruch Lifshitz, "Papyrus grecs du désert de Juda," *Aeg* 42 (1962) 240–56.

15 Asher Gulak, "סיקריקון," *Tarbiz* 5 (1934) 23–27.

16 Henry G. Liddell and Robert Scott, *A Greek-English Dictionary* (Oxford: Clarendon, 1968) *s.v.*; Rostovtzev, *Studien*, 313, 334.

17 Shmuel Safrai, "סיקריקון," *Zion* 17 (1952) 56–64; see also Judah Rokeaḥ, "*Heᶜarot kozbiyot*," *Tarbiz* 35 (1966) 126–31, who assumes that the term stems from *sica*, and he considers it to be the name of a supposed law, νόμος σικαρικῶν, "people who seized land by the sword"; and see 131, his conclusion, that "what we see before us is not an anti-Jewish legislation," but "the outcome of an internal conflict" emerging from the aspiration to find the best possible safeguard for private property. Daniel Sperber, *A Dictionary of Greek and Latin Legal Terms in Rabbinic Literature* (Ramat Gan: Bar-Ilan Univ., 1984) 120f., finds that the word means "confiscation by authorities," "purchase of confiscated property," the name of such property itself, while the confiscation

penalized according to the *lex Cornelia de sicariis et veneficiis*, some of them being put to death and others forced to abandon their land.

What is the gist of the information in the talmudic literature on this issue? One should note that the *tannaim* mention the *sīqorīqīn* together with the tenants, the share-croppers, and the land-robbers, and the *gemara* of the *Yerushalmi* explains that the law had to do with extensive confiscations of land.[18] There were those who became owners of such land (owners of *sīqorīqīn*).[19]

These traditions are included in discussions that relate to first fruits and priestly gifts, and the way they mention the *sīqorīqīn* is similar to the mention of share-croppers. It is clear that according to the *halakhah*, their status and rights were not axiomatic. By way of generalization it may be said that the *halakhah* did not recognize their rights. The main information is in the tractate *Giṭṭin*: in the Mishnah, the Tosefta, the *Yerushalmi*, as cited at the beginning of this article, in fragments A–C.

OUR SOURCES

According to the Mishnah (fragm. A), in the beginning there was no law of *sīqorīqīn* in Judaea regarding "those killed in the war," and we can understand that the source refers to people killed in the revolt, that is, the Bar Kokhba revolt, as is made clear in the continuation: "after the matter of those killed in the war there was *sīqorīqīn*." It appears obvious that the intention is not to people called *sīqorīqīn*, but to the law of *sīqorīqīn*.

Following is an explanation of the law as regards an earlier time, the essence of the matter being that the validity of the act of possession (or, so it seems, also the right of tenancy) was canceled as concerns those who had approached the holders of the *sīqorīqīn* lands. Only acts concluded with the real proprietor were valid; it may be assumed that those holders were approached because of the absence of the owner; clearly, if he was killed, or had run away, the actual holder had to be approached, while any agreement reached with him (by the Roman regime, presumably) was invalidated. "This is the first Mishnah," and there was another, later one, by the decision of the "later court." That "later court," was "convened by Rabbi."

The *Yerushalmi* (fragm. B) even explains well the essence of the change; it employs the term *šemad*, meaning the period of oppression during the revolt and afterwards, when they would "expropriate their fields and sell them to

was probably called: σικαρικόν derived from *sica*, *sicarius* (a murderer) and see his bibliographical list and also other different opinions. See also Joshua Schwartz, "*Ereṣ yehuda b'ᶜiq'vot dikkuy mered bar kokhba*," in Aharon Oppenheimer and Uri Rappaport, eds., *Mered bar kokhba, meḥkarim ḥadašim* (Jerusalem: Yad Ben-Zvi, 1984) 218–19; Menaḥem Mor, *Mered bar kokhba, ᶜoṣmato weheqqefo* (Jerusalem: Yad Ben-Zvi, 1991) 243–44.

18 *M.Bik.* 1:2; *y.Bik.* 1:63d (Jer. 349–50).

19 *T.Ter.* 1:6.

others." The (surviving) land owners who returned to their locations would seize them (*ṭorefim*, literally: devour), that is, annul, reclaim, the land from those who had purchased it, which we may understand as: they would appeal to the courts for the return of their land. However, since "the country was completely held (*ḥaluṭa*) under *sīqorīqīn*," and there was no way to arrange the matter, "(the courts) were disposed to abolish the *sīqorīqīn* in Judaea," apparently meaning: that there was a general cancellation of the validity of the purchases of lands such as these on the ground that they had been robbed. That is, at the start, shortly after the revolt and its consequences, the *sīqorīqīn* law was not enacted.

It was only done later, based upon what had already been practiced in Galilee a long time before: "In Galilee there has always been a law of *sīqorīqīn*." By what was enacted by the court set up by Rabbi the *sīqorīqīn* law was introduced in Judaea as well, valid "on everybody, so that justice should be universal." Here, the Mishnah (fragm. A above) informs us about the essence of the law: "he who bought from the *sīqorīqīn* gives the (primary) owner a fourth," that is, a fourth of the value of the land. In other words: they were forced into a compromise, but they added a condition, included in the Mishnah version, that if there is a possibility that the owners buy (or lease?) the land, "they have priority before anyone else."

According to the *Yerushalmi* (fragm. B above), there were some exceptions, when the *sīqorīqīn* law did not apply: 1. there was no compromise with people who seized "robbed" land, being descendants of families of "share-croppers for generations" (*ḥakhirei battei-avot*) that is, families which have rented that land generation after generation. It is reasonable to assume that the person who had replaced these tenants could not remain there because the owner of the land had received compensation, that of the "fourth," but had to vacate the location without compensation.

Also, 2. "whoever was displaced because of debts or because of taxes was not affected by *sīqorīqīn*." In other words, if the land was expropriated from the original owner because of an unpaid debt, or taxes not paid to the regime, the owner was not eligible for the compromise, the "fourth."

Here an additional enactment was introduced, a kind of alleviation for the person whose land was expropriated because he had not paid the tax: "in a case of (unpaid) tax, one awaits the owners for twelve months; R. Judah b. Pazi (mid-fourth century) said: "one keeps proclaiming during four Sabbaths [weeks] after the 12 months." It appears that the discussions relating to this issue were continuing from the end of the second century to the middle of the fourth, about 150 years.[20]

20 *M.Giṭ.* 5:6–7; y.*Giṭ.* 5:47b (Jer. 1076–77); the Mishnah text as quoted in the *Yerushalmi* has R. Yehoshuᶜa instead of Rabbi; Safrai, "סיקריקון," 57f., has already explained that the version Rabbi

There are a number of parallel versions of the Mishnah and the *Yerushalmi* with minor changes and additions. The Tosefta version (fragm. C) changes around the order, stating that the validity of the purchase used to be negated if the person first approached the owner and only later the holder of the *sīqorīqīn* (land), that is, the one who had seized the land.[21]

Comments about people killed by Romans and related matters are also found in the *Bavli*, where R. Judah, apparently the aforementioned R. Judah b. Pazi, is quoted, who explains, in line with the above-stated interpretation, that the Mishnah meant that in Judaea there was no *sīqorīqīn* law; this is followed by explanations (apparently distorted) about the gravity of the oppressive restrictions imposed by the Romans on Judaea.[22]

Another point that requires attention is the information in the *Yerushalmi* version that the situation in Galilee was different, which certainly suits the period of the Bar Kokhba revolt and later, when Galilee was relatively quiet: "In Galilee there has always been a law of *sīqorīqīn*"; in Galilee the courts were able to deal properly with cases of land seizure, and impose that compromise.

However, one may also interpret it in the opposite way, that the main meaning of *sīqorīqīn* law was to return the seized land to its owners without compromise, which might have been the main difference between Judaea, where compromise was required with the *sīqorīqīn* land, and Galilee, where there was no compromise. There is no clue about this unclear issue and its solution in our sources.[23]

A point we do find emphasized in the Tosefta version is the importance of the deed in such issues: "if the owner wrote him a deed, his purchase is valid." That is, the person who bought (or leased?) the land from the "robber" would prove, by a deed from the original owner, that he did not benefit from the seizure, but had purchased it legally. It may be that what is meant is the leasing of *sīqorīqīn* land that had been seized, which is valid if it was done legally; according to Samuel (the *amora*) the validity was improved if the deed was based also on a mortgage, having been done by a honorable person, who still has land of his own while at the same time leasing land.

is the correct one, which means that the discussions belonged to the end of the second century A.D., some two generations after the Bar Kokhba revolt. In the *Yerushalmi* version, a summary of the discussion about the advantage of reaching a compromise with the original owners follows; also cited is the opinion of Rav, explaining that a quarter (*revi^c*) might mean a quarter of the land or a quarter of its value, in cash. It also contains a garbled expression "*pywṭwt pryy*," apparently the remains of some Greek formula.

21 *T.Giṭ.* 5:1–2, and compare Shaul Lieberman, *Tosefta kif'shuṭah* (10 vols.; Jerusalem: Jewish Theological Seminary of America, 1955) 8:841–47.

22 *B.Giṭ.* 55b; the essence of the *sīqorīqīn* law was then apparently still clear to these Babylonian Sages.

23 See Mary Smallwood, *Jews under Roman Rule* (Leiden: Brill, 1976) 413, who writes about the relevance of the Jewish population of Galilee, which became the main component in the Jewish population after the revolt.

The Tosefta version, even though slightly corrupted, therefore contains the essence of the issue: in Judaea, the buyer (or lessee?) of land from the unlawful owner was in the beginning under no obligation to recompense the (lawful) owner with the "fourth," because there was an interest in settling Jews on land whose owners had been killed in the war (the Bar Kokhba revolt).

It would appear that this right of the buyer (or lessee?) was strengthened when there was a deed issued by the original owner ("he made for him *aḥarayut*," by which a deed with mortgage is meant). Only at a later time one had only to pay the original owner the "fourth," and, if he had rehabilitated himself, he had priority rights for one year. This was the meaning of enacting the *sīqorīqīn* law.[24]

The matter of the twelve-month wait for the original owners so that they can pay the taxes, and proclaiming on four Sabbaths in the synagogue that this is seized land, proves that the courts dissociated themselves from the tax collectors and would oppose a fictive purchase of land.[25]

The *Bavli* reports an event (in Babylonia) where one Gidal bar Re^cilai [R. Ilai (?)] had received land (in lease) from a family called B'nei Baga, people who had seized the land from its previous owner. For *ṭasqa*, it states there, and there is no way of knowing whether this means that the land was seized because of non-payment of taxes (the previous matter dealt with in the Talmud there discusses outstanding tax debt), or whether *ṭasqa* means here rental money.

Gidal had paid the lease sum three years in advance. The original legal owners then appeared and said to the tenant: you held the land for a year and enjoyed its produce, now we will pay (the *ṭasqa*) and the fruits will be ours. The original owners then asked Rav Papa to evict the B'nei Baga from the land; it would appear that Rav Papa agreed, and intended that the B'nei Baga's income for the first year be theirs, to which Rav Ḥuna b. Joshua disagreed. To his mind, the B'nei Baga had to understand that "they had put their money on a deer's horns [that is, a runaway horse]." What we see here is, that there was indeed a custom of making a proclamation for twelve months, and those original owners returned in time to make their claim.[26]

As to the preference given to the owners to reclaim their property after having been in *sīqorīqīn* hands for one year, one can find an early precedent in

24 *T.Giṭ.* 5:1; see also *b.B.Bat.* 47b, relying on the opinion of Rav: "This they [the *tannaim*, the sages of the Mishnah] said only in reference to [the case where the Romans] said, 'go seize [the land], [thus] you obtain ownership; but if [he presents] a deed his acquisition' [is valid]"; and the differing opinion of Samuel: "Even with a deed his acquisition is not [valid], unless [the person who bought the (land)] wrote a mortgage on property for him, before that" (that is, the buyer was already the owner of property that could assure fulfillment of the conditions of the transaction and actually mortgaged that property).

25 See also *y.Giṭ.* 5:47b (Jer. 1076).

26 *B.Giṭ.* 58b; compare Lieberman, *Tos. kif'sh.*, 8:845–47.

Hellenistic law, which continued into the Roman regime.[27] The preference of the prior owners was a kind of a general rule, as may be seen in the Mishnah: "(if) the owners say 'for twenty' and anybody else 'for twenty,' the owners are preferred."[28]

Here it should be noted that the extension of this rule is similar to the laws of preemption of contiguous neighbors, granting priority to the local villagers in the case of absentee owners, this is the προτίμησις rule extant in the Hellenistic and Roman world until it was annulled by the Christian emperors.[29]

A parallel expression connected to the *sīqorīqīn* law may be found in the matter of a slave being sold to *sīqorīqīn*, meaning to someone who held seized land; he is not entitled to manumission, while the law was that the sale of a slave to a gentile meant the slave's manumission. Similarly, the slave is not freed if he was sold because of a debt; he was included in the defrayment of a debt. The acceptance of the possibility that a slave be sold to someone who holds *sīqorīqīn* land not being freed by the act of sale, shows that the issue regards slaves sold to Jews who received land of the *sīqorīqīn* category and there was room for compromise in the issue. However, the continuation of this discussion in the *Bavli* emphasizes, as if contrary to the above, that if the slave was sold to a gentile *farhang* (some kind of a dignitary), the slave is freed.[30]

PARALLELS

This phenomenon of the Roman regime seizing derelict lands is well known from other countries under Roman rule. It was permitted to expropriate land abandoned by the *coloni*, the share-croppers, if it was not cultivated during two years. This situation was considered one of waiving rights, *cessio*, whether out of absence or an inability to continue cultivating the land. After two years of absence from the land, the owner, or the *colonus*, forfeited the land rights.[31]

27 Rostovtzev, *Studien*, 19, 144, 162; Horst Braunert, "Studien zur Bevölkerungsgeshichte des ptolemäischen Ägypten," *JJP* 9–10 (1955/56) 260.

28 *M.Nez.* 8:2. This *halakhah*, on the matter of consecrated properties, is certainly one of the earliest rules in the Mishnah, dating from the period when the Temple was still standing. The formulae utilized for the *sīqorīqīn* were obviously influenced by it. See also *b.Nez.* 27b, with additional discussion wherein the term *ḥryq* seems to me to be garbled, and it should be *ḥdyq*, meaning *patrimonium*, as it is in Syriac, and close to the Arabic *ḥadiqa*.

29 Francis de Zulueta, *De patrociniis vicorum* (Oxford: Clarendon, 1909) 72.

30 *B.Bat.* 44a; see the *ᶜArukh* under *'frhng*, said to be derived from the Persian *farhangadar*, judge; perhaps the official in charge of abandoned land (subject to *sīqorīqīn* law) is meant; a version with a more direct formulation of the matter of the sold slave is found in the *t.ᶜAbod. Zar.* 3:16: "If he [a gentile] took [the slave] as part of [the owner's] debt, or he was offered it as [part of] *sīqorīqīn*, he is freed."

31 Kehoe, *Economics*, 44, 124; Jerzy Kolendo, *Le Colonat en Afrique sous le haut-empire* (Paris: Belles lettres, 1991) 70. Formulation of agreements in the style of renunciation had been practiced for

This term, *cessio*, forfeit, originates in the rules of the *lex Iulia*, dating from the time of Augustus, pertaining to those who did not pay their debts and arrived to a *cessio bonorum*, a forfeit of their properties. The debtor was given the choice of voluntary forfeiture of property in favor of the creditor, thus maintaining his good name and not being considered a criminal offender; this was a great opportunity, an announcement of voluntary forfeiture being deemed sufficient: *In omni cessione sufficit voluntatis sola professio.*[32]

However, the *cessio* itself did not mean that the property passed over to the creditor. A *missio*, or writ of state seizure by the *praetor* was required, after which the creditor received his satisfaction through sale (*venditio*) out of the total property (*concursus bonorum*). Only at a later stage of legal development were certain properties in relation to the size of the debt set aside (*distractio bonorum*).

The Roman legal tradition benefited the debtor with much greater protection than in the Greek tradition, where the system of immediate forced seizure of property, by way of coercion (κατενεχυρασία) was the norm. The Hellenistic tradition was preserved even until the late empire, and the Roman custom never became uniform and obligatory throughout the empire. In Egypt, individual violent seizure held sway, and even the imprisonment of the debtor by the creditor, until the time of Justinian.[33]

Nevertheless, the Roman system spread, at the same time, to the east; that is, the system of the trustee, who held the property (*sequester*), and the forfeiture of the properties, the *cessio bonorum*, evidence of which is in the many documents of this type in the Egyptian papyri. In all events, this was the custom when the lender was a person of respected social standing, especially if a Roman citizen. This process proved itself efficient in tax collection; thus there was more and more disregard of the local legal tradition.

The seizure trustees were appointed from among the military in the partic-

---

many generations. See it for Elephantine, 464 B.C.: "withdrawal from land": Bezalel Porten, et al., *The Elephantine Papyri in English* (Leiden: Brill, 1996) 158–62, no. B24).

32 See *Codex Theodosianus*, 4.20: *qui bonis excedere possunt . . . qui lege Iulia cedere possunt* (who can give up their properties . . . who can give up, in accordance with *lex Iulia*), where the main aspects of this matter are included. See also Naphtali Lewis, "Why 'Parachoresis," *Symposion* 6 (1985) 31; Hannah M. Cotton, "The Archive of Salome Daughter of Levi," *ZPE* 105 (1995) 185, who explains συνκεχωρηκέναι as "cessation of property."

33 See discussions on the matters of collection of debts: Egon Weiss, "Execution," PWSup 6:56–64; Adolf Berger, "Lex Iulia," PW 12.2, 2389–91; "κατενεχυρασία" Egon Weiss, "Cessio bonorum," PW 10.2, 2495–512. See also Friedrich Preisigke, *Wörterbuch der griechischen Papyrusurkunden* (3 vols.; Berlin, published by his family, 1925–31) 1:481; Gunther Wesener, "Distractio bonorum," PWSup 9:27–32; Moriz Wlassak, "Cessio bonorum," PW 3.2, 1995ff.; Max Kaser, *Das römische Privatrecht* (2 vols.; Munich: Beck 1955–59) 1:403; Rudolf Sohm, *Institutionen, Geschichte und System des römischen Privatsrecht* (Munich: Duncker, 1917) 351.

ular province; proof, for example, is in an inscription from the third century A.D. from Tralles, in Asia Minor, south of Ephesos, enacted in the name of Aurelius Onesimos, a soldier of the first Illyrian legion, who was in charge of *cessio* affairs.[34]

THE LEGAL TERM: *CESSIO*, FORFEITURE

In light of the above, it may be argued that the term *sīqorīqīn*, as well, was initially derived from a legal situation that preceded the Bar Kokhba war, from processes of forfeiture of land. Here we feel a strong rejection of foreign systems. It was the rejection of an attempt to institute the Roman system of land forfeiture by the debtor, among the Jews of Judaea. This, along the accepted lines of Roman law. But, the Jewish rural community had its own customs and a venerable tradition of regulations regarding inter-personal relationships, the core of which was the wisdom in human relations, of the first *ḥasidim*, and the fear of Heaven. Impounding land because of debt was a very serious issue. True, the lender's rights were clear; if the debt was unpaid the land was "devoured." Yet the Jewish legal authority exercised strong measures only in clear cases of robbery on the part of the debtor, who took money, or its equivalent, and did not repay.

When the lender was a powerful figure and the debtor a local person whose family had been living on the land since the days of "Joshua bin Nun," and had become entangled in growing interest because of the tax burden, it was inconceivable that an official act of the seizure clerk, appointed over forfeitures, who actuated a note signed when credit was extended, could throw a person off his land and home. For according to *halakhah*, an act of the court was required, as was right of possession, which meant cultivating the land and enjoying its

34 See *ILS* 8875: Αὐρ. στρατιώτης Ἰλλυρικιανῆς καὶ τούτωρ κεσσιωνάριος; Naphtali Lewis, et al., *The Documents from the Bar Kokhba Period in the Cave of Letters, Greek Papyri* (Jerusalem: Shrine of the Book, 1989) 92f.; *cessio* and its corresponding word in Greek συγχωρήσις always contain the idea of concession, of giving up; often also of seizure, evacuation, taking possession; see Preisigke, *Wb. der griechischen Papyrusurkunden*, 2:501. Latin *cedere* is represented in the Greek legal terminology by derivatives of χωρεῖν; παραχωρεῖν is often used; so also in the Syrian law books, when it expresses the *in iure cessio hereditatis*; see Ernst Rabel, "Nachgeformte Rechtsgeschäfte," *Zeitschrift der Savigny-Stiftung* (Romanistische Abteilung) 27 (1907) 321. The *perfectum*, which contains the κ is quite current; see, for instance, the papyrus no. 7559, in Friedrich Preisigke, et al., *Sammelbuch griechischer Urkunden aus Ägypten* (Strassburg: Trübner, 1915, continued by others, editions vary), where in line 5 we find συνκεχωρηκέναι, and in line 22, garbled: συνκαιχωρηκαίναι; see also no. 7599 of A.D. 95, lines 9, 15, 28. In the agreement between Herakleia and Paponas (A.D. 56), P. Oxy. 271, line 17: συνκεχωρηκέναι and in line 43: συνκεχωρηκένε and see the editor's notes on pp. 92–93. See more on *cessio bonorum* in the article of Angelo Segrè, "Note sul documento esecutivo Greco-egizio," *Aeg* 9 (1928) 3–62, with a discussion focused on collection carried out "socially" as different from that carried out personally, as documented in papyri.

fruits for three years. The system dictated by the Romans did not ask that the creditor should show a right of possession (*ḥazaqa*), he could get legal satisfaction in ways considered robbery; especially when exorbitant interest was involved, contradicting the *halakhah*, and through recourse to a foreign and unfamiliar judicial system.

Nonetheless, Jewish scholars did see room for compromise, this is where the owners received a quarter of the value of their land, whether in terms of land or money. An echo of that essential contrast in the legal procedures reverberates in the discussion between R. Mana and Alexa, apparently a gentile judge. This is already the end of the fourth century A.D., and the *Gemara* was undoubtedly written later, in the fifth century; the differences, as described in that discussion, are fundamental. In the gentile view, of Alexa, sequestering land in the case of debt non-payment is virtually automatic. In contrast, the Jewish court is presented as more liberal; it proclaims, and does not expropriate except when there is a deliberation and a ruling. And if after the ruling, the debtor absconds, the court intervenes to execute the sentence and only after warnings are issued for three months. Then at last the court orders the debt paid from the property of the debtor.[35]

From the above, one may understand the term *sīqorīqīn* and I believe that it is a corruption of the Greek word meaning (land) that has been forfeited. This word derived from the verb συγχωρέω, which means to surrender (usually in an official manner, via a court) and from this we have συγχώρησις, which means an agreement to forfeit something, a writ of surrender (usually official) parallel to the Latin *cessio*. One should note the evidence of the Greek Egyptian papyri, which show that the ε and the η were pronounced: ī, and were in writing often replaced by a ι. This we find as early as in the first century A.D., as shown by Francis Gignac. Thus the word συγκεχωρηκένε (found in a Judaean Desert papyrus) was heard as: *sīqīḥorīqīni*; therefore what we have in our sources is *sīqorīqīn* (and not *sīqorīqōn*) – which is also the *lectio difficilior* – and is correct.

When was this term used in daily life? When property was surrendered in someone's favor; then undoubtedly the first owners, who received – according to the *sīqorīqīn* arrangements – a "fourth" of the land's value, would write a deed of resignation and the land would stay as the property of the one who seized it.

35 *Y.Ketub.* 9:33b (Jer. 1001). Alexa argues: "We do it much better than you. We write a final decision; if he (the debtor) comes, well and good; if not we sequester his properties. He (R. Mana) answered: 'we do the same; we track after him with three letters; if he comes, well and good; if not, we forfeit his properties'; (Alexa) said to him: 'Imagine that he was in some distant place'; (then, R. Mana says) we track him with three letters, the first after thirty days, the second after another thirty days, and the third after an additional thirty days; if he comes, well and good; if not, we sequester his properties. (Here) R. Mattaniah said: 'this happens if his case was in court and he fled; but if his case (still) has not been in court and he fled, we do not sequester but (first) proclaim.'"

There was undoubtedly such a writ for land which had belonged to those killed or made refugees by the Romans.[36]

On 19 June A.D. 130, very near the time of the Bar Kokhba revolt, Basa b. Yešu^ca, guardian of the orphans of Yešu^ca b. Khtousion, and Julia Crispina, who served also as guardian, authorized the surrender of a house in Ein Gedi, from among the properties of the grandfather Eleazar, in favor of Sh'lomṣiyon, Babatha's stepdaughter: "we acknowledge that we have conceded to you": συγκεχωρηκέναι σοι; this is about an αὐλή which the editor translated: a courtyard; but like חצר in Hebrew it meant a compound.[37] This term is also found in *cessio* documents from Egypt, such as that of A.D. 95, where Iulia Herakla gives away a parcel of land to her daughter.[38]

These are papyri of the συγχώρησις type, which constitute a well-known section in papyrus research; they usually open with the word συγχωρεῖ and are composed as a voluntary agreement between the sides which they then present to the court.[39]

From what was said until this point about the rules of *sīqorīqīn*, one sees that

36 See, for example, Samuel Krauss, *Griechische und lateinische Lehnwörter in Talmud, Midrasch und Targum* (Berlin: Calvary, 1898) 180: γενέσια = גינוסיא, 211; δεκουρίον = דיקוריון; as to the ε and the η in later Greek, see the evidence of the papyri: Francis T. Gignac, *A Grammar of the Greek Papyri of the Roman and Byzantine Periods* (2 vols.; Milano: La Goliardica, 1975) 1:235–37, 249–50; the second syllable of סיקריקין is what is called "an open one" and we may safely assume that even before the introduction of written vowels it was vocalized by a *qomeṣ* (not as in the Sephardic tradition); therefore the assumed pronunciation was *sīqorīqīn*, quite close to the Greek. Obvious traces of this *qomeṣ*, in open syllables, as well as in closed ones that were accentuated in the Hebrew of those generations, can be found in several biblical names cited by Flavius Josephus. For instance Χοδαμος, *Ant.* 1.220, for Hadad (Gen 36:35), Αροδος, *Ant.* 2.180, for Ard (Num 26:40); Ασοφον, *Ant.* 13.338, for Ṣafon (Josh 13:27); Χειρομος, *Ant.* 8.76 and more, for Ḥiram (2 Sam 5:11, and more); Οχοζιας, *Ant.* 8.420 for Aḥazyahu (1Kgs 22:40 and more); Αχονιος, *Ant.* 11.145–46, for Shekhanya (Ezra 8:3 and more); see also σφωθαι = שְׁפָתַי; εμωσην = אֲמְחָצֵם, in Einar Brønno, *Studien über hebräische Morphologie und Vokalismus* (Leipzig: Brockhaus, 1943) 354 (from Origenes' Hexapla; I am grateful to my colleague Prof. Abraham Tal, who proposed this book to me.) True, on the other hand there are cases where we find α where in our Hebrew there is a *qameṣ*; see the article of Alexander Sperber, "Hebrew Based upon Greek and Latin Transliterations," *HUCA* 12–13 (1937/38) 103–264, who uses mainly the Septuagint and the transcriptions of Hieronymus.

37 See the document edited by Lewis, *Documents*, no. 20. See Jacob Polotsky, "*Hate^cudot hay'waniyot mim'arat-ha'igarot*," *BIES* 26 (1962) 240. On αὐλή, see Moshe Gil, *Related Worlds*, Aldershot (2004) no. 3, 9f. See Lewis, *Documents*, 90, line 7 (and also further); see in the same document, line 7: συνκεχωρηκέναι; as also in line 27, where the scribe first intended to write παρακεχωρηκέναι and corrected it.

38 See P. Oxy. no. 273 (vol. 2, 258f.), line 17 (of A.D. 56), and also no. 272, lines 23, 27 (A.D. 66), and no. 279, line 4 (a petition with the request to receive a piece of land for sharecropping; A.D. 44–45); compare Hannah M. Cotton and Ada Yardeni, *Aramaic, Hebrew and Greek Documentary Texts from Nahal Hever and Other Sites*, DJD 27 (1997) 205.

39 See Ludwig Mitteis and Uri Wilcken, *Grundzüge und Chrestomatie der Papyruskunde* (Leipzig: Teubner, 1912) 65ff.

they dealt with lands confiscated from Jews. We may surmise that aside from what is connected to the Bar Kokhba revolt and conflicts on a political-military basis, in general, these rules were linked to situations where owners ran away because of a great tax burden, or fled and abandoned lands for whatever reason. The rules were meant to arrange the condition of the new owners. The original owners had priority when seeking to buy, or lease, the land. Over all this prevailed the strong hand of the Roman empire.

The Jewish Sages recognized both the rights of the original owners and those of the new buyers, or sharecroppers, and the *halakhah* they enacted was a compromise with realities. Priority rights were preserved for the original owners for one year, and they were eligible for the quarter payment except if debt and taxes had caused their absence.

However, at a later stage the rights of absentees, or escapees whose reason for having run away was non-payment of taxes, was also recognized. Changes occurred in these rules down the years, and it is unlikely that the original meaning of the *sīqorīqīn* laws or even the term itself, was still clear to the late Babylonian *amoraim*. The *geonim* also grappled with the term, and it would seem that the issue appeared unclear to them.[40]

40 The *geonim*: see Simḥa Assaf, *Tešuvot hag'onim mittokh hag'niza* (Jerusalem: Darom, 1929) 36f., no. 87, MS Antonin (the Antonin Geniza Collection in St. Petersburg) no. 866; Assaf, *Tešuvot hag'onim* (Jerusalem: M'qiṣei nirdamim, 1942) 82f., no. 73, TS 24.48.

The Earliest Texts of the *Birkat Haminim*

Uri Ehrlich
Ben Gurion University of the Negev

Ruth Langer
Boston College

The *birkat haminim* petitions God to doom groups of people deemed harmful to the Jewish community, both Jews and gentiles. The blessing's text consequently was often adapted to reflect new realities. Throughout its history, it has attracted attention from those, especially Christians, concerned about Jewish attitudes to them. This concern led to extensive censorship of the text. However, modern scholars pondering the early history of the blessing had only limited evidence for its actual formulations.

This article presents a panoramic study of the text of the *birkat haminim* from the earliest preserved manuscripts (from the Cairo geniza) until official Catholic censorship began in the sixteenth century. The six centuries plus of texts presented here allows us to document the medieval development of the blessing. Across the regional variants, we find an extremely stable structure together with significant openness to addition, deletion, or rearrangement of the parts. This data and its analysis provide a firm basis for understanding the prayer's subsequent developments and a firmer basis than previously available for reconstructing its earlier history. This evidence will serve, we hope, as a resource for scholarly discussion about the place of the *birkat haminim* in the complex array of relationships between Jews and gentiles.

In his classic work on Jewish liturgy, Ismar Elbogen begins his commentary on the *birkat haminim*[1] saying, "No benediction has undergone as many textual variations as this one, some through the natural effect of changing times, and others through censorship. It is most doubtful that we will ever be in a position to recover its original text."[2] Elbogen is neither original nor unique, either in his recognition that the text of this prayer has undergone numerous transformations or in his sense that reconstruction of an original text is perhaps not possible.[3] However, systematic research among the findings of the Cairo

1 Literally, the "benediction of the heretics," better but still inadequately translated as the "malediction of the heretics," the twelfth benediction of the weekday *ᶜamidah*, the central prayer of rabbinic communal liturgy.

2 Ismar Elbogen, *Jewish Liturgy: A Comprehensive History*, trans. Raymond P. Scheindlin (Philadelphia, Jerusalem, New York: Jewish Publication Society, Jewish Theological Seminary of America, 1993) 45; Heb. ed., p. 40, §9.b.12.

3 See, for example, the commentaries on this blessing of Seligmann Baer, *Seder ᶜavodat yisraʾel* (Roedelheim, 1868. Repr.; Tel Aviv: Schocken, 1957) 93–95; Joseph Hertz, *The Authorized Daily Prayer Book* (New York: Bloch Publishing Company, 1948, 1975) 143–44, and the literature on this blessing to be discussed below.

geniza and in later prayer book manuscripts and editions allows us today to understand much of the history of this blessing and its development. This article assembles and analyzes the medieval texts of this blessing beginning with the earliest texts of the blessing that have been preserved and suggests ways to understand its medieval history.

SCHOLARLY DISCUSSIONS

In 1898, Solomon Schechter published the first findings from the Cairo geniza, revolutionizing the study of Jewish liturgy.[4] In this short article, he included a selection of prayers of a rite, until then unknown. Scholars quickly came to recognize this as the rite of *ʾereṣ yisraʾel.*[5] This rite, although adhering to the basic structures and ideas of known rabbinic liturgy, differed significantly in its precise formulations of the individual prayers. Included among Schechter's geniza fragments were two versions of the *birkat haminim*, both of them deviating in significant ways from the familiar versions of the prayer. Although Schechter did not comment upon this in his brief article, most striking to his readers was that these versions of the *birkat haminim* explicitly included among the malefactors being cursed *noṣerim*, the common Hebrew term for Christians. Many through the centuries had understood the prayer to have been anti-Christian in its origins and ongoing intent. Scholars were aware that the Church fathers, and especially Justin Martyr (d. c. 165),[6] accused Jews of cursing Christians during prayers, and that Epiphanius (d. 403) and Jerome (d. 420) specifically identify this as a curse against Nazarenes, suggesting that the *berakhah* had included somewhere an explicit reference to *noṣerim.*[7] However, no previously discovered liturgical text of the blessing had included this precise language.

4 S. Schechter, "Geniza Specimens," *JQR* OS 10 (1898) 654–59; repr. in Jakob J. Petuchowski, ed., *Contributions to the Scientific Study of Jewish Liturgy* (New York: Ktav, 1970) 373–78. For the texts of the *birkat haminim*, see pp. 657, 659 and 376, 378 respectively. A geniza is a storehouse for Hebrew manuscripts that, although they are no longer useful, are considered too holy to be destroyed.

5 See, for instance, Emil Schürer, *Geschichte des jüdischen Volkes im zeitalter Jesu Christi*, Zweiter Band (Leipzig: J. C. Hinrichs, 1907. Repr.; Heidelberg: Georg Olms Verlagsbuchhandlung, 1964) 542–43. He, and most since, have referred to this rite as Palestinian. In today's English usage, "Palestinian" does not designate a Jewish culture. We will instead transliterate the Hebrew designation for the Land of Israel.

6 *Dialogue with Trypho*, esp. §96 and §137. There is no scholarly consensus on how many of Justin's references, if any, are actually relevant.

7 William Horbury, "The Benediction of the Minim and Early Jewish-Christian Controversy," *JTS* 33 (1982) 20–23 (repr. in his *Jews and Christians in Contact and Controversy* [Edinburgh: T&T Clark, 1998]) cites the relevant literature. The patristic texts are collected in A. F. J. Klijn and G. J. Reinink, *Patristic Evidence for Jewish-Christian Sects* (Leiden: E. J. Brill, 1973) 174–75, 200–201, 218–19, 220–21, 224–25. For the pre-Schechter discussions, see esp. S. Krauss, "The Jews in the Works

Once Schechter's article was noticed,[8] this blessing received renewed attention by both Jewish and Christian scholars as they began to try to understand the Jewish origins of Christianity and the history of the "parting of the ways."[9] According to rabbinic tradition, this blessing was added to the *ᶜamidah* at Yavneh.[10] This places the origins of the *birkat haminim* firmly in the late first century C.E. The explicit inclusion of *noṣerim* in the geniza text thus suggested that the addition of this blessing was a deliberate move to exclude Christians from the synagogue, an understanding reinforced by a late midrashic tradition that requires one leading the prayers who errs in the blessing to repeat it correctly, thus cursing himself.[11] Because of the perception, perhaps correct, that the early history of the *birkat haminim* sheds light on this critical moment in the emergence of Christianity onto the world scene, a huge literature has developed on the subject. Not only does the blessing receive independent treatment,[12] but it

---

of the Church Fathers," *JQR* OS 5 (1893) 130–34. Krauss, 133, speculates incorrectly as to which term of the known blessing texts had once been *noṣerim*. Adolf Schlatter, *Die Kirche Jerusalems vom Jahr 70 bis 130* (Gütersloh: Bertelsmann, 1898; repr. in *Synagoge und Kirche bis zum Barkochba-Aufstand: Vier Studien zur Geschichte des Rabbinats und der jüdischen Christenheit in den ersten zwei Jahrhunderten* [Stuttgart: Calwer Verlag, 1966]) 108–10, cites Krauss and offers his own speculation.

8 Schürer, in his 1907 revision of the second volume of his history, p. 543 f., is apparently the first to utilize this data. He understands *noṣerim* to designate all Christians. Neither Ismar Elbogen, "Geschichte des Achtzehngebets," *MGWJ* 46 (1902) 330–57, 427–39, 513–30 nor Emil G. Hirsch, "Shemoneh ᶜEsreh," *JE* (1905) 11:270–82 acknowledge the geniza materials. Hermann L. Strack, *Jesus, die Häretiker und die Christen nach den ältesten jüdischen Angaben* (Leipzig: J. C. Hinrichs'sche Buchhandlung, 1910) 64*–67*, cites the geniza text as support for S. Krauss's 1893 surmise. He provides detailed notes about the two different versions in Schechter's publication (p. 30). Adolf Harnack, "Judentum und Judenchristentum in Justins Dialog mit Trypho nebst einer Collation der Pariser Handschrift Nr. 450," *Texte und Untersuchungen zur Geschichte der altchristlichen Literature* 3.9 (1913) 80, cites only Schechter's main text in his discussion of Justin Martyr's report that Jews are cursing Christians in the synagogue and concludes that there must be something to Justin's claim. On p. 90, he lists this among the items that confirm the historicity of Justin's reports. This tendency to cite just Schechter's main text becomes widespread.

9 See the substantial literature cited by William Horbury in his analysis of Justin Martyr's references to Jews' cursing Christians, in his "The Benediction of the Minim," 20–23. For a more recent bibliography, see Pieter W. van der Horst, "The Birkat Ha-Minim in Recent Research," in P. W. van der Horst, ed., *Hellenism - Judaism - Christianity: Essays on their Interaction* (Kampen: Kok Pharos, 1994; 2nd enlarged ed.; Leuven: Peeters, 1998) 113–24.

10 *B.Ber.* 28b; *y.Ber.* 4:3 8a.

11 *Tanhuma Vayiqra* 2 (Warsaw ed.); Buber ed., *Vayiqra* 3. See, for instance, Elbogen's use of this text, §8.10, p. 32 (Eng.; p. 28 Heb.).

12 For the most comprehensive survey of the literature, see: van der Horst, "The Birkat Ha-Minim," 1994 ed.: 99–111; 1998 ed., 113–24. Widely cited studies focusing specifically on the blessing include: Reuven Kimelman, "*Birkat Ha-Minim* and the Lack of Evidence for an Anti-Christian Jewish Prayer in Late Antiquity," in E. P. Sanders, A. I. Baumgarten, and Alan Mendelson, eds., *Jewish and Christian Self Definition, Volume Two: Aspects of Judaism in the Graeco-Roman Period* (4 vols.; Philadel-

receives attention in histories of early rabbinic Judaism[13] as well as histories of early Christianity, particularly in works on the Gospel of John, explaining his references to the expulsion of Christians from the synagogues.[14]

However, in spite of the fact that additional geniza texts of the *ᶜamidah* including versions of the *birkat haminim* similar to Schechter's second version were published in English by Jacob Mann in 1925[15] and in Hebrew by Simcha Assaf in 1949,[16] the vast majority of these publications have presumed that Schechter's first version represents the authentic rite of *ᵓereṣ yisraᵓel*[17] and that it, rather than any other known version, was preserved intact from the earliest promulgation of the blessing. This is even more surprising because in 1925–26, two articles published in the English-language *Jewish Quarterly Review* demonstrated even greater variety in the earliest known texts of the blessing. A. Mar-

phia: Fortress Press, 1981) 2:226–44; William Horbury, *Jews and Christians in Contact and Controversy* (Edinburgh: T&T Clark, 1998) which collects several of his earlier articles on the subject; and David Flusser, "Some of the Precepts of the Torah from Qumran (4QMMT) and the Benediction Against the Heretics," *Tarbiz* 61 (1991–92) 333–74 (Heb.).

13 Influential studies include: Günther Stemberger, "Die sogenannte 'Synode von Jabne' und das frühe Christentum," *Kairos* 19 (1977) 14–21; Peter Schaefer, "Die sogenannte Synode von Jabne: Zur Trennung von Juden und Christen im ersten/zweiten Jh. n. Chr," *Studien zur Geschichte und Theologie des rabbinischen Judentums* (Leiden: E. J. Brill, 1978) 44–64; Gedaliah Alon, *The Jews in their Land in the Talmudic Age (70–640 C.E.)*, Gershon Levi, trans. and ed. (Jerusalem: Magnes, 1980. Repr.; Cambridge, Mass. and London: Harvard Univ. Press, 1989) 288–90; Johann Maier, *Jüdische Auseinandersetzung mit dem Christen in der Antike* (Darmstadt: Wissenschaftliche Buchgesellschaft, 1982) 138–39; Steven T. Katz, "Issues in the Separation of Judaism and Christianity After 70 C.E.: A Reconsideration," *JBL* 103 (1984) 43–76; Lawrence Schiffman, *Who Was a Jew? Rabbinic and Halakhic Perspectives on the Jewish Christian Schism* (Hoboken, N.J.: Ktav, 1985) 56–60; Richard Kalmin, "Christians and Heretics in Rabbinic Literature of Late Antiquity," *HTR* 87.2 (1994) 155–69; Daniel Boyarin, *Border Lines: The Partition of Judaeo-Christianity* (Philadelphia: Univ. of Pennsylvania Press, 2004).

14 John 9:22, 12:42, 16:2. J. Louis Martyn, *History and Theology in the Fourth Gospel* (3rd ed.; Louisville/London: Westminster John Knox Press, 2003) chap. 2, raised the issue in the most influential way. He received serious refutations from Stemberger, Schaefer, and Maier, cited in the previous note, and most recent scholars follow them rather than him. See also, among many others, Raymond E. Brown, *Introduction to the Gospel of John*, edited, updated, introduced and concluded by Francis J. Moloney, S.D.B., ABRL (New York: Doubleday, 2003) 68, n. 65; Adele Reinhartz, *Befriending the Beloved Disciple: A Jewish Reading of the Gospel of John* (New York/London: Continuum, 2001) chap. 3; Claudia Setzer, *Jewish Responses to Early Christians: History and Polemics, 30–150 C.E.* (Minneapolis: Fortress, 1994) 89–93; and Stephen G. Wilson, *Related Strangers: Jews and Christians 70–170 C.E.* (Minneapolis: Fortress Press, 1995) 176 ff.

15 Jacob Mann, "Genizah Fragments of the Palestinian Order of Service," *HUCA* 2 (1925) 296, 306, repr. in Petuchowski, *Contributions*, 406, 416.

16 "From the Order of Prayers in *ᵓEreṣ Yisraᵓel*," in Yitzhak Baer, Yehoshua Gutman, Moshe Schwabe, eds., *Sefer Dinaburg* (Jerusalem: Kiryat Sefer, 1949) 118 (Heb.).

17 Schürer, in 1907, already warned against presuming that the geniza text was original. An egregious recent example of this reliance on Schechter is David Instone-Brewer, "The Eighteen Benedictions and the *Minim* Before 70 CE," *JTS* 54.1 (2003) 25–44.

morstein's article entitled "The Amidah of the Public Fast Days,"[18] presented numerous geniza fragments, including, in the second half, a series of eighteen texts of the *birkat haminim* (from among the thirty manuscripts he checked). According to Marmorstein's summary of his data, he found ten different versions of the blessing. However, he makes no attempt to distinguish between texts originating in *ʾereṣ yisraʾel* versus Babylonia, or to distinguish between poetic elaborations on the prayer versus prose versions, or to establish relationships between the texts. The importance of Marmorstein's contribution thus lies primarily in his publication of data that gives witness to a much wider variety of possible texts of the *birkat haminim* in the period of the geniza than that suggested by Schechter.

Louis Finkelstein, in his "The Development of the Amidah,"[19] compared the texts of Schechter's versions with those of the *Seder Rav Amram Gaon* and the *Siddur Rav Saadia Gaon,*[20] both Babylonian geonic prayer books dated today to the late ninth and early to mid-tenth centuries respectively. In his notes, Finkelstein also compared these texts with exemplars of the known later rites. He therefore points to the coexistence of at least three contemporaneous rites. Regarding the *birkat haminim* specifically, his selection of texts suggests that only one rite, that of *ʾereṣ yisraʾel,* actually referred explicitly to *noṣerim*, and that of Saadia did not even include mention of the *minim*. His goal in this comparison was to discern shared elements and to reconstruct an original version, inevitably simpler than all known versions, from which all later rites evolved. However, even scholars who today posit a single original composition of the *ʿamidah* and especially of the *birkat haminim* find Finkelstein's methods questionable.[21]

18 *JQR* NS 15 (1924/5) 409–18; repr. in Petuchowski, *Contributions*, 449–58.

19 *JQR* NS 16 (1925/6) 156–57; repr. in Petuchowski, *Contributions*, 163–64.

20 In both cases, citing from manuscripts of these texts. The *Siddur Rav Saadia Gaon* was published only in 1941, from the Oxford manuscript (Neubauer 1096) that Finkelstein used through a photograph then available at the Jewish Theological Seminary. The *Seder Rav Amram Gaon* was in constant circulation from the late ninth century, but as is well known, scribes did not hesitate to make changes, particularly to its prayer texts. Finkelstein here relies on one of the best manuscripts, that of Salzburg, now found in the library of the Jewish Theological Seminary of America in New York, #4074. He himself relied on Alexander Marx's collection of the variants. See his notes, p. 132 (Petuchowski, *Contributions*, 139).

21 Form-critical study of the liturgy, as presented most persuasively by Joseph Heinemann, *Prayer in the Talmud: Forms and Patterns*, trans. Richard S. Sarason (Berlin and New York: Walter de Gruyter, 1977. Heb. ed., 1964) suggested that rabbinic liturgy evolved gradually from prayer forms common to various social settings in the pre-rabbinic world, meaning that the origins of the liturgy rarely lie in deliberate compositions. Ezra Fleischer, beginning with his article, "On the Beginnings of Obligatory Jewish Prayer," *Tarbiz* 59 (1989–90) 397–441 (Heb.), raised cogent challenges to this picture, arguing for a deliberate composition of the *ʿamidah* and other prayers at Yavneh in the late first century C.E. (For an English review of his writings, see Ruth Langer, "Revisiting Early Rabbinic Liturgy: The Recent Contributions of Ezra Fleischer," *Prooftexts* 19 [1999]

No further significant contributions[22] were made to our understanding of the textual development of the *birkat haminim* until 2000, with the publication of Yehezkel Luger's doctoral dissertation, *The Weekday Amidah in the Cairo Geniza*.[23] The many discussions published in the intervening years had mostly focused on Schechter's version of the blessing, ignoring almost entirely the contributions of Mann, Marmorstein, Finkelstein, and Assaf. Luger, on the other hand, returns directly to the geniza manuscripts. Among the sixty-five manuscripts of the *ᶜamidah* that Luger studies, he locates fifteen exemplars of the *birkat haminim*.[24] Among these fifteen, he discerns three discrete versions, the second of which he identifies as most characteristic of *ʾereṣ yisraʾel*.[25] However, he also suggests in his introduction that the boundaries between the rites of Babylonia and *ʾereṣ yisraʾel* are not as firm as had hitherto been believed. He characterizes separately each blessing within a manuscript as being either according to the rite of *ʾereṣ yisraʾel* or Babylonia and then offers a summary of the mixture found within each manuscript.[26] He therefore suggests a much broader variety in reality than these three rites, but does not offer a map of this variety. In his specific presentation of the *birkat haminim*, Luger is the first to demonstrate that Babylonian texts (five of his seven exemplars of version A) in the period of the geniza also included explicit reference to *noṣerim*.

THIS PROJECT

Methodical survey of all known manuscripts of the weekday *ᶜamidah* from the geniza as well as the earliest preserved manuscripts of the rites of the various Jewish diaspora communities suggests that the picture presented by all these scholars is significantly oversimplified. In what follows, we present the fruits of this research, first in a detailed discussion of Uri Ehrlich's much broader survey of the geniza materials, and then in a parallel discussion of Ruth Langer's survey of the medieval manuscripts of the European rites. Unfortunately, too few medieval manuscripts have been preserved from North Africa and the Middle East to allow legitimate conclusions to be drawn about those rites. What material exists will appear here only in comparison to the geniza texts which largely derive from that same world.

179–94 and "Controversy" in 20 [2000] 380–87.) Jewish liturgical scholars, including the authors of this article, have as yet reached no consensus on how to reconcile these two views.

22 Flusser, "Some of the Precepts of the Torah," contains several reconstructions of the blessing based on very limited data, ample guesswork, and questionable methodologies.

23 Yehezkel Luger, *The Weekday Amidah in the Cairo Genizah* (Jerusalem: Orhot Press, 2000) (Heb.).

24 Note that although Luger lists Marmorstein's article in his bibliography, he does not include the fragments that Marmorstein mentioned.

25 Luger, *Weekday Amidah*, 134–35.

26 Luger, *Weekday Amidah*, 17–21.

Based on this data, we offer a revised picture of the history of the *birkat haminim* in its formative stages. The results of this study go a long way to answering Elbogen's questions with which we opened. While we may never know what the original text of the blessing might have been (if there was only one), we now can trace much of its development and can map out its many and shifting formulations before Catholic censorship radically altered them in the sixteenth century.[27]

The Geniza Texts of the *Birkat Haminim*

METHODOLOGICAL ISSUES

Among the geniza manuscripts, 112 liturgical fragments include complete or partial texts of the *birkat haminim*. However, twelve of these have been excluded here because they are too fragmentary or in such poor physical condition that their exact contents are unclear. Nevertheless, the collection of manuscripts cited here is close enough to being exhaustive to provide data for an authoritative discussion of the text of the *birkat haminim* in the geniza period.[28]

Not all materials found in the geniza represent the "geniza period." The geniza contains a huge collection of manuscripts that were copied over a period of more than four hundred years (900–1300), and the liturgical materials typically are anonymous, making it very difficult to comprehend their history. The geniza also contains material that definitely or possibly originated elsewhere in the Jewish world, prayer books that emanated from other diaspora communities or that were copied under their influence. Consequently, each prayer book fragment requires paleographic analysis to provide an estimation of its date and hand. This information, partial and only preliminary though it is, allows a tentative chronological and geographic ordering of this material, at least within the approximately four centuries in which most of the manuscripts were written.[29] These criteria resulted in the elimination of an additional six manuscripts that were identified as not (or only doubtfully) Middle Eastern, i.e., from outside the geniza's own world. After sifting out these manuscripts, ninety-four fragments remained for inclusion in our discussion.

It is also critical to remember, even after identifying the useful manuscripts, that we have very little concrete contemporary evidence for how Jews prayed

27 On censorship, see Amnon Raz-Karotzkin, *The Censor, the Editor and the Text* (Jerusalem: Magnes, 2005) (Heb.). For the effects of censorship on the *birkat haminim* specifically, see Langer's forthcoming book.

28 This collection of texts of the *birkat haminim* is part of Uri Ehrlich's forthcoming synoptic edition of the geniza texts of the entire weekday *ʿamidah*.

29 Dr. Edna Angel performed this preliminary paleographic analysis, and the reservations about the results mentioned here are hers.

before this period. It is highly likely that significant elements of the development of rabbinic liturgy, even those reflected in the geniza manuscripts, are the product of a yet earlier period, sometimes centuries earlier than the dates when these manuscripts were produced. Therefore, simple analysis of the physical characteristics of these manuscripts is insufficient. In most cases, the actual language of the prayer text is a better key to its dating and provenance.

DISCUSSION OF THE TEXTS

The table on pages 10 and 11 presents seven versions of the *birkat haminim* found in the Cairo geniza. The list of manuscripts and a full discussion of the variants among the fragments of the various versions appears in the appendix at the end of this article.[30] The discussion that follows will be based on the data in the table and the primary variants in the appendix.

30 Among the manuscripts collected, two groups do not appear in this table, but are listed at the end of the Appendix A. One group, consisting of six manuscripts, has the following basic text: ומלכות זדון מהרה תעקר ותשבר ותכניע בימינו והמינים כרגע יאבדו ברוך אתה יי שובר אויבים ומכניע זדים (The empire of insolence quickly uproot, smash, and bring low in our day, and may the *minim* be destroyed in an instant. Blessed are you, Eternal, who breaks enemies and humbles the insolent.) There are two main variants within this group: one manuscript, instead of והמינים (and the *minim*), has והנוצרים והמינים (the *noṣerim* and the *minim*); and another lacks the entire phrase והמינים כרגע יאבדו (and may the *minim* be destroyed in an instant). This group is not included in the table because it is to all appearances an abbreviation of an eastern version of the prayer of unknown date or provenance. All of the manuscripts in this group also abbreviate the next blessing (*birkat haṣaddiqim*), beginning it with the words ותן שכר טוב וכו' (Give a good reward, etc.), and some of them also abbreviate the blessing for healing, beginning it with the words והעלה רפואה וכו' (Raise up healing, etc.). It is difficult to assess the reason for this abbreviation of the *birkat haminim*; it is possible that some considered the repetition in the language of the blessing to be improper.

The other group excluded from the table consists of two manuscripts whose language is: המינים והמלשינים (כולם) כרגע יאבדו וכל צוררי עמך ישראל ואויביהם וקמיהם וחושבי רעתם (ומלשיניהם) מהרה מארץ יכרתו ישברו ויאבדו ותכניעם במהרה בימינו ברוך אתה יי שובר אויבים ומכניע זדים "May the *minim* and the informers (all) be destroyed in an instant, and may all the oppressors of Your people Israel and their enemies and opponents and those who plan evil against them (and those who inform against them) be speedily cut off from the earth, may they be smashed and lost, bring them low speedily in our day. Blessed are You, Eternal, who breaks enemies and humbles the insolent." These two manuscripts are relatively late (thirteenth-fourteenth centuries). It is plausible that this language is also an abbreviation, perhaps because of an external or internal censor. On this text, see also L. Finkelstein, "The Development of the Amidah," *JQR* NS 16 (1925–26) 140; repr. in Petuchowski, *Contributions*, 147. Finkelstein copies this text from *Oṣar tov* (*Hebraïsche Beilage zum Magasin für die Wissenschaft des Judenthums*) 1 (1878) 10–13. There, that manuscript is identified as an Arabic rite prayer book manuscript from Rome. Its text for the *birkat haminim* is similar to the otherwise anomalous text that appears in MS Rome Casanatense 3085, an eastern rite siddur with Arabic instructions, dated to the fifteenth–sixteenth centuries. The publication in *Oṣar tov* does not identify its author or offer comment on the text.

Even on first glance, one can discern that the geniza texts, in their seven different branches, rest upon a shared textual foundation. All of the geniza manuscripts without exception begin with למשומדים אל תהי תקוה (May there be no hope for apostates).[31] The segment ומלכות זדון מהרה תעקר בימינו (may the empire of insolence be speedily uprooted in our day) appears, with the addition of a word or two, in all the branches except one (1). The petition, והנוצרים והמינים כרגע יאבדו (may the *noṣerim*[32] and the *minim*[33] immediately perish), with this wording or with slight variants, also appears in all but one branch (6). The eulogy of the blessing concludes without exception with the words מכניע זדים (who humbles the insolent). However, within this shared framework, there are identifiable characteristics that differentiate the various rites and their branches and that witness to the developmental history of the benediction.

Among the geniza texts, the most fundamental distinction is between the wording of the *birkat haminim* in the *ʾereṣ yisraʾeli* rite and in the Babylonian rite.[34] In all the *ʾereṣ yisraʾeli* rite prayer books, the blessing concludes with מכניע זדים (who humbles the insolent) alone, while in the Babylonian rite prayer books, the blessing concludes with a double eulogy, either as שובר רשעים ומכניע זדים (who breaks the wicked and humbles the insolent) or as שובר אויבים ומכניע זדים (who breaks enemies and humbles the insolent).[35] The *ʾereṣ yisraʾeli* rite is also unique in its citation at the end of the body of the blessing of Psalms 69:29, ימחו מספר חיים ועם צדיקים אל יכתבו (May they be blotted from the Book of Life and not be inscribed with the righteous). A third component that is distinctive in the rite of *ʾereṣ yisraʾel* is the words אם לא ישובו

31 Except the manuscripts mentioned in the previous note.

32 As discussed above, the appearance of *noṣerim* in Schechter's published geniza manuscripts was a source of much discussion. We will not translate the term here because its meaning is somewhat ambiguous. While the word is clearly derived from the Hebrew name of Nazareth, it is unclear whether this designates Christians in general (as is the contemporary meaning of the word), a category of Jewish-Christians (corresponding to the Greek and Latin for Nazarenes, and variants on this term), or something else entirely.

33 This term too will remain untranslated here. Literally, *minim* means "sectarians." Rabbinic texts use the term in a variety of ways to apply to various sorts of religious and philosophical opponents, some, but not all, of whom were Christians.

34 The differences between the wordings of the daily *ʿamidah* in the rites of *ʾereṣ yisraʾel* and of Babylonia are clear-cut and the existence of a few prayer books that mix the rites does not blur the boundaries. For some principle characteristics of the *ʿamidah* in the rite of the Land of Israel, see J. Mann, "Genizah Fragments of the Palestinian Order of Service," *HUCA* 2 (1925) 295–97.

35 The words מכניע זדים (who humbles the insolent) already serves as the name for the *birkat haminim* in the talmudic sources from *ʾereṣ yisraʾel*. See, for example, *y.Ber.* 5:3, 9c: לכל אין מחזירין אותו חוץ ממי שלא אמר מחיה המתים ומכניע זדים ובונה ירושלים אני אומר מין הוא (One does not make him [that is, a *sheliaḥ ṣibbur*] repeat [a prayer in which he has erred], unless he skipped "who resurrects the dead" or "who humbles the insolent" or "who rebuilds Jerusalem." I say that such a person is a *min*). For the language of the Babylonian eulogy, see *Midrash Psalms* 29 (Buber ed., 116b).

ʾEreṣ Yisraʾeli Rite		*Babylonian Rite*				
1 (8 MSS)	2 (2 MSS)	3 (8 MSS)	4A (21 MSS)	4B (17 MSS)	5 (6 MSS)	6 (24 MSS)
למשומדים אל תהי תקוה	למשומדים אל תהי תקוה	למשומדים אל תהי תקוה	למשומדים אל תהי תקוה	למשומדים אל תהי תקוה	למשומדים אל תהי תקוה	למשומדים אל תהי תקוה
אם לא ישובו לתורתך						
					וכל המינים כרגע יאבדו	
					וכל אויבי עמך מהרה יכרתו	
	ומלכות זדון מהרה תעקר בימינו	ומלכות זדון מהרה תעקר בימינו	ומלכות זדון מהרה תעקר ותשבר בימינו	ומלכות זדון מהרה תעקר ותשבר ותכניע בימינו	ומלכות זדון מהרה תעקר ותשבר בימינו	ומלכות זדון מהרה תעקר בימינו
הנצרים והמינים כרגע יאבדו	והנצרים והמינים כרגע יאבדו	והנצרים והמינים כרגע יאבדו	והנצרים והמינים כרגע יאבדו	והנצרים והמינים כרגע יאבדו		

לתורתך (if they do not return to Your Torah), that come to modify the harsh curse with which the blessing opens.[36] However, this component appears only in the more widespread branch of the *ʾereṣ yisraʾeli* rite (1), while in the other branch (2), a phrase which appears in all of the branches of the Babylonian rite replaces it, reading ומלכות זדון מהרה תעקר בימינו (Uproot the empire of insolence quickly in our days).

Quite distinct variations appear within the Babylonian rite. The manuscript evidence suggests that there were five separate branches of this rite, but with clear connections between several of them. It is quite simple to delineate the developmental process between branches 3, 4A, and 4B. The linguistic foundation of all of them is the language of version 3, to which version 4A adds the

36 Based on the fact that these words reflect back on and moderate the previous phrase, and because they are not found in the other version of the Land of Israel (2), Flusser, "Some of the Precepts," 347–48, concludes that they are a secondary addition.

ʾEreṣ Yisraʾeli Rite		*Babylonian Rite*				
1 (8 MSS)	*2 (2 MSS)*	*3 (8 MSS)*	*4A (21 MSS)*	*4B (17 MSS)*	*5 (6 MSS)*	*6 (24 MSS)*
ימחו מספר חיים ועם צדיקים אל יכתבו	ימחו מספר חיים ועם צדיקים אל יכתבו					
			וכל אויבי עמך וצורריהם מהרה יכרתו	וכל אויבי עמך וצורריהם מהרה יכרתו		
				ושבור עול הגוים מעל צוארינו ואל תתן תקומה לכל אויבי נפשינו		
ברוך אתה יי מכניע זדים	ברוך אתה יי מכניע זדים	ברוך אתה יי שובר רשעים ומכניע זדים	ברוך אתה יי שובר רשעים ומכניע זדים	ברוך אתה יי שובר אויבים ומכניע זדים	ברוך אתה יי שובר אויבים ומכניע זדים	ברוך אתה יי שובר רשעים ומכניע זדים

petition against enemies, וכל אויבי עמך וצורריהם[37] מהרה יכרתו (May all the enemies of Your people and their oppressors be speedily cut off),[38] and version 4B expands upon this addition, saying ושבור עול הגוים מעל צוארינו ואל תתן תקומה לכל אויבי נפשינו (and break the yoke of the gentiles off our necks and

37 The word וצורריהם (and their persecutors), functioning only as a synonym for אויבי עמך (the enemies of Your people), does not appear in four manuscripts of this version. The word is also absent in all the citations of this segment in version (5). It is possible that these four manuscripts of 4A point to the original form of the segment.

38 Apparently, the text of the *Siddur of R.Shlomo of Sigilmassa* belongs to branch 4A. The manuscript 4ל and the combination of manuscripts 22ק and 25ק (see Appendix A) are copies of this sage's *siddur* and their language belongs to this branch. One must remember that processes similar to those which shaped the great *siddurim* of the geonim, Rav Amram and Rav Saadia, also affected this highly esteemed siddur. Its usage by various communities in different periods caused the introduction of prayer texts into the manuscripts that were customary in those locales and that were not the original language of the *siddur*. This is how one should understand the text of the

grant no recovery to our enemies).[39] These two later additions function to designate additional enemies beyond the מלכות זדון (the empire of insolence). As is common in additions to existing liturgical texts,[40] these were inserted at the end and hence not in conjunction with the segment addressing ומלכות זדון (and the empire of insolence).

A similar developmental trajectory appears when we consider the verbs petitioning for the downfall of the empire. Branch 3 reads: ומלכות זדון מהרה תעקר בימינו (and uproot the empire of insolence speedily in our day). Only a few of its manuscripts add other verbs. In contrast to this, in branch 4A, the majority of manuscripts add the verb ותשבר (and smash) after תעקר (uproot), and in version 4B, in the majority of its manuscripts, the petition is three-fold תעקר ותשבר ותכניע (uproot and smash and bring low). The physical characteristics of the manuscripts support the suggestion that these are indeed later additions. There are more later manuscripts of branch 4B than of 3 and 4A. In addition, it was a text similar to version 4B, rather than its predecessors, that apparently influenced the later middle eastern rites.[41]

---

blessing that is published in the edition of Shmuel Haggai (Jerusalem 1995) that reads: למשומדים למינים ולזידים אל תהי להם תקוה ומלכות זדון מהרה תעקר ותשבר ותכניע ותאביד אויבינו מהרה כרגע יאבדו והזדים מהרה יכרתו ואל תתן תקומה לכל אויבי נפשינו וצררינו בא״י שובר רשעים ומכניע זדים "May there be no hope for the apostates and the *minim* and the insolent, and may the insolent empire be quickly uprooted and smashed and humbled and led astray, and may our enemies speedily immediately be lost, and may the insolent be quickly cut off and do not grant any recovery to our enemies and our oppressors. Blessed are You, Eternal, who breaks evildoers and humbles the insolent." This section of Haggai's edition is based on an early sixteenth-century manuscript of the *siddur*. See Yosef Tobi, "The Prayer Book of Rabbi Shlomo ben Nathan of Sigilmassa," in Zvi Malachi, ed., *Yad Leheiman: Memorbuch for A. H. Habermann* (Tel Aviv: Habermann Institute, 1984) 348. The text itself is definitely defective and to a certain extent one can recognize in it the influence of the Persian rite (see below, n. 41).

39 This addition is actually a combination of two separate passages. The last phrase, ואל תתן תקומה וכו׳ (and grant no recovery, etc.) is missing in about a third of the manuscripts of branch 4B, and it is possible that it is an even later addition that has the purpose of returning the language of the end of the blessing to a topic that is מעין החתימה (that reflects the topic and language of the concluding eulogy). Compare also the later eastern rites. In Persia, only the second phrase appears; in Aleppo, both phrases appear but in reversed order. On both rites see n. 41.

40 See, for example, the addition, לא יבושו לעולם קויך (May those who hope in You never be ashamed) that was added in many *ʾereṣ yisraʾeli* rite prayer books at the end of the *ʾavot* benediction; or the addition כהרף עין ישועה לנו תצמיח (May salvation sprout for us in the blink of an eye) at the end of the *gevurot* benediction. For these additions, see: Uri Ehrlich, "A Complete Weekday Amidah According to the Rite of the Land of Israel," *Qovez al Yad* NS 18 (2005) 18–21 (Heb.). See also the discussion of the addition in the next paragraph.

41 See also the Persian rite text (ENA 23, published by Shlomo Tal, *Nusaḥ hatefillah shel yehudei p'ras* [Jerusalem: Ben-Zvi Institute, 1980] 84): למשומדים ולמינים ולזדים ולכופרים ולרשעים אל תהי להם תקוה ותאוה ומלכות זדון מהרה תעקר ותשבר ותכניע ותאביד וכל אויבי עמך ישראל וצרריהם במהרה יכרתו וישמדו ויאבדו ואל תתן תקומה לכל אויבי נפשנו בא״י שובר אויבים ומכניע זדים "May there be no hope and desire for apostates and for *minim*, and for the insolent and for heretics and

This developmental picture helps us to evaluate the rest of the segments of this subset of branches. Here, the pairing of *noṣerim* with *minim* in the segment והנוצרים והמינים כרגע יאבדו (May the *noṣerim* and the *minim* immediately be lost), is very stable, hardly lacking in a single manuscript. The few texts that mention additional groups of evildoers, like מלשינים and מוסרים (both referring to informers), etc., are clustered in version 4B, which, as we saw, represents a somewhat later period than the others.[42] These additions to *noṣerim* and *minim* and certainly the substitution of other types of evildoers for one, the other, or both of them, not only appear in few manuscripts from the geniza period, but all such manuscripts are late.

This developmental claim also suggests that the Babylonian variant of the blessing's eulogy that reads שובר רשעים (who breaks evildoers) is earlier and that which reads שובר אויבים (who breaks enemies) is later. In most of the manuscripts of branches 3 and 4A, the eulogy reads שובר רשעים (who breaks evildoers), while in version 4B, the majority of the manuscripts read שובר אויבים (who breaks enemies). One might hypothesize that originally, the referent of the language שובר רשעים (who breaks evildoers) was internal Jewish sinners like apostates and *minim*, while the referent of מכניע זדים (who humbles the insolent) was to external enemies like the insolent empire. Thus, the Babylonian eulogy reflected the two main objects of the prayer. But with the addition of the new segment dealing with enemies at the end of the blessing, a process began of replacing the wording שובר רשעים (who breaks evildoers) with שובר אויבים (who breaks enemies) so that the language of the eulogy would reflect that of the body of the blessing.[43]

---

for the evildoers, and may You speedily uproot and smash and humble and set astray the empire of insolence, and may all the enemies of Your people Israel and their oppressors quickly be cut off and persecuted and lost, and do not give recovery to any of the enemies of our persons. Blessed are You, Eternal, who breaks enemies and humbles the insolent." See also the Aleppo rite text (MS Oxford Bodleian Library MS Marsh. 90 [1146] 28b): למינים אל תהי תקוה [והנצרים] והאויבים והזידים כולם כרגע יאבדו וכל אויבי עמך ישראל ולוחציהם ומבקשי רעתם כולם מהרה יכרתו וישמדו ואל תתן תקומה ואחרית לכל אויבי נפשינו אנא [ברחמיך הרבים] שבור עול הגוים מעל צורינו ומכף אויבינו ואל תמסרינו ומלכות זדון מהרה תעקר ותשבר בימינו ברוך אתה ה׳ שובר אויבים ומכניע זדים "May there be no hope for *minim* and may [the *noṣerim*] and the enemies and the insolent all immediately be lost, and may all the enemies of Your people Israel and their persecutors and those who seek ill of them all quickly be cut off and persecuted and do not grant any recovery or future to any of the enemies of our persons. Please [in Your great mercy], break the yoke of the nations from our necks, and from the hands of our enemies, and do not hand us over, and may You speedily uproot and smash the empire of insolence in our day. Blessed are You, Eternal, who breaks enemies and humbles the insolent."

42 In branch 3, a single manuscript reads *malshinim* instead of *noṣerim*, and this too is the latest manuscript of this version.

43 See also the ninth-century responsum of Rav Natronai Gaon (R. Brody, ed., *Teshuvot Rav Natronai bar Hilai Gaon* [2 vols.; Jerusalem: Ofeq, 1994] 1:137–38): וברכת המינים יש שחותם שובר

Finally, it is important to indicate that the linguistic core of this family of branches, found in version 3, is identical word for word to branch 2 of the rite of *ʾereṣ yisraʾel*, aside from the two characteristics that are unique to that rite. This suggests that there was a point of historical connection between the rites of *ʾereṣ yisraʾel* and Babylonia.

The majority of the Babylonian-rite manuscripts belong to this family of branches (3, 4A, 4B). Related to it is branch 5 which includes all the components of version 4A, but in a different order. Here, the petitions against *minim* and against enemies always directly follow the opening segment (against apostates) and precede the one against the insolent empire, which now concludes the body of the blessing.[44] A consequence of – and perhaps the reason for – this reorganization is that it makes the sequence of topics more logical and harmonious. It juxtaposes the segments against internal sinners, that is, the apostates and the *minim*, at the beginning of the blessing, leaving the segments that deal with external enemies (the enemies of Your people, and the empire of insolence) for the end. Most likely, the earlier order of the blessing's segments was that found in the Babylonian family of branches 3, 4A, and 4B, and the order found in version 5 developed from this, rather than the reverse. That the *ʾereṣ yisraʾeli* branch version 2 also reflects this earlier order underscores this supposition. If this determination is correct, then it is logical to hypothesize either that branch 5 separated from branch 4A which already included the basic version of the addition against enemies, or that it reflects a parallel development to that of branch 4A, constituting a different method of incorporating this addition.

In spite of its limited circulation among the communities represented in the geniza, branch 5 had a deciding and enduring influence on the development of the *birkat haminim* in later centuries. Its order of topics is the order in all

רשעים ויש [שחותם מכניע זדים] "There are those who conclude the *birkat haminim* with 'who breaks evildoers' and there are [those who conclude 'who humbles the insolent.']" *Midrash Psalms* 29 (Buber ed., 116b) does employ the eulogy שובר אויבים (who breaks enemies), but it is likely that this wording is the product of the influence of the later liturgical rite used in the place of the copyist. This claim is supported by the text itself, which reads: קול ה׳ יחיל מדבר. אלו הרשעים שמנוקים מכל מצוה כמדבר, והקב״ה מחלחל אותם, כנגד שובר אויבים "*The voice of God makes the desert tremble*: these are the *evildoers* who have been cleansed of all *miṣvot* like a desert, and the Holy One, blessed be He, makes them tremble, corresponding to 'who breaks enemies.'"

44 We must point out that the geniza contains twelve fragments of this version, not only the six that have been considered in our discussion here. The six that were excluded are either not in a middle eastern hand or are in a doubtfully middle eastern hand. Not a single one can be dated before 1250, and some are significantly later. (A list of these manuscripts may be found at the end of Appendix A). That these manuscripts belong to version 5 is not surprising, for all of the later western rites draw from the wording of this version. On this, see below. Like version 4B whose manuscripts are also mostly relatively late, these manuscripts include many variants in the segment against the *minim*.

European rites.[45] In contrast, the order of topics that was widespread in the Babylonian rite persisted only in the Middle East, but only until the arrival of Sefardi refugees and the imposition of the Sefardi rite.[46] The structure of the blessing in the European rites can probably be attributed to the *Seder Rav Amram Gaon*'s great influence on the development of prayer there.[47] In spite of the numerous differences among the manuscripts of the *Seder Rav Amram Gaon*, all of them present branch 5's organization of the components of the blessing.

Among the branches of the Babylonian rite, branch 6 is exceptional. Unlike all other Babylonian branches, it contains no segment against enemies, and unlike every other known version of the blessing, it omits entirely the segment against the *minim*. However, in spite of this, version 6 was very widespread among the liturgies of the communities represented in the geniza. This probably derives from the great authority given to the *Siddur Rav Saadia Gaon* by many early communities in the east. That this version received Rav Saadia Gaon's stamp of approval is certain: five of the geniza manuscripts of this version are definitely copies of his prayer book, including that which appears in the printed version. This authoritative source also accounts for the great stability in the wording of this version; there are relatively few variants found among the geniza manuscripts.

However, this version still presents a significant difficulty. How can a text of the *birkat haminim* lack the segment dealing with the *minim*, that which appears to be the heart of the blessing? One possibility is that an activist and authoritative Gaon like Saadia deliberately omitted this segment from a received Babylonian rite text like branch 3. This abbreviation, if he made it, is consistent with Saadia's predilection for short and concise texts. However, we have no proof that Saadia himself made such a change. Another authority might also have been responsible, if such a change in fact occurred.

It is possible to posit a reverse process, that this version was itself a received early text that Rav Saadia Gaon chose to adopt for his prayer book. If so, this could be an extremely ancient text, perhaps the earliest preserved. It would then be witness to the period before the addition of the explicit curse against

45 Maimonides' text, למשומדים אל תהי תקוה כל המינים כרגע יאבדו ומלכות זדון תעקר ותשבר מהרה בימינו בא״י שובר (רשעים) אויבים ומכניע זדים "May there be no hope for apostates, may all the *minim* immediately be lost, and may the empire of insolence be uprooted and smashed speedily in our day. Blessed are You, O God, who breaks [evildoers] enemies and humbles the insolent" also reflects this ordering of the segments. See E. D. Goldschmidt, "The Oxford MS of Maimonides' Book of Prayer," in his *On Jewish Liturgy: Essays on Prayer and Religious Poetry* (Jerusalem: Magnes, 1996) 199 (Heb.).

46 See n. 41.

47 No manuscripts have been preserved that might reflect the prayer customs of Jews in Europe preceding the arrival there of the *Seder Rav Amram Gaon*. It is therefore impossible to know for certain whether his Babylonian rite displaced a native rite, or whether it was only with the arrival of his text that European Jews began to adhere to rabbinic norms of prayer.

the *noṣerim* and *minim*.[48] As is well known, Lieberman and Heinemann suggest that the establishment or emendation of the *birkat haminim* that the Babylonian Talmud (*Ber.* 28b–29a) reports was not the composition of a blessing *ex nihilo*, but rather the introduction of the segment against the *minim* into an existing prayer.[49] This theory is based on a *baraita*:[50]

> שמונה עשרה ברכות שאמרו חכמים, כנגד שמנה עשרה אזכרות שבהבו לה׳ בני אלים כולל של מינים בשל פרושין, ושל גרים בשל זקנים ושל דוד בבונה ירושלם.
>
> The eighteen blessings that the sages decreed correspond to the eighteen mentions of the Divine Name in Psalm 29. [To achieve this number of blessings] one includes that of *minim* in that of the *paroshim*, and that of proselytes in that of the elders, and that of David in that for the rebuilding of Jerusalem.

As Lieberman suggests, the *paroshim* are those who separated themselves (פרשו) from the ways of the community, and these included apostates.[51] It is possible, then, that version 6 represents an early *birkat haparoshim* into which the Sages added the segment against the *minim*. According to this hypothesis, this addition accounts for the formulation of the two branches of the *ʾereṣ yisraʾeli* rite and also for the foundation of the majority of the Babylonian branches. The more common *ʾereṣ yisraʾeli* branch 1 combined the two parts, substituting the segment against the *minim* for the early segment against the empire of insolence. The *ʾereṣ yisraʾeli* branch 2 added the segment against the *minim* into the full text of its received wording, creating the three-fold blessing text. This same combination generates the body of the Babylonian rite text that is reflected in purest form in branch 3 and from which developed the rest of the branches of this rite (as described above). In Babylonia, though, a remnant of the early wording predating the addition of the segment against the *minim* also survived – in the text of version 6 adopted by Rav Saadia Gaon. However, in spite of the apparent popularity of this rite among the Jews who left their texts in the geniza, version 6 does not persist in any known rite.

Finally, we still need to explain the history of the term *noṣerim* in the texts of the blessing. This word appears in all the prayer books of the rite of *ʾereṣ*

48 This was apparently the opinion of Louis Finkelstein, who saw this wording as the "original text" of the blessing. See his "The Development of the Amidah," *JQR* NS 16 (1925–26) 157; in Petuchowski, *Contributions*, 164.

49 See Saul Lieberman, *Tosefta kifshutah, zera'im* (2 vols.; New York: Jewish Theological Seminary of America, 1955) 1:54; Joseph Heinemann, *Prayer in the Talmud: Forms and Patterns* (Berlin & New York: Walter de Gruyter, 1977) 225.

50 *T.Ber.* 3:25 and parallels.

51 See *Seder Olam Rabbah*, end of chap. 3.

yisraʾel, as it does in all but two of the forty-five exemplars of the Babylonian rite's branches 3, 4A and 4B. However, this is not the situation in branch 5. Although only the word *minim* appears in the text presented in the table, this reflects only half of the manuscripts. Three manuscripts read וכל המינים (and all the *minim*), two have both *noṣerim* and *minim*, and one reads וכל המינים וכל המלשינים (and all the *minim* and all the informers). In light of this, it is difficult to determine whether the early text of this branch was *minim* alone, and the term *noṣerim* was added through the influence of the more widespread branches, or perhaps it was the opposite and the early text read "*noṣerim* and *minim*" but the word *noṣerim* was eliminated.[52] However, in light of the general picture that emerges from the geniza findings, that so many manuscripts read both *noṣerim* and *minim*, always in this order with almost no exceptions, both in the rites of *ʾereṣ yisraʾel* and of Babylonia, it is more reasonable to conclude that the terms *noṣerim* and *minim* entered the blessing together. If one of them is early, then both are, and if one of them is late, then both are.

The evidence of the early prayer books suggests that the separation of the terms is a product of elimination of the word *noṣerim*, perhaps as a result of external pressures. While the meaning of *minim* retained some ambiguity, *noṣerim* became a term applied specifically to Christians, making it more politically sensitive. However it is no less logical to posit that this change reflected an internal shift in Jewish thinking about the gentiles among whom they were living. Perhaps Jews living in Muslim lands, alongside a defanged Christian minority, had no reason to call for their demise. Or, alternatively, dropping the specificity of *noṣerim*, retaining just the more general *minim*, allowed the inclusion of Muslims in the intent of the curse. Version 5 teaches that this process had already begun in the Babylonian rite at the beginning of the period witnessed in the Cairo geniza,[53] and it took on, from its beginning, just the form of the elimination of the word *noṣerim*.[54] Only slightly later, the additions of other groups of

52 A hint of such a process of elimination of the word *noṣerim* might be found in the addition of the word "all" before the word *minim* in this version. Such an addition would hint at what was no longer being stated explicitly.

53 Note that one of the manuscripts of this branch is dated around 900.

54 As was indicated above, the text that appears in the *Seder Rav Amram Gaon* belongs to this branch. However, it is difficult to determine whether Rav Amram himself included the word "*noṣerim*" or whether it had already been eliminated. The Oxford manuscript of the *siddur* reads והנוצרים והמינים יכלו כרגע (May the *noṣerim* and the *minim* be destroyed immediately) while the manuscript of the Jewish Theological Seminary reads והמינים כרגע יאבדו (May the *minim* be immediately lost). The text found in the manuscript of the British Library is a clear reworking of the wording of the blessing, which reads וכל הזדים כרגע יאבדו (May all the insolent be immediately lost). This manuscript also corrects the beginning of the blessing, reading למלשינים אל תהי תקוה (May there be no hope for informers). Both of these segments reflect language typical of texts rewritten after censorship was imposed in the early modern period.

sinners began.[55] In this context, it is important to recall again that in the early Babylonian rite, the version that did not include the segment against the *minim* at all was widespread and had the seal of Rav Saadia Gaon on it.

Later Medieval Versions of the *Birkat Haminim*

Methodological Introduction

The Cairo geniza may provide our earliest source of (post-Qumran) Jewish liturgical manuscripts, but its evidence can be fully evaluated only in comparison with the later liturgical materials that were collected and preserved in European and eventually also North American contexts.[56] Which manuscripts were collected and preserved was largely a matter of happenstance, dependent both on the whim of wealthy Christian collectors (whose collections often ended up in public or university libraries) and on the fate of the Jewish communities of various areas. As a result, there are rather rich collections of manuscripts preserved from Ashkenaz[57] and Italy, while very few manuscripts survived from Sefarad.[58] Enough survive from the Romaniot rite[59] that we include them here, but there are so few medieval texts surviving from the Jewish communities living in the domains of Islam and non-Byzantine eastern churches that no valid conclusions may be drawn about their native rites. What evidence exists has been noted in comparison with the geniza materials in the previous section.

This imbalance makes it necessary to treat each rite according to separate criteria, looking at all available manuscripts when only a relatively few survived, as in the case of the Sefardi, French and Romaniot rites; and looking primarily at those that survived the censor unscathed when there are hundreds of manuscripts, as in the case of the Italian rites. In all cases, there is some variety apparent within each rite. Jewish liturgical scholars are only beginning to under-

55 This also arises from the limited evidence that one can derive from the group of manuscripts described at the beginning of n. 30.

56 Fortunately for the scholar, microfilms of these manuscripts by the thousands have been systematically collected and made available in the Institute for Microfilmed Hebrew Manuscripts at the Jewish National and University Library in Jerusalem. The data and discussion that follow derives from Ruth Langer's study of this material. Her sabbatical work in 2001–2 was supported by a fellowship from the Yad Hanadiv/Beracha Foundation as well as by Boston College.

57 In medieval liturgical studies, this designation conventionally applies to the three distinct rites of northern France, the Rhineland, and the Canaanite or Slavic lands to the east.

58 That is, the rites of the Iberian peninsula and areas to which Iberian Jews transported their rites. In the period before the mass expulsions of Jews from Spain at the end of the fifteenth century, this especially included areas of North Africa, Italy, and various islands in the Mediterranean.

59 This rite is that of the medieval Byzantine empire. It encompassed the Balkans, Greece, southern Italy, and at least some of Asia Minor. Greek was the vernacular of this community; the rite is sometimes also called "Greek."

stand the characteristics of the regional branches of some European rites; this work has not progressed far enough to inform this study deeply.[60]

Two upheavals in the sixteenth century radically changed the map of texts of the *birkat haminim*, creating much of the informational gap that this article addresses. First, the expulsion of the Iberian Jews (1492 and 1497) and their dispersal throughout the Jewish world resulted in the submersion and disappearance of the local rites of North Africa, the Middle East, and the Balkans, in deference to the Castilian rite of the dominant group of Sefardi refugees. This is almost certainly a significant factor contributing to the disappearance of manuscripts of the native rites of these areas.[61] Second, the printing of Hebrew prayer books for the entire Jewish world was early dominated by the Italian presses, and these were placed under official Church censorship in the 1550's. These two factors resulted in an erasure of local rites and forced radical and universal changes to the texts of the *birkat haminim*, to the point that no one has yet retrieved their previous versions accurately or fully.[62]

This task is immensely complicated by the fact that Jewish sensitivity to Christian concerns about this prayer probably, and in some cases, certainly, resulted in a degree of self-censorship in Europe, even before the Church imposed changes. Even more significantly, the Counter-Reformation's concern about Hebrew texts was not limited to newly printed editions. The Church objected to the presence of heresy within its domain, including within existing books and manuscripts. These they systematically collected and expurgated or destroyed. Luckily, the relatively limited number of objectionable passages found in Jewish liturgy resulted in regular expurgation by blacking out or less frequently, erasing, the words deemed offensive to Christians and Christianity.[63] As a

60 Jonah Fraenkel is currently studying the Ashkenazi rites, including those of northern France. His conference presentations suggest a major contribution to the map of medieval liturgy.

61 Preservation of older unusable manuscripts would likely be done by an elite who could give space to "useless" books. However, in this instance, the elite was precisely the group most likely to accept the Sefardi rite. Local traditions of *piyyut* did continue to exist in manuscript form, but generally written as a supplement to the printed Sefardi statutory prayers. See the sources referenced in Langer, *To Worship God Properly: Tensions between Liturgical Custom and Halakhah in Judaism* (Cincinnati: HUC Press, 1998) 179 ff.

62 Various scholars have made attempts based on the few manuscripts and medieval texts about the prayers to which they had access. See for example, the commentary of Baer, *Seder ᶜavodat yisraʾel*, 93–94; or Hirsch, "Shemoneh ᶜEsreh," 11:281.

63 On the history of Christian censorship of Hebrew books, see Moshe Carmilly-Weinberger, *Censorship and Freedom of Expression in Jewish History* (New York: Sepher-Hermon Press with Yeshiva Univ. Press, 1977); Amnon Raz-Krakotzkin, "Censorship, Editing, and the Reshaping of Jewish Identity: The Catholic Church and Hebrew Literature in the Sixteenth Century," in Allison P. Coudert and Jeffrey S. Shoulson, eds., *Hebraica Veritas?: Christian Hebraists and the Study of Judaism in Early Modern Europe* (Philadelphia: Univ. of Pennsylvania Press, 2004) 125–55; and his *The Censor, the Editor and the Text* (Jerusalem: Magnes, 2005) (Heb.); and the sources they cite.

consequence, the majority of medieval European liturgical manuscripts contain texts of the *birkat haminim* whose words are illegible or have been rewritten with acceptable terms. However, we can also frequently guess from the size of the expurgation what might have been the original text. Because it is usually impossible to date a rewriting, we will have to presume that all such texts post-date our period of interest.

EUROPEAN RITES

The table on the opposite page presents single early exemplars of each of the European rites. Appendix B provides critical notes to the variants found in other uncensored manuscripts. Where appropriate, the following discussion will also draw on additional evidence that can be gleaned from censored manuscripts.

As is immediately evident and as has been suggested above, all European rites organize their segments according to Babylonian version 5, apparently according to the rite of the *Seder Rav Amram Gaon* that was so immensely influential in shaping European liturgical traditions. The variety among these rites lies in the specific words that they employ and not in the ordering or general intention of their segments. The Romaniot/Greek and Sefardi rites demonstrate a tendency to elaborate on that core structure, but not to the degree found in the Babylonian rite's branch 4B, its variants, and its clones in the Eastern Rites. All of these European rites functioned in territory that was either fully Christian or that had a significant Christian presence either before or during the period represented by these manuscripts.[64] It might seem noteworthy, then, that not a single manuscript contains a reference to the *noṣerim*. However, in medieval European Hebrew, the referent of the word *minim* was "Christians."[65] Christians were well aware of this and knew that the malediction was consistently interpreted as referring to them. The absence of *noṣerim* therefore does not signify all that much and may be more a product of its earlier elimination from the Babylonian branch 5 on which these rites depended.

Perusal of the variants listed in Appendix B will also demonstrate that not a single one of these rites has successfully imposed a fixed and authoritative text, in spite of the discussions of textual fixity spearheaded by the *ḥasidei ʾashkenaz*

64 All Sefardi manuscripts post-date the Reconquista, but we must presume that the Sefardi rite took shape in Muslim Spain, beginning at least from the point of their reception of explicit liturgical direction from the Babylonian *geonim* Natronai and Amram in the late ninth century. We know nothing about the worship traditions of Iberian Jews prior to this. Much of Balkan territory fell at times under Turkish Muslim control, and few manuscripts fully predate this. We have no evidence for the nature of Jewish worship in the rest of Europe before its Christianization.

65 See, for example, the use of the term in the Hebrew text (but not the translation!) of David Berger, *The Jewish-Christian Debate in the High Middle Ages: A Critical Edition of the* Nizzahon Vetus (Philadelphia: Jewish Publication Society of America, 1979).

Romaniot	*Italian*	*Ashkenazi*	*French*	*Sefardi*
למשומדים אל יהי להם תקוה	ולמלשינים בל תהי תקוה	למשומדים אל תהי תקוה	ולמשומדים אל תהי תקוה	למשומדים אל תהי תקוה
והמינים והמלשינים והכופרים והמסורים כולם כרגע יאבדו	וכל המינים כלם כרגע יאבדו	וכל המינים כרגע יאבדו	וכל המינים כרגע יאבדו	וכל המינים וכל המלשינים וכל המסורות כלם כרגע יאבדו
וכל אויבי עמך ישראל מהרה מארץ יכרתון	וכל גוים אויבי עמך ישראל מהרה יכרתו	וכל אויבי עמך מהרה יכרתון	וכל אויבי עמך בית ישראל מהרה יכרתון	וכל אויבי עמך ישראל [נ״א וכל אויבינו וכל שונאינו וכל מבקשי רעתינו] מהרה יכרתו
ומלכות זדון מהרה תעקר ותשבר [ותמגר] ותכניע אותם מהרה בימינו	ומלכות זדון במהרה תעקר ותשבר ותכניע אתם במהרה בימינו	ומלכות זדון מהרה תעקר ותשבר ותמגר ותכניע כל אויבינו במהרה בימינו	ומלכות זדון מהרה תעקר ותשבר ותמגר ותשפיל ותשמיד ותכניע כל איובנו במהרה בימינו	ומלכות זדון מהרה תעקר ותשבר ותמגר ותכניע ותשפיל ותפיל כל אויבינו וכל שונאינו ותכלם במהרה בימינו
בא״י שובר רשעים ומכניע זדים	בא״י שובר אויבים ומכניע זדים	בא״י שובר אויבים ומכניע זידים	בא״י שובר אויבים ומכניע זדים	בא״י שובר אויבים ומכניע זדים

and subsequently introduced into the halakhic texts of the Iberian peninsula by the Asherides. While the general structure of the *berakhah* is indeed stable, small details are far from stable and even larger details within the lists of nouns and verbs can vary significantly. We lack sufficient information about the provenance of most manuscripts to know whether these represent regional variants or, alternatively, some degree of fluidity in the language of the text. That clusters of variants do not appear together consistently in the same manuscripts suggests, though, that we are dealing with individual rather than regional decisions. Such variations include the matter of whether the *berakhah* begins with a conjunctive or not (ולמשומדים or למשומדים) where the French, Ashkenazi, and Romaniot rites demonstrate both, or the precise list of verbs and their objects in the segment directed against the government. As would be expected, the eulogy is largely stable, though the Babylonian variant, רשעים instead of אויבים, "evil ones" instead of "enemies," does appear in one Romaniot manuscript and in a few Sefardi censorship-era editions.[66]

Romaniot Rites. The earliest manuscripts of this rite show significant consistency in their texts. However, none predate the fourteenth century, and the single fourteenth-century manuscript has numerous small variants from the others. Therefore, the base text for our discussion is one dated slightly later, to the fourteenth or fifteenth centuries. As the rite was only printed twice[67] before the community adopted Sefardi-rite prayer books almost entirely, its preserved history is very short. Most exemplars of the Romaniot rite elaborate somewhat on their presumed Babylonian predecessor, adding emphasis to the opening segment with the word להם (for them) and to the second segment with an extended list of malefactors in addition to the *minim*. Although there are minor differences in grammar, spelling, and order among the manuscripts, the list itself is the same in each uncensored version.[68]

In the third segment of this rite, we see what appears to be a change over time, resulting in a unique text. In the fourteenth-century manuscripts, this segment is very similar to other rites. But starting by the fifteenth century, the prayer is that the enemies be cut off *from the earth* (מארץ יכרתון). In the sixteenth century, this addition becomes מארץ חיים (from the land of the living) forming an obvious allusion to Jeremiah 11:19, ונכרתנו מארץ חיים ושמו לא יזכר עוד "Let us cut him off from the land of the living, that his name be remembered no more" (NJPS).[69]

As in all the European rites except Italy, the earliest exemplar of the Romaniot rites (27) adds a second mention of enemies in the conclusion of the fourth segment. As a result, the final verb directed against the government in the geniza rites now applies to this added category. It is possible that this is a relic of the

66 See the editions printed in Venice 1564, 1565, and 1617 (סדר תפלות כל השנה כמנהג א"א ספרד ... [בית ייואני קאיון, שעז]), all three examined in the Jewish National and University Library, Jerusalem.

67 Venice 1586 and 1665, both under the aegis of the Catholic censor. (Jewish Theological Seminary, Very Rare Books, Reel 5, #5706 and #5708.)

68 The printed editions both substitute זדים (the arrogant) for the entire list. They also retrieve the להם (to them) which was omitted in the later manuscripts.

69 In addition to the manuscript listed in the appendix, this language appears in the two printed editions and in an uncensored seventeenth-century manuscript, MS Parma 2587 (947).

earlier organization of the *berakhah*, when this segment preceded that about the enemies, as in the Babylonian branches 4A and 4B, and because the boundaries between the segments were not fully clear, this segment retained some of what followed it in that organization. This gives added support to the hypothesis offered above that the reorganization characteristic of Babylonian branch 5 occurred after the emergence of branch 4A, but likely before the elaboration of that branch in 4B.[70] In all the other Romaniot exemplars, in Italy, and scattered exemplars elsewhere, this specific reference has become "them," a term that now can apply as well to the empire or perhaps all the preceding discussions of the prayer, thus creating a smoother text. There is no literary imperative to mention "enemies" at this point. The standard reference to the empire as "insolent," once appearing as the fourth segment of the blessing, fulfills any demand for a literary transition to the eulogy.

Italian Rites. A vast collection of liturgical manuscripts from Italy survived. However, they were routinely subject to censorship, both internal and external, to the point that it is difficult to discern the original versions of the *birkat haminim*. The earliest manuscript that shows no signs of censorship hails from the fourteenth century. The earliest preserved Italian liturgical manuscript is a bit earlier, from the thirteenth century, but this exemplar already includes suggestions of self-censorship – a self-censorship that did not prevent a more severe externally imposed censorship of this manuscript later. However, the Italian practice of self-censorship did generate a ready set of substitute terms that could be instituted once external censors found the original unacceptable. Because the overwhelming majority of early printed Hebrew prayer books emanated from Italy, these substitutions found their way into all other European rites.

Unlike in the Romaniot rite, the Italian-rite manuscripts show so much variety as to suggest the presence of regional subrites. However, the current state of research does not allow their identification.[71] While the critical notes in the appendix cover only the eight apparently uncensored manuscripts (of over 150 witnesses to the text of the *birkat haminim* examined that are dated before the imposition of external censorship), the discussion here will make reference, as appropriate, to the witness of the censored texts also.

The Italian rites are unique in that there is no surviving evidence that they ever addressed their opening segment to משומדים *meshummadim*, "apostates." The vast majority of manuscripts simply pray that there be no hope for מלשינים *malshinim*, "informers."[72] However, approximately a quarter of the manuscripts

70 See above, in the discussion following n. 44.

71 Even the most recent printing of the Italian-rite *maḥzor*, the *Siddùr Benè Romi* (Milan: Morashà, 2000–) contains variants according to the separate usages of Rome and Milan.

72 This included, apparently, the *Seder Ḥibbur Berakhot*, available today only in Solomon Schechter's

still contain – or show evidence that they once contained – an alternative opening, praying that there be no hope for *minim* and *malshinim*[73] (or in the reverse order).[74] We might speculate that in the period preceding our evidence, the Italian rites commonly began this way, but that the opening term *minim* was dropped, most likely in an act self-censorship, but possibly because of a consciousness that most other rites included it in the second segment. Although our handful of uncensored manuscripts include two that begin just with *minim*, directing the second segment to the *malshinim* instead, this is actually a rare variant. Though other exemplars may have been censored past recognition, it appears in only one other manuscript among those examined, and that one seems to represent a post-censorship version in every aspect except this opening word.[75]

Did the Italian rites once begin with an address to *meshummadim*? Here we can only speculate. Given the virtual universality of this opening line, not only in the geniza but in almost all other rites, this seems likely. The alternative text in the Italian rites would then be the product of an early act of self-censorship, one so early and universally accepted that no traces are left of the original in any known manuscripts. This self-censorship might logically have occurred together with the removal of the *noṣerim* from this rite. However, there is

copy (JTS MS 8402) of the only known manuscript, later destroyed in a fire in 1894. Thus, there is no longer a possibility of examining the text for signs of censorship. See Abraham I. Schechter, *Studies in Jewish Liturgy* (Philadelphia: Dropsie College, 1930) 85.

73 In addition to the manuscript listed as 8ט, see, for example: MS Paris Alliance Israelite Universelle 427, fourteenth century; MS Vatican Biblioteca Apostolica 331, fourteenth century; MS Parma Biblioteca Palatina Codice de Rossi 1754 (1056), Cremona 1479; MS Cambridge University Library Add. 491,1, fifteenth century; MS Parma Biblioteca Palatina Codice de Rossi 1739 (561), 1504. In all these, it is either fully obvious or there is strong reason to claim based on a partially legible word that the opening word was למינים. In a larger group, an initial word that was likely למינים has been expunged by the censor. See for example: MS Montefiore (Jews College, London) 217,1, thirteenth–fourteenth centuries; MS Paris Bibliotheque Nationale héb. 598, fourteenth–fifteenth centuries; MS Frankfurt a.M. Stadt- und Universitätsbibliothek Oct. 129, fourteenth–fifteenth centuries; MS Parma Biblioteca Palatina Codice de Rossi 1756 (236), fifteenth century; MS Parma Biblioteca Palatina Codice de Rossi 2740 (1212), fifteenth century; MS Zürich Zentralbibliothek Heidenheim 123, fifteenth–sixteenth centuries; MS Moscow Russian State Library MS Guenzburg 1693, sixteenth century. Such examples span the chronology of the available manuscripts, appearing as frequently in the sixteenth century as in the fourteenth.

74 This appears only in MS Parma Biblioteca Palatina Codice de Rossi 1775 (1060), early fifteenth century, and apparently in MS Cincinnati HUC 311, fifteenth century, where the second word has been expunged.

75 MS Parma Biblioteca Palatina 3504 Stern 25, dated to the fifteenth century. Here the *mal-shinim* receive no explicit mention. The second segment is directed to כלם (all of them). However, this is a typical post-censorship move, and the third and fourth segments show clear signs of censorship, suggesting that something is suspect about this initial reference to the *minim*.

evidence for a corresponding alternative opening in the rite of Aleppo, which begins with an address just to the *minim*,[76] as is found in a few Italian rite texts. As the second segment of the Aleppo text (which follows the thematic organization of Babylonian branch 5) preserves its reference to *noṣerim*, it is unlikely that the text there represents an act of self-censorship in the presence of Christians, and no other rites from Muslim countries show evidence of pressure to avoid references to apostates. Therefore, the possibility exists that there did indeed exist a version of the blessing, not represented in the geniza, that did not concern itself with apostates.

The Italian rites are also apparently unique in their universal use of בל instead of the common אל to express the negative in this segment.[77] This is perhaps simply a choice of the more poetic and hence more elevated form.

The address of the second segment in this rite is dependent on the address of the first. Thus, the few texts that address the first segment only to *minim* then address the second segment to *malshinim*. Texts that address the first segment to both present a variety of readings. A few repeat the reference to *minim* in the second segment, perhaps a relic of the deep historical positioning of the term here.[78] Many have been censored and simply present an erasure. However, others have simply closed the gap, leaving a line that reads וכולם כרגע יאבדו (and may they all immediately be lost). Alternatively, they replaced the original noun, probably usually *minim*, with זדים (insolent), a term that has the double virtue of appearing in the talmudically mandated eulogy of the prayer and of filling the physical space left by an erased "*minim*" quite simply. However, it is possible that self-censorship made this substitution original in some of the manuscripts. It is tempting to suggest that both forms, כולם and זדים, were generated initially in rites that addressed the opening segment to both *minim* and *malshinim*, and that did not want to repeat these terms here. However, these forms appear just as frequently in conjunction with opening segments addressed just to the *malshinim*.

A mere handful of texts preserve witness to what was likely the, or at least an,

76 MS Oxford Bodleian Marsh. 90 (1146), dated fourteenth–fifteenth centuries; MS Cincinnati, Hebrew Union College 407, dated 1410. Compare also MS Casanatense 3085, dated to the fifteenth–sixteenth centuries, of uncertain provenance except that the manuscript contains Arabic instructions, which simply lacks this opening line in all four appearances of the blessing.

77 MS Moscow Russian State Library MS Guenzburg 726, fifteenth century, is the only exception in an Italian text. It is also missing in the *Seder Ḥibbur Berakhot* (Schechter, *Studies*, 85).

78 An example of this may be MS Vatican Biblioteca Apostolica 331, fourteenth century, but the microfilm was not entirely legible. MS Cambridge University Library Add 491,1, fifteenth century does have this text, as did MS Parma Biblioteca Palatina Cod. Parm. 1354, fifteenth century, and MS Parma Biblioteca Palatina Codice de Rossi 1756 (236), fifteenth century, before they were censored. In this last case, the *minim* were apparently erased from the first line but not the second!

original wording of the third segment of this prayer in Italy, וכל גוים אויבי עמך ישראל.[79] This might be translated either "all the gentile nations who are the enemies of Your people Israel" or "all the gentile nations, the enemies of Your people Israel." This seems not to have mattered, for in the vast majority of exemplars, the reference to "gentile nations" did not survive censorship. "Enemies of Your people Israel" was not eliminated entirely, but was transformed to "Your enemies," a term that Christians (or Muslims) would not apply to themselves. From the earliest manuscripts, as represented in the critical notes in the appendix, an overwhelming majority of Italian manuscripts present this as their original text, while only a minority show gaps where the original terms were erased. The possibility thus exists that "all Your enemies" was indeed the original text of some Italian rites.

Similarly, relatively few Italian manuscripts preserve their witness to the full form of the fourth segment, calling for the downfall of the governing power. However, there is little basis on which to suggest an alternative original to that shown in our table. When censorship removed reference to the empire of insolence, this did indeed unsettle the text, and manuscripts beginning in the fourteenth century do show evidence of a tendency to omit this direct object entirely, leaving one or more of the verbs to refer to the subject of the previous segment, often with the pronominal third person plural suffix ם– attached to them. Thus, a typical Italian manuscript that was probably self-censored reads just ותכניע אותם,[80] or ותכניעם[81] (and humble them), or ותכניע אותם ותשבר[82] or תשברם ותכניעם[83] (and smash them and humble them) – speedily in our day. As in all the other parts of the Italian text of the *birkat haminim*, these changes occur even in the earliest preserved manuscripts, suggesting that Italian Jews did not hesitate to adjust this statutory prayer text to prevent Christian displeasure. We can only speculate to what degree this was a product of the Italian Renaissance-era intelligentsia's interest in Hebrew or, conversely, a self-protective measure among Jews subject to conversionary pressures and informing by former Jewish converts to Christianity.

79 In addition to ט1, see: MS Cluj Academia RSR MS O. 301, dated 1399; MS London Monte-fiore MS no. 212, fourteenth–fifteenth centuries; MS Moscow Russian State Library MS Guenzburg 726, fifteenth century; MS Moscow Russian State Library MS Guenzburg 741, fifteenth century; MS Parma Biblioteca Palatina Codice de Rossi 3135 (325), Imola 1458; and MS Paris Bibliothèque Nationale Heb. 609, Spello 1648. MS Cambridge University Library Add 491,1, fifteenth century, probably also represents this text, but the scribe skip-ped the word "enemies" in apparent error, leaving the nonsensical וכל גוים עמך ישראל (all nations Your people Israel).

80 For example, MS Cambridge Trinity College F. 12.122, fourteenth–fifteenth centuries.

81 For example, MS Parma Biblioteca Palatina Codice de Rossi 2891 (882), early fifteenth century.

82 For example, MS Parma Biblioteca Palatina Cod. Parm. 1793 (854), dated 1326.

83 For example, MS Rome Biblioteca Casanatense 2828, thirteenth–fourteenth centuries.

Ashkenaz. As with the Italian rites, a relatively wealthy collection of manuscripts survives from medieval Ashkenaz. However, while very few Italian manuscripts escaped the censor, close to half of the Ashkenazi manuscripts preserve their original text of the *birkat haminim* intact. As official Catholic censorship was imposed as part of the Counter-Reformation, it is possible that manuscripts then in Protestant lands fared better, but it is impossible to verify this. The text of the *birkat haminim* printed in Ashkenazi prayer books uniformly represents a post-censorship text from the mid-sixteenth century.[84] The Ashkenazi manuscript evidence is also richer in pre-fourteenth century materials than any other rite, including a number of texts from the thirteenth century. At least two branches of the Ashkenazi rite exist this early, the western Rhineland rite and the Canaanite (Slavic) rite, which become later the German and the Polish rites respectively.[85] These are easily identified by the latter's elaborate introduction to the Sabbath and Festival Torah procession,[86] but their texts of the *birkat haminim* are identical. The general uniformity in this rite may be ascribed to the insistence of the *ḥasidei ˀashkenaz* (twelfth-century Rhineland Pietists) on precise liturgical texts,[87] although not all the variants hew to their insistence that the number of words in the prayer must remain constant. Most of these variants appear to be borrowings from neighboring rites, suggesting that they come from border communities or immigrant groups where the rites were blending. There is essentially no evidence in Ashkenaz for self-censorship or change in this rite over this period.

Just under a third of our manuscripts include a conjunctive *vav* at the beginning of the *berakhah*, similar to the variety found in the French rites (see below). Only one of these, a fifteenth-century manuscript, also has adopted the Italian opening of *malshinim* instead of *meshummadim*,[88] that which will become universal in the wake of censorship. Otherwise, the Ashkenazi rites

84 This is a result first of the location of most early Hebrew presses in Italy, second of the need of printers even outside Catholic lands to sell to a wide geographical area, and later, of Russian government censorship too.

85 The rite of northern France is distinct and will be treated below.

86 See Ruth Langer, "Sinai, Zion and God in the Synagogue: Celebrating Torah in Ashkenazi," in Ruth Langer and Steven Fine, eds., *Liturgy in the Life of the Synagogue* (Winona Lake, Ind.: Eisenbrauns, 2005) 133 ff. This rite is represented on our list by manuscript numbers 16, 24, 26, 29, 31, and 37.

87 Their commentary with its insistence on 29 words appears in manuscript number 29, MS Jerusalem, Jewish National and University Library 8° 4199, dated 1410, quoting the tradition that this number corresponds to the number of punishments God will in the future extract from the evil Edom, that is, Rome. See Eleazar of Worms, *Perushei siddur hatefillah laroqeah*, eds. Moshe and Yehuda Alter Herschler (Jerusalem: Makhon Harav Herschler, 1992) §56, pp. 342–43.

88 MS Oxford Bodleian MS Opp. 156 (Neubauer 1114) – number 32א in our list. It is possible that this is a rewritten text, but it appears original on the microfilm.

universally address the first segment to *meshummadim* and the second to *minim*. There is a small but significant cluster of manuscripts in which "Your people" is given further specificity as "the house of Israel." This particular form is common in France, but all other European rites specify at least "Israel." In this, the dominant Ashkenazi form is the only one to preserve the Babylonian precedent which presumes that Israel need not be specified as the ones who are God's people. The tendency in Europe to add specificity might be understood as a response to Christian supersessionist claims to be the rightful heirs to Israel's relationship with God. The vast majority of Ashkenazi manuscripts maintain the general European pattern of specifying "all our enemies" a second time at the end of the fourth segment, though a significant cluster, like in the Romaniot rite, and a relatively late cluster, change this to "them."[89] The inclusion of additional verbs in this segment in a few manuscripts is an influence from the west typical of the French rites, to which we now turn.

France. Until recently, Jewish liturgists clustered the French rites as a subset of Ashkenaz. While the rites are closely related, there are clear lines of demarcation between the rites of northern France and of the Rhineland. However, because of the expulsion of Jews from all areas of France except the Papal States over the course of the fourteenth century, this rite ceases to exist as the émigrés blend into the communities in which they settle. The one exception is the northern Italian Piedmont communities of Asti, Fossano and Moncalvo (מנהג אפ"ם) which preserve the French traditions. No version of the northern French rite was ever printed.[90] The rites of southern France are, in general, distinct from those of northern France. However, their text of the *birkat haminim* is distinctively French, so we include them in this discussion. Although Provençal Jews were never expelled from the Papal States and maintained a continuous presence in cities like Avignon, Carpentras, and Lille, each of which preserved its own liturgical traditions, few of their liturgical manuscripts from this period were preserved and even fewer of these contain statutory prayer texts. Also included in this discussion is the single preserved exemplar from the British Isles from this period, from a manuscript written shortly before the expulsion of the Jews in 1295. The Jews of pre-expulsion England were closely tied to the Jews of northern France in their liturgical traditions, as is evident in the absence of significant variants here from our base text.

As in Ashkenaz, only about a third of the French exemplars begin with a conjunctive *vav*. While Jews lived in France, the second segment remained simple, but beginning in the late fourteenth century, expanded versions of this segment

89 See the discussion there.

90 See Stefan C. Reif, *Judaism and Hebrew Prayer: New Perspectives on Jewish Liturgical History* (Cambridge: Cambridge Univ. Press, 1993) 167. Jonah Fraenkel in his current work is addressing the specific characteristics of this rite.

begin to appear in both the northern and southern rites, adding *malshinim* and *mesorot* (two words for informers), as is common in Sefarad.[91] However, our evidence is too limited to suggest that there was indeed a deliberate or universal change to this dying rite. As discussed above, the French rites universally identify the enemies of the third segment as "enemies of the house of Israel," although three northern and both southern exemplars omit "house," making this segment identical with one of the versions found in Sefarad.[92]

The most characteristic element of the French rites is their elaboration on the list of verbs found in the fourth segment. Here, the first three verbs appear in consistent order: תעקר ותשבר ותמגר (uproot and smash and defeat). ותכניע (and humble) also appears on every list, after these, but additions precede and follow it. These four verbs are standard in Ashkenaz, the Romaniot rites, and Sefarad, while Italy omits ותמגר,[93] the verb represented in the geniza only in a few texts of branch 5. Although its precise location varies, every exemplar except the earlier Provençal text includes ותשפיל (and cast down).[94] Otherwise, we find two verbs added: ותשמיד (and utterly destroy) appears only in our base text and one other manuscript;[95] and ותכלה (and annihilate), another harsh synonym, appears in four differently ordered lists in five different northern French manuscripts,[96] more than a third of our exemplars. In Provence we find a third, ותפיל (and cast down), apparently a Sefardi influence.[97] It is possible that all these variants represent regional subrites.[98] This Sefardi

91 See the four French texts and the one Provençal text listed in the variants, all dated to 1394 or the fifteenth century. In addition, this version appears in MS Vatican Biblioteca Apostolica ebr. 324, dated to 1395. This manuscript was censored and then restored/corrected in a later hand.

92 In addition to the two manuscripts listed in the variants, see MS Moscow Russian State Library MS Guenzburg 189, fourteenth century. Given the imprecise dating of these manuscripts, these may also be post-expulsion changes from the same period as those just discussed. However, there is only partial overlap between the manuscripts involved.

93 This word is also absent in one French manuscript, MS Moscow Russian State Library MS Guenzburg 1665, fourteenth century. Here, the text of the *berakhah* is found inserted into a *piyyut* for Purim. As it contains some obvious errors, it is not included in the appendix.

94 And the censored MS Parma Biblioteca Palatina Codice de Rossi 3006 (654), from Tallard (southern France), 1304. However the text has been censored and parts have been rewritten. What appears now for this segment looks like a Sefardi text.

95 6צ, although the reading there is somewhat uncertain.

96 6צ, 7צ, 8צ, and 11צ. It also appears in the censored MS Vatican Biblioteca Apostolica ebr. 324, dated 1395, in a fifth variant: ותכניע ותשפיל ותכלה את.

97 In both exemplars. It also appears in MS Parma Biblioteca Palatina Codice de Rossi 3006 (654), from Tallard (southern France), 1304. As this and the earlier text are the two not including ותשפיל, one wonders whether this was a scribal omission of a single letter in these two manuscripts. However, the later Provençal text includes both terms, suggesting that ותפיל was authentically part of the Provençal rite.

98 None of the published halakhic texts of this world preserve an intact text of the *birkat haminim* (with the exception of the *Ez Hayyim*, included in the appendix). The Hurwitz edition of *Maḥzor*

influence is also evident in the addition of וכל שונאיך (all who hate You) to three manuscripts. That two of these are late[99] and the third is clearly censored[100] accounts for the shift from "our enemies and all who hate us" to "all Your enemies and all who hate You" which arguably excludes Christians. However, this language does appear in the censored manuscript from Tallard (Provence). In this text, some sensitive language has simply been censored and not replaced (*meshummadim, malkhut zadon*), but other terms like *minim* remain, suggesting the possibility that what is there represents original texts. Thus, the change to God's enemies instead of Israel's enemies, at least in the fourth segment, may date to the early fourteenth century. Alternatively, it is possible that just the pronominal suffixes of these words were rewritten. This is likely the case in the third segment where the words following "enemies," presumably "of Your people Israel," were indeed removed and a second person pronominal suffix added to make "Your enemies."

Sefarad. Of twenty-five Hebrew manuscripts containing the weekday *ᶜamidah* of the Iberian rites before the period of censorship, only eleven preserve enough data to enable recognition of their original texts of the *birkat haminim*, while a few others allow reconstruction of individual segments. In addition, two Ladino prayer books preserve translations from which we can reconstruct the Hebrew. These texts clearly represent several different subrites, but these cannot be identified with certainty. For example, among a cluster of texts that show significant similarity one to another, we find one catalogued as hailing from Catalon[101] in the extreme northeast on the one hand, and two catalogued as from Lisbon[102] in the extreme west of the peninsula, on the other. Several of these texts also show signs of censorship or self-censorship. That Sefardi Jews practiced self-censorship is evident in manuscripts, both liturgical and halakhic, that simply skip the *birkat haminim* entirely.[103]

Vitry (Nuremburg: J. Bulka, 1923) was based on a censored manuscript. The recent Goldschmidt edition (Jerusalem: Makhon Ozar Haposeqim, 2004) 113, presents an Ashkenazi text. I have not located others that include discussions of the language of the *berakhah*, with the exception of the *Perush hatefillot vehaberakhot* of R. Yehuda b"R. Yaqar, ed. Shmuel Yerushalmi (Jerusalem: Mᵓorei Yisrael, 1979). However, R. Yehuda comments only on elements of the *berakhah* common to all the rites. It cannot be determined from this text whether he is writing about his native Provençal rite or the rite of his later Spanish community.

99 8צ from northern France, dated 1470, 11צ from the Piedmont, dated 1533.

100 MS Parma Biblioteca Palatina Codice de Rossi 3006 (654), from Tallard (southern France), 1304.

101 2ס.

102 4ס, 5ס.

103 MS JTS 4067, SHF 1895:22, dated to the fifteenth century, simply says, ואומ' ברכת המינים (and recite the *birkat haminim*), without giving the text. The first printed edition of this rite, Napoli 1490, simply skips the *berakhah* without comment. Most manuscripts and printed editions of

We begin by noting that not a single Iberian exemplar of the *birkat haminim* begins with the conjunctive *vav*. The one text included here that does hails from Fez, Morocco and contains other unique details, like its inclusion of להם (to them) in this first segment.[104] However, because this text is otherwise mostly in continuity with the Sefardi rites, we include it here. The address of this segment to כופרים (theological heretics) in a Catalonian rite siddur is a product of a censored and rewritten text and therefore not of concern here. The Ladino texts translate *meshummadim* as "*reñegados*," a term that apparently did not carry the opprobrium of the Hebrew original as it continues to appear in Ladino translations for centuries, even where the Hebrew had changed.[105]

The Sefardi texts expand on the second segment of the *berakhah*. While most of the Hebrew texts add two categories of informers, *malshinim* and *mesorot*, a cluster omit this last term. This cluster includes two manuscripts identified as of the Lisbon rite, one identified as Catalonian, and the two Ladino texts. The Ladino texts, after translating *minim* into Spanish as "heretics," do not translate *malshinim* at all, leaving it as is when writing in Hebrew characters and writing *malsines* in Latin characters. The Hebrew word had entered Judeo-Spanish and is attested to in pure Spanish texts beginning in the fourteenth century.[106] Borrowed into Spanish, *malsines* comes to serve as a term of opprobrium without obvious specific application.

Most Sefardi texts expand upon our base text's version of the third segment. This same cluster of texts directs this curse to "all our enemies and all who hate us," or in the self-censored version found in the Ladino texts, "all Your enemies

---

David Abudarham's liturgical commentary delete his commentary on this *berakhah*, though it has been published now in Menahem Avraham Braun, ed., *Tehilah leDavid* (Jerusalem: Makhon Or HaSefer, 2001) 226–28. Most manuscripts of the *Ṣedah laderekh* have something similar to the printed edition, which speaks about the conjunction between the blessings before and after the *birkat haminim*, ignoring our text entirely. However, the fifteenth-century MS JTS 1117, ENA 1757, includes an extremely lengthy discussion of the *berakhah*, one that other copyists simply omitted.

104 סו.

105 See the prayer books printed for former *conversos*, called *Orden de las oraciones cotidianas* (with variations in the spelling of the last word), beginning in the late seventeenth century. The earliest examined was printed in 1695 in Amsterdam, the latest in 1771 in London. If *reñegados* carries the sense of "apostates" in these texts, we face a bizarre phenomenon of former apostates cursing their relatives and ancestors. However, none of the Spanish terms carry the necessary association with Christianity that is embedded in the Hebrew terms they replace.

106 We wish to express our thanks to Ruth Langer's colleague Dwayne Carpenter for his help with the Ladino texts. The data on the use of *malsin* in Spanish is according to Mark Davies, *Corpus del Español*, http://www.corpusdelespanol.org, search for *malsin** (December 15, 2005; August 23, 2006). Davies is professor of Corpus Linguistics at Brigham Young University. One of the fourteenth-century texts is a translation of Judah Halevi's *Sefer haKuzari*, where this term is paired with "*ereges*," the translation of *minim*. This would suggest that the oral life of this term is significantly older.

and all who hate You."[107] Another cluster adds to this, "all who seek ill for us."[108] However, the base text's version is equally well attested in this period,[109] and we also find versions that shorten it to "all our enemies" or "all Your enemies."[110]

We find a similar variety in the fourth segment. All open by praying that the empire of insolence תעקר ותשבר (be uprooted and smashed) and include ותכניע[ם] (and humble [them]) in their lists of verbs.[111] Three other versions each add only one word to this core, each different: ותכלה (and annihilate),[112] ותמגר (defeat),[113] and ותאבדם (cause them to be lost).[114] Another exemplar adds two verbs, reading ותמגר ותכניע ותשפיל (and defeat and humble and bring low).[115] Four more versions expand this list even further. These, instead of expanding the third segment to specify "all our enemies and all those who hate us," place this phrase as the object of this expanded list of verbs here in the fourth segment.[116] One text only adds ותכלם (and utterly destroy them) after these enemies.[117] Our base texts adds another verb introducing the enemies, ותפיל (and cast down). Another variant reorganizes these verbs, adds ותכריע (subdue), and intensifies the call for urgency with כרגע (immediately);[118] another adds only ותשמיד to the three common verbs listed above.[119] Thus, in contrast to the other rites, the situ-

107 Also in MS JTS 5445 SHF 1903:16, third quarter of fourteenth century, Portugal (censored and rewritten with acceptable words).

108 In MS Biblioteca Palatina Parm. 29, fourteenth century (heavily censored except for this segment); MS Biblioteca Palatina Cod. Parm. 2207, dated 1439 (in poor condition and censored); and 8ס, 9ס, and 11ס.

109 In addition, it appears in MS Moscow Russian State Library MS Guenzburg 1419, fifteenth century (heavily censored); MS JTS 4112 SHF 1563:13, fifteenth century, probably North African (in poor condition), as well as 7ס and 10ס.

110 MS Oxford Bodleian Library MS Opp. Add. Oct. 17 (Neubauer 1135), fourteenth century. The post-censorship text reads אויביך. See also 4ס, probably self-censored, and 6ס, which maintains אויבינו.

111 Except 3ס. This text was censored, but it also contains numerous peculiarities suggesting that this may be a scribal error. 5ס is the only manuscript to contain only this core.

112 2ס plus the Ladino texts which follow this rite closely.

113 4ס, 8ס, and the earlier but heavily censored MS Oxford Bodleian Library MS Opp. Add. Oct. 17 (Neubauer 1133), fourteenth century.

114 11ס.

115 6ס. A similar text appears in 9ס, but the text is not fully legible. There may have been an additional verb and the last two incorporate the direct object "them." Compare also MS Biblioteca Palatina Cod. Parm. 1917, fifteenth century, which in its current state lists תכלה תמגר תשבר תעקר, that is, in reverse order from usual and without the conjunctives connecting them.

116 Not all Sefardi rite texts include this language. See 4ס, 6ס, and the less certain evidence from the censored texts: MS Oxford Bodleian Library MS Opp. Add. Oct. 17 (Neubauer 1133), fourteenth century, and MS Biblioteca Palatina Cod. Parm. 1917, fifteenth century. Note, though, that none include this phrase twice.

117 MS JTS 4112 SHF 1563:13, fifteenth century, probably from North Africa, not censored but in poor condition.

118 7ס.

119 10ס.

ation in Spain is one of extreme fluidity with a wide variety of details expressed within the common structure of the prayer. The calls of Asher b. Yehiel and after him Jacob b. Asher for a text of twenty-nine words, following the dictum of the *ḥasidei ʾashkenaz*, went essentially unheeded.[120]

Conclusions

Until recently, a comprehensive study of the texts of the *birkat haminim* of the kind we have offered here simply was not feasible. The texts of the Cairo geniza have recently been made much more accessible to scholars.[121] Consequently, it is now possible to reconstruct the prayer texts that were common among the Jewish communities of the Middle East between the ninth and thirteenth centuries. Medieval Hebrew manuscripts, scattered among the libraries of the world, have been microfilmed and made available in one centralized collection in the Institute for Microfilmed Hebrew Manuscripts at the Jewish National Library in Jerusalem. This makes comprehensive study of later medieval Jewish rites achievable, especially for those communities for which ample evidence was preserved. In both periods, where scholars earlier drew conclusions based on one or two manuscripts, we now often bring dozens and sometimes hundreds to the table.

As is clear from this study, by the time of the earliest preserved liturgical evidence, there were multiple co-existent texts of the *birkat haminim*. Among the manuscripts of these texts we find a profusion of smaller and larger differences within what is recognizably the same prayer. Analysis of our fuller collection of the geniza evidence allows us to organize these texts into a new and more certain classification as the rites of *ʾereṣ yisraʾel* and Babylonia and to identify their subdivision into discrete branches.

A focus on the significant number of shared characteristics among the branches suggests the plausibility of positing a shared literary source. We cannot with any certainly reconstruct the precise language of this source, but the analysis of the different texts suggests the very tentative hypothesis that Babylonian branch 3 and *ʾereṣ yisraʾeli* branch 2 (without its citation of Ps 69:29) are the closest to it.

Was this the text formulated by those "establishing" the text at Yavneh or was this a text that emerged at some later date, or was this the product of some general consensus, either at Yavneh or later, about the proper thematic and linguistic

120 *Shut HaRosh* 4:20; *Tur* OH 118.

121 In 2003, the Israeli National Academy of Sciences and Humanities founded the Jewish Liturgy Project (*Mifʿal hatefillah*) in order to collect and catalogue the texts of the early *siddur*. This project, headed by Uri Ehrlich, is located at Ben-Gurion University and makes its materials available to scholars of liturgy by request.

structure of the blessing? We hesitate to answer this question here. This question can only properly be addressed, not with specific reference only to the *birkat haminim*, but within the much wider context of the problem of the emergence of statutory rabbinic prayer, at the heart of which lies the *ᶜamidah* in which the *birkat haminim* is embedded. This itself has been a matter of heated scholarly dispute in recent years,[122] and its resolution requires a much broader engagement with the relevant historical sources for the period.

In the *geniza*, all versions of the malediction first cursed the apostates, those who betrayed the Jewish community by conversion, the *meshummadim*, by asking God to remove their "hope," presumably of salvation. This segment persists unchanged in medieval Europe, with the exception of in Italy, where only the alternative of *malshinim*, "informers," sometimes together with *minim*, ever appears in the manuscripts. Given the centrality of salvific claims in Christian missionary address to Jews, it is easy to understand how this language might have resulted from an act of self-censorship to avoid antagonizing the Church. The non-Italian European rites only drop this address to *meshummadim* after the sixteenth century when Catholic censorship forces its removal from the printed and written texts.

The earliest texts of the *birkat haminim* seem also to have included a curse of *noṣerim* and *minim*, applying a single verb, יאבדו (may they be lost) to both. Whether or not these were initially two discrete categories of people is unclear. These terms are already attested to by the Church fathers Jerome and Epiphanius, around 400 C.E., who tell us that Jews were cursing Christians, three times a day in their synagogues, referring to Christians or Jewish-Christians as Nazarenes in a blessing called "Minaeorum."[123] The formulation of this segment in the geniza texts is extremely stable, always placing *noṣerim* before *minim*. Consequently, it is logical to conclude that the word *noṣerim* is not a later addition to this phrase (as has been suggested by some scholars)[124] but rather an integral part

122 The essential dispute is between the methods of Joseph Heinemann and Ezra Fleischer. See Heinemann's *Prayer in the Talmud: Forms and Patterns*, trans. Richard S. Sarason (Berlin, New York: Walter de Gruyter, 1977) chaps. 1, 2, and 9; and Fleischer's "On the Beginnings of Obligatory Hebrew Prayer," *Tarbiz* 59 (1990) 397–441 (Heb.). For discussions of Fleischer's challenge to Heinemann, see among others, Ruth Langer, "Revisiting Early Rabbinic Liturgy: The Recent Contributions of Ezra Fleischer," *Prooftexts* 19, no. 2 (1999) 179–94, and Uri Ehrlich, "On the Early Texts of the Blessings 'Who Rebuilds Jerusalem' and the 'Blessing of David' in the Liturgy," *Peᶜamim* 78 (1999) 16–43 (Heb.).

123 See the evidence collected, among others, by Horbury, "The Benediction of the Minim." Many, including Horbury, understand Justin Martyr (*Dialogue with Trypho*, mid-second century C.E.) also to give witness to the *birkat haminim*. However, Justin's statements are much more ambiguous and scholars do not agree on whether they refer to the *birkat haminim* or to some other synagogue-based Jewish cursing of Christians.

124 See, for example, Kimelman, "*Birkat Ha-Minim*."

of its original formulation. If this segment of the blessing is early, then the word *noṣerim* is early, and if it is all later, then the word *noṣerim* is also later. Therefore, one's reading of the liturgical history must also intersect with an understanding of the relationships between Christians (or at least Jewish-Christians) and Jews in the periods in question.

However, the geniza also contains evidence for the beginnings of the process of removing the word *noṣerim* from the blessing. This process finds expression in several manuscripts of branch 5,[125] the branch that was received by the European rites. It is possible that the form adopted there already lacked this term; *noṣerim* does not appear in a single European manuscript of the *birkat haminim*. In any case, there is no reason to presume that the removal of *noṣerim* from the text of the blessing was the product of official external censorship. It is among the earliest documented omissions from the language of the blessing. This may well have been the result of a change in the historical circumstances of the worshippers, who saw no continuing need to mention *noṣerim* explicitly. Jews living in the realm of Islam may have found the more general term *minim* sufficient. However, this could also have originated as an act of internal Jewish censorship to avoid explicit cursing of their Christian neighbors. If this was the case, then the result was ironic. Medieval European Jews understood the remaining term "*minim*" to refer quite explicitly to their Christian neighbors.[126]

All of the geniza versions except branch 1 (from the Land of Israel) and all later medieval texts also call on God to bring down the gentile government. Such an outcome is a logical necessity for the steps towards messianic redemption that the weekday *ᶜamidah* petitions for at this point. As such, this is a key element of this malediction, but one that functions independently of the curses of internal Jewish malefactors. Its importance is evident in its appearance as the second segment of the blessing in all the geniza versions except Babylonian branch 5, the one that spreads to Europe through the agency of the *Seder Rav Amram Gaon*. The verbs of this segment were a favored locus for intensifying the malediction, and we find significant variety in the expansions of the list. It is only early modern censorship that forces this segment to lose its reference to the "empire of insolence."

As the geniza evidence demonstrates, there were communities that continued to elaborate upon the themes of the *birkat haminim*. Most significant was the apparent addition of a specific malediction calling for Israel's enemies "to be cut off" (יכרתו). It may be the addition of this segment that leads to the reorganization of the segments of the blessing evident only in branch 5 from the geniza, but absolutely universal in Europe. The resultant text curses first

125 As regards the *Seder Rav Amram Gaon*, see above, n. 54.

126 This usage can be documented as early as Rashi, i.e., about as early as any European Hebrew texts.

Jewish malefactors (apostates and heretics, if that is the meaning of *minim*) and then gentiles, instead of interspersing the two categories as is common in the earlier rites.

This malediction of enemies was also a favorite locus for elaborating upon the curse, as is evident already in geniza branch 4B. On the other hand, the text of the *Seder Rav Amram Gaon* included only a basic form of this segment; only some of the European rites intensify this language. Of course, this language was also sensitive in Christian Europe; external censorship and sometimes self-censorship leads to a consistent rephrasing of this segment so that it curses God's enemies, not Israel's enemies.

Thus, while Elbogen is correct that we cannot in any absolute sense "recover" the original text of the *birkat haminim*, there is much that we can reconstruct given the textual evidence at hand today. We do know what the European texts were, in all their complexity, before the advent of Christian censorship, and we know how they fit into the picture left to us by the manuscripts preserved in the Cairo geniza. These manuscripts give us significant clues as to the development of this prayer, at least in the geonic period and perhaps even before.

Appendices

Following the text of each version we give the critical apparatus indicating the additions or deletions to that text found in the various manuscripts. After this, in the list identifying the source of each manuscript, we give brief notes indicating any physical lacunae in its text of the *berakhah*. These lacunae do not appear in the apparatus. We have not included here information about graphical variants like abbreviations or errors unless they seemed of significance and we do not note corrections or additions made by the scribe himself. We have also not included details about how the scribe recorded the statutory blessing formula. *Note:* נ׳ = נוסף; ח׳ = חסר.

Appendix A
Variants of the *Birkat Haminim* in the Geniza Manuscripts[127]

ᵓ*EREṢ YISRA*ᵓ*ELI* BRANCH 1

למשומדים אל תהי תקוה
אם לא ישובו לתורתך
הנצרים והמינים כרגע יאבדו
ימחו מספר חיים ועם צדיקים אל יכתבו
ברוך אתה יי מכניע זדים

לתורתך | נ17 בתורתך.|| ימחו | א3, נ2 וימחו.|| חיים | א3, ק12 החיים.|| ימחו מספר חיים | ק72 ח׳.

Manuscripts

א3 Oxford, Bodleian Heb. d. 55.33–34, a word is missing between ועם and אל.

נ2 Jewish Theological Seminary ENA 694.10, several words are missing between יכתבו and זדים.

נ13 Jewish Theological Seminary ENA 3027.7–8, complete.

נ17 Jewish Theological Seminary ENA 3810.4–5, the beginning of the text is missing, up to the word תהי; approximately three words are missing between בתורתך and יאבדו; several words are missing between צדיקים and זדים.

ק12 Cambridge, T-S 8 H 24.5, a word is missing between תהי and אם, and between יי and זדים.

ק32 Cambridge, T-S H 18.3, complete.

127 We would like to express our thanks to Vered Raziel-Kretzmer for her help in preparing this presentation of the Geniza texts.

34ק Cambridge, T-S K 27.18, approximately seven words are missing between אל and והמינים; approximately five words are missing between ימחו and יכתבו; the concluding benediction is missing after the word יי.

72ק Unidentified Schechter 1; information based on Schechter's description.[128]

ᵓEREṢ YISRAᵓELI BRANCH 2

למשומדים אל תהי תקוה
ומלכות זדון מהרה תעקר בימינו
והנצרים והמינים כרגע יאבדו
ימחו מספר החיים ועם צדיקים אל יכתבו
ברוך אתה יי מכניע זדים

בימינו | ק31 ח׳.|| והנצרים | ק31 הנצרים.

Manuscripts

31ק Cambridge, T-S Glass 20.57, a word is missing between מספר and ועם.

35ק Cambridge, T-S K 27.33, complete.

BABYLONIAN BRANCH 3

למשומדים אל תהי תקוה
ומלכות זדון מהרה תעקר בימינו
והנצרים והמינים כרגע יאבדו
ברוך אתה יי שובר רשעים ומכניע זדים

מהרה | ק33 ח׳.|| תעקר | ק23, ק26, נ׳ ותשבר. ק6, נ׳ ותשבר ותכניע. ק47 נ׳ ותשבר תכניע.|| והנצרים | ק26 הנצרים.|| והנצרים והמינים | ק47 והמינים והמלשינים כולם.|| יאבדו | ק47 נ׳ וישמדו. ק5, ק57 נ׳ ימחו מספר החיים ועם צדיקים אל יכתבו.|| רשעים | ק6, ק38 אויבים.

Manuscripts

5ק Cambridge, T-S 8 H 9.12, a word is missing between למשומדים and תהי, and between זדון and תעקר.

6ק Cambridge, T-S 8 H 10.2, complete.

23ק Cambridge, T-S AS 104.168, complete.

26ק Cambridge, T-S AS 105.105, two words are missing between למשומדים and תקוה.

33ק Cambridge, T-S H 18.6, complete.

38ק Cambridge, T-S NS 120.89, three words are missing between למשומדים and ומלכות; two words are missing between בימינו and כרגע; a word is missing between כרגע and ברוך.

128 S. Schechter, "Geniza Specimens," JQR OS 10 (1898) 659.

ק47 Cambridge, T-S NS 151.96, complete.

ק57 Cambridge, T-S NS 196.5a, the beginning is missing, up to the word ומלכות.

BABYLONIAN BRANCH 4A

למשומדים אל תהי תקוה
ומלכות זדון מהרה תעקר ותשבר בימינו
והנצרים והמינים כרגע יאבדו
וכל אויבי עמך וצורריהם מהרה יכרתו
ברוך אתה יי שובר רשעים ומכניע זדים

תקוה | ק28 נמחק: אם לא ישובו לתורתך. || ומלכות...בימינו | ק7 ח׳. || מהרה | ל1, ק21, ק22, ק25, ק33 ח׳. || ותשבר | נ16, ק51, ק55, ק63, ק65 ח׳. נ14, פ2, ק19, ק28, ק48 נ׳ ותכניע. ק53 נ׳ ותכניע מהרה. || בימינו | ל2 ח׳. || והנצרים...יאבדו | ק55 ח׳. || והנצרים | ל2, ק19 הנצרים. ק7 וכל הנוצרים. ק51 נ׳ כלם. || אויבי | ק51 צוררי. || וצורריהם | ק7, ק19, ק51, ק55 ח׳. ק20, ק48, ק53, ק63 נ׳ כולם. || מהרה | ל1, ק20, ק53, ק63, ק65 במהרה. ל2 המה. || יכרתו | ק20, ק48, ק53, ק63, ק65 יכרתון. ל4, נ1, נ14, נ16, פ2, ק25 נ׳ וישברו. ק28 נ׳ ביד אחר: ושבור עול הגוים מעל צאורינו. || שובר רשעים | ק7 ח׳. || רשעים | נ14, ק6, ק38 אויבים. ק25 נ׳ במקומו אויבים.

Manuscripts

ל1 British Library Or. 5557 O 12, complete.

ל2 British Library Or. 5557 Z 15–16, complete.

ל4 British Library Or. 12378.6, complete.[129]

נ1 Jewish Theological Seminary ENA 694.5–6, very fragmentary: the first word is missing; several words are missing between ומלכות and ותשבר; two words are missing between והנצרים and יאבדו and between עמך and יכרתו; a number of words are missing between ברוך and זדים.

נ14 Jewish Theological Seminary ENA 3240.18, complete.

נ16 Jewish Theological Seminary ENA 3774.9, complete.

פ2 Paris, Collection Jacques Mosseri VIII, 82.2, two words are missing between למשומדים and תקוה; a word is missing between ברוך and רשעים.

ק7 Cambridge, T-S 8 H 10.6, complete.

ק19 Cambridge, T-S AS 103.17, two words are missing between ברוך and שובר.

ק20 Cambridge, T-S AS 103.73, two words are missing between למשומדים and תקוה.

129 We would like to express our thanks to Avi Shmidman for drawing this manuscript to our attention.

21ק Cambridge, T-S AS 103.97, very fragmentary: several words are missing between למשומדים and ומלכות, between תעקר and והמינים, between עמך and ברוך, and between אתה and זדים.

22ק Cambridge, T-S AS 103.277, continuous with T-S AS 105.103 (25ק).

25ק Cambridge, T-S AS 105.103, continuous with T-S AS 103.277 (22ק).

28ק Cambridge, T-S AS 108.4, a word is missing between ברוך and יי.

48ק Cambridge, T-S NS 152.30, complete.

51ק Cambridge, T-S NS 153.161, complete.

53ק Cambridge, T-S NS 155.3, complete.

55ק Cambridge, T-S NS 157.67, complete.

56ק Cambridge, T-S NS 157.193, incomplete at the end, after the word והנצרים.

63ק Cambridge, T-S NS 271.106, complete.

65ק Cambridge, T-S NS 271.234, a word is missing between אתה and שובר.

BABYLONIAN BRANCH 4B

למשומדים אל תהי תקוה
ומלכות זדון מהרה תעקר ותשבר ותכניע בימינו
והנצרים והמינים כרגע יאבדו
וכל אויבי עמך וצורריהם מהרה יכרתו
ושבור עול הגוים מעל צוארינו
ואל תתן תקומה לכל אויבי נפשינו
ברוך אתה יי שובר אויבים ומכניע זדים

ומלכות | נ10 מלכות. || ותשבר | נ6 ומשביר. || ותכניע | ק54 נ׳ ותאביד מהרה. || והנצרים והמינים | נ6 והנוצרים ומינים. נ10 נ׳ והמלשינים וכל בעלי זרוע. ק3 נ׳ והמלשינים והמוסרים כולם. ק15, ק64 נ׳ כולם. ק27 נ׳ והכופרים וכל בעלי זרוע. ק54 והמינים והנצרים והכופרים וכל בעלי זרוע כולם. ק58 הנצרים והמינים והמלשינים והמוסרים כולם. ק60 נ׳ ובעלי זרוע. ק62 נ׳ והמלשינים והמוסרים. || כרגע...וצורריהם | נ10 ח׳. || כרגע יאבדו | ק27, ק60 ח׳. || יאבדו | ק15 ח׳. || אויבי | ק60 אויבנו ואויבי. || עמך | ק54, ק60 נ׳ ישראל. || וצורריהם | ק3 ושונאיהם וצורריהם ומבקשי רעתם. ק15 נ׳ כולם. ק27 נ׳ ומבקשי רעתם כולם. ק54, ק60 נ׳ ומבקשי רעתם. ק58, ק64 נ׳ ושונאיהם ומבקשי רעתם כולם. ק69 נ׳ ושונאיהם כולם. || מהרה | ק15, ק24, ק37 במהרה. ק64 ח׳. || מהרה יכרתו | נ6 ח׳. || יכרתו | נ10 נ׳ ויאבדו וישמדו. ק3 יכנעו וישמדו. ק27 נ׳ וישברו וישמדו ויאבדו. ק54, ק58, ק69 נ׳ וישמדו ויאבדו. ק60 נ׳ ויאבדו. ק64 ישמדו וישברו. || ושבור | נ10, ק3, ק69 שבור. ק27, ק54 אנא למען שמך שבור. ק60 אנא למענך שבור. || הגוים | ק42, ק54, ק69 נ׳ מהרה. || ואל...נפשינו | נ6, ק8, ק18, ק24, ק37, ק61 ח׳. || ואל | נ10 אל. || תקומה | ק42, ק54 נ׳ ואחרית. || נפשינו | ק3 נ׳ ומבקש רעתנו. ק42 נ׳ ומבקשי רעתנו בכף אויבנו אל תמסרינו. ק27, ק54 נ׳ וביד (ק54: וכף) אויבנו אל תמסרינו. || אויבים | ק8, ק18, ק24, ק27 רשעים. ק42, ק54 רשעים ואויבים.

Manuscripts

- 6נ Jewish Theological Seminary ENA 2168.28–32, the fragment ends after the word אויבים.
- 10נ Jewish Theological Seminary ENA 2527.8, complete.
- 3ק Cambridge, Or. 1080 3.2, complete.
- 8ק Cambridge, T-S 8 H 10.12, complete.
- 15ק Cambridge, T-S Arabic 36.12, complete.
- 18ק Cambridge, T-S AS 102.110, complete.
- 24ק Cambridge, T-S AS 104.228, a word is missing between יכרתו and עול, and between מעל and ברוך.
- 27ק Cambridge, T-S AS 107.111, the beginning of the text is missing, up to the word והכופרים.
- 37ק Cambridge, T-S NS 120.87, complete.
- 42ק Cambridge, T-S NS 124.109, the beginning is missing, up to the phrase מהרה מעל צוארינו.
- 54ק Cambridge, T-S NS 156.7, complete.
- 58ק Cambridge, T-S NS 196.7, two words are missing between ואל and לכל; a word is missing between אתה and שובר.
- 60ק Cambridge, T-S NS 197.60, several words are missing between נפשינו and שובר.
- 61ק Cambridge, T-S NS 271.2, complete.
- 62ק Cambridge, T-S NS 271.44, incomplete at the end, after the word והמוסרים.
- 64ק Cambridge, T-S NS 271.157, a word is missing between עמך and ושנאיהם, and between וישברו and עול; incomplete at the end, after the word עול.
- 69ק Cambridge, T-S NS 273.67, the beginning is missing, up to the word ושונאיהם.

BABYLONIAN BRANCH 5

למשומדים אל תהי תקוה
וכל המינים כרגע יאבדו
וכל אויבי עמך מהרה יכרתו
ומלכות זדון מהרה תעקר ותשבר בימינו
ברוך אתה יי שובר אויבים ומכניע זדים

תהי | ק13 נ׳ ביד אחר: להם. || וכל המינים | נ3 והנוצרים והמנים. ק5 וכל המינים וכל המלשינים. ק39 וכל הנוצרים והמינים. || וכל ... יכרתו | נ3 ח׳. || וכל | נ5 כל. || וכל אויבי עמך | ק17 וכל שנאיך. || אויבי עמך | נ5 אויבינו וכל שונאינו. ק39 נ׳ וקמיהם. || תעקר ותשבר | נ5 נ׳ ותכלם ותכניעם. ק40 נ׳ ותכניע. ק17 נ׳ ותמגר ותכניע. ק13 ותשבר נמחק ביד אחר ונ׳: ותמגר. ק39 תעקר תשבר ותכניע. || אויבים | ק13 נמחק ביד אחר ונ׳: רשעים.

Manuscripts

- נ3 Jewish Theological Seminary ENA 920.14–15, the last word of the concluding benedictory formula is missing.
- נ5 Jewish Theological Seminary ENA 1314.1–6, a word is missing between תכניעם and בימינו, and between שובר and ומכניע.
- ק13 Cambridge, T-S 10 H 1.5, complete.
- ק39 Cambridge, T-S NS 120.105, a word is missing between מהרה and תשבר; several words are missing between בימינו and אויבים.
- ק40 Cambridge, T-S NS 121.37, a word is missing between תקוה and המינין, between מהרה and ומלכות, and between ומלכות and מהרה; 2 words are missing between ותכניע and אתה.
- ק71 Cambridge, T-S NS 289.1, complete.

BABYLONIAN BRANCH 6

למשומדים אל תהי תקוה
ומלכות זדון מהרה תעקר בימינו
ברוך אתה יי שובר רשעים ומכניע זדים

ומלכות | ק11, ק67 מלכות. || זדון | נ15 נ׳ תעקר. || תעקר | א4, ס1, ק9, ק45, ק49 נ׳ ותשבר. ק59 נ׳ ביד אחר ותשבר. ל3 נ׳ ותשבר במהרה. || בימינו | נ15, ק14, ק45 ח׳. ק59, ק68 נ׳ ביד אחר: הנצרים (ק68: והנצרים) והמינים כרגע יאבדו וכל אויבי עמך וכל צורריהם מהרה (ק68: וצורריהם כלם במהרה) יכרתו. || רשעים | א1, ל3 אויבים. ק43 זידים, ותוקן ביד אחר: רשעים.

Manuscripts

- א1 Oxford, Bodleian Heb. d. 51.73–78, complete.
- א2 Oxford, Bodleian Heb. d. 55.15–16, complete.
- א4 Oxford, Bodleian Hunt. 448, complete (not a genizah fragment).

ל3 British Library Or. 6197.33, a word is missing between ומלכות and מהרה, and between בימינו and אתה.

נ4 Jewish Theological Seminary ENA 964.3–10, complete.

נ11 Jewish Theological Seminary ENA 2527.9, complete.

נ12 Jewish Theological Seminary ENA 2947.2–3, complete.

נ15 Jewish Theological Seminary ENA 3751.3, two words are missing between למשומדים and תקוה; a word is missing between תעקר and אתה.

ס1 Cincinnati, Hebrew Union College Acc. 1246, a word is missing between למשומדים and תהי; two words are missing between ומלכות and תעקר.

פ1 Paris, Alliance Israélite Universelle IV.A.2, incomplete at the end, after the word בימינו.

ק9 Cambridge, T-S 8 H 10.17, complete.

ק11 Cambridge, T-S 8 H 11.3, complete.

ק14 Cambridge, T-S Arabic 36.11, complete.

ק16 Cambridge, T-S Arabic 36.54, complete.

ק36 Cambridge, T-S NS 38a.33, complete.

ק43 Cambridge, T-S NS 149.140, complete.

ק45 Cambridge, T-S NS 150.41, complete.

ק46 Cambridge, T-S NS 150.188, complete.

ק49 Cambridge, T-S NS 152.235, complete.

ק52 Cambridge, T-S NS 154.26, several words are missing between ומלכות and בימינו; the closing benedictory formula is missing, after the word שובר.

ק59 Cambridge, T-S NS 196.24, complete.

ק66 Cambridge, T-S NS 272.30, complete.

ק67 Cambridge, T-S NS 272.65, the beginning is missing, up to the word מלכות; a word is missing between מהרה and בימינו, and between שובר and ומכניע.

ק68 Cambridge, T-S NS 272.77, two words are missing between למשומדים and תקוה; a word is missing after תעקר.

BABYLONIAN MANUSCRIPTS NOT INCLUDED IN THE VARIANTS ABOVE

Manuscripts with the Abbreviation ומלכות זדון וכו'.[130]

Cambridge, University Add. 3160.8

Cambridge, University Or. 1081 2.77A

Cambridge, T-S 8 H 10.20

Cambridge, T-S AS 109.83

Cambridge, T-S NS 122.50

Cambridge, T-S AS 105.136

Manuscripts with the Abbreviation והמינים והמלשינים וכו'.[131]

Cambridge, T-S AS 102.60

Cambridge, T-S NS 278.151

Manuscripts that are not eastern, are doubtfully eastern, or late that were excluded above

Jewish Theological Seminary ENA 2219.11

Jewish Theological Seminary ENA 2321.1–10

Jewish Theological Seminary ENA 2431.11–14

Cambridge, Westminster College Lit. II.9–13

Cambridge, T-S AS 108.56

Cambridge, T-S NS 150.17

Appendix B
Variants of the *Birkat Haminim* in the Medieval European Rites

While manuscripts in Appendix A have been numbered primarily by their libraries of origin, here they are identified first by their rite (Hebrew letter). In all cases, the first manuscript listed is the text presented. Except in rare instances, censored manuscripts have not been included in the variants.

ROMANIOT[132]

למשומדים אל יהי להם תקוה
והמינים והמלשינים והכופרים והמסורים כולם כרגע יאבדו
וכל אויבי עמך ישראל מהרה מארץ יכרתון

130 See above, n. 30.

131 See above, n. 30.

132 Included here are all the exemplars of this rite that predate the Sefardi influence and the censor.

ומלכות זדון מהרה תעקר ותשבר [ותמגר] ותכניע אותם
מהרה בימינו
בא״י שובר רשעים ומכניע זדים

למשומדים | ר2 ולמשומדים. ר3 נמחק וכתוב מחדש ולמלשינים. || יהי | ר2, ר3, ר4, ר5 תהי. || להם | ר4, ר5 ח׳. והמינים ר2 וכל המינים. || והכופרים | ר2, ר3 והכופרנים. || והמסורים | ר2, ר3 והמסורות. || והכופרים והמסורים | ר4 והמסורות והכופרנ׳. || מארץ | ר2 ח׳. ר5 נ׳ חיים. || יכרתון | ר4, ר5 יכרתו. || ותמגר | ר1 ח׳. || ותכניע אותם במהרה | ר2 ותכניע ותשפיל כל אויבינו מהרה. || רשעים | ר2, ר3, ר4 אויבים.

Manuscripts

- ר1 Paris, Bibliotheque Nationale héb. 596, fourteenth–fifteenth century.
- ר2 British Library Or. 9150, fourteenth century.
- ר3 Biblioteca Palatina Codice Parma de Rossi 1782 (89), 1485, Lecce.
- ר4 Paris, Alliance Israélite H.58.A, fifteenth century.
- ר5 Paris, Bibliotheque Nationale héb. 616, 1523, Akarnania.

ITALIAN[133]

ולמלשינים בל תהי תקוה
וכל המינים כלם כרגע יאבדו
וכל גוים אויבי עמך ישראל מהרה יכרתו
ומלכות זדון במהרה תעקר ותשבר ותכניע אתם במהרה בימינו
בא״י שובר אויבים ומכניע זדים

ולמלשינים | ט2, ט7 ולמינים. ט8 ולמינים ולמלשינים. || המינים | ט2, ט7 המלשינים. || וכל גוים אויבי עמך ישראל | ט8 אויבי ח׳. ט2, ט3, ט4, ט5, ט6, ט7 וכל אויביך. || ומלכות זדון... ותשבר | ט5 ח׳.

Manuscripts

- ט1 Biblioteca Palatina Codice Parma de Rossi 1901 (1024), fourteenth century.
- ט2 Paris, Bibliotheque Nationale MS héb. 595, fourteenth century.
- ט3 Leeds, Brotherton Library MS Roth 58, fifteenth century.
- ט4 British Library Or. 13260, fifteenth century.
- ט5 Moscow Russian State Library MS Guenzburg 679, fifteenth century.
- ט6 Biblioteca Palatina Codice Parma de Rossi 1924 (1149), fifteenth century.

Because the earliest manuscript differs significantly from the others, it has not been used as the base text.

133 There are hundreds of medieval Italian liturgical manuscripts preserved. In my sampling of these, I collected over two hundred texts of the *birkat haminim*, but most of these show signs of censorship. Presented here are the eight manuscripts that seem to have survived relatively uncensored. The discussion in the main text makes reference to the evidence that can be gleaned from the rest and that gives these manuscripts a broader and more accurate context.

ט7 Florence, Biblioteca Medicea Laurenziana Conv. Sopp. 33, fifteenth century.

ט8 Cambridge, University Library Add 491,1, fifteenth century.

ASHKENAZI[134]

למשומדים אל תהי תקוה
וכל המינים כרגע יאבדו
וכל אויבי עמך מהרה יכרתון
ומלכות זדון מהרה תעקר ותשבר ותמגר
ותכניע כל אויבינו במהרה בימינו
בא״י שובר אויבים ומכניע זידים

למשומדים | א12, א13, א14, א16, א17, א20, א22, א23, א24, א29, א30, א31, א34, א35 ולמשומדים. א32 ולמלשינים || אויבי עמך | א5, א14, א19, א23, א27, א33, נ׳ בית ישראל. א35 נ׳ מהרה בית ישר׳ (כנראה בטעות). א36 נ׳ ישראל. || מהרה | א2 במהרה. || יכרתון | רוב כ״י יכרתו. || ותכניע כל אויבינו | א7, א8, א39 ח׳ כל. א5 נ׳ את. א9, א20, א31 ח׳ כל אויבינו. א10, א16, א22, א31, א32, א34 ותכניעם. א2 ותשפיל ותכניע ותכלה כל אויבינו. א18 ותשמיד ותכניע ותשפיל ותכלה כל אויבינו. א19 ותכניע ותשפיל כל אויבינו. || במהרה | א4, א6 מהרה.

Manuscripts

א1 Amsterdam, Universiteitsbibliotheek MS Rosenthal 609, 1236, Esslingen.

א2 Oxford, Bodleian MS Michael 200 (Neubauer 1121), thirteenth century.[135]

א3 University of Toronto MS Friedberg 3–015, thirteenth century, Worms; the end of the word יכרתו is illegible; text between זדון and ותמגר and between ברוך and ומכניע is illegible.

א4 Munich, Bayerische Staatsbibliothek Cod. hebr. 410, thirteenth–fourteenth century.

א5 Oxford, Bodleian MS Michael 548, 1308.

א6 Cincinnati, Hebrew Union College 389, 1314.

א7 Oxford, Bodleian MS Opp. 758 (Neubauer 1105), early fourteenth century.

א8 London, Bet Din and Bet Hamidrash 36, 1392.

א9 Oxford, Bodleian MS Michael 327–28 (Neubauer 1107–8), fourteenth century.

א10 Oxford, Bodleian MS Opp. 643 (Neubauer 1109), fourteenth century.

134 Over eighty manuscripts from before the sixteenth century contain the *birkat haminim*. More than half, however, have been censored. The Ashkenazi rite preserved a stable text with few variants until censorship forced changes.

135 According to Jonah Fraenkel, this thirteenth-century manuscript is a particularly unique mix of French and Ashkenazi rites (private correspondence).

11א Oxford, Bodleian MS Opp. 647 (Neubauer 2274/1), fourteenth century.

12א Oxford, Bodleian MS Opp. 649 (Neubauer 1102), fourteenth century; rite of Frankfurt am Main.

13א Oxford, Bodleian Library MS Michael 161–62 (Neubauer 1110–11), fourteenth century.

14א Hamburg, Staats- und Universitätsbibliothek Hebr. 129, fourteenth century.

15א Vatican, Biblioteca Apostolica ebr. 333, fourteenth century.

16א British Library Add. 26954, fourteenth century.

17א Leipzig, Universitätsbibliothek 1108, fourteenth century.

18א Munich, Bayerische Staatsbibliothek Cod. hebr. 381, fourteenth century.

19א Cambridge, University Library Add. 379/1, fourteenth century.

20א Oxford, Bodleian MS Opp. 646 (Neubauer 1106), fourteenth–fifteenth century.

21א Hamburg, Staats- und Universitätsbibliothek Cod. hebr. 105, fourteenth–fifteenth century.

22א Hamburg, Staats- und Universitätsbibliothek Cod. hebr. 219, fourteenth–fifteenth century.

23א Vienna, Oesterreicher Nationalbibliothek Cod. Hebr. 12A, fourteenth–fifteenth century.

24א Vienna, Oesterreicher Nationalbibliothek Cod. Hebr. 77, fourteenth–fifteenth century.

25א Warsaw, Uniwersytet, Inst. Orientalistyczny 258, fourteenth–fifteenth century.

26א Vatican, Biblioteca Apostolica Ebr. 325, fourteenth–fifteenth century.

27א Cambrai, Bibliotheque municipale A. 946, fourteenth–fifteenth century.

28א Vatican, Biblioteca Apostolica ebr. 318, 1402.

29א Jerusalem, Jewish National & University Library 8⁰4199, 1410.

30א Oxford, Bodleian MS Canon Or. 110 (Neubauer 1124), 1482.

31א Israel Museum 180/53, approximately 1460.

32א Oxford, Bodleian MS Opp. 156 (Neubauer 1114), fifteenth century.

33א Oxford, Bodleian MS Opp. 650 (Neubauer 1128/1), fifteenth century.

34א Oxford, Bodleian Opp. 777 (Neubauer 1131), fifteenth century.

35א Berne, Burgerbibliothek A423, fifteenth century.

36א Hamburg, Staats- und Universitätsbibliothek Cod. hebr. 42, fifteenth century.

37א Hanover, Kestner-Museum MS 3953, fifteenth century.

38א British Library Or. 12281, fifteenth century.

39א Karlsruhe, Badische Landesbibliothek Cod. Reuchlin 11, fifteenth century.

FRENCH

ולמשומדים אל תהי תקוה
וכל המינים כרגע יאבדו
וכל אויבי עמך בית ישראל מהרה יכרתון
ומלכות זדון מהרה תעקר ותשבר ותמגר ותשפיל
ותשמיד ותכניע כל איובנו במהרה בימינו
בא״י שובר אויבים ומכניע זדים

ולמשומדים | צ3, צ4, צ5, צ7, צ9, צ10, פ1, פ2, אנ1 למשומדים.|| וכל המינים | צ5, צ8, צ10, צ11, פ2 נ׳ והמלשינים ומסורות כולם.|| יאבדו | צ3 יאבדון.|| עמך בית ישראל | צ3, צ4, צ11, פ1, פ2 ח׳ בית.|| יכרתון | צ2, צ3, צ5, צ8, צ11, פ1, פ2 יכרתו.|| ותמגר | צ11 ח׳.|| ותשפיל ותשמיד ותכניע | צ2, צ3, צ5 ותשפיל ותכניע. צ4 ותכניע ותשפיל. צ9, צ10, אנ1 ותכניע ותשפיל את. צ6 ותכניע ותשפיל ותכלה ותשמיד את. צ7 ותשפיל ותכניע ותכלה את. צ8 ותשפיל ותכניע ותכלה. צ11 ותכניע ותשפיל ותכלה. פ1 ותכניע ותפיל. פ2 ותכניע ותשפיל ותפיל.|| כל איובנו | צ8, צ11 כל איוביך וכל שונאך.|| במהרה | צ2 מהרה.

Manuscripts (צ = צפון צרפת, פ = פרובנס, דרום צרפת, אנ = אנגליה)

1צ Oxford, Corpus Christi College 133, twelfth century.

2צ University of Toronto MS Friedberg 3-014, thirteenth century?

3צ Oxford, Bodleian MS Opp. 759 (Neubauer 1118), thirteenth–fourteenth century.

4צ Biblioteca Palatina Codice Parma de Rossi 2766 (961), thirteenth–fourteenth century.

5צ Oxford, Bodleian MS Opp. (336 (Neubauer 1129/1), approximately 1394.

6צ Oxford, Bodleian MS Opp. 335 (Neubauer 1130/1), fourteenth century.

7צ Columbia University x 893 J 51 Q, fourteenth century.

8צ Biblioteca Palatina Codice Parma de Rossi 1902 (403), 1470.

9צ Oxford, Bodleian Or. 24 (Neubauer 1122), fourteenth–fifteenth century.

10צ Warsaw, Zydowski Instytut Historyszny 254, fourteenth–fifteenth century.

11צ Jewish Theological Seminary 4079/6, 1533, rite of Asti, Fossano, and Moncalvo.

אנ1 Rabbi Jacob Hazan of London, *ᶜEṣ Ḥayyim*, ed., Israel Brody (Jerusalem: Mossad HaRav Kook, 1962) 1:90, according to MS Leipzig, Universitaetsbibliothek B.H.Qu.40, end of the thirteenth century.

פ1 Paris, Bibliothèque Nationale Heb. 637, thirteenth–fourteenth century.

פ2 Biblioteca Palatina Codice Parma de Rossi 1923 (1117), fifteenth century.

SEFARDI

למשומדים אל תהי תקוה
וכל המינים וכל המלשינים וכל המסורות כלם כרגע יאבדו
וכל אויבי עמך ישראל מהרה יכרתו
ומלכות זדון מהרה תעקר ותשבר ותמגר ותכניע ותשפיל
ותפיל כל אויבינו וכל שונאינו ותכלם במהרה בימינו
ברוך אתה ה׳ שובר אויבים ומכניע זדים

למשומדים | ס11, ולמשומדים. ס2 לכופרים.|| תהי | ס11 נ׳ להם.|| וכל המלשינים | ס3, ס4, ס5, ס6, ס7, ס10 והמלשינים.|| וכל המסורות | ס2, ס4, ס5, ל1, ל2 ח׳. ס6, ס7, ס10 והמסורות. ס8 וכל האפיקורסים. ס3 נמחק ואחריו עוד מילה שלא ניתן לקרוא לגמרי, וה-----ים. ס9 וכל המסרים. ס11 וכל המוסרים.|| כלם | ס3, ס4, ס5, ס8, ס9 ח׳.|| וכל אויבי עמך ישראל | ס2, ס3, ס5 וכל אויבינו וכל שונאינו. ס8, ס9, ס11 וכל אויבינו וכל שונאינו וכל מבקשי רעתינו. ס6 וכל אויבינו. ס4 וכל אויביך. ל1, ל2 וכל אויביך וכל שונאיך.|| תעקר ותשבר | ס3 ח׳.|| ותמגר...תכלם | ס2, ל1, ל2 ותכלה ותכניעם. ס3 תכלה. ס4, ס8 ותמגר ותכניע. ס5 ותכניע. ס6 ותמגר ותכניע ותשפיל. ס9 ותמגר [---] ותכניעם ותשפילם. ס7 ותמגר ותכניע ותכריע ותפיל ותשפיל כל אויבינו וכל שונאינו ותכלם כרגע. ס10 ותמגר ותכניע ותשפיל ותשמיד בכל אויבנו וכל שונאינו. ס11 ותאבדם ותכניעם.|| שובר | ס3 משבר.

ל1 אלוס דירייניגאדורי[ש] נון אלייא אישפראנשה
אי טודוש לוש איריג׳יש אי טודוש לוש מלשינים קומו פונטו שי דיפירדיראן
אי טודוש טוש אינימיגוש אי טודוש טוש אבורישיינטיש אליינא שיראן טאג׳אדוש
אי ריינו די סובריורייו אליינה אראנקאראש, אי קיבראנטארא[ש],
אי אטימאראש, אי אבאטירלושאש איליינה אין נואישטרוש דילייאש
בינדיג׳ו טו ה׳, קיבראנטאן אינימיגוש אי אבאטיין סובירווייווש.

ל2 A los reñegados no sea esperança,
y todos los herejes y todos los malsines como punto (2: momento) seran (2: sean) perdidos.
Y todos tus enemigos y todos tus aborricientes ayna seran tajados
y reyno dela soberuia (2: malicia) ayna arrancaras, y quebrantaras, y atermaras, y quebrantarlos as ayna (2: presto) en nuestros dias.
Bendicho tu, Adonay, quebrantán enemigos y sojuzgan (2: quebrantán) soberuios.

Manuscripts

1ס Jewish Theological Seminary 4601–3602, ENA 861–82, fourteenth–fifteenth century.

2ס Biblioteca Palatina Codice Parma de Rossi 1738 (386), fourteenth–fifteenth century; Catalonian rite (the MS shows signs of censorship).

3ס Hamburg, Staats- und Universitätsbibliothek Cod. hebr. 205, fifteenth century (censored, but the stricken text is mostly legible).

4ס Jerusalem, Ben Zvi Institute, S19 2048, fifteenth century; Lisbon rite.

5ס Jerusalem, Jewish National & University Library Heb. 8° 844, fifteenth century; Lisbon rite.

6ס Biblioteca Palatina Codice Parma de Rossi 1752 (975), fifteenth century.

7ס Cambridge, University Library Add. 438(5), fifteenth century.

8ס Cambridge, University Library Add. 1204(6), fifteenth century.

9ס London, School of Jewish Studies 32, fifteenth–sixteenth century.

10ס Florence, Biblioteca Medicea Laurentiana Plut. II. 52, fifteenth–sixteenth century.

11ס Leiden, Bibliotheek der Rijksuniversiteit Cod. Or. 4814, sixteenth century, Fez.

1ל Paris, Bibliotheque Nationale hebr. 668, first half of the fifteenth century; published by Moshe Lazar and Robert Dilligan, *Siddur Tefillot: A Woman's Ladino Prayer Book* (Culver City, Calif.: Labyrinthos, 1995) 44–47.

[1]2ל Cincinnati, Hebrew Union College, Moshe Lazar and Robert J. Dilligan, eds., *Libro de oracyones: Ferrara Ladino Siddur (1552)* (Lancaster, Calif.: Labyrinthos, 1995) 61.

[2]2ל Cincinnati, Hebrew Union College, Moshe Lazar and Robert J. Dilligan, eds., *Libro de oracyones: Ferrara Ladino Siddur (1552)* (Lancaster, Calif.: Labyrinthos, 1995) 90.

The Blemished First-Born Animal

A Case Study in Tannaitic Sources

Tzvi Novick
Yale University

Recent synoptic studies comparing the Mishnah with the Tosefta and (to a lesser extent) with the tannaitic *midrashim* have shown that the Mishnah, far more often than has generally been assumed, reworks sources that are attested, in their original (or at least pre-mishnaic) form, in these other works. The current essay identifies a more complicated instance of "late" Mishnah. The list of animal blemishes in *m.Bekorot* chapter 6 appears to modify an original list, reflected in *t.Bekorot* chapter 4, by integrating materials attested in *Sifre Deuteronomy* and especially in the *Sifra*. The Mishnah's changes may have been motivated by the desire to adapt the list to the changed legal circumstances of the post-Temple period, and to synthesize different traditions about disqualifying blemishes.

Recent studies of synoptic parallels in tannaitic literature demonstrate that the Mishnah, far more often than has generally been assumed, reworks sources that are attested, in their original (or at least pre-mishnaic) form, in the Tosefta and the tannaitic *midrashim*.[1] Two book-length treatments venture that redacted compositions identical with or basically equivalent to the Tosefta and the *Sifra*, respectively, served as sources for the Mishnah.[2] The current essay takes

1 Shamma Friedman, in such works as "Mishnah and Tosefta Parallels (1) – Shabbat 16:1," *Tarbiz* 62 (1993) 313–38 (Heb.); "Mishnah and Tosefta Parallels (2) – Rabban Gamaliel and the Sages (Shabbat 13, 14)," *Bar-Ilan* 26–27 (1995) 277–78 (Heb.); and *Tosefta Atiqta, Pesaḥ Rishon: Synoptic Parallels of Mishna and Tosefta Analyzed with a Methodological Introduction* (Ramat-Gan: Bar-Ilan Univ. Press, 2003) (Heb.), has spearheaded the search for "old" (pre-mishnaic) Tosefta. In his introduction to *Tosefta Atiqta*, Friedman traces the awareness of old Tosefta among nineteenth and twentieth century scholars. Alberdina Houtman's doctoral dissertation (published as *Mishnah and Tosefta: A Synoptic Comparison of the Tractates Berakhot and Shebiit*, TSAJ 59 [Tübingen: J. C. B. Mohr, 1996]) likewise demonstrates that the Mishnah reworks sources reflected in the Tosefta. The project of identifying sources of the Mishnah in the tannaitic *midrashim* has won fewer adherents, but see below at n. 2.

2 On the Tosefta, see Judith Hauptman, *Rereading the Mishnah: A New Approach to Ancient Jewish Texts*, TSAJ 109 (Tübingen: Mohr Siebeck, 2005). According to Hauptman (*Rereading*, 1–2), "the Tosefta existed as an ordered collection prior to the time of the Mishnah; many of its paragraphs served as building blocks of the Mishnah. That is, the redactor of the Mishnah rewrites, reconceptualizes, and reorders the Tosefta collection, and other old materials, to produce his own work." Where the Tosefta seems to be commenting on our Mishnah, it is in fact, argues Hauptman (*Rereading*, 20), commenting on an "*ur*-Mishnah." On the *Sifra*, see R. Reichman, *Mishna und Sifra: Ein literarkritischer Vergleich paralleler Ueberlieferungen*, TSAJ 68 (Tübingen: J. C. B. Mohr, 1998). Reichman contends (*Mishna*, 2) that the Mishnah is dependent on "einem schriftlich fixierten Werk, das viel-

an agnostic stance on broad claims of this sort, but claims to identify another instance of secondary Mishnah. The example I have found, *m.Bekh.* 6:1–13 (a list of animal blemishes), differs from most others in two respects. First, in most other examples, there is a binary relationship between the mishnaic version in question and its parallel(s): the parallel is original, and the mishnaic version an adaptation thereof. The example below triangulates Mishnah, Tosefta, and tannaitic *midrash*: I show that the Mishnah reworked an earlier source reflected in the Tosefta by splicing into it sources preserved in the *Sifra* and *Sifre Deuteronomy*. The Aramaic translations (*targumim*) to the biblical blemish lists are also utilized (with due caution) as a control. The interaction of these different bodies of literature sheds new light on the extent and method of the Mishnah's editorial practices. Second, synoptic studies typically focus on a single pericope. I undertake here to examine an entire chapter. The wider perspective permits one to discern editorial interventions that might otherwise have gone unnoticed.[3] It is hoped that this essay will make a methodological contribution by encouraging the synoptic comparison of larger blocks of text.

The Law of Blemishes

The biblical law of blemishes is concentrated in Leviticus 21–22. Leviticus 21:16–23 lists blemishes that disqualify priests from serving in the Temple. Blemishes that disqualify animals from being sacrificed upon the altar are detailed in Lev 22:18–25. The prohibition against sacrificing blemished animals occurs again in Deuteronomy 17:1. Deuteronomy 15:21–22 legislates concerning the blemished firstborn animal.[4] According to the understanding of these biblical sources

---

leicht nicht wesentlich anders als der uns bekannte Sifra war"; or, in a slightly different formulation (*Mishna*, 237): "Es ergibt sich, dass bei der Mishna-Redaktion eine Sifra-Vorlage benutzt wurde." A pioneer proponent of early *Sifra*, Solomon Gandz ("Die altere Mishna im Sifra," in *Rahmer's Juedisches Literaturblatt* (Berlin: S. Cronbach, 1912) 108, cited in Reichman, *Mishna*, 12) proposed an ur-Mishnah theory quite similar to Hauptman's account of the relationship between the Mishnah and the Tosefta: "Die im Sifra gebrachten Mischna-Zitate stammen aus einer älteren Halachaquelle, höchtwarscheinlich der älteren Mischna, die unserer, der Rabbi's, als Grundlage gedient hat."

3 The benefits of considering large blocks of texts are (at least) two. First, differences in large-scale structure between parallel texts become noticeable. On this see also Chaim Milikowsky, "*Vayiqra Rabba*, Chapter 28, Sections 1–3: Questions of Text, Redaction and Affinity to *Pesiqta d'Rav Kahana*," *Tarbiz* 71 (2001–2) 17 (Heb.). Second, local changes in specific pericopes may form mutually reinforcing patterns. For example, the possibility that the Mishnah introduces new leg blemishes that constitute doublet renderings of terms in the biblical blemish list (see the section below entitled *Leg Blemishes* [p. 10]) is bolstered by the fact that the Mishnah appears to do the same thing in connection with eye blemishes (see the section below entitled *Eye Spots* [p. 12]).

4 On the threefold law of blemishes (Leviticus 21 on priests, Leviticus 22 on animals donated to the Temple, Deuteronomy 15 on the firstborn), see Rava's question in *b.Bekh.* 43a: למה לי דכתב רחמנא מום באדם מום בקדשים מום בבכור "Why need the Merciful One have written [about] blemishes for man, blemishes for designated animals, blemishes for firstborns?"

that is, to my knowledge, explicit or implicit in all rabbinic treatments of the subject, there are two kinds of animal blemishes. If an animal designated for sacrifice incurs a *less* severe blemish, it may not be sacrificed, but it also cannot be redeemed for personal consumption. (The animal must therefore be allowed to graze unmolested.) If a *more* severe blemish is incurred, then the animal may be redeemed. Thus, to take the example that will be of interest to us, the firstborn male animal of certain species is, from birth, designated for sacrifice. Parts of the firstborn must be offered on the altar; priests consume the remainder. If the firstborn has a blemish of the more severe sort, the priest may privately slaughter and consume it like any other animal. If the blemish is less severe, the animal may neither be sacrificed on the altar nor slaughtered for private consumption. With respect to priestly blemishes, there is no distinction between more or less severe blemishes, for such blemishes have only a single consequence: disqualification of the priest from serving in the Temple.[5]

A list of animal blemishes appears in *m.Bekhorot* 6 (*t.Bekhorot* 4).[6] In the Mishnah, the main list (6:1–12) identifies more severe blemishes, that is, blemishes that permit the animal to be slaughtered for personal consumption, and an appendix (6:13) identifies less severe blemishes, that is, blemishes that disqualify the animal for sacrifice but do not license personal consumption.[7] The main list divides in two. The first part (6:1–8) records blemishes about which there is no disagreement (save in details), while the second part (6:8–12) is populated by blemishes not universally recognized. The transition between the two parts of the main list occurs in the report of a discussion at Yavneh between the Sages and Aiala, an expert in animal blemishes (compare *m.Bekh.* 4:6).[8]

5 In employing the terms "less severe" and "more severe," I purposely refrain from defining these categories by anything other than their legal consequences; for the principles that determine whether a given blemish is less or more severe are murky. The view that permanent blemishes are more severe while transient blemishes are less severe is widely attested. The notion that internal blemishes are less severe is also attested, but much less commonly. Moreover, some seem to take the view that internal blemishes do not have the legal status of blemishes at all. See *t.Bekh.* 4:5 (on the debate between R. Joshua and R. Hananiah); *b.Bekh.* 39a (on missing internal limbs); *b.Bekh.* 37a–b (which seems to imply, in connection with the animals of Leviticus 27, that only transient blemishes, not internal blemishes, constitute less severe blemishes).

6 Throughout this essay I use the text and numbering of MS Kaufman for the Mishnah, and cite variants only when they are germane to the argument. For the Tosefta, I use Zuckermandel's edition (Jerusalem: Bamberger and Wahrmann, 1937), based for tractate *Bekhorot* on MS Vienna.

7 I do not mean to imply through the use of the term "appendix" that *m.Bekh.* 6:13, or its counterpart in the Tosefta (4:15–16), is a secondary addition, or secondary in importance, to the first list. I call the first list the "main list" and the second list the "appendix" simply because, in their redacted forms, the first is much longer than the second. "First list" and "second list" would serve adequately, but "main list" and "appendix" are more distinctive, and thus facilitate the analysis of what is an intricate and to many an unfamiliar corpus.

8 The first part of *m.Bekh.* 6:8 provides the last of the more severe blemishes. The pericope continues by noting that the blemishes collected in 6:1–8 were recited to the Rabbis at Yavneh by Aiala

The Tosefta chapter also divides into a main list (4:1–14) and an appendix (4:15–16). As in the Mishnah, the main list first identifies universally recognized blemishes (4:1–10) and then, through the conversation between the Sages and Aiala, transitions into contested blemishes (4:11–14). The main lists of the Mishnah and the Tosefta overlap extensively, but the headers differ. In the Tosefta, the main list does not, according to the header, restrict itself, as in the Mishnah, to blemishes on account of which "one slaughters (שוחטין) the firstborn" (*m.Bekh.* 6:1), that is, severe blemishes, but rather covers blemishes that "nullify (פוסלין) . . . the firstborn" (*t.Bekh.* 4:1). As animals are nullified, or barred from the altar, in virtue of more and less severe blemishes alike, one or more items on the Tosefta's main list could, according to the Tosefta, constitute less severe blemishes. The Tosefta's appendix diverges from the Mishnah's both in header and content. The items that it includes constitute, according to its header, not less severe blemishes, as in the Mishnah, but defects that do not constitute blemishes at all. Thus, while the Mishnah contrasts more severe blemishes (main list) to less severe blemishes (appendix), the Tosefta contrasts blemishes (main list) to non-blemishes (appendix).

This difference already raises the suspicion that the Mishnah chapter constitutes a secondary form of the list attested in the Tosefta. For the distinction underlying the Mishnah, namely that between more severe and less severe blemishes, is precisely that aspect of the law of firstborn blemishes that remained relevant to daily life after the cessation of sacrifice. It no longer mattered then whether the imperfection was less severe, or no blemish at all; in either case, the animal could only be left to graze until it had developed a more severe blemish, at which point it could be slaughtered and consumed. The Tosefta's list, by contrast, is organized with the Temple cult in mind: the main list describes imperfections that prohibit sacrifice, while the appendix describes imperfections that do not. It is therefore possible that, in the aftermath of the Temple's destruction, an original blemish list more or less like that of the Tosefta was modified to suit the changed legal circumstances. This hypothesis, admittedly speculative, will not be addressed directly in the discussion below. I offer it here to motivate a

(איילא in Kaufman, איילה in Cambridge). Aiala wished to add three items to the list, but the Rabbis disagreed with him. The disagreement between Aiala and the Rabbis provides the Mishnah the occasion to shift from the first part of the list (universally recognized blemishes) to the second part (debated blemishes). The anonymous voice in the *Bavli* discerns the basic structure of the main list: תנא שלשה הוסיף ואמרו לו לא שמענו את אלו וקתני ואתי דיחידאה "It teaches, 'He added three . . . and they told him: these we have not heard,' and then it continues to teach individual opinions" (*b.Bekh.* 41a). In MS Vienna of the Tosefta (4:11), the animal expert is identified as אמלה. Whatever the correct name – Tal Ilan, *Lexicon of Jewish Names in Late Antiquity, Part I: Palestine 330 B.C.E.–200 C.E.* (Tübingen: Mohr Siebeck, 2002) 361, does not decide – the variation is probably due to scribal error, for the double י in Kaufman and Cambridge looks strikingly like a מ.

more detailed examination of the relationship between the Mishnah's and the Tosefta's blemish lists. The first part compares the items in the two appendices, and the second part, the items in the main lists. The evidence collected in both parts confirms the secondary character of the Mishnah's version.

The Appendices

The Tosefta's appendix (4:15) has the following header: יש דברים שהן כמומין ושוחטין עליהן במקדש ואין שוחטין עליהן בגבולין "There are things that are like (but are not actually) blemishes, so we slaughter on their account in the Temple, but we do not slaughter on their account in the provinces." In other words, because the items in the appendix are not blemishes, the animal (whether it had been designated for sacrifice by a voluntary act, or, as in the case of the firstborn, from birth) must be sacrificed on the altar. Four examples are given: הנימוס הצומח והצומים ונקבה שיש לה קרנים. The Tosefta proceeds to explain (4:16) that the נימוס is a (male) animal without horns, that is, the inverse of the final item on the list, the female with horns.[9] The terms צומח and צומים describe animals with ear blemishes.[10] The Tosefta then records a discussion about androgynous firstborns. R. Ishmael asserts that androgyny is a blemish. The Sages contend that androgynous animals do not acquire firstborn status in the first place.[11]

9 See likewise *t.Menaḥ.* 13:6, where the נימוס is contrasted with the קירון "horned." The context of this pericope also confirms that the נימוס may indeed be offered on the altar. Marcus Jastrow, *Dictionary of the Targumim, Talmud Babli, Talmud Yerushalmi, and Midrashic Literature* (New York: Judaica Press, 1992 [1903]), s.v. גמם, would emend נימוס to גמום "worn away" (compare *m.Bekh.* 6:4 שניגממו). Zuckermandel cites in his apparatus a similar variant from a printed edition. Jacob Levy, *Wörterbuch über die Talmudim und Midraschim* (Berlin: B. Harz, 1924), s.v. נימוס, rejects the Tosefta's explanation of the term. Instead, he derives נימוס from Greek νομή "pasture," and thus translates "wild animal." It is also possible that נימוס derives from נינוס by dissimilation. The word would thus be a variant on ננס "dwarf." This etymology is not necessarily incompatible with the Tosefta's definition, for the Greek equivalent, κολοβός "docked, stunted," when used in connection with animals, can refer to the absence of horns. See H. G. Liddell and R. Scott, *Greek-English Lexicon* (9th ed.; Oxford: Oxford Univ. Press, 1996), s.v. κολοβός.

10 Each term appears differently in *t.Bekh.* 4:15 and 4:16, and it is difficult to know which, if either, is correct. In referring to these blemishes, I use the text of 4:15 because it receives confirmation from the quotation of this passage in *b.Bekh.* 44a. This quotation is itself noteworthy. It occurs after the formula תניא נמי הכי, in support of R. Ḥisda's statement, עז שאין לה קרנים ורחל שיש לה קרנים כשרים לגבי מזבח "A goat without horns and a ewe with horns are fit for the altar." In the quotation, the Tosefta's list reads thus: עז שאין לה קרנים ורחל שיש לה קרנים והצימח והצימם. In accordance with the general trend identified by Judith Hauptman, *Development of the Talmudic Sugya* (New York: Univ. Press of America, 1988), the *Bavli* appears to have modified the vocabulary and order of 4:16 so that the quotation matches the preceding amoraic statement.

11 There are legal differences between the two positions. For example, though a blemished firstborn is available for personal consumption, it may not be sheared. Thus, R. Ishmael would permit eating but not shearing, while the Sages would permit both eating and shearing.

R. Shimon appears to cite a verse in support of the Sages.[12]

The Mishnah's appendix (6:12) opens with the following header: אילו שאין שוחטין עליהן לא במקדש ולא במדינה "On account of the following we slaughter neither in the Temple nor in the provinces." The Mishnah's appendix is thus dedicated to less severe blemishes, ones that prevent the animal from being sacrificed on the altar but do not license its profane consumption. These blemishes are listed below, in the Mishnah's order, but grouped, for reasons that will become clear, into four sets:

1. חוורוור והמים שאינן קבועין (transient whiteness and transient water, two types of eye blemishes), חיטיו הפנימיות שנפגמו ושנגממו (damaged inner teeth)

2. בעל גרב (an animal with scurf), בעל ילפת (an animal with warts), בעל חזזית (an animal with lichen), זקן (an old animal), חולה (a sick animal), מזוהם (an animal emitting an offensive odor)

3. שנעבדה בה עבירה (an animal used to commit sin), שהמית את האדם (an animal that killed a person)

4. טומטום (*tumtum*), אנדרגינס (androgyne)

None of these items occurs in the Tosefta's list of non-blemishes. The items in the fourth set, intersexual animals, are the subject of the last part of the Tosefta's appendix, although the Tosefta cites no one who one espouses the position that intersex is a less severe blemish. The Mishnah continues, as in the Tosefta, with R. Ishmael asserting (here in contrast to the first, anonymous opinion) that intersex is a blemish of the more severe variety (and hence licenses consumption of the animal outside the Temple), while the Sages say that the intersexual animal does not have firstborn status in the first place.

How are we to account for the fact that the two appendices overlap with respect to intersexual animals, but otherwise not at all? One possibility is that the Tosefta's material on intersexual animals arose as a commentary to a Mishnah-like list including intersex among less severe blemishes. On this account, the Tosefta's appendix must be understood as an amalgam of two different sources, the first a list of non-blemishes, without any direct relationship to the Mishnah, and the second a commentary on the intersexual animals in the Mishnah's list of less severe blemishes. But in fact, there is a natural connection between the Tosefta's list of non-blemishes and its material on intersexual animals: the occurrence of two *cross*-sexual animals (the male without horns and the fe-

12 Note that while the debate between R. Ishmael and the Sages concerns the androgyne alone, R. Shimon's exegetical comment speaks of both androgynes and *tumtums*. I thank the anonymous readers for pointing out this discrepancy.

male with horns) on the list of non-blemishes leads easily into a discussion of *inter*sexual animals. This associative link suggests that the discussion of intersexual animals is original to the Tosefta. Moreover, the Mishnah's characterization of intersex as a less severe blemish is suspicious. This position is not represented in the Tosefta's discussion, and is intrinsically improbable, since the usual markers of less severe blemishes, namely transience and interiority, do not characterize intersexual animals.[13] There is thus a basis for supposing that the author of the Mishnah replaced the Tosefta's appended list of non-blemishes with his own list of less severe blemishes, and transitioned to the closing discussion of intersexual animals (the only component that remained from the original appendix) by adding intersex animals as the final item on his list.[14]

The hypothesized reconstruction finds support in the fact that the Mishnah's appended list is a composite whose sources are, for the most part, identifiable. The first set of items was generated from the main list, which counts permanent whiteness, permanent water, damaged outer teeth, and uprooted inner teeth as more severe blemishes (3–4). The implication, drawn in the appendix, is that transient whiteness, transient water, and damaged inner teeth constitute less severe blemishes.[15]

The second and largest set of items is directly paralleled in two pericopes in *Sifre Deuteronomy*. First, in commenting on Deut 15:21, *But if it has a blemish, lameness or blindness, any ill blemish, you shall not sacrifice it to the Lord your God*, the *Sifre* (section 126) reasons:

> מנין לבעל גרב ובעל יבלת ובעל חזזית וזקן וחולה ומזוהם תלמוד לומר מום כל מום רע לא תזבחנו לה׳ אלהיך יכול לא ישחט עליהם במקדש אבל ישחט עליהם בגבולים תלמוד לומר פסח או עור פסח ועור בכלל היו ולמה יצאו להקיש אליהם מה פסח ועור מיוחדים מום שבגלוי ואינו חוזר אף אין לי אלא מום שבגלוי ואינו חוזר

> Whence that one afflicted with scurf, warts, or lichen, or one that is old, or sick, or emitting an offensive order (is blemished)? From: "any blemish … any ill blemish, you shall not sacrifice it to the Lord your God."

13 On these markers, see above, n. 5, and the text below at n. 16.

14 It is important to realize that the Mishnah's deletion of the Tosefta's appended list does not imply or require a legal challenge to it. The items in the Tosefta's list are, after all, imperfections that are *not* animal blemishes. By eliminating them from Chapter Six, the Mishnah, likewise, implicitly asserts that they are not animal blemishes. In fact, the Mishnah transfers the two middle items on the list, צומה and צומים, to 7:4, the list of imperfections that constitute blemishes for priests but not for animals. It naturally does not transfer the first and last items, since these, insofar as they concern horns, are inapplicable to humans.

15 The first two blemishes are less severe because they are transient, and the third because it is interior.

Perhaps they may not be slaughtered on account of these in the Temple, but they may be slaughtered on account of them in the provinces? Therefore it says: "lame or blind." Lame and blind were in the general category (of blemishes), so why were they singled out? To compare to them: Just as the lame and blind are distinct insofar as their blemish is visible and intransient, so the rule (of disqualification) applies only to blemishes that are visible and intransient.[16]

According to the above exegesis, the six listed blemishes render a firstborn animal ineligible for sacrifice (because they count legally as blemishes) but also ineligible for ordinary consumption (because, unlike the explicitly listed blemishes of blindness and lameness, they are either interior or transient). The same six items appear in the *Sifre*'s commentary (section 147) on Deut 17:1, *You shall not sacrifice to the Lord your God an ox or a sheep that has a blemish, any ill thing*:

אשר יהיה בו מום אין לי אלא שנולד תם ונעשה בעל מום נולד בעל מום ממעי אמו מנין תלמוד לומר מום כל דבר רע מנין בעל גרב בעל יבלת ובעל חזזית תלמוד לומר מום כל דבר רע מנין לזקן וחולה ומזוהם תלמוד לומר שור ושה כל דבר רע

"That has a blemish" (Deut 17:1): This refers only to one that was born whole and became blemished. Whence (the disqualification of) one blemished from the womb? Therefore it says: "blemish, any ill thing." Whence (the disqualification of) one afflicted with scurf, warts or lichen? Therefore it says: "blemish, any ill thing." Whence (the disqualification of) one that is old, sick, or emitting an offensive odor? Therefore it says: "ox or sheep, any ill thing."

Thus Deut 17:1 teaches that the six items are blemishes (*Sifre* 147), while Deut 15:21 classifies them among the less severe variety (*Sifre* 126).

It is difficult to suppose that *Sifre* 126 is dependent on *m.Bekh.* 6:12, for there is no obvious feature that characterizes all and only the members of the second set in the Mishnah's list, and that could thus explain why the *Sifre* singled out just that set for mention.[17] The vector of dependence seems to run rather in the opposite direction. The Mishnah adopted *Sifre* 126, or a teaching substantively identical to it, and integrated it into the chapter by inserting, at the beginning

16 The Hebrew text for this and the next excerpt is taken from the critical edition of Louis Finkelstein, *Sifre on Deuteronomy* (New York: Jewish Theological Seminary of America, 2001). The translations are based on Reuven Hammer, *Sifre: A Tannaitic Commentary on the Book of Deuteronomy*, Yale Judaica Series 24 (New Haven: Yale Univ. Press, 1986) 171.

17 Such selectivity would also be unexpected given the tendency of *Sifre Deuteronomy* closely to follow the mishnaic text when it does quote from it. On this tendency see Menahem Kahana, עוללות מכילתא, *Tarbiz* 59 (1990) 239–40, and the sources cited in 239 n. 27.

of the appended list, the three items generated from earlier pericopes in the chapter. After the six entries borrowed from the *Sifre*, the Mishnah added two cases (the third set of items in the appendix) in which the blemish is not visible: an animal that has been utilized in a forbidden fashion and one that has killed a person.[18] The hypothesized reconstruction explains why the first set in the Mishnah's appended list is comprised of blemishes, while the second set is comprised of blemished *animals*. If the Mishnah were the original context for the items in the second set, one might have expected them to appear as blemishes (והגרב והילפת והחזזית "and scurf and warts and lichen," etc.), like the members of the first set. That they appear instead as kinds of animals (בעל גרב "one with scurf," etc.) suggests that they originated in a list, like that of the *Sifre*, in which *all* the items are animals rather than blemishes.[19]

The Main Lists

As noted above, the main list (*m.Bekh.* 6:1–11, *t.Bekh.* 4:1–14) divides into two parts: the first (6:1–8/4:1–10) records uncontested blemishes, and the second (6:9–11/4:11–14), contested blemishes. The first part is more carefully constructed than the second. In particular, the first part traces the anatomy of the animal from top to bottom: from the ear (6:1/4:1), which peeks out above the animal's body, to the eyes (6:2–4/4:2–4), the nose (6:4/4:4), the teeth (6:4/4:5), the trunk/genital area (6:5–6/4:6–9) and finally to the legs (6:7–8/4:9–10).[20]

18 In the Vilna edition of the *Bavli*, these two items reappear in the final pericope of *m.Bekh.* 7, under the category of פסולין בבהמה. They are omitted in the manuscripts (Kaufman, Cambridge, Parma A, Munich).

19 A final point in favor of the secondary character of the Mishnah's appendix: R. Ishmael and the Sages speak, in the Mishnah as in the Tosefta, in the singular: "there is no *blemish* greater than *this*" (R. Ishmael); "*it* is not a firstborn" (the Sages). This is appropriate for the Tosefta, where only a single anomaly, androgyny, is under discussion (until R. Shimon's statement, on which see above n. 12). But the fourth set in the Mishnah includes both the androgyne and the *tumtum*. Therefore, R. Ishmael and the Sages ought to speak in the plural. The singular is explainable as a carryover from the Tosefta. One could, however, maintain the Mishnah's independence from the Tosefta and still explain the solecism by supposing that the Mishnah's appendix itself originally included only the androgyne, and that the *tumtum* entered at a later stage.

20 The anatomical sequence recollects the *waṣf*s of Canticles, which hymn the various parts of the lover's body in order, from head downward (4:1–7, 5:11–16, 6:4–7). (The praise proceeds once [7:1–10] from feet upward, but the reversal in this case may be attributed to the fact that the object of the *waṣf* is dancing [7:1], so that attention is first drawn to the feet.) On the genre see David Bernat, "Biblical *Waṣf*s Beyond Song of Songs," *JSOT* 28 (2004) 327–49. There are intriguing echoes of the *waṣf* of Canticles 4 in particular: the frequent comparison of the lovers' parts to animals; the reappearance of two of the rare anatomical words from the *waṣf* of Canticles 4 in the blemish list, מתאימות (Cant 4:2, 6:6 and *m.Bekh.* 6:4/*t.Bekh.* 4:5) and מדבר (Cant 4:3 and *m.Bekh.* 6:8/*t.Bekh.* 4:11); the *waṣf*'s conclusion, in which the man describes the woman as unblemished (Cant 4:7 ומום אין בך "there is no blemish in you").

The second part does not betray any such organizing principle. The following discussion concentrates on the first part of the main list, since, given its tighter structure, the differences between the Mishnah and the Tosefta are easier to discern and account for. For a summary, in table form, of the entries analyzed below, please see the Appendix.

LEG BLEMISHES

At the beginning of its section on leg blemishes, the Mishnah (6:7) lists בעל חמש רגלים ושאין לו אלא שלוש "One with five legs or with only three." The parallel Tosefta pericope (4:9) runs as follows: איזה יתיר כל שיש לו שלש עינים וחמש רגלים החסר שלש רגלים ועין אחת "What is an 'excessive' (יתיר)? One that has three eyes or five legs. A 'defective' (חסר)? Three legs and one eye." The questions indicate that the Tosefta is commenting on a blemish collection that contained the terms יתיר and חסר. Intriguingly, R. Huna's remark (*b.Bekh.* 40a) on *m.Bekh.* 6:7 utilizes the same terms, even though they do not occur in the Mishnah: "This (the Mishnah's classification of five or three legs as a blemish) applies to one that has too few (חסר) or too many (יתר) *fore*legs. If (this is the case for) *hind* legs, it is also moribund." R. Huna was evidently aware of the tradition associating these terms with the blemish of five and three legs. A targumic tradition old enough to be attested both in the Babylonian branch (*Onqelos*) and in the Palestinian (*Neofiti*, *Pseudo-Jonathan*) uses יתיר and חסר to render the animal blemishes שרוע and קלוט in Lev 22:22.[21] In the *Sifra*'s commentary on the animal blemish list in Lev 22:22, there is no mention of extra or missing limbs.[22] The *Sifra* interprets שרוע and קלוט differently (*Emor* 7b:6):

> שרוע שנשמטה ירכו וקלוט פרסת רגלו דומה לשל סוס פרסת רגלו דומה לשל חמור
>
> שרוע: (One) whose thigh(-bone) slipped (from its socket). וקלוט: The hoof of its leg is similar to that of a horse, the hoof of its leg is similar to that of an ass.

21 In *Onqelos*, יתיר corresponds with שרוע, and חסר with קלוט. The order in *Neofiti* is reversed. In light of the fact that these translations are not narrowly literal, and that, in rendering שרוע in Lev 21:18 (in the list of human blemishes), the two *targumim* offer different, divergent approaches, it is fair to identify, in the translations of שרוע and קלוט in Lev 22:23 (in the list of animal blemishes), a common targumic tradition, rather than the convergence of independent traditions. For an important methodological discussion of the problems involved in distinguishing cases of genetic relationships among targums from cases of coincidental convergence, see Paul V. M. Flesher, "The Translations of Proto-Onqelos and the Palestinian Targums," *JAB* 3 (2001) 75–100.

22 For quotations from the *Sifra*, I use the edition of Isaac Weiss (Vienna: Hirsch, 1862), and supplement it with manuscript evidence, especially from MS Assemani 66, only when there are meaningful differences. Since Weiss' edition has two chapters "3" and two chapters "7" in *Emor*, I refer to them as 3a and 3b, and 7a and 7b, respectively. On the textual witnesses to the *Sifra* see Reichman, *Mishna*, 22.

Neither the words שרוע and קלוט nor the blemishes that the *Sifra* identifies with these words occurs in the Tosefta. In the Mishnah (6:7), however, the entry about five- and three-legged animals is followed by these two items:

ושרגליו קלוטות כשלחמור והשחול... אי זה הוא השחול שנישמטה יריכו

> And whose legs are drawn in like those of an ass, and a dislocated (animal)... What is a dislocated (animal)? (One) whose thigh (bone) slipped (from its socket).

The first item closely parallels קלוט according to the definition of the *Sifra*, while the second item is defined precisely as the *Sifra* defines שרוע.

The above data are best explained by positing that the Tosefta witnesses an early version of the blemish list that included only יתיר and חסר. These items were associated with the biblical animal blemishes שרוע and קלוט, as indicated by the unanimous targumic tradition. A different approach to these terms, one attested in the *Sifra*, was introduced by the Mishnah into the blemish list.[23] The first four items in *m.Bekh.* 6:7 (five legs, three legs, ass-like legs (hooves), and slipped thighbone) constitute, as it were, doublet translations of the words שרוע and קלוט in Lev 22:23.[24] Other explanations of the data are of course possible. A joint ancestor of the Tosefta and the Mishnah might have included all four items. The Mishnah would have preserved this list unchanged, while the Tosefta would have omitted two. But the fact that the *targumim* record only the two items that occur in both the Tosefta and the Mishnah (that is, excessive and defective), while the *Sifra* records only the two items that occur in the Mishnah but not in the Tosefta (that is, ass-like legs and slipped thighbone), suggests that the Mishnah innovated by synthesizing two independent traditions, only one of which (the one attested in the *targumim*) had occurred in the earlier version of the list.[25]

23 The Mishnah cannot, however, have borrowed from the *Sifra* passage in its current form, for the Mishnah identifies the blemish by the term שחול, while the *Sifra* simply attaches its description of the blemish to the biblical term שרוע.

24 The Mishnah further modified its antecedent by eliminating the Tosefta's second interpretation of יתיר and חסר, that is, an animal with three eyes or one eye. The Mishnah would have deleted this interpretation to avoid violating the list's top-down organizing principle.

25 I should emphasize that the role of the targumic tradition in this argument does not depend on dating a particular targum, or a stratum thereof, earlier than the redacted Mishnah, Tosefta, or *Sifra*. The *targumim* simply provide further reason to think that the Tosefta's inclusion of יתיר and חסר and its exclusion of שרגליו קלוטות כשל חמור and שנישמטה יריכו are not merely the result of chance, or of some selection principle employed by the Tosefta vis à vis its sources. Insofar as they manifest the same pattern of inclusion and exclusion as the Tosefta, the *targumim* rather suggest that the Tosefta faithfully follows a tradition about animal blemishes that includes only יתיר and חסר. Clearly the targumic tradition is of no evidentiary value if it is dependent on the Tosefta itself, but there is, to my knowledge, no basis for positing such dependence.

EYE SPOTS

A similar development may be reconstructed at another point in the list of animal blemishes. Leviticus 21:20 disqualifies priests on account of the two blemishes דק ותבלל בעינו. Among the Tosefta's collection of eye blemishes for firstborn animals, the items דוק and חלזון (probably spots of different shape or color) occur in sequence (4:2).[26] All extant *targumim* to Lev 21:20 (*Onqelos*, *Neofiti*, *Neofiti* margin, *Fragmentary Targum*, *Pseudo-Jonathan*) define תבלל בעינו as one whose eye contains a חלזון. It is therefore likely that the Tosefta's דוק and חלזון correspond to the biblical דק and תבלל.[27] The Mishnah (6:2) also includes דוק and חלזון, but in between these two items it inserts תבלול, which it defines as a condition in which the white of the eye breaches the pupil. The *Sifra* to Lev 21:20 (*Emor* 3a:13) offers the same definition of תבלל בעינו. It appears that the original list of animal blemishes, attested by the Tosefta, included only חלזון, which, as in the *targumim*, was deemed to correspond with the biblical blemish תבלל בעינו. The Mishnah introduced a second tradition about תבלל בעינו, one attested in the *Sifra*, and thus produced another doublet.

An alternative interpretation of the absence of תבלול from the Tosefta should be considered. It may be that *t.Bekh.* 4:2 is a commentary on *m.Bekh.* 6:2: it explains every term in the latter (דוק, חלזון, נחש, and עינב) save תבלול, because תבלול is the one item that *m.Bekh.* 6:2 itself explains.[28] This possibility cannot be excluded, but it can be challenged. For why, on this approach, does *m.Bekh.* 6:2 in fact explain only תבלול? On the interpretation I have advanced, an answer readily suggests itself: תבלול is a secondary addition, and came with its own explanation.

RELATIVE-CLAUSE CONSTRUCTION

The Mishnah's blemish list employs, at four points, a distinctive construction characterized by an anatomical header followed by one-word relative clauses in quick succession. In connection with eye blemishes (6:2), the Mishnah includes חריץ שלעין שניקב שניפגם שניסדק "the groove of the eye that was pierced, that

26 According to MS Vienna, the Tosefta actually has רוק "spittle," not דוק. But the occurrence of דוק in the same position in the Mishnah (on which see below), and the fact that רוק is not (to my knowledge) elsewhere employed as a blemish term, establish that רוק is a misspelling for דוק.

27 The *targumim* offer different renderings of דק. *Onqelos* (like *Sifra Emor* 3a:12, and compare the LXX) has דוקא, that is, a spot in the eye. It evidently interprets Lev 21:20 so that בעינו modifies not only תבלל but also דק. The Palestinian *targumim* link דק not with תבלל בעינו, the blemish that follows in the verse, but rather with גבן, the blemish that precedes it. These *targumim* have two renderings of both גבן and דק. On one account, גבן is a hunchback and דק is a dwarf. On another account, גבן is one whose eyebrows cover his eyes, while דק is one who has no eyebrows. Two of the Palestinian *targumim* (*Neofiti*, *Fragmentary Targum* V, and compare the Peshitta) record both renderings of each term.

28 I owe this suggestion to one of the anonymous readers.

was defective, that was slit." After finishing with the eye blemishes, the Mishnah moves down the body to the nostrils, lips, and teeth (6:4):

> חוטמו שניקב שניפגם שניסדק שפתו שניקבה שניפגמה שניסדקה חיטיו החיצונות שניפגמו שניגממו הפנימיות שנעקרו
>
> Its nostril that was pierced, that was defective, that was slit; its lip that was pierced, that was defective,[29] that was slit; its outer (front) teeth that were defective, that were worn, its inner (back) teeth that were uprooted.

The Tosefta does have something different to say about pierced nostrils (on which see below), but otherwise both the construction and the particular blemishes quoted above are absent from the Tosefta. A detailed consideration of these differences suggests that here, as above, the Mishnah has innovated by introducing a tradition attested in the *Sifra*.

The first item, חריץ שלעין, occurs as such only in two *Bavli* manuscripts (Vat 120 and France II I 9–7). Other manuscripts have ריס, הריס, or הרים.[30] ריס "eyelash" is, however, almost certainly incorrect, for the *Bavli* (*Bekh.* 38b) wonders about the anatomical reference of the term in the Mishnah, while ריס is a perfectly common term that would not, so to speak, have raised an eyebrow. (The appearance of ריסי עיניו "his eyelashes" in *m.Bekh.* 7:3 indeed goes without comment from the *Bavli* [*Bekh.* 43b–44a].) Moreover, ריס "eyelash" elsewhere occurs only in the plural and in construct with עינים; the singular and של are unique. Most likely, then, ריס, הריס and הרים are orthographic or phonetic variants of חריץ.[31] A blemish in the חריץ שבעין is also attested in one witness to *b.Giṭ.* 56a.[32] The term probably refers to the upper eyelid, or to the upper ridge thereof. The anatomical distance from ריס "eyelash" is thus small, but the lexical

29 In MSS Kaufman and Munich, שניפגמה "defective" is missing. In the former, there is space at the end of the line (which also marks the end of the column) for the word. The word appears in MSS Cambridge and Parma A.

30 See MSS Kaufman, Cambridge, Parma A, and Munich (ריס); Vat 120 and Vilna edition (הריס); Brit. Lib. ADD. 25717 (402) and Venice edition (הרים).

31 The variation on the initial ח is a result of the weakening of gutturals in rabbinic Hebrew. See Shim'on Sharvit, "Gutturals in Rabbinic Hebrew," in Menahem Zvi Kaddari and Shim'on Sharvit, eds., *Studies in the Hebrew Language and the Talmudic Literature, Dedicated to the Memory of Dr. Menahem Moreshet* (Ramat-Gan: Bar-Ilan Univ. Press, 1989) 226–33 (Heb.). The variation between חריץ and ריס (*t.Bekh.* 4:3) is parallel to that between חוורוור (*m.Bekh.* 6:2) and ווריר (*t.Bekh.* 4:2, 4:4). Likewise, הסחוס (*m.Bekh.* 6:1) derives from the Aramaic word חסחוס. On the latter see Moshe Bar-Asher, "The Noun Pattern פְּעוּל in Mishnaic Hebrew," *Lešonenu* 66 (2004) 66 (Heb.). See also Moshe Bar-Asher, "The Different Traditions of Mishnaic Hebrew," in David M. Golomb, ed., "*Working With No Data*": *Semitic and Egyptian Studies Presented to Thomas O. Lambdin* (Winona Lake, Ind.: Eisenbrauns, 1987) 28 and n. 153.

32 See Alexander Kohut, *Aruch Completum* (2nd ed.; Vienna: Menorah, 1926), see חרץ. S.v also Jastrow, *Dictionary*, s.v. חריץ.

difference is important for understanding the parallel pericope in the *Sifra* (*Emor* 7a:12), which defines the item חרוץ in the biblical list of animal blemishes (Lev 22:22) as follows:

> ריס של עיניו שניקב שנפגם ושנסדק שפתו שנקבה ושנפגמה ושנסדקה חיטיו החיצונות שנפגמו ושנגממו ופנימיות שנעקרו
>
> Its ריס that was pierced, that was defective, and that was slit, its lip that was pierced, and that was defective, and that was slit, its outer teeth that were defective and that were worn down, and inner (teeth) that were uprooted.

The *Sifra* understands חרוץ in Lev 22:22 to describe an animal blemished in the ריס of the eyes, in the lip, or in the teeth. The biblical prooftext offers further reason to believe that the original form of the *Sifra* (not witnessed in any of the manuscripts I have seen), as of the Mishnah, read חריץ rather than ריס, for the exegetical link to biblical חרוץ (Lev 22:22) then becomes clear. It is noteworthy that R. Pappa, a fourth-century *Amora*, identifies the חריץ of the eye as תורא ברא דעינא "the outer row of the eye" (*b.Bekh.* 38b), and, in commenting on the lips of *m.Bekh.* 6:4, notes: תורא ברא דשיפתיה "the outer row of its lip" (*b.Bekh.* 39a). Did R. Pappa know of a tradition involving the anatomical part חריץ של שפתו?

In any case, there are several indications that the original list, as attested by the Tosefta, did not contain the blemishes of the eye groove, etc., in *m.Bekh.* 6:2, 6:4, and that the Mishnah introduced them from the *Sifra* or from a source like it. Since no Palestinian *targum* save the late *Pseudo-Jonathan* is available for Lev 22:22, the *targumim* cannot help us decide whether the Mishnah added the blemishes or the Tosefta omitted them.[33] Probably the most important evidence occurs in connection with the nostril blemish. Of the four instances of the relative-clause construction in the Mishnah, the only one not paralleled in the *Sifra* passage is the one that concerns the nostril. The nostril blemish is also the only one that has any sort of parallel in the Tosefta: in 4:6, nostrils that pierce one into the other are said to license profane consumption, so long as the piercing occurs on the surface of the nose. If the unique status of the nostril blemish with respect to both the *Sifra* and the Tosefta is something other than a coincidence, the following reconstruction best explains it. The original list, as attested by the Tosefta, contained only the nostril blemish, in the form given in 4:4. The Mishnah imported the eye groove, lip, and tooth blemishes from the *Sifra*, or from a source like it, and split off the eye groove entry from the lip and teeth entries in order to accommodate the top-down logic of its list: the eye groove blemishes were inserted in *m.Bekh.* 6:2, before blemishes

33 *Onqelos* renders פסיק "broken." *Pseudo-Jonathan* probably echoes the *Sifra* in rendering לקויין ריסוי "its eyelashes are afflicted."

of the eyeball, while the lip and teeth blemishes found a place in *m.Bekh.* 6:4, after the blemishes of the nostril. The nostril entry was then modified to match its new neighbors.

The secondary quality of the Mishnah's eye groove, lip, nose and teeth blemishes is supported by the resemblance between חריץ "eye groove" and the biblical חרוץ, which suggests an origin in *midrash*. It is also noteworthy that in both the Mishnah and the *Sifra*, the blemishes of eye groove, nostril (in the Mishnah), and lip are ordered "pierced, defective, slit." At the top of the animal list in both the Mishnah (6:1) and the Tosefta (4:1), ear blemishes of the same three kinds occur, but in a different order. In the Mishnah, the order is "defective, slit, pierced," and in the Tosefta, "slit, defective, pierced." Though the oral quality of rabbinic study and transmission, and the textual variability consequent thereto, caution against easy inference from minor, non-substantive divergences, the shift in the Mishnah itself from the ear blemishes (ordered "defective, slit, pierced") to the eye groove, nostril, and lip blemishes (ordered "pierced, defective, slit") offers further support for the claim that the two sets of blemishes derive from different sources.[34]

BROKEN LIMBS

The last item on the first (undisputed) half of the Mishnah's main list is נשבר עצם ידו ועצם רגלו אף על פי שאינו ניכר "a bone of its foreleg or a bone of its hindleg broke, even though it is not noticeable" (6:8). The Mishnah here borrows from the biblical list of priestly blemishes, which includes שבר רגל או שבר יד "broken of foot or broken of hand" (Lev 21:19). The Tosefta (4:10) ends not by including broken limbs as blemishes but by excluding broken ribs:

> נשתברו רוב צלעותיו או שהיה בו מום מבפנים אינו מום שנ׳ עור ופסח מה עור ופסח המיוחדין מום שבגליו ואינו חוזר
>
> If most of its ribs broke or it had an internal blemish, it is not a blemish, for it says, "blind and lame" (compare Deut 15:21): blind and lame are singled out insofar as they are visible and intransient blemishes.

It is possible that the Mishnah and Tosefta trace to a common source that explicitly accepted broken limbs as blemishes and rejected broken ribs. The

34 For a thoughtful discussion of the kinds of variations characteristic of oral performance, see Elizabeth Shanks Alexander, "The Fixing of the Oral Mishnah and the Displacement of Meaning," *Oral Tradition* 14 (1999) 100–139. A note is in order here on the relationship of the arguments advanced in this paper to recent developments in the study of rabbinic orality. Alexander and other scholars of orality, most notably Martin Jaffee, *Torah in the Mouth: Writing and Oral Tradition in Palestinian Judaism, 200 B.C.E.–400 C.E.* (Oxford: Oxford Univ. Press, 2001), have suggested that the question of priority is often misplaced, and that synoptic parallels should, as a general

Mishnah would have retained broken limbs (and have omitted the discussion of broken ribs, perhaps because it preferred to mention only flaws that *do* count as blemishes), while the Tosefta would have retained the discussion of broken ribs (and have omitted broken limbs, perhaps because it had nothing to say about them).

But it is also possible that the Tosefta reflects the original form of the list. The mention of broken ribs may be understood in light of the context of 4:10: having just indicated that protruding loins count as a blemish, the list's author cautions that internal anomalies count as blemishes *only* if they protrude, and thus become visible; broken ribs therefore do not count as blemishes. The Mishnah would then have modified this entry by inserting broken limbs. The introduction of broken limbs from the priestly blemish list to the animal blemish list is paralleled in the *Sifra* (*Emor* 7a:11), which provides the following account of the animal blemish שבור "broken" (Lev 22:22):

> שבור מה תלמוד לומר לפי שנאמר שבר יד או שבר רגל שיכול אין לי אלא שנשברה ידו או נשברה רגלו מנין לרבות שבר זנב תלמוד לומר או שבור או יכול שאני מרבה שבר צלע תלמוד לומר שבר יד או שבר רגל מה אילו מיוחדים שמומן בגלוי ואין חוזרים יצא שבר צלע שאין מומו בגלוי
>
> שבור "broken": Why is this said? For it says "broken of hand or broken of foot" (Lev 21:19),[35] and I might have thought, only broken of hand or broken of foot. Whence to include broken of tail? From: "broken." Or perhaps I should include broken of rib? Therefore it says "broken of hand or broken of foot": As these are distinct insofar as their blemish is visible and permanent, this excludes broken of rib, whose blemish is invisible.

One argument for the influence of the *Sifra* (or a similar midrashic source) on the Mishnah is the peculiarity of the term יד in the context of animal blemishes. All four animal limbs would more naturally fall under the term רגל, unless one had a reason for distinguishing forelegs from hind legs. The occurrence of יד in *m.Bekh.* 6:8 indicates close reliance on the biblical list of human

---

matter, be understood as different performative versions of the same tradition. In my view, it is methodologically preferable first to attempt to explain differences between parallel versions by identifying one as more conservative (although not necessarily original), and the other as a conscious or unconscious reworking of the first. Only if such a reconstruction is not forthcoming should the parallels be understood as equally authentic performances. This methodological preference is grounded in the traditional notion of parsimony: the performative hypothesis posits additional entities, insofar as it assumes that multiple versions of a given tradition circulated, of which the extant ones are merely the lone survivors.

35 Strangely, all witnesses of the *Sifra* that I have examined (Assemani 66, Vat 31, and the Venice *editio princeps*) quote the verse in this order, even though the biblical verse has foot before hand. The LXX also puts hand before foot.

blemishes, and thus possibly on a midrashic intermediary, such as the *Sifra* passage above, that adverts to the human blemish שבר יד in its discussion of animal blemishes. Nevertheless, the evidence in this case is far from conclusive. Indeed, the *Sifra* passage, with both includes broken limbs as blemishes and excludes broken ribs, is precisely the sort of text from which both the Mishnah (which includes broken limbs but does not exclude broken ribs) and the Tosefta (which excludes broken ribs but does not include broken limbs) might independently have derived.

MAIN LIST DIFFERENCES SUMMARIZED

The above discussion covers every blemish present in the first part of the main list in the Mishnah but absent from the corresponding part of the Tosefta. Only two items occur in the Tosefta but not the Mishnah. The first is יבלת "wart" (*t.Bekh.* 4:2). Given the analysis of the appendices in the second section of this essay, the absence of this item from the Mishnah is readily understandable. Having introduced יבלת into its new appendix under the influence of *Sifre Deuteronomy* 126 (or a parallel source), which counts it as a less severe blemish, the Mishnah was forced to delete יבלת from the main list, which is comprised, in the Mishnah's reworking, only of more severe blemishes. The second entry that appears in the Tosefta but not the Mishnah is ניטלו קרנים וטלפים והזכר עמהם "the horns and hooves were removed together with the marrow" (*t.Bekh.* 4:8). I have no adequate explanation for the absence of these items from the Mishnah.

The comparison of the main lists in the Mishnah and the Tosefta thus indicates that most of the differences involve mishnaic pluses, that is, items found in the Mishnah but not the Tosefta. All of these pluses are paralleled in the *Sifra*. At the same time, the set of items common to the Mishnah and the Tosefta is absent from the *Sifra*, but partially paralleled in the *targumim*. Or, in schematic terms, the common core of the main lists in the Mishnah and Tosefta is a set of items X (partially paralleled in the *targumim*). The Tosefta contains only the set of items X, the *Sifra* only the set of items Y, and the Mishnah X+Y. The reasonable conclusion is that the Tosefta witnesses an original blemish list with ties to the targumic tradition, while the Mishnah inserts additions associated with the midrashic (*Sifra*) tradition.

A final category of evidence from the main list for the secondary character of the Mishnah should be considered here. We observed above that, while the Tosefta's header indicates that the main list is comprised of blemishes that would prohibit sacrifice, the Mishnah takes the view that the main list includes only blemishes that would license profane consumption, that is, only more severe blemishes. If the Tosefta is original, then it is possible that some of the items in the portion of the main list common to the Mishnah and the Tosefta ought to be characterized, despite the Mishnah's claim, as less severe blemishes.

It is clear that many, if not most, of the items in the main list are permanent, and thus presumably more severe; thus, for example, an animal with three legs (*m.Bekh.* 6:7, *t.Bekh.* 4:9) will never obtain a fourth. Indeed, for most of the blemishes in the first half of the main list, the Tosefta indicates explicitly that one may (profanely) slaughter the animal. The tail blemishes (6:5/4:7), however, constitute a notable exception. While the Mishnah lists them without comment, and thus implies that they license profane slaughter, the Tosefta explicitly indicates that animals with such blemishes may *not* be slaughtered outside the Temple. It is possible, however, that the Mishnah simply has its origin in a different opinion about the tail blemishes.

Conclusion

The arguments marshaled above indicate that *m.Bekhorot* chapter 6 adapted an earlier list witnessed in the Tosefta, in part by incorporating traditions witnessed in the *Sifra* and *Sifre Deuteronomy*. It should be clear that this conclusion does not, by itself, permit any generalizations about the relative chronology of the Mishnah, the Tosefta, and the tannaitic *midrashim* as a whole. Nor, indeed, does the above discussion require that the parts of the Mishnah's list paralleled in the *Sifra* and the *Sifre* have derived from these very works. Indeed, the sometimes significant lexical differences between the parallel passages in the Mishnah and in the tannaitic *midrashim* generally preclude the possibility of direct borrowing. But some of the additions do seem, on internal grounds, to originate in biblical exegesis (see, for example, the discussion of the חריין שלעין), and the material on animal blemishes in the *Sifra* and *Sifre* shows, as a general matter, little connection to the material common to the Mishnah and Tosefta. It is therefore best to speak of the Mishnah supplementing the earlier list by (among other things) adverting to an independent midrashic tradition. The Mishnah's changes need not all be assigned a single motive. In introducing an almost entirely new appendix, the Mishnah may have wished to reshape the earlier list so that it addressed the changed legal circumstances of the post-Temple period, when the crucial distinction was not between blemishes and non-blemishes (as in the Tosefta), but between more severe blemishes and less severe blemishes. The additions to the main list seem motivated by the ideal of comprehensiveness: to the traditional list of blemishes inherited from the source attested in the Tosefta, the Mishnah added blemishes from other sources.

I thank Professors Moshe Bar-Asher and Judith Hauptman for their helpful comments on earlier drafts of this essay. Special thanks to Professor Christine Hayes, who was kind enough to read two drafts.

Appendix

The table below summarizes the differences between the Mishnah and Tosefta with respect to the main list.

Mishnah	*Tosefta*
חריץ שלעין שניקב שניפגם שניסדק "the groove of the eye that was pierced, defective, or slit" (6:2)	
תבלול "blending" (6:2)	
	יבלת "wart" (4:2)
חוטמו שניקב שניפגם שניסדק "its nostril that was pierced, defective, or slit" (6:4)	נקבו חוטמיו זה לתוך זה "its nostrils were pierced one into the other" (4:4)
שפתו שניקבה שניפגמה שניסדקה "its lip that was pierced, defective, or slit" (6:4)[36]	
חיטיו החיצונות שניפגמו שניגממו הפנימיות שנעקרו "its outer (front) teeth that were defective or worn, or its inner (back) teeth that were uprooted" (6:4)	
בעל חמש רגלים ושאין לו אלא שלוש "one with five legs or with only three" (6:7)	איזה יתיר כל שיש לו שלש עינים וחמש רגלים החסר שלש רגלים ועין אחת "What is an 'excessive'? One that has three eyes or five legs. A 'defective'? Three legs or one eye." (4:9)
ושרגליו קלוטות כשלחמור "and whose hooves are drawn in like (those of) an ass" (6:7)	

table continues

36 See above, n. 29.

Mishnah	*Tosefta*
השחול ... אי זה הוא השחול שנישמטה ירכו "and a dislocated (animal).... What is a dislocated (animal)? (One) whose thigh (bone) slipped (from its socket) (6:7)	
	ניטלו קרנים וטלפים והזכר עמהם "the horns and hooves were removed together with the marrow" (4:8)
נשבר עצם ידו ועצם רגלו אף על פי שאינו ניכר "a bone of its foreleg or a bone of its hindleg broke, even though it is not manifest" (6:8)	נשתברו רוב צלעותיו או שהיה בו מום מבפנים אינו מום שנ׳ עור ופסח מה עור ופסח המיוחדין מום שבגליו ואינו חוזר "if most of its ribs broke or it had an internal blemish, it is not a blemish, for it says, 'blind and lame' (compare Deut 15:21): blind and lame are singled out insofar as they are visible and intransient blemishes." (4:10)

Justification by Deed

The Conclusion of *Sanhedrin-Makkot* and Paul's Rejection of Law

DEVORA STEINMETZ
Jewish Theological Seminary

Many have noted the coincidence in the last *sugya* of *b.Makkot* and the Pauline letters of the idea of law being reducible to a single commandment or principle as well as the citation in the *Makkot sugya* of Habakkuk 2:4, which is also highlighted in the Pauline letters.

In this article, I argue that the parallels between the last *sugya* in *Makkot* and the Pauline letters go beyond that. Specifically, both the Pauline letters and this *sugya* address the problematic asymmetry inherent in a worldview that demands fulfillment of commandments and adherence to prohibitions: violating even a single prohibition constitutes a failure to live the life that God has demanded that a person lead, even if the person has otherwise followed the requirements of God's law nearly all of the time. Since every person, as an imperfect creature, will fail to follow God's law perfectly, how can human beings hope to live before God?

Paul's answer to this question is well known. I argue in this article that the extended *sugya* which concludes *Sanhedrin-Makkot* addresses this same question – with, not surprisingly, a very different answer, and yet with striking similarities to many of Paul's arguments and with a striking coincidence of verses interpreted in the service of the respective arguments.

In addition to comparing the *sugya* with Paul's arguments, I look at the passage within its literary context and discuss its meaning as the conclusion of *Sanhedrin-Makkot* and its connection to core ideas in the final chapter of *Makkot*. Finally, I analyze the *sugya* from the perspective of legal philosophy and psychology, using the lens of the writings of Herbert Morris on "shame morality" and "guilt morality."

The final *sugya* (talmudic literary unit) in the Babylonian Talmud tractate *Makkot* includes several famous passages. Perhaps the most well known is the statement by Rabbi Simlai that there are 613 *miṣvot*, 248 positive commandments corresponding to the limbs of a human being and 365 negative commandments corresponding to the days of a solar year, followed by an extended homily about the progressive reduction of this great number of *miṣvot* to eleven, six, three, two and, finally, one: וצדיק באמונתו יחיה – *but the righteous shall live by his faith[fulness]* (Hab 2:4).[1] This passage is famous not only as the source

1 For a discussion of this passage in relation to partial parallels in *Tanḥuma* Buber *Shoftim* 10, *Midrash Tehillim* 15, and *Berešit Rabbah* 48:6, see Yaakov Gartner, "*ᶜIbud bavli shel derašat Rabbi*

of the idea that there are 613 *miṣvot* but also because of the intriguing idea of reducing the number of *miṣvot* to a small number of core behaviors or, perhaps, principles. The passage has drawn attention not only because of its inherent interest but because of elements that can be seen as parallels to two different ideas that occur in the New Testament: the notion of fulfilling the law through a single commandment, in the case of the New Testament through the commandment to love your neighbor as yourself (Galatians 5:14 and Romans 13:8–10;[2] see also James 2:8–11), and the idea that Hab 2:4 encapsulates the path to life (Gal 3:11 and Rom 1:17).

In this article, I will revisit this passage from a variety of perspectives and within a variety of contexts. I will look at the passage within its literary context: both its immediate context – the *sugya* of which it is a part – and its broader context – the chapter and tractate-pair[3] of which the *sugya* in which this passage is embedded forms the conclusion. I will also look at the passage in comparison with passages from the Pauline letters which, it turns out, not only bear the parallels noted above, but have striking similarities to what I will argue is the central problem that this passage addresses as well as to verses cited in this passage and to interpretations offered and rejected in this passage. And, finally, I will look at this passage within its literary context from the perspective

Simlai ᶜal taryag miṣvot," *Sinai* 96 (1985) 236–49. The word *emunah* in the Habakkuk verse is often translated as "faith," but *emunah* in biblical texts is most accurately construed as "faithfulness" or "trustworthiness." The rendering "faith(fulness)" is meant to retain the biblical meaning of the word while reflecting later interpretations, such as Paul's, which read in this verse the idea of faith. See n. 51, below, for references to scholarly discussions of Paul's rendering of the verse and n. 66 for the distinction between faith and faithfulness. It should be noted that the understanding of *emunah* that is reflected in the homily in *b.Makkot* is most probably "faithfulness" or "trustworthiness," given the emphasis in the preceding sections of the homily on qualities of justice and righteousness.

2 See also Matt 22:39, Mark 12:31, and Luke 10:27. These passages have been discussed also in relation to the teaching of Rabbi Akiva in *Sifra* on Lev 19:18.

3 *Sanhedrin* and *Makkot* originally comprised a single tractate. See Saul Lieberman, *Hilkhot hayerushalmi lerabbenu Moshe ben Maimon z"l* (New York: Jewish Theological Seminary of America, 1947) app. 1 (p. 67, n. 8) for *Makkot* as the final three chapters of *Sanhedrin* in the *Yerushalmi*, an arrangement that is reflected, as well, in the Parma and Kaufmann manuscripts of *m.Makkot*. While the *Bavli* knows *Makkot* as a separate tractate (see *b.Šebu.* 2b and compare *b.Mak.* 2a), it is not clear at what point in time *Sanhedrin-Makkot* came to be seen as separate tractates. It is possible that, at early stages of the *Bavli*'s development, *Makkot* and *Sanhedrin* were still seen as a single tractate. But, even if the two tractates became separated in Babylonian tradition early on, it is still appropriate to see the final *sugya* of *Makkot* as the coda of *Sanhedrin-Makkot*, since the two tractates are clearly continuous both thematically and stylistically. See Tamás Turán, *Talmud Bavli, Tractate Makkoth, Chapter Three (Elu Hen Ha-Loqin): A Critical Edition and a Critical Commentary* (Ph.D. diss.; New York: Jewish Theological Seminary of America, 2004) 31–32, for references to passages from *geonim* and *rishonim* that reflect a view of some or all of *b.Makkot* as part of *b.Sanhedrin*.

of legal philosophy and psychology, especially using the lens of the writings of Herbert Morris on "shame morality" and "guilt morality."

The passage occurs in the middle of a *sugya* on the last *mishnah*[4] of *Makkot* (*b.Mak.* 23b–24a). The *mishnah* reads as follows:

כל חייבי כריתות שלקו נפטרו ידי כריתתם שנאמר ונקלה אחיך לעיניך – כשלקה הרי הוא כאחיך – דברי ר׳ חנניא בן גמליאל.

אמר ר׳ חנניא בן גמליאל: מה אם העובר עבירה אחת נוטל נפשו עליה העושה מצוה אחת על אחת כמה וכמה שתינתן לו נפשו.

ר׳ שמעון אומר: ממקומו הוא למד שנאמר ונכרתו הנפשות העושות וגו׳ ואומר אשר יעשה אותם האדם וחי בהם – הא כל היושב ולא עבר עבירה נותנין לו שכר כעושה מצוה.

רבי שמעון בר רבי אומר: הרי הוא אומר רק חזק לבלתי אכול הדם כי הדם הוא הנפש וגו׳ – ומה אם הדם שנפשו של אדם קצה ממנו הפורש ממנו מקבל שכר גזל ועריות שנפשו של אדם מתאוה להן ומחמדתן הפורש מהן על אחת כמה וכמה שיזכה לו ולדורותיו ולדורות דורותיו עד סוף כל הדורות.

רבי חנניה בן עקשיא אומר: רצה הקדוש ברוך הוא לזכות את ישראל לפיכך הרבה להם תורה ומצות שנאמר ה׳ חפץ למען צדקו יגדיל תורה ויאדיר.[5]

4 I am referring to the final *mishnah* according to the *mishnah* division in the *Bavli*; this corresponds to the final two *mishnayot* in texts of the Mishnah: *m.Makkot* 3:15–16. For the purposes of the discussion here, I will consistently refer to this passage as the final *mishnah* of *Makkot*.

5 Yaakov Naḥum Halevi Epstein, *Mavo lenusach hamishna* (2 vols.; Jerusalem: Magnes Press, 2000) 2:977–78, writes that Ḥananiah ben Aqashia's teaching appears to be a later addition to the *mishnah*, and the view that this teaching is an aggadic addition to the end of *m.Makkot* has become commonplace. Epstein brings no evidence in support of this conjecture, however; he bases it solely on the fact that this teaching is added to the end of the sixth (extra-mishnaic) chapter of *ʾAbot* (and, in liturgical practice, to the end of each chapter of *ʾAbot*) as well as on the addition of a teaching of Ḥananiah ben Aqashia to the end of *m.Qinnim*. As Epstein notes, however, the teaching appears and is discussed in a Geniza fragment of *y.Makkot* (the text can be found in Lieberman, *Hilkhot hayerushalmi*, 67); working with the assumption that the teaching is not integral to the *mishnah*, Epstein suggests that it is, in fact, a *baraita* that the *Yerushalmi* cites in relation to the *mishnah*. Absent any evidence to support the contention that the teaching is a late addition to the *mishnah* (and especially given that the Geniza fragment can well be taken as evidence to the contrary); given that the mishnaic context is already aggadic and, even without Ḥananiah ben Aqashia's teaching, would end the tractate on a positive note (and thus the idea that Ḥananiah ben Aqashia's teaching was added to the *mishnah* in order to end on a positive note is less compelling than similar arguments about other such endings); and noting (as will be discussed below) that Rabbi Simlai's teaching about 613 *miṣvot* can well be seen as appearing in the *sugya* in relation to Ḥananiah ben Aqashia's teaching about the plurality of *miṣvot*, I will be working on the assumption that this teaching was part of the *mishnah* as it appeared before the redactor of the *Bavli sugya* (which does not mean, of course, that it could not have been added at some point later than the original redaction of the Mishnah).

All those who are liable for *karet* (excision) who have been flogged become exempt from their *karet*, as it says: *and your brother shall be dishonored* (niqleh*) before your eyes* – once he receives *malqot* (lashes), he is like *your brother* – the words of Rabbi Ḥananiah ben Gamliel.

Rabbi Ḥananiah ben Gamliel said: If one who transgresses a single transgression loses his life on account of it, one who performs[6] a single commandment – how much more so that his life will be given to him.

Rabbi Shimon says: It can be learned from its proximate location [that is, a nearby verse], as it says [*For whoever does any of these abominations*], *the souls who do shall be cut off* [*from the midst of their people*] (Leviticus 18:29) and it says [*And you shall keep my statutes and my judgments*] *which a person shall do and live by them* (Lev 18:5) – thus anyone who sits and does not commit a transgression is given reward as one who performs a *miṣvah.*

Rabbi Shimon ben Rabbi says: Behold it says *Only be steadfast that you do not eat the blood, for the blood is the life. . . .* [*Do not eat it, in order that it be good with you and with you children after you when you do what is right in the eyes of God.*] (Deuteronomy 12:23–25) – If [regarding] blood, by which a person's soul is repulsed, one who separates from it receives a reward, then [regarding] robbery and forbidden sexual relationships, which a person's soul desires and covets, how much more so will one who separates from them gain merit for himself and for his descendents and for the descendents of his descendents until the end of all the generations.

Rabbi Ḥananiah ben Aqashia says: The Holy Blessed One wanted to give merit to Israel, therefore he multiplied for them Torah and *miṣvot*, as it says *God desires for the sake of his righteousness to make the Torah great and to glorify it.* (Isaiah 42:21)

Here is the *Bavli* passage, which includes a brief *aggadah* embedded within the extended homily on the reduction of the number of *miṣvot*:[7]

דרש רבי שמלאי: שש מאות ושלש עשרה מצות נאמרו לו למשה: שלש מאות ושׁשים וחמש לאוין כמנין ימות החמה, ומאתים וארבעים ושמונה עשה כנגד איבריו של אדם.

אמר רב המנונא: מאי קרא? תורה צוה לנו משה מורשה – תורה בגימטריא שית מאה וחד סרי הוי; אנכי ולא יהיה לך מפי הגבורה שמענום.

6 ᶜ*oseh*, literally "does." This meaning, while less idiomatic in English, will become crucial for our discussion of Paul below.

7 Text and translation follow the Vilna edition; significant variants are discussed in the notes.

בא דוד והעמידן על אחת עשרה דכתיב: מזמור לדוד ה' מי יגור באהלך מי ישכון בהר קדשך הולך תמים ופועל צדק ודובר אמת בלבבו לא רגל על לשונו לא עשה לרעהו רעה וחרפה לא נשא על קרובו נבזה בעיניו נמאס ואת יראי ה' כבד נשבע להרע ולא ימיר כספו לא נתן בנשך ושוחד על נקי לא לקח עושה אלה לא ימוט לעולם.

הולך תמים – זה אברהם דכתיב: התהלך לפני והיה תמים;

פועל צדק – כגון אבא חלקיהו;

ודובר אמת בלבבו – כגון רב ספרא;

לא רגל על לשונו – זה יעקב אבינו דכתיב: אולי ימושני אבי והייתי בעיניו כמתעתע;

לא עשה לרעהו רעה – שלא ירד לאומנות חבירו;

וחרפה לא נשא על קרובו – זה המקרב את קרוביו;

נבזה בעיניו נמאס – זה חזקיהו המלך שגירר עצמות אביו במטה של חבלים;

ואת יראי ה' יכבד – זה יהושפט מלך יהודה, שבשעה שהיה רואה תלמיד חכם היה עומד מכסאו ומחבקו ומנשקו וקורא לו רבי רבי מרי מרי;

נשבע להרע ולא ימיר – כר' יוחנן דא"ר יוחנן: אהא בתענית עד שאבא לביתי;

כספו לא נתן בנשך – אפילו ברבית עובד כוכבים;

ושוחד על נקי לא לקח – כגון ר' ישמעאל בר' יוסי.

כתיב: עושה אלה לא ימוט לעולם – כשהיה ר"ג מגיע למקרא הזה היה בוכה, אמר: מאן דעביד להו לכולהו הוא דלא ימוט, הא חדא מינייהו ימוט! אמרו[8] ליה: מי כתיב עושה כל אלה? עושה אלה כתיב – אפילו בחדא מינייהו. דאי לא תימא הכי, כתיב קרא אחרינא: אל תטמאו בכל אלה – התם נמי הנוגע בכל אלה הוא דמטמא, בחדא מינייהו לא? אלא לאו באחת מכל אלה, הכא נמי באחת מכל אלו.

בא ישעיהו והעמידן על שש דכתיב: הולך צדקות ודובר מישרים מואס בבצע מעשקות נוער כפיו מתמוך בשוחד אוטם אזנו משמוע דמים ועוצם עיניו מראות ברע.

הולך צדקות – זה אברהם אבינו, דכתיב: כי ידעתיו למען אשר יצוה וגו';

ודובר מישרים – זה שאינו מקניט פני חבירו ברבים;

מואס בבצע מעשקות – כגון ר' ישמעאל בן אלישע;

נוער כפיו מתמוך בשוחד – כגון ר' ישמעאל בר' יוסי.

אוטם אזנו משמוע דמים – דלא שמע בזילותא דצורבא מרבנן ושתיק, כגון ר"א ברבי שמעון;

ועוצם עיניו מראות ברע – כדרבי חייא בר אבא, דאמר ר' חייא בר אבא: זה שאינו מסתכל בנשים בשעה שעומדות על הכביסה.

וכתיב: הוא מרומים ישכון וגו'.

בא מיכה והעמידן על שלש דכתיב: הגיד לך אדם מה טוב ומה ה' דורש ממך כי אם עשות משפט ואהבת חסד והצנע לכת עם אלהיך.

עשות משפט – זה הדין;

אהבת חסד – זה גמילות חסדים;

והצנע לכת – זה הוצאת המת והכנסת כלה. והלא דברים קל וחומר: ומה דברים

8 MS Munich has "Rabbi Akiva said" instead of "they said." See the parallel in *b.Sanh.* 81a and the discussion of these two passages below.

שאין דרכן לעשותן בצנעא אמרה תורה והצנע לכת, דברים שדרכן לעשותן בצנעא על אחת כמה וכמה.

חזר ישעיהו והעמידן על שתים שנאמר: כה אמר ה׳ שמרו משפט ועשו צדקה.

בא עמוס והעמידן על אחת שנאמר: כה אמר ה׳ לבית ישראל דרשוני וחיו.

מתקיף לה רב נחמן בר יצחק: אימא דרשוני בכל התורה כולה!

אלא בא חבקוק והעמידן על אחת שנאמר: וצדיק באמונתו יחיה.

Rabbi Simlai expounded: Six hundred thirteen *miṣvot* were given to Moses: three hundred sixty-five negative commandments, corresponding to the number of days in a solar year, and two hundred forty-eight positive commandments, corresponding to the number of limbs of a person.

Rav Hamnuna said: What is the scriptural source? *Moses commanded us the Torah as an inheritance* (Deut 33:4) – Torah in *gematria* equals six hundred eleven. *I* [*am the Lord your God*] and *you shall have no* [*other gods*] we heard from the Almighty.

David came and reduced them to eleven, as it is written: *A psalm of David: God, who may live in your tent? Who may dwell in your holy mountain? One who walks in perfectness and works righteousness and acknowledges truth in his heart; has no slander on his tongue, has not done evil to his fellow, and has not borne reproach for* [*his acts toward*] *one who is close to him; in whose eyes a contemptible person is repulsive and who honors those who fear God; who swears to his detriment without retracting; who does not give out his money with interest, and does not take a bribe against the innocent. One who acts thus will never be shaken* (Psalm 15).
One who walks in perfectness – this is Abraham, as it is written: *Walk before Me and be perfect* (Genesis 17:1);
works righteousness – like Abba Ḥilqiyahu;
and acknowledges truth in his heart – like Rav Safra;
has no slander on his tongue – this is our father Jacob, as it is written: *if my father feels me, I shall appear to him as a deceiver* (Gen 27:12);
has not done evil to his fellow – that he did not infringe on his fellow's trade;
and has not borne reproach for [*his acts toward*] *one who is close to him* – this is one who brings his relatives near;
in whose eyes a contemptible person is repulsive – this is King Hezekiah, who dragged the bones of his father on a bier of ropes;
and who honors those who fear God – this is Yehoshafat, king of Judah, who, when he would see a scholar, would stand from his throne and embrace him and kiss him and call him "my teacher, my teacher, my master, my master";

who swears to his detriment without retracting – like Rabbi Yoḥanan, for Rabbi Yoḥanan said: "I will remain fasting until I come to my home";
who does not give out his money with interest – even interest from an idolater;
and does not take a bribe against the innocent – like Rabbi Yishmael son of Rabbi Yose.

It is written: *One who does these will never be shaken.* When Rabban Gamliel would reach this scriptural passage he would cry. He said: "It is only the person who does *all* of these who will not be shaken, thus [the person who does] *one* of them will be shaken!"
They (MS Munich – Rabbi Akiva) said to him: "Is it written 'one who does *all* of these'?! *One who does these* is written – even by means of *one* of them.
"For if you do not say this, another scriptural verse is written: *Do not become defiled by means of any* (*kol* – which can mean 'any' or 'all') *of these* (Lev 18:24) – there too, is it the one who touches *all* of these who is defiled, but [one who touches] any *one* of them not?! Rather, no, [a person is defiled] by means of any *one* of all of these – here, too, by means of any *one* of all of these."

Isaiah came and reduced them to six, as it is written: *One who walks in righteousness and speaks uprightly, spurns profit from fraudulent dealings, waves away bribery instead of grasping it, closes his ear against listening to infamy, and shuts his eyes against seeing evil* (Isa 33:15).
One who walks in righteousness – this is our father Abraham, as it is written: *For I have known him that he will command* [*his children and his household after him and they will keep the way of God to do righteousness and justice*] (Gen 18:19);
and speaks uprightly – this is one who does not embarrass his friend in public;
spurns profit from fraudulent dealings – like Rabbi Yishmael son of Elisha;
waves away bribery instead of grasping it – like Rabbi Yishmael son of Rabbi Yose;
closes his ear against listening to infamy – that he did not hear a derogatory remark about a rabbinic disciple and remain silent, like Rabbi Eleazar son of Rabbi Shimon;
and shuts his eyes against seeing evil – in accordance with the teaching of Rabbi Ḥiyya son of Abba, for Rabbi Ḥiyya the son of Abba said: "This is one who does not look at women while they are standing over the laundry."
And it is written: *He will dwell on high . . .* (Isa 33:16).

Micah came and reduced them to three, as it is written: *He has told you,*

O human, what is good and what God seeks of you: only doing justice and loving kindness and walking humbly with your God (Micah 6:8).
doing justice – this is judgment;
loving kindness – this is performing acts of kindness;
and walking humbly – this is taking out the dead [for burial] and bringing in the bride [for marriage]. And isn't this an *a fortiori* argument: If, concerning matters that customarily are not done in private, the Torah says *and walk humbly*, in matters that customarily are done in private, how much more so.

Isaiah came again and reduced them to two, as it says: *Thus said God: Observe justice and do righteousness* (Isa 56:1).

Amos came and reduced them to one, as it says: *Thus said God to the house of Israel: Seek me and live* (Amos 5:4).

Rav Naḥman son of Isaac challenged: I could say "seek me" by means of all of the Torah! Rather –

Habakkuk came and reduced them to one, as it says: *but the righteous shall live by his faith[fulness]* (Hab 2:4).

Elu hen haloqin
"These are the Ones Who are Flogged"

M.Makkot 3:15 resumes the topic that was introduced implicitly at the beginning of the chapter of Mishnah – the idea that those whom the Torah says are punished by *karet*[9] (excision) are subject to *malqot* (flogging). The first *mishnah* of the third chapter of *Makkot* lists violators of law who are subject to flogging. The first group of laws in this list are those about which the Torah says that the violator is cut off – *krt*.[10] The *gemara* on that *mishnah* (*b.Mak.* 13a–b) points

9 This formulation suggests that *karet* is a sanction that is imposed on the person, which does not necessarily correspond to the biblical concept of a person being cut off from his people; see below about the variety of understandings of this biblical idea. I am using this formulation here as an approximation of the term *ḥayvei karet* – a term that assimilates *karet* to a system of punishments for which one may be liable or from which one may be exempt.

10 See Rashi s.v. *ʾelu hen haloqin* and Tosafot s.v. *veʾelu hen haloqin habaʾ ʿal ʾaḥoto* for attempts to account for the list of violations in this *mishnah* and for the point that the *mishnah* includes violations subject to *karet* in order to teach that those subject to *karet* are flogged. See Aharon Shemesh, *ʿOnšim veḥaṭaʾim: Min hamiqra lesifrut ḥazal* (Jerusalem: Magnes Press, 2003) 178–204 for a detailed discussion of the components of the list in *m.Mak.* chapter 3. See Steinmetz, "Crimes and Punishments, Part 2: Noachide Law, Brother-Sister Intercourse, and the Case of Murder," *JJS* 55 (2004) 278–305 for a discussion of the prohibition against brother-sister intercourse, the first crime listed in this *mishnah* and the source of the position of one of the *tannaim* in the three-

out that the mishnaic list accords with the view of Rabbi Akiva. The *gemara* introduces a three-way tannaitic dispute about violators of which laws are subject to flogging. Rabbi Akiva holds the position that those who are liable for *karet* are subject to flogging, corresponding to the list of liable violators of law in the *mishnah*, while one of the opposing positions includes even those who are liable for criminal execution as subject to flogging, and the other excludes those who are liable for *karet* from being subject to flogging.

Turning back to focus on the violator of law who is subject to flogging, the final *mishnah* of the tractate begins with the astonishing statement that anyone who is liable for *karet* becomes exempt from this punishment by means of suffering the punishment of flogging. This teaching goes well beyond the implication of the first *mishnah* of the chapter, which includes those subject to *karet* under the rubric of those who suffer the sanction of flogging, but which does not make the claim that this sanction exempts them from suffering *karet*.

The teaching of Rabbi Ḥananiah ben Gamliel in this final *mishnah* invites comparison with the position of Rabbi Akiva introduced in the *gemara*'s discussion of the first *mishnah* in the chapter: "Rabbi Akiva says: Those who are liable for *karet* are included in the category of those subject to forty lashes, for if they repent the heavenly court forgives them."[11] Rabbi Akiva's teaching can be read in two very different ways. The first has to do with a legal technicality: the principle that one cannot be liable for two punishments for one violation of law. Rabbi Akiva can be understood to be explaining that, even though one is generally not subject to two punishments, one can be flogged for a sin that the Torah says results in *karet* because it may well happen that the person will ultimately not be subject to *karet*. If the person repents, then the heavenly court forgives him, and he will not suffer *karet*; thus, imposing lashes does not violate the principle of not inflicting two punishments for a single violation of law.[12]

---

way dispute introduced by the *gemara* in relation to this *mishnah*, as the locus of principles of law within rabbinic texts.

11 See the discussion of Rabbi Ḥananiah ben Gamliel's position on *b.Mak.* 23b and the comments of Rabbi Zerachia Halevi, Nachmanides, and Rabbi Yom Tov Ishbili (Ritva). For a brief discussion about the relationship between Rabbi Akiva's and Rabbi Ḥananiah ben Gamliel's teachings and for summaries of some classical and contemporary approaches to this question, see Shemesh, *ᶜOnšim veḥaṭaʾim*, 89 and n. 97.

12 This is the element of Rabbi Akiva's argument on which the *gemara* focuses in its discussion of the *baraita* (*b.Mak.* 13b–14a). The focus of the *gemara*'s discussion is on understanding the rationales behind the three different positions in the *baraita*. It takes Rabbi Akiva's teaching, which follows the position of Rabbi Yishmael in the *baraita*, that a person subject to judicial execution incurs the penalty of flogging, to be articulating not only why the person subject to *karet* does receive lashes but also why the person subject to judicial execution should *not* receive lashes. Even if this understanding of Rabbi Akiva's teaching is accepted, it does not rule out a further explanation of why the person subject to *karet* should receive lashes. That is, this aspect of Rabbi Akiva's teaching explains only why it is not a violation of the rules of judicial punishment for a per-

An alternative, though not mutually exclusive,[13] reading understands Rabbi Akiva not to be explaining why the court *may* impose flogging in a case where one is subject to *karet* but, rather, why the court *should* impose flogging in such a case. Rabbi Akiva can be understood to be saying that the court should impose flogging because the person who is subject to *karet* has an opportunity to be absolved from that dire consequence of his actions. If the person repents, then he will be exempt from *karet*. According to this reading, Rabbi Akiva is taking the court's imposition of flogging as creating an opportunity for the person to repent and thus to avoid the penalty of *karet* – a penalty that, without this opportunity, would be the inevitable consequence of his violation of law.[14]

Such a position might be seen as differing from the teaching of Rabbi Ḥananiah ben Gamliel in the final *mishnah* of *Makkot*, in that Rabbi Akiva seems to be focusing on the need for repentance,[15] while Rabbi Ḥananiah ben Gamliel's teaching might suggest that flogging itself, even without repentance, exempts the person from *karet*. It is also possible that the two teachings are consistent with each other, with both Sages understanding flogging as an opportunity for repentance, even though Rabbi Ḥananiah ben Gamliel does not say this.[16] In fact, the idea of repentance, and even of atonement, is completely absent from the Mishnah's discussion of flogging, which focuses on legal categories of liability and exemption.[17] It is certainly possible that Rabbi Ḥananiah ben Gam-

---

son subject to *karet* to be flogged, but it does not explain why the person *should* receive lashes. There is more than one possible answer to this question; one possibility not discussed here is that Rabbi Akiva believes that it is essential for a human court to impose punishment on the violator of law, perhaps in order to enact the community's condemnation of the person who violates law, or for some other reason.

13 That is, the first reading sees Rabbi Akiva's teaching as explaining only why the court *may* inflict flogging on the person subject to *karet* but as silent as to why the court *should* do so. The second reading takes Rabbi Akiva's teaching to speak to why the court not only *may* but *should* inflict flogging on the person who is subject to *karet.*

14 See Shemesh's discussion of Rabbi Akiva's position in relation to *Sifre Bamidbar* 112 in *ᶜOnšim veḥaṭa᾽im*, 88–89.

15 And so might well maintain that exemption from *karet* can occur even without flogging, if the person repents on his own, though it is possible that he sees flogging as essential, as well. See Shemesh, *ᶜOnšim veḥaṭa᾽im*, 89.

16 See n. 11, above. Note that the question of whether flogging itself brings atonement or whether it is an opportunity for repentance, and it is repentance that brings atonement, is reflected in halakhic literature on the custom of flogging before Yom Kippur. See Tur, *Oraḥ Ḥayyim*, 607 and Karo, *Beit Yosef* (though the issue there is complicated by the fact that the flogging that was practiced did not fulfill the legal requirements of flogging, a concern that was a factor in the *semikhah* controversy in which R. Yosef Karo was involved – see Jacob Katz, "*Maḥloqet hasemikhah bein Rabbi Yaᶜaqov berav vehaRalbaḥ*," *Zion* 16 [1951] 28–45). See Shemesh, *ᶜOnšim veḥaṭa᾽im*, 97–98. For descriptions of the custom, see Daniel Sperber, *Minhagei Yisra᾽el: Meqorot vetoldot* (7 vols.; Jerusalem: Mossad Harav Kook, 1990–2003) 7:252–97.

17 Shemesh, *ᶜOnšim veḥaṭa᾽im*, 98 n. 110, notes that the mention of the recitation of "*vehu raḥum*" in

liel's position presupposes that repentance accompanies flogging and is essential for atonement and for exemption from *karet*, even though his teaching in the *mishnah* is silent on this point.[18]

Whether or not we see Rabbi Akiva's and Rabbi Ḥananiah ben Gamliel's teachings as reflecting identical positions, their teachings are certainly aligned in two ways. First, both sages see *karet* as not inevitable; the cutting off from the people that the Torah describes as the inevitable consequence of certain actions is, in the eyes of these two Sages, avoidable. Second, the teachings of these two Sages both mandate flogging for those who are subject to *karet*, a position that is reflected as well in the opening *mishnah* of the third chapter of *Makkot*.

But, as noted, Rabbi Ḥananiah ben Gamliel's teaching at the end of *m.Makkot* goes beyond the implication of the *mishnah* with which the chapter begins. If the court imposes flogging on those whom the Torah says are subject to *karet*, as the first *mishnah* suggests, and if the imposition of flogging exempts the sinner from *karet*, as Rabbi Ḥananiah ben Gamliel teaches in the final *mishnah*, then the Torah's mandate of *karet* for violations of law is effectively nullified. The court's action in inflicting flogging trumps God's ability to act in response to violation of God's law, and the Rabbis' teaching about flogging overturns the rule of the Torah.[19]

Karet

What the Torah means by the sanction of *karet* – which appears in the Torah in verbal forms: the soul or person is cut off – is disputed both in classical sources and in modern scholarship. Interpretations range from premature death (the person's life is cut off) to death of the soul (the person is permanently cut off, even after life is over) to excommunication (the person is cut off from his people in the sense of permanent expulsion from the community), among others.[20] The passive form of the verb[21] also leaves unclear whether *karet* is a penalty that

---

m.Mak. 3:4 is a late addition to the *mishnah*, probably influenced by the Yom Kippur eve tradition that is reflected in Moses Issertes' Rema's comment, *Darkhei Moshe* 4 on Tur, *Oraḥ Ḥayyim* 607.

18 Compare the discussion in *m.Yoma* 8:8 and *b.Yoma* 85b–86a about the interplay of repentance and other means (such as sacrifices, Yom Kippur, and suffering and death) in the attainment of atonement.

19 See Shemesh, *ᶜOnšim veḥaṭaʾim*, 90–91, 96–97.

20 For a brief overview of the range of traditional and contemporary opinions, see Jacob Milgrom, *The JPS Torah Commentary: Numbers* (Philadelphia and New York: Jewish Publication Society, 1990) 405–8. See also William Horbury, "Extirpation and Excommunication," *VT* 35 (1985) 13–38.

21 The verb nearly always occurs in passive forms (*venikhretah*, *venikhrat*, *venikhretu*, and *hikaret tikaret*, the last appearing only in Num 15:31), although active forms with God as the subject appear in Lev 17:10 and 20:3, 5, and 6. See also the active form of the verb in a command addressed to Moses and Aaron: *Do not cut off* (Num 4:17, in reference to the Qehatites), followed by *But thus do to them, that they may live and not die* (4:18).

is imposed on the person – and, if so, whether it is a punishment imposed by God or by human beings – or whether it is the natural and inevitable consequence of the person doing a deed that removes him from inclusion within the community (in life or, perhaps, even after death).[22]

It is also not fully clear for what sins people are subject to *karet* in the Torah. While we tend to think of *karet* as a sanction for specific sins, it is possible to read the Torah as suggesting that a person is subject to *karet* for any purposeful violation of a prohibition.[23] A general statement about *karet* appears in the context of the atoning sacrifices that people bring if they violated God's law inadvertently. Following the rules for inadvertent violations of law, the Torah says this about intentional violations of law: *But the soul that acts with a high hand . . . he has blasphemed the Lord, and that soul shall be cut off from the midst of its people. Because he has despised the word of the Lord and broken his command – that soul shall be surely cut off; its iniquity is in it* (Numbers 15:30–31). Aharon Shemesh has argued that this passage refers to the purposeful violation of any commandment.[24] While for an inadvertent violation the person can achieve forgiveness by means of an atoning sacrifice, for a purposeful violation the person is cut off. The purposeful violation of law, in the view of the Torah, constitutes dishonor to God and despising of God's word; the person bears his sin and is cut off from his people.

Classical rabbinic interpretation limits the scope of this passage in Numbers to the sin of idolatry, partly to address the exegetical problem posed by an apparent inconsistency between the sacrifice mandated for unintentional sin

22 See Shemesh, *ᶜOnšim veḥaṭaʾim*, 58–59, and see Milgrom, *Numbers*, 405–6. Milgrom argues that *karet* is a divinely-imposed sanction, which is also the classical rabbinic view.

23 Even one for which the Torah specifies a different sanction, as in Exod 31:14, concerning Shabbat. Note that the passage immediately following the passage about *karet* in Num 15:30–31 is the story of the person who gathers wood on Shabbat (Num 15:32–36). He is executed by the people, but the juxtaposition of this story with the rules concerning unintentional and intentional violation of law, the latter of which results in *karet*, suggests that the wood-gatherer's violation of Shabbat is an illustration of intentional sin that results in *karet*. Thus, this passage is consistent with the assignment of both execution and *karet* to Shabbat violation in Exod 31:14, supporting the possibility that *karet* might well be the consequence of any intentional sin. For a discussion of the wood-gatherer passage in relation to the *karet* passage, see Milgrom, *Numbers*, 408–10. Milgrom (407–8) sees the passage about Shabbat as well as the passage about *molekh* in Lev 20:2–3 as support of the idea that *karet* is a divine punishment which can be conjoined with human punishment. Classical rabbinic interpretation, though, sees the Torah's mandate of *karet* for sins for which there is judicial execution as applying only if the court is unable to execute the sinner. But see the passage about the wood-gatherer in *Tanḥuma* Buber *Bamidbar* 28, on Num 4:17 (on this verse, see n. 21, above; see Shemesh's brief reference to the *Tanḥuma* passage in *ᶜOnšim veḥaṭaʾim*, 90, n. 98). This passage juxtaposes *karet* and execution and also suggests the possibility that violation of any command leads to *karet*.

24 Shemesh, *ᶜOnšim veḥaṭaʾim*, 60, 80, 91–96.

here and the sacrifice mandated for unintentional sins in Leviticus 4,[25] though perhaps also in an attempt to limit the category of those who fall under the rubric of this harsh penalty. Once this passage is read as referring only to the sin of idolatry, we are left with a conception of *karet* as applicable only to the sin of idolatry and to other specific sins in relation to which the Torah explicitly says that the violator will be cut off.[26] These sinners, and these only, according to rabbinic interpretation, are subject to *karet*.[27]

The limitation of *karet* to specific sins goes hand-in-hand with the conception of *karet* as a sanction that is imposed, rather than as a consequence of sin. *Karet*, in rabbinic texts, appears as a specific penalty that is imposed by God, parallel to but different from other penalties that are imposed by human courts in response to violations of specific laws, such as judicial execution.[28] Thus, rabbinic texts can talk of one who is liable for (or exempt from) *karet* – which is now a noun, not a (passive) verb – just as they talk of those who are liable for or exempt from judicial punishments and penalties.

Nevertheless, the possible (and perhaps most likely) meaning of this biblical passage raises an important problem which, indeed, can be raised even without the support of any other biblical passage. If the Torah requires adherence to laws, isn't it the case that any violation of law puts into question the person's ability to live as a member of God's people?[29]

In fact, a similar question arises in any system that requires adherence to rules or to norms of behavior. When a parent gets a call from a teacher saying that Johnny spit on the child next to him at circle time, the parent doesn't (or, at least, isn't expected to) ask, "Well, was Johnny good *most* of the day?" If you are arrested for committing murder, you can't go before the judge and say, "Hey, I adhere to the law *most* of the time, so I deserve to go free."

While classrooms and courtrooms are hardly comparable systems, my point in bringing these two examples is to illustrate a problem. There is an inherent asymmetry between good and bad behavior in *any* system, with a single bad deed (or at least a single really bad deed) outweighing all the things you don't do wrong and even all the things that you do right. Leaving aside the murderer for a moment, and moving back to Johnny – why *is* it absurd for the parent to challenge the teacher's concern based on whether Johnny behaved appropriately in class for most of the day? Maybe Johnny didn't spit or hit or kick anyone all day except for this one unfortunate incident at circle time. Maybe Johnny

25 Shemesh, *ʿOnšim veḥaṭaʾim*, 59, 91–92.

26 See *m.Ker.* 1:1.

27 But see below, n. 35.

28 See, for example, the contrasting terms *behikaret* and *biydei adam* in *b.Mak.* 23b.

29 Whether *karet* implies death or/and some form of being cut off from the people, either in life or after death – or both in life and after death, as in *Sifre Num.* 112 and *b.Sanh.* 90b.

even did all the work that the teacher assigned and cleaned up at clean-up time. Maybe he even stepped forward to help a child or assist a teacher once or twice during the course of the day.

Later we'll return to why a single bad act might call into question Johnny's place in the classroom community despite Johnny's general adherence to the norms of that community, as well as look at what Johnny might have to do to regain his place in that community. But for now, I want simply to emphasize the asymmetry that Johnny and his parents have to contend with;[30] an asymmetry that holds even in the relatively forgiving world of the kindergarten classroom. How much more so within a religious system that focuses so extensively on law and on the consequences of violating law – which is, after all, the subject of the greater part of *Sanhedrin-Makkot*. A single intentional violation of law could well call into question the person's continuing to live as a member of the community. Whether one looks to the model of the biblical passage concerning *karet*, to other biblical passages concerning communal acceptance of norms and the consequences of breach of the commandments,[31] or to biblical passages that stress the life-giving nature of the *miṣvot* –"which a person shall do and live by them" (Lev 18:5)[32]– one could well worry that sin will lead to the sinner's being cut off from life within God's community.[33]

And yet, we all recognize that there is no one who never sins: כי אין אדם אשר לא-יחטא (1 Kings 8:46). If sin leads to being cut off, and if everyone sins, then how can we live?

This problem is the cause of Rabban Gamliel's despair in our passage: "It is only the person who does *all of these* who will not be shaken. . . !"[34] Rabban Gamliel's despair is inevitable from within a worldview that sees living be-

30 Modern psychology research supports the idea that people's judgments of a person's morality are asymmetrical with respect to good and bad deeds. See Glenn D. Reeder, "Trait-Behavior Relations and Dispositional Inference," *Personality and Social Psychology Bulletin* 19 (1993) 586–93.

31 Such as the covenantal blessings and curses of Deuteronomy 27–29; see esp. 29:17–20.

32 The life-giving quality of the *miṣvot* is a common theme in Deuteronomy in particular; see, for example, 30:15–20.

33 It should be noted that the standard sanction in the Dead Sea texts is exclusion from the community. Depending on the nature of the violation and on whether the violation was done intentionally, exclusion could be temporary or permanent. Shemesh sees the biblical sanction of *karet* and the biblical linkage of covenant and exile as two different models on which the sect built its penal code, the former generating the idea of permanent exile from the sect (Shemesh notes, in particular, the term *beyad rama* that occurs in the biblical passage about *karet* – Num 15:30 – and in sectarian passages about exile from the sect – for example, 1QS 8:22–9:2) and the latter generating the idea of temporary exclusion; see *ᶜOnšim veḥaṭaʾim*, 60–82. Whether or not *karet* and covenant/exile serve as distinct models for the Dead Sea sect, though, I am treating the range of biblical ideas about the consequences of sin – *karet*, exclusion from the covenantal community, and not meriting life – as a single cluster, any element of which evokes the whole idea of the sinner being cut off from life within God's community.

34 Note the parallel to this passage in *b.Sanh.* 81a, where Rabban Gamliel responds to a passage from

fore God as predicated on fulfilling God's law and that sees every person as necessarily failing to fulfill God's law. I want to emphasize this point because, from our current vantage point within the history of Judaism, the cause for this despair is not obvious. Contemporary Jews have emphasized so much the importance within Jewish tradition of repentance, forgiveness, and atonement that it is hard for them to imagine why Rabban Gamliel is crying. But the point is that the emphasis on repentance and methods to achieve atonement are responses to a problem. These responses are usually taken so much for granted that it is hard to see the seriousness of the problem. But the problem is there, and *b.Makkot* gives voice to it by inserting the Rabban Gamliel anecdote in this final *sugya*.

We return to our look at the final *sugya* of *b.Makkot*, then, by noting a link between the Rabban Gamliel anecdote and the opening of our *mishnah*. If sin cuts one off, and everyone sins, then how can we hope to live before God? The *mishnah* offers one response to that problem: "All those liable for *karet* who receive lashes are exempt from their *karet*, as it says: *and your brother shall be dishonored (*niqleh*) before your eyes* –"once he receives lashes (*malqot*), he is like *your brother* – the words of Rabbi Ḥananiah ben Gamliel."

Of course, the *mishnah* is speaking specifically of those who are liable for *karet* within the rabbinic understanding of the limited scope of that sanction.[35] My focus above on the idea that *karet* can be seen as a cutting off that is the consequence of *any* intentional violation of God's law suggests, though, that this teaching about *karet* can be read as responding to more than the limited situations in which one has violated a law that the Rabbis understand to be punishable by *karet*. Similarly, while the Rabbis see *karet* as a particular punishment that is imposed by God, the range of possible significations of the Torah's passages about being cut off that I reviewed above suggests that a teaching about *karet* and its revocation relates to more that just the person becoming legally exempt from this divinely-imposed punishment. The issue of the revocation of *karet* raises the question of whether the consequences of sin are inevitable or

Ezekiel, which is working with Lev 18:5, וחי בהם. Here Rabban Gamliel says: "It is only the person who does *all of these* who will live . . . !" See n. 59, below. I will return below to Rabbi Akiva's response in the *b.Mak.* and *b.Sanh.* passages, as well as to a closer look at the verses that prompt Rabban Gamliel's despair in each of these passages.

35 Though Shemesh, *ᶜOnšim veḥaṭaʾim*, 92–96, argues that rabbinic texts retain the idea that *karet* is applicable to any purposeful violation of God's law, and he suggests that Rabbi Ḥananiah ben Gamliel's teaching about flogging and *karet* reflects this position, since Rabbi Ḥananiah ben Gamliel's second teaching in the *mishnah* talks about *any* transgression. According to Shemesh, the list of violations in *m.Ker.* 1:1 is not meant to limit the applicability of *karet*, but rather to indicate for what non-deliberate violations of law one must bring a *ḥaṭat* sacrifice. The subject of *m.Ker.* is really the *ḥaṭat*, while the subject of *m.Mak.* chap. 3 is *karet*, Shemesh suggests, for *m.Mak.* chap. 3 is the final chapter of a tractate (*Sanhedrin-Makkot*) that discusses sanctions in order of increasing severity.

whether the person who has sinned can somehow alter the consequences of his action – can he ever be fully reincorporated into the community from which he has been cut off? That is, the situation of *karet* can be seen as paradigmatic for the distancing of the sinner from God and from God's people, the inability to live before God when one violates God's life-giving commandments. And, thus, a teaching that stresses the revocable nature of *karet* can be read as responding, not only to the problem of those who have violated one of a particular group of laws that have *karet* as a sanction, but also to the problem of anyone who tries to live as a member of God's community, bound by God's law, but who inevitably fails to follow that law perfectly. And so, what I am suggesting is that the appearance of the anecdote about Rabban Gamliel in this *sugya* extends (or restores) the field of significance of *karet*. The anecdote raises (or discloses), in the context of the *mishnah*'s legal teaching about the punishment of *karet* and exemption from that punishment, the universal problem of the inevitability of sin and its consequences.

Revoking *Karet*

This *mishnah*'s teaching –"once he receives lashes, he is like 'your brother'"– resonates with an insight of Herbert Morris, to whose philosophy of punishment we will return below. Distinguishing between what he calls a "shame morality" and a "guilt morality" (more on what he means by these terms later), Morris says: "A shame morality leads to casting outside the community, exile; a guilt morality, to suffering in order to be accepted back within. We only trouble to punish those we still care about and respect."[36] The *mishnah*, in Morris' terms, mandates suffering in order to enable the violator of law to be accepted back within.[37]

It is important to recall, though, that the ideas that everyone who is subject to *karet* receives lashes and that the punishment of flogging exempts the sinner from *karet* have no support from the Torah, where *karet* is portrayed as the inevitable consequence of sin (or at least of certain sins). This teaching is a prime example of rabbinic *derashah* overriding the clear rule of the Torah

36 Herbert Morris, *On Guilt and Innocence: Essays in Legal Philosophy and Moral Psychology* (Berkeley and Los Angeles: Univ. of California Press, 1976) 62.

37 See *b.Sanh.* 90b and the parallel in *Sifre Bamidbar* 112, where *teshuvah* serves this same function; through an exegesis of Num 15:31, *that soul shall surely be cut off; its iniquity is in it*, the Sages determine that the soul is only permanently cut off if its iniquity is still in it – that is, if the person has not repented. See also the discussion above of Rabbi Akiva's teaching in the *baraita* at the beginning of the third chapter of *b.Makkot*, which says that repentance exempts one from *karet* and which can be understood as suggesting that flogging is an opportunity for repentance.

and, in parallel, of human activity (court-imposed flogging) subverting divine activity (*karet*).[38]

Indeed, consideration of this teaching propels the *gemara* into a series of passages about the capacity of human beings to determine outcomes through their own power of exegesis or judgment.[39] In fact, I think that this can be seen as the core idea knitting together all of the passages in the final *sugya* of *Makkot*: Abaye's reassurance of Rav Yosef that one can determine that the *halakhah* is in accordance with Rabbi Ḥananiah ben Gamliel without ascending to heaven but rather by means of *derashah*;[40] the tradition of Rabbi Yehoshua ben Levi, invoked by Abaye, about enactments of human courts to which the heavenly court assented; the teaching of Rabbi Eleazar about the times when a heavenly voice supported human determinations; the Rabbi Simlai passage, in which human beings reduce the number of God-given commandments, into which is inserted Rabbi Akiva's rereading of a biblical passage in order to comfort the despairing Rabban Gamliel; the teaching of Rabbi Yose bar Ḥaninah about the decrees of Moses that were overturned by later prophets; and, finally, the two stories in which Rabbi Akiva reinterprets by means of hermeneutical rules, not a biblical text, but rather the devastating reality that confronts him and his colleagues.[41]

38 See Shemesh's *ʿOnšim veḥaṭaʾim*, 96–97 and his reference to *b.Šebu.* 21a, where the very final כי לא ינקה ה׳ is interpreted thus: "*God* will not cleanse, but the court below flogs him and cleanses him."

39 Compare Rava's statement about Sages in relation to Torah scrolls in *Makkot* 22b, also concerning flogging: "How foolish are the other people who stand before a Torah scroll but do not stand before a great man, for in the Torah scroll it says 'forty' [lashes] and the Rabbis came and reduced them by one."

40 See Shemesh, *ʿOnšim veḥaṭaʾim*, 90–91.

41 It is noteworthy that the parallel to the Rabban Gamliel/Rabbi Akiva anecdote in *Midrash Tehillim* 15 conflates that story with elements that appear in the two stories about Rabbi Akiva at the end of this *sugya*. In *Midrash Tehillim*, Rabban Gamliel is crying but Rabbi Akiva laughs, as in the stories about Rabbi Akiva and the Sages at the end of *b.Makkot*, and the passage ends with Rabban Gamliel saying "You have comforted us, Akiva, you have comforted us," as the Sages say at the end of this *sugya*. The passage in *Midrash Tehillim* seems clearly to be dependent on the *Bavli*, especially because it mentions Rabban Gamliel crying both in relation to Psalm 15, as in *b.Mak.* 24a, and in relation to Ezekiel 18, as in *b.Sanh.* 81a, and it would seem that the composer of this passage noted the connection between the story of Rabbi Akiva's response to Rabban Gamliel's despair and the stories at the end of the *sugya* of Rabbi Akiva's responses to the despairing Sages. Gartner, "*ʿIbud bavli*," notes links between the Rabbi Simlai passage, including the anecdote about Rabbi Akiva and Rabban Gamliel, and the last two sections of the *sugya*. Note, too, the similarity between Rabbi Akiva's argument in the first of the two stories at the end of the *sugya* – "If for those who violate his will it is thus, how much more so for those who perform his will"– and Rabbi Ḥananiah ben Gamliel's second teaching in the *mishnah* –"If one who transgresses a single transgression loses his life on account of it, one who performs (does) a single commandment – how much more so that his life will be given to him."

If so, then this final *sugya* of *Makkot* makes a critical point. The issue of sin and its consequences is not just a legal issue; it is a question of whether human beings – the sinner and/or the community – can shape their destiny, can alter the course of their lives, or whether, once an action is taken, the future is determined and is out of human hands. The *sugya* conflates the ability of the Rabbis to reread Torah and the ability of human beings to shape reality. It does this in its discussion of the *mishnah*'s teaching about flogging, where *derashah* overrides Torah law just as the action of the court subverts God's actions. And it does this in the range of passages in the final *sugya* that I just inventoried – where exegesis and destiny go hand in hand, where prophets overturn fateful Torah teachings, where the actions and decisions of human beings gain God's assent, and where Rabbi Akiva, the master of exegesis, applies his skill to offer an interpretation of reality in which what *is*, rather than signifying the fateful judgment of what *will be*, is instead read to yield a radically hopeful vision of the future.

What I am arguing is that this final *sugya* in *Makkot* offers an understanding of the person: human beings and human communities determine who they are and what their future will be – they are not only creative readers of Torah but creative shapers of self and of the community's future. This is a particular view of the person, a view which is antithetical to the idea that, once a critical juncture is taken, there is no turning back. It is, in essence, a rejection of that view of human behavior and its consequences of which the irrevocable sanction of *karet* is paradigmatic. In making *karet* revocable, in suggesting that human action trumps *karet*, the passage rejects the notion that what the future seems to hold is ever inevitable, sealed by the past.

Transgressions and *Miṣvot*

I want to leave aside for awhile the teaching about flogging and *karet* and its relation to the larger *sugya* and return to the core problem – the asymmetry between good and bad deeds, between following the law and violating the law. Rabbi Ḥananiah ben Gamliel, the author of the teaching in the *mishnah* about lashes superceding *karet*, goes on in the *mishnah* to articulate a teaching that is very similar to that of Rabbi Akiva in response to Rabban Gamliel's despair: מה אם העובר עבירה אחת נוטל נפשו עליה, העושה מצוה אחת על אחת כמה וכמה שתינתן לו נפשו – "If one who transgresses a single transgression loses his life on account of it, one who performs a single commandment how much more so that his life will be given to him." Now, this teaching actually makes no sense. If you lose your life for transgressing a single commandment, then you cannot gain your life by fulfilling a single commandment. This teaching tries to restore the symmetry between good and bad deeds, but it leads to a paradox when applied to the real lives of ordinary mortals. Since we all do some good and some bad, even perhaps mostly good and a little bad, do we merit life?

The same paradox characterizes Rabbi Akiva's teaching in response to Rabban Gamliel's expression of despair:

> Is it written "one who does *all* of them"?! *One who does them* is written – even by means of *one* of them. For if you do not say this, another scriptural verse is written: *Do not become defiled by means of any* (בכל) *of these* (Lev 18:24) – there too, is it the one who touches *all* of these who is defiled, but [one who touches] *one* of them not?! Rather, no, [a person is defiled] by means of *one* of these – here, too, by means of *one* of these.

A verse that appears just a bit later in the same Leviticus passage that Rabbi Akiva cites makes the point even more clearly: כי כל-אשר יעשה מכל התועבת האלה ונכרתו הנפשות העשת מקרב עמם – *For whoever does any of these abominations, the souls who do so shall be cut off from the midst of their people* (Lev 18:29). Here, the Torah clearly is saying that even one of the sins mentioned in the passage causes the sinner to be cut off from his people. This verse, in fact, is cited in the *mishnah* in relation to yet another verse from the same passage: *You shall keep my statutes and my judgments, which a person shall do and live by them* . . . (Lev 18:5). In the *mishnah*, Rabbi Shimon cites these two verses to support the teaching of Rabbi Ḥananiah ben Gamliel, which, as noted, is very similar to Rabbi Akiva's argument.

The clear message of the Leviticus passage to which Rabbi Akiva refers in his response to Rabban Gamliel, and to which Rabbi Shimon refers in his argument in support of Rabbi Ḥananiah ben Gamliel's teaching, is that violating *any* law leads one to be cut off. Rabbi Akiva's argument, then, seems to make sense as exegesis: he argues from the clear implication of the Torah about the consequences of negative actions to demonstrate that the Torah's promises, like the Torah's warnings, are contingent on a single act. But, as applied to real life, the argument makes no sense at all. If the Torah says that violating even a single law cuts one off, then it is quite impossible to say, as Rabbi Akiva does here and as Rabbi Ḥananiah ben Gamliel does in the *mishnah*, that doing even one good deed grants life![42]

42 To Rabbi Akiva's response and to Rabbi Ḥananiah ben Gamliel's teaching compare *t.Qidd.* 1:13: "Whoever performs a single *mitzvah* . . . and whoever transgresses a single transgression. . . ." The formulation in *m.Qidd.* 1:10 is less clear and potentially less paradoxical: "Whoever performs a single *mitzvah* . . . and whoever does not perform a single *mitzvah* . . . ." The *mishnah* may be saying the same thing as the passage in the Tosefta (see Shamma Friedman, "The Primacy of Tosefta to Mishnah in Synoptic Parallels," in Harry Fox and Tirzah Meacham, eds., *Introducing Tosefta: Textual, Intratextual, and Intertextual Studies* [New York: Ktav, 1999] 120–21), or it may

The problem of symmetry is even clearer in the biblical passage quoted in a parallel to the Rabban Gamliel/Rabbi Akiva anecdote in *b.Sanh.* 81a:

דרש רב אחא ברבי חנינא: מאי דכתיב אל ההרים לא אכל – שלא אכל בזכות אבותיו.
ועיניו לא נשא אל גלולי בית ישראל – שלא הלך בקומה זקופה.
ואת אשת רעהו לא טמא – שלא ירד לאומנות חבירו.
ואל אשה נדה לא קירב – שלא נהנה מקופה של צדקה,
וכתיב צדיק הוא חיה יחיה.

כשהיה רבן גמליאל מגיע למקרא הזה היה בוכה, ואמר מאן דעביד לכולהו – הוא דחיי, בחדא מינייהו – לא.
אמר ליה רבי עקיבא: אלא מעתה אל תטמאו בכל אלה – הכי נמי בכולהו אין, בחדא מינייהו לא? אלא באחת מכל אלה, הכי נמי באחת מכל אלה.

Rav Aḥa beRabbi Ḥaninah expounded: What is meant by that which is written *upon the mountains he did not eat* (Ezekiel 18:6)? – that he did not eat through the merit of his ancestors;
and to the idols of the house of Israel he did not lift up his eyes – that he did not walk with an upright [haughty] posture;
and his neighbor's wife he did not defile – that he did not infringe upon his neighbor's trade;
and a menstruant woman he did not approach – that he did not benefit from the charity fund;
and it is written: *He is righteous; he shall surely live* (Ezek 18:9).

When Rabban Gamliel would reach this scriptural passage he would cry and say: "It is only the one who does all of these thing who will live, thus by means of [only] one of them – not!"

Rabbi Akiva said to him: If so, *Do not become defiled by means of any of them* (Lev 18:24) – also means, by means of all of them, yes [he is defiled], by means of one of them not?! Rather [just as Lev. 18:24 meant], by means of one of all of these, so too here [in Ezek 18:9], by means of one of all of these."

Here, Rabban Gamliel cries in response to a passage from Ezekiel 18: *He walks in my statutes and keeps my judgments to do the truth; he is righteous – he shall surely live* (Ezek 18:9). This chapter clearly is commenting on Lev 18:5: *You shall keep my statutes and my judgments, which a person shall do and live by them...*, the verse which is cited by Rabbi Shimon in our *mishnah*. Ezekiel 18 sets out opposing visions of the good and bad person. The bad person is guilty of a variety of sins, while the righteous person commits none of them. The bad person is subject to death; the righteous person gains life.

It is noteworthy that Ezekiel 18 is cited further on in the *Makkot sugya* as one of the examples of a prophet overturning Moses' decree. While the Torah teaches that the sons are implicated in the sins of the fathers (Exodus 34:7), Ezekiel declares that each person lives or dies based only on his own actions: *the soul that sins – it shall die; the son shall not bear the iniquity of the father, and the father shall not bear the iniquity of the son; the righteousness of the righteous shall be upon him, and the wickedness of the wicked shall be upon him* (Ezek 18:20). The juxtaposition of the Exodus and Ezekiel verses in this passage highlights the idea that I argued above links together all of the parts of the final *sugya* of *Makkot*. As in Rabbi Ḥananiah ben Gamliel's teaching about flogging, the ability of the prophet to overturn the words of the Torah corresponds to a declaration of the freedom of each person to shape his own future irrespective of the past deeds of his father or even of his own past deeds.

But Ezekiel 18 raises a problem as well. The chapter uses the rhetoric of extremes; it speaks of the evil person who will die based on his own actions and the righteous person who will live based on his own actions.[43] The chapter does not describe the standard person, the person who mostly does good and desists from evil, but who sometimes sins. It describes wholly good people who become wholly evil and wholly evil people who become wholly good, thus emphasizing the possibility and power of *teshuvah*, but it does not offer a vision of the regular person, the person whose actions combine some bad with the good.

It is this problem that animates the *mishnah* in *Makkot* and the Rabban Gamliel anecdote (as it appears both in the final *sugya* of *Makkot* and in the parallel in *b.Sanhedrin*). Both the second teaching of Rabbi Ḥananiah ben Gamliel in the *mishnah* and Rabbi Akiva's response to Rabban Gamliel in the anecdote in the *gemara* make an outrageous and, I have argued, paradoxical claim. The fact that a single violation causes a forfeiting of life, rather than being a cause for despair, leads to the conclusion that a single positive act (indeed, according

---

be saying something different: the antithesis in the *mishnah* may be between someone who performs even a single *miṣvah* and someone who does not perform even one *miṣvah*. If one accepts the latter reading, the *mishnah* avoids the paradox generated by the Tosefta's formulation (how can the teaching apply to someone who performs some *miṣvot* but who also sins – that is, everyone?) and offers a teaching consistent with Rabbi Akiva's message – that doing even a single *miṣvah* grants life (even if the person also sins). See the conflicting *derashot* of Ben Azai and Rabbi Akiva in *y.Qidd.* 1:10/61d, and note that both the *Yerushalmi* and *b.Qidd.* 39b–40b discuss the *mishnah* in *Qiddušin* in relation to the *mishnah* in *Makkot* (note that both Talmuds interpret the teaching about a single *miṣvah* in relation to the *balance* of *miṣvot* and transgressions, a single *miṣvah* being able to tip the balance in a person's favor; see also *t.Qidd.* 1:14). See the discussion in E. P. Sanders, *Paul and Palestinian Judaism* (Minneapolis: Fortress Press, 1977) 128–39.

43 Moshe Greenberg notes the "black-and-white terms" of Ezekiel's description of the righteous and wicked person and discusses the lists of righteous deeds here and in other biblical passages in relation to New Testament and rabbinic texts, including the Rabbi Simlai passage, in *Ezekiel 1–20*, AB 22 (1983) 340–47.

to Rabbi Shimon's explication of Leviticus 18 in the *mishnah*, even desisting from negative acts) merits life.

But how can one live through the performance of *miṣvot* if one forfeits life by violating even a single one of God's commands? The claim only becomes sensible if it is accompanied by a mechanism to erase or atone for violations in this life, since there is no person, no matter how righteous, who never sins. Hence, the teaching of Rabbi Ḥananiah ben Gamliel with which the *mishnah* begins[44] asserts that the system has within it a way to undo the effects of sin, to trump the cutting off that sin brings in its wake. The suffering caused by the human-imposed punishment of flogging (possibly along with the opportunity for forgiveness and atonement that it offers, as discussed above) undoes the forfeiting of life that sin brings, allowing life to be gained through the performance of *miṣvot*.

I want to return now to the classic essay by Herbert Morris that was quoted above and which will be discussed at greater length below. In "Persons and Punishments,"[45] Morris makes the claim that people have a *right* to punishment – that punishment is a *benefit* in that, among other things that he spells out, it enables people to be restored to their place in the community. Morris lays out what he presents as two contrasting visions of morality: what he calls a "shame morality" and a "guilt morality." In the former, misdeeds are construed as evidence of something fundamentally wrong with the person. In the latter, misdeeds are conceived of as deviations from a rule, deviations that require some sort of penalty or punishment in order to set things right.

Morris lays out a number of striking contrasts between the two models; for the moment, I will quote just two short passages:

> . . . shame links essentially to worth concepts and guilt does not. We may react to the shameful person with contempt; to the guilty we react with condemnation. With shame there is an inevitable derogation in one's status as a person; with guilt one's status is intact but one's relationship to others is affected. The shameful is not worthy of association; the guilty is still worthy but a price must be paid. Abandonment by others is the spontaneous result that follows upon knowledge of a contemptible nature; punishment is not a spontaneous response but a price paid for restoration. A shame morality leads to casting outside the community, exile; a guilt

44 And similar teachings elsewhere about the power of repentance, such as the one in *b.Sanh.* 90b, discussed in n. 37, above. See also the inventory of means of atonement in *b. Yoma* 86a, mentioned in n. 18, above.

45 The essay was reprinted along with three additional brief essays under the title "Persons and Punishments" in *On Guilt and Innocence*, 31–88. My discussion focuses on the main essay along with the first addendum, entitled "Guilt and Shame."

> morality, to suffering in order to be accepted back within. We only trouble to punish those we still care about and respect.[46]
>
> . . . it may well be that, everything considered, we should prefer the pain and suffering of a system of punishment to a world in which we only experience shame on the doing of wrong acts, for with guilt there are relatively simply ways of ridding ourselves of the feeling we have, that is gaining forgiveness or taking the punishment, but with shame we have to bear it until we no longer are the person who has behaved in the shameful way. . . .[47]

I am not interested here in the validity or general applicability of Morris' definitions of shame and guilt; I want, rather, to use his construction of these categories as a heuristic device. Above, I suggested that the imposition of flogging in place of *karet* is parallel to the substitution, in Morris' terms, of a guilt morality for a shame morality. Rather than being cast out of the community, as *karet* mandates, the person is punished and, by means of this punishment, reinstated within the community – he is, once again, *your brother*. Thus, rather than violation of God's law being seen as evidence of a person's fundamental unworthiness, sin is seen as a deviation that requires imposition of a penalty in order to set things straight again.

But what happens if we take the alternative point of view? That is, what happens if we retain the notion that sin renders one fundamentally unworthy? And what if we then acknowledge that there is no person who does not sin – that sin is part of the human condition? In that case, we are thrown back into the core asymmetry between good and bad deeds. *Any* bad deed makes a person fundamentally unworthy to live before God – or demonstrates the person's fundamental unworthiness – in much the same way that Johnny's spitting on his classmate called into question Johnny's place in the classroom community. And thus, since we all sin, we are all unworthy to live before God.

Paul

This problem is the starting point of Paul's argument about law in the two letters in which he addresses this subject most comprehensively, Galatians and Romans. I want to make it clear at the outset – though I will return to this point later on, when I locate this discussion in the context of the contemporary debate about Paul – that by "starting point" I do not mean what motivates Paul's position or what is the core problem for Paul. I am not taking a stand here about what led Paul to his views about law or about whether a problem with law was the

46 Morris, *On Guilt and Innocence*, 62.

47 Morris, *On Guilt and Innocence*, 45.

core problem for Paul. Rather, by "starting point" I mean that Paul takes the following as a premise of much of his argument: if a person gains life (is justified)[48] by means of obeying the law, all people will inevitably fail to gain life, since no person can avoid sinning.

I cannot analyze, in the context of this study, all of the passages in which Paul articulates this problem and works out his solution, but I want to look at a few passages that strike me as particularly interesting in light of the *Makkot* passage and the verses that are interpreted there. I will begin by looking briefly at two famous passages in Galatians and move on to discuss the broad contours of the argument in Romans.

GALATIANS

In Chapter Three of Galatians, Paul has been arguing that justification is by faith and that Gentiles are included in God's promise to Abraham. Having supported the notion of justification by faith by quoting Gen 15:6, והאמן ביהוה ויחשבה לו צדקה, *Abraham believed God, and it was reckoned to him as justice*[49] (Gal 3:6), Paul argues that blessing comes through faith (Gal 3:9), while law brings a curse:

10 For as many as are of the works of the law are under a curse. For it is written: *Cursed is every one who does not abide in all things which are written in the book of the law to do them.*
11 But that in the law no man is justified with God is manifest, because *the just man will live by faith.*
12 But the law is not of faith, rather *he that does those things shall live by them.*
13 Christ redeemed us from the curse of the law, becoming a curse for us, for it is written: Cursed is every one that hangs on a tree.

21 Is the law then against the promises of God? May it not be! *For if a law had been given which could give life*, indeed justice would have been by the law.

48 See n. 51, below.

49 E. P. Sanders, *Paul, the Law, and the Jewish People* (Philadelphia: Fortress Press, 1983) 13–14, n. 18 discusses the problem of how to translate words with the root *dik-* in such a way that neither obscures Paul's argument by translating different uses of the root differently nor prejudices a reading of Paul by using a translation that favors one over another interpretation of Paul. Sanders prefers "be made righteous" over "be justified," because the latter tends to connote to "be declared or found innocent," while Sanders feels that "the question is precisely whether or not Paul has shifted the meaning beyond that of the law court"; see n. 51, below. In the translations that I offer here, I translate words with the root *dik-* consistently as "just, justice, be justified," in order to preserve the connection between all of the words with the root *dik-*. In discussion, however, I use forms of "just" and "righteous" interchangeably.

22 But the Scripture has shut up all under sin, that the promise by the faith of Jesus Christ might be given to those who believe.
23 But before the faith came, we were kept under the law, shut up to the faith which was to be revealed.
24 Therefore the law was our pedagogue in Christ, that *we might be justified by faith.*

This passage juxtaposes Lev 18:5, אשר יעשה אתם האדם וחי בהם ..., with Hab 2:4, וצדיק באמונתו יחיה .... These two verses are quoted in Gal 3:11 and 3:12 and are referred to again in 3:21 and 3:24[50] (the verses and the references to them are italicized in the passage above). These two verses, for Paul, contrast the notions of gaining life through adherence to law and of living (or being justified) by faith.

The Habakkuk verse, for Paul, offers a clear, concise statement of the point that he wants to make.[51] As we will see below, Paul uses this same verse to launch his extended argument about faith and law in Romans. The three components of the Habakkuk quotation (expressed in the three words of the clause in the Hebrew) link together the main elements that Paul uses in his extended argument:

50 Note that 3:24 can also be seen as working off Gen 15:16, as does 3:8. But Paul is identifying the teaching of the Genesis verse and the Habakkuk verse in relation to justification, so it makes most sense to see him as referring in 3:24 to both the Genesis verse and the Habakkuk verse, rather than as referring to one or the other. I am stressing the echo of Habakkuk here to highlight the structure of 3:21–24 in relation to 3:10–13.

51 There is significant scholarly discussion about Paul's presentation of Hab 2:4 here and in Rom 1:17 in relation to the MT and LXX versions of this verse as well as about how to construe the syntax of the verse as Paul presents it. See, for example, James D. G. Dunn, *Romans 1–8*, WBC 38A (1988) 44–46; Richard N. Longenecker, *Galatians*, WBC 41 (1990) 118–19; Sanders, *Paul*, 484, n. 38; Sanders, *Law*, 53, n. 23; Richard B. Hays, *Echoes of Scripture in the Letters of Paul* (New Haven: Yale Univ. Press, 1989) 202, n. 14. The two possible ways of construing the syntax of *ek pisteōs* generate the following possible translations: "The one who is righteous by faith shall live" and "The righteous one shall live by faith." If, however, one sees righteousness/justification in Paul as essentially coterminous with gaining life, the issue of deciding between these constructions is much less significant. (For a similar argument, see Richard B. Hays, *The Faith of Jesus Christ: An Investigation of the Narrative Substructure of Galatians 3:1–4:11* [Chico: Scholars Press, 1983] 150–51. Contrast Sanders, who rejects the judicial meaning of *dik-* in Paul, and who thus can accept the idea of being justified through something without that thing granting life. Thus, Sanders can understand Romans 10:5 as saying "that the Jews might have righteousness by doing the law, but that one does not 'live' thereby." [*Law*, 63, n. 132]). Daniel Boyarin, *A Radical Jew: Paul and the Politics of Identity* (Berkeley and Los Angeles: Univ. of California Press, 1994) 117, argues that justification should be understood in terms of the Hebrew יצדק, "which means both to be just or righteous and to be *declared* or *recognized* as just or righteous." The term justification "refers to the situation of the believer at her last judgment (whether eschatological or merely after death is irrelevant here), where the question is: Will I be acquitted by the divine court? Justification means acquittal." From this perspective, being justified is equivalent to living before God, and thus I have used the terms interchangeably throughout my discussion.

justification, faith, and life. Paul shapes his argument by linking this verse with other verses that contain some of these key elements: the Genesis verse, which includes the elements of faith and justice, and the Leviticus verse, which talks of how a person gains life.

In the section quoted above, as noted, Paul introduces the Habakkuk and Leviticus verses as offering two contrasting pathways to life. Paul must argue that the model of Lev 18:5 cannot work; for him, the idea that one can gain life through observing (doing) the law (3:12) is incompatible with the idea that it is faith that justifies/grants life (3:11). And so, to mediate between these two verses, Paul introduces another verse, Deut 27:26 (3:10) and offers an argument based on this verse (3:21–22). The following outlines the structure of the passage in relation to the verses that Paul cites and to the argument that he makes based on these verses (the intervening verses as well as 3:23 relate to the argument about the promise to and blessing of Abraham and to an argument about why the law was given if it cannot bring blessing):

3:10 Deuteronomy 27:26 (the mediating verse)

3:11 Habakkuk 2:4 (the verse that expresses Paul's point)

3:12 Leviticus 18:5 (the verse that offers what Paul presents as contradicting the point of Habakkuk)

3:21 argument in relation to Leviticus 18:5

3:22 argument in relation to Deuteronomy 27:26, which shows why the model of Leviticus 18:5 can't work

3:24 conclusion in relation to Habakkuk 2:4

In order to dismiss the possibility that one can gain life through the law, as Lev 18:5 says, Paul states simply that all people sin (Gal 3:22). Thus, even though doing the law *could*, in theory, grant life, in fact – given that all sin – there can be no law which gives life, and thus justification cannot be by law (Gal 3:21).

Paul introduces this point by quoting Deut 27:26, a verse that talks of the curse that comes from disobedience to law, in stark contrast to the blessing that Paul had argued comes to Abraham and to his descendants through faith.[52] Paul quotes Deut 27:26 in a way that differs slightly from the Masoretic text, although it conforms to the LXX. While the Masoretic text reads: ארור אשר לא-יקים

52 Sanders, *Law*, 21 argues that Paul was compelled to cite Deut 27:26 because he needed a verse that connects the law with a curse, in order to set up the contrast with the blessing that is promised to Abraham through faith. (See Heikki Räisänen, *Paul and the Law* (Philadelphia: Fortress Press, 1986) 95, n. 13 and Boyarin, *A Radical Jew*, 139.) Thus, Sanders argues that other terms of Paul's rendering of Deut 27:26 are incidental to the main thrust of Paul's use of the verse, and therefore that significance should not be attributed to the word "all"– see next note.

את-דברי התורה-הזאת לעשות אותם ..., Paul renders: "Cursed is every one who does not abide in *all* things which are written in the book of the law to do them" (3:10). Paul's inclusion of the word "all" suggests that everyone is under a curse *because* no one fulfils all of the law.[53] The life promised in Lev 18:5[54] depends on doing the law (אשר יעשה אתם), but curse devolves upon those who do not fully do the law (לעשות אותם, Deut 27:26).[55] Since all sin, law cannot bring life, and there must be an alternative to justification by law – living by faith (3:11).

This passage offers a striking parallel to the *Makkot* passage, both in the juxtaposition of the verses and in the exegesis offered. The Rabbi Simlai passage about the number of *miṣvot* appears in this *sugya* as a commentary on the *mishnah*'s emphasis on the power of *miṣvot* (and even of desisting from sin) to grant life. This is first articulated in Rabbi Ḥananiah ben Gamliel's second teaching in the *mishnah*: "If one who transgresses a single transgression loses his life on account of it, one who performs (does) a single commandment how much more so that his life will be given to him." It is further worked out in Rabbi Shimon's exegesis of Lev 18:5, אשר יעשה אתם האדם וחי בהם, in relation to Lev 18:29, ונכרתו הנפשות העושות מקרב עמם (which returns to the issue of *karet* with which the *mishnah* begins). And, finally, it is emphasized in Rabbi Ḥananiah ben Aqashia's statement about God giving so many *miṣvot* in order to give merit to Israel[56] (note the use of צדק in the verse cited in this final teaching, to be discussed below).

The capstone of the Rabbi Simlai passage is the citation of Hab 2:4, וצדיק באמונתו יחיה. Whatever exactly the homilist intends by saying that בא חבקוק

53 This point is much discussed and much contested in the scholarly literature. See, for an example of an opposing argument, James D. G. Dunn, *Jesus, Paul, and the Law: Studies in Mark and Galatians* (Louisville: Westminster/John Knox Press, 1990) 226 (and see the secondary literature cited on 234, n. 41) and, for an example of a supporting argument, Räisänen, *Paul and the Law*, 95 (and see the secondary literature cited on p. 94, n. 2). Räisänen, like others, cites Gal 5:3 as confirmation of the idea that Paul is pointing to the problematic nature of the need to obey *all* of the law; interpretation of this verse is, like interpretation of 3:10, a point of scholarly disagreement. See, further, the secondary literature cited in Longenecker, *Galatians*, 118 and Sanders, *Law*, 52–53, n. 22. And see n. 60, below. For a parallel to the understanding of Gal 3:10 that is suggested here, see James 2:10: *And whoever keeps the whole law, but stumbles in one thing, has become guilty of all.* While James' overall argument about law is radically different from Paul's, his articulation of the idea that imperfect obedience to the law makes one *a transgressor of the law* (2:11) suggests that this idea may well have been commonplace. See below on Paul's exegesis of Eccl 7:20 in Romans 3.

54 Shlomo Naeh, "Why Did Rabban Gamliel Cry? Some Aspects of the Last Mishna of *Makkot* and its Sugya in the *Bavli*," presented at the conference in tribute to Professor David Weiss-Halivni (New York, May 30, 2005), notes that the word "all" appears in LXX for Lev 18:5: *And you shall keep all of my statutes and all of my judgments and do them, which a person shall do and live by them*, as it does in MT in similar verses, such as Lev 19:37.

55 In relation to Paul's emphasis on *doing* the law, see the discussion of Rom 10:5, below.

56 See n. 5, above.

והעמידן על אחת, his message is certainly different from the teaching of Paul, who presents Habakkuk as offering a paradigm that supersedes the notion of gaining life through obedience to law. Yet, like Paul, the *sugya* juxtaposes the Habakkuk verse with Lev 18:5, which is introduced by Rabbi Shimon in the *mishnah*[57] and which, I have argued, encapsulates the problem that the *mishnah* is addressing: how can we live, rather than be cut off, if we will inevitably fail to follow the law by which we are told we gain life?[58]

In the middle of the Rabbi Simlai passage, as I discussed above, Rabban Gamliel gives expression to the hopelessness of meriting life by means of good behavior. Earlier, I discussed Rabbi Akiva's difficult response which, I noted, is similar to Rabbi Shimon's argument in the *mishnah* in that both cite a verse from Leviticus 18 about sinning in order to make a point about the ease of gaining life by doing good or by not sinning. But here I want to call attention to Rabban Gamliel's argument: מאן דעביד להו לכולהו הוא דלא ימות, הא חדא מינייהו ימות! (in the *b.Sanhedrin* parallel, the verse in question is Ezekiel's restatement of Lev 18:5: צדיק הוא חיה יחיה, and Rabban Gamliel worries: מאן דעביד לכולהו הוא דחיי, בחדא מינייהו לא!).[59] Rabban Gamliel worries that the verse is saying that, in order to attain life, one has to keep *all* of the law, and that requirement is simply impossible to fulfill. Rabbi Akiva responds: מי כתיב „עושה כל אלה"? עושה אלה כתיב. Rabban Gamliel's understanding corresponds precisely to Paul's rendering of Deut 27:26: "Cursed is every one who does not abide in *all* things which are written in the book of the law to do them." Rabbi Akiva's response is a sharp rejection of such an interpretation – he points out that the verse does not say "all," precisely the word that Paul includes in Deuteronomy's curse of the person who does not fulfill the law.[60] Rather, Rabbi Akiva argues,

57 Naeh, "Why Did Rabban Gamliel Cry?," argues that originally the *mishnah* ended with Rabbi Shimon's citation of this verse.

58 See the comment of Rabbi Yom Tov Ishbili (Ritva), s.v. "*ba ḥavaquq veheᶜemidan ᶜal ᵓaḥat*," which understands the Habakkuk citation in relation to Lev 18:5, though it is not clear that the Ritva is drawing this connection in relation to the *mishnah*'s citation of the Leviticus verse.

59 Naeh, "Why Did Rabban Gamliel Cry?," points out that MS Munich has this version of Rabban Gamliel's statement in *b.Makkot*. Naeh argues that the original story was told in relation neither to the Ezekiel verse, as in *b.Sanhedrin*, nor to the Psalms verse, as in *b.Makkot*, but in relation to Lev 18:5: *which a person shall do and live by them*. (And, as noted above, n. 54, the LXX of 18:5 includes the word "all," exactly the reading that Rabban Gamliel assumes and that Rabbi Akiva argues against.) Whether or not one accepts Naeh's reconstruction, it is noteworthy that his source-critical argument leads to the same idea that I am arguing here from a literary/theological perspective – that Rabban Gamliel despairs in relation to the Torah's promise that one gains life through obedience to God's commandments. See nn. 119 and 120, below, though, about different implications of the two approaches in relation to the place of this story within the larger *sugya*.

60 It is noteworthy that the word "all" *does* appear in Deut 28:58; this and the following verse are read, according to *m.Mak.* 3:14, while the person who is liable for lashes is flogged. See Longe-

much like Rabbi Ḥananiah ben Gamliel in the *mishnah*, doing even a single *miṣvah* grants life.

And so, the *Makkot* passage and the Galatians passage bear striking similarities. Both address the problem of Leviticus 18 – does law grant us life, or do we inevitably fail to fulfill the law and thus are cut off from God? Both introduce Hab 2:4 as the passage that holds the key to the extended argument. And both attempt to resolve the conflict between the promise that law grants life and the reality that no one is perfectly obedient to the law by citing a verse that relates to the question of whether one can gain life only if one obeys *all* of the law.

The arguments of the two passages, though, could not be more different. The *Makkot* passage (that is, the *mishnah* along with the extended Rabbi Simlai passage) emphasizes that even partial obedience to the law grants life and that disobedience does not inevitably cut one off, since human beings have a way to bring the sinner back in. Paul, in contrast, uses the fact of imperfect obedience to dismiss the possibility that obedience to law can grant life. For him, the faith of Hab 2:4 offers a necessary alternative to achieving life through law.

In the preceding chapter of Galatians, Paul cites another biblical passage that includes the elements of faith, justice, and life, the same elements that appear in the Habakkuk, Genesis, and Leviticus verses on which Paul builds his argument in Galatians 3. Paul works out the implication of this passage in relation to the fact of Christ's death in order to present the notion of justification by faith and to address the question of how one might live. The passage on which he builds his argument is Ps 143:1–2 (LXX: 142:1–2): ... באמנתך ענני בצדקתך ואל-תבוא במשפט את-עבדך כי לא-יצדק לפניך כל-חי, ... *in your faithfulness answer me in your justice. And do not enter into judgment with your servant, for none living will be just before you.*

Here is Paul's argument in Galatians 2 (again, omitting verses that make a point not germane to the central argument):

16 But knowing that man is not justified by the works of the law, but by *the faith of Jesus Christ*, we too believe in Christ Jesus, that we may be *justified by the faith of Christ*, and not by the works of the law, *because by the works of the law no flesh shall be justified.*

19 For I, through the law, died to the law, that I may live to God: with Christ I have been crucified.

20 And no longer do I live, but Christ lives in me. And that which I now live

necker, *Galatians*, 117, who cites these verses in relation to Paul's quotation of Deut 27:26 in Gal 3:10. Hays, *Echoes of Scripture*, 43, sees Gal 3:10 as conflating Deut 27:26 with Deut 28:58; he also notes Deut 28:15, a verse that introduces the curses that will come upon the one who does not do "all" of the commandments.

in the flesh, I live in the faith of the Son of God, who loved me, and gave himself up for me.

21 I do not set aside the grace of God. For if justice be by the law, then Christ died in vain.

Since the law brings a curse, as Paul will demonstrate later by quoting Deut 27:26 (Gal 3:10), Christ was made a curse for us and died on a tree as one accursed (Gal 3:13). Not only did Christ die for us, but, Paul now argues, we die *in* Christ, by means of faith in him. Thus, we both achieve atonement through the death of Christ and enter, through his death, into a new life in faith, freed from the law (Gal 2:19–21).

For Paul, then, there is no way to live in the flesh under the law. Law brings death – thus, we die in Christ. And we can achieve life only in a new existence, freed from the law – thus, we are dead to the law and reborn into a life lived by faith.

Note that in Gal 2:16 Paul doubly recasts Ps 143:2.[61] First, he emphasizes that it is *by law* that no person can be justified. Second, he renders "one living" as "flesh." Paul is suggesting that it is one's incarnation in flesh that makes it impossible not to do evil. He makes this claim explicitly and graphically in a variety of passages, such as Gal 5:16–24 as well as Rom 3:10–18, Rom 6:13 and 6:19, and Rom 7:23–25. His argument here is continuous with the argument in Galatians 3. One *can* be justified, Paul argues, but not through law, since our fleshly existence makes it impossible not to sin (2:16). Since we cannot obey the law, law brings death (2:19; rather than the life of Lev 18:5 – see Gal 3:21), but our death with Christ (2:19) brings us new life in faith (2:20).

Justification by the faith of Christ (2:16) is Paul's understanding of Ps 143:1: באמנתך ענני בצדקתך.[62] As Paul construes this phrase, it fits perfectly which

61 This is noted and discussed by Dunn, *Jesus, Paul, and the Law*, 199 and *Romans 1–8*, 153–55. My discussion diverges from Dunn's interpretation of these elements, which rests heavily on his understanding of Paul as criticizing observances that mark Jews "as distinctively God's people," an understanding that, in turn, rests on Sanders' work on Paul and the law (see *Romans 1–8*, lxiv–lxxii).

62 It is a commonplace that Paul is working with Ps 143:2 here, but the preceding verse is not usually discussed in this context (one exception is Boyarin, *A Radical Jew*, 118–19). I present the masoretic parsing of 143:1, which takes באמנתך as connected with ענני בצדקתך; taking באמנתך, alternatively, as concluding the preceding clause does not affect the suggestion that Paul is reading in this verse the idea of justification through the faith of Christ, since in such a construction of the verse the words באמנתך and בצדקתך are parallel. Dunn, *Romans 1–8*, 133 (on God as "true" in Rom 3:4) points out that *emunah* in Psalms is generally translated as ἀλήθεια in LXX, as opposed to as πίστις when it occurs elsewhere; nevertheless, he suggests that "there is a Hebraic connection of thought" between these two words as used by Paul. See Hays, *Echoes of Scripture*, 202, n. 8, for Paul's use of ἀλήθεια with "covenantal connotations." My interpretation of Gal 2:16 as working with Ps 143:1 as well as with the following verse rests on the assumption that Paul is

his understanding of Hab 2:4, וצדיק באמונתו יחיה, the verse around which he builds his argument in the passage from chapter 3 discussed above. The third element of the Habakkuk passage – life – appears in the following verse in Psalms, a verse which, as noted, Paul renders as saying that no one can be justified through the works of the law. Taken together, as Paul reads them, the two verses argue for the necessity of justification by faith: since the law brings death to those who live in the flesh, only faith in the crucified Christ can bring life.

ROMANS

The broad contours of Paul's argument about faith and law in Romans are structured around the same verses as is his argument in Galatians. Paul introduces Hab 2:4 early in this letter: "For the justice of God is revealed therein, from faith unto faith, as it is written: *The just man lives by faith*" (Rom 1:17).[63] As in Galatians, Paul plays out the implications of this teaching in relation to other verses that include the elements of justice and faith, especially Ps 143:1–2 and Gen 15:6, and in relation to Lev 18:5, וחי בהם.

Chapter 3 of Romans is constructed around Ps 143:1–2: באמנתך ענני ... בצדקתך ואל-תבוא במשפט את-עבדך כי לא-יצדק לפניך כל-חי. Paul quotes this passage in 3:20, though his argument earlier in this chapter, and even as early as chapter 1, echoes this passage as he is interpreting it.[64] Paul cites Ps 143:2 in Romans 3 in the same way that he does in Gal 2:16, inserting "by the works of the law" and rendering "one living" as "flesh":[65]

20 Because *by the works of the law no flesh shall be justified before him*, for through the law is the knowledge of sin.
21 But now without the law the justice of God has been made manifest, being witnessed by the law and the prophets.
22 That is *the justice of God, through faith of Jesus Christ*, to all those who believe....

---

understanding *emunah* here as suggesting "faith." See n. 64, below, on Paul's use of "truth" in the opening chapters of Romans.

63 See Dunn, *Romans 1–8*, 46: "To expound his theme with Hab 2:4 understood thus is the task he sets himself in this letter."

64 See n. 62, above, on *emunah* as ἀλήθεια as well as πίστις. The use of "truth" in Romans 1 is probably a working out of the meanings of *emunah*; thus, Paul is probably juxtaposing Hab 2:4 with Ps 143:1–2 already in Rom 1:17–18, where God's justice (Ps 143:1) and human *in*justice (Ps 143:2) are juxtaposed, as are faith (*emunah* in Hab 2:4) and truth (*emunah* in Ps 143:1). See n. 70 below for references to Ps 143:1–2 earlier in Romans 3.

65 The reference to "flesh" is particularly apt here given the preceding catena composed of verses that describe sinfulness largely in reference to body parts: throat, tongues, lips, mouth, feet, and eyes (Rom 3:13–18). See further below on body parts as sinning or as doing good.

It should be noted that Paul is working not only with Ps 143:2 but also with the end of the preceding verse, as I have suggested is the case with Paul's reference to justification by the faith of Christ in Gal 2:16. Here, Paul is contrasting the justice of God (צדקתך), which comes through faith in Jesus[66] (באמנתך), with the justification of people through the works of the law, which is impossible (כי לא-יצדק לפניך כל-חי).[67]

As in Galatians 3, Paul here works out his contention that justification can come only through faith and not through law by reference to human beings' sinfulness. Paul frames the central section of this chapter with another verse that includes the root צדק: כי אדם אין צדיק בארץ אשר יעשה טוב ולא יחטא (Eccl 7:20).[68] Paul cites the first part of the verse in 3:10 in order to support his claim,

66 See Dunn, *Romans 1–8*, 166–67 and Longenecker, *Galatians*, pp. 87–88 on whether the genitive in this frequently-appearing phrase should be construed as Christ's faith(fulness) or as faith in Christ. See also the argument for the former reading in Hays, *The Faith of Jesus Christ*, 157–76 and the argument for the latter reading in Stephen Westerholm, *Israel's Law and the Church's Faith: Paul and his Recent Interpreters* (Grand Rapids: Eerdmans, 1988) 111–12, n. 12, and see Boyarin, *A Radical Jew*, 119 and 294–95, n. 27.

67 Compare Phil 3:9: "... not having a justice of my own, which is of the law, but that which is through the faith of Jesus Christ, the justice from God, based on faith." See n. 85, below.

68 It is instructive to contrast Paul's use of this verse with the occurrence of this verse in a story about Rabbi Akiva in *b.Sanh.* 101a. Rabbi Akiva and his colleagues go to visit their teacher, Rabbi Eliezer, who is ill. As in the stories at the end of *b.Makkot*, the other disciples cry while Rabbi Akiva laughs. Rabbi Akiva explains that he is happy because Rabbi Eliezer's pain demonstrates that his merit has not been exhausted – that is, he is being punished in this world but will merit eternal life. In response to Rabbi Akiva's interpretation of his suffering, Rabbi Eliezer argues that he has not neglected any of the Torah. Rabbi Akiva responds by quoting Eccl 7:20 as a teaching of Rabbi Eliezer himself.

As in the *b.Makkot* stories, Rabbi Akiva is able to see something different in the reality that confronts him from what is apparent to his colleagues. But here, in addition, Rabbi Akiva cites his teacher's teaching to teach his teacher something that his teacher has not understood. While in the mouth of Rabbi Eliezer the verse from Ecclesiastes might have been a pessimistic teaching (see Hans Joachim Schoeps, *Paul*, trans. H. Knight [Philadelphia: Westminster Press, 1961] 185), Rabbi Akiva employs it to teach a salvific message. In fact, the teaching is very much in line with that about flogging and *karet* in relation to Rabbi Akiva's reply to Rabban Gamliel in *b.Makkot*. The fact that there is no one who does not sin does not mean that life is unattainable through human action; at the same time, the fact of sin requires means of atonement, so that people can merit life through (even incomplete) fulfillment of *miṣvot*. Rabbi Eliezer's suffering, much like flogging, is an essential component of a view that asserts that life can be merited through *miṣvot* but that takes human imperfection seriously. (The difference, of course, is that Rabbi Eliezer's suffering is attributed to God, while flogging is imposed by the human court; as discussed above, the power of human action and human self-determination is central to the *b.Makkot sugya*.) Thus, while Paul sees Eccl 7:20 as denying the possibility of justification through deeds, Rabbi Akiva uses it to explain the necessity of human suffering in such a way that affirms the capacity of human beings to merit life through fulfillment of *miṣvot*.

It is noteworthy that the story in *b.Sanhedrin* is paired with a similar story in which Rabbi Akiva celebrates suffering as a catalyst for repentance. See the discussion above on whether flogin the previous verse, that "all are under sin" (3:9): "As it is written: *There is none just, not one.*" This citation launches a catena of scriptural references, beginning, in 3:11–12, with a reference to Ps 14:2–3, which ends with "*there is none that does good, not even one.*" Paul, it seems, is working through the Ecclesiates verse bit by bit: first he cites the beginning of the verse verbatim: "*There is none just*" (3:10); then, he echoes the second part of the verse through quoting Ps 14:3: "*there is none that does good*" (3:12); finally, he returns to the theme of sin that led to citation of this verse by stating that "all have sinned" (3:23), echoing the final part of the verse. Thus, the claim in 3:9 that "all are under sin" is substantiated in 3:10 through 3:23 through a breakdown of Ecclesiates 7:20 in reference to other biblical verses that vividly portray human beings' sinfulness. It is toward the end of this central section of the chapter that Paul quotes Ps 143:2: "by the works of the law no flesh shall be justified before him" (3:20). The structure of the argument, the interweaving of Ps 143:1–2 with Eccl. 7:20[69] and related verses,[70] makes it clear that Paul is saying that it is *because* of universal sinfulness that no one can be justified by the works of the law – and, thus, that humans beings need the justice of God by faith.

If it is indeed the case that Paul is working through each part of Eccl 7:20 (and it should be noted that my analysis of Paul's argument about sinfulness and the impossibility of justification through deeds does not depend on this point), then it is worth pausing to note how Paul is reading this verse and what other possible way there is to read it. Taken as a unit, the verse can simply mean that there is no one who is completely righteous – so righteous that he *only* does good and *never* sins.[71] Paul, though, breaks the verse into three parts and applies the negative of the first part separately to each individual part. This process generates the following three statements: "There is none just" (3:10); "there is none that

ging brings atonement in and of itself or whether it brings atonement by spurring the sinner to repent.

69 Psalms 143:1–2 is juxtaposed with Eccl 7:20 also in *Midrash Tehillim* 143. The *midrash* illustrates the impossibility of a human being being vindicated (*zkh/ṣdq*) in judgment before God since all human beings sin, citing 1 Kgs 8:46 (*When they sin before you – for there is no person who does not sin. . . .*) and Eccl 7:20. The *midrash* is probably taking the word *ṣadiq* in the latter verse as connoting "one who is declared just/who is vindicated" in the judicial sense (see n. 49, above), as it takes *yiṣdaq* in Ps 143:2 as meaning "is declared just/is vindicated" in judgment.

70 The interweaving is more complex than this summary indicates, given the subtle references to Ps 143:1–2 throughout this chapter. The central section, which establishes universal sinfulness (3:9–23), comes after a passage that is knit together by "the faith of God," "the justice of God," and "the truth of God" (3:2–7) (see Dunn, *Romans 1–8*, 136 and see nn. 62 and 64, above, on *emunah* as both "faith" and "truth"), the first two of which recur in the verses that immediately follow this section (3:24–26). Thus, overt or more subtle references to Ps 143:1–2 are truly interwoven with the demonstration of universal sinfulness – supporting the idea that the latter is essential for Paul's argument that justification can only come through faith.

71 This is how, for example, Ibn Ezra understands the verse: "*who does good* always *and does not sin* ever."

does good" (3:12; quoting Ps 14:3, but, in so doing, expressing the negative form of the second part of the verse from Ecclesiastes, as if it said אין אשר יעשה טוב); "all have sinned" (3:23; taking the negative form of the negative final part of the verse, as if it said אין אשר לא יחטא, and expressing it as a positive assertion).

Fragmenting the verse in this way nuances each part in a far more negative way and generates a very different reading of the verse from the one that seems to emerge from reading it as a single unit. In this fragmented reading, no one does good, everyone sins, and thus no one is righteous. It is this reading that allows Paul to use this verse as a demonstration that "all are under sin" (3:9). The difference between the two possible readings of this verse is that, in one, the verse is saying that no one is wholly righteous (only doing good and never sinning)[72] while, in the other, the verse is saying that no one is righteous in that no one does good and all have sinned. Thus, for Paul, all are in the power of sin.[73]

Paul's construction of this verse encapsulates what I have argued characterizes Paul's understanding of why justification cannot be through works of the law: the fact that there is no one who does *only* good and *never* sins is equivalent, for Paul, to no one doing good and everyone sinning – to being under sin. And so it is the impossibility of perfectly fulfilling the law which underpins Paul's contention that justification cannot come through the works of the law.

Chapter 4 of Romans concludes the main part of Paul's argument in this letter that justification is by faith, not by works.[74] Here, as in Galatians 3, Paul introduces Gen 15:6, והאמן ביהוה ויחשבה לו צדקה (Rom 4:3),[75] though the argument that Paul makes based on this verse is different in Romans than in Galatians. In Romans 4, Paul introduces Gen 15:6 to set up a stark distinction between faith and works. Analyzing the word ויחשבה, Paul argues that reckoning functions differently for those who work and for those who believe but do not work. The faith of the latter is reckoned for justification through God's grace (4:5), while the works of the former are reckoned in terms of debt (4:4).

As many commentators have suggested,[76] Paul is using this distinction to set

72 This is how Rabbi Akiva understands the verse in the story discussed in n. 68, above.

73 For sin as a power in Romans, see Dunn, *Romans 1–8*, 148–49 and Beverly Roberts Gaventa, "The Cosmic Power of Sin in Paul's Letter to the Romans: Toward a Widescreen Edition," *Int* 58 (2004) 229–40.

74 Thus, chap. 5 begins with the assumption that justification by faith has been established. Chapter 5 serves as the conclusion of chaps. 1–4 and as the introduction to chaps. 6–11 (for a discussion of views of the structure of the letter and the place of chap. 5 within this structure, see Dunn, *Romans 1–8*, 242–44).

75 Paul, in fact, sets the stage for the explicit introduction of this verse in chapter 4 in 3:28: "For we account a man to be justified by faith, without the works of the law." Paul here introduces the notion of accounting, חשב, which he works out in the following chapter in relation to Gen 15:6.

76 Sanders, *Paul*, 484, understands Paul's use of Gen 15:6 in Galatians in this way: "Righteousness *cannot* be by law, *since it is by faith. . . .*" For Sanders, the antithesis is alone enough to prove that righteousness cannot be by law, since, if it could be, then Christ died in vain. Paul's view of the

up an antithesis between faith and works (similar to his antithesis between grace and works in Rom 11:6). But Paul seems to be going further, to be setting up the *impossibility* of works being reckoned for justification. Paul does this by introducing another biblical passage that includes the verb "to reckon," but in which there is a shift in the object of the verb: "*Blessed are they whose lawless deeds have been forgiven, and whose sins have been covered. Blessed is the one whose sin the Lord will not reckon* [יחשב]" (Rom 4:7–8, quoting Ps 32:1–2 [LXX 31:1–2]). Paul characterizes this passage as talking about the blessedness of the person "to whom God reckons justice without works" (4:6), which follows directly from his contrast between reckoning for the person who works and reckoning for the person who has faith (4:4–5). But whereas the contrast with which Paul begins suggests that one *could* gain reward through works, the passage that Paul now introduces suggests quite the opposite: that, if God *were* to reckon works, the person would be found to be sinful. Thus, Paul is not only setting up an antithesis between faith and works; he is suggesting that a person *cannot* be justified through works.

Having established in chapters 1–4 that justification is by faith, not by works, Paul goes on in chapters 6–8 to a new theme, the link between law, sin, and death.[77] The theme of death versus life is introduced in chapter 5, to be discussed below, and is resumed in chapter 10, when Paul explicitly cites Lev 18:5 (Rom 10:5). But Paul clearly is working with the Leviticus passage even before he introduces it explicitly. For example, Paul declares that "we have died to sin" (6:2): "For we are buried together with him [Christ] through baptism into death, that as Christ was raised from the dead through the glory of the Father, so we also may walk in newness of life" (6:4). This is in clear contrast to walking in the commandments (ללכת בהם, Lev 18:4) and living by them (וחי בהם, Lev 18:5). Because of sin, failure to obey the commandments, death has come (5:12–13);[78] by dying with Christ, through faith in him,[79] we achieve life. Paul works with the idea of Lev 18:5 also in his striking portrayal of sin itself as being dead or coming to life, in inverse relationship to the person: ". . . For without the law sin was dead. And I lived then without the law. But when the commandment

---

law, according to Sanders, is prompted by Paul's conviction of the necessity of the Christ-event; see, for example, *Paul*, 482. Sanders sums up this understanding in his famous statement that Paul worked backwards, "from solution to plight" (see, for example, *Law*, 68 and see the discussion below).

77 Dunn, *Romans 1–8*, 301–2.

78 The relationship between law and the accounting of sin in 5:13 resonates with the idea of reckoning in chap. 4.

79 Paul describes the relationship of the person of faith to the death of Christ in a variety of ways, including the idea that Christ's death is an atoning sacrifice (for example, Rom 3:25) and the idea that one dies with Christ (for example, Gal 2:19).

came, sin came to life. And I died. And the commandment that was for life, itself was found to be for death to me" (7:8–10).

Finally, returning to the theme of law versus faith at the end of chapter 9 and the beginning of chapter 10,[80] Paul cites Lev 18:5 explicitly to contrast "the justice which is of the law" with "the justice which is of faith" (10:5–6). Of the former, says Paul, "Moses wrote . . . the one that shall do it shall live by it" (10:5). Paul contrasts this with "the justice of faith" into whose mouth Paul puts an astonishing inversion of Deuteronomy's promise that the commandments,[81] which one might find inaccessible, are in fact well within reach (Deut 30:11–14):

> 6 But the justice which is of faith speaks thus: Say not in your heart, Who shall ascend into heaven? That is, to bring Christ down.
> 7 Or who shall descend into the deep? That is, to bring up Christ from the dead.
> 8 But what does it say? The word is near you, in your mouth and in your heart. This is the word of faith, which we preach.

The Deuteronomy passage talks about commandment (Deut 30:11) and concludes its denial of the commandment's inaccessibility with the assertion that it is indeed near: "in your mouth and in your heart" *to do it* (Deut 30:14). Paul omits the opening reference to commandment and offers an interpretation of the passage in relation to Christ. He goes on to cut off the quotation just before the end. In place of the words "to do it," Paul appends an explication of הדבר – the word or thing that the biblical passage asserts is near – as referring to "the word of faith."[82] Thus, what is near is not the commandment, but rather faith. Faith, says Paul, "comes from hearing" (10:17); to achieve the justice which is

80 Dunn, *Romans 1–8*, 302, notes that the word πίστις does not occur in chaps. 6 through 8 of Romans.

81 The passage in Deuteronomy uses the word *miṣvah* in the singular. While the word can be taken to connote the commandments in general, Nachmanides offers an alternative interpretation, that the word refers specifically to the commandment of repentance, taking *vehasheivota* and *veshavta* earlier in the chapter (Deut 30:1–2) as commands (rather than as indicative of what will happen in the future). (I am indebted to David Silber for calling this interpretation to my attention in relation to this discussion of the Romans passage.) The possibility of reading Deut 30:11 in relation to repentance raises the intriguing possibility that Paul's reinterpretation of the passage not only suggests that doing the commandments is an unattainable goal (as I discuss shortly) but that repentance for those who fail to fulfill the commandments is also unattainable (on the absence of repentance in Paul's writings, see below). It should be noted that the link between 30:11–14 and repentance likely would have been salient for Paul whether or not he understood the word *miṣvah* in 30:11 to refer to repentance, since the entire preceding section (30:1–10) talks about repentance, and since the biblical passage juxtaposes the idea of repentance with the idea of the commandments being accessible/fulfillable. The biblical passage emphasizes the capability of the person to fulfill the *miṣvot* as well as to repent of failure to fulfill the commandments; Paul denies both.

82 My discussion of this passage to this point is heavily indebted to Hays, *Echoes of Scripture*, 78–

of faith (which "speaks," 10:6), one must simply hear, believe (with the heart), and confess (with the mouth) (10:8–10).

It seems clear that Paul is contrasting here the *doing* of Lev 18:5 (Rom 10:5) with the hearing of the word of faith.[83] It is important to note that, since the Deuteronomy passage explicitly responds to the concern that the commandments are unfulfillable, Paul's inversion of this passage not only replaces the reference to the commandments with faith, but, in so doing, leaves the problem to which the Deuteronomy passage is responding unanswered. That is, by wiping out Deuteronomy's answer to the concern that the commandments are not within reach, Paul subtly suggests that, indeed, the problem to which the Deuteronomy passage is responding is simply unsolvable. Doing the commandments *is* an inaccessible goal. Thus, the promise of Lev 18:5 is not within reach, while the word of faith is near (10:8) and, thus, can bring justification (10:4,[84] 10).

The contrast between *doing* the law and *hearing* the word of faith aligns with Paul's contrast between "the justice of God" and "their own" (Rom 10:3). "The justice of God" is that which comes through faith; "their own" is the attempt to achieve justification through doing the law.[85] Not only is the first accessible (it

---

82. Hays comments that Paul's choice of this biblical passage "is daring and perhaps deliberately provocative. It would not be easy to find another text in the Old Testament that looks less promising for Paul's purposes." On the other hand, Paul needs to address this passage, since it explicitly responds to the concern that the commandments are unfulfillable. See below on the force of Paul's erasure of Deuteronomy's answer to the problem of the commandments' inaccessibility.

83 Romans 2:13, "For not the hearers of the law are just before God, but the doers of the law shall be justified," supports the idea that Paul is focusing on the problem of *doing* the law. Law requires doing, while faith requires merely hearing. Thus, in Romans 10, faith is attainable (it speaks and need merely be *heard*), while the law is out of reach (as it must be *done*).

That the focus in Rom 10:5 and in Gal 3:10, 12 is on *doing* the law (and on what the implication of such a focus might be) is much disputed; see, for example, James D. G. Dunn, *Romans 9–16*, WBC 38B (1988) 601. For Sanders' view, see *Paul*, 483, n. 37 and *Law*, 54, n. 30. Sanders rejects the idea that Paul addresses the problem of unfulfillability, the impossibility of *doing* the law. For Sanders, Paul rejects the very premise of Lev 18:5, that law could (at least in principle) bring life, since, for Paul, justification can only be achieved through faith. For the alternative view advanced here, that law could bring life were people able to fulfill the law, see, for example, Brendan Byrne, *'Sons of God'–'Seed of Abraham'* (Rome: Biblical Institute Press, 1979) 152 and 231 and Byrne, *Romans*, SP 6 (1996) 317 and 321.

84 For *telos* in 10:4 as connoting both "goal/fulfillment" and "end," see Dunn, *Romans 9–16*, 589–91. Westerholm, *Israel's Law*, 130, argues for the meaning "end," working with the understanding adopted here that Paul accepts the potential life-giving capacity of the law along with the actual inability of law to grant life because people cannot fulfill the law. Thus, Westerholm sees this passage as saying that now, with the possibility of justification through faith in Christ, there is no further need for law. See also Räisänen, *Paul and the Law*, 53–56.

85 The implication of "their own" has been a point of great scholarly dispute. For summaries of and responses to the Lutheran view, see, for example, Dunn, *Jesus, Paul, and the Law*, 223; Sanders, *Law*, 38; Boyarin, *A Radical Jew*, 293–94, n. 23. The interpretation offered here coincides with that of Westerholm, *Israel's Law*, 130 and 172.

need simply be heard) and the second out of reach, but, Paul emphasizes, the first is offered by God while the second must come from the person. The contrast in Rom 10:3–4 between justification from God, through faith, and (the failed attempt to achieve) justification through the person's own action once again recalls Paul's interpretation of Ps 143:1–2: ...באמנתך ענני בצדקתך ואל־תבוא במשפט את־עבדך כי לא־יצדק לפניך כל־חי.[86]

Habakkuk 2:4, then, sets out the agenda for Paul's main line of argument in Romans. After introducing this passage in chapter 1, Paul works out the relationship between its components, focusing on justification and faith in chapters 4 and 5 and on life in chapters 6 through 8, and finally bringing all three components together in the bold argument of chapter 10. As in Galatians, Paul sets Hab 2:4 in opposition to Lev 18:5 in relation to the question of how one gains life, mustering Ps 143:1–2 and Gen 15:6, with their association of faith and righteousness, to work out why life/justification must be by faith and not by works. Paul's argument, in essence, can be reduced to a demonstration that Hab 2:4 wins out over Lev 18:5,[87] since the life promised in the latter through obeying the law is unattainable.

The final *mishnah* in *Makkot* along with the Rabbi Simlai passage, I have noted, are structured around the same two biblical verses. And, I have argued, they address the same question – is it possible to live by law if we inevitably fall short of fully obeying the law? For Paul, the answer is a clear no. That the law is not perfectly fulfillable leads to the conclusion that law cannot bring life. In contrast, the *mishnah* as well as the Rabbi Akiva passage argue that even partial obedience grants life. Thus, inability to perfectly fulfill the law may require punishment (or other vehicles of atonement), but it does not lead to despair of gaining life through *miṣvot*.

Justification through Deeds

I want now to turn to the final teaching in the *mishnah*, that of Rabbi Ḥananiah ben Aqashia: רצה הקדוש ברוך הוא לזכות את ישראל לפיכך הרבה להם תורה ומצות שנאמר ה׳ חפץ למען צדקו יגדיל תורה ויאדיר (ישעיה מ״ב), "The Holy Blessed One wanted to give merit to Israel, therefore he multiplied for them Torah and *miṣvot*. . . ."[88] *Lezakot* should be understood here as meaning to justify, to declare righteous.[89] Rabbi Ḥananiah ben Aqashia is reading the verse from Isaiah

86 See the discussion of Romans 3, above, and esp. nn. 64 and 67.

87 As in Gal 3:11–12 and the ensuing argument.

88 See n. 5, above.

89 Compare the parallels in *Šemot Rabbah* 9:1; *Vayiqra Rabbah* 31:8; *Bamidbar Rabbah* 14:10, 15:2, and 17:5; *Tanḥuma Vayeira* 8 and *Tazria* 9; *Tanḥuma* (Buber) *Vaʾeira* 11, *Behaʿalotekha* 2, and *Šelah* 28; and *Pesiqta Rabbati* 40. These parallels make it clear that *lezaqot* is interchangeable with

as saying that God wanted to justify Israel (no doubt reading the word צדקו as *ṣadeqo*, "to declare righteous") and so made Torah great – that is, made a lot of law. Thus Rabbi Ḥananiah ben Aqashia is claiming not only that performance of *miṣvot* is the path to life, but that God made many *miṣvot* in order that Israel can be justified.

Paul makes the opposite claim toward the end of a rhetorically striking passage in Romans 5, the chapter that serves as the conclusion to the argument about justification through faith rather than through works and that introduces the idea of law bringing death and faith bringing life. Rather than law being an opportunity for justification – and the more law the better – Paul declares: "Now the law entered in, that trespass might abound" (Rom 5:20). The passage is knit together by a series of comparisons and how-much-more-so arguments:

> 15 But not as the trespass, so also the effect of grace. For if by the trespass of one, many died, how much more the grace of God and the gift by the grace of one man, Jesus Christ, has abounded to many.
> 16 And not as the one who sinned, the gift. For judgment was from one to condemnation, but the effect of grace is from many trespasses, to justification.
> 17 For if by the trespass of one, death reigned through one, how much more those who receive abundance of grace and of the gift of justice shall reign in life through one, Jesus Christ.
> 18 Therefore, as through the trespass of one, unto all men to condemnation, so also through the just act of one, to all men to justification of life.
> 19 For as through the disobedience of one man, many were made sinners, so also through the obedience of one, many shall be made just.
> 20 Now the law entered in, that trespass might abound. But where sin abounded, grace overflowed in abundance.
> 21 That as sin has reigned to death, so also grace might reign through justice to eternal life, through Jesus Christ our Lord.

The final *mishnah* in *Makkot* includes a similar rhetorical strategy, leading up to Rabbi Ḥananiah ben Aqashia's teaching about the multiplicity of laws providing an opportunity for justification:

> Rabbi Ḥananiah ben Gamliel said: If one who transgresses a single transgression loses his life on account of it, one who performs (does) a single commandment – how much more so that his life will be given to him.

lehaṣdiq, both referring to vindication in judgment and to granting life. See Herbert W. Basser, *Studies in Exegesis: Christian Critiques of Jewish Law and Rabbinic Responses 70–300* C.E. (Leiden: Brill, 2000) 123–24.

> . . . Rabbi Shimon ben Rabbi says: Behold it says *Only be steadfast that you do not eat the blood, for the blood is the life. . . .* [*Do not eat it, in order that it be good with you and with you children after you when you do what is right in the eyes of God.*] (Deut 12:23–25) – If [regarding] blood, by which a person's soul is repulsed, one who separates from it receives a reward, then [regarding] robbery and forbidden sexual relationships, which a person's soul desires and covets, how much more so will one who separates from them gain merit for himself and for his descendents and for the descendents of his descendents until the end of all the generations.

As we have seen, Rabbi Ḥananiah ben Gamliel reverses the core asymmetry between good deeds and bad deeds, claiming rather paradoxically that, if violating a single law causes one to lose life, then how much more so does fulfilling a single *miṣvah* cause one to gain life. Rabbi Shimon ben Rabbi makes a rhetorically similar argument, showing that, if keeping from a forbidden thing for which one has no desire grants merit, how much more so does keeping from forbidden things which one greatly desires. These two teachings lead up to Rabbi Ḥananiah ben Aqashia's teaching that God desired to justify Israel and that the multitude of God's laws are designed to give Israel an opportunity for justification.

The passage from Romans, rhetorically so similar, makes an opposite claim, though one that is also based on the notion that the good is greater than the bad: if the sin of one man (here, Adam, prefiguring Christ) brings death, then how much more so does the grace of God through Jesus bring "justification of life." Justification cannot come through law: rather, "the law entered in, that sin might abound." Law is an opportunity for disobedience and death; "justice unto life everlasting" must come in a different way.

It should be noted that the Rabbi Simlai passage, which begins with Rabbi Simlai's teaching about the number of *miṣvot*, appears in this *sugya* as a commentary on Rabbi Ḥananiah ben Aqashia's teaching: "God wanted to bring merit to Israel and *therefore* multiplied for them Torah and *miṣvot*."[90] Rabbi Simlai, in the context of this *mishnah*, is saying: how much did God multiply *miṣvot*?

90 The connection between Isa 42:21 and the idea of 613 *miṣvot* is made explicitly in *Šemot Rabbah* 14:10. Alternatively, one could see Rabbi Simlai's homily as included here in relation to the *mishnah*'s teaching about doing even one *miṣvah* (Shlomo Naeh, oral communication); the focus, according to such a reading, is not on the great number of *miṣvot* with which the homily begins, but rather on the idea of the *miṣvot* being reduced to one. See below on Rabbi Akiva's response to Rabban Gamliel echoing both the *mishnah*'s teaching about doing one *miṣvah* and the culmination of Rabbi Simlai's homily about the reduction of the *miṣvot* to one. It is noteworthy that both Rabbi Simlai's homily and the *mishnah* talk of both many *miṣvot* and a single *miṣvah*, the *mishnah* moving from the idea of one to the idea of many and the homily moving from many to one.

How many *miṣvot* did God give Israel as an opportunity for justification? It is perhaps noteworthy that the number of positive commandments offered corresponds to the number of a person's limbs. In effect, Rabbi Simlai is saying that every limb of a person can be called upon to perform *miṣvot*, the opposite of Paul's repeated argument that one's fleshliness inevitably entraps one in sin – "But I see a different law in my members . . . captivating me by the law of sin which is in my members" (Rom 7:23) – so that life cannot come through law.[91]

Paul and the Law

It is important to point out that the readings of Paul that I have offered stand in stark opposition to much of the "New Perspective" on Paul that has developed in the wake of Sanders' revolutionary work on Paul and contemporary Judaism.[92] Sanders has argued that it was not a problem with law that led Paul to the conclusion that justification is through faith in Christ. Indeed, for Sanders, Paul is arguing "from solution to plight"[93] – that is, it is the fact of the Christ-event[94] (along with, Sanders stresses in later formulations, the need to offer salvation to the Gentiles)[95] that motivates any argument that Paul makes in relation to law versus faith.

Further, Sanders argues against the view of contemporary Judaism as a religion of works-righteousness. For Sanders, salvation within Judaism is not dependent on obedience to the law; rather, Sanders' notion of "covenantal nomism"[96] encapsulates a view of Judaism in which covenant election and salvation precede obedience to the law and in which obedience is a response to "being in" (rather than a way of "getting in") the covenant.[97]

As a corollary to this, Sanders and his followers argue that Paul is not setting justification through faith over against works of the law in the sense of attacking the attempt to achieve salvation through obedience to the law or the attempt to achieve justification through one's own effort instead of through God's free grace.[98] And, further, it is argued that no Judaism of the time expected perfect

91 Compare the catalogue of sinning body parts in Rom 3:13–18.

92 For a recent summary of the main points of the New Perspective, as well as a critique of some of those points, see Brendan Byrne, "Interpreting Romans: The New Perspective and Beyond," *Int* 58 (2004) 240–52.

93 See, for example, *Paul*, 474 and *Law*, 27.

94 See *Paul*, 482 and the formulation in *Paul*, 552: "In short, *this is what Paul finds wrong in Judaism: it is not Christianity.*"

95 Sanders, *Law*, 47.

96 See esp. *Paul*, 75 and 236.

97 See, for example, *Law*, 6–10.

98 The latter position is that of Bultmann; for a summary of Bultmann's view, see Westerholm, *Israel's Law*, 71–75.

obedience to the law or was concerned with the problem of the law being unfulfillable and, accordingly, that the issue of human inability to fulfill the law is not a core problem for Paul.[99]

This is not the place for an extensive engagement with the New Perspective on Paul, but a few comments are in order in relation to the readings of passages from Galatians and Romans that I have offered. First, I think it is important to distinguish between what might have motivated Paul to come to the conclusions to which he came and what Paul sets out as a core premise of his argument. That is, while I would not argue that what actually led Paul to his conclusion about justification through faith was a problem with law,[100] I think it is clear that Paul does pose a problem with law as a core premise of his arguments in Galatians and Romans about the inadequacy of law to grant life and the necessity of faith as the path to justification.[101]

Second, I think it goes without saying that the Judaism of Paul's time, in continuity with biblical tradition, sees obedience to the law as the means of attaining life. Sanders' important arguments against a Lutheran understanding of Jewish legalism does not exclude, as Westerholm and Byrnes have argued,[102] a more nuanced understanding of obedience to law as central to the Jewish conception of righteousness and salvation – in short, of *miṣvot* as life-giving.

Finally, the fact that Jews acknowledged that people fail to obey the law perfectly and the fact that rabbinic Judaism (again, in continuity with biblical traditions) emphasized that repentance and atonement are available do not mean that rabbinic Jews had no problem with the fact that we all fail to live up to the requirements of the law. The fact that rabbinic texts offer a solution does not mean that they don't see a problem. My reading of the *Makkot* passage shows that they *do* see a problem and, in fact, it seems strikingly close to the problem that Paul is addressing. Paul's solution, in fact, *is* to set up justification through faith over against justification through works – Hab 2:4 over against Lev 18:5. It is in the particular solution that Paul offers that he differs with rabbinic Judaism. Thus, the similarities that I have pointed out between the *Makkot* passage and passages from Galatians and Romans argue for a reevaluation of the post-Sanders perspective on Paul and the law.

99 See *Law*, 27–28 and Boyarin, *A Radical Jew*, 138. Sanders writes (28): "All the rabbis whose views are known to us took the position that all the law must be accepted.... No rabbi took the position that obedience must be perfect. Pharisees and rabbis of all schools and all periods strongly believed in repentance and other means of atonement in the case of transgression." But this seems to confuse the fact that the Rabbis emphasize a solution with the idea that they do not perceive a problem; see below.

100 Though this is certainly possible.

101 As opposed to Sanders' idea that Paul simply reasons that, if justification is by faith, then it cannot be by law; see n. 76, above.

102 Westerholm, *Israel's Law*; Byrnes, "Interpreting Romans." See also Byrnes' review of Sanders, *Paul* in *'Sons of God,'* esp. 229–31.

Let me sum up the main points of my argument so far, before going on to address what I think are the different philosophical underpinnings of the rabbinic and Pauline texts.

I have argued that the *Makkot* passage (the *mishnah* along with the *gemara*) addresses a problem posed by the core texts and core premises of Judaism and that Paul is addressing the same problem in his arguments about law and justification. I am not suggesting that any of the statements in the *mishnah*, any of the traditions cited in the *gemara*, or the *Bavli sugya* itself are responding directly to Paul's teachings, although I am not sure that such a possibility should be ruled out. It is possible that the correspondences emerge independently from reflection upon shared biblical texts and the apparent relationship between those texts, from shared hermeneutics, from shared ideas (such as that the good with which God governs the world exceeds the bad), and from shared human concerns within the shared context of a religious tradition based on law.

I have also argued that, within its broad literary context, the final *mishnah* of *Sanhedrin-Makkot* and the Rabbi Simlai passage serve as a counterpoint to a tractate-pair the greater part of which addresses the severe consequences of violation of law. I have suggested that the final *sugya* asks how we ordinary people – the majority of us who do mostly good but who occasionally fail to fulfill the Torah's precepts – can hope to live. I did not fully address the extended homily concerning the reduction in the number of *miṣvot*, culminating in the citation of Hab 2:4, which poses intriguing difficulties. But I did suggest that Rabbi Akiva's teaching, inserted into the center of the extended homily, offers a solution to the problem, a solution that is both based on law and that demands a mechanism of atonement for violations of law, such as the mechanism suggested in the *mishnah*'s teaching about flogging.

In addition, I have suggested that the *mishnah*'s teaching about flogging propels the idea that unifies all of the sections of this final *sugya*: that we are masters of our own fate and that human action as well as human interpretation define reality. It is this point to which I want to return now.

"Guilt" versus "Shame": *Makkot* and Paul

Earlier, I presented two brief passages from Herbert Morris' classic essay on punishment, in which he argues in favor of a system of punishment, of what he calls a "guilt morality," and presents the claim that people have "a right to punishment." Morris lays out a range of benefits which he feels are offered by a system based on guilt and punishment, rather than alternative systems, such as one based on the notion of illness and therapy or one based on shame. One of the benefits was mentioned above: a guilt morality, Morris argues, allows a person to pay the price of his misdeed and thus to be accepted back into the community. I suggested that the *mishnah*'s teaching about the person who receives the penalty of flogging becoming exempt from *karet* fits Morris' model of a guilt morality –"once he receives lashes, he is like 'your brother'"– that is, not only is the person exempt from a more severe punishment, but the person is reincorporated into the community.[103]

But another benefit of a guilt morality, according to Morris, is that it takes the person seriously as a moral agent. In a system of punishment, Morris argues, "The punishment associated with these primary rules paid deference to an individual's free choice by connecting punishment to a freely chosen act violative of the rules, thus giving some plausibility to the claim . . . that what a person received by way of punishment he himself had chosen."[104] A legal system that holds people accountable for their choices, for Morris, fits with a view of human beings "as capable . . . of creating, among other things, ourselves."[105] Thus, punishment is connected with a claim about human responsibility that implies both freedom of choice and self-determination.

These ideas intersect in our *sugya*, the closing passage of the tractate-pair that deals with the subject of punishment and the legal system that determines guilt and innocence and inflicts punishment on the guilty. The final teaching about punishment in Mishnah *Sanhedrin-Makkot* is the teaching of Rabbi Ḥananiah ben Gamliel about those who are liable for *karet* achieving exemption through the court-imposed punishment of flogging. This teaching, as I discussed above, combines the notion of the possibility of the sinner's reincorporation into the community with the idea of human beings' power to shape their destiny. The latter is expressed through the substitution of a human-imposed punishment for *karet*, whether *karet* is seen as a cutting off from the people naturally consequent upon the sinner's violation of God's command or as a punishment inflicted on the sinner by God's hand. The court's action, as envisioned in the Mishnah, trumps what would appear to be the inevitable consequence of sin, just as the exegesis of the Sages overrides the law of the Torah. And, as I pointed out, this notion of human decision-making and human interpretation as determining future reality, despite scriptural passages or historical reality to the contrary, is the theme that knits together all of the parts of this final *sugya*. Thus, perhaps counterintuitively, it is in connection with the idea of the legal

103 Note that rabbinic texts assert that even those who are condemned to execution are not permanently cut off; see *m.Sanh.* 6:2, on the purpose of confession before execution (compare *b.Yoma* 86 on suffering and on death effecting atonement even for the most egregious sins).

104 *On Guilt and Innocence*, 41; see also 47–48. See the argument about *hatraʾah* (the formal warning that must be issued and accepted in order for a person to be punishable for violating a prohibition) in Steinmetz, "Crimes and Punishments, Part 1: *Mitot Beit Din* as a Reflection of Rabbinic Jurisprudence," *JJS* 55 (2004) 81–101 (at 99–100). On whether the notion of punishment as something that is "chosen" is appropriate in an *educational* setting (school or family), see the reference in n. 108, below.

105 *On Guilt and Innocence*, 42.

institution of punishment that the *gemara* lays out a vision of human freedom and self-determination, in Morris' words, the idea that human beings are "capable . . . of creating, among other things, ourselves."

It is noteworthy that it is Rabbi Akiva, the Sage who is known as the master of exegesis and who applies his interpretive skill at the very end of our *sugya* to reinvision the future reality, who assures Rabban Gamliel that human beings are not doomed to failure, that even less-than-perfect people who obey God's law less than perfectly can live before God. As discussed above, this teaching, combined with the teachings of the Mishnah, suggests that failings can be atoned for, through the actions of human beings, and that human actions are redemptive, as performing even a single *miṣvah* brings life.

I want now to return to Johnny, the child who spit on his classmate. And I want to look at what happens to Johnny in two different kinds of classrooms. One of the classrooms, perhaps the one more familiar to most of us, is a classroom in which rules are clear; rules are communicated clearly to the children and, perhaps, a list of rules is displayed prominently in the classroom. The rules include things like "no hitting," "no name calling," "no knocking down other children's structures." When a child breaks a rule, there is a clear and consistent response. Perhaps the child sits in the time-out chair for five minutes, or perhaps the child is asked to apologize to the classmate whom he has hurt, or perhaps the child is not allowed in the block corner for the rest of the day. After that – after the five minutes, or the apology, or the end of the day – the child is accepted back as a full participant in the class. In fact, barring a pattern of rule-breaking behavior, the child's parents might never be called to be told what the child did. And at parent-teacher conferences the parents will certainly hear about all the ways in which the child does what he is supposed to do: completes his work, cleans up at clean up time, and is generally cooperative and helpful.

But Johnny could be a student in a different kind of classroom. In this classroom, specific rules are not articulated, and there is no list of rules posted on the bulletin board. Teachers in this classroom tell children simply that everyone is to behave in a way that allows everyone to learn and to feel safe and comfortable. The idea is for the children to embrace this ideal and to shape their behavior to align with this broad goal. The expectation is that children strive to be as good as possible, not that they merely follow the teachers' instructions and don't violate the classroom rules that have been articulated. If Johnny spits in this classroom, the teacher does not tell him that he has broken a rule and that he needs to do such-and-such and then rejoin the group. When Johnny spits, the teacher tells Johnny that he has behaved in an unacceptable way. The point is for Johnny to feel that he had done something that violates the core principle of this classroom; he has not behaved in a way that allows everyone to learn and to feel safe and comfortable. The teacher calls Johnny's parents, because she is concerned about Johnny – there must be something wrong with Johnny if he spits on another child during circle time. The teacher will be watching Johnny, and it might take some time until Johnny is able to demonstrate to his teacher and to his classmates that he isn't a kid who spits. Meanwhile, his place in the classroom community is compromised – all is not the same as it was before he spat.

These two illustrations, which, in fact, represent radically different educational philosophies, are offered here to illustrate what Morris' conception of a "guilt morality" and a "shame morality" might look like in real life.[106] Here is a

106 It should be noted that Morris himself raises the question of setting, asking in what settings and under what conditions a guilt or a shame model might be more appropriate (*On Guilt and Innocence*, 62–63):

> A clue here is that guilt finds a natural role within the law. . . . The law is concerned primarily with maintaining a certain balanced distribution of freedom and does this by ordering relationships among individuals through rules that set up a system of reciprocal rights and duties. There are a number of implications to such arrangements that provide useful leads in answering the question I have raised. . . . First, in law our major concern is the maintenance of a minimum level. Second, the concern is that conduct, relating to values sought to be protected, reach a minimum. Third, relatively precise guides and rules are seen as assuring maintenance of the distribution of value in the community. Fourth, there is a recognition that strong inclinations operate against compliance and there is the need for incentives. Fifth, there is an absence of concern for motives, with purity of heart, grandeur of soul. Diminishing harm to others is the predominant goal. Sixth, there is incentive put forward for restoring relationships. Finally, the relations are between individuals who do not ordinarily have close ties that would, apart from obligations or a sense of obligation, provide strong motives for satisfying the interests of others. It is, I think, whenever interests of this kind predominate that one is pulled to responses that generate the conception of guilt. It will be, for example, when we view as pre-eminently important a certain balanced distribution of freedom that we shall think in terms of rights and duties and move to concepts of wrongdoing and guilt. Shame will arise when our concern is achieving more than a minimum, when our concern is that individuals realize to the fullest what they have within them, when what one is takes priority over a nice balance in relations with others with respect to particular types of conduct.

While I am using classroom settings to illustrate Morris' contrasting models, it is important to point out that the goals of schooling are not identical to the goals of law, and that the models of guilt and shame, as Morris notes, fit with different goals as well as with different kinds of social relationships (or different assumptions about what relationships ought to be fostered) within different settings. Similarly, it goes without saying that, while we talk about "law" in Judaism, the role and nature of law within a religious system is not identical to that within a secular, political framework. Thus, even if we accept Morris' correlation of a guilt model with law, the question of whether a guilt model fits sufficiently well with *miṣvot* is still open. See the concluding discussion of the *b.Makkot sugya*, below.

list of differences that Morris spells out as distinguishing a shame morality from a guilt morality, the last part of which I quoted above in relation to the substitution of flogging for *karet*:

> First, [in a shame morality] conduct is evaluated through comparison and contrast with a certain model identity. It is not criticism that employs the concepts of disobeying an order or violating a rule. . . . Second, the shame morality is a scale morality not, like guilt, a threshold morality. There is the conception of a good toward which we may have traveled some distance but not the whole way. The critical concept associated with shame is failure, shortcoming, not violation. With guilt one has either done wrong or not; it is not a concept admitting of degrees of realization. Third, connected with this contrast between the conception of a scale and a threshold is the fact that with shame we may focus on failure to achieve an ideal, perfection, some maximum whereas with guilt it is a minimum demand that has not been met. Fourth, shame, unlike guilt, is not essentially tied to fault. Fault is connected with blame and blame is connected with failing to meet demands that others might reasonably place on one because they would place it upon themselves in like situations. Shame, however, may arise through failure to do the extraordinary. . . . Fifth, what is valued in a shame morality is an identity of a certain kind and not, as is necessary with guilt, a relationship with others. The whole focus in a shame scheme where relationships are valued is the question "Am I worthy of being related to the other?" With guilt we have a conceptual scheme of obligations and entitlements. . . . With shame what is crucial is a failing to correspond with the model identity. We shall feel shame, then, in situations where we do not conceive of ourselves as damaging a relationship with others. And where the maintaining of that relationship is an element in one's model identity, the shame response focuses on failing to be a worthy person as one conceives it, rather than on failing to meet one's obligations to others and needing to restore the relationship. An act could only restore the relationship if it revealed that one was worthy of the relationship but paying the price is not alone adequate for restoration. The disposition is to be the kind of person one values. One is not forgiven one's shame and punishment does not divest one of it. Sixth, feeling shame because of what we have done, we naturally see ourselves as shameful persons and the steps that are appropriate to relieve shame are becoming a person that is not shameful. Shame leads to creativity; guilt to restoration. Seventh, . . . With shame, the disposition is to hide, to vanish; with shame we want to sink into the ground, we cannot stand the sight of ourselves.

> Eighth, shame links essentially to worth concepts and guilt does not. We may react to the shameful person with contempt; to the guilty we react with condemnation. With shame there is an inevitable derogation in one's status as a person; with guilt one's status is intact but one's relationship to others is affected. The shameful is not worthy of association; the guilty is still worthy but a price must be paid. Abandonment by others is the spontaneous result that follows upon knowledge of a contemptible nature; punishment is not a spontaneous response but a price paid for restoration. A shame morality leads to casting outside the community, exile; a guilt morality, to suffering in order to be accepted back within. . . .[107]

The first classroom that I portrayed corresponds to Morris' guilt morality. In this classroom, a child who conforms to the rules governing interactions with others is good enough. There is only a problem if the child fails, in some way, to adhere to the minimum expectations of the classroom. If the child has violated those demands in some way, then the child has to do something to restore his relationship with his classmates. His act of restoration compensates for or counterbalances his act of violation. Just as his act of violation is understood by the teacher as a choice that rightfully compromises the child's place in the classroom community, his act of paying back is presented by the teacher as the consequence of the child's choice and as necessary to restore the child's place among his classmates.[108]

But the second classroom is based on a different assumption. This classroom corresponds to Morris' shame morality. In this classroom, a child is to strive to be the best that he can. Rather than setting out a minimum set of expectations or rules, the teacher sets out an ideal toward which children are to strive. In this classroom, the best of the children is never good enough, because one never reaches the ideal that has been set out. And Johnny, the child who spit, is shameful. His act casts doubt on his identity as a worthy person, and he can't change that simply by undergoing a punishment that has been laid out as the consequence of spitting. In order to regain his place in the classroom, Johnny must become a person who is not shameful. He needs to change who he is, to recreate himself so that he is no longer a child who spits on other children.

The first classroom, illustrative of Morris' guilt morality, corresponds to the view of human nature and human capacity for restoration in the final *sugya* of *Makkot*. The second classroom, illustrative of Morris' shame morality, corre-

107 Morris, *On Guilt and Innocence*, 60–62.

108 For one perspective on using the language of "choice" in relation to the punishment imposed by the adult, rather than in relation to the action that the child did, see Alfie Kohn, *Punished by Rewards: The Trouble with Gold Stars, Incentive Plans, A's, Praise, and Other Bribes* (Boston and New York: Houghton Mifflin, 1993) 238–39.

sponds for the most part to the view of Paul. But here is where we encounter a problem. The child in the second classroom, we have seen, needs to transform himself. In Morris' words, "Shame leads to creativity; guilt to restoration." Yet it is the first model, the model of *Makkot*, that embodies the notion of creativity, of human beings' ability to transform themselves and their destiny.[109] The restoration of the person who is liable for *karet* is dependent on creativity, on human interpretation and human action.

In contrast with the *Makkot* model, Paul's letters do not suggest the possibility of human beings recreating themselves. As scholars have noted, Paul does not talk about repentance.[110] The possibility of repentance is predicated on a person's capacity to change – or, alternatively, on the idea that sin does not attest to a person's true nature, that a person who has sinned can return to a pre-sin state. But Paul seems to assume an alternative view of human nature, a view that is largely deterministic. Once Johnny has spit, he has shown himself to be a spitter. For Paul, sin demonstrates human beings' essential sinfulness, and so there is no possibility of restoration short of entering into a wholly different existence predicated on different terms of salvation – terms that, it should be noted, need to be offered from the outside.[111] If sin attests to a sinful nature, then, according to Paul, human action cannot restore the person to a state of living before God.

What separates Paul from rabbinic Judaism, I have argued, is not his concern with the human propensity toward sin or the idea that human sinfulness poses a challenge to our ability to live before God. These concerns, in fact, are shared by Rabban Gamliel in our *sugya* and, I have suggested, underlie the teachings in our *mishnah*. The radical disjunction between Paul and rabbinic Judaism, rather, lies in the different answers offered in response to this problem. And, I am now suggesting, the different answers that are offered in the final *sugya* of *Makkot* and in the Pauline letters rest on different assumptions about human nature.[112]

109 Thus, as noted above, the citation in this *sugya* of a verse from Ezek 18 not only rejects the notion of children dying for the parents' sins (the explicit reason for the verse's citation) but also affirms the idea that each person determines his own nature and has the power to change it at any time (the fundamental theme of this chapter of Ezekiel).

110 See Schoeps, *Paul*, 187–88; George Foot Moore, *Judaism in the First Centuries of the Christian Era: The Age of the Tannaim* (3 vols.; Cambridge, Mass.: Harvard Univ. Press, 1959) 3:150–51; Sanders, *Paul*, 499–501.

111 See the discussion of Gal 3:20–22 and of Rom 10:3, above, and nn. 67 and 85.

112 With correspondingly different assumptions about the nature of law – Paul perhaps reflecting a natural law conception and rabbinic law being fundamentally positivist. (The issue of Paul and natural law is too complex to be addressed here; for a brief review, see Michael B. Crowe, *The Changing Profile of the Natural Law* [The Hague: Martinus Nijhoff, 1977] 52–57.) On a natural law conception as having natural consequences that do not admit to mitigation based on repentance or excuses, see Steinmetz, "Vineyard, Farm, and Garden: The Drunkenness of Noah in the Con-

Rabbinic Judaism's embracing of law – of *miṣvah*, human action, as the path to life – is intertwined with the idea of human self-determination. Paul's rejection of law is embedded in a deterministic view of human nature.[113]

"GUILT" AND "SHAME" IN *MAKKOT*

There is one more point that Morris makes that I think raises an intriguing feature of the *Makkot sugya*. In the first through fourth distinctions that he draws between the guilt and shame models in the passage quoted above, Morris works out the idea of a threshold, or a minimum demand, characterizing the guilt model, in contrast with a maximum, an ideal toward which one strives and in relation to which one can feel shame even if one merely fails to do the extraordinary. Clearly, the former correlates with a system based on law. As Morris says, "With guilt, one has either done wrong or not." A system of dos and don'ts allows one to measure clearly whether one has failed to do what one must do or has done what one is forbidden to do. The latter, in contrast, relates to ideal qualities or characteristics or modes of behaving, not to specific behaviors that one either must or must not do.[114]

Turning a final time to the *Makkot sugya*, it should be noted that, while I have presented Rabban Gamliel as crying in relation to the impossibility of doing *miṣvot*, the anecdote's place within the *sugya* suggests the need for a more com-

text of Primeval History," *JBL* 113 (1994) 193–207. On the idea that the rabbinic view of *miṣvot* is starkly positivist, and that rabbinic texts portray an awareness of this conception of law as contrasting with alternative, natural law conceptions (which apply to those not commanded at Sinai), see Steinmetz, "Crimes and Punishments, Part I" and "Crimes and Punishments, Part II." I hope to develop the idea of the positivist rabbinic conception of law as related to the idea of human freedom in future work.

113 It should be noted that, within Dead Sea texts, the standard sanction of expulsion from the community correlates with a deterministic view of human nature as well; see Shemesh, *ᶜOnšim veḥaṭaʾim*, 3 and 61–62. See n. 33, above, for the idea that expulsion is a realization of *karet* – thus, the sanction of expulsion represents the antithesis of the *mishnah*'s teaching about flogging reincorporating into the community the one who would be "cut off." For recent discussions of Paul's "anthropology" that emphasize Paul's deterministic view of human nature, see Timo Laato, *Paul and Judaism: An Anthropological Approach* (Atlanta: Scholars Press, 1995) and Timo Eskola, *Theodicy and Predestination in Pauline Soteriology* (Tübingen: Mohr Siebeck, 1998).

114 Note Paul's contrast in Gal 5:19–23 between the (negative) "works of the flesh" and the (positive) "fruit of the Spirit." The latter list consists entirely of virtues, that is, qualities that may inform behavior but that are not, in themselves, behaviors. The former, as Paul's category "works" implies, includes behaviors as well as qualities. (Some of the items in the list of "works of the flesh" are not simple to categorize as behaviors or qualities. See Longenecker, *Galatians*, 253 for this first list as including both singular and plural nouns and for the tendency of many scribes to recast the singular nouns in this list as plurals. Longenecker notes: "Greek abstract nouns are often, though not always, used in the plural to signify manifestations or demonstrations of the quality denoted in the singular, and thus to mean 'displays of' or 'actions expressing' that quality.")

plex reading. Rabban Gamliel is presented as crying in response to the passage from Psalm 15,[115] a passage that lists a series of general qualities – such as walking perfectly and acting justly – as well as a few specific actions that the person has desisted from doing – such as lending money with interest or taking a bribe against the innocent. The *sugya* presents Rabban Gamliel's response after a systematic interpretation of each characteristic of the righteous person described in the psalm. Notably, the interpretations of the specific behaviors elevate the demand well beyond the simple meaning of the scriptural passage. It is not enough not to take bribes (can one be considered righteous for simply desisting from violating this prohibition?!) or not to violate the biblical prohibition of lending with interest; the *gemara* offers illustrations that go beyond the requirements of the law, generating a portrait of the person who "dwells in God's tent" as a person who is righteous in the extreme.[116] It is then that the *sugya* interposes the story of Rabban Gamliel crying. Coming from the *gemara*'s reading of Psalm 15, we can indeed understand why Rabban Gamliel cries. The portrait offered by the psalm, along with the *gemara*'s elaboration of the attributes listed by the psalmist, offers a model of the righteous person that is impossible to emulate. If it is only *such* a person that "dwells in God's tent," then none of us can live before God.

The *sugya* has made a subtle and curious move. Rabbi Simlai's homily states that Moses was given 613 *miṣvot* but that a series of later figures reduced the number progressively. A reduction of the number of *miṣvot* can be seen as a reduction in the requirements that a person must fulfill.[117] But, in fact, the progressively smaller list of requirements are progressively more focused on broad attributes that the *gemara* identifies with mythically righteous figures and that seem impossible to aspire to. In a sense, the extended homily moves from Morris' minimalist model (though one that has 613 requirements) to his maximalist model (though it has only a single demand), from a threshold model in which one either has or has not obeyed the rules to a model in which one can only aspire to become more and more like the ideal person but in which one will always fall short. It is when this second model is introduced that the *gemara* presents Rabban Gamliel weeping with despair.

The situation is similar in the parallel passage about Rabban Gamliel crying in *b.Sanhedrin*. Ezekiel 18:10–12 is first cited in this passage in relation to the

115 See n. 119, below.

116 The *sugya*'s linking of several of these characteristic to mythically righteous figures of the biblical and rabbinic pasts, such as Abraham and Abba Ḥilqiyah, enhances the sense of the unachievability of the righteousness portrayed in the psalm – you would need to have the outstanding characteristics of Abraham *plus* of Abba Ḥilqiyah and of other such figures in order to fulfill the vision of the psalm!

117 See Rivan (R. Yehuda ben Natan), s.v. *veheᶜemidan ᶜal ʾaḥat ᶜesrei*.

mishnah's teaching about a person who violates more than one capital offence. The list of offences in the passage is first taken literally: *a shedder of blood* means a murderer; *his neighbor's wife he defiled* means that he has committed adultery; *to the idols he has lifted up his eyes* means that he is an idolater. A person who does these things, says Ezekiel, *shall not live; all of these abominations he has done; he shall surely die....* (18:13) But the *gemara* soon moves on to look at the verses in Ezekiel that describe the opposite person: *upon the mountains he did not eat, and to the idols of the house of Israel he did not lift up his eyes, and his neighbor's wife he did not defile, and a menstruating woman he did not approach... He is righteous; he shall surely live* (18:6, 9). Rav Aḥa beRabbi Ḥaninah offers an interpretation of each of the acts that Ezekiel describes the righteous person as not doing: *upon the mountains he did not eat* – that he did not eat through the merit of his ancestors; *and to the idols he has not lifted up his eyes* – that he did not walk with an upright [haughty] posture; *and his neighbor's wife he did not defile* – that he did not infringe upon his neighbor's trade; *and a menstruating woman he did not approach* – that he did not benefit from the charity fund.[118]

It is at this point that the anecdote about Rabban Gamliel crying appears. And, indeed, it is really only at this point that it makes sense. It would not be at all difficult to imagine someone who keeps all the laws that the *gemara* has cited from the Ezekiel passage – someone who neither murders, nor commits adultery, nor worship idols.[119] It is only after the introduction of Rav Aḥa's homily, which transforms the idea of the righteous person who achieves life from one who keeps the rules to one who meets lofty aspirations of personal con-

118 This interpretation might well be based on the idea that one cannot be righteous simply by desisting from doing the (particularly egregious) sins listed in this verse (see next note). In addition, the Ezekiel passage soon goes on to list positive behaviors that could well be seen as markers of a righteous person – such as clothing the naked and doing true justice (18:7–8) – so perhaps the interpretation is partially motivated by a quest to see these first elements in the passage as similarly describing positive behaviors that define a person as righteous.

119 Naeh, "Why Did Rabban Gamliel Cry?" notes the difficulty of seeing Rabban Gamliel as despairing in relation to this biblical passage. In fact, Naeh notes, in a parallel to the final *mishnah* of *Makkot* in *Sifre Devarim* 286, Rabbi cites the Ezekiel passage and comments on it – "But what did he do?!" (that is, he merely desisted from sinning) – leading to the conclusion that one who desists from sinning is rewarded as if he had fulfilled a *miṣvah*. Rabbi's reading of the passage fits well with Ezekiel's list of ways in which one desists from sin and highlights the lack of fit between Rabban Gamliel's despair and the Ezekiel passage, according to the passage's plain meaning. Thus, Naeh argues that the anecdote about Rabban Gamliel crying could not originally have been told in relation to the Ezekiel passage (he makes a similar argument in relation to the Psalms passage, which also appears in the *Sifre* parallel); see n. 59, above. My goal here, it should be noted, is not to reconstruct the original anecdote about Rabban Gamliel crying in relation to a biblical passage, but rather to understand the anecdote as it appears within the *Bavli sugyot*. Naeh, in contrast, describes the anecdote's placement within the extended Rabbi Simlai homily in *b.Makkot* as "*bediᶜavad*." See next note.

duct, that it makes sense for Rabban Gamliel to weep in despair.

In both the *Makkot* and *Sanhedrin* passages, then, the *gemara* introduces the story of Rabban Gamliel weeping only once there has been a shift from a focus on specific laws that one must obey to a focus on broad qualities that shape a righteous person's behavior. In Morris' terms, each of these *sugyot* shifts from a guilt morality to a shame morality. Rabban Gamliel's despair over the impossibility of achieving life, then, is expressed not in relation to the plenitude of law but in relation to a maximalist demand of righteous behavior.

More specifically, in the *Makkot sugya* the anecdote about Rabban Gamliel interrupts the flow of Rabbi Simlai's extended homily. It appears at the moment after Rabbi Simlai has made the initial shift from a focus on *miṣvot*, the element that links this homily to the *mishnah*, to a focus on qualities of personal conduct. The anecdote hovers between the two poles of the homily – the minimalist, guilt model and the maximalist, shame model. The interpretation that I offered earlier reads the anecdote in relation to the minimalist pole; on this reading, Rabban Gamliel despairs of the possibility of fulfilling all of the *miṣvot*. But we might alternatively read the anecdote in relation to the maximalist pole; on this reading, it is in relation to the aspiration to be perfectly righteous that Rabban Gamliel sees everyone as necessarily failing.

Rabbi Akiva's response, too, can be read in relation both to the *mishnah*'s teaching about *miṣvot* and to the conclusion of Rabbi Simlai's homily. The first of these readings, which is the one that I have been working with up to now, sees Rabbi Akiva's response as entirely consistent with Rabbi Ḥananiah ben Gamliel's teaching in the *mishnah* about gaining life through the performance of even a single *miṣvah*. The alternative reading sees Rabbi Akiva's response as anticipating the conclusion of the homily, the reduction of the *miṣvot* to a single quality. Let's take each of these readings of Rabbi Akiva's teaching in turn and see how it can fit as a response to Rabban Gamliel's despair, recalling that we have just offered two different understandings of the cause of Rabban Gamliel's despair, as well. We will begin with our initial understanding of R. Akiva's teaching.

If we read Rabban Gamliel as crying because of an acute awareness that there is no person who does not sin, then Rabbi Akiva is saying that one achieves life nonetheless through the performance of even a single *miṣvah*. This is the reading that I developed earlier, a reading that situates both Rabban Gamliel and Rabbi Akiva squarely within the "guilt" pole of the *sugya*. And, as discussed earlier, it is the paradoxical nature of Rabbi Akiva's teaching and of Rabbi Ḥananiah ben Gamliel's similar teaching in the *mishnah* that necessitates a mechanism for undoing the consequences of sin, such as the mechanism described in the first teaching of the *mishnah*, the teaching that flogging undoes the consequences of an act that could cut one off.

If, though, we understand Rabban Gamliel's crying in relation to the *sugya*'s shift to a maximalist/shame model, then we might read Rabbi Akiva as forcing a shift back to the minimalist/guilt model. It is as if Rabban Gamliel is working with a model in which no one is ever good enough, and Rabbi Akiva responds with a model in which, though you can't be a perfect human being, you *can* be good enough. Indeed, the suggestion that the performance of even one *miṣvah* is sufficient can be seen as a hyperbolic affirmation of a minimalist model in response to the extreme maximalism suggested by the portrait of the righteous person in Psalm 15, as elaborated by the *gemara*.[120]

On the other hand, as I just suggested, Rabbi Akiva's response itself can be read in relation to the conclusion of Rabbi Simlai's homily. While Rabbi Akiva's claim about "even by means of *one* of them" echoes the teaching of the *mishnah* about one who performs even *one miṣvah*, it also resonates with the end of the extended homily, in which a prophet comes and reduces all of the *miṣvot* to just *one* quality. If we read Rabbi Akiva's response to Rabban Gamliel as anticipating the culmination of Rabbi Simlai's homily, then Rabbi Akiva is affirming the aspirational, maximalist model toward which the homily has been moving, the model which, on our new reading, has precipitated Rabban Gamliel's despair. Nevertheless, even within this model, Rabbi Akiva is suggesting, righteousness is within reach of the human being.

The question that I am raising is how do we read the tradition about Rabban Gamliel's weeping and Rabbi Akiva's response within the context of the *sugya* in which it appears. While Rabban Gamliel weeps in response to different biblical passages in *Makkot* and in *Sanhedrin*, in both cases he weeps in response to a passage that has just been presented in the *gemara* as aspiring to the extraordinary, within a larger *sugya* that begins as a discussion about law. In *Makkot*, the situation is even more complicated, because Rabbi Akiva's response resonates both with the minimalist teaching of the *mishnah* about *miṣvot* and with the climax of the homily about the reduction of *miṣvot* to maximalist principles or qualities. The shift within the *sugya*, the place of the anecdote in the middle of the homily, and the echo of Rabbi Akiva's statement with both the "one" of the *mishnah* and the "one" at the end of the homily raise intriguing questions

120 It goes without saying that the readings of the *sugya* that I am offering approach the *sugya* synchronically, that is, as an integrated literary unit in which the interplay of the parts may be read as generating significance independent of the textual histories of those parts. From such a perspective, we can speak of Rabban Gamliel's despair in relation to the *gemara*'s elaboration of the Psalms passage quoted in the Rabbi Simlai homily, whether or not the anecdote about Rabban Gamliel originated in relation to the passage from Psalms and granting, of course, that the *gemara*'s elaboration of this passage postdates Rabban Gamliel by hundreds of years. That is, I am asking neither (the historical question) "why did Rabban Gamliel cry" nor (the source-critical question) "in relation to what biblical passage did the original version of the story portray Rabban Gamliel crying" but, rather, "what is the meaning of Rabban Gamliel's despair and Rabbi Akiva's response within the context of the *Bavli sugya* on the final *mishnah* of *Makkot*."

of interpretation and call into question a reading of the *sugya* that focuses too exclusively on law as the path to living before God.

Perhaps, ultimately, we should not choose between the alternative interpretations of the cause of Rabban Gamliel's despair and the meaning of Rabbi Akiva's response that I have just laid out. Perhaps, rather, we should read the multiple resonances of this anecdote as complementing each other, highlighting the problems and promises of a religious life that is grounded in specific actions and yet that accepts the challenge of aspiring to moral perfection.

The anecdote about Rabban Gamliel weeping and Rabbi Akiva's response to his despair hovers between the "guilt" and "shame" poles of the *sugya*, between the *mishnah*'s teachings about performing *miṣvot* (along with Rabbi Simlai's teaching about the great number of *miṣvot*) and the ending of the extended homily of Rabbi Simlai about the progressive reduction of *miṣvot* and the attendant transformation to a focus on an aspirational model of religious life. I have suggested that the thrust of the final *mishnah* and *sugya* affirms a vision in line with Morris' description of a "guilt morality," with its assertion of human responsibility, freedom, and self-determination. The Rabbi Simlai homily, though, introduces a maximalist, aspirational perspective, and the appearance of the Rabban Gamliel anecdote in the middle of the homily highlights the challenges that this perspective poses to the person who would live before God. The resonance of Rabbi Akiva's teaching with both poles of the *sugya* suggests, perhaps, that the fundamental belief in human self-determination – in *miṣvah*, human action, as the path to life – makes living before God possible even within the impossibly maximalist view of the religious life.

The Economics of Jewish Childhood in Late Antiquity

Amram Tropper
Ben-Gurion University

Jewish children in late antiquity lived in a pre-industrial agrarian society in which the household served as the primary unit of both production and consumption. Children were active participants in the strategies families developed to maintain and care for their members as well as beneficiaries of their household economy. The current inquiry seeks to contribute to the study of Jewish children and childhood in late antiquity by exploring numerous ways in which household economics influenced the lives of children and contributed to the construction of ideas of childhood. By analyzing the economic setting, the structure of the average Jewish family, the costs and benefits of rearing children, the beating of children, the distribution of food within the family, child minding, formal education, professional training, marriage and parent-child tensions, I have constructed a model of childhood rooted in household-economics. I compare the features of this model to contemporary features of the Graeco-Roman world in order to ascertain the ways in which Jewish childhood was similar or different to the portrait of childhood which emerges from the evidence left by other groups in the Roman Empire.

Jewish children in late antiquity lived in a pre-industrial agrarian society in which the household served as the primary unit of both production and consumption.[1] Children were active participants in the strategies families developed to maintain and care for their members as well as beneficiaries of this household economy. The economic function of the family certainly lost some of its prominence with the coming of the industrialization, specialization and urbanization of modernity,[2] but in the pre-industrial economy of late antiquity, producing the means of subsistence for its members still functioned as a central and vital role of the family. In light of the important function of the household economy in the ancient Jewish setting, the current inquiry seeks to contribute to the study of Jewish children and childhood in late antiquity by exploring the many ways in which household economics influenced the lives of children and contributed to the construction of ideas of childhood.

1 See Jack Goody, *The European Family: An Historico-Anthropological Essay* (Oxford: Blackwell, 2001) 2; Miriam Peskowitz, "Family/ies in Antiquity: Evidence from Tannaitic Literature and Roman Galilee Architecture," in S. J. D. Cohen, ed., *The Jewish Family in Antiquity* (Atlanta: Scholars Press, 1993) 31–34.

2 See Michael Mitteraeur and Reinhard Sieder, *The European Family* (Oxford: Blackwell, 1982) 78.

Sources and Methodology

The sources for the study of Jewish life in late antiquity consist of actual remains of the past preserved in situ and literary works that were copied and transmitted over time.[3] In this article, I seek to illuminate the economics of Jewish childhood in late antiquity by exploring the wealth of information relating to Jewish social history contained within one literary corpus transmitted over the centuries, namely rabbinic literature. Scholars today agree that rabbinic texts should not to be taken at face value since the laws and ethos they prescribe may not have been widely practiced or shared[4] and the stories they tell are often fictitious. Nonetheless, rabbinic texts have much to reveal about childhood in antiquity. The rabbis were embedded within the social and economic reality of their times and therefore their texts inevitably reflect this ambient environment.[5] Regardless of the ideological dimensions of rabbinic literature, inadvertent comments and implicit presuppositions in rabbinic texts often shed light on the broader social reality of late antiquity. In addition, rabbinic texts convey their authors' explicit ideals and expectations in reference to children. Many of the ideas and values expressed in rabbinic literature were probably limited to the educated rabbinic elite, but scholars now recognize that rabbinic literature also preserves folk elements and popular literary motifs that appar-

3 Social scientific approaches, which compare ancient Jewish culture and society to other cultures and societies, offer important insights into Jewish life but do not depend on any additional sources from the ancient Jewish world.

4 The manifest overlap between rabbinic law and the practices of the Jews attested in legal documents found in the Judean desert demonstrate, however, that rabbinic law was intimately related to more popular Jewish practices and should not be viewed entirely as a creation of the rabbis themselves. See Hayim Lapin, "Maintenance of Wives and Children in Early Rabbinic and Documentary Texts from Roman Palestine," in C. Hezser, ed., *Rabbinic Law in its Roman and Near Eastern Context* (Tübingen: Mohr Siebeck, 2003) 191; Martin Goodman, "Josephus and Variety in First-Century Judaism," *Proceedings of the Israel Academy of Sciences and Humanities*, 7:6 (2002) 208–13; Goodman, "Josephus, the Pharisees and Ancestral Tradition," *JJS* 50 (1999) 17–20; Hannah M. Cotton, "The Rabbis and the Documents," in M. Goodman, ed., *Jews in a Graeco-Roman World* (Oxford: Oxford Univ. Press, 1998) 167–79.

5 The social and economic status of the rabbis is still a matter of dispute amongst scholars. While Hezser supported Urbach's view that Palestinian *tannaim* and *amoraim* came from all levels of society, others have argued that the rabbis emerged as an urban elite during the early third century. See Catherine Hezser, *The Social Structure of the Rabbinic Movement in Roman Palestine* (Tübingen: Mohr-Siebeck, 1997) 23–36; Martin Goodman, *State and Society in Roman Galilee, A.D. 132–212* (Totowa, N.J.: Rowman and Allanheld, 1983) 93; Hayim Lapin, "Rabbis and Cities in Later Roman Palestine: The Literary Evidence," *JJS* 50 (1999) 187–207; Hayim Lapin, "Rabbis and Cities: Some Aspects of the Rabbinic Movement in its Graeco-Roman Environment," in Peter Schäfer and Catherine Hezser, eds., *The Talmud Yerushalmi and Graeco-Roman Culture* (3 vols.; Tübingen: Mohr-Siebeck, 2000) 2:51–80; Michael L. Satlow, *Jewish Marriage in Antiquity* (Princeton and Oxford: Princeton Univ. Press, 2001) 20.

ently represented the ideas of a far larger segment of the Jewish population.[6] Consequently, though rabbinic literature was produced by an educated elite, it nonetheless illuminates the ambient social reality of late antiquity and, at times, it expresses popular norms and common conceptions representative of a wider Jewish population. When exploring a topic such as children and childhood, one should be attentive to the possibility that rabbinic texts may reflect popular notions of childhood (a possibility that is strengthened by the presence of similar notions amongst other contemporary groups), while seeking to delineate the dimensions of childhood in rabbinic literature that appear to be distinctively rabbinic.

The earliest rabbinic composition, the Mishnah, was edited in Palestine during the early third century C.E. though it includes much earlier material. The latest rabbinic compositions of Palestinian provenance regularly cited in this study were edited in the fifth century, though these texts also include earlier material. Due to the span of time covered by this corpus, it is tempting to try to reconstruct a history of social change or development, a diachronic account of the economics of childhood in the early centuries of the Common Era. For the most part, however, the nature of the evidence precludes such an attempt. As Richard Saller noted in a related context, "To trace change in social relations with confidence requires a series of comparable evidence over time. The uneven preservation of material from antiquity largely frustrates the historian's search for a time series of evidence of tolerable quality."[7] For our purposes, rabbinic literature simply does not provide sufficient evidence of changing social patterns over time and therefore a diachronic approach seems for the most part unpromising. Instead, a synchronic approach that stresses continuities over time and constructs a heuristic model of the economics of childhood shows more potential. Indeed, the reliability of this model is strengthened by the likelihood that the Jewish household-economy did not undergo drastic transformations during this period.

Geographically, the primary focus of this paper is Roman-Byzantine Palestine and accordingly the bulk of rabbinic sources cited below emerged within

6 See Galit Hasan-Rokem, *Web of Life, Folklore and Midrash in Rabbinic Literature*, trans. Batya Stein (Stanford: Stanford Univ. Press, 2000). Even though rabbis, and especially those in Babylonia, may have sought to distance themselves from their non-rabbinic neighbors (see Richard Kalmin, *The Sage in Jewish Society of Late Antiquity* [London and New York: Routledge, 1999] 5–14), they were still intimately familiar with the ambient social and cultural setting, or as Hasan-Rokem put it, they "were concerned with the comprehensive ethnographic recording of their culture" (Hasan-Rokem, *Web of Life*, 2). See also n. 4.

7 Richard P. Saller, *Patriarchy, property and death in the Roman Family* (Cambridge: Cambridge Univ. Press, 1994) 4. See also Mark Golden, *Children and Childhood in Classical Athens* (Baltimore and London: Johns Hopkins Univ. Press, 1990); compare Sarah B. Pomeroy, *Families in Classical and Hellenistic Greece: Representations and Realities* (Oxford: Clarendon Press, 1997) 1–16.

this locale. However, one contemporary rabbinic composition edited outside of Palestine also appears repeatedly in my analysis and it serves as a secondary focus of this inquiry. The Babylonian Talmud, which includes earlier materials but was redacted only in the sixth or seventh century C.E., was produced by rabbis in Sassanian Persia and reflects a Jewish community living in an overarching political and cultural climate quite unlike that of Roman Palestine. Thus when unattested in Palestinian sources, social phenomena adduced from the *Bavli* may be said to represent a Jewish community outside of Palestine and the Roman Empire. However, since the *Bavli* also contains literary materials that originated in Palestine, at times it can be employed to corroborate or strengthen a portrait independently derived from Palestinian sources. In short, although the *Bavli* must be handled with care, it serves important corroborative and comparative purposes.

In illuminating the nature of Jewish household economics and the texture of Jewish childhood(s), cross-cultural comparisons to Graeco-Roman society and other similar pre-industrial societies are deployed below. The value of these external sources is threefold: the similarities to rabbinic texts help confirm the plausibility of a claim otherwise based on Jewish sources; the information provided by these sources help fill in lacunae when the Jewish evidence turns up short;[8] and the Graeco-Roman evidence, at least, depicts the overarching socio-economic, political and cultural environment within which Jews of the Roman Empire lived.

The Economic Setting[9]

The vast majority of people in under-developed pre-industrial agrarian societies, such as that of Roman Palestine, lived at or near subsistence levels.[10] Whether in cities, towns or small villages, most people worked in agriculture and only a small elite (probably not more than ten percent of the population in the Mediterranean basin) could live off the food surplus.[11] Food in the Mediterranean consisted primarily of cereals in porridge or bread form, dry legumes, olives,

8 See Satlow's valuable articulation (*Jewish Marriage*, xxv) of these methodological issues.

9 For a helpful bibliography and an insightful analysis of the state of scholarly discussion regarding the economic setting of Palestine in late antiquity, see Philip A. Harland, "The Economy of First-Century Palestine: State of the Scholarly Discussion," in Anthony J. Blasi, Jean Duhaime and Paul-Andre Turcotte, eds., *Handbook of Early Christianity: Social Science Approaches* (Walnut Creek, Calif.: Alta Mira Press, 2002) 511–27.

10 See Peter Garnsey, "The Land," in Alan K. Bowman, Peter Garnsey and Dominic Rathbone, eds., *The High Empire, A.D. 70–192*, CAH 11 (2nd ed.; Cambridge: Cambridge Univ. Press, 2000) 679; Peter Garnsey and Richard Saller, *The Roman Empire: Economy, Society and Culture* (Berkeley and Los Angeles: Univ. of California Press, 1987) 43.

11 See Peter Garnsey, *Food and Society in Classical Antiquity* (Cambridge: Cambridge Univ. Press, 1999) 23–25; Jack Pastor, *Land and Economy in Ancient Palestine* (London and New York: Routledge, 1997) 10–11; Michael Avi-Yonah, *The Jews Under Roman and Byzantine Rule* (Jerusalem:

grapes and other assorted fruits. Meat was rarely eaten and most large animals were primarily kept for farm work.[12] Large-scale industry was not usually a viable alternative to agriculture and most non-agricultural goods were produced at home or by local artisans. Industry was also severely handicapped by the limited technology of the time, the absence of an entrepreneurial class and the great risks and costs involved in long-distance trade. Long-distance trade in surplus produce and commodities certainly existed,[13] but local trade, often performed by the producing and consuming households themselves, was a more pervasive element in the commercial life of cities and towns.[14] In short, the average household strove to provide food, shelter and clothing for its members with self-sufficiency (rather than export) as an ideal if unobtainable goal; for wealthy aristocrats, land was the most steady, secure and prestigious investment.

The fate of the average family in Roman Palestine was dependent on its ability to produce food in a region plagued with food crises.[15] Drought was a familiar if not frequent occurrence and other natural disasters such as crop diseases and outbreaks of pestilence often threatened these ancient agriculturalists. A farmer left part of his crop-land fallow in order to replenish the fertility of the soil and thereby reduced the size of his productive land. In a similar vein, the Sabbatical year would have been a daunting challenge for those who did not work the land during its course.[16] Wars, bandits and other disturbances were also bound to diminish productivity and deprive a farmer of his crops.[17] Eking a minimal subsistence out of the land was therefore no small affair and in order

---

Magnes Press, 1984) 20–21; Bruce J. Malina and Richard L. Rohrbaugh, *Social Science Commentary on the Synoptic Gospels* (Minneapolis: Fortress Press, 1992) 7.

12 See Peregrine Horden and Nicholas Purcell, *The Corrupting Sea: A Study of Mediterranean History* (Oxford: Blackwell Publishers, 2000) 175–230; Garnsey, "The Land," 681, 688–89; Ze'ev Safrai, *The Economy of Roman Palestine* (London and New York: Routledge, 1994) 104–214; Gildas Hamel, *Poverty and Charity in Roman Palestine: First Three Centuries* C.E. (Berkeley, Los Angeles and Oxford: Univ. of California Press, 1990) 8–29; J. David Schloen, *The House of the Father as Fact and Symbol: Patrimonialism in Ugarit and the Ancient Near East* (Winona Lake, Ind.: Eisenbrauns, 2001) 100–104.

13 See Safrai, *The Economy*, 429; Ze'ev Safrai, "The Influence of Demographic Stratification on the Agricultural and Economic Structure during the Mishnaic and Talmudic Periods," in A. Kasher, A. Oppenheimer and U. Rappaport, eds., *Man and Land in Eretz Israel in Antiquity* (Jerusalem: Yad Izhak Ben Zvi, 1986) 22 (Heb.); Seth Schwartz, "Historiography on the Jews in the 'Talmudic Period' (70–640 CE)," in Martin Goodman, ed., *The Oxford Handbook of Jewish Studies* (Oxford: Oxford Univ. Press, 2002) 93–95; W. V. Harris, "Trade," in Bowman, *The High Empire*, 710–13.

14 See Garnsey and Saller, *The Roman Empire*, 43–44; Hayim Lapin, *Economy, Geography, and Provincial History in Later Roman Palestine* (Tübingen: Mohr Siebeck, 2001) 113–22, 138; Malina and Rohrbaugh, *Social Science Commentary*, 8.

15 See Hamel, *Poverty*, 44–52; Peter Garnsey, *Famine and Food Supply in the Graeco-Roman World: Responses to Risk and Crisis* (Cambridge: Cambridge Univ. Press, 1988) 272.

16 See David A. Fiensy, *The Social History of Palestine in the Herodian Period* (Lewiston: Mellen, 1992) 5–6.

17 See Jack Pastor, *Land and Economy*, 2–3, 57–58 (and references in n. 26).

to reduce the risks posed by an unreliable environment, subsistence farmers in antiquity sought to disperse their landholdings, diversify their produce and store the surplus.[18]

Although subsistence farmers aimed for self-sufficiency and not profits, the production of a food surplus was of tremendous importance. A surplus could be used to purchase goods that a family did not produce and a stored surplus might help offset future shortfalls. Farmers could pay taxes or repay their debts with surplus produce, and if they were tenants, they could cover their rents.[19] In short, subsistence farmers not only needed to produce enough food to meet the dietary demands of their families, they needed to produce enough to buy necessary items, to cover taxes and rents, and to repay debts. Surplus in the form of taxes and rents also sustained the urban-based elites who consumed most of it and invested the rest.[20]

In filling the gap left over by agriculture, many households would have complemented their agricultural activity with non-agricultural economic activities

18 See Garnsey, *Famine and Food Supply*, 271; Horden and Purcell, *The Corrupting Sea*, 201–9. Our evidence for the location of individual ancient Jewish landholdings is quite minimal, but it stands to reason that Jewish farmers with sufficient means would have sought to acquire land in different locations. The *Bavli* (*B.Meṣ.* 107a) reports that the Palestinian *amora* R. Yoḥanan recommended that a farmer divide his holdings between cereals, olives and vines, and *Lev. Rab.* 30:1 (ed. M. Margulies [repr.; New York and Jerusalem: Maxwell Abbell Publication Fund and The Jewish Theological Seminary of America, 1993. Jerusalem: Qeren Yehudah Leib u-Mini 'Epsḥtayn, 1953–60] 688–89) relates a story in which the very same R. Yoḥanan notes that he had once owned a field, an olive orchard and a vineyard (see Daniel Sperber, *The City in Roman Palestine* [New York and Oxford: Oxford Univ. Press, 1998] 190–91; S. Applebaum, "Economic Life in Palestine," in S. Safrai, et al., eds., *The Jewish People in the First Century: Historical Geography, Political History, Social, Cultural and Religious Life and Institutions* [2 vols.; Assen/Maastricht and Philadelphia: Van Gorcum and Fortress Press, 1974–76] 2:651; Shimon Dar, "Agriculture and Agricultural Produce in Erez-Israel in the Roman-Byzantine Period," in A. Kasher, et al., eds., *Man and Land in Eretz Israel in Antiquity* [Jerusalem: Yad Izhak Ben Zvi, 1986] 144 [Heb.]). In a similar vein, an analysis of the farmland in western Samaria suggests that the average family farm consisted roughly of 52 percent grains, 25 percent olives, 22 percent vines, ten to fifteen head of sheep and one or two head of cattle (Dar, "Agriculture"). By diversifying, families not only sought to accommodate their varied needs, but they minimized the farm's dependence on any single crop (see also Pomeroy, *Families*, 142). In respect to storage, the archaeological remains of ancient homes as well as our literary sources indicate that surplus produce and other valuable goods were stored within the home (S. Safrai, "Home and Family," in Safrai, *The Jewish People in the First Century*, 2:732, 743–74; Yizhar Hirschfeld, *The Palestinian Dwelling in the Roman Byzantine Period* [Jerusalem: Franciscan Printing Press and Israel Exploration Society, 1995] 27, 50, 264; Pomeroy, *Families*, 33).

19 See Garnsey, *The Roman Empire*, 51–52; Keith Hopkins, "Taxes and Trade in the Roman Empire (200 B.C.–A.D. 400)," *JRS* 70 (1980) 104; Hamel, *Poverty*, 142–63.

20 See Garnsey, *The Roman Empire*, 44–45; Garnsey, *Food and Society*, 33; Hopkins, "Taxes and Trade," 122.

such as trade, manufacturing or construction.[21] This non-agrarian sector of the economy would have been stronger in settlements with larger populations and markets, and the commercialized sector of the economy would have probably been centered on cities.[22] Although the role of agriculture was of equal importance in the lives of most city or village dwellers, urbanites would have had easier access to larger markets, superior services and a wider network of social and economic relations.[23] The commercial lives of the cities would have also been strengthened by their role in the overarching imperial economy.[24] One small group of urbanites, the wealthy elites, would not have actually produced food or commodities, but rather on the basis of their legal claims to rents and taxes, they would have derived their maintenance and wealth from the exploitation of productive farmlands around the city.[25]

The elites and altogether about a third of the population in Roman Palestine lived in cities.[26] The rest, and therefore the bulk of the population, lived in towns and small villages.[27] The population in Palestine increased during the late Roman and Byzantine periods and at its height the land probably contained about a million inhabitants of which approximately a quarter were Jewish.[28] The peace that reigned for much of this period, the intensification and specialization in agriculture, the development of new industry and the growing emphasis on export enabled this population increase. Urbanization went hand in hand with a larger population and cities were instrumental forces in the commercial world which helped maintain the population. In other words, demographic pressures created financial pressures which in turn led to the pursuit of new avenues for economic growth. The growing economic success of the period might lead one to think that families of this period enjoyed a higher standard of living as Palestine became more urbanized and commercialized, but rabbinic sources

21 See David J. Mattingly and John Salmon, eds., *Economies Beyond Agriculture in the Classical World* (London and New York: Routledge, 2001) 4. Hopkins, "Taxes and Trade," 101–25.

22 Lapin, *Economy*, 5.

23 Safrai, *The Economy*, 430; Garnsey, *The Roman Empire*, 56; Lapin, *Economy*, 119; Hamel, *Poverty*, 30–43.

24 Hopkins, "Taxes and Trade," 101–16. (One need not assume, however, that the imperial economy was well integrated.)

25 Garnsey, *The Roman Empire*, 44–49; Horden and Purcell, *The Corrupting Sea*, 205–8.

26 See Magen Broshi, "The Population of Western Palestine in the Roman-Byzantine Period," *BASOR* 236 (1979) 5.

27 See Safrai, "Home and Family," 728; Yuval Portugali, "The Settlement Pattern in the Western Jezreel Valley," in Kasher, *Man and Land in Eretz Israel*, 13–14 (Heb.).

28 See Portugali, "The Settlement Pattern," 7–19; Broshi, "The Population of Western Palestine," 1–10; Broshi, "Demographic Changes in Ancient Eretz-Israel: Methodology and Estimates," in Kasher, *Man and Land in Eretz Israel*, 49–56 (Heb.); Lawrence E. Stager, "The Archaeology of the Family in Ancient Israel," *BASOR* 260 (1985) 5.

indicate otherwise. Many Jews apparently experienced the economic pressures of the time while being unable to translate the fruits of their labors into a higher standard of living.[29] Urbanization, population growth, intensification, specialization and access to imperial trade routes indicate that Palestine experienced aggregate economic growth. However, the absence of extensive technological innovations suggests that productivity (or per capita growth) was only moderately enhanced.[30]

This short sketch of the ancient economy portrays some central features of the economic setting in Roman Palestine. The average Jew was a subsistent farmer who desired self-sufficiency while only a small minority of Jews amassed wealth and joined the local elite. In Babylonia as well, most Jews worked the land and strove to be self-sufficient. Babylonia was considered a highly fertile region in ancient sources and the Sassanians invested heavily in a sophisticated irrigation system.[31] As in Palestine, much of the surplus production in Babylonia went towards rents and taxes. Babylonian Jews also engaged in manufacturing and commerce alongside agriculture, and the Tigris and Euphrates rivers served as important trade routes akin to Roman roads and Mediterranean sea-lanes.[32] In addition, Babylonia apparently also underwent a process of urbanization in the third century C.E.[33] However, it bears noting that unlike their counterparts in the Roman Empire, Babylonian Jews were not integrated into the overarching commercial community of the Roman Empire[34] and the political and social order they inhabited was quite unlike that in the west.[35]

Although my primary interest in this article revolves around the economic dimension of the family, we should keep in mind that households in the

29 See Safrai, "The Influence of Demographic Stratification," 20–48; Safrai, *The Economy*, 436–58; Doron Bar, *Changes in the Rural Population of Palestine and its distribution from the Bar-Kokhba Revolt to the Arab Conquest* (Ph.D. diss.; Jerusalem: Hebrew Univ., 2001) (Heb.).

30 See Garnsey, *The Roman Empire*, 51–63; Richard Saller, "Framing the Debate over Growth in the Ancient Economy," in W. Scheidel and S. von Reden, eds., *The Ancient Economy* (Edinburgh: Edinburgh Univ. Press, 2002) 251–69.

31 See Jacob Neusner, *A History of the Jews in Babylonia: I. The Parthian Period* (Leiden: E. J. Brill, 1969) 1–3; Isaiah Gafni, *The Jews of Babylonia in the Talmudic Era: A Social and Cultural History* (Jerusalem: Zalman Shazar, 1990) 130–31 (Heb.). On the perception of the fertility of Palestine in the ancient world see Pastor, *Land and Economy*, 177 n. 56.

32 See Moshe Beer, *The Babylonian Amoraim: Aspects of Economic Life* (Ramat-Gan: Bar Ilan Univ., 1982) 15, 158 (Heb.); Gafni, *The Jews of Babylonia*, 133. Though it has been suggested that commerce formed the primary economic activity amongst Jews in Babylonia, our sources imply that agriculture reigned supreme (Beer, *The Babylonian Amoraim*, 23) and comparisons to other preindustrial economies indicate the same.

33 Beer, *The Babylonian Amoraim*, 57; Jacob Neusner, *A History of the Jews in Babylonia: II. The Early Sassanian Period* (Leiden: E. J. Brill, 1966) 10–12; Kalmin, *The Sage in Jewish Society*, 7–14.

34 See Safrai, "The Influence of Demographic Stratification," 21.

35 See Gafni, *The Jews of Babylonia*, 126–27.

ancient world were not purely rational economic organizations designed to maximize productivity. Though economic considerations were of great importance in family decisions, social status, cultural expectations and other non-economic considerations also influenced these decisions.[36] In other words, the household sought to employ its resources in order to efficiently attain its goals, but these goals were not purely monetary.[37] Thus in constructing a model of childhood in light of the ancient Jewish household economy, I focus on financial considerations but evaluate these considerations alongside ancient social norms and cultural expectations.

One highly significant cultural dimension of the ancient Jewish household economy was the idea of the patrimony, the ancestral-land (*naḥalah*) which every generation of the family was supposed to maintain and then pass on to the next generation. In biblical times, the patrimony was an "essentially inalienable piece of land possessed solely by a gentilic unit, whether large or small; hence, this land could not, at least in theory, be sold to any would-be purchaser, and its transfer from one owner to another could only be effected through inheritance."[38] In practice, of course, many families lost their patrimonies due to factors such as financial pressures, hostile political forces and exile, but the portrayal of Naboth's unwillingness to sell his plot to Ahab attests to the strength and importance of the patrimony ideal amongst ancient Israelites.[39] Landholding families sought to preserve their patrimonies at all costs since, in a certain sense, the patrimony did not really belong to them. Rather, the patrimony was considered the property of a much larger timeless family which extended far into the past and indefinitely into the future. Current landholders were therefore viewed simply as the contemporary custodians of the patrimony.[40]

The ideology of the patrimony not only flourished during the ancient past, but it continued to persist into the rabbinic period.[41] The following description of a dramatic custom is just one of the rabbinic texts which illustrates the importance of the patrimony in rabbinic eyes.

> When a person sold his patrimony, his relatives would bring barrels and fill them with parched grains and nuts, and break them before children. And the children would gather them up and say, "So and so has been cut off from his patrimony." And when he brought it back (literally:

36 See M. Finley, *The Ancient Economy* (Berkeley, Los Angeles and London: Univ. of California Press, 1999) with Ian Morris's important foreword.

37 See Jon Elster, *The Cement of Society: A Study of Social Order* (Cambridge: Cambridge Univ. Press, 1989).

38 Stager, "The Archaeology of the Family," 22.

39 See 1 Kgs 21; Stager, "The Archaeology of the Family," 23.

40 See Pastor, *Land and Economy*, 18, 169. See also Pomeroy, *Families*, 141.

41 See Fiensy, *The Social History*, 7–15.

returned it), they would do likewise and say, "So and so has returned to his patrimony.[42]

Even if this custom was a creation of the rabbinic imagination, the description of the custom testifies to the importance of the patrimony for the rabbis. The smashing of the barrels symbolized perhaps the break with the past the patrimony seller's relatives wished to address and the subsequent declaration indicates that the selling of the patrimony was considered a betrayal of the family in its broadest sense. Perhaps then the high profile of the children in this ceremony would have served to evoke in the seller the realization that the selling of his patrimony was a betrayal of his future descendents since it deprived them of their rightful inheritance.

It bears stressing, however, that the continued importance of an ideology of patrimony in the rabbinic period does not mean that Jews in Roman Palestine worked tribal lands which had actually been owned by their own families since biblical times. In the wake of exile, invasions, famines, debts and the redistribution of the land by political forces, Jews in Palestine undoubtedly were removed from their tribal lands long before late antiquity.[43] In a related vein, Hayim Lapin argues that even the farming of ordinary (non-tribal) patrimonies presupposes a long-term stability of both kinship structures and practices of property distribution yet the extent that land changed ownership in

42 *Y.Qidd.* 1:5 60c (Daniel Sperber, trans., *Roman Palestine: 200–400: The Land*, 174–75 [152 n. 32]). See also *y.Ketub.* 2.10 26d; compare *b.Ketub.* 28b. The very same ceremony is ascribed to a man who married an unsuitable woman and this alternative setting is presented immediately after the text cited here. The juxtaposition of these two settings for the ceremony emphasizes that in both cases the ceremony addresses a betrayal of the family. (Compare this ceremony to the Greek custom of showering nuts, fruits and assorted foods on wives and slaves when they entered their new home (Pomeroy, *Families*, 71; Cheryl Anne Cox, *Property, Marriage Strategies, and Family Dynamics in Ancient Athens* [Princeton, N.J.: Princeton Univ. Press, 1998] 191 n. 109); to the Roman custom of scattering nuts at a wedding (Beryl Rawson, *Children and Childhood in Roman Italy* [Oxford: Oxford Univ. Press, 2003] 84); and to the Jewish custom of throwing assorted food before a bride and groom at a wedding (Nissan Rubin, *The Joy of Life: Rites of Betrothal and Marriage in the Talmud and Midrash* [Tel-Aviv: Hakibutz Hameuchad, 2004] 200–215 [Heb.]; Daniel Sperber, *Minhagei Yisrael* [7 vols.; Mossad Harav Kook: Jerusalem, 1989–2003] 4:150–56 [Heb.]. Moshe Benovitz has suggested to me that perhaps the custom described here never actually existed but was an anachronistic application of wedding/divorce traditions to historical "wedding/divorce" from land). Perhaps due to the importance of social status in Babylonia or owing to the absence of a *naḥalah* ideology in Babylonia, the *Bavli* does not mention the patrimony selling setting and refers only to the unsuitable marriage setting (compare Shalom Albeck, "The History of the Modes of Acquisition in the Talmud," *Bar-Ilan* 9 [1972] 263–64). Parenthetically, it is worth noting that children are portrayed here as the custodians of the collective memory of the group in that they ensure that the ceremony will be remembered long into the future.

43 Daniel Sperber's conservative estimation is that true tribal properties, as opposed to ordinary patrimonies, did not exist by the end of the Second Temple period (*Roman Palestine*, 174 n. 49).

ancient Palestine is actually unknown.[44] Although the strong attachment to the patrimony found in rabbinic literature[45] suggests that a small landholder in Roman Palestine may have viewed his privately owned land as an inheritance from the ancient past, it is unlikely that many patrimonies would have remained in the same family for centuries on end.[46]

Moreover, from as early as the monarchic period in ancient Israel and down through the Roman period, it is thought that much and perhaps most of the land in Palestine was owned by the crown and wealthy aristocrats.[47] On the basis of rabbinic literature, however, Daniel Sperber disagrees and argues that much of the Jewish population in Palestine owned its own land during the first two centuries of the Common Era. Only from the third century onwards, he argues, did the majority of farmers become tenants on the estates of powerful overlords.[48] Although later rabbinic sources certainly seem to portray a gloomy picture in comparison to earlier sources as Sperber argues, it is questionable whether the evidence of the earlier sources actually indicates that a majority of the Jews in Palestine were private landholders. Josephus never states that most Jews worked their own privately held lands; the Gospels seem to reflect a situation in which the elites already controlled much of the land during the first century C.E.;[49] and tannaitic assumptions regarding landholding may not be representative of Jewish society as a whole. These assumptions may portray an idealized abstraction[50] or may simply reflect the concerns of a landed rabbinic class.[51] In truth, we actually do not know what proportion of the land was owned by free peasants[52] and the gloomy picture in later sources may be the

44 See Lapin, *Economy*, 2–5.

45 See references in Sperber, *Roman Palestine*, 179 n. 49.

46 Consider also Martin Goodman's argument on the diminution of family plots due to the successive division of the plots by more than one heir (Martin Goodman, *The Ruling Class of Judaea: The Origins of the Jewish Revolt Against Rome A.D. 66–70* (Cambridge: Cambridge Univ. Press, 1987) 61–62; Pastor, *Land and Economy*, 7–8).

47 See Pastor, *Land and Economy*, 9, 13 n. 1, 21, 170.

48 See Sperber, *Roman Palestine*, 3–6, 135. See also Avi-Yonah, *The Jews*, 21.

49 See Douglas E. Oakman, "Cursing Fig Trees and Robbers' Dens: Pronouncement Stories Within Social-Systemic Perspective in Mark 11:12–24 and Parallels," *Semeia* 64 (1993) 258–63. See also Fiensy, *The Social History*, 60.

50 See Jacob Neusner, *The Economics of the Mishnah* (Chicago and London: Univ. of Chicago Press, 1990) 51–53. Consider the similar state of affairs in Xenophon's *Oeconomicus* where the *oikos* is generally presented as based on landed wealth though Xenophon recognizes the existence of non-landed occupations as well (Xenophon, *Oec.* 6.13–14; Cox, *Household Interests*, 131).

51 See Neusner, *The Economics*, 136; Hayim Lapin, *Early Rabbinic Civil Law and the Social History of Roman Galilee: A study of Mishnah Tractat Baba' Mesia'* (Atlanta, Georgia: Scholars Press, 1995) 232–41; Seth Schwartz, *Imperialism and Jewish Society 200 B.C.E. to 640 C.E.* (Princeton and Oxford: Princeton Univ. Press, 2001) 113, 160.

52 See Applebaum, "Economic Life," 656.

product of the pressures created by the urbanization and population growth of the period.[53] Though we may not assume that most Jews owned land during the Roman period, cultural traditions regarding patrimony nonetheless continued to resonate.[54] In addition, it seems fair to say that regardless of ownership, the average plot was small and run by a family.[55]

The Familial Setting

The average family was part of an overarching household which was defined rather broadly in the Graeco-Roman world. The Greek *oikos*, for example, was comprised of father, mother, children, slaves and property[56] and the Roman *domus* included the house, father, mother, children, slaves, freedmen, freedwomen, more distant relatives, boarders and friends.[57] Similarly, the householder in rabbinic literature is the *baal habayit*, the master of the house "who manages and controls the personnel and property of the house."[58] The presence of non-kin household members, such as slaves, must have had important ramifications for home life in general and the lives of children in particular.[59]

53 See Safrai, "The Influence of Demographic Stratification," 48 n. 100. It has also been suggested that climactic changes led to famines in the middle decades of the third century (Günther Stemberger, *Jews and Christians in the Holy Land: Palestine in the Fourth Century*, trans. R. Tuschling [Edinburgh: T & T Clark, 2000] 14), though Bar argues that the supposed evidence for an economic decline in the third century stratum of rabbinic literature is unconvincing and does not differ significantly from the evidence of other strata (Bar, *Changes in the Rural Population*, 165–77). See also Schwartz, "Historiography," 93.

54 See Pastor, *Land and Economy*, 169.

55 "By and large, agricultural plots in later Roman Palestine tended to be small . . . the distribution of land plots plausibly has been associated with a pattern where the unit of production was something like the household farm (whatever the structure of that household)" (Lapin, *Economy*, 103). See Lapin's references in n. 74 and Shimon Dar, "Agriculture and Agricultural Produce," 144–48; Sperber, *Roman Palestine*, 4–5; Applebaum, "Economic Life," 656; Pastor, *Land and Economy*, 8–10. Though some scholars question whether we can truly ascertain the size of the average agricultural plot in Roman and Byzantine Palestine (M. Broshi, "Agriculture and Economy in Roman Palestine According to Babatha's Papyri," *Zion* 55 [1990] 280 [Heb.]; Pastor, *Land and Economy*, 9), there seems to be no reason to doubt that many small landholders and tenant farmers developed small plots suitable for a household farm.

56 See W. K. Lacey, *The Family in Classical Greece* (Ithaca, N.Y.: Cornell Univ. Press, 1968) 15–16; Pomeroy, *Families*, 23–33; Cox, *Household Interests*, 130–215.

57 Thomas Wiedemann, *Adults and Children in the Roman Empire* (New Haven and London: Yale Univ. Press, 1989) 143; Suzanne Dixon, *The Roman Family* (Baltimore and London: Johns Hopkins Univ. Press, 1992) 11; Keith R. Bradley, *Discovering the Roman Family: Studies in Roman Social History* (New York and Oxford: Oxford Univ. Press, 1991) 9–10; Garnsey, *The Roman Empire*, 128. On the word *familia* see Dixon, *The Roman Family*, 2–3.

58 Neusner, *The Economics*, 51–69. See also Catherine Hezser, *The Social Structure of the Rabbinic Movement*, 310–11; Satlow, *Jewish Marriage*, 20–21.

59 Garnsey, *The Roman Empire*, 128.

For the purposes of the current discussion, however, let us consider the nature of the family (in our modern sense), that is the matrix of kin relatives which populated this household.

Certain scholars assume that the Jews of Roman Palestine lived primarily in homes inhabited by their extended families. As S. Safrai put it, "the extended family often lived together in one house, including the father and the families of his married sons."[60] The extended family, however, does not consistently fulfill a clearly defined role in rabbinic law and in its stead, the nuclear family, consisting of a conjugal couple with their children, pervades rabbinic law. On the basis of this and other considerations, other scholars have concluded that the nuclear family was the standard family in the Jewish home of the rabbinic period.

It has also been argued that the extended family served as the primary Jewish family structure in previous eras and that the demise of the extended family went hand in hand with the weakening of ties between small landholders and the land. This shift has been dated alternatively to the rise of the monarchy in ancient Israel,[61] to the early Second Temple period[62] and to the Hellenistic and Roman periods.[63] Population increase, growing urbanization, persecution, heavy taxes and the division of patrimonies in inheritance have all been adduced as factors which decreased the ties of the small landholders to the land and enhanced the role of the nuclear family.[64] Indeed, it has even been suggested that the rise of the nuclear family in the early rabbinic period is the Jewish counterpart to the high profile of the Roman nuclear family during the first few centuries of the Common Era.[65]

In truth, the developmental scheme in which the extended family in an ancient agrarian context makes way for the urban nuclear family is familiar from other fields as well. Greek historians used to argue that the historical society of the polis was preceded by a society based on clans (that is, extended families), Roman historians viewed the extended family run by the *paterfamilias*

60 Safrai, "Home and Family," 732. See also Dar, "Agriculture," 144.

61 See discussion and critique in S. Bendor, *The Bet-Ab in Israel from the Settlement to the End of the Monarchy: The Social Structure of Ancient Israel* (Israel: Oranim, Poalim and Hakibutz Hameuchad, 1986) 11, 40, 81–82 (Heb.).

62 E. E. Urbach, "Inheritance Laws and after-life," *Fourth World Union of Jewish Studies* (1967) 1:133–41 (Heb.).

63 See Nissan Rubin, "For Whom Does One Mourn? A Sociological Analysis of Talmudic Sources," *Bar Ilan* 10 (1972) 111–22 (Heb.); Rubin, *The End of Life: Rites of Burial and Mourning in the Talmud and Midrash* (Israel: Hakibutz Hameuchad, 1997) 11–22, 87–102 (Heb.); Fiensy, *The Social History*, 121–46.

64 See Urbach, "Inheritance Laws"; Rubin, "For Whom Does One Mourn?"; Ze'ev Safrai, "Family Structure during the Period of the Mishna and the Talmud," *Milet* 1 (1983) 129–56; John Cooper, *The Child in Jewish History* (Northvale, N.J. and London: Jason Aronson Inc., 1996) 58–70.

65 See Adiel Schremer, *Male and Female He Created Them: Jewish Marriage in Late Second Temple, Mishnah and Talmud Periods* (Jerusalem: Zalman Shazar, 2003) 336–38.

as the predecessor to the nuclear family and social scientists employed an abstract evolutionary model of family history which posited the shift from extended to nuclear family structures.[66] However, this evolutionary view of family history has been convincingly refuted and I attempt to demonstrate elsewhere why the extended family was never the average type of family in the ancient Jewish world.[67] Echoing demographic studies of other societies, I argue that the high mortality rate along with virilocal residence (and a relatively late average age of first marriage for Jewish men in Roman Palestine) ensured that three generations of a family would have only lived together in a home for a limited period of time.[68] In addition, the high child mortality rate made a family with more than two adult children uncommon[69] and if, on average, at least one of the family's adult children was female, it is clear that most families would not have produced two married brothers to live together. Thus, the notion that Jews in antiquity usually lived in large, multi-generational families composed of co-resident married brothers is demographically impossible.[70]

In place of the large extended family, the average family was apparently comprised of four to five members[71] and was more closely related to the model of the nuclear family as it progressed through the life-course. Typically, the family was nuclear (married couple and children), sometimes with an aged (grand) parent, and would change as its children grew up and left for work or marriage.[72] In addition, due to high mortality rates, divorce and remarriage, many complex variations on the nuclear family were bound to appear. Thus, most Jewish families in late antiquity, as in earlier eras, were variations on a nuclear

66 See Cynthia B. Patterson, *The Family in Greek History* (Cambridge, Mass. and London: Harvard Univ. Press, 1998) 5–26.

67 See Amram Tropper, "Children and Childhood in Light of the Demographics of the Jewish Family in Late Antiquity," *JSJ* 37 (2006) 299–343.

68 See Mitterauer, *The European Family*, 34; Stager, "The Archaeology of the Family," 20; compare Bendor, *The Bet-Ab*, 82–84. In places such as Babylonia where the average age of first marriage for men was around twenty, the average period in which three generations could have lived together would have been longer than in places like Palestine and the Western Diaspora where the average age of first marriage for men was closer to thirty. On ages of first marriage for men and women, see Schremer, *Male and Female*, 73–125; Satlow, *Jewish Marriage*, 40, 105–9; Rubin, *The Joy of Life*, 35–72; G. H. R. Horsley, ed., *NewDocs* 4 (1987) 221–27.

69 Tim Parkin, *Demography and Roman Society* (Baltimore and London: Johns Hopkins Univ. Press, 1992) 112; Stager, "The Archaeology of the Family," 18–20.

70 See Mitterauer and Sieder, *The European Family*, 24–47.

71 See Nathan Schur, "The Numerical Relationship between the Number of Households and the Total Population in the Cities of Eretz Israel During the Ottoman Period," *Cathedra* 17 (1980) 102–6 (Heb.); Israel Finkelstein, "A Few Notes on Demographic Data from Recent Generations and Ethnoarchaeology," *PEQ* 122 (1990) 47–52; Stager, "The Archaeology of the Family," 18–20.

72 See Dixon, *The Roman Family*, 6; Bradley, *Discovering the Roman Family*, 156–76; Ross S. Kraemer, "Jewish Women in the Diaspora World of Late Antiquity," in Judith R. Baskin, ed., *Jewish Women in Historical Perspective* (2nd ed.; Detroit: Wayne State Univ. Press, 1998) 61.

theme.[73] Nonetheless, it bears stressing that extended families certainly existed even though they were not the norm.[74] Moreover, values such as filial piety and laws that bolstered patriarchal authority demonstrate that even though elderly grandparents were not all that common, their cultural weight and legal status were not in proportion to their numbers.

The Costs and Benefits of Raising Children

In light of the above description of the economic function of the household, let us consider the role of the young child in this ancient setting. First and foremost, since the family was the locus of production, children worked far more in antiquity than they do in modern western countries. Adults had heavy workloads and children were employed to lessen this burden.[75] Children would not have been able to work in jobs which demanded a great deal of strength, yet they were nonetheless involved in agriculture and a wide variety of handicrafts and services. They fulfilled household and domestic chores, worked in fields and shops, served as messengers, and purchased and sold goods.[76] In cities, the diversified urban economy would have offered more financial opportunities for children than the predominantly agricultural work available in rural areas.[77] Some of these forms of child labor would have been important for the direct contributions made to household income, while others would have been valued for the time they freed up for other family members who were involved in the primary production of food.[78] In short, the average Jewish household in late antiquity needed every able-bodied worker it could enlist in order to ensure that it would remain a viable economic entity.

In *b.Mo^ced Qaṭ.* 24b one finds two rabbinic traditions which may shed further

73 On the serial marriages and complex families of Josephus, Berenice and Babatha, see Ross S. Kraemer, "Typical and Atypical Jewish Family Dynamics: The cases of Babatha and Berenice," in David L. Balch and Carolyn Osiek, eds., *Early Christian Families in Context: An Interdisciplinary Dialogue* (Grand Rapids, Mich.: Eerdmans, 2003) 142–45.

74 See Roger S. Bagnall and Bruce W. Frier, *The Demography of Roman Egypt* (Cambridge: Cambridge Univ. Press, 1994) 63; Dixon, *The Roman Family*, 7–8.

75 See Beatrice B. Whiting and Carolyn P. Edwards, *Children of Different Worlds: The Formation of Social Behavior* (Cambridge, Mass.: Harvard Univ. Press, 1988) 101–2.

76 In reference to the Roman world in general see Bradley, *Discovering the Roman Family*, 144; Wiedemann, *Adults and Children*, 153–57. Rabbinic sources corroborate the Roman portrait of the working child and assume that children worked in various fields. See, for example, *m.ᶜErub.* 3:2, *m.Giṭ.* 5:7; *m.B.Meṣ.* 7:6, *t.Giṭ.* 3:12; *t.Maᶜaś.Š.* 4:9, *y.Maᶜaś.Š.* 4:2 51b.

77 See Beryl Rawson, "Adult-child Relationships in Roman Society," in Beryl Rawson, ed., *Marriage, Divorce, and Children in Ancient Rome* (Canberra and Oxford: Humanities Research Centre and Clarendon Press, 1992) 28.

78 See Mark Golden, *Children and Childhood in Classical Athens* (Baltimore and London: The Johns Hopkins Univ. Press, 1990) 32.

light on the economic role of children in antiquity. Though these traditions are attributed to Palestinian sages, they are not found in Palestinian sources and therefore perhaps express the sentiments of Babylonian sages.

> And what is the rule in respect of making lamentation for them? R. Meir in the name of R. Ishmael says: In the case of the poor lamentation is made for a child of three and in the case of the rich for a child of five. R. Judah speaking in his [R. Ishmael's] name says: With the poor [they make a lament] for children of five; with the rich for children of six.[79]

Although the specific ages in these two traditions attributed to R. Ishmael vary, the poor consistently are said to lament for a child deemed too young to be lamented by the rich. The poor already lament a child of three while the rich only start to lament a child of five, or the poor lament a child of five while the rich only begin to lament at six.[80] Commentators agree that poor parents lament very young children because the tragedy of a child's death is considered more severe for them than for wealthy couples. They differ, however, on pinpointing the precise rationale underlying this class difference.[81] Rashi, for example, suggested that since the poor lack other sources of joy, they mourn their deceased children more than the wealthy mourn theirs and R. Joseph ibn Ḥaviva argued that the poor come to love their children more than the rich since they suffer hunger and starvation to feed their children.[82] I would like to suggest that the likely importance of child labor amongst the poor would have engendered a high valuation of even very young children in impoverished families.[83] The great demands placed on an impoverished family would have required its children to start working as soon as humanly possible and consequently the young child was of more financial value to a poor family than to its wealthy

79 Trans. H. M. Lazarus (London: The Soncino Press, 1938). Compare rabbinic notions to the Roman practice of gradually increasing the mourning period for children between ages three and ten (see Rawson, *Children and Childhood*, 104).

80 Compare *Sem.* 3:4 where the ages differ but the poor also lament for younger children than do the rich.

81 See Shlomo Josef Zevin, ed., *Talmudic Encyclopedia* (26 vols.; Jerusalem: Talmudic Encyclopedia Publishing, 1947–2004) 9:610.

82 See Rashi s.v. *ʿaniyim* and *Nimmuqe Yosef* on Alfasi, 17b (on the identity of the author of this commentary, see Yaakov S. Spiegel, "*Nimmuqe Yosef* by Rabbi Joseph Haviva," *Sidra* 4 [1988] 135–38) (Heb.).

83 For a similar position, see the manuscript attributed to Rashi, s.v. *ʿaniyim* (Efraim Kupfer, ed., *R. Salomon Izhaqi: Commentarius in tractum Moʿed Qatan* [Jerusalem: Mekize Nirdamim, 1961] 78–79. See also Adiel Schremer, "On the Commentaries of Moʿed Qatan Attributed to Rashi," in Daniel Boyarin, et al., eds., *Atara L'Haim* [Jerusalem: Magnes Press, 2000] 534–54 [Heb.]). On the possibility that even very young children, including children under five years old, are able to work, see, for example, Bradley, *Discovering the Roman Family*, 115–16; Russell Freedman and Lewis Hine, *Kids at Work: Lewis Hine and the Crusade Against Child Labor* (New York: Clarion Books, 1998) 2; Whiting, *Children of Different Worlds*, 101.

counterpart which had the leisure to delay the child's initiation into the work force to a much later date.[84] The immediate financial loss incurred by the death of a child as well as the long-term loss of a potential family worker meant that the financial repercussions of the death of a very young child was felt most strongly amongst the poor. Thus, perhaps the different lamentation practices noted above do not reflect different levels of sentimentality amongst the poor and the wealthy, but rather different levels of economic dependency on children. The poor, who were heavily dependent on child labor, were said to lament even very young children while the rich, who were not dependent on child labor, only were thought to lament older children whom they apparently considered more developed persons and worthy of lamentation. Lamentation, in other words, was linked to economic dependency only amongst families that needed their children to be productive.

For the truly wealthy who did not depend on child labor, the economic contribution of young children to the family was probably not of significance. While children in poorer families emerged rather quickly into adulthood since the labor demands placed upon them would have introduced them to the adult world at a relatively young age, the young children of the wealthy would have had the luxury of a relatively work-free childhood. Thus, from the young child's perspective, one's family's economic status would have been a critical factor in determining the extent to which one spent one's days laboring strenuously, performing simple chores, studying or playing. From the parents' perspective, the economic well-being of the family would help determine whether a child was viewed primarily as a costly economic necessity or as a luxury item (akin to a "pet"), desired primarily for its companionship or other non-economic functions.[85]

The flipside of the financial benefits a family accrued through the labor of its children was the costs of raising these children. The rabbis viewed the raising of children as a terrible burden[86] and referred to "the pain of rearing children."[87] The Bible limited Eve's physical punishment to a painful pregnancy and childbirth, yet the rabbis saw fit to expand Eve's punishment to include "the pain of rearing children" which denotes financial costs amongst other things.[88] Similarly,

84 See Rawson, "Adult-Child Relationships in Roman Society," 28; Bradley, *Discovering the Roman Family*, 116.

85 See Wiedemann, *Adults and Children*, 26.

86 See, for example, *Gen. Rab.* 45:4 (eds. J. Theodor and Ch. Albeck [repr.; Jerusalem: Shalem, 1996. Berlin: M. Poppeloyer, 1903–36] 451); *y. Taᶜan.* 2:2 65b–c (*b. Taᶜan.* 16a; *b. Yebam.* 63a).

87 See, for example, *Gen. Rab.* 20:6 (Theodor-Albeck, 190) and *Lamentations Rabbah, Petiḥta* 24 (ed. S. Buber [repr.; Tel-Aviv: s.n., 1967. Vilna: Romm, 1899]) 27; *b. Šabb.* 89b. More generally, earning a living was said to be more difficult than the splitting of the Red Sea (*Gen. Rab.* 97:3 [Theodor-Albeck, 1245; compare *b. Pesaḥ.* 118a]) and the *Bavli* claimed that it was more painful than childbirth and redemption (*b. Pesaḥ.* 118a).

88 See *Gen. Rab.* 20:16 (Theodor-Albeck, 190; *b. ᶜErub.* 100b); Judith R. Baskin, *Midrashic Women:*

the rabbis argued that the children of Merab bore Michal's name since Michal raised them.[89] Psalm 77, according to a statement attributed to R. Eleazar, refers to the "children of Jacob" as "the children of Joseph" because though Jacob begot them, Joseph supported and sustained them. Halakhic texts discuss the possibility that a father might starve or steal in order to feed his children (and slaves) and it seems likely that these hypothetical legal cases actually reflect a dire social reality in which some fathers were driven to take these extreme measures in order to maintain their families.[90] In sum, the cost of raising children in the ancient world was quite substantial and was probably considered onerous by the majority of the population, who were living at or near subsistence levels. As a position attributed to R. Eleazar the son of R. Simeon declared, "it is easier to raise a legion of olives in Galilee than a child in the land of Israel."[91]

The costs and benefits of children for the family are significant not only because they illustrate the economic role of the young child in the family, but because they enhance our understanding of the economic factors involved in the decision to beget and raise children. In the short-term, the introduction of a child into a family had both costs and benefits. The family would have to feed an additional mouth as well as expend its limited resources on caring for and raising the new family member. However, the family would also benefit from the labor of the new addition whose contributions to the household income would increase as the child grew. In weighing these short-term costs and benefits, scholars reason that the costs generally outweighed the benefits and children, on average, consumed more than they produced. As Clark Nardinelli put it, the "consensus from the development literature, then, is that throughout history children have not been profitable investments in agricultural societies."[92] Thus, the economic welfare of the family in the short-term did not serve as an incentive for having children and, moreover, it probably served as a severe disincentive among impoverished Jewish families. Some Jewish families were so poor that they could not afford to maintain their children and in such cases, families might have tried to limit the number of their offspring through various means such as contraception, abortion, exposure, infanticide or the selling of their children into slavery.[93] However, while Greek philosophers such

---

Formations of the Feminine in Rabbinic Literature (Hanover and London: Brandeis Univ. Press, 2002) 74–79.

89 See *y.Sanh.* 6:7 23d; (compare *b.Sanh.* 19b where this reasoning is also applied to Moses and Obed son of Ruth).

90 See *t.B.Qam.* 10:21; *t.B.Meṣ.* 8:2.

91 See *Gen. Rab.* 20:6 (Theodor-Albeck, 190).

92 Clark Nardinelli, *Child Labor and the Industrial Revolution* (Bloomington and Indianapolis: Indiana Univ. Press, 1990) 48.

93 On exposure see, for example, *m.Qidd.* 4:2; *m.Mak.* 2:7; *t.Mak.* 1:8 (ed. M. S. Zuckermandel [repr.: Jerusalem: Wahrmann, 1963. Passewalk, Germany: Yiśśakhar Yiṣḥaq Me'ir, 1880] 674); *Gen. Rab.* 51:1 (Theodor-Albeck, 532); (*b.Qidd.* 73a–b). On sterilization as contraception, see *t.Yebam.* 8:4;

as Plato and Aristotle allowed and even recommended infant exposure under certain circumstances, rabbis and other Jewish intellectuals condemned exposure and infanticide.[94]

In truth, however, the economic factors involved in the decision to raise a child were not limited to short-term costs and benefits alone but included long-term considerations as well. Most important of these considerations was the hope that a family's offspring would live a long life and thereby serve the family's financial interests in the future. These future interests consisted primarily of the support of elderly family members and the transmission and redistribution of family wealth through inheritance and dowry.[95] In light of these long-term benefits, Alison James, Chris Jenks and Alan Prout note that from "the point of view of each household, survival and prosperity depended on maximizing the number of children and optimizing their productive activity."[96] Since children in the ancient world worked and were generally not furnished with an expensive education, the long-term intergenerational wealth flow favored the parents and therefore justified maximizing the number of children.

In respect to the redistribution of wealth, the family sought to transmit its property and wealth to the next generation much as it sought to perpetuate itself through biological reproduction.[97] Hence families with property or other

---

(*b.Yebam.* 65a) (Judith Hauptman, *Rereading the Rabbis: A Woman's Voice* [Boulder, Colorado and Oxford: Westview Press, 1998] 131–38). On the enslavement of children, see *t.B.Bat.* 7:3; *y.B.Bat.* 8:8 16b; (*b.B.Bat.* 127b). On the exposure and sale of children more generally, see Adele Reinhartz, "Philo on Infanticide," *SPhilo* 4 (1992) 42–58; Lapin, "Maintenance of Wives and Children," 142–45, 183; C. Hezser, "Slaves and Slavery in Rabbinic and Roman Law," in C. Hezser, ed., *Rabbinic Law in its Roman and Near Eastern Context* (Tübingen: Mohr Siebeck, 2003) 142–45; Hezser, "The Exposure and Sale of Infants in Rabbinic and Roman Law," in K. Herrmann, M. Schlüter and G. Veltri, eds., *Jewish Studies Between the Disciplines/Judaistik zwischen den Disziplinen* (Leiden and Boston: Brill, 2003) 3–28; V. Vuolanto, "Selling a Freeborn Child: Rhetoric and Social Realities in the Late Roman World," *Ancient Society* 33 (2003) 169–207; Daniel R. Schwartz, "Did the Jews Practice Infant Exposure and Infanticide in Antiquity?" *SPhilo* 16 (2004) 61–95.

94 See Schwartz, "Did the Jews Practice Infant Exposure," 63–64.

95 See Saller, *Patriarchy*, 155, 224; Nardinelli, *Child Labor*, 36–57. On the dowry in Jewish circles see Adiel Schremer, *Male and Female*, 216–80.

96 Allison James, Chris Jenks and Alan Prout, *Theorizing Childhood* (Cambridge: Polity Press, 1998) 117.

97 See Peskowitz, "'Family/ies' in Antiquity," 20–21. Peskowitz also notes that the functional notion of the family in which families exist in order to transmit family holdings and pedigree is somewhat circular. From an evolutionary perspective, however, the function of the family is more complex. The family is a mechanism "designed" to help propagate people just as, in a certain sense, people and other organisms are mechanisms "designed" to propagate genes (see Linda A. Pollock, *Forgotten Children: Parent-Child Relations from 1500 to 1900* [Cambridge: Cambridge Univ. Press, 1983] 33–43; R. Dawkins, *The Selfish Gene* [London: Oxford Univ. Press, 1976]). The family thus enhances the reproductive success of its members and the selective advantages of many features of family life, such as caring for children and ensuring their success in future life by teaching them trades and bequeathing them inheritances, are readily apparent. However, there is no reason to interpret all aspects of family life only in terms of their adaptive significance since

wealth desired children in order to create heirs to the family inheritance.[98] Methods existed in rabbinic and Roman law to bequeath one's property to non-family members, but the dominating role of family members in biblical and rabbinic inheritance laws and stories indicate that inheritances usually remained within the Jewish family.[99] As R. Akiva is reported to have said, "a father endows his son with beauty, strength, wealth, wisdom and years"[100] and as R. Yoḥanan is said by the *Bavli* to have stated in the name of R. Simeon b. Yoḥai, "The Holy One blessed be He, is filled with anger against any one who does not leave a son to be his heir."[101] Thus children and particularly boys were valued as potential heirs,[102] while the dowry given to daughters served as an alternative channel of wealth redistribution (especially in Babylonia where dowries were quite substantial).[103]

In respect to the support of elderly family members, it bears stressing that most parents in antiquity would not have had enough resources to pay for care or support in their old age and children were viewed as the solution to this serious problem. Graeco-Roman sources indicate that children were widely viewed as a parental investment in their future well-being[104] and certain rabbinic sources also articulate this long-term economic role of children.[105]

---

more proximate levels of causation involving social and cultural forces can easily complement the explanations of ultimate causation offered by evolutionary theory. Moreover, many features of family life, such as adoption for example, may not necessarily have any selective advantages (see Steven J. Gould and R. C. Lewontin, "The Spandrels of San Marco and the Panglossian Paradigm: A critique of the Adaptationist Programme," *Proceedings of the Royal Society of London, B*, 205 [1979] 581–98).

98 See Dixon, *The Roman Family*, 24; Rawson, *Children and Childhood*, 108.

99 For a similar state of affairs in Roman life, see Dixon, *The Roman Family*, 26. In reference to rabbinic laws, see Reuven Yaron, *Gifts in Contemplation of Death in Jewish and Roman Law* (Oxford: Clarendon Press, 1960); Joseph Rivlin, *Inheritance and Wills in Jewish Law* (Ramat-Gan: Bar-Ilan Univ. Press, 1999).

100 *M.ᶜEd.* 2:9.

101 *B.B.Bat.* 116a (trans. I. W. Slotki [London: The Soncino Press, 1935]).

102 The overriding preference for male sons in rabbinic literature is due, at least in part, to the fact that inheritance passed primarily through male progeny (see L. J. Archer, *Her Price is Beyond Rubies: The Jewish Woman in Graeco-Roman Palestine* [Worcester, England: Sheffield Academic Press, 1990] 17–29).

103 See Schremer, *Male and Female*, 265–71. On the possibility of bestowing gifts in contemplation of death to daughters, see Hauptman, *Rereading*, 184–87.

104 Tim Parkin, "Out of Sight, Out of Mind: Elderly Members of the Roman Family," in Beryl Rawson and Paul Weaver, eds., *The Roman Family in Italy: Status, Sentiment, Space* (Canberra and Oxford: Humanities Research Centre and Clarendon Press, 1997) 123–25; Pomeroy, *Families*, 193–94.

105 For example, *y.Qidd.* 1:7 61a states that just as fathers endow their sons with five qualities (beauty, strength, wealth, wisdom and years), sons are required in turn to supply their fathers with food, drink, clothing, shoes and care. In a similar vein, R. Eliezer interpreted a dream in which the lintel in the dreamer's house was broken to mean that the dreamer will have a son who shall serve as her lintel, that is, take care of her (*y.Maᶜaṣ.Ṣ.* 4:6 55c [Roger Brooks, *The Talmud of the Land*

In *Gen. Rab.* 36:7[106] we hear that while in the ark (and prohibited from sexual relations), Noah was disturbed that he did not have a young son to take care of him in his old age. Moreover, later on when Ham castrated his father, Noah once more rued that he would not have a young son care for him in his old age. Similarly, the following halakhic text from the *Bavli* demonstrates not only that some rabbis viewed children as a form of insurance for a parent's old age, but that they were willing to take uncharacteristically strong legal measures on behalf of this principle.

> Now, what is the decision?[107] Come and hear what R. Aḥa b. Ḥanina stated in the name of R. Abbahu in the name of R. Assi: Such a case once came before R. Yoḥanan at the Synagogue of Caesarea, and he decided that the husband must divorce her and also pay her the amount of her *kethubah*. Now, if it be suggested that a woman is not subject to the commandment, how could she have any claim to a *kethubah*? It is possible that this was a case where she submitted a special plea; as was the case with a certain woman who once came to R. Ammi and asked him to order the payment of her *kethubah*. When he replied, "Go away, the commandment does not apply to you," she exclaimed, "What shall become of a woman like myself in her old age!" "In such a case," the Master said, "we certainly compel [the husband]."
>
> A woman once came [with a similar plea] before R. Naḥman. When he told her, "The commandment does not apply to you," she replied, "Does not a woman like myself require a staff in her hand and a hoe for digging her grave!"[108] "In such a case," the Master said, "we certainly compel [the husband]."[109]

In the latter two stories cited here, rabbis, supposedly from both Palestine and Babylonia, uncharacteristically compel the termination of barren marriages at the request of wives who desire children to care for them in their old age. In the final story, the wife not only expects her child to care for her, but also to bury her when she passes away. Thus, these rabbinic sources apparently reflect the widespread expectation, shared by Jews, Greeks and Romans, that children would

---

of Israel: Maaser Sheni (Chicago and London: Univ. of Chicago Press, 1982) 145–46]). Compare Gerald Blidstein, *Honor Thy Father and Mother: Filial Responsibility in Jewish Law and Ethics* (New York: Ktav, 1975) xi–xii, 10.

106 Theodor-Albeck, 341.

107 The Talmud is answering the question of whether a woman is obligated to procreate.

108 The woman's argument is that she needs children to maintain her during her lifetime and then bury her when she dies.

109 *B. Yebam.* 65b (trans. I. W. Slotki, London: *The Soncino Press*, 1936). Compare *y. Yebam.* 6:6 7d and see Hauptman's discussion, *Rereading*, 132–38.

take care of their parents as they aged and after they died. Yet, a broader analysis of rabbinic discussions of filial piety reveals that even if the rabbis recognized this instrumental dimension of parental expectations, rabbinic discourse highlighted the religious dimension of filial piety, viewing it as "a shaping, directing value that contributes to the meaning of life in society."[110]

In contrast to the short-term economic disincentives for having children, the potential for children to inherit family patrimonies and their role as insurance for their parents' old age would have served as strong incentives for bearing children. These factors, however, would not have assumed a constant level of importance within different sectors of the population. Many poor couples would not have needed to produce heirs since they would not have had much of an inheritance to transmit while very rich couples might have had sufficient wealth to purchase sustenance and care in their old age so that they would not need children as care-takers.[111] In addition, although the high mortality rate in late antiquity probably ensured that only a small percentage of (inheriting) males would ever reach maturity, small landholders might still have sought to limit the number of their offspring so as not to divide their patrimony amongst too many heirs and thereby lower the family's socio-economic status.[112] Yet despite these economic reasons to limit the number of children in a family, it nonetheless appears that the overall financial benefits of child-bearing to the household, namely additional labor, the production of caretakers for elderly household members and the creation of heirs for the family fortune, usually would have been considered sufficient compensation for the costs of raising children.

Let us turn now to other aspects of the experience of childhood influenced by economic factors. The beating of children by parents and teachers was common in ancient Greece and Rome[113] and rabbinic literature provides ample evidence for a similar state of affairs in Jewish circles.[114] The rabbis promoted the popular wisdom of the time which asserted that moderate child-beating was an effective and desirable educative tool.[115] In this vein, *Sifre Zuṭa* tellingly

110 See Blidstein, *Honor Thy Father and Mother*, 1 (xi–xii, 10).

111 See Rawson, "The Roman Family," 7; Parkin, "Out of Sight," 135.

112 Keith Hopkins, *Death and Renewal* (Cambridge: Cambridge Univ. Press, 1983) 43, 74–78, 98–99, 195. Goodman, *The Ruling Class*, 61–62 argues that Jews would have considered the notion of limiting children to a certain maximum to be "ideologically odious," but at times social and financial pressures might have worked against this ideology.

113 See Wiedemann, *Adults and Children*, 27–30.

114 See, for example, *m.Ned.* 3:2; *t.Giṭ.* 3:5; *t.Sukkah* 2:6; *Sifre Deut.* 45 (ed. L. Finkelstein [repr.; New York and Jerusalem: The Jewish Theological Seminary of America, 1993. Berlin: Gesellschaft zur Förderung der Wissenschaft des Judentums, 1939] 103); *Sifre Num.* (ed. H. S. Horovitz [repr.; Jerusalem: Wahrmann, 1966. Liepzig: Gustav Fock, 1917] 103); *Gen. Rab.* 48:6 (Theodor-Albeck, 480); *Lam. Rab., Petiḥta* 2 (2) (Buber, 4); *Lam. Rab.* 4:11 (Buber, 148); (*b.Ber.* 32a; *b.Sukkah* 29a; *b.B.Bat.* 21a).

115 For a positive attitude towards child beating see *m.Mak.* 2:2; *Mekhilta, Mishpatim* 4 (H. S. Horo-

refers to the father who administers a violent chastisement as "he who beats out of love."[116] From a sociological point of view, beating children served as a physical expression of the imbalance of power in the adult-child relationship[117] and Thomas Wiedemann has suggested that the economic setting of the ancient world made a quick and efficient means of parental control necessary. "The beating of children," writes Wiedemann, "is characteristic of a peasant society" and "was essential for the functioning of the household as an economic unit." The economic pressures in antiquity were so severe, Wiedemann argues, that parents resorted to physical violence in order to ensure the cooperation of their children.[118] This underlying economic factor is never made explicit in Jewish sources, yet it seems not unlikely that the harsh ancient economy contributed to the atmosphere in which physical violence was viewed as a compelling form of child disciplining.

The Distribution of Food

The distribution of food was another important dimension of the experience of children that was also heavily influenced by economic factors. Jews, like most ancients, felt a moral obligation to feed their children and Palestinian rabbis even transformed this value into law during our period.[119] Rabbinic ideals for

---

vitz and I. A. Rabin, eds., *Mekhilta de Rabbi Ishmael* [repr.; Jerusalem: Shalem, 1997. Frankfurt am Main: J. Kauffmann, 1931] 263); *Sifre Deut.* 182 (Finkelstein, 224); *Lam. Rab.* 1:3 (Buber, 64); *Tanḥuma, Shemot* 1 (Enoch Zundel ben Yosef commentator [repr.; Jerusalem: Levin-Epshtayn, 1969. Szczecin: E. Shrenttsel, 1863] 62a–63a); *Exod. Rab.* 1:1 (ed. Avigdor Shinan [Tel-Aviv: Dvir, 1984] 35–39). On the importance of moderation see *t.B.Qam.* 9:11; *y.Moᶜed Qat.* 3:1 81d; (*b.Moᶜed Qat.* 17a; *b.Ḥul.* 107b; *b.Giṭ.* 36a; *b.Mak.* 16b; *b.Bek.* 46a).

116 *Sifre Zuṭa* 35:22 (ed. H. S. Horowitz [repr.; Jerusalem: Wahrmann, 1966. Leipzig: Gustav Fock, 1917] 333).

117 See Wiedemann, *Adults and Children*, 27; Richard Saller, "Corporal Punishment, Authority and Obedience in the Roman Household," in Beryl Rawson, ed., *Marriage, Divorce, and Children in Ancient Rome* (Canberra and Oxford: Humanities Research Centre and Clarendon Press, 1992) 144–65. John J. Pilch interpreted severe parental discipline among Jews in antiquity in light of Mediterranean cultural norms arguing that in a community which viewed human nature as a mixture of good and evil tendencies, adults distrusted children and therefore the standard parenting style relied on physical punishment as a major strategy in controlling children and teaching them self control ("Beat His Ribs While He is Young. Sir 30:12: A Window on the Mediterranean World," *BTB* 23 [1993] 101–13). See also Meir Bar-Ilan, "The Battered Jewish Child in Antiquity," (Ramat-Gan: Bar-Ilan Univ., January 2003) http://faculty.biu.ac.il/~barilm/battered.html, September 26, 2006.

118 See Wiedemann, *Adults and Children*, 30.

119 Regarding the history of the father's legal obligation to feed his children, see Elimelech Westreich, "A Father's Obligation to Maintain his Children in Talmudic Law," *JLA* 10 (1992) 177–212; H. Lapin, "Maintenance of Wives and Children"; Mordechai Akiva Friedman, *Jewish Marriage in Palestine: A Cairo Geniza Study* (2 vols.; Tel Aviv and New York: Tel-Aviv Univ. and JTS, 1980) 1:356–91; Moshe S. HaCohen, "The Jewish Law of Child Maintenance Payments – Its Formation,

the maintenance of children, however, did not necessarily translate into social reality and it is important for us to consider how the distribution and division of food within the household actually took place.

In many cases, caretakers, such as nurses, pedagogues and teachers would have been the ones actually overseeing the child's diet and ensuring that he or she ate properly, though parents would have assumed the ultimate responsibility and concern for the child's sustenance. In this vein we find a king parable in which the king interrogates his servant every single day regarding his son's eating and drinking habits.[120] Such parental concern is similarly expressed in the following text:

> A parable of a king of flesh and blood who entrusted his son to a pedagogue. He [the king] would sit and order him [the pedagogue], saying to him, See to it that he [my son] not eat any bad food, and that he not drink any bad drink. The son was so upset with his father that he said, Not because he loves me [he limits me so], but because he cannot stand for me to eat.[121]

While the king commands the pedagogue to ensure that his son not eat or drink anything bad for him, the son interprets these limitations as evidence that his father does not want him to eat at all. In this particular case it seems that the son disregards, perhaps willfully, his father's good intentions, but at times a parent might have truly desired to deprive his child of food. For example, the king in the following parable intentionally deprives his children and slaves of food.

> A parable of a king of flesh and blood with many children and servants who were nourished and maintained from his hand. The keys to the storehouse were in his hand; when they did his will he opened the storehouse and they ate and were satiated, but when they did not do his will, he locked the storehouse and they died of starvation.[122]

This text demonstrates how a father might have used the allocation of food within the family as leverage in an attempt to assert his authority and will over his dependents. As head of the family and controller of its resources, the fa-

---

Development and Circumstances" (Ph.D. diss.; Ramat-Gan: Bar-Ilan Univ., 1998); Israel Zvi Gilat, *The Relations Between Parents and Children in Israeli and Jewish Law* (Tel-Aviv: Choshen Lamishpat, 2000) 155–248; Schwartz, "Did the Jews Practice Infant Exposure," 77–91. See also *Let. Aris.* 248.

120 See *Lev. Rab.* 2:5 (Margulies, 43–44).

121 *Sifre Num.* 87 (Horovitz, 87).

122 *Sifre Deut.* 40 (Finkelstein, 83). See also parable in *Sifre Num.* 89 (Horovitz, 90).

ther was in a position to use these resources to strengthen his hold over his immediate family and other dependents.

The following *baraita* from the *Bavli* illustrates yet another reason why a father might have deprived his children of food.[123]

> Our Rabbis taught. . . . The guests may not give from what is set before them to the son or daughter of the host, unless they have the host's permission to do so. It once happened that a man in a time of scarcity invited three guests to his house and he only had three eggs to set before them. When the child of the host entered, one of the guests took his portion and gave it to him, the second guest did likewise, and so did the third. When the father of the child came and saw him stuffing one [egg] in his mouth and holding two in his hands, he [in rage] knocked him to the ground so that he died. When the child's mother saw this she went up to the roof and threw herself down and died. He went up to the roof and threw himself down and died.[124]

During a time of scarcity, the host in this story fed his guests before his own child. The guests, however, pitied the child and fed him, and when the father saw his son eating the food reserved for the guests he was enraged. For him, the social expectation that he feed his guests was so strong that he first neglected to feed his own son and later on attacked him when the child ate the guests' food. The tragic conclusion of the story indicates that the storyteller disapproves of the father's extreme reaction, but for our purposes, this story illustrates how a child's diet might be effected by competing demands placed on the family. More generally, other cultural and ethical demands existed which might come into conflict with the maintenance of children. Thus, for example, we find in both Babylonian and Palestinian sources the notion that the maintenance of orphans should ideally precede even that of one's own family.[125]

Moreover, the division and distribution of food even in the context of the family itself did not generally favor children. Peter Garnsey has argued that the distribution of food within the ancient family was determined by the confluence of three factors: productivity, status and power. Male adults, for example, would have been considered important producers with both high status and much power and hence they would have received substantial portions of

123 Parts of this *baraita* are paralleled in chapter six of *t.B.Bat.*, but since the story does not appear in any Palestinian source, it is not certain whether it is of Palestinian or Babylonian origin. See also *Der. ʾEr. Rab.* 8:2, 9:7 (Marcus van Loopik, *The Ways of the Sages and the Way of the World* [Tübingen: Mohr-Siebeck, 1991] 122–24, 135–36).

124 *B.Ḥul.* 94a.

125 See *Lev. Rab.* 37:2 (Margulies, 856–60); *b.Tanḥ.* 24a.

the available food. Children might have been viewed as the future producers of the family, but their food allocation would have suffered greatly due to their lowly social status and meager power. Girls would have probably been even worse off than boys since males in general were valued more highly than females.[126] On the basis of this analysis, Garnsey concludes that, as in developing countries today, malnutrition would have been predominantly an affliction of young children. Not all young children, however, would have faired the same since the children of the wealthy would have enjoyed a superior diet as compared with those of the poor. In addition, older children would have usually received a larger allocation of food than younger children since they would have been viewed as relatively valuable producers with a moderate level of social status (though still minimal power).[127]

Perhaps this difference between older and younger children explains the logic of a question posed in a story that appears in *b. Taᶜan.* 23a–b.

> Abba Ḥilkiah was the grandson of Ḥoni the Circle-Drawer and whenever the world was in need of rain the Rabbis sent a message to him and he prayed and rain fell. Once there was an urgent need for rain and the Rabbis sent to him a couple of scholars [to ask him] to pray for rain. . . . He sat down to eat but he did not say to the scholars, "Join me." He then shared the meal among his children, giving the older son one portion and the younger two. . . . When he came down he said to the scholars, Why have you scholars come here? They replied: The Rabbis have sent us to you, Sir, [to ask you] to pray for rain. . . . We know that the rain has come on your account, but tell us, Sir, the meaning of these mysterious acts of yours, which are bewildering to us. . . . Why did you give, Sir, one portion to the older son and two portions to the younger? He replied: Because the one stays at home and the other is away in the Synagogue [the whole day].[128]

I suspect that the sages in this story are not troubled by the fact that Abba Ḥilkiah did not treat his sons equally because if that were the case the story would not have informed the reader which child was older and which younger. Rather, the sages cannot understand why Abba Ḥilkiah allocated a double por-

126 Compare Cooper, *Child*, 48.

127 See Garnsey, *Food and Society*, 49, 100–112. On the preference for males over females in the rabbinic world see Nissan Rubin, *The Beginning of Life: Rites of Birth, Circumcision and Redemption of the First-born in the Talmud and Midrash* (Israel: Hakibutz Hameuchad, 1995) 38–40 (Heb.).

128 Trans. J. Rabbinowitz (London: The Soncino Press, 1938). See also *y. Tanḥ.* 1:4, 65b–c. On the actions of Jewish holy men such as Abba Ḥilkiah which apparently violate normal social conventions, see Richard Kalmin, "Holy Men, Rabbis, and Demonic Sages in Late Antiquity," in Richard Kalmin and Seth Schwartz, eds., *Jewish Culture and Society Under the Christian Roman Empire* (Leuven: Peeters, 2003) 228–34.

tion to the younger child when it is the older child in their view who should have received the larger portion. Since older children were more productive than younger children and retained a higher social status, the natural expectations of the sages and the ancient audience of this story is that the older child should receive the larger portion of food.

In a similar vein, one halakhic position argues that the obligation to maintain boys precedes the obligation to maintain girls since males studied Torah, or in other words, since boys were accorded a higher social status than girls. Interestingly, a second position contends that the maintenance of girls should actually precede that of boys since the moral integrity of Jewish daughters might be compromised by their need to beg. This latter position does not contradict the notion that boys should be favored owing to their higher social status, but rather argues that the moral ramifications of favoring boys are simply unacceptable.[129]

Although ancient Jews recognized that there was a pecking order in respect to the allocation of food, at times they sought to neutralize this hierarchy in favor of a more equitable system. In the context of a halakhic analysis of activities permitted at the Sabbath dinner table, the Mishnah states that "one may cast lots with his sons and the members of his household on the table [regarding the order in which the portions of food are distributed] so long as one does not intend to change a large portion into a small one because of [the prohibition against] dice [that is, gambling]."[130] On the same legal issue, the Tosefta permits a wedding party to cast lots on the Sabbath even in respect to the size of the portions and it permits the casting of lots amongst a host's guests though only in respect to the order of distribution.[131] Although the rabbis sought to discourage certain types of food lotteries, the nature of these cases reveal that, at times, Jews in Palestine would cast lots in order to determine the order in which people were served as well as the size of their individual portions. Both the order and size of portions reflected the importance of the diners so that a random lottery system offered a more equitable system than the divvying up of portions by the householder or host. The cases discussed in the Tosefta reflect public occasions, even religious banquets, in which it seems that the lottery was part of an attempt to promote a sense of brotherhood and equality much like

129 See *t.Ketub.* 4:8; *y.Ketub.* 4:8 28d; *b.Ketub.* 49a–b. See also Ross S. Kraemer, "Jewish Mothers and Daughters in the Greco-Roman World," in S. J. D. Cohen, ed., *The Jewish Family in Antiquity* (Atlanta: Scholars Press, 1993) 107–8. On the importance of preserving a girl's virginity until marriage within rabbinic culture, see Judith Romney Wegner, *Chattel or Person: The Status of Women in the Mishnah* (New York and Oxford: Oxford Univ. Press, 1988) 20–28.

130 *M.Šabb.* 23:2.

131 *T.Šabb.* 17:4 (*b.Šabb.* 149a–b). See Saul Lieberman, *Tosefta Ki-Fshutah: A Comprehensive Commentary on the Tosefta: Shabbat* (10 vols.; New York: Jewish Theological Seminary, 1955–88) 3:283–84; Rubin, *The Joy of Life*, 284.

the way ancient Greeks insisted that the meat of a sacrificial banquet would be evenly divided amongst the citizens of the city.[132] The lottery amongst the members of the household discussed in the Mishnah, however, was not designed to enhance the social harmony of the community at large, but focused on the internal dynamics within the family. Perhaps a father would have been pressured by his family, or by ethical ideals, to administer a lottery in order to avoid the unfairness of a "natural" distribution based on factors such as productivity, status or power. Younger children, of course, would have profited from such equalizing modes of food distribution.

Child-Care and Education

Let us consider now the economic dimensions of three additional aspects of childhood: child-minding, formal education and professional training. Though children were naturally cared for by their relatives, non-kin such as slaves, wet-nurses, pedagogues, teachers and day-laborers also took care of children.[133] These child-minders were not even necessarily Jewish yet they sometimes became such long-term,[134] essential and loved members of the household that children would call them "father so-and-so" or "mother so-and-so."[135] Wealthy Jewish parents would have had ample resources to pay for caretakers, but poor families might have also employed help in order to enable parents to work without disruption or in emulation of the upper classes.[136] In addition, a non-kin guardian might be placed in charge of an orphan's inheritance which he was supposed to maintain until the child came of age.[137] In short, many families depended on

132 See Garnsey, *Food and Society*, 131–38; N. Loraux, "La cité comme cuisine et comme partage," *Annales ESC* 36 (1981) 618–20.

133 See, for example, *t.Šabb.* 17:26; *t.ʿAvod. Zar.* 3:1–3; *Gen. Rab.* 31:7 (Theodor-Albeck, 280); (*b.Ned.* 37a–b). See also Catherine Hezser, "The Impact of Household Slaves on the Jewish Family in Roman Palestine," *JSJ* 34 (2003) 375–424.

134 See Bradley, *Discovering the Roman Family*, 27.

135 See *y.Nid.* 1:4 49b (*b.Ber.* 16b) for rabbinic disapproval of this practice. See also Bradley, *Discovering the Roman Family*, 76–102. (In reference to Abbaye, see *b.Qidd.* 31b; Charlotte Elisheva Fonrobert, *Menstrual Purity: Rabbinic and Christian Reconstructions of Biblical Gender* [Stanford: Stanford Univ. Press, 2000] 151–53.)

136 See Parkin, *Demography and Roman Society*, 129–32; Bradley, *Discovering the Roman Family*, 16–19, 61–63. Catherine Hezser has argued that since the term pedagogue only appears in king parables (but see *Gen. Rab.* 1:1 [Theodor-Albeck, 1]), one may conclude that only non-Jews or the wealthy employed them (C. Hezser, *Jewish Literacy in Roman Palestine* [Tübingen: Mohr Siebeck, 2001] 59–60). It is not certain, however, that king parables reflect only an aristocratic setting (see David Stern, *Parables in Midrash: Narrative and Exegesis in Rabbinic Literature* [Cambridge, Mass. and London: Harvard Univ. Press, 1991] 19). If we focus on the custodial rather than educative role of the pedagogue, it is not unlikely that lower class Jews, like their Roman counterparts, employed male child-minders (see Bradley, *Discovering the Roman Family*, 47).

137 See, for example, *m.Giṭ.* 5:4; *m.B.Qam.* 4:4; *t.B.Meṣ.* 5:20; *Gen. Rab.* 65:16 (Theodor-Albeck, 728–

non-kin workers, both slaves and paid employees, who fulfilled critical roles in the protection, socialization and education of their children.

Biblical and Second Temple texts indicate that instruction in Jewish values, beliefs and customs was a central role of the family from time immemorial[138] and early rabbinic texts continue to view the parent, or more precisely the father, as responsible for the education of his sons.

> "And teach them to your children (or sons)" [*beneikhem*] (Deut 11:19); "your sons" and not "your daughters" are the words of R. Yose b. Akiva. Hence they said that when an infant begins to speak, his father should speak to him in the holy language and teach him Torah. Should he not speak with him in the holy language nor teach him Torah, it is as if he had buried him as it is said, "And teach them to your sons, reciting them"; if you teach them to your sons, "to the end that you and your children (or sons) may endure" (Deut 11:21), and if not, to the end that your days will be shortened. For in this manner the words of Torah are interpreted, from the positive [we understand] the negative, and from the negative, the positive.[139]

Greek was naturally taught to Jewish children living in the Greek-speaking diaspora and rabbinic sources indicate that some (and perhaps many) Jewish children in Palestine learned Greek at home as well.[140] R. Abbahu apparently encouraged teaching one's daughter Greek and his contention that Greek was an ornament for a young woman (that would enhance her value on the marriage market) reflects a social environment that viewed knowledge of Greek in a

---

29); (*b.Pesaḥ.* 49b). See also H. M. Cotton, "The Guardianship of Jesus son of Babatha: Roman and Local Law in the Province of Arabia," *JRS* 83 (1993) 94–108.

138 See O. Larry Yarbrough, "Parents and Children in the Jewish Family of Antiquity," in Shaye J. D. Cohen, ed., *The Jewish Family in Antiquity* (Atlanta: Scholars Press, 1993) 42–49; Josephus, *C. Ap.* 2.178; Philo, *Legat.* 210; S. Safrai, "Education and the Study of Torah," in Safrai, *The Jewish People in the First Century*, 2:947; John M. G. Barclay, "The Family as the Bearer of Religion in Judaism and Early Christianity," in Halvor Moxnes, ed., *Constructing Early Christian Families: Family as Social Reality and Metaphor* (London and New York, Routledge, 1997) 68–72.

139 *Sifre Deut.* 46 (Finkelstein, 104). See also *m.Qidd.* 1:7; *t.Qidd.* 1:11; *Mekhilta, Bo* 18 (Horovitz and Rabin, 72–73); *Mekhilta de Rashbi* 20 (J. N. Epstein and E. Z. Melammed, eds., *Mekhilta de Rabbi Simeon b. Yohai* [Jerusalem: Mekize Nirdamim, 1955] 150); (*b.Ber.* 21b; *b.Qidd.* 29a–30b).

140 Rabbinic sources explicitly state that Greek was taught in the patriarch's household and the rabbinic prohibition against teaching one's children Greek suggests that parents did teach Greek to their children. See *m.Soṭah* 9:14; *t.Soṭah* 15:8; *y.ʿAbod. Zar.* 2:2 41a; Saul Lieberman, *Greek in Jewish Palestine* (New York: Jewish Theological Seminary, 1942) 1–67; Lieberman, *Hellenism in Jewish Palestine* (New York: Jewish Theological Seminary, 1950) 100–114; Lieberman, "How Much Greek in Jewish Palestine?" in Alexander Altmann, ed., *Biblical and Other Studies* (Cambridge, Mass.: Harvard Univ. Press, 1963) 123–41; compare G. Alon, "S. Lieberman, *Greek in Jewish Palestine*," *KS* 20 (1943) 76–95 (Heb.).

favorable light.[141] In short, the home was an important setting in which families taught their children Jewish, and perhaps Graeco-Roman, culture and values.

Home schooling was a financially efficient way to educate one's children, but alternative and more costly educational routes existed as well. Tutors and schoolteachers had been employed in the Greek world for centuries and Graeco-Roman primary schools must have existed even in Palestine during the early centuries of the Common Era though perhaps not in small, Jewish villages. Tutors in Jewish studies were also employed during this period and rabbinic legal sources discuss whether one was permitted to hire a Samaritan or non-Jew to teach one's child to read and whether it was prohibited to hire an instructor on the Sabbath.[142] Scholars have traditionally maintained that a centralized network of Jewish schools was already established in late Second Temple Palestine.[143] It is unlikely, however, that a centralized network existed at such an early date and a more critical reading of rabbinic sources suggests that the type of primary school promoted by the rabbis only became widely available during the third century C.E.[144] Thus, for many Jews during our period, school was simply not an option and children would have been taught either by family members or by hired tutors. When rabbinic schools became more available in the third century, more families presumably would have taken advantage of their services.

From a household economic perspective, it is worth considering the economic factors underlying the family's decision to hire a tutor for its child or to send its child to school in Roman Palestine. Children would begin their formal studies at around age six or seven and their studies would often continue into their early teens.[145] During these years, the family not only would have to fund its child's tuition, but it would also lose many productive hours which the child could have otherwise spent working.[146] For the wealthy, the costs of a child's formal education were not significant while the benefits were clearly desirable. Children in Graeco-Roman schools would acquire the cultural identity cards needed to succeed in the wider social world of the Roman Near East and especially religious families might attempt to enhance their sons' knowledge of Judaism and positions in the educated Jewish elite by means of a formal Jewish education.[147] For the poor masses, the costs of a formal education would

141 See *y.Pe*ʾ*ah* 1:1 15c; *y.Šabb.* 6:1 7d; *y.Soṭah* 9:15 24c.

142 See *y.Pe*ʾ*ah* 8:9 21b; *t.*ʿ*Abod. Zar.* 3:1–2; (*b.Šabb.* 12a, 150a; *b.Ketub.* 5a, 111b; *b.*ʿ*Abod. Zar.* 15b).

143 See, for example, S. Safrai's overview in "Education and the Study of Torah," 948.

144 See *y.Ketub.* 8:11 32c; *b.B.Bat.* 21a; David Goodblatt, "The Talmudic Sources on the Origins of Organized Jewish Education," *Studies in the History of the Jewish People and the Land of Israel* 5 (1980) 83–103; Hezser, *Jewish Literacy*, 39–109. Interestingly, the education of children at Qumran may have been organized by the community (see 1QSa I, 6–9).

145 See *m.*ʾ*Abot* 5:21; *Gen. Rab.* 63:9 (Theodor-Albeck, 692–93); *b.Ketub.* 50a.

146 See Hezser, *Jewish Literacy*, 67.

147 See Hezser, *Jewish Literacy*, 109; Keith Bradley, "Children and Dreams," in Suzanne Dixon, ed.,

have served as a very serious disincentive for sending a child to school. Many simply would not have been able to afford the expenses entailed by a formal education and perhaps this economic reality explains why some women refused to bring their children to the synagogue for schooling saying, "if he (my son) is fit to learn, then he will learn (even without the schooling)."[148] Yet some highly pious or ambitious lower and middle class families may have reasoned that the social opportunities and religious teachings offered by the schools more than justified severe financial sacrifices on the part of the family.

If at least some Jewish boys enjoyed a formal primary education, most girls received no formal education of any sort.[149] Fearing for the safety and chastity of their daughters, parents would not have been inclined to send their daughters to educational institutions out of the home. Moreover, families may not have felt the need to enhance the image of their daughters with a formal education since women probably played a relatively minor role in the public life of this patriarchal society. From an economic perspective, it was probably considered unwise to invest much in a daughter's education since girls, who generally left home upon marriage, were not going to be long-term contributors to the family income.[150] Indeed, *Lamentations Rabbah* views sons as the pillars of the house and daughters as birds who fly away from home when they marry.[151] The practical and cultural knowledge girls needed to know would be acquired at home and perhaps a trustworthy adult, such as a parent, might teach a girl additional knowledge or skills (such as Greek) in order to improve her chances of attracting a wealthy or upper class suitor.

Like transmitting a cultural education to one's progeny, training one's sons in a craft or profession was also a traditional obligation of Jewish parents. This training followed a child's early cultural education and generally began at around the age of twelve or thirteen.[152] Early Greek legislators transformed this parental obligation into law and also stated that in return for the training

---

Childhood, Class and Kin in the Roman World (London and New York: Rouledge, 2001) 46.

148 *Y.Ḥal.* 1:1 57b.

149 While the rabbis elaborated upon a father's legal obligations to his young son, they stressed the father's legal rights over his daughter. See, for example, *Mekhilta de Rashbi* 20 (eds. Epstein-Melammed, 150), which lists the duties a father has towards his son and the privileges he maintains over his daughter. See also Archer, *Her Price*, 86–101; Wegner, *Chattel or Person*, 20–39; Kraemer, "Jewish Women in the Diaspora," 49–50; Judith R. Baskin, "The Separation of Women in Rabbinic Judaism," in Yvonne Y. Haddad and Ellison B. Findly, eds., *Women, Religion, and Social Change* (Albany: State Univ. of New York Press, 1985) 3–18.

150 See James, *Theorizing Childhood*, 138.

151 See *Lam. Rab.* 1:1 (Buber, 47).

152 The order of the duties the father owes his son listed in *t.Qidd.* 1:11 suggests that a child learned a craft after he learned Torah and before he got married. (See also *b.Ketub.* 50a according to R. Nathan ben R. Yehiel and Alexander Kohut, *Aruch Completum* [8 vols.; Berlin: Menorah, 1926] 3:376. For a similar age in the Roman world, see Bradley, *Discovering the Roman Family*, 108.)

his parents afforded him, a son was obligated by law to support his parents in their old age.[153] The rabbis similarly transformed this parental duty into law and the juxtaposition of the "duty of the son towards his father" with "the duty of the father towards his son" in rabbinic texts suggests that the rabbis also conceptualized this legal relationship in reciprocal terms.[154] The rabbis, however, did not imbue this reciprocity with the same legal weight it received in Greek law where a son's obligation to support his elderly father was voided in cases where his father had neglected to oversee his training in a craft.

The rabbis not only discuss a father's obligation to oversee his son's training in a craft, they also recommend certain professions and oppose others. R. Meir, for example, was said to have recommended teaching one's son a simple and clean craft. The Mishnah prohibited bachelors and women from becoming elementary school teachers and in their attempt to prevent promiscuity and reinforce gender roles, the sages discouraged training one's son in a craft practiced amongst women. Abba Guria is cited as opposing training one's son to be an ass driver, a camel driver, a barber, a sailor, (a potter), a shepherd or a storekeeper since these professions involve thievery and a position attributed to R. Judah highlighted the evils involved in the practice of medicine and being a butcher.[155] In general the rabbis expressed a positive attitude towards agriculture and artisanship and a negative attitude towards commerce.[156] These attitudes are reminiscent of the traditional values of a land-based aristocracy which felt threatened by successful merchants whose source of wealth rested on enterprise and skill rather than on land.[157]

Rabbinic literature also supplies evidence of the apparently widespread folk wisdom that a child should ideally learn the profession of his forbearers or as R. Meir was said to have declared: "One can make a living in any situation, [nonetheless] happy is the person who sees his parents in an excellent occupation; woe to the person who sees his parents in a lowly profession."[158]

153 See Pomeroy, *Families*, 141; A.R.W. Harrison, *The Law of Athens, I: The Family and Property* (repr.; London, Indianapolis and Cambridge: Gerald Duckworth and Hackett Publishing, 1998) 77; Golden, *Children and Childhood*, 92.

154 See *m.Qidd.* 1:7; *t.Qidd.* 1:11; *y.Qidd.* 1:7 61a; (*b.Qidd.* 29a); Gerald J. Blidstein, "Master and Parent: Comparative Aspects of a Dual Loyalty (Mishnah Baba Meziah 2:11 and Mark 3:31–35)," in Alan J. Avery-Peck and J. Neusner, eds., *The Mishnah in Contemporary Perspective* (Leiden: Brill, 2002) 255–66; Philo, *Decal.* 106–20; Yarbrough, "Parents and Children," 50–53; Adele Reinhartz, "Parents and Children: A Philonic Perspective," in S. J. D. Cohen, ed., *The Jewish Family in Antiquity* (Atlanta: Scholars Press, 1993) 77–81; Bezalel Porten, *Archives from Elephantine: The Life of an Ancient Jewish Military Colony* (Berkeley and Los Angeles: Univ. of California Press, 1968) 229.

155 *M.Qidd.* 4:13–14. See also *t.Qidd.* 5:14–16 (Lieberman, *Tosefta Ki-Fshutah: Kiddushin*, 983); *y.Qidd.* 4:11 66b; (*b.Qidd.* 82a–b).

156 See Safrai, *The Economy*, 304–12.

157 Compare Garnsey, *The Roman Empire*, 45.

158 *Y.Qidd.* 4:11 66b. See also references in n. 155.

R. Meir's saying presupposes that a person had a vested interest in his parents' occupation since it was common for parents to train their offspring in their own professions. Echoing R. Meir's presupposition, R. Yoḥanan, according to the *Bavli*, sought to reveal the biblical text which proves why "a person should not change his occupation or the occupation of his forefathers."[159] In an urbanizing world where numerous and variegated crafts and occupations grew in importance, a patrimony was not only the land or wealth parents bestowed upon their children, but also the tools of the trade that parents bequeathed to their children. Just as Hellenistic mercenaries bequeathed their horses and armor to their sons,[160] rabbinic literature relates that a carpenter would give his tools to his son who came of age and a physician would give his medicine chest to his son who came of age.[161]

Tools of the trade passed down from parent to child, however, were not necessarily material objects. Specialized skills and knowledge were also transmitted within the family. Inscriptions in Palestinian synagogue mosaics from the fifth century C.E. reveal that Marianos and his son Aninas were craftsmen who built synagogue mosaics together.[162] In a similar vein, the rabbis portrayed the house of Garmu as the family of specialist bakers who supplied the Temple with the showbread and the house of Abtinas as the family who prepared the incense for the Temple. These families, according to the Tosefta, maintained the detailed practices of their family-trade as a secret, and when the sages sought and failed to find alternative vendors in Egypt, the houses of Garmu and Abtinas doubled their prices.[163] Although these stories about the houses of Garmu and Abtinas might not have transpired as narrated in the Tosefta, they indicate nonetheless that a family business may well have transmitted trade secrets among its members and manipulated prices when it was clear that it monopolized the market. Like other craftsmen, communal leaders and functionaries also

159 See *b.ᶜArakh.* 16b.

160 See Pomeroy, *Families*, 158–59 n. 58.

161 See *y.Roš Haš.* 1:3 57b. In reference to the transmission of rabbinic leadership from father to son, see Gedalyahu Alon, *Jews, Judaism and the Classical World*, trans. Israel Abrahams (Jerusalem: Magnes, 1977) 446 n. 27; Ephraim E. Urbach, "Class-Status and Leadership in the World of the Palestinian Sages," in Robert Brody and Moshe D. Herr, eds., *Collected Writings in Jewish Studies* (Jerusalem: Magnes, 1999) 460–61; Moshe Beer, "The Hereditary Principle in Jewish Leadership," *Bar Ilan* 13 (1976) 149–57 (Heb.); Beer, "The Sons of Eli in Rabbinic Legend," *Bar Ilan* 14–15 (1977) 79–93 (Heb.); Isaiah Gafni, "'*Shevet umehokek' – Al defusei manhigut ḥadashim betekufat hatalmud beeretz yisrael ubebavel*," in Isaiah Gafni and Gabriel Motzkin, eds., *Priesthood and Monarchy: Studies in the Historical Relationships of Religion and State* (Jerusalem: Zalman Shazar, 1987) 79–91 (Heb.); Avraham Grossman, "From Father to Son: The Inheritance of the Spiritual Leadership of the Jewish Communities in the Early Middle Ages," *Zion* 50 (1985) 189–91 (Heb.).

162 See Lea Roth-Gerson, *The Greek Inscriptions from the Synagogues in Eretz Israel* (Jerusalem: Yad Izhak ben Zvi, 1987) 29, 33 (Heb.).

163 See *m.Šeqal.* 5:1; *m.Yoma* 3:11; *t.Yoma* 2:5–6. See also Mark Wischnitzer, *A History of Jewish Crafts and Guilds* (New York: Jonathan David, 1965) 23.

sought to transmit their professions to their sons and a Jerusalem synagogue inscription from the late first century B.C.E. or early first century C.E. refers to a Theodotus who was a third generation archisynagogus.[164] Gedalyahu Alon has shown that it was customary for the sons (or eldest sons) of rabbis and other functionaries to succeed their fathers[165] and the patriarchate is probably the most obvious example of an important rabbinic family which maintained a leading role in rabbinic affairs for generations.[166] Even the repetition of certain names in the patriarch's family across the generations (like Gamaliel and Simeon) may reflect the attempt to "create an expectation of success"[167] for a career in rabbinic leadership. Yet for the majority of the population, the hereditary quality of job selection also worked to the disadvantage of young boys by impeding their social advancement.[168]

Although the sources discussed above indicate that bequeathing one's occupation to one's children was an ideal and probably a common social reality as well, it was not always the case. For example, a parable in *Genesis Rabbah* portrays a blacksmith whose son is a goldsmith and a story in *Lamentations Rabbah* describes a man who has four sons each working in different professions (and a fifth son still in school).[169] Various factors such as the nature of each individual's inherent talents, the demand in local markets, the number of children in a family and the ambitions of parents for social or financial betterment must have led many parents to have their children trained in occupations they themselves did not follow. In addition, the early demise of many parents would have ensured that by the time they reached the appropriate age, many children would not have had a living father or mother to train them.[170]

Rabbinic laws regarding apprenticeship and instruction in Torah are similar in many respects. Like hiring an instructor to teach Torah in *loco parentis*, a father could also hire a substitute craftsman to fulfill his obligation to teach his son a craft. Similarly, just as the rabbis discussed whether a child's instructor may be a Samaritan or a non-Jew and whether he may be hired on the Sabbath, they also considered the very same propositions in reference to a master craftsman. A third similarity between instruction and apprenticeship seems to be that even though rabbinic legal texts always relate to the legal obligations to educate and train one's son as paternal obligations, other rabbinic sources indi-

164 See Roth-Gerson, *The Greek Inscriptions*, 76. See also *t.Menaḥ.* 13:21.

165 See Alon, *Jews, Judaism and Classical World*, 436–57. See also *Sifre Deut.* 162 (Finkelstein, 212–13); *Pesikta de Rav Kahana* 11:22 (ed. B. Mandelbaum [New York: Jewish Theological Seminary, 1962] 196–98).

166 However, see the new revisionist interpretation of Sacha Stern, "Rabbi and the Origins of the Patriarchate," *JJS* 54 (2003) 193–215.

167 Pomeroy, *Families*, 157.

168 See Bradley, *Discovering the Roman Family*, 109–12.

169 See *Gen. Rab.* 84:5 (Theodor-Albeck, 1005); *Lam. Rab.* 1:9 (Buber, 72).

170 See Tropper, "Children and Childhood," 326.

cate that the social reality was more complex. In reference to the education of one's young children, mothers were considered responsible for ensuring that their children went to the synagogue to study.[171] In a similar vein, the following stories demonstrate how a mother might have arranged her son's apprenticeship with a master-craftsman.

> "My life was bereft of peace, I forgot what happiness was" (Lam 3:17). R. Eleazar b. R. Yose said in the name of R. Ḥananiah b. R. Abbahu: There is a story of a woman in Caesaria who brought her son to a baker to teach him a craft. He said to her, let him stay with me for five years and I will teach him five hundred confections of wheat.... There is a story of a woman who took her son to a cook in Caesaria to teach him a craft. He said to her, let him stay with me and I will teach him five hundred ways of preparing an egg. He stayed with him and at the end of five years she came to take him [home]. Said he [the cook] to her, let him stay with me for another five years and I will teach him another hundred ways to prepare an egg. Rabbi heard and said, we have never seen such luxury [in the post-Temple era]![172]

These two stories, purportedly from Second Temple times, reveal how a mother in Roman Palestine could have arranged her son's apprenticeship. Moreover, they offer evidence that the apprenticeship contracts from Roman Egypt reflect a type of apprenticeship arrangement that was apparently practiced in Roman Palestine as well.[173]

Keith Bradley analyzed the apprenticeship documents from Egypt in depth and it is worth noting some of his observations here. Bradley noted that legally responsible adults contracted children as apprentices and the rabbinic evidence discussed above indicates that the same was the case amongst Jews in Palestine. Bradley also noted that free females never appear in the Egyptian contracts and he concluded that free girls learned traditional domestic jobs at home or crafts from family members. Girls do not appear as apprentices in rabbinic law or literature but certain rabbinic texts reveal that women were also artisans and involved in non-domestic work activities. Thus, for example, R. Meir's statement cited above refers to one's parents' occupation rather than one's father's occupation, thereby intimating not only that women practiced crafts but that husbands and wives may have often worked together in a single occupation.[174] In respect to the economic value of apprenticeships, Bradley reasoned that an

171 See *b.Ber.* 17a; *b.Soṭah* 21a; *Pesiq. Rab.* 43 (ed. Meir Ish-Shalom [repr.; Tel-Aviv: Esther, 1963 Vienna, s.n., 1880]) 182a–b.

172 *Lam. Rab.* 3:17 (Buber, 129–30).

173 See Bradley, *Discovering the Roman Family*, 103–24.

174 See also Peskowitz, "Family/ies in Antiquity," 31–32; Lapin, "Maintenance of Wives and Children,"

apprentice's earnings would have supplemented his family's immediate income and in the long term, the apprenticeship would have granted the apprentice the means to provide for himself, his future family and his elderly parents. Though the rabbinic portrayal of professional training as a father's duty to his son underscores the advantages the son accrued from his apprenticeship, in some cases the son's training would have offered immediate benefits to his parents as well. On the other hand, contracting one's son to be an apprentice meant losing a family laborer and might have even entailed a financial investment on the part of the family.[175]

The following discussion from *y.B.Bat.* 9:3 17a seems to reflect the type of legal and social complications that could arise in the aftermath of a professional training.

> R. Ḥiyya the Great said, "In general, brothers are considered partners up to three generations." R. [Abbah] bar [A]bun said, "R. Hamnuna also taught so." R. Ammi said, "A son who was seen [doing business] on his own during his father's lifetime, what he acquired he has acquired for himself [and not for the father's estate]." Like the [following case of a] man who became a scribe. His brothers wanted to divide [his salary] with him. The case came before R. Ammi who said, "Thus do we say, 'A man who found an object – do his brothers divide it with him?'" [Obviously not.][176]

According to the legal principle that brothers are partners (attributed to R. Ḥiyya the Great), brothers possess equal shares in the (as yet undivided) family estate. The brothers in the case cited above clearly believed wholeheartedly in this principle and wished to apply the principle even to income earned independent of family resources. Even though their brother apprenticed as a scribe (quite possibly at the expense of the family estate[177]) and then earned his

---

181. See also Eric M. Meyers's "The Problems of Gendered Space in Syro-Palestinian Domestic Architecture," in David L. Balch and Carolyn Osiek, eds., *Early Christian Families in Context: An Interdisciplinary Dialogue* (Grand Rapids, Mich. and Cambridge: Eerdmans, 2003) 44–69, where he argues that "the material world of Roman-period Palestine clearly shows that women participated more fully in crafts, daily household labors and management, and hence had a much higher degree of recognition and responsibility than one might infer from literary sources alone" (68).

175 See W. L. Westermann, "Apprentice Contracts and the Apprentice System in Roman Egypt," *CP* 9 (1914) 295–315.

176 See also *t.B.Bat.* 10:3–5; (*b.B.Bat.* 143b–44b).

177 According to the Penei Moshe s.v. *ʾit ʿavid*, the brothers' claim rested on the fact that their father financed the scribe's training. Legally, according to this reading, the argument between the scribe and his brothers revolved around whether his tuition was to be seen as an investment or as a gift from their father. The underlying rationale for the brothers' position was that their father's moneys should be viewed as family funds and since family funds financed the scribe's tuition, the family should share in its profits. The Talmud, however, does not mention that the father financed

living on his own, they viewed his income as family income and therefore argued that his salary should be divided amongst them as well. The family, according to this view, is not unlike the modern kibbutz in which every member's income, even if earned outside of the kibbutz, is considered communal wealth. The scribe clearly disagreed with his brothers and when the case was brought before R. Ammi, he adjudicated that income earned independent of family resources was the private income of the working individual and not part of the family estate. Though R. Ammi did not decide in favor of the brothers, this case illustrates how a family might have viewed an apprenticeship not simply as the future profession of an individual family member but rather as an investment for the family as a whole. In addition, similar stories in the continuation of this talmudic pericope suggest that the scribe's family was not at all unusual but rather was expressing an apparently widespread understanding of the nature of the family estate.

Let us consider now some further social dimensions of apprenticeship in the ancient world. Apprentices would have had to work very hard and would have even been beaten by their masters at times, but Bradley is probably correct in reasoning that the exploitation and abuse of apprentices would have been moderated by a desire to maximize their productivity.[178] Indeed, Roman epitaphs indicate that a close bond sometimes formed between master and apprentice and one Latin inscription records how one master loved his apprentice Florentius even more than he loved his own son.[179]

The apprentice was subject to the authority of his master, but his very role as an apprentice was determined by parental control. As Bradley put it, "When parents chose occupations for their children, they were able to maintain control over their offspring in a society fundamentally patriarchal in character and to limit the emergence of individual independence inimical to the interests of familial cohesiveness."[180] Most children would have obediently become apprentices in line with their parents' wishes, but from time to time the attempt to control and direct the lives of teenage children would have encountered difficulties. In mid-second century C.E. Syria, the teenage Lucian of Samosata was sent to apprentice in the family profession as a mason. During his first day of work, Lucian broke a stone and hence was beaten. He fled to his mother and subsequently dedicated himself to culture, never returning to work as an apprentice.[181] This story, like the evidence adduced above from rabbinic literature, indicates

the scribe's tuition. Moreover, the overarching context and the cases brought in the continuation of the pericope suggest that regardless of who paid the scribe's tuition, the brothers believed that the scribe's salary belonged to the family estate until the estate was divided amongst the heirs.

178 See Bradley, *Discovering the Roman Family*, 110–11.

179 See *CIL* 6 (1882) n. 10013; Bradley, *Discovering the Roman Family*, 116.

180 Bradley, *Discovering the Roman Family*, 118.

181 Lucian, *Somn.*

that the apprentice contracts from Roman Egypt are probably representative of the entire region. Indeed, the striking parallels between Lucian's story and the following parable from *Midr. Sam.* 13:5[182] indicates that the social complications surrounding apprenticeships were similar throughout the region.[183]

> "But the people refused to listen to Samuel's warning. . ." R. Huna and R. Jeremiah in the name of R. Samuel b. R. Isaac [said], since it is written "How long will you refuse [to obey me]?" (Exodus 16:28), therefore it is written "But the people refused to listen." [This may be compared] to [a parable of] a butcher who died and left behind a son. His mother would bring him to [study] a craft and he would flee. She would bring him to the synagogue [to study Torah], and he would flee. She said, To conclude the matter I will have him taught the craft of his father. She went and brought him to a colleague of his father and said to him, Here, teach him the craft of his father. He would bring him in and would say to him strip (the hide) off the [corpse's] head! He would strip it off its legs. Strip it off its legs! And he would strip it off its head. He went and brought him to his mother and said to her, Here he is, bury him for he rejects the craft of his father. Since it is written "How long will you refuse" therefore it is written "But the people refused."[184]

The mother of the fatherless child in this parable makes three attempts to find an appropriate educational framework for her son but he spurns all her efforts. He flees from an apprenticeship, absconds from his studies in the synagogue and when she apprentices him in his deceased father's profession, he intentionally makes himself a nuisance. This parable is designed to illustrate Israelite behavior in the time of Samuel, but it also describes a social reality akin to that which Lucian faced in his own childhood. Children with gumption or guile, who were dissatisfied with the apprenticeship chosen for them by their parents, would seek and perhaps find ways to circumvent or change the plans which had been laid out for them.

Lucian's preference to study versus his family's desire for him to train in a craft reveals another tension in the world of antiquity, the tension that existed

182 Ed. S. Buber (repr.; Jerusalem: s.n., 1965. Cracow: Y. Fisher, 1893) 84–85.

183 Even though *Midrash Samuel* was edited in the Middle Ages (probably no earlier than the eleventh century), it preserves much earlier Palestinian material (see Jacob Elbaum, "Midrash Samuel," *EJ*, 11:1518). Thus it is possible that our specific text is of amoraic origin and the attribution to Palestinian *amoraim* here strengthens that possibility. Alternatively, it is also possible that our text is late and reflects the fact that apprenticeships were also practiced in the early middle ages.

184 *Midr. Sam.* 13:5 (Buber, 84–85). For the translation and preferred reading of the term *qatzav* (butcher) and the latter portion of this citation, see Michael Sokoloff, *A Dictionary of Jewish Palestinian Aramaic* (Ramat-Gan: Bar Ilan Univ. Press, 1900) 204, 500.

between pursuing a higher education and an apprenticeship, or more generally, between culture and craftsmanship, study and work. A similar type of tension surfaces in rabbinic literature as well, though with one important difference. Rather than studying the Greek classics as Lucian did, a rabbinic education involved studying *halakhah* and Jewish lore. This tension resounds in a statement attributed to R. Nehorai which closes a mishnaic analysis of the appropriate and inappropriate crafts to teach one's son.

> I leave aside all the crafts in the world and teach my son only Torah, for a person enjoys its reward in this world and the capital remains for him in the world to come while all other crafts are not so.[185]

In a complete contrast to R. Nehorai, Aḥer, the ultimate heretic in rabbinic literature, disrupts a schoolhouse and encourages the students to pursue crafts rather than Torah study.[186] In short, a higher education, whether in rhetoric, philosophy or Jewish culture, could come into conflict with professional training, but the average family would not have been able to afford sending its teenage son to any higher education institution.

Marriage

Like the economic dimensions of child labor, of schooling and of professional training, that of marriage was also of tremendous importance in the lives of children and young adults in antiquity.[187] Though many individuals would have married sufficiently late that we would no longer consider them to have been children, marriage nonetheless signified the final transition into adulthood and hence serves as a helpful (if not exactly accurate) dividing line between childhood (broadly defined) and adulthood.[188] The negotiations over money and resources at the start of a marriage reflected the desires of the families of the bride and groom to provide for the new couple's future while minimizing their own costs. As far as the *halakhah* was concerned, the father was responsible

185 *M.Qidd.* 4:14.

186 See *y.Ḥag.* 2:1 77b. See also Alon Goshen-Gottstein, *The Sinner and the Amnesiac: The Rabbinic Invention of Elisha ben Abuya and Eleazar ben Arach* (Stanford: Stanford Univ. Press, 2000) 81–88.

187 See Schremer, *Male and Female*, 261–92.

188 See David Kraemer, "Images of Childhood and Adolescence in Talmudic Literature," in D. Kraemer, ed., *The Jewish Family: Metaphor and Memory* (New York and Oxford: Oxford Univ. Press, 1989) 67, 74. Kraemer chose to terminate his study of childhood at the age of marriage, but he was of the opinion that most Jewish men married around the age of twenty. Since it appears that Jewish men (at least in Palestine) married much later, we must acknowledge that many men may have physically matured long before they married. (On the average age of marriage for men and women in Jewish antiquity, see n. 68 and the references listed there.)

to marry off his son,[189] but the social reality was more complicated. The high mortality rate would have meant that many children would have lost their fathers before they were ready to marry and both the *Bavli* and Roman sources reveal that mothers might have also participated in choosing a spouse.[190] In any event, most youths were married in unions contracted primarily on the basis of social and economic considerations.

Parent-Child Tensions

I have explored above the role of the child in the household economy, beginning with the financial considerations that informed the decision to procreate and then following the child through the life course until marriage. Before concluding, let us consider the economic dimension of one additional element relating to the child's role in the household economy, namely parent-child tensions. Unlike the issues discussed above, parent-child tensions are not limited to any particular stage in the life-course and the financial dependency of adults upon their parents suggests that conflicts persisted (and perhaps even intensified) as children became middle-age adults and their parents entered old age. Thus, my final discussion extends beyond childhood itself, exploring the economic dimension of parent-child conflicts throughout the life-course.

Family life probably involved a fair mixture of harmonious interaction and conflicts. Thus, almost every aspect of childhood discussed above was probably also a potential source of friction between child and parent. An infant might throw tantrums when forced to stop breastfeeding[191] and a growing child might complain about the diet allocated to him.[192] A child might ignore or disobey his parents and possibly even fight back when they disciplined or beat him.[193] A student might flee his school, an apprentice his apprenticeship and a bride or groom might resent his or her parents for their choice of a spouse.[194] In later periods in life, caring for an elderly parent not only could have been a trying experience emotionally but it would have also often involved substantial expenses on the part of the children who may have resented the burden.[195] In short, most areas of parent-child interaction were potential sources of fric-

189 See n. 139.

190 See, for example, *b.Ber.* 56a; *b.Ned.* 23a; *b.Qidd.* 45b. Roman mothers also arranged marriages although they did not have the legal right to do so. See Dixon, *The Roman Family*, 36.

191 See *Sifre Num.* 89 (Horovitz, 89–90); (*Sifre Zuṭ.* 11:8 [Horovitz, 270]).

192 See n. 121.

193 See *b.Moᶜed Qaṭ.* 17a where it is argued that beating one's son may cause him to rebel and hit back.

194 See n. 182; *Gen. Rab.* 48:6 (Theodor-Albeck, 480); *Lam. Rab.* 1:3 (Buber, 64); *Sifre Deut.* 290 (Finkelstein, 309); (*b.Sanh.* 76a).

195 See *Mekhilta*, Jethro 8 (Horovitz and Rabin, 231–32); *Mekhilta, Mishpatim* 1 (Horovitz and Rabin, 248); *Mekhilta de Rashbi* 13 (Epstein-Melammed, 46); *Mekhilta de Rashbi* 20 (Epstein-Melammed, 152); *y.Peʾah* 1:1 15c; (*b.Qidd.* 31a–b).

tion and in keeping with my focus on the household economy, I shall focus on the role of family wealth in parent-child conflicts.

In the subsistence agrarian economy of the Roman Empire, most families owned little property and all members of the household were dependent on the family's land and income. Use of family wealth was a major element in family dynamics and a father, as legal head of the family, was able to use his control over this wealth as leverage against his children. Thus, one aggadic motif consists of the parable of the father who commands his children's caretakers to provide for his children only when they comply with his will.[196] In a similar vein, the *halakhah* states that a father could utter a vow that would prohibit his child from deriving any benefit from his property[197] and the *Bavli* reports a case in which a man who disapproved of his son's thievery was said to have pronounced such a vow.[198] The rabbis also describe how, in Temple times, a father could dedicate all his wealth to the Temple[199] and a *baraita* in the *Bavli* tells a story about a father who did so in order to punish his son for not studying Torah.[200] In short, these laws and stories illustrate one way in which a father could use his control over the family wealth as a means of ensuring the obedience of his children.

An alternative form of financial control over children involved the threat to disinherit a child but before describing the nature of this threat, let us first consider some aspects of inheritance in the Jewish context. Transmitting wealth or the patrimony to the next generation through inheritance was a central function of the family and parents took comfort in knowing that an inheritance would enrich the family in the future.[201] Jewish daughters, who left home upon marriage, generally were not heirs, though resources were set aside to provide for the maintenance of unmarried girls still living at home. Inheritances were traditionally split amongst sons who eventually used the wealth to raise their own families.[202] Rabbinic sources indicate that a son's personal worth might

196 See, for example, *Sifre Deut.* 306 (Finkelstein, 331) and the references in n. 122.

197 See *m.B.Qam.* 9:10.

198 See *b.Ned.* 48b. See also *b.Ketub.* 62b–63a; *b.Ned.* 50a.

199 See *t.ᶜArakh.* 4:23.

200 See *b.Šabb.* 127b.

201 A mother might also view the inheritance as a means of ensuring care for her old age. In a story in *Lam. Rab.* 1:1 (Buber, 48), a mother tells her son that since she and her husband were not able to have a child, she produced a son through an extramarital union. This child was so important to her because she viewed her own flesh and blood as a more dependable source of support for her old age than her dead husband's relatives. Interestingly, other rabbinic texts reflect the husband's concern that he might be cuckolded and then he would pass on his inheritance to non-family members. See, for example, *Mekhilta de Rashbi* 20 (Epstein-Melammed, 154); *b.B.Bat.* 58a.

202 Naturally, the division of an inheritance among heirs sometimes led to disputes. In addition, despite the importance usually ascribed to inheritance, it is worth noting that *Sifre Deut.* 309 (Finkelstein, 349) states that a person loves land that he purchased on his own more than land he received as an inheritance.

improve considerably upon the death of his father[203] and the rabbis believed that shortly after hearing that his father had died, an heir recited the blessing designated to be said upon the hearing of good tidings immediately after he recited the blessing reserved for bad tidings.[204] The following story even illustrates (in rather comical fashion) the lengths to which sons might go in order to ensure that their alcoholic father did not drink away their inheritance.

> R. Aḥa said: There is a story of a man who would sell his household goods and drink wine with the proceeds; he sold the beams of his house and drank wine with the proceeds. His sons complained and said, our old father will depart from the world and leave us nothing after his death. What shall we do with him? Let us go, ply him with drink and make him drunk. [Then] let us carry him and take him out [of town] and let us say that he died and we shall lay him in his grave. They did as follows. They took him, plied him with drink, made him drunk, took him out, and placed him in a cemetery. Wine merchants [then] passed the gate of the cemetery and hearing that a seizure for public service was to take place in the province, they said come and let us unload these skin bottles in this grave and flee. They did thus, unloading their loads in the cemetery and [then] they went to see the uproar in the province. The man [mentioned above] was there and they saw him but thought he was dead. When he woke from his sleep, he saw a skin bottle placed above his head. He untied it, placed it in his mouth and began to drink. Once he was drunk, be began to sing. Three days later his sons said, should we not go and see what our father is doing, whether he is dead or alive? They went and found him with the skin bottle placed in his mouth, sitting and drinking. They said to him, even here amongst the dead, your Creator has not abandoned you, will he abandon you amongst the living? Since Heaven gives you [wine] we do not know, what we shall do with you. Come, let us take him [into the house] and make an allocation for him. They made an arrangement for him and each day a different son would provide him with drink.[205]

In sum, the traditional function of inheritance in the family, a function also enshrined in the biblical limiting of potential heirs to family members, ensured that sons usually inherited their parents.

Rabbinic law, however, developed legal techniques which circumvented the limitations set in biblical law as understood by the rabbis. By bequeathing a

203 See *m.ʿArakh.* 4:3; *t.ʿArakh.* 2:17.

204 See *y.Ber.* 9:2 14a; (*b.Ber.* 59b).

205 *Lev. Rab.* 12:1 (Margulies, 245–47; translation based in part on J. Israelstam, *Midrash Rabbah* [London: The Soncino Press, 1939]).

present or composing a will, a father was able to "violate" biblical limitations and allocate his wealth as he saw fit. As the Mishnah states, "He who writes his property to others and neglected his sons, what is done is done, but the sages are not pleased with him. Rabban Simeon ben Gamaliel says, if his sons were acting improperly, then he is remembered for the good."[206] Mishnaic law thus not only allows for disinheritance, but Rabban Simeon ben Gamaliel, echoing Graeco-Roman practice, even argues that improper behavior on the part of one's children calls for disinheritance.[207] Similar sentiments reappear in various other places in rabbinic literature and let us consider two instructive examples.

> R. [E]Liezer's brothers were once ploughing in the plain, while he was ploughing on the mountain. His cow fell and was maimed and this proved fortunate for him. He fled and went to R. Yoḥanan ben Zakkai where he ate clods of earth until his mouth emitted an offensive odor. They went and told R. Yoḥanan ben Zakkai that the breath from R. Eliezer's mouth smelt foul and he said to him: "As the smell of your mouth became unpleasant for the sake of Torah, so will the fragrance of your learning be diffused from one end of the world to the other." After some time, his father came up to disinherit him and found him sitting and lecturing with the greatest of the city sitting before him. . . . Said his father to him, "My son I came up only to disinherit you from my property; now, however, all my property is given to you as a gift." "Behold," he replied, "let it be *herem* [accursed] to me; I will take only an equal share with my brothers."[208]

In the light of issues discussed above, this first example is edifying because it illustrates the high value ascribed to family professions by non-rabbinic families in Palestine and the low value ascribed to Torah study. For current purposes, however, this story is significant because it demonstrates how a father could punish his son with disinheritance and reward him with a disproportionate share in the inheritance. In a similar vein, the following parable makes it evidently clear how a father could write his son out of his will if his son mistreated or disrespected him.

> Another interpretation: Do you requite the Lord? (Deut 32:6): A parable: To what may this be likened? To one who stood up in the forum and insulted his own father. The bystanders said to him, "You stupid fool! Whom

206 See *m.B.Bat.* 8:5.

207 In both ancient Greece and the Roman Empire, "dishersion of a son was abnormal and a result of bad behavior" (Garnsey, *The Roman Empire*, 142 ff.; Barry S. Strauss, *Fathers and Sons in Athens: Ideology and Society in the Era of the Peloponnesian War* [London: Routledge, 1993] 65).

208 *Gen. Rab.* 41:1 (Theodor-Albeck, 397–99 [with parallels cited in commentary]; translation based largely on H. Freedman, trans., *Midrash Rabbah* [London: The Soncino Press, 1939] 340).

> are you insulting? It is your own father! How he labored for your sake, how much weariness he suffered for your sake! If you did not honor him in the past, surely you should honor him now, lest he should will all his possessions to others." So also did Moses say to Israel, "If you do not remember the miracles and mighty deeds that the Holy One, blessed be He, performed for you in Egypt, at least consider how many good things He plans to grant you in the world to come."[209]

In short, by depriving his children of his wealth during his own lifetime and by threatening them with disinheritance upon his death, a father was empowered with two important methods for encouraging his children to obey him.

Conclusion

The economic setting of the Jewish household in Roman Palestine supplies us with a helpful model for analyzing economic influences on childhood. Within a pre-industrial under-developed agrarian society, most families needed all the help they could get and hence families expected children, like all other members of the household, to contribute to the family income. Even young children were expected to work as soon as they were deemed capable, whether in the house, the market, the field or the shop. As children grew, their economic contribution increased and parents would seek to train their sons in a craft, or arrange an apprenticeship for them, and train their daughters at home in domestic chores or in a craft. The financial hardships involved in raising children most certainly underlay rabbinic complaints about raising children, but the long-term financial benefits children offered would have made most parents consider their efforts well rewarded. The child was not only a source of family income, but also served as insurance for his parents' old age and an heir to the family patrimony.

If from the family's perspective, the child was the object of current investments and hopes for the future, the child's perspective was rather different. The child did not control the family resources and hence was subject to the power of others. Parents made the important decisions in a child's life, such as those regarding food-allocation, education, choice of profession and choice of spouse, and they enforced these decisions with physical force or other means of coercion. The activities and opportunities available to a child would have been constrained further by the financial status of his family and the type of settlement in which he lived. Gender differences would have created a distinct childhood

209 *Sifre Deut.* 309 (Finkelstein, 348–49; Reuven Hammer, trans., *Sifre* [New Haven and London: Yale Univ. Press, 1986]). See also *Lam. Rab.* 1:1 (Buber, 41–42); *Exod. Rab.* 1:1 (Shinan, 35–39).

for girls as for boys and the different economic roles boys and girls assumed in the family would have inevitably influenced the treatment children of each gender received. In short, the household economic perspective suggests that most Jewish children were not coddled as pets or treated as incompetent little adults, but rather were viewed as developing family members who were to be educated and trained so that they could enhance the financial status of the family in the present and in the future.

The many comparisons to the ambient Graeco-Roman environment made above suggest that the economics of childhood as it emerges from rabbinic literature reveals a model of childhood that in many respects was not limited to the rabbis themselves and was representative of Jews more generally.[210] Singular features of rabbinic culture, however, suggest that the rabbinic construction of childhood would have been distinctive in certain ways. For example, in contrast to common Roman sensibilities, rabbis (and other Jewish intellectuals) had a highly negative attitude towards the exposure of children, and the rabbinic understanding that procreation was a religious commandment would have challenged even the poorest of rabbinic families to beget and raise children. In a similar vein, knowledge of Torah was such an integral component of rabbinic identity that even impoverished rabbinic families would have had a very strong incentive to arrange a formal education for their male offspring. Indeed, the high evaluation of Torah study amongst the rabbis would have led them to encourage their sons to pursue a higher education and perhaps even a long-term commitment to Torah study while many non-rabbinic Jews would have questioned the profitability of such pursuits. In respect to the family as a lived experience, the instrumental value of children especially as caretakers for their elderly parents was clearly significant amongst Jews in late antiquity, but the rabbis chose to emphasize instead the religious dimension of filial piety. In short, the household economic perspective strengthens the portrait of Jewish families as embedded within the gentile world of late antiquity while pointing to rabbinic culture as a setting within which notions of childhood uncommon in late antiquity flourished.

210 See S. J. D. Cohen, "Introduction," in S. J. D. Cohen, ed., *The Jewish Family in Antiquity* (Atlanta: Scholars Press, 1993) 2; Kraemer, "Typical and Atypical Jewish Family Dynamics."

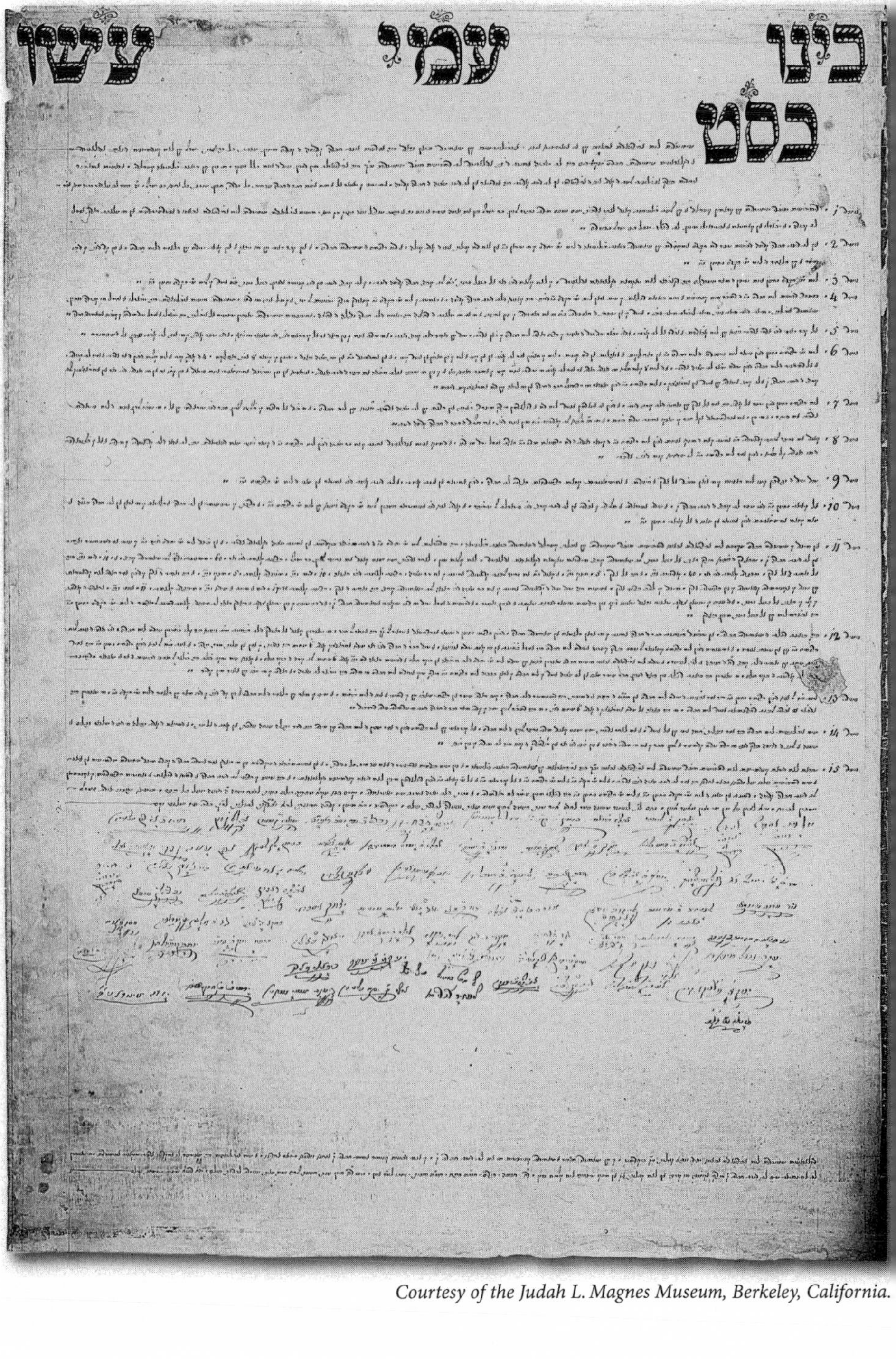

Courtesy of the Judah L. Magnes Museum, Berkeley, California.

The Constitution of the Burial Society of the Bucharest Sephardic Community April 30, 1850

ISAAC JERUSALMI
Hebrew Union College-Jewish Institute of Religion

The Judah L. Magnes Museum in Berkeley, California, has recently acquired the Ladino manuscript of the Constitution drafted in 1850 for the Burial Society of the two Sephardic Synagogues in Bucharest, Rumania. We already knew that the first Constitution of that Burial Society had been written in 1819 by Haham Eliezer Papo, originally from Sarajevo, when he became the spiritual leader of Rumanian Jewry. Documented revisions took place in 1821, 1833, 1837, 1849 and 1878, but no trace of the 1850 revision was available until the present, imposing document came to light. By its contents and structure, it seems to have provided answers to financial and disciplinary issues, such as introducing three classes of funerals, with specific fees, as well as shifting the washing of the deceased from the Burial Society to the *Bikḳur Ḥolim*. For reasons still unknown, this document slipped out of the Society's possession until 1903, when a dated endorsement on its *verso* states that it was "donated" by Albert and Dina Zwiebel to the Spanish Community in Bucharest. As such, it represents a "missing" link in the long chain of organized good deeds performed by the Sephardic Community of Bucharest.

In 1994, Mr. Seymour Fromer, the now director emeritus of the Judah L. Magnes Museum in Berkeley, California, purchased an extremely unusual document from a Hassidic antiquarian in London dealing in Judaica. It started with the three Hebrew words found usually on title-pages בינו עמי ועשו, "understand," "my people," and "do," about 15 cm. apart. The actual text started with the three letters בסט in large text size to give it the appearance of a *ketubba* or "marriage contract." On the right side, it had a sequence of Arabic numerals from 1 to 15, each one preceded by the word נומירו, or "number," and yet no one was able to read the forty long lines of text written on linen paper in this elegant, but puzzling Hebrew cursive. Additionally, like a *Torah Scroll,* it was attached to a single wooden rod, framed with a red ribbon, and protected in a box covered with dark green leather, tooled and gilded, with two clasps (one is now missing). Mr. Fromer added that the owners had it in their family for decades and would have liked to continue owning it, if only someone could identify its contents! Failing that, they had decided to part from it for a decent price.

Mr. Former was as puzzled as the Hassidic owners at the sight of this impressive document. But taking a chance, he purchased it as a potentially "valuable" manuscript for the Judah L. Magnes Museum in Berkeley. The few scholars who saw it there opined that it was written in a stylized Ladino cursive quite difficult to read by the untrained eye. It took 6 separate, 8" x 10" black and white photographs, to put together a composite, readable picture of the entire document which I received for an evaluation. In the course of our efforts to pin down the language of the document in front of us, my wife and I, both born in Turkey, assumed that we would inevitably encounter vocabulary hurdles caused by Rumanian, Bulgarian or even Serbian loanwords.[1] Twice we almost gave up not because of any frustration with Rumanian, Bulgarian or Serbian words of which there were none, but on account of the unfamiliar nature of the script. As a matter of fact, the ten or so Turkish words[2] we identified convinced us that it was a Sephardic piece written by Ottoman Jews. Thus our perseverance was rewarded on our third try.

In sum, this majestic looking manuscript, 80 cm. long and 60 cm. wide (the actual text is 53 cm.) was the Constitution of the חברה קדושה, or Burial Society, of the Sephardic Community in Bucharest, Rumania, dated 18 Iyyar 5610 (April 30, 1850), duly signed by about 70 individuals, and formally enacted on 1 Sivan 5610 (May 12, 1850) with a two line addendum 10 cm. below the main text. Not being an historian, and even less familiar with Rumanian Jewry, I was reluctant to take the next step of publishing it. I shared my reservations with Dr. Herbert Paper, former editor of the *Hebrew Union College Annual*, who immediately said, "documents like these are best grasped by people of the same culture. Read and translate it, and let the scholars of Rumanian history take it from there; their gratitude will surprise you."

As part of the Ottoman Empire, Rumania was situated in the North Central part of European Turkey, with Ottoman Crimea to the East and Ottoman Hun-

1 The language of Sephardic Ottoman Jews has been recently raised to the level of a separate academic discipline. Because Sephardic Jews lived for centuries in the vast domains of the Ottomans, now transformed into Rumania, Bulgaria, Serbia, Greece, etc., it has become fashionable to assume that there is a concomitant Rumanian, Bulgarian, Serbian and Greek "influence" on Ladino. Such influences, if any, are negligible, having rarely penetrated the printed Ladino literature, except for Turkish whose impact was indeed pervasive from the very beginning. As for a name for this language, almost half a dozen are under consideration. Now that a *National Authority for Ladino* has been established in Israel by an Act of the Knesset, with budgetary resources from the State, thanks to the efforts of the Hon. Isaac Navon (fifth president of Israel, who now heads that organization), it no longer makes sense to "balkanize" our terminology. That is why the term *Ladino* is used throughout this presentation.

2 The following is a list of all Turkish words occurring in the Magnes Museum text of 1850 (words in parenthesis reflect their Modern Turkish spelling): *çirak* (*çırak*), "apprentice," *djivan* (*civan*), "young helper," *fener*, "lantern," *grosh* (*kuruş*), "piaster," *kabbar bashi* (*başı*), "chief" grave-digger, *kiaya* (*kâhya*), "steward," *para*, 1/40 of a *kuruş*, *sira* (*sıra*), "turn," *tefter* (*defter*), "note-book."

gary to the West. The earliest Sephardic influx to the Balkans came soon after the expulsion from Spain in 1492, as they settled first in Salonika and from there spread to Ruse (Rusçuk), Nikopolis (Niğbolu), Shumen (Şumnu), Sarajevo (Bosnasaray), and across the Danube to the provinces of Walachia (Eflâk) and Moldavia (Buğdan),[3] constantly mentioned as problem areas in late Ottoman history. Soon, Jews from Istanbul, Vienna and even Amsterdam joined them in their business and financial ventures. Over the years, they established two Sephardic Synagogues in Bucharest called the *Kahal Grande*, and later on, the *Kahal Chico.* A brief summary of their foundation and ultimate destruction runs as follows:

> [T]he two Synagogues in question are the *Kahal Grande* and the *Kahal Chico.* The *Kahal Grande,* also known as *Kahal Kadosh Gadol,* was apparently erected in 1814, as stated in a license granted to the community by Prince Ioan Caragea. In 1853, the building was reconstructed in Moorish style borrowing details from the Synagogue *del Transito* in Toledo, Spain. In 1891, a big Rieger Jaegerdorf organ was brought in from Leipzig, and the place soon started hosting concerts by A. I. Ivela (Halevy), the great choir conductor, whose brilliant personality attracted many other prominent musicians, Jewish as well as gentile, to the Synagogue. Ivela, a rabbi's son, who lost his eyesight as a student, "dedicated his entire life to music and the strengthening of Judaic life." He composed for the Spanish Synagogue a splendid collection of religious songs, *Juval,* and turned the site into a famous concert venue, thus exploring yet another potential function of the synagogue as a house of music. Shattered by a major earthquake in 1940, the *Kahal Grande* was torched a year later by the Legionaries, then razed in 1955. The *Kahal Chico* was built in the 19th century and reconstructed in 1864, and again in 1948, but ended up under the wrecker's ball to make room for a municipal project.[4]

The first known Constitution of the Bucharest Sephardic Burial Society was drafted by the famous Haham Eliezer Papo, author of the *Pelé Yoeṣ,*[5] who arrived from Sarajevo in 1819 and settled there. In 1983, Jacob Geller of Tel Aviv

3 Eugen Denize, "The Sephardic Jews in Walachia and Moldavia between the Sixteenth and Nineteenth Centuries," in Paul Cernovodeanu, ed., *History of the Jews in Romania* (5 vols.; Tel Aviv: Tel Aviv Univ., 2002) 1:51–62.

4 See Streja Aristide and Lucian Schwarz, *Synagogues of Romania* (Tel Aviv: Hasefer Publishing House, 1997) 64–65. For a picture of the *Templul Sefarad*, see Carol Iancu, *Les Juifs de Roumanie* (Aix-en-Provence: Editions de l'Université de Provence, 1978) doc. no. 4.

5 אליעזר פאפו, ספר פלא יועץ (קושטנדינה, 1823/5584). A new, vocalized edition was published in Jerusalem by "*Tushiyya* Publications" in 1987.

University published a short history of the Jews of Bucharest.[6] In his research, he worked indirectly on Ladino documents that had been previously translated into Rumanian in 1911 by a certain Sephardic teacher called Y. D. Bali;[7] and Geller now translated all of these 1911 Rumanian translations into Hebrew which by then didn't reflect the Turkish vocabulary interspersed within the text.[8] He also listed additions to, or revisions of, the First Constitution of 1819 which took place in 1821, 1833, 1837, 1849.[9] Yet, our 1850 text, now housed in the Magnes Museum, was clearly missing from his study. Was it because it was never translated into Rumanian or perhaps because it wasn't even available to Y. D. Bali in 1911 who translated all the other original Ladino texts into Rumanian? Before discussing a few salient historical data, it will be useful to review briefly the contents of the 1850 Magnes Museum scroll which is the obvious "missing link" in this almost two centuries old tradition of a written Constitution in cemetery governance.

Summary of the 1850 Magnes Museum Text

The preamble stresses a unanimous decision to constitute a *Ḥevra Ḳeḏosha* of *Ḳabbarim* or "grave-diggers" whereby a signatory and his son will be called a *ḥaver* or "Associate" for life, morally bound to perform certain duties stated below.

Article 1 Everyone must be involved in the funeral arrangements of any Jew by preparing a grave, carrying the dead to the cemetery and performing the burial.

6 Geller, Jacob, *The Sephardic Jews of Rumania, the Rise and Decline of the Sephardic Community in Bucharest* (Tel Aviv: Tel Aviv Univ., 1983) 91–98. Geller's study is the most comprehensive to date. All references to his work will be introduced as Geller.

7 About Bali, Geller writes, הן תורגמו מהמקור לשפה הרומנית, בשנת 1911, על-ידי המורה י. ד. באלי. אני מפרסם כאן לראשונה את התקנות הללו בשלמותן בעברית, כפי שתרגמתי אותן מהשפה הרומנית, "they were translated from the original into Rumanian in the year 1911 by the teacher Y. D. Bali. I am publishing here these articles in their entirety for the first time in Hebrew, as I translated them from Rumanian," see Geller, *The Sephardic Jews*, 90.

8 Geller writes: התקנות הללו... נכתבו במקורן בלאדינו, בתוספת מלים עבריות וביטויים שכיחים במסורת הספרדים, הכל בכתב-יד עברי ספרדי (ראה להלן צילום דף התקנות). Therefore, when he says, "these articles . . . were originally written in Ladino with the addition of Hebrew words and expressions found in the Sephardic tradition, entirely in the Sephardic Hebrew script (see further down the photo of a page of articles) . . . ," the reader is in the dark as to the language of "these expressions found in the Sephardic tradition" which are probably traditional Turkish phrases so common among Ladino speakers! His only reference to a Turkish word is *baş kabbar* which he correctly translates as הקברן הראשי, "chief grave-digger." Also the promised "photo of a page of articles" was never incorporated into his book! See Geller, *The Sephardic Jews*, 90.

9 Geller cites the 1878 and 1880 Constitutions, with one new article for each, but these concern the *ḥevra ḳeḏosha li-reḥiṣa*, not the *ḥevra ḳeḏosha* proper, Geller, *The Sephardic Jews*, 98.

Article 2 The officers are: two *peḳiḏim* or "presidents" chosen from among the members of the two Congregations; two *parnasim* or "managers" chosen from among the members of the Burial Society, helped by other hired people.

Article 3 Fees[10] to be collected from the next of kin for a separate Cemetery Fund.

Article 4 Members promise to abide by the instructions of the two presidents. Victims of a contagious disease will be buried only after "ritual washing" has taken place by the *ḥevra li-reḥiṣa.*

Article 5 Duties of the chief grave-digger.

Article 6 Procedures to follow in drawing lots to determine a fair distribution of duties and fines for those disobeying orders.

Article 7 One of the two managers must always accompany a casket to the cemetery. Any member, exempted up to three times after an unexcused absence, may be dropped from membership on his fourth absence.

Article 8 Procedures to follow when the deceased is a child and fine for failure to abide by them.

Article 9 Storage procedures for funeral paraphernalia.

Article 10 The duty of the *kiaya* or "steward" to keep a ledger of incomes and expenditures.

Article 11 Establishing three classes of funerals and their respective fees, with provisions for the indigent or people of "worthy ancestry."

Article 12 Organizing an annual banquet to honor worthy members.

Article 13 Procedures for the installation of new officers once a year.

Article 14 Special arrangements for the funeral of members of the Society and fine for failure to show up.

Article 15 Exhortation to fully carry out all these duties, so that no other group may create another Burial Society in Bucharest. The date of enactment: 18 Iyyar 5610 [April 30, 1850]

Approximately 70 signatures.

10 Fees and penalties are recorded in an assortment of currencies. Beside the Ottoman *grosh* and *para*, worth 1/40 of a *grosh*, the *firfiriḳ* (פֿירפֿיריק) (*vier Pfennig*) and the *esfanṣiḳ* (איספֿאנציק), presumably two Austrian coins, occur side by side with the French *frank* and the Rumanian *lei*. To what extent these represent actual diverse currencies or possibly just names of former curren-

Ratification of this document occurred on 1 Sivan 5610 [May 12, 1850] by the *yeḥiḏim*, "members" and *gabbayim*, "treasurers" of both Sephardic Congregations in Bucharest, supporting this Burial Society and its rights to raise funds independently for its needs.

From the first Constitution in 1819 to the fifth in 1849, the name of the Society was החברה הקדושה לרחיצה וללויה, the Burial Society for רחיצה, "washing" and לויה, "accompanying" (the dead). The 1850 Magnes Museum text is not a mere revision of the previous ones, but a new beginning with a new name, as it now calls itself simply a חברה קדושה, or Burial Society. The "job description" of its חברים, or *associates* consisted solely in digging a grave, carrying the deceased to the cemetery, and burial. For members of the Society only, it also included conducting services at the home of the deceased, but the רחיצה, or "washing" of the dead and the *guevo* or the "mourners' meal" after the burial were not expected.

The 1819 Constitution had 7 articles and 48 signatures. Subsequent constitutions built on these articles and added to them: Article 8 in 1821, ratified by 14 signatures; Article 9 in 1833 with 54 signatures; Article 10 in 1837 with the signatures of 5 *parnasim*. The 1849 Constitution rewrites the same 10 articles of the 1837 version, but significantly shortens them. Why, then, was there a need for a brand new constitution a year later, in 1850, with 15 articles?

A careful reading of this 1850 Magnes Museum text suggests that it may have been drawn up in response to a crisis, if not a mini-revolt, on the part of members who may have resented the harsh fines mentioned in almost every article of previous Constitutions from 1819 up to 1849, to punish those members who didn't abide by the rules in performing their funeral duties, among them absenteeism. The revised text of 1837 was especially harsh in that respect. Article 10 specifies that public discussion concerning the appointment and dismissal of *parnasim*, the induction of a new *associate*, and the assessment of a monetary fine, etc. must be avoided. Anyone who transgresses these articles shall be punished,[11] even if it means erasing his signature[12] from the Constitutional

cies applied to actual ones, is always an intriguing problem. For a long time Jews in Greece referred to the Greek *drachma* as a *frank*, just as Turks in New York today, when dealing with fellow Turks, refer to the US dollar as a (Turkish) lira! One point is clear, there is no mistake in Article 11, where the casket fee is given numerically as 17.20 *grosh*, and in full letters as seventeen and a HALF *grosh*, based on a *grosh* having 40 *paras*! Similarly, the 1 *esfanṣiḳ* fine per absence mentioned in Article 6, "with the Fund contributing 1 matching *esfanṣiḳ*," for a total of 2 *esfanṣiḳ*s or 40 *pfennig* could also be loose usage for 40 *paras* or 1 *grosh*! Differently said, since a *grosh* is 40 *paras*, 20 *paras* represent 1 *esfanṣiḳ*, just as 2 *esfanṣiḳ*s correspond to 40 *paras*!

11 Examples of similar harsh fines and punishments at early American Sephardic Congregations

Document of the Burial Society. It is clear that open criticism was no longer tolerated and that in extreme cases the punishment could go as far as "erasing a member's signature from the Constitutional Document of the Burial Society." In the 1850 Constitution, on the other hand, the "fine clauses" have been confined to Articles 6, 8 and 14.

Up to 1850, there seems to have been one type of funeral; and apparently people weren't getting their money's worth of service. For the first time in 1850, we notice the introduction of 3 classes of funerals: for the rich, the poor and the people in-between.

Furthermore, between 1819 and 1849, the emphasis in every single Constitution was on the rights and privileges of the Society's *own* members, the *associates* or חברים, even though their purported primary task was to take care of the Congregational members or יחידים, not the other way around. In the brand new, 1850 Magnes Museum text, there is a dramatic overhaul of priorities, with only the last article dealing with the חברים or *associates*, while everywhere else the obvious emphasis is on serving the יחידים or members, as implied in the statement, "we take upon ourselves the full obligation of serving the *yeḥiḏim*...."

Conclusion

All these reasons may explain why such a sumptuous looking Constitution for a Burial Society, professionally written by a scribe, drafted also by someone versed in the lessons of the past, was conceived in anticipation of a more stable, less polemical future. As a perpetual reminder of some past conflict, was it designed to hang in a Synagogue office, or was it rolled up in its box, for display on rare occasions only? We do know that Isak Lazar is the one who provided the ornate box in which the scroll was originally housed. Lazar's name and the year 1857 are still clearly stamped in gold on the binding. But we would probably never have known the exact motivation behind this strange enterprise, without one additional observation.

---

are: *Shearith Israel* Congregation in New York City with a $250 fine in its 1805 Constitution for insulting the *parnas*; *Mikveh Israel Congregation* in Philadelphia with a $25 fine in its 1824 Constitution for unruly behavior during services. Also at *Mikveh Israel*, "no person deceased shall be entitled to an *hashkava*... until the sum required by the Constitution be paid to the *Gabay*." See Daniel J. Elazar, Jonathan Sarna and Rela G. Monson, *A Double Bond, The Constitutional Documents of American Jewry* (Lanham: Univ. Press of America, 1992) 108 and 127–28, respectively.

12 A similar case of "name erasing" is found in New York's *Shearith Israel Congregation*'s 1761 Constitution as punishment for not conforming to the rules of the Congregation. An even harsher punishment of denying burial rights is imposed on those who break disciplinary rules or haven't paid their financial obligations in Charleston's *Beth Elohim Congregation*'s 1820 Constitution. See Elazar, *A Double Bond*, 105 and 116, respectively.

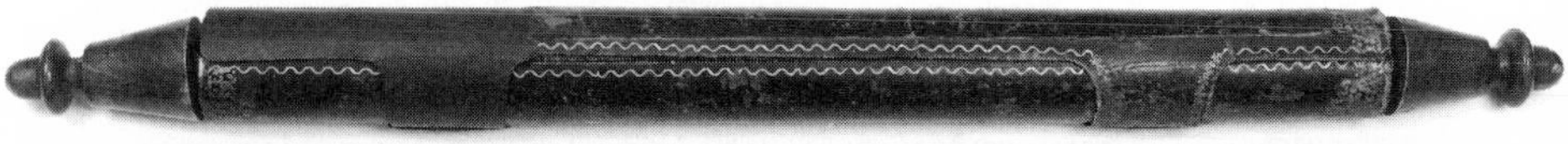

On the upper left side of the verso, there is an intriguing handwritten comment that reads:

Photography by Sibila Savage, Emeryville, California.

Donat de noi Comunații Spaniole
Albert și Dina Zwiebel
in 6/19 Decenbre 1903
Bucuresci

Donated by us to the Spanish Community
Albert and Dina Zwiebel
6/19 December 1903
Bucharest

If in 1903, Albert and Dina Zwiebel donated a document signed in 1850 to the Spanish Community, it seems that the document somehow slipped out of the Community between those two dates and was returned by the Zwiebels as a gift. Apparently it was a prized possession and wasn't even made available to the individual who translated the other Constitutions from Ladino into Rumanian in 1911. In the intervening 80 to 90 years there must have been other revisions, but none survived, or if they did, they were never translated into Rumanian.[13]

13 Thus in terms of note 5 above, the text of the 1850 Magnes Museum Constitution represents the "last written word" for the Rumanian Sephardic Burial Society tradition.

What survived are listings of *peḳiḏim*, "presidents," from 1820 to 1912, and *parnasim*, "managers," from 1812 to 1893,[14] with some time gaps in between. For the former, the gap is between 1836 and 1852, for the latter, the gap is between 1846 and 1852. Does this 1850 Constitution, signed on April 30 of that year, make sense without a general election before its enactment?

Therefore, this "missing link," with its sesquicentennial life-span, represents a worthy memorial to Rumanian Sephardic Jewry. For a while, this *ketubba*-like document was relegated to the "lost and found" category. But in the end, it triumphed as it migrated to the West and gained citizenship in America at the Judah L. Magnes Museum in Berkeley, California.

I have the distinct pleasure of expressing my grateful thanks to Mr. Seymour Fromer for his efforts in assuring the survival of this unique document published here. He and Mr. James Leventhal, the present Development Coordinator at the Magnes Museum, have opened the doors of their Institution for the completion of this project. I hope their patience will be rewarded.

14 See Geller, *The Sephardic Jews*, 99.

Transcription

בינו **עמי** **עשו**

בס״ט מוזוטרוס לוס אפֿירמאדוס אבאשו קון אה אונאמיינטו אונו. אינבֿילו[נ]טימוס קון מואיסטרו בואין גראדו פור אזירמוס אונה חברה קדושה די קברים סיגון מנהג כל תפוצות ישראל קון לאס קונדיסייוניס דיגֿאס אדילאנטרי אי דיקלאראמוס מוזוטרוס חברים מקשיבים פור לה מצוה איסטה דיגֿה אדילאנטרי לה ריסיבֿימוס סובֿרי מוזוטרוס יב״ך פור אפֿירמארלה סין דינגון מודו די אונס כלל ועיקר. סי נון קון בואינה בֿילונטאד קומפלידה. אי דאמוס אסאבֿיר אטודוס פורקי אינבֿילונטי אלמה די קאדה אונו די אפֿירמארסי אין לא דיטה קארטה פור אינריזייאר אין לה דיטה מצוה די חברה קדושה. אי סי טייני קי ייאמאר איל אי סוס איזֿוס חבר די חברה עד סוף כל הדורות סיגון מנהג כל אחינו בני ישראל ו״ה יעזור לנו על דבר כבוד שמו אכי״ר.

נומירו 1. ריסיבֿימוס סובֿרי מוזוטרוס קון קוראסון קומפלידו אי קון אלמה בֿילונטוזה קואנדו לאחר אריכות ימים ושנים סירה נפטר אלגון בר ישראל בין איש ואשה עשיר או עני גר או תושב מגדול ועד תינוק בן יומו. סומוס אובֿליגאדוס מוזוטרוס לוס אפֿירמאדוס אבאשו די אינטרימיטירמוס אין סו מלאכה פארה אזירלי לה קבורה אי ייבֿארלו אין קואיסטאס אי אינטיראրלו סיגון לה ריגלה מכל בני ישראל הכשרים.

נומירו 2. אין לה דיטה חברה קדושה דיבֿימוס טיניר דוס פקידים איסקוזֿידוס קון מואיסטרה בואינה בֿילונטאד די לוס שי׳ יחידים קי סי טופאן הי״ו אין לאס דוס קהלות אונו די קאדה קהילה . אי דוס פרנסים די מוזוטרוס חברים . אי און קבר באשי קון סו גֿיבאן אי און קיאייאה טודוס קון פלאזיר דילוס חברים. אי נון קירי דיגֿו קי דיבֿי סיאיר אי קון פלאזיר די לוס ש״י פקידים הזמן הי״ו.

נומירו 3. לוס שי׳ פקידים הזמן אייוס טיינין די סיאיר משתדלים פור ריקאבֿדאר לאס טאקסאס דיקלאראדאס אדילאנטרי. קי לאס קואלאס דיבֿי דאר איל בעל המת ב״מ אלה קופה חברה קדושה דיטה. קי לה קופה דיטה נון דיבֿי קונוסיר אדינגון בעל המת ב״מ אוטרו קי לוס ש״י פקידים הזמן הי״ו

נומירו 4. סיינפרי דיבֿימוס לוס חברים הי״ו די ריסיבֿיר סוס קונסיזֿוס אי סוס בואינאס ריגלאס קי מוס אראן לוס שי׳ פקידים הי״ו דיגֿוס פור קואינטו דילה דיטה חברה קדושה. אי באסטה קי לוס שי׳ פקידים הי״ו קומאנדין פורקי ייבֿימוס אל מת אי קי סילי אגה סו ריזֿו. מוזוטרוס סומוס אובֿליגאדוס פור ייבֿארלו אי אזירלי סו קבורה סיגון מואיסטרו אובֿליגו. סייאה דיאה סייאה נוגֿי סייאה לובֿייאה סייאה נייבֿי. אוטרו קי אין טיינפו די חאזינורה ב״מ סי איס חאזינורה קי נון אפיגה אי סי אזי סו מלאכה די רחיצה פור מאנוס דילה חברה גדולה די רחיצה. איסטונסיס מוזוטרוס טאנביין טינימוס איל אובֿליגו פור ייבֿארלו אי אזירלי טודו סו ריזֿו קי קונבֿייני אמואיסטרה חברה.

נומירו 5. איל קבר באשי דיבֿי אירסי אריבֿה 5ונטו קון לוס קאבֿאדוריס אי אבֿריר איל לה קאבֿה. אי דיבֿי ייבֿאר טודו מודו די גאסטי קי פרימי פארה לוס חברים קי בֿאן

אריב̆ה. טודו קין גאסטה דילה קופה דיטה. אי סי טירנה אונס קי נון פואידי איר איל קבר באשי דיג̆ו דיב̆י מאנדאר סו ג̆יראק. אי דיב̆י טיניר קארגו קיסי אגה לה קאב̆ה סיגון איל דימיניסטיר.

נומירו 6. לוס שי׳ פרנסים הזמן דיב̆ין נוטאר לוס נומבריס די לוס חברים הי״ו אין פאפיליקוס אי איג̆ארלוס אין דוס קוטיס. לוס קי סאב̆ין אזיר לה קאב̆ה אין און קוטי אי לוס קי נון סאב̆ין אין אוטרו קוטי. אי אין אסודיסיינדו ב״מ און מת, מצוה גראנדי טיינין קי קיטאר 8 אוג̆ו פאפיליקוס. 4 די קאדה קוטי אי לוס קואלוס דיב̆ין די איר אריב̆ה אי אזיר לה קבורה. אי איל ריסטאנטי דילוס חברים דיב̆ין טודוס ייב̆אר לה מצוה אריב̆ה. אי די לוס 8 קיליס סאלייו סו דאנדה פארה איר אזיר לה קאב̆ה סי טירנה אונס קומו קי איסטה חאזינו ב״מ או קי נון סי טופה אינלה סיב̆דאד איס פטור די דיטה דאנדה. אינטאנטו אין נון טוב̆יינדו אסימיז̆אנטי אונס נוטאדו אי נון קיג̆ו איר אין סו דאנדה דיב̆י דאר און איספ̆אנציק אלה קופה די דיטה חברה ק׳ אי לה קופה אייודארה קון אוטרו און איספ̆אנציק. אי לוס פרנסים הי״ו דיב̆ין מאנדאר סו פריסונאל חבר די חברה אין סו לוגאר קון דוס איספ̆אנציקיס דיטוס.

נומירו 7. לוס פרנסים הזמן דיב̆ין טיניר איל קארגו פור אזיר איל ארון קון גאסטי דילה קופה דיטה. אי דיב̆ין אה אונארסין אינטרי לוס דוס אי ריגלארסין פורקי סיינפרי ב̆אייגה און פרנס קון לה מצוה אריב̆ה ג̆ונטו קון לוס חברים. אי סי ב̆ידו איל פרנס קי פ̆אלטו אלגון חבר דיב̆י טופארסי קון איל. סי טוב̆ו אלגון אונס די לוס נוטאדוס אריב̆ה איס פטור. אי סי נון. איס אינפריזינטאדו אקיל חבר קי מאנקו אסטה טריס ב׳יזיס. אי סי ח״ו פ׳אלטו אלה קוארטינה ב̆יז סין אונס דיג̆ו. איס סאלידו די חבר די חברה קדושה דיטה.

נומירו 8. קואנדו איס נפטר אלגונה קרייאטורה ב״מ אסטה קי איס די סינקו אנייוס דיב̆ין לוס פרנסים הי״ו די קיטאר דאנדה די דוס פריסונאס חברים הי״ו פארה אזירלי טודו סו ריז̆ו. אי די סינקו אנייוס אינדילאנטרי אסטה קי איס בר מצוה דיב̆ין לוס פרנסים הי״ו די קיטאר ג̆ינטי מאס דימאזייאדוס כפי לה אידאד דילה קרייאטורה קי סירה אי איל קי פ̆אלטארה די סו דאנדה קי לי סאלייו. דיב̆ין אזיר לוס פרנסים הי״ו לו מידיזמו קנס דיג̆ו אריב̆ה.

נומירו 9. טודו מודו די תכריכין קומו לוס פאנייוס קי סי איג̆אן סוב̆רי איל ארון אי פ̆ינירים אי אסימיז̆אנטיס קוזאס פרימורוזאס פארה לה חברה. דיב̆ין איסטאר אין אונה קאשה. אי לה דיטה קאשה דיב̆י איסטאר אין מאנו די לוס שי׳ פרנסים הי״ו.

נומירו 10. איל קיאייאה הזמן הי״ו דיב̆י טיניר לה קופה די דיטה חברה ק׳. אי טודה אינטראדה אי סאלידה קי אב̆רה אין לה דיטה קופה דיב̆י נוטארלה אל טיפ̆טיר. אי קאדה אנייו דיב̆י אמוסטראר חשבון אלוס שי׳ פקידים ג̆ונטו קון לוס שי׳ פרנסים הי״ו. אי פרוכת קי טינימוס אין לה חברה אי פלאטאס קי סי אראן אין לא חברה בע״ה אי מאס קוזאס אסימיז̆אנטיס דיב̆ין איסטאר אין מאנו די איל קיאייאה הזמן הי״ו.

נומירו 11. אין סיינדו קי מוזוטרוס חברים מקשיבים לוס אפ̆ירמאדוס אבאשו ריסיב̆ימוס סוב׳רי מוזוטרוס קון אוב̆ליגו קומפלידו די מואיסטרה בואינה ב̆ילונטאד.

פור סירבֿירלוס אלוס ש״ר יחידים הי״ו די דיטה סיבֿדאד בוקורישט אין איסטה מצוה דיקלאראדה אריבֿה. אי אין בֿיינדו לוס ש״׳ יחידים דיגֿוס הי״ו קי מוסי אזי דימיניסטיר גאסטי אין לה דיטה חברה ק׳. טופארון די גֿוסטו פורקי פאגי איל בעל המת אלה מואיסטרה קופה סיירטאס טאקסאס דיקלאראדאס אדילאנטרי. לאס קואלאס סון. לאחר אריכות ימים ושנים קואנדו איס נפטר אלגון בר ישראל. פרימה קלאסה דיבֿי דאר „60״ סיסינטה גרוש׳ אלה מואיסטרה קופה. אי „10״ דייס גרו׳ פור איל גאסטי די איל ארון. סיגונדה קלאסה דיב״י דאר „40״ קוארינטה גרו׳. אי פור איל ארון „5״ סינקו גרו׳. אי קואנדו ב״מ איס נפטר אלגונה קרייאטורה אסטה קי איס בר מצוה. פרימה קלאסה דיבֿי פאגאר „10״ דייס גרו. סיגונדה קלאסה „5״ סינקו גרו׳. אי פור גאסטי די ארון קי דיבֿין אזיר פארה לאס קרייאטוראס קון טודו קי אקונטיסירה קרייאטורה קי נון פרימירה ארון. סיינדו קי אלרובֿ פרימי ארון. איזימוס פור טודו מודו די קרייאטורה אסטה קי איס בר מצוה דיבֿי פאגאר אלה מואיסטרה קופה פור גאסטי די ארון. פרימה קלאסה „17.20״ דייס אי סייטי אי מידייו גרו׳. סיגונדה קלאסה „11״ אונזי גרו׳ אפארטי די קארוסה קי קאלי קי פאגי איל בעל המת. אי די עניים קי טומאן צדקה טאנטו גראנדי טאנטו גֿיקו נון פואידימוס טומאר דינגונה טאקסה ני דינגון גאסטי. אי דיבֿימוס די אזירלי טודו סו ריזֿו טוקאנטי אמואיסטרה חברה ק׳. אי די בני טובים קי נון טומאן צדקה ני פואידין פאגאר לה סיגונדה קלאסה ריסטה אל פאריסיר די לוס ש״׳ פקידים הזמן הי״ו פור אבֿינירסילוס קון איל בעל המת סיגון פואידין.

נומירו 12. פור בואינה ריגלה די מואיסטרה חברה. אין טובֿיינדו פֿייסטה חבר די חברה איסטה קי סי אראן פלאטאס אין מואיסטרה חברה. דיבֿין פרנסי הזמן די טומאר אינפריסטאדו אי טראייר אל ק״ק פור אונראר אל חבר. סי טאנביין קואנדו איל פאטרון דילה פֿייסטה ייבֿה גוסטו פור קילו בֿיזֿיטין טודוס לוס חברים. דיבֿי דארסי די נוטה אלוס פרנסים הי״ו קון און טיינפו אנטיס. אי איסטונסיס דיבֿין לוס פרנסים קומאנדאר אל שמש פורקי קומבידי אטודוס לוס חברים פור אזירלי בֿיזֿיטה אין סו קאזה טודוס אינגֿונטו. אי טודו חבר די חברה דיבֿי דאר מידייו איספֿאנציק קאדה 6 מיזיס פור נדבות קי אזין אין עליות ספר תורה. אי אונה בֿיס אל אנייו דיבֿין פרנסים הזמן הי״ו פור אזיר [און]ה מ[יז]ה קון גאסטי דילה קופה ר״ח די חנוכה או ל״ג לעומר. אי טודוס לוס אפֿירמאדוס אבאשו סומוס חברים טאנביין גֿונטו קון טודוס לוס ש״׳ יחידים דילה סיבֿדאד אין ביקור חולים אי דיבֿימוס פאגאר דוס גרו׳ קאדה 6 מיזיס אלה קופה די בקור חולים. אי קואנדו מוס טוקה בֿילה פור בֿילאר אל חאזינו דיבֿימוס די איר או מאנדאר פריסונה [קון ל]ה קארטה די בקור חולים. סי טאנביין פור בואינה ריגלה נון פואידי דינגון חבר מיטיר מאנו אין לה מצוה אוטרו קי לוס חברים קי אראן בכבוד לוס פרנסים הי״ו פורקי טוקי אטודוס לוס חברים סו סירה פור ייבֿאר לה מצוה . אי פארה קי סי ייבֿי קון אונור סין קוריר.

נומירו 13. אונה בֿיז אל אנייו דיבֿין פרנסים הזמן הי״ו פור אזיר אגֿונטה די טודוס לוס חברים אין חוה״מ די פסח או די סוכות פור דימיניסטיר דילה חברה. קומו פארה מיטיר און פרנס מואיבֿ׳ו קון קי ריסטי אי אונו די לוס בֿייגֿוס. אי טייני קי סיאיר קון פלאזיר דילוס חברים אי נון קירי דוגֿו קי דיבֿי סיאיר קון פלאזיר דילוס ש״׳ פקידים הי״ו. סי טאנביין פור אדובֿאר סי אבֿרה אלגונה (ר)[ד]יפֿירינסייאה אינטרי לוס חברים.

סי פור פאגאר איל מידייו איספֿאנציק די קאדה **6** מיזיס דיגֿו. סי פור ריסיבֿיר אלגון יחיד קי קירי סיאיר חבר די חברה דיטה סי מיריסירה סירה ריסיבֿידו.

נומירו 14. מוס אובֿליגאמוס לוס חברים פור אזיר גמילות חסד אונו קון איל אוטרו. אי איס לאחר אריכות ימים ושנים קואנדו סירה נפטר אלגון די לוס חברים. איל קבר באשי קון לוס פרנסים דיבֿין די אזיר מנין די לוס חברים קון סירה פור דיזיר תפילה מנחה ערבית אין קאזה די איל מת. אי דיספואיס די קאדה תפילה סי דיבֿי די מילדאר תהלים אי משנה אי אלגו די דרשה פורקי דיגה סו יורש טריס קדישים. אי אלגון חבר קי איס סו סירה די בֿיניר אי נון בֿינו דיבֿי דאר און פֿירפֿיריק די קנס פור לה סירה קי נון בֿינו.

נומירו 15. טודאס לאס דיטאס קונדיסייוניס לאס ריסיבֿימוס סובֿרי מוזוטרוס לוס אפֿירמאדוס אבאשו יב״ך פור אפֿירמארלאס קון מואיסטרה בואינה בֿילונטאד. אי נון מוס פודימוס אריפינטיר די אייאס עד סוף כל הדורות. אי אין איסטה סיבֿדאד די בוקורישט נון סי פואידין אזיר אוטרה חברה די קברים סיינדו מוזוטרוס מיריסימוס אין אייאה אי מוס ריסיבֿימוס עלינו ועל ירשינו הבאים אחרינו פור אזיר לה דיטה מצוה דיגֿה אריבֿה. אי לוס שי׳ פקידים הי״ו אי לוס שי׳ פרנסים הי״ו אי איל קבר באשי הי״ו אי איל שי׳ קיאייאה הי״ו דיבֿין ריגלארסין סיגון לאס דיטאס קונדיסייוניס דיקלאראדאס. אי פור שמש קי פרימי אלה דיטה חברה אי ריסטו די ריגלאס אי גאסטיס פרימורוזוס קי אקונטיסיראן אלה דיטה חברה קדושה. ריסטה אין מאנו די לוס שי׳ פקידים הזמן הי״ו אילוס שי׳ פרנסים הזמן הי״ו פור ריגלאר סיגון מיזור ליס פאריסירה. אי זכות דילה מצוה איסטה מוס מאמפאראר‍ה. יקויים בנו מקרא שכתוב בילע המות לנצח ומחה ה׳ דמעה מעל כל פנים. ובימינו תיושע יאודה וישראל ישכון לבטח. ובא לציון גואל וכן יהי רצון ונאמר אמן. ביום ל״ג לעומר שמונה עשר לחדש אייר שנת חמשה אלפים ושש מאות ועשרה לבריאת עולם. בוקורישט „בא סימן״ קרובה ישועתי לבא וצדקתי להגלות לפ״ק ברוב עוז ושלום. וקים.

[Approximately 70 signatures.]

דיקלאראמוס מוזוטרוס לוס אפֿירמאדֿוס אבאשו יחידי וגבאי קהלות ה״ק בוקורישט קי קון מואיסטרו סאבֿיר אי מואיסטרה קונטינטיס סי איזו לה דיטה חברה ק׳, קי אנסי דיבֿימוס קונוסיר איסטה חברה ק׳ אנחנו וזרעינו הבאים אחרינו. אי מוס אובֿליגאמוס פור מאנטיניר לו איסקריטו אריבֿה טוקאנטי אמוזוטרוס, סי טאמביין לה ליסינסייה טייני לה דיטה חברה ק׳ פורקי אקוזגה סו קופה אין לאס קהלות ה״ק אין סינקו טיינפוס לוס קואלוס סון ר״ח חנוכה. פורים. חוה״מ פסח. חוה״מ סוכות. ויזכו לש״ר אמן. ביום ר״ח סיון שנת חמשת אלפים ושש מאות ועשרה לבריאת עולם, יהא רעוא שיהיו בשמחת עולם.

Transliteration

עשו עמי בינו

BSṬ Mozotros, los afirmados abasho, kon a unamyento[15] uno, envelu[n]timos kon muestro buen grado por azermos una *ḥevra ḳedosha* de *ḳabbarim* sigun *minhag kol tefuṣoth Yisrael* kon las kondisyones dichas adelantre. I deklaramos mozotros, *ḥaverim maḳshivim,* por la *miṣva* esta, dicha adelantre, la risivimos sovre mozotros, ke mos bendiga a todos, por afirmarla sin dingun modo de *ones kelal ve-ᶜiḳḳar,* si non kon buena veluntad kumplida. I damos asaver a todos porke envelunte alma de kada uno de afirmarse en la dita karta por enrezyar en la dita *miṣva* de *ḥevra ḳedosha.* I se tyene ke yamar el i sus ijos *ḥaver* de *ḥevra ᶜad sof kol ha-doroth,* sigun *minhag kol aḥenu bene Yisrael, va-A' yaᶜazor lanu al devar kevod shemo, amen ken yehi raṣon.*

Numero 1. Risivimos sovre mozotros kon korason kumplido i kon alma veluntoza kuando, *le-aḥar arikhuth yamim ve-shanim,* sera *nifṭar* algun *bar Yisrael, ben ish ve-isha, ᶜashir* o *ᶜani, ger* o *toshav, mi-gadol ve-ᶜad tinok ben yomo,* somos ovligados mozotros, los afirmados abasho, de entremetermos en su *melakha* para azerle la *ḳevura,* i yevarlo en kuestas, i enterrarlo sigun la regla *mi-kol bene Yisrael ha-kesherim.*

Numero 2. En la dita *ḥevra ḳedosha* devemos tener dos *peḳidim* eskojidos kon muestra buena veluntad de los Srs. *yeḥidim* ke se topan, *hy"v,*[16] en las dos *ḳehilloth* – uno de kada *ḳehilla* – dos *parnasim* de mozotros, *ḥaverim,* i un *ḳabbar bashi* kon su *djivan,* i un *kiaya.* Todos kon plazer de los *ḥaverim,* i non kere dicho ke deve seer i kon plazer de los Srs. *peḳidim ha-zeman, hy"v.*

Numero 3. Los Srs. *peḳidim ha-zeman* eyos tyenen de seer *mishtaddelim* por rekavdar las taksas deklaradas adelantre, ke las kualas deve dar el *baᶜal ha-meth, b"m,* ala *kuppa ḥevra ḳedosha* dita, ke la *kuppa* dita non deve konoser adingun *baᶜal ha-meth, b"m,* otro ke los Srs. *peḳidim ha-zeman, hy"v.*

Numero 4. Syenpre devemos los *ḥaverim, hy"v,* de risivir sus konsejos de sus buenas reglas ke mos aran los Srs. *peḳidim, hy"v,* dichos por kuento dela dita *ḥevra ḳedosha.* I basta ke los Srs. *peḳidim ha-zeman, hy"v,* komanden porke yevemos al *meth* i ke sele aga su rijo. Mozotros somos ovligados por yevarlo i azerle su *ḳevura* sigun muestro ovligo seya diya, seya noche, seya luvya, seya niyeve, otro ke en tyenpo de hazinura *b"m.* Si es hazinura ke non apega i se aze

15 The word division of the Ladino expression אה אונאמיינטו אונו, *a unamyento uno* for "unanimously," looks clumsy, but quite common in the written literature. At times these defy Spanish norms, while frequently they follow Hebrew habits, such as *deel* in one word for *de el* analogous to the Hebrew ממנו.

16 The recurring acronym הי"ו *may the Lord bless and keep him* (*them*) appears as *hv"y* in both the romanized Ladino version as well as in the English translation.

su *melakha* de *reḥiṣa* por manos de la *ḥevra gedola* de *reḥiṣa*. Estonses, mozotros tanbyen tenemos el ovligo por yevarlo i azerle todo su rijo ke konvyene amuestra *ḥevra*.

Numero 5. El *ḳabbar bashi* deve irse ariva djunto kon los kavadores i avrir el la kava, i deve yevar todo modo de gaste ke preme para los *ḥaverim* ke van arriva; todo ken gasta, de la *kuppa* dita. I si terná *ones* ke non puede ir el *ḳabbar bashi* dicho, deve mandar su *çirak* i deve tener kargo kese aga la kava sigun el demenester.

Numero 6. Los Srs. *parnasim ha-zeman* deven notar los nombres de los *ḥaverim, hy"v,* en papelikos i echarlos en dos kutis: Los ke saven azer la kava en un kuti, i los ke non saven en otro kuti. I en asodesyendo,[17] *b"m,* un *meth, miṣva* grande tyenen ke kitar 8 ocho papelikos, 4 de kada kuti, i los kualos deven de ir arriva i azer la *ḳevura*, i el restante delos *ḥaverim* deven todos yevar la *miṣva* arriva. I de los 8 keles salyo su danda para ir azer la kava, si terná una kesha ke esta hazino *b"m,* o ke non se topa enla sivdad, es *paṭur* de dita danda. Entanto, en non tuvyendo asemejante *ones* notado, i non kijo ir en su danda, deve dar un *esfanṣiḳ* ala *kuppa* de dita *ḥevra ḳedosha* i la *kuppa* ayudara kon otro un *esfanṣiḳ*, i los *parnasim, hy"v,* deven mandar su personal *ḥaver* de *ḥevra* en su lugar kon dos *esfanṣiḳes* ditos.

Numero 7. Los *parnasim ha-zeman* deven tener el kargo por azer el *aron* kon gaste dela *kuppa* dita, i deven a unarsen entre los dos[18] i reglarsen, porke syempre vayga un *parnas* kon la *miṣva* arriva djunto kon los *ḥaverim*. I si vido el *parnas* ke falto algun *ḥaver*, deve toparse kon el. Si tuvo algun *ones* de los notados arriva, es *paṭur*. I si non, es enprezentado akel *ḥaver* ke manko asta tres vezes. I si *ḥ"v* falto ala kuartena ves sin *ones* dicho, es salido de *ḥaver* de *ḥevra ḳedosha* dita.

Numero 8. Kuando es *nifṭar* alguna kriyatura *b"m*, asta ke es de sinko anyos, deven los *parnasim, hy"v,* de kitar danda[19] de dos presonas *ḥaverim, hy"v,* para azerle todo su rijo. I de sinko anyos endelantre asta ke es *bar miṣva* deven los *parnasim, hy"v,* de kitar djente mas demazyados *ke-fi* la edad dela kriyatura ke sera. I el ke faltara de su danda kele salyo, deven azer los *parnasim, hy"v,* lo medezmo *kenas* dicho arriva.

Numero 9. Todo modo de *takhrikhin*, komo los panyos ke se echan sovre el *aron*, i *feneres*, i asemejantes kozas premurozas para la *ḥevra*, deven estar en una kasha, i la dita kasha deve estar en mano de los Srs. *parnasim, hy"v.*

17 *Asodeser*, "to occur," is by now archaic, or dialectal at best, see Joseph Nehama, *Dictionnaire du Judéo-Espagnol* (Madrid: Consejo Superior de Investigaciones Cientificas, 1977) 62a.

18 "Both must meet" to translate the Ladino *deven a unarsen* (in 2 words) *entre los dos*.

19 The origin of the word *danda* could not be established. Contextually, there is no doubt that *kitar danda* means "to draw lots."

Numero 10. El *kiaya ha-zeman, hy"v,* deve tener la *kuppa* de dita *ḥevra ḳedosha.* I toda entrada i salida ke avra en la dita *kuppa* deve notarla al *tefter.* I kada anyo deve amostrar *ḥeshbon* alos Srs. *peḳidim* djunto kon los Srs. *parnasim, hy"v.* I *parokheth* ke tenemos en la *ḥevra* i platas ke se aran en la *ḥevra b"h,* i mas kozas asemejantes deven estar en mano de el *kiaya ha-zeman, hy"v.*

Numero 11. **En syendo** ke mozotros, *ḥaverim makshivim* los afirmados abasho, risivimos sovre mozotros kon ovligo kumplido de muestra buena veluntad por sirvirlos a los Srs. *yeḥidim, hy"v,* de dita sivdad Bukuresht en esta *miṣva* deklarada arriva; i **en vyendo** los Srs. *yeḥidim* dichos, *hy"v,* ke mose aze demenester gaste en la dita *ḥevra ḳedosha,* **toparon** de djusto porke page el *baᶜal ha-meth* ala muestra *kuppa* syertas taksas deklaradas adelantre, las kualas son: *le-aḥar arikhuth yamim ve-shanim,* kuando es *nifṭar* algun *bar Yisrael,* **prima klasa** deve dar 60 sesenta groshes ala muestra *kuppa,* i 10 dyez gro. por el gaste de el *aron.* **Sigunda klasa**, deve dar 40 kuarenta gro., i por el *aron* 5 sinko gro. I kuando *b"m* es *nifṭar* alguna kriyatura asta ke ẹs *bar miṣva,* **prima klasa** deve pagar 10 gro., **sigunda klasa** 5 sinko gro. I por gaste de *aron* ke deven azer para las kriyaturas kon todo ke akontesera, kriyatura ke non premerá *aron,* syendo ke al *rov* preme aron, izimos por todo modo de kriyatura asta ke es *bar miṣva* deve pagar ala muestra *kuppa* por gaste de aron **prima klasa** 17.20 dyez i syete i medyo gro., **sigunda klasa,** 11 onze gro., aparte de karosa ke kale ke page el *baᶜal ha-meth.* I de *aniyyim* ke toman *ṣedaka,* tanto grande, tanto chiko, non puedemos tomar dinguna taksa ni dingun gaste, i devemos de azerle todo su rijo tokante a muestra *ḥevra ḳedosha.* I de *bene ṭovim* ke non toman *ṣedaka,* ni pueden pagar la sigunda klasa, resta al pareser de los Srs. *peḳidim ha-zeman, hy"v,* por avenirselos kon el *baᶜal ha-meth* sigun pueden.

Numero 12. Por buena regla de muestra *ḥevra,* en tuvyendo fyesta *ḥaver* de *ḥevra* esta, ke se aran platas en muestra *ḥevra,* deven *parnasé ha-zeman* de tomar enprestado i trayer al *ḳ"ḳ* por onrar al *ḥaver.* Si tanbyen kuando el patron dela fyesta yeva gusto por kelo vijiten todos los *ḥaverim,* deve darse de nota alos *parnasim, hy"v,* kon un tyenpo antes. I estonses deven los *parnasim* komandar al *shammash* porke kombide atodos los *ḥaverim* por azerle vijita en su kaza, todos endjunto. I todo *ḥaver* de *ḥevra* deve dar medyo *esfanṣiḳ* kada 6 mezes por *nedavoth* ke azen en *ᶜaliyoth sefer Tora.* I una ves al anyo, deven *parnasim ha-zeman, hy"v,* por azer [un]a m[ez]a kon gaste dela *kuppa rosh ḥodesh* de *ḥanukka,* o *Lag la-ᶜOmer.* I todos los afirmados abasho somos *ḥaverim,* tanbyen dju-to kon todos los Srs. *yeḥidim* dela sivdad en *biḳḳur ḥolim.* I devemos pagar dos groshes kada 6 mezes ala *kuppa* de *biḳḳur ḥolim.* I kuando mos toka vela por velar al hazino, devemos de ir o mandar presona [kon l]a karta de *biḳḳur ḥolim.* Si tanbyen por buena regla non puede dingun *ḥaver* meter mano en la *miṣva* otro ke los *ḥaverim* ke aran *be-khavod* los *parnasim, hy"v,* porke toke atodos los *ḥaverim* su *sira* por yevar la *miṣva* i para kese yeve kon onor, sin korrer.

Numero 13. Una vez al anyo, deven *parnasim ha-zeman, hy"v,* por azer adjunta de todos los *ḥaverim* en *ḥol ha-moᶜed* de *Pesaḥ* o de *Sukkoth* por demenester dela *ḥevra*, komo para meter un *parnas* muevo, kon ke reste i uno de los vyejos, i tyene ke seer kon plazer delos *ḥaverim,* i non kere dicho ke deve seer kon plazer delos Srs. *peḳidim, hy"v,* si tanbyen por adovar si avra alguna (r)[d]iferensya entre los *ḥaverim*; si por pagar el medyo *esfanṣiḳ* de kada 6 mezes dicho; si por risivir algun *yaḥid* ke kere seer *ḥaver* de *ḥevra* dita, si meresera, sera risivido.

Numero 14. Mos ovligamos, los *ḥaverim*, por azer *gemiluth ḥesed* uno kon el otro, i es: *le-aḥar arikhuth yamim ve-shanim,* kuando sera *nifṭar* algun de los *ḥaverim*, el *ḳabbar bashi* kon los *parnasim* deven de azer *minyan* de los *ḥaverim* kon *sira* por dizir *tefilla, minḥa, ᶜarvith* en kaza de el *meth*. I despues de kada *tefilla,* se deve de meldar *tehillim* i *mishna* i algo de *derasha* porke diga su *yoresh* tres *kaḏḏishim*. I algun *ḥaver* ke es su *sira* de vinir i non vino, deve dar un *firfiriḳ* de *kenas* por la *sira* ke non vino.

Numero 15. Todas las ditas kondisyones, las risivimos sovre mozotros, los afirmados abasho, ke mos bendiga El a todos, por afirmarlas kon muestra buena veluntad, i non mos podemos arepintir de eyas *ᶜad sof kol ha-doroth*. I en esta sivdad de Bukuresht, non se pueden azer otra *ḥevra* de *ḳabbarim* syendo mozotros meresimos en eya i mos risivimos *ᶜalenu ve-al yorshenu ha-baim aḥarenu* por azer la dita *miṣva* dicha arriva, i los Srs. *peḳidim, hy"v,* i los Srs. *parnasim, hy"v,* i el *ḳabbar bashi, hy"v,* i el Sr. *kiaya, hy"v,* deven reglarsen sigun las ditas kondisyones deklaradas. I por *shammash* ke preme ala dita *ḥevra,* i resto de reglas, i gastes premurozos ke akonteseran ala dita *ḥevra ḳedosha*, resta en mano de los Srs. *peḳidim ha-zeman, hy"v,* i los Srs. *parnasim ha-zeman, hy"v,* por reglar sigun mijor les paresera, i *zakhuth* dela *miṣva* esta mos mamparara. יקויים בנו מקרא שכתוב בילע המות לנצח ומחה ה׳ דמעה מעל כל פנים. ובימינו תיושע יאודה וישראל [ירמ. 23:6] ישכון לבטח. ובא לציון גואל, וכן יהי רצון ונאמר אמן. ביום ל״ג לעומר שמונה עשר לחדש אייר שנת חמשה אלפים ושש מאות ועשרה לבריאת עולם. בוקורישט „בא סימן״ קרובה ישועתי לבא וצדקתי להגלות לפ״ק [יש. 56:1] ברוב עוז ושלום. וקים.

[Approximately 70 signatures.]

Deklaramos mozotros los afirmados abasho *yeḥide ve-gabbaye ḳehilloth ha-ḳ' Bukuresht* ke kon muestro saver i muestra kontentes se izo la dita *ḥevra ḳ,'* ke ansi devemos konoser esta *ḥevra ḳ' anaḥnu ve-zarᶜenu ha-baim aḥarenu*, i mos ovligamos por mantener lo eskrito ariva tokante amozotros. Si tambyen la lesensya tyene la dita *ḥevra ḳ'* porke akojga su *kuppa* en las *kehilloth h"ḳ* en sinko tyenpos los kualos son ר״ח חנוכה, פורים, חוה״מ פסח, חוה״מ סוכות, ויזכו לש״ר אמן. ביום ר״ח סיון שנת חמשת אלפים ושש מאות ועשרה לבריאת עולם, יהא רעוה שיהיו בשחמת עולם.

Translation

עשו עמי בינו[20]

BSṬ.[21] We, the undersigned, of our own free will, agree unanimously to constitute ourselves into a *Ḥevra Ḳedosha*[22] of *ḳabbarim*,[23] (Burial Society of grave-diggers) according to the *minhag* of Jewish communities in the Diaspora and in compliance with the terms stipulated below. Concerning this *miṣva* stated below, we, the concurring[24] *associates*, state that we – may God bless us all – take it upon ourselves to fulfill it with no compulsion whatsoever, but rather by complete consent. We have also informed everyone, so that each person may freely sign this document in order to strengthen the *miṣva* of having a *Ḥevra Ḳedosha* (Burial Society), whereby any signatory and his sons will be called an "*Associate* of the *Ḥevra*" in perpetuity, according to the *minhag* of all our Jewish brethren. May He help us honor His name, and may this be favorable, Amen.

Article 1. With perfect heart and willing soul, we, the undersigned, take upon ourselves the obligation of taking care of the funeral arrangements[25] of any Jew who has passed away[26] – hopefully at a ripe old age – whether man or woman, rich or poor, foreign or local, adult or a baby one day old, by preparing his grave, carrying him on our shoulders,[27] and burying him according to the custom of observant Jews.

20 The three words בינו עמי עשו "understand, my people, do" are separate acronyms frequently used on documents and title-pages. בינו stands for: בעזרת ה' נתחיל ונגמור, *With God's help let us start and finish.* עמי, עשו, stand for עזרי מעם ה' עשה שמים וארץ, *My help is from the Lord, Who made heaven and earth* (Ps 121:2), see T. Schrire, *Hebrew Amulets* (London: Routledge & Kegan Paul, 1966) 43.

21 The acronym BSṬ is for בסימן טוב, *Besimman ṭov* or בסימנא טבא *Besimmana ṭava* which mean, "under the auspices of a good omen."

22 For "Burial Society," the Sephardic tradition prefers the Hebrew *Ḥevra Ḳedosha* to its Aramaic counterpart *Ḥevra Ḳaddisha.*

23 While the Hebrew word for *grave-digger* is קַבְּרָן, *ḳabberan*, the customary Sephardic term is קַבָּר, *ḳabbar*, built on the pattern of the standard *nomen professionis.*

24 The Hebrew word מקשיבים literally means "listening," or "attentive."

25 The specific funeral arrangements required in this 1850 draft include: 1. digging a grave, 2. carrying the deceased and 3. burial, but no רחיצה or "ritual washing" which was formerly part of the 1819 Constitution, see Geller, *The Sephardic Jews*, 91.

26 Etiquette requires Jewish languages to use the word נפטר, "parted" instead of "died." In common Ladino parlance, "my uncle died yesterday" would be "*mi tiyo fue niftar ayer.*"

27 Accompanying the dead, including carrying the bier "on shoulders," was a special *miṣva*, if not all the way to the cemetery, at least up to a certain agreed point. *Hahamim* were carried *en palmas*, "on the palms" of those participating in the funeral procession based on Ps 91:12, על-כפים ישאונך, "they will carry you on the palm of their hands."

Article 2. In said *Ḥevra Ḳeḏosha,* we must have: two *peḳiḏim,*[28] freely chosen from among the *yeḥiḏim,*[29] *hy"v*, from the two *Ḳehilloth*, one from each, two *parnasim*[30] from among us, the *associates*, a *Ḳabbar Bashi*[31] with his *Djivan,*[32] and a *Kiaya.*[33] All of the above will serve with the approval of the *associates*. Needless to say it must also be with the approval of the current[34] *peḳiḏim*, may God bless and keep them.

Article 3. The current *peḳiḏim* must endeavor to collect the fees listed below which the next of kin of the deceased – far be it from us – shall pay to the Fund[35] of said *ḥevra ḳeḏosha*. This Fund shall not deal with the next of kin except through the current *peḳiḏim* – may God bless and keep them.

28 Each of the two Sephardic Congregations in Bucharest chose one *paḳiḏ* from among its *yeḥiḏim* or members to act as its congregational President. Geller seems justified in equating the office of the *paḳiḏ* with that of President based on the *paḳiḏ*'s role in the Congregational structure. See Geller, *The Sephardic Jews*, 26. Thus in the context of the Burial Society, the role of these two *peḳiḏim*, as two co-Presidents, must have been to monitor *ex-officio* the *parnasim* of the *beth ha-ḥayyim* on behalf of each synagogue.

29 A *yaḥiḏ* is an individual who customarily attends services at a synagogue of his choice and makes donations to it. As such, he can be described as a "member" of that synagogue, even though the strict notion of membership with annual dues was viewed until recently as a Western custom. Actually, the "annual dues" in early Sephardic Congregations were levied when members had to buy seat tickets for the High Holidays. In Charleston's *Beth Elohim Congregation* members who refused to buy a seat for their wives could lose their rights and privileges. See Elazar, *A Double Bond*, 114.

30 The Aramaic loan-word *parnes* signifies "provide/manage." As a provider/manager, the *Parnas*, especially as a *Parnas Presidente*, was still the title given to the President of the Congregation in Charleston's *Beth Elohim*, see Elazar, *A Double Bond*, Rule III, 114. This explains why in Charleston there is additionally a *Parnas* of *beth ha-ḥayyim* or "Cemetery Manager," see Elazar, *A Double Bond*, Rule V, 114. In Izmir, too, the Administrator of *Ḥevra Ḳeḏosha of Orphan Girls* was called a *Parnas*. See ספר דילה חברה קדושה די יתומות (Kostandina: Binyamin de Moshe Rosi, 1755) 3b. In Rumania, however, the two *parnasim* were chosen from among the Associates of the Burial Society, with a role similar to that of the *Parnas* of *beth ha-ḥayyim* in Charleston.

31 The word *Ḳabbar Bashi* is obtained by combining the Turkish *bash*, "head," with *ḳabbar*, "grave-digger": to create a title for "Chief Grave-digger," similar to *Ḥaham Bashı*, "Chief Rabbi."

32 *Djivan* is a Turkish (Persian) word meaning "young." In this context, it refers to a "young helper" for the chief grave-digger.

33 *Kiaya* reflects the Ladino pronunciation of the Turkish word *kâhya*, "steward."

34 I translated הזמן as "current." The two expressions פקידים הזמן and פרנסים הזמן, which occur 14 times, are obvious Hebrew mistakes for פקידי-הזמן and פרנסי-הזמן, where הזמן means "in office" or "current." In the 1728 Constitution of *Shearith Israel* in New York, the term used is "*Parnaz* then in Being," while in Charleston, *Temple Beth Elohim*, still retained the old term *Parnas Presidente* brought over from Europe. See, Elazar, *A Double Bond*, 103 and 114, respectively.

35 The old term *kuppa*, "charity box" or "communal fund," is used here specifically for the Cemetery Fund which was created under Article 3 of the first Constitution of 1819, which calls it a "separate Fund," see Geller, *The Sephardic Jews*, 91. Conversely, the *Biḳḳur Ḥolim* Fund was men-

Article 4. We, the *associates, hy"v*, must always welcome the advice of the current *peḳiḏim, hy"v*, and abide by their ruling on behalf of said *ḥevra ḳeḏosha.* It shall be sufficient for the *peḳiḏim* to issue instructions for us to carry the deceased in compliance with all the requirements. We are indeed obligated to carry him and dig his grave, according to our duty, by day or by night, in rain or in snow, except in times of disease – far be it from us. If it is not a contagious disease,[36] then the *reḥiṣa* preparations will be carried out by the great *ḥevra* of *reḥiṣa*. We, then, have the obligation to carry him and fulfill all the requirements necessitated by our *ḥevra*.

Article 5. The *ḳabbar bashi* must go to the cemetery[37] with the grave-diggers to dig the grave, taking charge of all expenses incurred by the *associates* going to the cemetery; also any out-of-pocket expenses must be defrayed from said Fund. In an emergency, when the *ḳabbar bashi* cannot go, he must send his apprentice[38] to make sure the grave is dug properly.

Article 6. The current *parnasim* must write down the names of the *associates, hy"v*, on pieces of paper, putting them in two boxes: one box for those who know how to dig a grave, and another box for those who do not know. In the event of a death – far be it from us – it is a great *miṣva* for them to draw 8 pieces of paper, 4 from each box, for those who must go to the cemetery and dig the grave, with the remaining *associates* carrying the deceased[39] to the cemetery. Anyone of the 8 whose allotment it was to dig a grave and who has an excuse such as being sick – far be it from us – or being out of town, is exempt from his allotment. However, in the absence of a valid excuse, he must pay one *esfanṣiḳ* to the Fund of said *ḥevra ḳeḏosha* for his reluctance to carry out his allotment, while the Fund will contribute one matching *esfanṣiḳ*, and the *parnasim, hy"v*, will send a substitute *ḥaver* from the *ḥevra* with the two *esfanṣiḳs* mentioned above.

Article 7. The current *parnasim* are responsible to provide a casket paid from said Fund, and both must meet to make arrangements, so that one *parnas* will

tioned by its full name in Article 10 of the *Biḳḳur Ḥolim* Constitution, see Geller, *The Sephardic Jews*, 89.

36 Article 7 of the first Constitution of 1819 specifically mentions "cholera" as חולי רע, Geller, *The Sephardic Jews*, 93, Article 6.

37 Depending on context, *ir ariva* or "to go up" is used for going to the cemetery. In hilly Istanbul, most cemeteries are located on steep terrain and the expression *ir ariva* is an obvious choice for that setting.

38 *Çirak* is a Turkish word meaning "apprentice."

39 By metonymy, the word *miṣva* or "commandment" refers to the body of the dead person, or even the funeral itself. Hence *yevar la miṣva ariva* means "to carry the deceased to the cemetery," and *kuando va ser la miṣva* means "when is the funeral?"

always go with the *associates* to the cemetery accompanying the funeral. If the *parnas* notices the absence of an *associate*, he must have a meeting with him. In case of an excuse of those specified above, he is exonerated. If not, that *associate* may still be exempted up to three times. But if – God forbid – he is absent a fourth time without a valid excuse, he is removed from membership in said *ḥevra ḳeḏosha*.

Article 8. When a child up to five years old passes away – far be it from us – the *parnasim, hy"v*, must draw lots to appoint two individuals from the *associates, hy"v*, to make all necessary arrangements. However, from age five up to the age of *bar miṣva*, the *parnasim, hy"v*, must designate more people proportionate to the age of the child involved. Anyone who misses the allotment assigned to him is penalized by the *parnasim, hy"v*, with the same fine mentioned above.

Article 9. Any kind of shroud, as well as cloth coverings placed on the casket, lanterns, and similar items needed by the *ḥevra* must be stored in a case under the supervision of the *parnasim* – may God bless and keep them.

Article 10. The current *kiaya* must manage the Fund of said *ḥevra ḳeḏosha*. He must record on a ledger all income to, and expenditures from said Fund. Every year, he is subject to an audit by the *peḳiḏim* and the *parnasim* – may God bless and keep them. So, too, the *parokheth* which we have in the *ḥevra*, as well as the silver pieces which – with God's help – will belong to the *ḥevra*, and other similar objects must be under the supervision of the current *kiaya*.

Article 11. **Whereas**, we, the undersigned concurring *associates*, freely take upon ourselves the full obligation of serving the *yeḥiḏim, hy"v*, of said city of Bucharest in this *miṣva* stipulated above; and **whereas** the above mentioned *yeḥiḏim, hy"v*, noticed the need for us to pay for the expenses of said *ḥevra ḳ'*, **they decided** that the next of kin of the deceased should pay certain fees to our Fund specified below, as follows: When after ripe old age, a Jew shall pass away, the **first class** fee is 60, sixty, *grush* for our Fund, plus 10, ten, *grush* for the cost of a casket; the **second class** fee is 40, forty, *grush*, plus 5, five, *grush* for the casket. But when a child – far be it from us – up to *bar miṣva* age shall pass away, the **first class** fee is 10 *grush*, the second class is 5, five, *grush*, plus the cost of a casket especially made for a child, most of whom need such a casket, even though only a few can do without it. That is why we have decided that the casket fee to be paid to our Fund for all children up to *bar miṣva* age is: **first class**, 17.20, seventeen and a half, *grush*; **second class**, 11, eleven, *grush*, exclusive of the carriage fee to be paid by the next of kin of the deceased. However, from the indigent who receive charity, we may collect no fee or expense for the burial of adults or children, and are obligated to carry out all arrangements incumbent on our *ḥevra ḳedosha*. "People of worthy ancestry"[40] who are neither *ṣedaḳa* recipients, nor can afford to pay **second class** fees, are left to the discretion of the current *peḳidim* who shall reach a workable agreement with the next of kin of the deceased.

Article 12. For the welfare of our *ḥevra*, when an *associate* of this *ḥevra* has a celebration, because[41] silver objects[42] will be available in our *ḥevra*, the current *parnasim* should borrow and bring them to the *Ḳ"Ḳ* in honor of the *ḥaver*. Likewise, if it pleases the honoree of the celebration for the *associates* to pay him a visit, advance notice should be given to the *parnasim* – may God bless and keep them. Then, the *parnasim* should instruct the *shammash* to invite all the *associates*, as a group, to pay him a visit at his residence. Each *associate* of the *ḥevra* must give half an *esfanṣiḳ* every 6 months for the donations they make when they are called to the *sefer Tora* during an *aliya*. Once a year, on *rosh ḥodesh Ḥanukka* or *Lag la-ᶜOmer*, the current *parnasim* must organize a banquet[43] at the expense of the Fund. All of us, the undersigned *associates*, together with all the *yeḥidim* of the city, shall serve in *Biḳḳur Ḥolim*. We must also pay 2 *grush* every 6 months to the Fund of the *Biḳḳur Ḥolim*. Whenever it is our turn "to hold a wake"[44] over a [dying] sick person, we must either go personally or send someone with the *biḳḳur ḥolim* card. Also, for the general welfare, no *associate* may touch a recently deceased person, except those *associates* whom the *parnasim*, *hy"v*, will have designated for this honor,[45] so that all *associates* may take a turn in carrying the deceased person, and also for the procession to take place honorably, without rush!

Article 13. Once a year, during *ḥol ha-moᶜed Pesaḥ* or (*ḥol ha-moᶜed*) *Sukkoth*, the current *parnasim*, *hy"v*, shall hold a meeting of all the associates to take care

40 The *bene ṭovim* or "people of worthy ancestry" is a reference to formerly wealthy families who have lost their fortune and are embarrassed to even apply for help from the community.

41 Similar to what happens in Mishnaic Hebrew with the conjunction ... ש for ... מפני ש, in Ladino, too, a "dry" *ke* often stands for *porke*, "because."

42 Article 7 of the first Constitution of 1819 specifically lists these valuable objects that can be "borrowed" to honor a member of the *ḥevra*. They are: the splendidly embroidered *mappa*, the silver vessels and ornaments, and the scrolls of the law which belong to the *ḥevra ḳedosha*, see Geller, *The Sephardic Jews*, 93.

43 In the previous Constitution, unexcused absence from this annual party was punishable by a fine, see Geller, *The Sephardic Jews*, 93.

44 Behind these semantically similar sounding concepts, the two customs of "holding a wake" and that of *velar la vela* are not at all comparable. The *vela* describes the "watch" that takes place when a sick person goes into an agony that may last for a few days. Following the death and the "ritual washing" or רחיצה of the deceased, *la vela del muerto* continues until the funeral. In the case of a Haham, a *ḥavura* or "group" of pious individuals assemble around the deceased to read Psalms and other appropriate texts.

45 The expression *azer be-khavoḏ* or "give an honor" is used when an individual is "extended an honor" to perform a liturgical task.

of the needs of the *ḥevra*, such as: installing a new *parnas*, with the incumbent *parnas* staying in office at the pleasure of the *associates*, and, also needless to say at the pleasure of the current *peḳiḏim*; mediating any disagreement among the *associates*; receiving payment of the half *esfanṣiḳ* due every six months; inducting any *yaḥiḏ* who wishes to become an *associate* of said *ḥevra*. If deserving, such a person shall then be inducted.

Article 14. We, the *associates*, obligate ourselves to do acts of "lovingkindness" towards each other.[46] When one of the *associates* – hopefully at a ripe old age – shall pass away, the *ḳabbar bashi*, in cooperation with the *parnasim*, shall organize a *minyan* of *associates* who shall take turns holding morning, afternoon and evening services at the home of the deceased. Following each morning service, Psalms, Mishna and some *derasha* shall be read so that the heir of the deceased can say three *ḳaddishim*.[47] Any *associate* who misses his turn to attend must pay a fine[48] of one *firfiriḳ* for the turn he missed.

Article 15. We, the undersigned – may He bless us all – take upon ourselves to fulfill all these conditions in good faith; we cannot back down from them in perpetuity. In this city of Bukuresht, let there be no other *ḥevra* of *ḳabbarim*, since we have established here a priority by taking upon ourselves and our heirs who shall come after us to fulfill the *miṣva* mentioned above. Therefore, the *peḳidim*, *hy"v*, and the *parnasim*, *hy"v*, and the *ḳabbar bashi*, *hy"v*, and the *kiaya*, *hy"v*, must comply with all the conditions stipulated above. As for the *shammash* needed for said *ḥevra*, as well as the remaining disbursements and necessary expenditures that may occur to said *ḥevra ḳeḏosha*, these are at the discretion of the current *peḳiḏim* and the current *parnasim* to pay out as best they deem appropriate, May the merit of this *miṣva* protect us! May the following verses from Scripture be fulfilled on our behalf: *He will destroy death forever. My Lord God will wipe the tears away from all faces* (Isa 25:8), *in our days, Judah shall be delivered and Israel shall dwell securely* (Jer 23:6), *He shall come as redeemer to Zion* (Isa 59:20). On the 33rd day of the ᶜOmer, the 18th of the month of Iyyar, in the year 5610 of the creation of the world, Bucharest. The sign[49] [date] is: *soon my salvation shall come and* DELIVERANCE [5610] *be*

46 For the funeral of an *associate*, the 1819 Constitution adds two rituals: prior to the funeral, *ṭevila* for the *roḥaṣim* themselves; and during the funeral, the ritual of *rodeos*, or "seven circuits" around the bier just before burial at the cemetery (See, Da Sola Pool, ed., *Book of Prayer According to the Custom of the Spanish and Portuguese Jews* (4 vols.; New York: Union of Sephardic Congregations, 1966) Vol. 1, *Daily and Sabbath*, 462–64.

47 The קדיש דרבנן is the particular doxology recited after a למוד or "study session" of religious texts in honor of a deceased person.

48 For the same offense, the 1819 Constitution recommends the expulsion of the defiant member from the Society, see Geller, *The Sephardic Jews*, 92, Article 5.

49 The expression בא סימן, "the sign comes," is used to introduce a verse in which the numerical

revealed (Isa 56:1), according to the short computation, with great strength and peace.... It is established.

[Approximately 70 signatures][50]

We, the undersigned, the *yeḥiḏim* and *gabbayim* of the Holy Congregations of Bucharest declare that this *Ḥevra Ḳ'* was established with our knowledge and consent. Therefore, we and our descendants who will follow us must recognize this *Ḥevra Ḳ,'* and pledge to keep its written statutes concerning us. Also this *Ḥevra Ḳ'* will have the authority to collect funds[51] from both Congregations during the following five times: *Rosh Ḥodesh Ḥanukka, Purim, Ḥol ha-Moᶜeḏ Pesaḥ, Ḥol ha-Moᶜeḏ Sukkoṯ* [5th is missing], and may they deserve abundant peace, amen. On *Rosh Ḥoḏesh Sivan* 5610 of the creation of the world. May it be favorable in eternal joy.

value of certain letters represents the date of a book or document. In this case, the word וצדקתי, with the numerical value of 610, is singled out according to the "short" computation, or 5610 according to the "full" computation. The full Jewish date is 18 Iyyar 5610 corresponding to April 30, 1850.

50 Names such Abraham, Isaac, Jacob, Moses, Aaron, Yeuda, Binyamin, David, Solomon, Eliezer, Mordehay, Gabriel, etc., are legible, but beyond Franko, Mitrani, Nahmias, Papo, Sisa and Varon, most family names are difficult to decipher.

51 Same provision in the 1819 Constitution, Article 3, see Geller, *The Sephardic Jews*, 91.

Abraham Firkovich and the Dedication Inscription of the Aleppo Codex

Yosef Ofer
Bar-Ilan University

The letters of Abraham Firkovich, the well-known Karaite leader and traveler, shed light on a strange historical affair, centering on the Dedication Inscription of the Aleppo Codex, written in the eleventh century. In the sixteenth century this inscription was copied, without indication of its origin, at the end of *Tiqqun Sofrim* (unvocalized Bible), sent to Krakow (Poland). The same inscription was copied at the end of another Bible Codex, which was in the Karaite synagogue in Jerusalem. But in this inscription the writing of the Bible was ascribed to the Karaite scholar Shelomo ben Yeroḥam, and not to Shelomo ben Buya'a, as in the origin.

Some scholars have already assumed that the last inscription is a forgery, done by Firkovich. The way in which Firkovich formulated this inscription and his motivations are clarified in this article, by examining the wording of some versions of this inscription, the Hebrew press of the period and Firkovich's own sayings in his letters.

This article treats a strange historical affair, centering on an inscription and three ancient manuscripts of the Bible. The inscription is the Dedication Inscription of the Aleppo Codex, which was inscribed at the end of the Codex in the eleventh century. The inscription was copied over in the sixteenth century at the end of a *Tiqqun Sofrim* in the town of Krakow (Poland) that was attributed to R. Moses Isserlis. The inscription was also copied over at the end of a Bible manuscript dating from 1322, which was called *Miqdash-yah* and located in the Karaite Synagogue in Jerusalem. The version copied over in *Miqdash-yah*, however, contains a number of changes from the original version in the Aleppo Codex. The most prominent of these changes is the name of the scribe who wrote the Aleppo Codex, Shelomo ben Buya'a, which was replaced by a well known Karaite name, Shelomo ben Yeroḥam.[1]

This matter has been dealt with by many.[2] However, in light of the Firkovich

1 On Shelomo ben Yeroḥam (or Salmon ben Yeruḥim) see "סלמון בן ירחם," *Encyclopaedia Hebraica* 26 (1974) 94.

2 These include: Paul Kahle, *Masoreten des Westens* (2 vols.; Stuttgart: W. Kohlhammer, 1927) 1:3; Itzhak Ben-Zvi, "The Codex of Ben Asher," *Textus* 1 (1960) 12–13; Aron Dotan, "האמנם נקוד כתר חלב בידי אהרן בן אשר?" (Was the Aleppo Codex Actually Vocalized by Aharon ben Asher?), *Tarbiz*

letters which have been found over the past few years, a number of points can be clarified. Copyist errors and suspected forgery mingle here. The main events described hereunder took place in the nineteenth century; additional events which occurred in the twentieth century will be mentioned later.

Abraham Firkovich (*Even Reshef*; 1787–1874), a well-known Karaite leader who traveled throughout the East collecting manuscripts, journeyed from Jerusalem to Aram Zova, that is, Aleppo (Halab) in Syria, late in 1863. Before he left, R. Ya'aqov Sapir of Jerusalem handed him a page containing a copy of the Dedication Inscription of the Aleppo Codex. This copy had been made for Sapir a few years earlier by an emissary whose name was Ya'aqov Ze'ev (*RYZ*). Firkovich took the page, traveled to Aleppo, and upon his return gave the page, with marginal corrections, back to Sapir. Sapir, who relates the entire story in his book *Even Sapir*, examined the corrections and was very surprised: some of the corrections seemed reasonable and acceptable, but he was unable to understand one central emendation. According to the Codex Dedication Inscription, the name of the scribe who wrote the manuscript was Shelomo ben Buya'a, whereas Firkovich had amended this and written "Shelomo ben Yeroḥam." Sapir was amazed:

> I cannot understand how *RYZ*, the first copyist, had confused these two names which are in no way similar to one another! Perhaps because there appears in Karaite literature one Solomon ben Yeroḥam, the famed antagonist of R. Saadya Gaon, *Even Reshef* thought that this was he? But this is no copyist's error, for the name written is Buya'a.[3]

Sapir does not say explicitly that he did not believe Firkovich, but he makes a point of stressing that the emissary R. Ya'aqov Ze'ev who had copied the inscription over for him had done so in good faith and was not to be suspected of ulterior motives.[4] From our standpoint, Firkovich's ulterior motives are well known, his forgeries having been revealed and proved while he was still alive.[5]

---

34 (1965) 151–53; Jordan S. Penkower, "Maimonides and the Aleppo Codex," *Textus* 9 (1981) 100–110, 119–24 (and see in his article the lengthy and detailed discussions of the Krakow manuscript); Yosef Ofer, "כתר ארם צובה לאור רשימותיו של מ״ד קאסוטו" (M. D. Cassuto's Notes on the Aleppo Codex), *Sefunot* ns 4 [19] (1989) 285–91.

3 Ya'aqov Sapir, אבן ספיר (2 vols.; Lyck: M'kize Nirdamim, 1866) 1:12b, n. 2.

4 Sapir notes also that this copy was made even before the argument broke out over the question if the scribe of the Codex was a Karaite (that is, before the debate to be described hereunder, which was carried by the *Ha-Maggid* newspaper starting from November 1857; Sapir, אבן ספיר, 19b).

5 For Firkovich's forgeries and other deeds, see: the annotations by Abraham Elijah Harkavy in the margins of Tsevi Graetz, ספר דברי ימי ישראל, Part 3 (Warsaw: Alapin Press, 1908. Photo-edition: Jerusalem: Makor, 1972) 175, 195, 485, 489 (and also in his book: Abraham Elijah Harkavy, *Altjuedische Denkmaeler aus der Krim* [St. Petersburg: Commissionnaires de l'Academie imperiale

Nevertheless, the matter seems extremely strange: what made Firkovich forge the name of the scribe who wrote the Aleppo Codex, while the original inscription could still be found in Aleppo and anyone who saw it would realize the other was a forgery?

Firkovich's own notes, which have recently[6] come to light, tell the exciting story of Firkovich's own biased historical research, forgeries brought to attest to the theories he raised, the affair becoming complicated as a result of new discoveries and Firkovich's searches for a way out of the maze.

As already noted, the name *Shelomo ben Yeroḥam* is also located in another copy of the Dedication Inscription of the Codex, which was copied over at the end of a biblical manuscript dating from 1322,[7] found in the Synagogue of the Karaites in Jerusalem and called *Miqdash-yah*. The inscription begins as follows (in translation):

---

des sciences, 1876]); Hermann Leberecht Strack, *Abraham Firkovitsch und seine Entdeckungen* (Leipzig: J. C. Hinrichs, 1876); Efrayim Dainard, תולדות אב״ן רשף (Warsaw: Goldman Press, 1875); David Kahana, ספר מעשי אבן רשף (Vienna: George Brag Press, 1884); Ya'akov Bakhrakh, אשתדלות עם שד״ל (2 vols.; Warsaw: Shuldberg Press, 1897) 2:203–18. The first to voice suspicion concerning Firkovich seems to have been Simcha Pinsker (with whom Firkovich cooperated to a large extent): "I cannot deny that that entire list seems suspect to me . . . though I have seen it with my own eyes and examined it as much as possible"– לקוטי קדמוניות (Vienna: Adalbert della Torre, 1860) 18 in a footnote.

6 Firkovich's letters are kept in the National Library of Russia at St. Petersburg, and are marked F.946, Lichnyj arhiv A. S. Firkovicha. I am indebted to Prof. Menahem Ben-Sasson and to my friend, Ze'ev Elkin, who provided me with a copy of his letter to *Hakham* Naḥamu Babovich (no. 605), which describes his trip to Aleppo, and enabled me to publish the fragments adduced hereunder. For Firkovich's letters see also: Tapani Harviainen, "The Cairo Genizot and other sources of the second Firkovich collection in St. Petersburg," in Ernest John Revell, ed., *Proceedings of the Twelfth International Congress of the International Organization for Masoretic Studies* – Masoretic Studies 8 (1996) 25–36; Tapani Harviainen, "Abraham Firkovich," in Meira Polliack, ed., *Karaite Judaism: A Guide to its History and Literary Sources* (Leiden: Brill, 2003) 875–92. In another article, Harviainen discussed Firkovich and the Dedication Inscription of the Codex. See: Tapani Harviainen, "Abraham Firkovich, the Aleppo Codex and its dedication," in Judit Targarona Borrás and Angel Sáenz-Badillos, eds., *Jewish Studies at the turn of the Twentieth Century* (2 vols.; Leiden: Brill, 1999) 1:131–36.

7 The manuscript is today to be found in the National Library in Jerusalem (its number is Heb 4° 780), but Mr. Raphael Weiser, the director of the Manuscript Department of the Library informed me that the manuscript was damaged by a fungus, and that it is kept isolated and it is impossible to consult it. I thus studied a photocopy of the manuscript made years ago, in which the inscription written at the end of the manuscript is barely legible. According to Weiser, the condition of the manuscript is even worse than that reflected by the photocopy. Richard Gottheil, who described this manuscript, read the date of its inscription on the colophon (with the assistance of David Yellin): "the [hundred and] eighty second year of the sixth [millen]ium," and according to his reconstruction the Bible had been written in the year 1422 (Richard Gottheil, "Some Hebrew MSS in Cairo," *JQR* o.s.17 [1905] 649–52). Yet Ben-Zvi and others read it: שנת שמונים ושתים

I said to copy the precious list from the end of the precious Bible called *Miqdash-yah* in Jerusalem which is inscribed in it from a book called *The Writ of Jerusalem* which was dedicated to the Jerusalem synagogue of Egypt.

This is the entire manuscript of twenty-four books written by our teacher R. Shelomo Ben Yeroḥam, the rapid scribe [...].

This inscription was first published in 1905 by Gottheil. In 1927 Kahle hinted that it had been forged by Firkovich.[8] Strong evidence of this is the textual similarity

לפרט האלף הששי "the eighty second year of the sixth millennium," and determined accordingly that the manuscript had been written in the year 1322. See Itzhak Ben-Zvi, "מקדשיה׳ הירושלמי," (The Jerusalem *Miqdash-yah*), *Azkara* 5 (1937) 556–58. See the description of manuscript in: Collette Sirat and Malachi Beit-Arié, אוצר כתבי-יד עבריים מימי הביניים בציוני תאריך עד שנת ה'ש (A treasury of dated Hebrew manuscripts from the Medieval Period until 1540), Part 1: "Descriptions" (Paris: Centre National de la Recherche Scientifique, and Jerusalem: Académie Nationale des Sciences et des Lettres d'Israel, 1972) MS I, 31.

8 See Kahle, *Masoreten des Westens* 1:3. The first known description of the ms is that of Ludwig August Frankl, who arrived in Palestine in 1856 and published in German his impressions of the journey two years later: Ludwig August Frankl, *Nach Jerusalem* (3 vols.; Leipzig: Nies'sche Buchdruckerei (C. B. Lorck), 1858) 2:65. In 1860 the book was published in a Hebrew translation (L. A. Frankl, ירושלימה! - ספר המסע [To Jerusalem! – the journey logbook], translated into Hebrew by Mendl Stern (Vienna: Knöpflmacher, 1860. Photo-edition; Jerusalem: Ariel Publishing, 1999]). Frankl visited the Karaite synagogue, where he was told that the Karaite community had only 32 members. Frankl describes the MS, saying: "The Torah is not rolled as a scroll the way it is in our books, but rather is made in the form of a book with processed calf leather plates, with colorful pictures and gold ornamentation all around. On the last plate there is the following inscription: '*I, Moshe b. Menahem*' [etc.]" (Frankl, ירושלימה!, 186). Frankl makes no mention of any other inscription on the manuscript. The colophon that he cites was written, as he says, "on the last plate."

Further evidence on the manuscript postdates Firkovich's visit. Abraham Elijah Harkavy viewed the MS in 1886, and briefly mentions it in חדשים גם ישנים 6 (1895) 3 (MS 24). Gottheil studied the manuscript before 1905 (as mentioned in the previous footnote). In the early thirties of the twentieth century, Pinhas Grayevsky described the manuscript and copied the colophon which the scribe of the manuscript had written (לוחות אבני זכרון - אבני קדש בירושלם, Part VIII [Jerusalem: Zukerman Press, undated] 15–16).

In 1937, Ben-Zvi published the inscription at the end of *Miqdash-yah*. Ben-Zvi makes no mention at all of Firkovich, and says: "Perhaps the copyist did not copy them from the original (the Aleppo Codex), but rather from some other scribe, but these changes show no clear sign of being forged ... The very fact he saw fit to copy it and add it to the colophon of *Miqdash-yah* demonstrates the admiration the Karaites had showed from time immemorial to the Aleppo Codex" (Ben-Zvi, *Miqdash-yah*).

However, in his article of 1960 (Ben-Zvi, *The Codex*, 12–13), he says (following Kahle): "At the end of מקדשיה [...] this same colophon was added in a modern Karaite script which was no part of the original MS; this was apparently the work of the notorious Karaite scholar Firkovich who introduced various changes and distortions into the original version in order to prove its Karaite origin."

between it and the "emendations" in the Dedication Inscription that Firkovich handed over to Sapir.[9]

A few years ago I carried out a detailed examination of the various copies of the Dedication Inscription made over the generations, and this examination brought to light a surprising finding:[10] in many textual details a relationship was revealed between Firkovich's two versions and the text copied in 1570 at the end of the Krakow *Tiqqun Sofrim* ascribed to R. Moses Isserlis. This text was published in 1857 by Mordechai Weismann Hayyut, in the newspaper *Ha-Maggid.*[11]

From the comparison it seems that the book called *The Writ of Jerusalem*, which is mentioned at the beginning of the Inscription of the *Miqdash-yah* Bible, never actually existed, and is no more than the result of an error. Hayyut copied over from the Krakow *Tiqqun Sofrim* one of the inscriptions copied into it from the Aleppo Codex, an inscription beginning in Arabic and telling of the redeeming of the Codex from booty taken from Jerusalem, for a synagogue called *Kanisat Yerushalayim*. The reference here is to the redeeming of the Codex from the Seljuks or from the Crusaders who had conquered Jerusalem, captured the Codex, and allowed members of the Rabbanite community in Fostat, Egypt, to redeem it for an exorbitant price.[12] The following is the text of the inscription (in translation):

> Transferred by virtue of its redemption from the booty of Jerusalem [*to this point in Arabic*], the Holy City, may it be rebuilt, to the community

9 This claim was raised by Penkower, "Maimonides and the Aleppo Codex," 124. For a detailed comparison of the Firkovich versions and other versions, see Ofer, "M. D. Cassuto's Notes," 287–91.

The question of the forgery of the Inscription requires a discussion, for the writer here states explicitly that he is copying over the inscription from another source: "I said to copy the precious list from the end of the precious Bible called *Miqdash-yah* in Jerusalem which is inscribed in it from a book called *The Writ of Jerusalem* which was dedicated to the Jerusalem synagogue of Egypt." From the context it appears that the writer is declaring that he is copying onto *Miqdash-yah* an inscription the source of which is in *The Writ of* Jerusalem. The forgery is thus not in the copying itself, but rather in two aspects: first, the copying was not carried out directly from *The Writ of Jerusalem*, but rather by means of the Krakow *Tiqqun Sofrim* and the newspaper *Ha-Maggid* (in actual fact, there never was such a thing as *The Writ of Jerusalem*, as demonstrated below); secondly, the copyist was not satisfied with copying the inscription precisely, but rather added and emended the text as he saw fit in difficult or doubtful places.

However, according to a precise reading of the beginning of the Inscription, it may be talking of yet another copying: the Inscription may have first been copied over from *The Writ of Jerusalem* to *Miqdash-yah*, and now the scribe was copying it over from there. It is thus strange to find the list at the end of *Miqdash-yah* itself, if it is supposed to be a copy of it.

10 See Ofer, "M. D. Cassuto's Notes," 284–91.

11 *Ha-Maggid*, Year 1, Issue 47 (November 13, 1857) 187; the continuation was published in Issue 48.

12 Ben-Zvi, "The Codex," 6–7. For the redeeming of Torah scrolls and other manuscripts, see: Moshe Gil, ארץ ישראל בתקופה המוסלמית הראשונה (634–1099) (Palestine during the First Muslim Period:

> of Egypt for the *Kanisat Yerushalayim* synagogue, may it be rebuilt in the lifetime of Israel. May its protector be blessed, and accursed is he who steals it, and he who sells it and he who pawns it. May it not be sold or redeemed for all time.[13]

The text of the inscription became corrupted either when it was copied into the Krakow *Tiqqun Sofrim* or when it was copied from there by Hayyut.[14] The copyist was completely unaware that the words before him were in Arabic, and so wrote as follows:[15] "Copied with the help of God and prepared from *Hakham* ... from the *Writ of Jerusalem*, the holy city etc."[16]

The Arabic word בחכם (by virtue) was read as a Hebrew word, מחכם, and the Arabic word נהב (booty) - as the Hebrew word כתב. In other words, the *Hakham* who prepared the copy and the *Writ of Jerusalem* from which the inscription was copied were nothing but the result of the confusion which befell the stages of transmitting and copying the inscription. This shows that the scribe who copied over the inscription at the end of the Karaite Bible in Jerusalem and claimed that he had copied it from a "book called *the Writ of Jerusalem*" actually copied it from Issue 47 of the newspaper *Ha-Maggid*. Undoubtedly, this has been done by Abraham Firkovich, who is known to have had a propensity for forging dedication inscriptions and dates of manuscripts so as to prove historical theories glorifying the actions of the Karaites.[17]

To comprehend the development of the affair, an important fact must be noted: at the time of the publishing of the inscription from Krakow, the Dedication Inscription of the Aleppo Codex has not been published yet, and the connection between the Krakow inscription and the Aleppo Codex was still unknown. Those who dealt with the inscription were unaware of it having been copied from another source and of it not being related to the *Tiqqun Sofrim* in which

---

634–1099) (Tel-Aviv: Tel Aviv Univ. and Israel Ministry of Defense Publishing, 1983) Part I, 670–72, and Part III, Cairo Geniza Documents nos. 573, 588.

13 אנתקל בחכם אלאפתכאך מן נהב ירושלים עיר הקדש תבנה ותכונן לקהל מצרים לכניסת הירושלים תבנה ותכונן בחיי ישראל ברוך שומרו וארור גונבו וארור מוכרו וארור ממשכנו לא ימכר ולא יגאל לעולם ועד

14 The *Tiqqun Sofrim* was lost in the Holocaust. See Ben-Zvi's call: "The fate of this Codex after the European holocaust and its present whereabouts are unknown to me. *Any one who possesses such information is requested to communicate with me. B-Z.*" (Ben-Zvi, "The Codex," 12, n. 27). And see Yehuda Leib Bialer, "קראקא – עיר סגולה" (Krakow – Special City), in Arieh Leib Bauminger, et al., eds., ספר קראקא – עיר ואם בישראל (The Book of Krakow, a Jewish metropolis) (Jerusalem: The Rav Kook Institute, 1959) 159–66.

15 The points following the quotation were printed that way in the original and will be discussed below.

16 נעתק בעזהשי"ת ונתקן מחכם.... מן כתב ירושלים עיר הקודש תבנה ותכונן לקהל מצרים לכניסת הירושלים (?) תבנה ותכונן בחיי ישראל...

17 For Firkovich's actions and forgeries see above, n. 5.

it was inscribed.[18] The publication of the inscription echoed throughout the Jewish world, especially after Hayyut asked his readers a series of questions and asked them to investigate the historical identity of the figures mentioned in the inscription he had published.[19] In retrospect, it can be stated that the debate which was stirred up about the family of Ben Asher and its connections with the Karaites and the Karaite faith was one of the initial phases in the modern study of the Masora and its development.[20]

In Issue 50 of *Ha-Maggid*[21] the publishers made public their reply to Hayyut's invitation. They brought the response of "our wise writer, Rabbi B. G. of Paris" (Ber Goldberg):[22] "With regard to the *Tiqqun Sofrim*, that was mentioned in *Ha-Maggid* in connection with Krakow's history, it was compiled by a Karaite *hakham*[.] The family, the names of whose members appear at the head of the book and at its end, is a well known Karaite one[,] and wherever the words[23] are obscured there was a Karaite name written there which was erased by chance or deliberately."

18 Hayyut himself sums up in 1861 his opinion on the subject and his attitude towards the reactions he had received (in the newspaper *Ha-Mevasser*, 160). He indicates two inconsistencies between the inscription he had published and the *Tiqqun Sofrim* in which it was inscribed. The inscription refers to "24 books" while "before us we only have the five books of the Pentateuch and one Scroll"; the inscription states that R. Aaron b. Mar Rav Asher vocalized the manuscript, while "before us there is no vocalization." Nevertheless, he traces the history of the manuscript before him taking the inscription into account, saying that Ben Asher was no Karaite, and that's why the Karaites had given the Rabbanites permission to study it, and R. Yosef Karo retrieved it from the Karaites.

It should furthermore be noted that the inscription of Krakow actually states at the beginning that it is copied from some other source. This is the meaning of the first two words of the inscription: נעתק בעזהשי"ת, which precede the quotation of the inscription from the Codex. However, the mistakes which had taken place in the interpretation of the Arabic words at the beginning of the inscription led to these two words being read in sequence with the continuation (נעתק בעזהשי"ת ונתקן מחכם etc.) and their meaning changing.

19 "I sincerely hope that one of the scholars engaged in uncovering the history of our people in the light of their studies note . . . who the princes 'Josiah and Hezekiah' were and when they lived, and what the phrases 'the community of Egypt and *Kanisat Yerushalayim*' and 'the colonies and communities in the Holy City' and so on refer to" (*Ha-Maggid*, Year 1, Issue 48 [November 20, 1857] 190 [continued from Issue 47]).

20 The newspaper *Ha-Maggid* was the first newspaper to appear in Hebrew. It came out in the town of Lyck and was edited by Eliezer Lippman Silbermann. The important role played by *Ha-Maggid* in this affair should be stressed – as a link between the scholars and sages throughout the Jewish Diaspora. A similar role was played also by the newspaper *Ha-Levanon*, the first Hebrew newspaper to appear in Palestine: in its first year (1863) Sapir published in it, in serial form, a description of the Aleppo Codex and details of the spelling and vocalization of the Codex.

21 *Ha-Maggid*, Year 1, Issue 50 (December 4, 1857) 197.

22 *Maskil* and research scholar (1799–1884), who worked in Berlin, London and Paris.

23 The Hebrew text here ובכל מקום נקוד וטלוא בכתבים is a play on words, referring to the biblical verse נקד וטלוא בעזים וחום בכשבים (Gen 30:33) and to the Ashkenazi pronunciation which renders the two words כתבים and כשבים homonymic.

In his final sentence Goldberg is referring to a number of places where Hayyut was unsuccessful in reading or in comprehending the inscription he had published, and so he marked them with dots and wrote in parenthesis at the beginning of his statement: "Wherever I was unable to read the text I marked dots like this. . . ." Goldberg thus assumes that these are not words obscured by time, but rather a deliberate erasure of Karaite names. The publishers back up Goldberg's opinion, and adduce a number of quotations from the Karaite composition *Dod Mordechai* which contain the names of the leaders mentioned in the inscription from Krakow.

Hayyut responded in Issue 16 of *Ha-Maggid*, Year 2, and listed a number of biblical variants found in the *Tiqqun Sofrim* and in a Torah scroll attributed to R. Moses Isserlis. Hayyut disagrees with Goldberg about the identity of the scribe and the Masorete, claiming that there is no evidence that they were Karaites:

> Scholars should now examine accordingly whether it really was a Karaite that prepared the inscription and tested it. The scholar who has decided on this (no. 50), should now produce proof [. . .] and if it is as he says, and those leaders who dedicated it [. . .] were not of the Rabbanites [. . .] nevertheless its honor will not be diminished.

It now seems that there was someone who accepted Goldberg's opinion and tried to take another step in that direction: wherever Hayyut showed dots, he tried to reconstruct the missing words in accordance with the context and on the basis of Goldberg's view that the dots represent deliberate erasures of Karaite names: the scribe who wrote the manuscript, "Shelomo . . . ," is Shelomo ben Yeroḥam, the well known Karaite scholar. Similarly, all the other places marked by dots were reconstructed according to their context. This reconstructed text is the text which was copied over into the Karaite Codex in Jerusalem, and is reflected in the emendations Firkovich gave Sapir in the margins of the page he handed him. It is not hard to guess who was behind these two sources.

I already assumed in the past[24] the essence of what has been presented here, but the details are now revealed explicitly in the recently uncovered Firkovich letters.[25]

> [. . .] The *Keter* (Crown, that is, biblical codex) in which there was the inscription of which there remained a copy at the end of the *Keter* called *Miqdash-yah* here in Jerusalem, in this synagogue of ours, we Karaites [. . .] is the very one at present in the city of Krakow, in the synagogue of

24 Ofer, "M. D. Cassuto's Notes," 289–90.

25 Firkovich's statements were written after he had already viewed the Aleppo Codex and compared its Dedication Inscription to the one of Krakow. For the purposes of this discussion, however, I have ignored this comparison in that stage of discussion and quoted only the sentences dealing with the *Miqdash-yah* and Krakow inscriptions.

> the Rabbanites, which was brought there from the town of Safed. And the reason that they erased in that inscription the name of the scribe which had been written there, Shelomo ben Yeroḥam, is that it will not be discovered that he was a Karaite scribe. They also erased the name Bozra, so that it will not be revealed that he who dedicated it was also a Karaite, for Bozra was an important center of Karaite Jews as mentioned above. Anyone interested in seeing the great argument amongst scholars of our generation on the subject of the inscription in the Codex in the Rabbanite synagogue of Krakow should look through the pages of *Ha-Maggid*, Year [ ] in the column *Ha-Zofe*, where he will see how those who wish to distort the facts can distort even something straight, while those who prefer the truth admit it. For there are many signs that they see that the names were not erased for no purpose and dots placed instead of them as a hint. And perhaps now that they see the text of the inscription of that Bible (of Krakow) which has survived in its entirety, at the end of the *Keter* called *Miqdash-yah* here in Jerusalem – perhaps those stubborn people will now admit the truth for it is well-founded.

Firkovich reveals the connection between the inscription he "found" in the Karaite synagogue and the *Tiqqun Sofrim* in Krakow. He mentions the argument which was carried on in the pages of *Ha-Maggid* (in the column named *Ha-Zofe*), and his support for Goldberg "who prefers the truth" and his reservations from Hayyut who "distorts" things. Firkovich also has strong evidence supporting Goldberg's argument: the text copied at the end of the *Keter* called *Miqdash-yah* is identical with that in Krakow, except that in it there are none of the deliberate erasures obscuring its Karaite origin.[26].. This, therefore, was the object of Firkovich: to bolster up his hypotheses concerning the original text of the inscription, and to transform it, as it were, into a textual fact.

In light of all this one special emphasis in Firkovich's statement will now be properly understood:

> I found the text of an inscription [...] at the end of the Bible known as *Keter* as well, but its name is *Miqdash-yah* and it was copied over from a book called *The Writ of Jerusalem* which was dedicated to the Jerusalem synagogue of Egypt. *And I already saw it in 1830 and copied it over at the end of my travel log book.*

26 One can interpret the words "the names were not erased for no purpose and dots placed instead of them" as an accusation of forgery directed at Hayyut himself (Goldberg never intended to do so, of course, but was referring to the erasures made in the manuscript over the generations). It is, however, possible that Firkovich did not intend to accuse Hayyut, but rather did not understand properly the significance of the dots or did not remember exactly what was written in the newspaper which was not available to him at that time.

Firkovich is trying to emphasize that he *found* the inscription (and did not create it), and that this discovery is nothing new: it already took place during his first trip to the East in 1830, long before the Krakow inscription was made public (in the year 1857).

The turning-point in this affair occurred, of course, when the Dedication Inscription of the Aleppo Codex was discovered. Sapir seems to have had a copy of this inscription as early as 1855,[27] but it was first made public in the *Ha-Levanon* newspaper in 1863 (Year 1, p. 23).

Sapir was aware of the debate which had raged in the pages of *Ha-Maggid* in 1857, and commented on it in his book *Even Sappir* which was published a few years later (Lyck 1866). Sapir quoted the Dedication Inscription of the Aleppo Codex, and then adduced in full the argument between Hayyut and Goldberg, claiming that the decision reached by the latter was mistaken, "for the erased and obscured words in the *humash* of Krakow appear clearly and explicitly in the whole Bible manuscript in Aleppo (from which the inscription in the *humash* [of Krakow] was copied), and there is no room for doubt" (p. 14a).

As for Firkovich, he received from Sapir the copy of the Dedication Inscription of the Codex when he came to Jerusalem in 1863. Firkovich realized immediately the similarity between the Krakow inscription (which he himself had reconstructed and completed) and the Dedication Inscription of the Codex. Did he consider the possibility that the Aleppo inscription was the original of the Krakow inscription? Sapir put this statement in brackets, casually as it were, and seems to have considered this self-evident. However, had Firkovich accepted it, he would have had to admit that Goldberg's claim of a forgery was unfounded, and that the reconstruction he himself had proposed for the Krakow inscription – a reconstruction he strove to perpetuate on the Karaite *Keter* in Jerusalem as well – was groundless.

Such a step was too difficult for Firkovich, and he sought and found a way out of the maze: in his opinion, we have before us two original inscriptions belonging to two different manuscripts. The inscription of the Aleppo Codex mentions "Shelomo known as ben Buya'a," while the Krakow inscription was indeed written by "Shelomo ben Yeroḥam." Furthermore, these two descriptions may very well be referring to a single person, whose father's name was Yeroḥam and whose nickname was "ben Buya'a." And so he wrote in his letter to his son-in-law:

27 This date is to be deduced from the manuscript of Me'orot Nathan, the list of questions Sapir sent to Aleppo. See: Refael Yitzchak (Singer) Zer, "מאורות נתן לר׳ יעקב ספיר" (R. Ya'aqov Sappir's Meoroth Nathan [MS JTS L 729]), *Leshonenu* 50 (1986) 151–213; Ofer, "M. D. Cassuto's Notes," 286 and n. 17.

> Now, my dear son-in-law, see what I have found: the text of an inscription similar to the previous inscription here in Jerusalem, may it be speedily rebuilt, at the end of the Bible known as *Keter* as well, but its name is *Miqdash-yah* and it was copied over from a book called *The Writ of Jerusalem* which was dedicated to the Jerusalem synagogue of Egypt.
>
> We have before us two inscriptions, in both of which the scribe of the two Bible texts is called "Our Teacher, R. Shelomo, the rapid scribe." The one is called "ben Yeroḥam," and he is R. Salmon ben Yeroḥam the Karaite, the great writer and antagonist of R. Saadya Gaon, while the other's father is not mentioned, so we do not know whose son he was. We only know that he was "known as ben Buya'a," a name we have now heard for the first time. We have no way of knowing whether ben Yeroḥam, the scribe of the Bible text (of Krakow) whose inscription is here in Jerusalem at the end of the *Keter* called *Miqdash-yah* or *Nezer Ha-Qodesh*, is himself the man known as "ben Buya'a" or not, but this is very probable, for the texts of the two inscriptions show that they were both poured out of the same mold, for they were both written by the same scribe.

In Firkovich's opinion, the two similar inscriptions belong to two ancient manuscripts which underwent similar stages of development: they were both written by Karaites and were then forcibly transferred to the possession of Rabbanite Jews. The Aleppo Codex returned to Karaite hands in Egypt (who were, in his opinion, the owners of the *Kanisat Jerusalem* synagogue in Cairo), while the second manuscript reached Krakow.

Let us now return to the annotations written by Firkovich in the margins of the page Sapir gave him. These notes were nothing but a comparison of the reconstructed inscription he had in his possession with the version Sapir had given him. Contrary to what Sapir understood, Firkovich had apparently not intended to claim that this was the text of the inscription in the Aleppo Codex. The way Firkovich saw it, he was using Sapir's page to compare two similar inscriptions found in two different manuscripts: the one in Aleppo and the one in Krakow.[28] In some places, Sapir's text is corrupt and that of Firkovich is more

28 Sapir's exact words were: "Before the aforementioned *Even Reshef* left Jerusalem to travel to Aleppo, I put in his hand a copy of [the inscription copied by] the aforementioned *RYZ*, for him to see there if the text is authentic. And when he returned to Jerusalem he gave me back the letter with a few emendations he had made in it according to what they had copied over for him in Aleppo or according to his own understanding (for he did not see it with his own eyes)" (*Even Sapir*, 12b, n. 2). Sapir does not say explicitly that Firkovich claimed that his emendations represented the text of the Aleppo Codex. He only says that Firkovich returned the page to him with emendations in its margins!

precise and matches the original more closely. Of course, wherever the text was reconstructed, the Sapir version is the one that matches the original.

When exactly did Firkovich write the inscription on the Karaite Bible in Jerusalem? There is a difficulty here. It seems that this inscription was written during the short period of time that Firkovich was in Jerusalem prior to his trip to Aleppo, that is, in October 1863.[29] During this brief visit, Firkovich and Sapir met, the former telling of his intention to journey to Aleppo, and the latter handing him in response a copy of the Dedication Inscription of the *Keter*. Were the text as written by Firkovich entirely dependent on the Krakow inscription as published in the *Ha-Maggid* newspaper, it is likely that Firkovich had copied over this inscription even before he heard of the Dedication Inscription of the Aleppo Codex, and only after completing this did he receive the copy of the inscription from Sapir. However, surprisingly, there are in Firkovich's inscription certain textual details which do not match the Krakow inscription; neither can they be deduced on the basis of logical reasoning alone.[30]

29 Firkovich's second (and last) trip to the East was in the years 1863–65 (when he was 76–78 years old!). He began his trip on the 6th day of Tishri, 5624 and arrived in Jerusalem on the 29th of Tishri. From there he traveled *via* Jaffa to Beirut and to Aleppo, after which he visited Antioch, Alexandretta and Beirut, returning to Jerusalem on the 12th of Tevet. It follows that his stay in Jerusalem before he traveled to Aleppo lasted only a very few days. See: Ze'ev Elkin and Menahem Ben-Sasoon, "אברהם פירקוביץ וגניזות קהיר" (Abraham Firkovich and the Cairo Genizot), *Pe'amim* 90 (5762/2002) 60–62; Harviainen, "The Cairo Genizot."

The dates mentioned here come from Firkovich's letters and are based on the Karaite Calendar. Hanna Firkovich, Abraham Firkovich's wife, erected an inscription in the Karaite synagogue in Jerusalem, which read as follows: "I arrived here in the Holy City of Jerusalem, may it be speedily rebuilt, on Tuesday, the 29th day of Tishri 5624, from the city of St. Petersburg" (Pinhas Grayevsky, "מחיי הקראים בירושלם" [On Karaite Life in Jerusalem] [Jerusalem: Zukerman Press, 1927] at the end of the booklet). This apparently refers to October 12, 1863, which is the 30th of Tishri 5624 according to the common Jewish calendar.

30 I have dealt thoroughly with all the textual details in my article: Ofer, "M. D. Cassuto's Notes," 287–91, and there is no need to repeat that discussion here. I shall stress only three points: 1. the home town of the person who dedicated the Keter, Bozra, does not appear in the Krakow inscription, instead of which dots are printed. It would seem that Firkovich reconstructed this detail by means of Sapir's copy; 2. the version החסיד השר (replacing החסיד הישר in the Keter – 287, line 9) appears here. This is where Firkovich abandoned the version of the Keter which appeared precisely in the Krakow copy, preferring Sapir's version. This shows that it really was Sapir's copy that served as a source for Firkovich; 3. a fascinating detail I did not mention in my previous article: Hayyut discussed the Dedication Inscription in the first issue of *Ha-Mevasser* (1861) 160, where he mentioned that the leaders of the Karaites permitted the Rabbanites to view the Keter "but not to read or study it." This shows that he had before him the correct version "not to read or study." But because of a printing error he printed in his first article לראות ולהשכיל ולהבין לה לקרות ולדרוש. However, this printing error led Firkovich to create the phrase לראות בו ולהשכיל ולהבין להם לקרות ולדרוש (*sic* in the *Miqdash-yah* inscription). In his annotations to the Sapir text he wrote להם לא לא, that is, the word לא does not appear, and in its place there appears the word להם.

There is thus no escaping the assumption that Firkovich was assisted by the inscription he received from Sapir, and on the basis of this he introduced certain corrections into the text he already had. Only afterwards did Firkovich copy over the text he had reconstructed at the end of the *Miqdash-yah* manuscript in the Karaite synagogue.

In Sapir's copy Firkovich discovered an important supplement that he had difficulty in reconstructing: the home town of Israel ben Simha, who had dedicated the Codex, is "the town of Bozra." This detail may have strengthened his belief that data linking the Krakow manuscript with the Karaites had been deliberately erased from it. Firkovich wrote: "They also erased the name Bozra, so that it not be revealed that he who dedicated it was also a Karaite, for Bozra was an important center of Karaite Jews."

Regarding the other textual variants, a significant fact reflected in Firkovich's letter should be emphasized: when he mentions the discussion in the *Ha-Maggid* newspaper, he does not have the paper before him. He refers interested parties to the *Ha-Zofe* column in *Ha-Maggid* (יעיין בעלי המגיד שנה [ ] בהצופה), but leaves a space for the year of publication. Firkovich does have before him, of course, a copy of the inscription published in *Ha-Maggid*, but it is possible that he only had the reconstructed version of it, and is consequently no longer able to distinguish between what he copied from the original and what he reconstructed logically. The frequent differences between the copy of the Krakow inscription he had and the copy of the Codex inscription Sapir had given him might well have strengthened his impression that two different inscriptions were involved. Thus, Firkovich never abandoned his belief that the scribe of the Krakow inscription was Shelomo ben Yeroḥam the Karaite, nor did he give up his intention to perpetuate on the ancient copy of the Bible the reconstructed inscription he had himself created.

Epilogue

Firkovich's opinion of the two inscriptions remained implicit in what he wrote, and was never made public. Sapir's opinion, that the Krakow inscription is a copy of the Aleppo Codex, has been accepted by scholars as self-evident,[31] and the variant "ben Yeroḥam" is considered a strange Firkovich forgery.

31 See, for example, Heinrich Graetz, "Die beiden Ben-Ascher und die Masora," *MGWJ* 20 (1871) 5–7; Ben-Zvi, "The Codex," 12. Christian David Ginsburg (*Introduction to the Massoretico-Critical Edition of the Hebrew Bible*, with Prolegomenon by Harry M. Orlinsky[2] [New York: Ktav Pub. House, 1966] 242) made a strange error: he mistakenly thought that the inscription in the *Ha-Maggid* newspaper was identical to the Cairo MS of the prophets (copied over in Sapir's book next to the Dedication Inscription of the Aleppo Codex), and concluded from this that the Krakow manuscript was copied over from the Cairo manuscript!

A last word about the sad epilogue of the affair: it is well known that the Aleppo Codex was damaged in the rioting of 1947, and the Dedication Inscription it included was lost. The *Tiqqun Sofrim* of Krakow disappeared during the Holocaust, and its present whereabouts are unknown. The fate of the third manuscript was no more favorable: after the fall of the Old City of Jerusalem in 1948, it was stolen; years later it was redeemed secretly and brought to the National Library in Jerusalem. The years it spent in captivity, however, had their effect: the manuscript was damaged by a fungus, its letters have become obscure, and at the present time it is in isolation and cannot be studied.

I delivered a lecture on the main points considered in this paper on August 12, 2001 at the Sixteenth Congress of the International Organization for Masoretic Studies (IOMS), which was held as part of the Thirteenth World Congress of Jewish Studies in Jerusalem.

An Exploratory Study on the Use of a Phylogenetic Algorithm in the Reconstruction of Stemmata of Halachic Texts

AVISHAI YORAV
Jerusalem

TAL DAGAN
Heinrich-Heine Universität, Düsseldorf

DAN GRAUR
Tel Aviv University and University of Houston

Until recently, philological-historical analyses of ancient texts were based almost exclusively on the know-how of experienced scholars. The main disadvantage of this approach is the lack of a methodological means for resolving conflicting conclusions reached by different researchers. Additional problems arise when the amount of data that needs to be considered is too large to be dealt with manually, or when the evidence precludes a simple description of the ancestry of the various versions. This article describes the analysis of several halachic texts through the use of a phylogenetic algorithm called maximum parsimony, which was originally designed for the study of biological data. Hundreds of textual variants occurring in various manuscript witnesses of three halachic texts were used in conjunction with the maximum parsimony procedure to derive phylogenetic trees from encoded data. Group patterns produced by this algorithm were found to be fairly similar to some results obtained through conventional philological-historical research conducted on the same texts. In a significant number of cases, however, particular stemmatic statements were not supported by maximum parsimony. Our conclusion is that phylogenetic methodology may be useful to historical-philologists in reconstructing the stemmata of text traditions or the ancestry of halachic manuscripts. Computerized phylogenetic algorithms are expected to outperform the traditional manual approach especially as far as long documents are concerned, as well as in cases in which a proliferation of text witnesses needs to be considered.

The scientific tradition in the humanities differs in several ways from that in the natural and exact sciences. This is not only true of the divergent character of the subject matter, but also regarding the techniques employed for data organization and the methodology for deriving inferences. This essay explores the interdisciplinary use of a methodological tool from evolutionary biology in philological-historical research.[1] In particular, we shall study the efficiency with which the history of ancient halachic text witnesses can be reconstructed correctly by maximum parsimony.

One of the principal tasks of historical philology as far as investigating texts is concerned is the arrangement of text witnesses in stemma form. Until recently, the standard methodology for stemmatic reconstruction was mainly based on the insights, know-how, and intuition of experienced scholars. The main disadvantage of this approach is the lack of a methodological means for resolving conflicting conclusions reached by different researchers. Additional problems arise when the amount of data to be considered is too large to be dealt with manually, or when inconsistencies due to contamination preclude the unequivocal description of the ancestry of the various text witnesses. The accuracy of inferred hierarchical clusterings of text witnesses increases with the number of paragraphs that are common to the textual variants under study. However, the number of possible combinations (stemmata) rises as well, and as a result so does the difficulty to reach properly integrated inferences. Manual resolution is only possible when the number of text witnesses is small, but becomes successively more difficult as these proliferate. A typical drawback of human intuition is the tendency to ignore evidence pertaining to negative relationships, that is, the assessment that links between two elements are *not found*. Phylogenetic algorithms can evaluate negative information as easily as positive information.

Here, we attempt to complement the traditional methodology with a computerized algorithm capable of clustering what might otherwise be indefinite or uninformative data. For convenience, we assume that the conventional analyses represent the "truth." The reliability of the algorithm is, then, evaluated according to the level of congruence exhibited between its output and the "truth." In general, we seek algorithmic assistance to human deduction. Under the reasonable assumption that it is impossible to program all the plethora of considerations necessary for philological-historical analysis, stemmatic reconstruction cannot be automated in its entirety. In general, we seek to draw on quantitative concepts, rather than be "restricted" by them.

Since the late 1960s, sophisticated methods for the reconstruction of the evolutionary history of biological species on the basis of molecular data (DNA and proteins) have been developed. Many of these methods have been implemented as computer software and are publicly available. In fact, this field of study, which is known as *molecular phylogenetics*,[2] has matured into a well established

1 This essay constitutes a second stage in the development of a methodology for the analysis of hierarchical relationships among halachic text witnesses. The first treatment of the subject was: Avishai Yorav, *Serial Norm for Comparison of Textual Variants* (Heb.) (August 2003) http://www.daat.ac.il/daat/toshba/mechkar/norma-2.htm.

2 For an introduction to the subject of molecular phylogenetics, see: Walter M. Fitch and Emman-

discipline mathematically, algorithmically, and biologically. Some of these reconstruction methods, that is, molecular phylogenetics, utilize textual information written either in the four-letter alphabet of DNA sequences or the 20-letter alphabet of proteins. In principle, therefore, these methods may be exapted for use on texts other than molecular sequences. There are many similarities between the development of text traditions and the evolution of biological entities. In both cases, information is transmitted by "descent with modification." In living organisms, the information is contained in the genetic material, transmitted by replication of the genetic material, and modified by mutation. In text traditions, the information is the text, transmitted by copying, and modified by error or deliberate change. The similarities between biological and textual evolution have been noted in the 1970s.[3] Beginning with the late 1990s, molecular phylogenetic methodology has been used to reconstruct the stemmata of text traditions and ancestor-descendant status of literary texts.[4]

---

uel Margoliash, "Construction of phylogenetic trees," *Science*, 155 (1967) 279–284; Dan Graur and Wen-Hsiung Li, *Fundamentals of Molecular Evolution* (2nd ed.; Sunderland, Mass.: Sinauer Associates, 2000); Joseph Felsenstein, *Inferring Phylogenies* (Sunderland, Mass.: Sinauer Associates, 2003); Simon Whelan, Pietro Lió, and Nick Goldman, "Molecular Phylogenetics: State-of-the-art Methods for Looking into the Past," *Trends in Genetics* 17 (2001) 262–72; David L. Swofford. *PAUP*. Phylogenetic Analysis Using Parsimony (*and other methods)* (Sunderland, Mass.: Sinauer Associates, 2001); Roderic D. M. Page and Edward C. Holmes, *Molecular Evolution: A Phylogenetic Approach* (Oxford: Blackwell Science, 1998); Willi Hennig, *Phylogenetic Systematics* (Urbana: Univ. of Illinois Press, 1966); Ian J. Kitching, Peter L. Forey, Christopher Humphries, and David M. Williams, *Cladistics: The Theory and Practice of Parsimony Analysis*, Systematics Association, Publication 11 (Oxford: Oxford Univ. Press, 1998); Naruya Saitou and Masatoshi Nei, "The Neighbor Joining Method: A New Method for Reconstructing Phylogenetic Trees," *Molecular Biology and Evolution* 4 (1987) 406–25.

3 Norman I. Platnick and Howard Donald Cameron, "Cladistic Methods in Textual, Linguistic, and Phylogenetic Analysis," *Systematic Zoology* 26 (1977) 380–85.

4 Adrian C. Barbrook, and others, "The Phylogeny of *The Canterbury Tales*," *Nature* 394 (1998) 839; Christopher J. Howe, and others, "Manuscript Evolution," *Trends in Genetics* 17 (2001) 147–52; Matthew Spencer and Christopher J. Howe, "Estimating Distances Between Manuscripts Based on Copying Errors," *Literary and Linguistic Computing* 16, 4 (2001) 467–84; Linne R. Mooney, and others, "Stemmatic Analysis of John Lydgate's Verse Chronicle '*The Kings of England Sithen William the Conqueror*,'" *Revue d'Histoire des Texts* 31 (2003) 277–99; Arthur R. Lee, III, "Numerical Taxonomy Revisited: John Griffith, Cladistic Analysis and St. Augustine's *Quaestiones in Heptateuchum*," StPatr 20 (1989) 24–32; Peter M. W. Robinson, "Computer-Assisted Stemmatic Analysis and 'Best-Text' Historical Editing," in Pieter van Reenen and Margot van Mulken, eds., *Studies in Stemmatology* (Amsterdam: Benjamins, 1996); Peter M. W. Robinson and Robert J. O'Hara, "Cladisitic Analysis of an Old Norse Manuscript Tradition," in Susan Hockey and Nancy Ide, eds., *Research in Humanities Computing* (Oxford: Oxford Univ. Press, 1996) 4, 115–37; Stephen C. Carlson, "A Phylogenetic Approach to N.T. Textual Criticism" (December 1, 2002) http://www.mindspring.com/~scarlson/tc/. An interesting forerunner to the use of phylogenetic methodology in the humanities is the field of glottochronology, which deals with the evolution of languages. For an early short review of the subject, see Robert B. Lees, "The Basis of Glottochronology," *Language*, 29 (1953) 113–27. The last few years have also witnessed the emergence of a "post-modernistic"

So far, however, no Hebrew or Aramaic manuscripts have been subjected to phylogenetic analysis.

Our paper has two goals. The first is to apply the phylogenetic methodology to rabbinic texts. The second is to compare deductions derived from traditional studies with those derived from quantitative phylogenetic analyses. This comparison may give us some clues on the extent with which computerized phylogenetic algorithms, which were obviously designed for distinctively unrelated purposes, may be of assistance to philological historians interested in rabbinic texts.

Phylogenetic trees for the different versions of a manuscript were inferred using maximum parsimony. Maximum parsimony is a method of evolutionary inference in which the phylogenetic tree with the least number of changes is chosen as the most likely one.[5] How evolutionary change is measured depends on the particular variant of the parsimony employed. In this study, we used the simplest parsimony method, called Wagner parsimony.[6] Our data was coded into binary character states: 1 for presence, 0 for absence. The algorithm can also process a modest amount of "no data" input. The Wagner parsimony criterion assumes that each character can be either inserted (0 changes to 1) or deleted (1 changes to 0).[7] We count the number of changes during the "evolution" of a manuscript for any possible tree. The most parsimonious tree is the one that requires the smallest number of changes.

The Wagner maximum parsimony algorithm (as well as other variants of maximum parsimony) yields unrooted phylogenetic trees. In such a tree, the distances between items and their relative arrangement on it represent an estimate of the affinities among the items. The algorithm identifies pairs of related items (sister taxa), and associates them with other items or clusters. In this study we opted for unscaled trees, that is, trees in which the lengths of the branches do not provide a quantitative estimate of the number of changes along the branch. The affinity between items or groups of items (degree of similarity) is graded by the number of branches separating them. Since the tree is unrooted, the direc-

---

approach. Followers of this trend are no longer concerned with the "original text," but rather treat each text witness as a distinct entity. Steering clear of any ideological discussion on this issue, we will only comment that our present study deals with situations in which it is safe to assume that the text witnesses have, in fact, "evolved" from an ancestral *urtext*.

5 For the reconstruction of the trees, we used the MIX software within the PHYLIP package. Joseph Felsenstein, "Parsimony in Systematics: Biological and Statistical Issues," *Annual Review of Ecology and Systematics* 14 (1983) 313–33.

6 Joseph Felsenstein, "PHYLIP – Phylogeny Inference Package (Version 3.2)" *Cladistics* 5 (1989) 164–66. Newer versions, such as the one used by us, can be obtained from Joseph Felsenstein at the Department of Genetics, University of Washington, Seattle (http://evolution.genetics.washington.edu/phylip.html).

7 The more common variant (character state) was assigned a value of zero; the other was assigned a value of one.

tion of an affinity is unspecified. That is, neighboring items may not necessarily have a common ancestor or be descended from one other. To determine the direction of a tree, that is, to produce a real historical stemma-like diagram, a particular item or group of items should be identified as the root of the phylogenetic tree.[8] Following the selection of a root, a directional (or rooted) tree is produced. This tree represents one evolutionary path from the root, via intermediate (mostly hypothetical) items, to the texts under study, which appear as terminal nodes.[9] Specifying the true root requires knowledge that is extraneous to the texts under study (for example, the ages of the manuscripts or testimony pertaining to the order in which the most ancient versions within a group have been copied). Alternatively, a trial-and-error system may be used, in which the researcher designates a particular item or group of items as a root, and then makes an expert decision on the likelihood of the resulting rooted tree based on external considerations. In the absence of any ability to root the tree unequivocally, unrooted trees may be used to test certain hypotheses concerning the relationships among manuscripts.

The number of possible trees that can be built depends on the number of textual variants under consideration. This number increases quite rapidly with the number of text witnesses,[10] and may become even larger in datasets with missing characters or indefinable character states. We note that the resulting tree may contain errors; however, by using such statistical methods as bootstrapping, one can ascertain which branches are reliable and which are not.

Application of a method from such an unrelated discipline as molecular evolution highlights a series of assumptions of conventional philological methodology, some of which are at odds with those used in maximum parsimony. For example, when studying copies of a text, one must allow for multiple identical errors or corrections of independent origin. This process of babelization[11] in the evolution of texts is analogous to the occurrence of homoplasies (reversals, parallelisms, and convergences) in DNA or proteins. Due to these processes,

8 It is important to note that the root must be uniquely specified. Therefore, a stemma with two or more elementary branches cannot be produced. Hybrid products in either evolutionary biology or philology cannot be analyzed with a methodology designed to produce binary graphs.

9 Inferred (or hypothetical) items on the diagram appear as internal nodes. The actual texts under study appear as terminal nodes and are indicated in this study by Hebrew letters.

10 The number of bifurcating unrooted trees for n textual variants is very large, $(2n-5)!/[2^{n-3}(n-3)!]$. The number of rooted trees is even larger, $(2n-3)!/[2^{n-3}(n-3)!]$. Given the staggering number of possible trees, only about 25 textual variants can be dealt with by exact maximum parsimony algorithms. When the number of variants exceeds 25, tree reconstruction requires heuristic approximations.

11 Babelization or "babylonization" has been shown to be the cause of similarities between a tenth-century text from Italy, a fourteenth-century text from Spain, and a seventheenth-century text from Germany, independently of any common textual substrate. See, Avishai Yorav, *Serial Norm for Comparison of Textual Variants.*

similar character states may not always constitute evidence of a genealogical link between text-witnesses. Methods of phylogenetic reconstruction, including maximum parsimony, are ill equipped to deal with homoplasious or babelized character states. Moreover, the one-root-only and the binary-bifurcation-only rules may be too stringent for dealing with the evolution of texts.

Complete reconstruction of relationships among text witnesses consists of two steps: the grouping phase (that is, construction of an unrooted phylogenetic tree) and determination of directional ancestral-descendant relationships (that is, rooting the unrooted tree). Phylogenetic methodology can only assist in the first step of the process. It is important to emphasize that the phylogenetic analysis is purely morphological and does not deal with the different meanings of the textual variants. Moreover, phylogenetic analysis can only be used to study stemmatological relationships within a set of textual variants. It cannot be used to aid in the resolution of questions pertaining to version traditions prior to the consolidation of the definite version of a text.

In this study, three halachic texts composed in late-antiquity or early medieval times and transcribed during the Middle Ages were investigated. The surviving text witnesses had been studied and documented extensively using traditional methods. Meticulous encoding of the textual variants was carried out according to a standardized scale.[12] Trivial textual variants at level 1 of the scale[13] were not used. Verification studies were not conducted; our basic premise was that the published text witnesses are errorless. The text witnesses were positioned as "taxa" and the textual variants as "characters."

First Case Study
Sefer Hilkhot Harif ᶜal Massekhet Pesaḥ Rishon

The editor of *Sefer hilkhot harif ᶜal massekhet pesaḥ rishon*[14] studied 14 manuscripts and a number of early printed editions. His conclusion was that all the printed editions were derived from the Constantinople edition (ד) and, therefore, it is the only printed edition that needs to be considered in a stemma. Moreover, one of the manuscripts (ז) is thought to have been derived from the printed editions and may, therefore, be excluded from further consideration.

12 See Yorav, *Serial Norm*. A detailed list of all the textual variants used in this study will be presented in a separate report. In the course of encoding, we were compelled to make several assumptions regarding the nature of the texts. Indeed, the encoding method and the hypotheses intrinsic to it may have added unrealistic elements to the study. For example, the assumption that variations within sentences or paragraphs are independent of one another may be problematic.

13 Level-1 variants include minor variations, such as alternations between complete and partial spellings or the use of very similar letters.

14 R. Hillel Hyman, *Sefer hilkhot harif ᶜal massekhet pesaḥ rishon* (Jerusalem: Jewish Theological Seminary, 1990).

The editor suggests that the text witnesses can be clustered into three groups[15] (hypothesis 1). The first group consists of ח, ט, י, and כ (hypothesis 2), the second of ל, מ, נ, ס, and ר (hypothesis 3), and the third of ע, פ, צ, ק, and ר (hypothesis 4). He further conjectures that manuscript נ was copied from ס (hypothesis 5), and ל and מ are to some extent related to the first group (hypotheses 6 and 7). ד is the most recent of the text-witnesses and was influenced to some degree by all the groups (hypothesis 8). ע is somewhat closely related to the second group (hypothesis 9). פ, צ and ק are said to more closely related to one another than any of them is related to either ע or ר (hypotheses 10 and 11, respectively). Of these eleven hypotheses, some are untestable by maximum parsimony (for example, hypothesis 8); others, such as hypotheses 3 and 6, are contradictory in the phylogenetical sense (that is, they cannot both be true). Moreover, some hypotheses, for example, hypothesis 2 may be partially correct and partially wrong. Finally, some hypotheses, for example, hypothesis 1, may only be tested against the rooted tree.

We applied the maximum parsimony algorithm to fourteen text witnesses consisting of thirteen manuscripts (ז was excluded) and one printed edition (ד). The textual variants in the first three chapters, consisting of approximately half of the text, were used. A total of 611 non-trivial variations was found. The resulting unrooted phylogenetic tree is shown in *Figure 1*. A rooted tree with ד as root is shown in *Figure 2*.

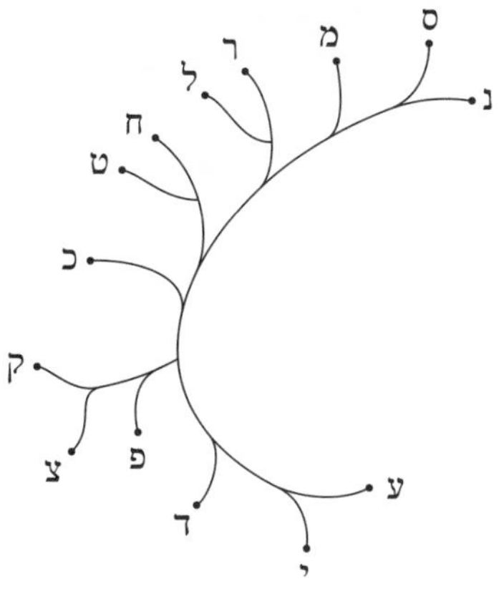

Figure 1. Unscaled unrooted phylogenetic tree for 14 text witnesses of *Sefer hilkhot harif ᶜal massekhet pesaḥ rishon.*

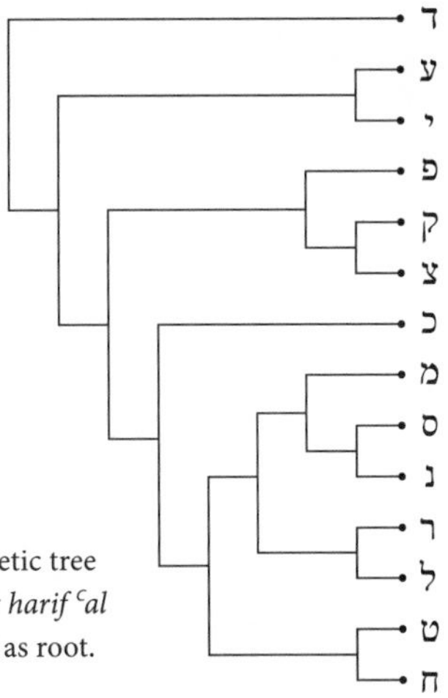

Figure 2. Unscaled rooted phylogenetic tree for 14 text witnesses of *Sefer hilkhot harif ᶜal massekhet pesaḥ rishon.* ד was used as root.

15 Hyman, *Hilkhot harif*, 11–14.

Let us first test several hypotheses against the unrooted phylogenetic tree. Hypothesis 2 is only very partially supported by the phylogenetic analysis, with ח and ט emerging as sister taxa. Hypothesis 3 is partially supported by the tree, if ו is excluded and ד is included. Hypothesis 4 is partially supported by the tree, if ו is included and י and ד are excluded. Hypothesis 5 is strongly supported by the tree. In the matter of the weak hypothesis 9, no support was garnered for a link between ע and the group containing ח, ט, י, and כ, although we recovered a close relationship between ע and י.

An inspection of the rooted tree in *Figure 2* indicates that it is impossible to divide the tree into three monophyletic groups of any kind, let alone into the particular tripartite division envisioned by R. Hillel Hyman. Moreover, the choice of the root does not matter, as the unrooted tree in *Figure 1* also is impervious to tripartition. We must, therefore, conclude that in the strict sense of the word, our results are incongruent with those of the editor.

Second Case Study
The Aramaic Text of the *Targum of Job*

The editor of the *Targum of Job*[16] examined fourteen manuscripts and two early printed editions. In his opinion, one of the manuscripts (ד) reflects two variant traditions. The first of these is found in chapters 1–13 (1ד); the second in chapters 14–42 (2ד). In total, there were 17 text witnesses. The editor identifies four basic groups, with certain links between them.[17] A simplified rendition of this stemma is shown in *Figure 3*.

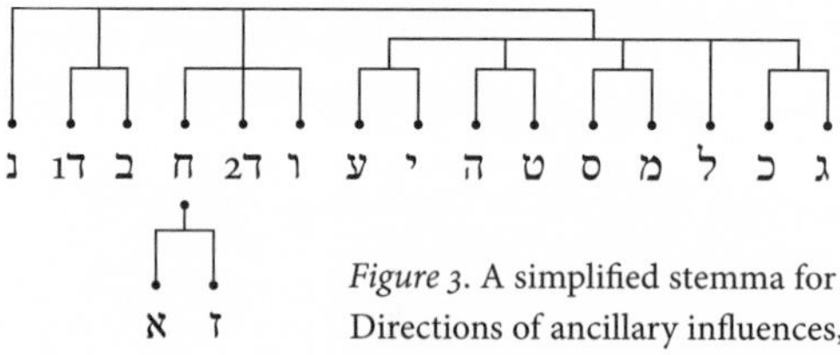

Figure 3. A simplified stemma for 17 text witnesses of *Targum of Job*. Directions of ancillary influences, degrees of certainty, and "group" influences are not shown.

Maximum parsimony was applied to the textual variants of chapters 1–6 and 14–19 (approximately 30% of the text). A total of 788 variations was found. The unrooted tree is shown in *Figure 4*. We have considered several possible rootings for the tree, for example, א and ו.[18] In the end, we opted for a rooted tree that maximizes the iconographic similarity to the traditional stemma (*Figure 5*).

16 David M. Stec, *The Text of the Targum of Job* (Leiden: Brill, 1994).

17 Stec, *Targum of Job*, 84.

18 ו is noteworthy in that it is the only manuscript from North Africa; the others are from Spain, Germany, or Italy. א is the most recent of the text witnesses.

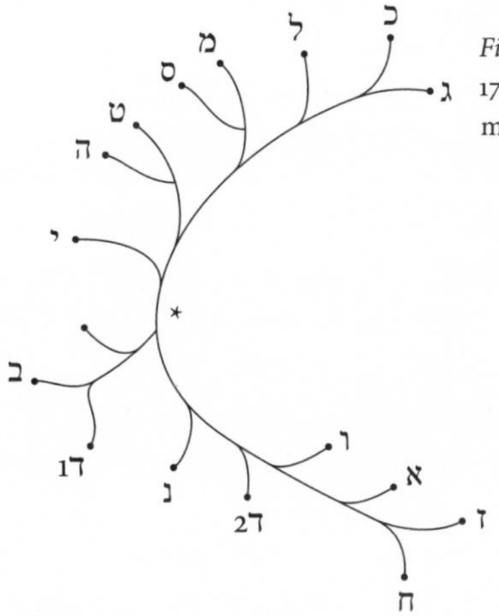

Figure 4. Unscaled unrooted phylogenetic tree for 17 text witnesses of *Targum of Job*. An asterisk marks the position of the root used in *Figure 5*.

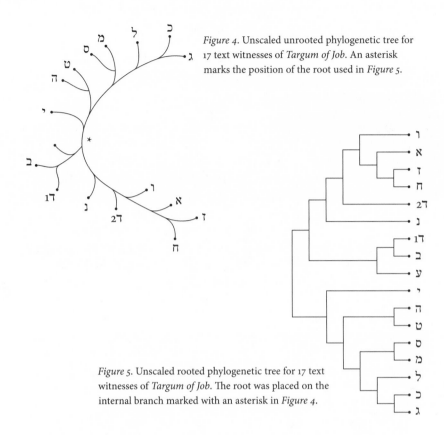

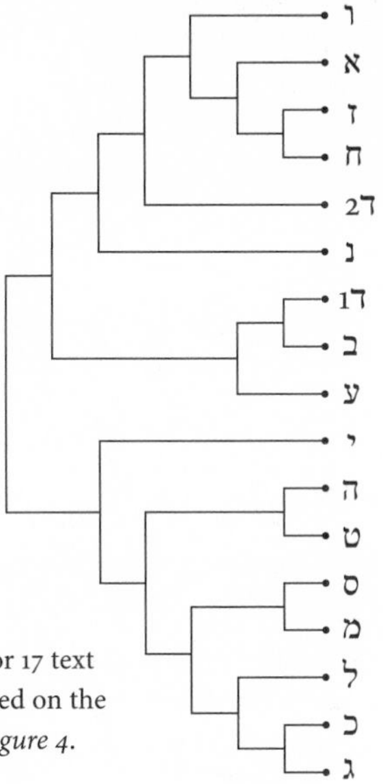

Figure 5. Unscaled rooted phylogenetic tree for 17 text witnesses of *Targum of Job*. The root was placed on the internal branch marked with an asterisk in *Figure 4*.

A comparison of the stemma with the maximum parsimony rooted reconstruction reveals a truly extraordinary degree of congruence. Four basal groups are recovered. The first groups consisting of ג, כ, ל, מ, ס, ט, ה, and י it is almost identical with the group proposed by David Stec. The only differences between the phylogenetically inferred group and the one in the stemma concerns the position of ע, which in the maximum parsimony tree clusters with the correctly identified groups consisting of ב and 1ד. In fact, even for the position of ע it is not possible to claim total error, because ע is suspected to have been affected by multidirectional influences. The internal relationships within the basal ג-כ-ל-מ-ס-ט-ה-י group were also identified correctly, with ג clustering with כ, מ clustering with ס, and ט clustering with ה. The algorithmic reconstruction confirms the grouping of ב with 1ד, and strongly supports the editor's decision to separate ד into two independent text witnesses, 1ד and 2ד. The algorithmic reconstruction also confirms the clustering of ז, ח, א, ו, and 2ד. In the stemma, נ appears as a group by itself. The phylogenetic analysis indicates a distant affinity with the ז-ח-א-ו-2ד cluster.

Third Case Study
Tractate *Pesaḥim* Chapters 3 and 4

The fact that chapters 3 and 4 of *tractate Pesaḥim* in Talmud Bavli have been annotated and edited independently by two researchers in two academic institutions on different continents,[19] allows us to pursue two types of comparative research. The basic assumption (with very rare exceptions) is that two chapters derived from the same manuscript represent a single integral textual unit. Therefore, if the phylogenetic algorithm works without error and if the various text witnesses do not contain hybrid parts, then the phylogenetic tree based on one chapter is expected to be identical to the phylogenetic tree based on the text of the other chapter. In other words, the text-witness groupings should be identical in both trees. Our first comparison will, therefore, contrast the inferred tree based on the textual variants of chapter 3 with the inferred tree based on the textual variants of chapter 4. We will, thus, be able to identify which parts are congruent between the two trees, that is, have been reliably reconstructed, and which are not. Our second sets of comparisons will contrast the trees derived by maximum parsimony with those derived by traditional means, whose technical details are oftentimes unspecified and frequently unspecifiable.[20] We note that in this type of analysis it is possible to evaluate (or grade) the "relative worth" of different scholars working in the conventional philological-historical tradition. We shall abstain from using maximum parsimony to raise personal philological criticisms. Rather, we shall use these comparisons to discuss the consistencies of the general conclusions of the editors.

The editor of chapter 3 of *Pesaḥim*[21] examined ten manuscripts, a printed edition (ונציה), and seven Genizah fragments. The editor provides a fairly detailed account of the methods employed in his stemma arrangement.[22] He distinguishes between "significant differences," "widespread significant differences," and other differences (but does not specify the criteria for the classification). He lists 128 variations between the text witnesses. His stemma consists of two main branches and an indeterminate group. Simply put, the typical representative of branch I is 125 'וט. א134 'וט, 109 'וט, and ונציה belong to this branch. 109 'וט, and ונציה represent later additions. Branch II is epitomized by 1608 'סמ.

19 It is important to note that the studies were indeed independent; there was no cooperation between the researchers, and at times competition was implied.

20 For example, Hyman, *Hilkhot harif*, 14, states: "Ultimately I must admit that an important part of the arrangement [of the text witnesses] into families was based on a sense born of hundreds of hours of work and experience . . ."

21 Shmuel Yosef Wald, *Talmud Bavli, Tractate Psachim, Third Chapter* (Jewish Theological Seminary; Jerusalem, 2000).

22 Wald, *Psachim*, 318–26.

Other descendants of branch II are מינכן 6, ששון, גניזה 1, אוקספורד, and מינכן 95. אוקספורד and מינכן 95 are somewhat more distantly related to branch II. סמ' 1623 and קולומביה, which are Yemenite manuscripts, are said to be closely related to each other, but their relationship to the other two groups was not determined. *Figure 6* presents a schematic and simplified summary of the stemma. The stemma rests on a very elaborate system of considerations. After delineating which text witnesses are viewed as distinctively representative of the two branches, and claiming that the other text witnesses are "heterogeneous," the editor presents 20 two-dimensional tables[23] quantifying the degree of agreement between the various "heterogeneous" text witnesses and the representatives of the two branches. Such meticulous statistical processing is unusual in philological-historical editing and analysis. Nevertheless, decisions based on traditional analyses are sometimes arbitrary.[24] The placement of ונציה and וט' 109 is especially problematic. Shmuel Yosef Wald appended them to branch I in the graphical stemma,[25] but his detailed tables[26] appear to indicate a branch-II affiliation.[27] No explanation for this contradiction is provided. The above clearly demonstrates that "general impressions" may influence experts more than tabulations of concrete quantities.

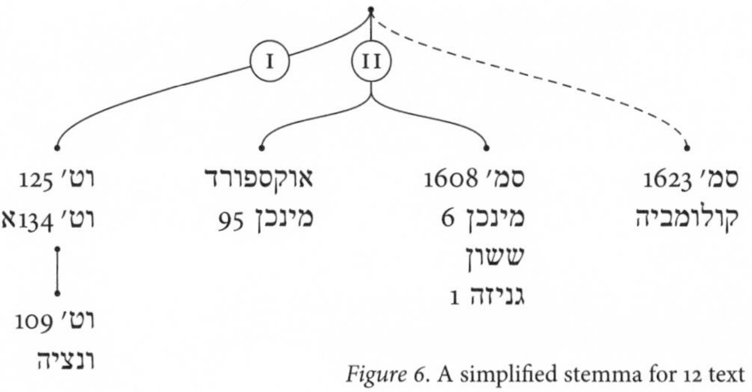

Figure 6. A simplified stemma for 12 text witnesses of chapter 3 of *Pesaḥim*.

23 Wald, *Psachim*, 319–25.

24 All the analyses start with a dichotomic division, whereby two text witnesses are identified as "opposite poles." Subsequently, all the other text witnesses are compared separately to the two opposites to determine how similar or dissimilar they are to the two poles. וט' 125 was chosen as main representative of branch I and סמ' 1608 was selected as main representative of branch II. Surprisingly, no reason is provided for this fundamental assertion, other then claiming that contradictions between the text variants were found in 95–98% of the cases.

25 Wald, *Psachim*, 283.

26 Wald, *Psachim*, 323, 325.

27 In the tables, there is a 39% match of וט' 109 to branch I and a 56% match to branch II. ונציה has a 30% match to branch I and a 67% match to branch II.

For chapter 3, we performed a maximum parsimony analysis on twelve text witnesses consisting of ten manuscripts, a printed edition, and a Genizah fragment (גניזה 1). One of the manuscripts (וט' 134א) encompasses only approximately 75% of the text. גניזה 1, which is the largest of the Genizah fragments available for analysis, contains only about 12% of the text. Hence our analysis contained a considerable fraction of missing data. We identified 353 non-trivial variations. The unrooted maximum parsimony tree is shown in *Figure 7*. The first and foremost observation is that Wald's tripartite division of the text witnesses cannot be recovered from the unrooted tree no matter which node or internal branch is chosen as root. Moreover, of the many groups and subgroups identified in the stemma in *Figure 6*, the only clustering that is recovered by the maximum parsimony phylogenetic algorithm is that of the Yemenite manuscripts קולומביה and סמ' 1623. מינכן 6 and סמ' 1608 were found to be closely related, as in the stemma, but without either ששון or גניזה 1. At this point it is not clear whether or not the lack of congruence between the stemma and the phylogenetic tree for chapter 3 is solely due to the fragmentary nature of וט' 134א and גניזה 1.

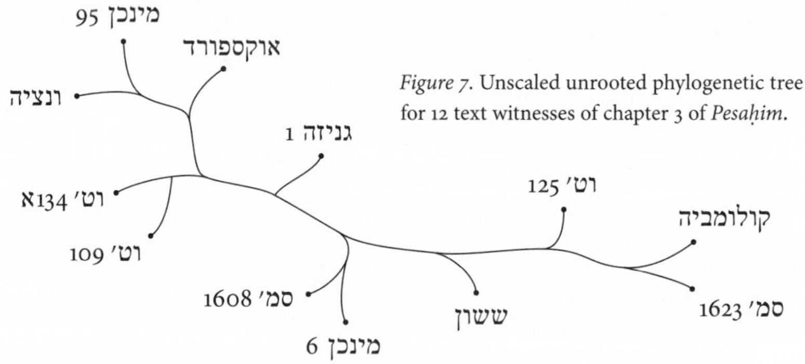

Figure 7. Unscaled unrooted phylogenetic tree for 12 text witnesses of chapter 3 of *Pesaḥim*.

The editor of chapter 4[28] examined 12 large text-witnesses and 11 additional Genizah fragments.[29] He identifies two main branches. Branch I is most distinctively represented by וט' 125; branch II by מינכן 6. Aaron Amit does not present a graphic stemma, but claims that סמ' 1608 (in 75% of the cases) and וט' 109 (in 60% of the cases) agree with branch II. The remaining text-witnesses are claimed to be heterogeneous. Manuscript וט' 134א was identified as composed of two unequal parts, each of which originated from a different text witness. There are only very minor variations between קולומביה and סמ' 1623. The editor does not say anything explicit regarding the arrangement of the other

28 Aaron Amit, "Makom sheNahagu, Talmud Bavli, Tractate Pesachim, Fourth Chapter" (masters thesis; Bar-Ilan Univ., Ramat Gan, 1995).

29 Not including גניזה 1 (mentioned in the previous section) as it lacks text from the fourth chapter.

text witnesses, nor does he offer verification for his contentions, except for directing the reader in general terms to an elaborate apparatus of textual variant comparisons in the thesis.

The maximum parsimony algorithm was run on thirteen text witnesses of chapter 4 (134 'וט was divided into א134 'וט and ב134 'וט). The Genizah fragments were excluded from the analysis. There were 586 non-trivial variations throughout the chapter. The unrooted maximum parsimony tree is shown in *Figure 8*.

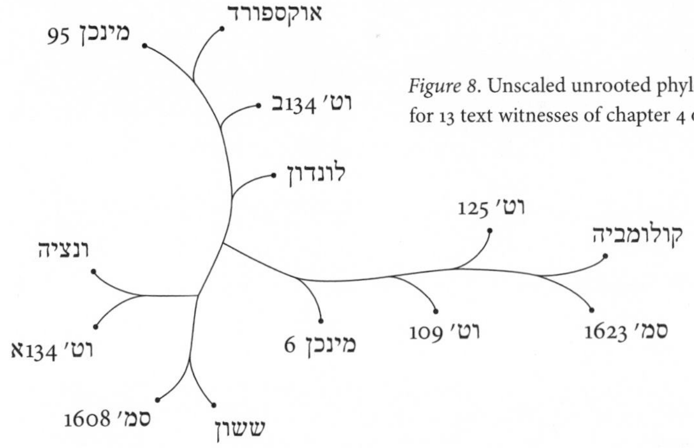

Figure 8. Unscaled unrooted phylogenetic tree for 13 text witnesses of chapter 4 of *Pesaḥim*.

Aaron Amit provided almost no strong arguments in favor of or against certain groupings. As a result it is difficult to contrast his claims with those obtained through maximum parsimony. All that can be said is that the grouping of קולומביה with 1623 'סמ is confirmed. On the other hand, the phylogenetic tree does not support a link between 6 מינכן and 1608 'סמ or 109 'וט.

In the main, the conclusions reached by the editor of chapter 4 of *Pesaḥim* agree with those of the editor of chapter 3.[30] Unfortunately, Amit does not list his considerations, other then discussing the differences between 125 'וט and 6 מינכן and providing a series of examples of textual variations between the two branches.[31] Of the 10 examples from category I, which he regards as most significant, he lists קולומביה and 1623 'סמ as exhibiting strong similarities to branch I, and 1608 'סמ, ונציה, אוקספורד, 134 'וט, and ששון to branch II, with no clear resolution regarding 109 'וט and 95 מינכן. If we accept this sample as representative – in practice, the examples were merely meant to illustrate the basic division between the two branches rather than arrange the text witnesses – then there

30 Both Wald and Amit select 125 'וט as the main representative of branch I. The editor of chapter 3 prefers 1608 'סמ to represent branch II, while the editor of chapter 4 prefers 6 מינכן. The two text-witnesses are 85% similar according to Wald, and 75% similar according to Amit.

31 Amit, "Makom sheNahagu," 19–37.

are several discrepancies between the conclusions of the two editors. According to the editor of chapter 3, וט' 134א belongs unequivocally to branch I, whereas Amit assigns it to branch II. According to the editor of chapter 3, קולומביה and סמ' 1623 are hybrids with a slight tendency toward branch II. The editor of chapter 4 agrees with the hybrid status, but sees a greater similarity to branch I. Wald assigns וט' 109 and ונציה to branch I (although, as we have previously observed, in his tables he places them closer to branch II). According to Amit they are closer to branch II.

To compare the two traditionally derived stemmata with the results of the maximum parsimony algorithm, as well as assess the source of incongruity between the phylogenetic trees for chapters 3 and 4, we combined the data from the two chapters into a single database. The eleven text witnesses that contain both chapter 3 and chapter 4 were used in the combined analysis.[32] וט' 134 was identified as a composite of two separate documents,[33] one from the thirteenth century and one from the fifteenth. For the combined analysis, we only used the later document that contains both chapters. This "pruning" of fragmentary and hybrid text witnesses is likely to improve our chances of reconstructing a less ambiguous tree than the previous ones. In total, 940 non-trivial textual variations were used.

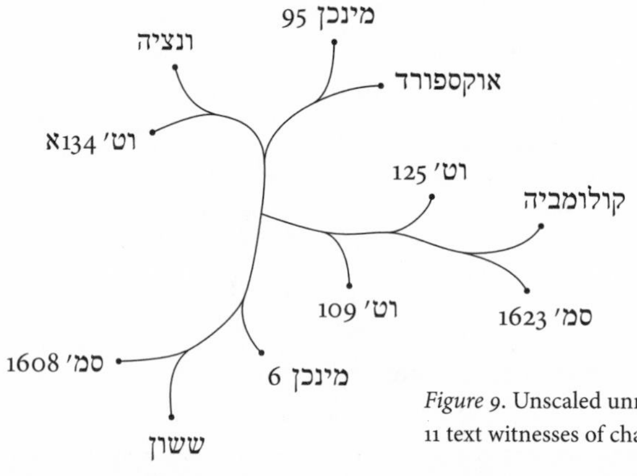

Figure 9. Unscaled unrooted phylogenetic tree for 11 text witnesses of chapters 3 and 4 of *Pesaḥim*.

The unrooted maximum parsimony tree for the combined data is shown in *Figure 9*. The first observation is that it is impossible to partition the tree into the two branches advocated by the traditional studies. The putative representatives

32 For example, the לונדון manuscript (extant in chapter 4 alone) and גניזה 1 (only partially extant in chapter 3) were excluded.

33 Pages 5b–11a and pages 54b to the end are from the earlier document (Germany, thirteenth century?); pages 15a to 54b, except pages 45b–48a, were completed by a later scribe (Germany, fifteenth century?).

of branch I (125 'וט, א134 'וט, 109 'וט, and ונציה) are scattered throughout the tree, so that no matter where we place the root the monophyly of the two branches cannot be recovered. On the other hand, the maximum parsimony tree strongly supports a monophyletic clade consisting of the principal members of branch II (1608 'סמ, 6 מינכן, and ששון). אוקספורד and 95 מינכן are clustered, but they have no relationship to branch II. קולומביה and 1623 'סמ are clustered as predicted by both traditional stemmata. Interestingly, they are intimately related to 125 'וט, which is the typical branch-I representative. The algorithm links א134 'וט to ונציה with no affinity to either branch I or branch II. This is in contradiction to the claim by the editor of chapter 3, who assigned both א134 'וט and ונציה to branch I. The editor of chapter 4 regards these text witnesses as "composites." The intermediate position of ונציה and א134 'וט supports this contention. The maximum parsimony algorithm's product places 109 'וט as a sister taxon of 125 'וט and the קולומביה and 1623 'סמ clade. The editor of the third chapter assigned it (with some reservation) to branch I, while the editor of the fourth chapter assigned it to branch II (with reservations as well).

Evaluation of the Maximum Parsimony Algorithm in Reconstructing Stemmatic Relationships among Halachic Text Witnesses

An exhaustive evaluation of the relationships between the products of two methodologies from such distant disciplines is an impractical endeavor. The best we can do is to look at the degree of congruence between the methods and assess the usefulness of the maximum parsimony algorithm as an aid in the reconstruction of stemmatic relationships among halachic text witnesses. The facts, as outlined above, are that in some cases we obtain surprising degrees of congruence between the phylogenetic algorithm and tradional methodology. For example, in the case of the Aramaic *Targum of Job*, a truly extraordinary degree of congruence was observed. Basal and distal groups were identified correctly, and even differences could be explained by hybridization and multidirectional influences. In fact, in the case of *Targum of Job*, several new relationships (clades) have been discovered on which traditional methods had nothing to say. We believe that these relationships should be further investigated. Admittedly, the congruence between the two methods is far from perfect, and in some cases there was very little in common. We think, however, that despite the inconsistencies discovered between the methods, the computerized algorithm may be of significant aid to conventional research. Had the editors of the four texts seen the phylogenetic outputs, they might have concentrated their efforts and restricted themselves to examining a limited number of "suspect" groups. It is quite possible that the phylogenetic results would have allowed them to settle doubts, refine groups, and possibly improve upon their final conclusions. Of course, binary trees derived through phylogenetic methodology can never be "true" in the absolute sense of the word, since it is universally accepted that all the text witnesses in our exploratory study have been subject to some degree of contamination.[34]

Traditional philological-historical studies require the researcher to approach his subject free of prejudice, but not without prior knowledge. However, sometimes the number of alternatives that a philologist may be required to consider is simply too large, and the task of stemmatic reconstruction becomes an impossible one. For example, the editor of the *Targum of Job* considered 17 text witnesses. Thus, in theory, he should have considered 6, 190, 283, 353, 629, 375 unrooted arrangements and 191, 898, 783, 962, 510, 625 rooted ones.[35] Given these mind-boggling numbers, a computer program is likely to be of great value by focusing the attention of the researcher on particular subsets of text witnesses.

One can only consider what it would take to build a stemma for the *Maimonides Code* (*Mishneh Torah*), which consists of approximately 800,000 words and for which there are several hundreds of text witnesses (mostly in fragmentary form). Can this task be even contemplated by using "manual" labor?

34 A similar problem exists in phylogenetic reconstruction of bacteria that have experienced horizontal gene transfer (textual contamination) in their past. See Hervé Philippe and Christophe J. Douady, "Horizontal Gene Transfer and Phylogenetics," *Current Opinion in Microbiology* 6 (2003) 498–505. Several phylogenetic methods have been proposed in the literature to deal with such "contamination," for example, Patricia Escobar-Páramo, and others, "Decreasing the Effects of Horizontal Gene Transfer on Bacterial Phylogeny: The *Escherichia Coli Case Study*," *Molecular Phylogenetics and Evolution* 30 (2004) 243–50. It is not inconceivable that this class of methods may one day be adopted to identify multidirectional influences in text witnesses.

35 Graur and Li, *Fundamentals of Molecular Evolution*, 173.

Jewish Biblical Theology Whence? Why? And Whither?

ZIONY ZEVIT
University of Judaism

In the early 1980's, some Jewish and Christian biblicists promoted the idea that Jewish scholars should develop an academic discipline that would become the Jewish equivalent of Biblical Theology. Since the late 1980's, a small number of Jewish scholars responded to the idea in very different ways. Those responding positively may become the vanguard of scholars who will shape the discipline of Jewish Biblical Theology should it emerge. This article points to serious intellectual, terminological, and practical problems with the whole undertaking and seeks to illustrate what they are, why they exist, and to propose how they may be overcome. It also attempts to clarify elements in the ethos of American biblical studies that have influenced the new interest in Jewish Biblical Theology.

The proposition that there can and should be a discipline "Jewish Biblical Theology" that will become part of or ancillary to (Christian or General) Biblical Theology, long considered a desideratum by non-Jewish scholars, is being promoted seriously by a number of Jewish scholars. As a consequence of almost twenty-five years of occasional remarks and publications and the efforts of a dedicated few, the proposition was elevated onto the public agenda through the constitution of a panel at the 2003 Annual Meeting of the SBL.[1]

Moshe Goshen-Gottstein was the first Jewish scholar to formally write on the idea. In 1981, he issued a call for Jewish biblical theology in a Hebrew article published in Israeli journal *Tarbiz* where it languished for lack of interest; in 1987, he reissued the call in an English article.[2] Biblicists, mostly Jewish and Israeli, who read Goshen-Gottstein's Hebrew article considered his proposal unscientific and odd. The abridged English version, however, appearing in a Festschrift dedicated to Frank Moore Cross of Harvard, lent the idea

1 I. Kalimi, one of the coordinators of this panel, announced that he is editing some of the papers presented at the SBL along with other invited studies for publication by Eisenbrauns as a collection. Panel members were: M. Z. Brettler, Brandeis University; M. Gruber, Ben Gurion University of the Negev; S. T. Kamionkowsky, Reconstructionist Rabbinical College; B. D. Sommer, Northwestern University; and Z. Zevit, University of Judaism.

2 M. H. Goshen-Gottstein, "Jewish Biblical Theology and the Study of Biblical Religion," *Tarbiz* 50 (1981) 37–64 (Heb.); "Tanakh Theology: The Religion of the Old Testament and the Place of Jewish Biblical Theology," in P. D. Miller, P. D. Hanson, S. Dean McBride, eds., *Ancient Israelite Religion: Essays in Honor of Frank Moore Cross* (Philadelphia: Fortress, 1987) 614–44.

greater credibility and helped it take root in the minds of some who thought it a possibility.[3]

What is new is the seriousness with which some Jewish scholars relate to the proposition and the somewhat intensive discussions that it has instigated in hall-conversations at the national meetings of both the Society of Biblical Literature and the Association for Jewish Studies since 2000.

It is not that Jewish biblical theology doesn't exist. Jewish and general bookstores are filled with books applying Bible lessons homiletically to the issues of everyday life in order to foster healthy attitudes and well-being. These works usually cite rabbinical sources (and, most recently, even Kabbalistic texts) to generate theological support for whatever interpretation they have decided to advance. Furthermore, in the USA alone approximately 3000 formally untrained Jewish biblical theologians share their thoughts regularly on Sabbaths and Jewish holidays when they teach or preach about whatever Torah portion or selection from the Prophets is read that day. Although the overwhelming majority of these are rabbis, in many congregations, educated and insightful laypersons are invited to either share or fill this role in the regular service on a rotating basis. But the new call is for something different.

It seeks something much more formal than less, more disciplined than off-the-cuff, more methodologically self-aware than traditionally patterned, something that can be described by the adjective hermeneutic rather than homiletic, something that communicates to an absent anonymous readership through books and journals rather than to familiar faces in their regular seats and, I suspect, something that will sit well in the ostensibly non-confessional non-denominational academy even if it cannot find a seat in the synagogue.

For scholars to establish a new discipline, it is necessary that they define its subject matter, that is, that they clarify and circumscribe what it is determined to study; that they determine a research agenda stating what they know, how they know it, and what they want to know in the future. It is also desirable that they outline and define acceptable methodologies that enable them not only to pose and research significant questions but also to recognize when important questions have been answered correctly, or at least not incorrectly. Since these tasks are executed simultaneously, not sequentially, early discourse in a new discipline will often be ill-defined and somewhat fuzzy. Disciplines and subdisciplines of biblical studies that emerged in the final decades of the twentieth century such as feminist hermeneutics, ecological hermeneutics, and rhetorical criticism all underwent this process. In the first decade of the twenty-

3 Most readers of the first article were Israelis working in an extremely secularized climate; the second article, directed to those in American or European contexts, was read by many in a climate where biblical studies are conducted in a mixed secular-religious one.

first century, discussions of Jewish biblical theology are characterized by their "ill-definedness."

At first observation, it is unclear why this should be the case because "biblical theology" has a long history in the Western intellectual tradition. Reflection, however, suggests that not only does the adjective "Jewish" lack clarity when attached to the expression "biblical theology," but that there are serious questions about the meaning of the two other components in the discipline's name that have been addressed only superficially in a Jewish context. Moreover, with two notable exceptions discussed below, little contact exists between the proposed discipline and the well-established one.

The broad objectives of this study are to introduce some clarity to the ongoing discussions by defining a series of critical, somewhat innocent, terms and by illustrating how they have different meanings in different institutional, rhetorical, and religious settings; to establish a typology of biblical theologies as currently practiced by non-Jews and to map Jewish biblical theologies onto this typology; to discuss the problem of Jewish biblical theology in secular academic settings, and finally, to suggest a protocol for the proposed discipline.

Jewish biblical theology potentially may have a profound affect on contemporary Judaism and Christian-Jewish dialogue. My intentions in this study are to catalyze discussions that will bring some order to the proposed, but as yet unestablished, discipline that will enable scholars to evolve a theoretical, analytical framework for the undertaking, and that will promote methodological self-consciousness beyond what has already been demonstrated. To do so, I analyze the problematic of the proposed discipline under the following broad rubrics and questions:

I. The semantics of the three components selected to denominate it independently and in various combinations: Jewish, biblical, theology, biblical theology, and finally, Jewish biblical theology.

II. Typologies of Christian biblical/Old Testament theologies

III. Calls for Jewish biblical theology and the typologies that they promote

IV. Why should Jews in secular academic settings want to undertake projects in Jewish biblical theology?

V. Whither Jewish biblical theology?

My reasons for determining these rubrics are the following:

1. *Jewish, biblical,* and *theology* have a restricted range of meanings in regular academic discourse and a somewhat different range in the inner-Jewish dialogue.

Advocates for the new discipline do not address this. Clarification of the distinctions between Jewish and non-Jewish uses of these terms focuses attention on what is and is not being addressed by the scholars involved.

2. So too, insofar as biblical theology is a well established Christian discipline, the analysis under rubric II proposes a typology of such theologies, sometimes ignoring as somewhat irrelevant distinctions between Catholic and Protestant biblical theologies and between conservative and liberal ones. The analysis is intended to provide a convenient, provisional matrix for the classification of the types of theologies that Jewish scholars propose under rubric III. This is necessary because there are essential ways in which Jewish undertakings cannot be like Christian ones.

3. Writers write for reasons within social and intellectual contexts. Under rubric IV, I consider the disadvantages accruing to Jewish scholars who chose to engage in the proposed discipline and speculate as to the catalysts in the contemporary American academic ethos that may have precipitated interest in it. Of necessity, this section has a journalistic, impressionistic quality because it considers very recent matters that have not been studied formally by social scientists.

I. The Semantics and Implications of the Key Terms

1. JEWISH

The term "Jewish" invites complicated questions. Does it refer to the status of individuals as recognized members of the Jewish people? Their status in only some part of the faith community? To a body of knowledge? Or to some admixture of the three?

The term may be intended to refer to individuals recognized as such according to normative Jewish standards: a person born of a Jewish mother or converted according to *halakhah*. This definition leaves unattended the question of whether or not those converted by non-orthodox rabbis who may or may not claim to follow orthodox standards are considered Jewish. But, allowing for the most liberal of definitions, including that of patrilineal descent by which one born of a Jewish father, but not a Jewish mother, is Jewish, this is the most trivial of the problems, but one to which I return below.

In the context of the *academy*, "Jewish" often refers to specific bodies of knowledge related to both Judaism and the Jewish people. Among scholars of the American or European or Australian Association for Jewish Studies or of Jewish Studies Institutes, "Jewish" includes minimally control of biblical and tannaitic Hebrew and refers more to the ability to read and comprehend basic texts than to their technical linguistic analysis, and, of course, Modern Hebrew for access to the volumes of research published solely in Hebrew. It includes familiarity with all and competency in some of the following: 1. history of the Jews and Judaism from the Hellenistic through the modern period; 2. *machshevet yisrael*, that is, the intellectual culture of Jews and Judaism in major historical periods – this consists primarily of philosophy, theology, metaphysics as known through texts, as well as what might be labeled legal, social, economic and political theory; 3. Jewish biblical commentary from the medieval through the early modern period; and 4. the Jewish liturgical calendar and life-cycle events as well as the texts and some folkways associated with them. It includes a specific area of expertise and specialization. Perhaps a working definition of competency in Jewish studies might be the ability of individuals to understand presentations and to participate actively in at least some sections reflecting disciplines other than those in which they specialize at meetings of a Jewish Studies society.

If "Jewish" refers only to the academic definition, then it is clear that many non-Jews might be able to do Jewish biblical theology while many Jews, say those knowledgeable only in the Bible and Ancient Near Eastern studies or the Bible and Archaeology paradigms, could not. An example of the former are the study guides to the weekly Torah reading posted on its website by the Bat Kol Institute of Jerusalem. Authors of these guides, whose names and institutional affiliations are provided, are described online as "Christians studying the Bible within its Jewish milieu using Jewish sources." In most guides, nothing in the exegesis or theological comments hints that the authors are not Jewish.

The academic definition might be strongly supported by the Association for Jewish Studies which views Jewish Studies as academic fields of inquiry and creativity in which all qualified scholars, no matter their religion, participate. I do not know, however, if it would be acceptable to those advocating the development of Jewish biblical theology.

2. BIBLICAL

Three questions relative to this second adjective merit consideration:

1. Is the canon considered for Jewish Biblical Theology restricted to the Tanakh, or may it be extended to include Ben Sirah, a composition highly regarded by some Rabbis? Books in the apocrypha and pseudepigrapha? Sectarian texts from Qumran? Some New Testament writings such as Matthew, the Pauline epistles, and Hebrews? The writings of Philo and Josephus? The Talmud and midrashic collections?

2. Should interpretive translations such as the LXX, Syriac, and the Aramaic targums be considered biblical in some broad or restricted way?

3. In considering the backgrounds of ideas, should any or all of the following cultures be considered essential and allowed to find shelter under the adjective: ancient Near Eastern, Persian and Hellenistic, Roman, medieval and post-medieval European and Middle Eastern?

These questions are precipitated by the following data: The Bible is a collection of religio-didactic writings produced, transmitted, and curated by ancient Israelites; Judaism is a religion that emerged out of Israelite religion during the Persian and Greco-Roman periods and, after molding by the rabbis, is characterized fairly as the religion of the two torahs: one written and one oral. In view of these, the three questions may be considered facets of the following major question: Does or should Jewish Biblical Theology cover the Bible as interpreted, taught, and preached by Jews in post-biblical periods or will it be restricted to evaluating only what is in the Hebrew Bible written from ca. 1200 to ca. 150 B.C.E.?

The case for a broad definition is made by Jon D. Levenson whose "Jewish Bible" includes more than the Hebrew Bible. Avigdor Shinan and Yair Zakovitch, developing notions of Umberto Cassutto, advance a history of literature argument claiming that if the more inclusive understanding is disallowed, much in the Hebrew Bible itself cannot be comprehended in its fullest since only some parts of Israel's originally oral traditions are found written in the Bible. Other parts, equally biblical and originating in the same period, are preserved only in younger documents. For example, the tale of what happened to Sarah in Pharaoh's palace (Gen 12:10–20) lacks some details preserved in Josephus (ca. 100 C.E.), others mentioned in the Talmud of the Land of Israel (ca. 400 C.E.), and still others presented in *Midrash Tanhuma* (ca. 600 C.E.) that were once part of the original story.[4]

4 J. D. Levenson, *Sinai and Zion: An Entry into the Jewish Bible* (Minneapolis: Winston Press, 1985) 3–12; A. Shinan and Y. Zakovitch, *Lo' kach katuv batanakh* (That's Not What the Good Book Says) (Tel Aviv: Yedioth Ahronoth Books, 2004) 15–25, 205–11; J. Kugel, *The Bible As It Was* (Cambridge, Mass.: Belknap Press, 1997) 1–48. Shinan and Zakovitch differ from Levenson and Kugel in that the former argue that information in younger sources does not represent motific development or the elaboration of details in the Bible, but rather that it was part of the original biblical story suppressed late in the biblical period. Theirs is an interesting, albeit a minority, opinion which has become widely disseminated through their book which was on best-seller lists in Israel through most of 2005.

E. S. Frerichs, a non-Jewish scholar, remarks that the quality of understanding of biblical texts, as expressed through translation or commentary, is much influenced by preknowledge and that for traditional Judaism, this cannot exclude the corpus of classical rabbinic literature. See Frerichs, "The Torah Canon of Judaism and the Interpretation of Hebrew Scripture," *HBT* 9 (1987) 13–15, 19–21.

3. THEOLOGY

"Theology" as a term in the semantic field of religious discourse. Initially, it is useful to consider "theology," one of many terms delimiting the semantic field of contemporary, Western religious discourse, along with five other common ones from within the same field: philosophy of religion, apologetics, polemics, argument and dialogue. All six denote different types of religious discourse that, no matter their rhetorical flourishes, claim to employ logical proofs and reasonable arguments. They differ, however, in their objectives, their *a priori* assumptions, and in the particular *Sitz im Leben* of each person advancing arguments vis-à-vis a particular religion/denomination/sect.

Philosophy of religion, or of religion X, takes its stance *outside* of the religion or denomination and considers religion an object of inquiry. One philosophical program may attempt to understand the questions for which religion (or religion X) is an answer, or for which its practitioners believe it an answer; or it attempts to discern how and why religion (or religion X) arrived at the answers that it provides to specific questions. Philosophical investigators generally understand themselves to be objective outsiders asking questions and seeking answers, whatever they may be. Philosophy sets for itself the goal of discovering truthful answers to its questions and it must and can debate the pros and cons of whatever conclusions it reaches.

Apologetics takes its stance *within* religion X and considers some element of the religion a subject requiring explanation for outsiders. It employs the language and jargon of the outside audiences to which it addresses itself in order to make itself clear and comprehensible in their terms. It's objective is to instill a sympathetic and even empathetic understanding of itself in others by means of reason and evidence. Occasionally, apologetics disguises itself as philosophy of religion. Sometimes, its objective is limited to fostering understanding; in missionizing religions, however, its objective often is to win converts.

Polemics takes its stance *within* the religion and presents itself as one side of an argument against an outsider. The language of polemics is that of the inside group. Whatever it comprehends of the other, or of the real or perceived attack of the other, is reduced to insider language, analyzed in insider categories, and demonstrated to be wrong. The actual objective of polemics, however, is to bolster the religion from within and to defend it from whatever may be construed as significant (and successful) attacks of its self-justifications for belief, doctrine, and/or practice. The major audience of polemics is not necessarily outsiders, but insiders. Polemics is an intellectual form of "whistling in the dark." If conducted cordially, polemics may give rise to conversations characterized by apologetics and hence to some mutual understanding or to conversion. Often, the analyses underlying polemics may be recast into apologetics and become the basis of intellectually fulfilling dialogues between alternative worldviews.

Argument takes its stance *within* the religion and is akin to polemics except that each side in the controversy recognizes the other as speaking from within the same tradition. It occurs between those who perceive themselves as sharing much in common while disagreeing over some (very) significant matters. Argument can ripen into factional polemics and blossom into schisms within a religion.

Dialogue, takes its stance *between* parties who recognize each other as speaking from within different (competing or opposed or other) alternative traditions. It is characterized by polite apologetics and its stated objective is to develop mutual understanding about that which the traditions share and that over which they disagree. It attempts to understand the origins of both common and disparate positions. Its primary purpose is educational. In some cases, it may be the discourse that precedes negotiating ruptures between groups; in others, it may be a pretext for missionizing.

Theology takes its stance *within* religion X, considers a particular religion a subject (never "religion" in the abstract or in general), and is directed to others within the religion. Although it may function like philosophy and employ the same terminology, eventually it loops back on itself not only because its questions are influenced, even determined, by the religion from within which it operates, but also because the parameters within which its answers must fall are pre-determined by the religion, either explicitly or implicitly. Both authors and audience know approximately where it will end up and both are aware of lines that cannot be crossed. When innovative, it pushes the envelope from within. Evaluations of its conclusions, the pros and cons, are severely restricted by the aforementioned parameters.

Because many theologians are trained in philosophical methods and integrate academic philosophy into their theology, and because many are committed to the proposition that reason and revelation converge, they often prefer to present themselves as philosophers, if only because that terms connotes objectivity. Theologians sometimes defend this practice, arguing that since philosophers too have *a priori* positions, preferences, and prejudices, so long as all is laid out, there is no difference between the two.[5]

5 L. E. Cady and D. Brown, for example, challenge the widely held distinction made between Religious Studies viewed as an objective social science that belongs in the university and Theology viewed as a spiritual instruction that belongs in religious institutions concerned with personal formation. They argue that whereas the distinction may have been (or may have appeared) valid under modernist paradigms, it collapses in post-modern conceptions that break down earlier lines of demarcation (Introduction to "*Religious Studies, Theology, and the University: Conflicting Maps, Changing Terrain*," *BCSR* 31:4 [2002] 96–98). Their article, actually the introduction to a book, cites theologians who argue that given the breakdown of borders between disciplines, some or all forms of theology or something called "academic theology" should be included in university curricula (100–101).

There is, however, a difference. Whereas both theologians and philosophers measure the validity of answers to questions by the rigor of the inquiry and analysis, theologians are constrained by their transcendent commitments to employ additional touchstones in proposing answers and evaluating their validity, touchstones related to confessional systems. Protestant theologians in particular work between the central tenets of *sola scriptura*, scripture alone, and *sola fide*, by faith alone.

Another distinction between philosophy and theology may lie in the questions that they pose. One can easily imagine a theologian writing a book "Philosophy as a Jewish (or Christian) Problem," but only a philosopher would write *Religion as a Philosophical Problem.*[6]

Theology as a term in general usage. As a general term in American parlance, *theology* involves four, sometimes five, different entities: 1. God, 2. people in some recognizably organized community, 3. an explicit or implicit communication usually via an esteemed or sacred text, and 4. an interpreter or exegete capable of "translating" the communication into a form that can be understood and applied by (members of) the community. 5. The fifth entity may be disciplines in the humanities or social sciences whose insights (or truthful findings) are deemed significant and/or a threat to religious thought, for example, economics,

---

R. Hindery, responding to their article advocates that academic theology, defined as the study of "that which matters most," should be integrated into academe when it remains "loyal to scientific freedom and methods such as, disclosing presuppositions, and testing assumptions, arguments, and conclusions against plural or conflicting viewpoints and positions. He excludes explicitly confessional works from academic theology in that it "hides its presuppositions or else refuses to present them in the context of viable alternatives," possibly because it may be likened to the passionate advocacy of other ideologies such as existentialism, postmodernism and economic theories. Nevertheless, Hindery recognizes that subjecting faith-based presuppositions to critical inquiry is a problem that has yet to be resolved both at the theological and practical levels ("Advocacy in Academe: Academic versus Confessional Theology," *BCSR* 32:1 [2003] 18–19). This is clear only when it is admitted that the adjective "faith-based" indicates that, though real, the beliefs lack any basis in verifiable, unequivocal evidence, when a distinction is made between the objects of the words *know* and *believe*. It is less clear, however, when the adjective is taken – as it is by many – as referring to matters whose objectivity is vouchsafed through the authentic faith experiences of many in the community. Hindery appears to be calling for theological advocacy accompanied by polemics and apologetics.

L. Orye argues that there is no scientific model to be followed by theology; see his "To Be or Not To Be Scientific Is Not the Question: A Science Scholar's Challenge for the Study of Religion," *BCSR* 34:1–2 (February, April, 2005) 14–15, 17, and the discussion below of the culture of the SBL/AAR Annual Meeting.

6 I. Klein, *Hadat keba'ayah filosofit* (Religion as a Philosophical Problem) (Jerusalem: Bialik Institute, 2004). See Klein's distinction between the philosophical, theological, and scientific – by which term he refers to social sciences and anthropological approaches – to the study and analysis of religion, p. 10.

anthropology, sociology; and/or they may be aspects of contemporary life such as public welfare, ecology, war, racism and the like.

Whatever its specific content, theology is understood to inform belief and attitudes and actions, even as its parameters are delimited by them. Theology involves attitudes towards, thoughts about, and reflections on the relationship between individuals in the faith community, their official texts, traditions of the religion and unanswered questions. It is concerned with questions about what belief and practice can and ought to be in living reality rather than what they were in the past. It proposes solutions at the intellectual level and works out their implications for understanding and living in a community.[7] Within the faith community, it is commonly understood that like vegetables and fruit, proper theology makes a difference. It is good for you.

Anselm of Canterbury (1033–1109) provides an expression that serves as a useful definition for theology: "faith seeking understanding." This comprehension works itself out differently in the many Christian seminaries and divinity schools that pepper North America, as should be expected. As a process, theology starts with something real but ineffable – faith, understood as the objectification of what is initially experienced or encountered subjectively – and seeks language that can give name and expression, clearly though abstractly, to the contents and contours of that which by its inherent nature is not easily expressible.

The following examples illustrate how the term is used in some institutional settings: At University of Note Dame, the following disciplines are listed under Theology: Hebrew Bible, New Testament, Christianity and Judaism in Antiquity. In addition there is a Moral Theology track and a Systematic Theology one, the latter covering philosophical theology, trinitarianism, ecclesiology, anthropology, christology, and spirituality. At Union Theological Seminary, New York, Theology covers systematics (which attends to different approaches to theology and their impact on liberation theologies, women, black theology, womanist dogmatics, the thought of Barth and Neibuhr), Christian ethics, and ecumenical studies.

Theology's questions are for the present. It is always renewing itself because today's present is tomorrow's past and each tomorrow brings new questions and challenges.[8] In religions with explicit or implicit doctrine enshrined in official texts, theology can draw on traditions, reinterpreting old answers so that they respond to contemporary questions. Sometimes, of course, today's questions are old ones, asked before and answered satisfactorily.

7 R.W. Moberly, *The Old Testament of the Old Testament* (Fortress: Minneapolis, 1992) 152. Moberly presents this as a classical understanding of the term.

8 H.W. Stone and J.O. Duke, *How to Think Theologically* (Philadelphia: Fortress, 1996) 4–6.

At its most general, *theology* is applied to just about anything related to religion. As used by Christians nowadays, the theological study of the Bible is based on three related notions: 1. the word is eternal, unchanging in meaning, 2. human understanding is time-bound, linked to the worldview and circumstances of the interpreter of the written word, and 3. theologians bridge this gap by explicating the eternal in their particular time and place. The translation presented by theologians succeeds in uncovering or describing what is there already and reinvigorating the word for the changed circumstances and new intellectual climates.

As a term in popular culture, *theology* can be applied to religious lessons learned from various aspects of the general culture such as sports, politics, movies, and so on. Focusing somewhat, some institutions of higher learning such as Notre Dame deem languages, linguistics, history, archaeology, text study, hermeneutics, and exegesis, that is, everything that can be related to the study of the (Hebrew) Bible under this term, because each of these poses or implies questions traditionally deemed grist for the theological mill.[9]

Biblical theology. Biblical theology is a recognized discipline in Christian institutions of higher learning. To catch the tone, I cite selected lines from some course descriptions:

> Denver Seminary, OT 550–559, Studies in Selected Books
> "Studies in depth for exegetical and theological insights which can speak to today's world."
>
> Denver Seminary, OT 661, Old Testament Theology and Religion
> "How have modern believers tried to organize the teaching of the varied texts of the Old Testament and relate them to the New Testament? "
>
> Trinity International University, BL 334, Old Testament Theology
> "An examination of the message of the Old Testament, with special emphasis of Jesus in the Old Testament and topics such as law and grace, Israel and the church, promise and fulfillment, and covenant and faith."
>
> Union Theological Seminary, New York, ST 341, The Bible and Theology
> "An Analysis of scripture in Christian dogmatics and the issues posed for theology today."

9 See Z. Zevit, "The Biblical Archaeology Versus the Syro-Palestinian Archaeology debate in Its American Institutional and Intellectual Contexts," in J. K. Hoffmeier and A. Millard, eds., *The Future of Biblical Archaeology: Reassessing Methodologies and Assumptions* (Grand Rapids, Mich./ Cambridge: Eerdmans, 2004) 12–19. For an example, see S. Coakley, "Pleasure Principles: Toward a Contemporary Theology of Desire," *Harvard Divinity Bulletin* (Autumn, 2005) 21–33.

In contrast to Christian institutions, *theology* is almost absent from course descriptions in centers of Jewish higher learning and rabbinical training.

The Jewish Theological Seminary of America, world center of Conservative Judaism, one of two Jewish institution to have *theology* in its name, offers a catalogue featuring hundreds of courses.[10] According to a recent catalogue, only six courses employ *theology* or *theological* in their titles or descriptions, and these six are all taught in the department of philosophy that lists 30 courses. One course, "Theological Tradeoff: Reason or Faith?" (Phil 7133) examines the role of reason and rationality in the development of modern Jewish thought; a second, "Faith after the Holocaust," studies philosophical thinking after the Holocaust and its relationship to the possibility of faith. These courses promise to discuss "post-Holocaust" theologians. Both reveal a historical orientation to theology. They are about theology or particular theologians subjected to a philosophical critique. The only course that appears to relate to the term as useful for informing life and thought is "Translating Jewish Theology for Educational Settings" (Phil 5525). There is no *theology* in course descriptions of the department of Bible and Ancient Semitic Languages that offers 50 courses. The closest that department comes is in "Biblical Literature & Religion" which includes a survey of the literature of the Bible with special emphasis on its "religious ideas."[11]

At Hebrew Union College (Cincinnati), Bible 521, Genesis 1–11, is described as "The Bible's introduction to theology, anthropology, and philosophy of history" but the course work is described primarily as a comparison of narratives and genealogies to cuneiform epics and onomastics. HUC has a Dept. of Philosophy and Theology whose theology components are described muddily: "God concepts," "theological self-expression," and "medieval Jewish polemics and apologetics."[12]

The Reconstructionist Rabbinical College has one bible course, Isaiah 1–39, whose description mentions that it covers "the theological message" of the book

10 The other is the Hebrew Theological College of Chicago, an Orthodox institution.

11 *Jewish Theological Seminary Academic Bulletin 2002–2004* (New York: JTS, 2002) 113–19, 164–69. The Philosophy department also offers "Theological and Ideological Tensions in Conservative Judaism" and "Theology of Mesekhet Berakhot." Ismar Schorsch, Prof. of Jewish History and former Chancellor of the Jewish Theological Seminary traces his institution's involvement with biblical theological issues to the 1950's after a number of faculty members accepted and championed the general conclusions of Yehezkel Kaufman's eight volume *Toledot ha'emunah hayisraelit* (The History of Israelite Religion) (Tel Aviv: Mosad Bialik and Dvir, 1937–56). His article also provides an interesting insight on how W. F. Albright, an important figure in the Biblical Theology movement in the United States, was tutored in Kaufman's work during his two-year appointment at JTS as a Visiting Research Professor in 1957–59. See I. Schorsch, "Coming to Terms with Biblical Criticism," *Conservative Judaism* 57 (2005) 3–5, 8–9, 12.

12 *Hebrew Union College-Jewish Institute of Religion, Catalogue 2001–04*, pp. 70–71.

against the backdrop of the historical period from which it emerged. Elsewhere, it is mentioned twice in courses taught in the "Religious Studies Program," but not at all in classes taught under the rubric, "Courses in Reconstructionist Judaism." Again, *theology* is rarely used in course descriptions.[13]

At Yeshiva University, bastion of American centrist and slightly right-of-center Orthodox Judaism, no course's title features the word. *Theology* occurs only in some descriptions of courses taught in the Bible Department, always in the following two expressions: "an analysis of literary techniques and theological concepts" or "literary and theological analysis." In the descriptions it appears to refer to key ideas or themes.[14] With regard to its use of theology in the context of biblical studies, Yeshiva University is similar to the other Jewish institutions considered above and very different from the Christian ones.

In Jewish institutional use, the word only refers loosely and vaguely to "religious ideas," not to a disciplined, focused study of such ideas in origin or application.

II. Typologies of Christian Biblical Theologies

1. Some Christian Approaches to Biblical Theology

Although Christian approaches to biblical theology reflect many different perceptions of and attitudes toward biblical literature and theology, the diversity masks a definable range of shared understandings about what biblical theology entails. For example, in a recent dictionary of biblical theology produced by Catholic scholars, L. J. Hoppe lists "five principles that guide the development of biblical theology":

1. Authentic biblical theology is based on the text of the Bible defined as normative for faith by the Church.

2. An authentic biblical theology considers the centrality of Jesus throughout and relates the Old and New Testaments.

3. Since the Bible considers ethical performance more important than religious belief, as is most obvious in the parables of Jesus, a biblical

13 Information from the online catalogue at http://www.rrc.edu/site/c.iqLPIWOEKrF/b.1453937/k.B97A/View_Our_Catalogue.htm, Jan. 21, 2007.

14 Information from the online catalogue of men's courses: http://www.yu.edu/yeshivacollege/departments/bible/index.asp?id=2146, Jan. 18, 2007. I observed also that *theology* is used in only one course description in the Bible program offered in the Bernard Revel Graduate School, in *Chronicles*. The term "ideological" does service to indicate religious thought in courses on Deuteronomy, 1 Samuel, and Amos, while "religious sentiments" is used for a course in Psalms, http://www.yu.edu/Revel/bible.asp, Jan. 18, 2007.

theology "ought to lead to an evaluation or clarification of the propriety of these ethical affirmations for the contemporary world."

4. Biblical theology recognizes that some of the God-language in the Bible is ideological rhetoric that is historically conditioned. Accordingly, this has to be accounted for when drawing conclusions.

5. Since the Bible offers several ways of understanding life with God, and since the tradition is the product of human imagination and experiences that are partial, limited, and relative, material collected and collated from the Bible itself does not suffice to produce a coherent philosophical system.[15]

Hoppe's second point, which distinguishes between the two testaments, reflects a significant conceptual change in biblical theology first proposed in 1796 under the influence of the newly emerging discipline of history. Then, G. L. Bauer distinguished between the two, warning against backreading Christian ideas into the Old Testament: "Christianity is the offspring of Judaism, and an accurate knowledge of the theology of the New Testament can be attained by those only who are acquainted with the theology of the Old Testament."[16]

Bauer's distinction influenced how scholars perceived the "Old Testament" and how they studied it. Once the Hebrew Bible was no longer conceived (only) as a source of proof-texts for dogmatics, scholars sensed that its character differed from that of the New Testament. Consequently, academic interests shifted away from the theological toward philological and historical studies for most of the nineteenth and twentieth centuries.[17] These developments reinforced the validity of Bauer's distinction. The growing sense that each canon was unique though both were bundled between the same covers managed to maintain itself somehow among theologians participating in fundamentalist backlashes against the higher criticism that became prominent at the end of the nineteenth century. It was maintained by scholars of more liberal stripe writing after World War I and has remained the norm since then, despite the tension that it introduces for many who address the issue of how, as committed Christians, they understand its usefulness and significance.[18]

15 L. J. Hoppe, "Biblical Theology," in C. Stuhlmueller, ed., *The Collegeville Pastoral Dictionary of Biblical Theology* (Collegeville, Minn.: Liturgical Press, 1996) liii–lv.

16 G. L. Bauer, *The Theology of the Old Testament: A Biblical Sketch of the Religious Opinions of the Ancient Hebrews from the Earliest times to the Commencement of the Christian Era extracted and Translated from Theologie des alten Testaments* (London: Charles Fox, 1839. Leipzig: Weygand, 1796 [Ger.]) not numbered. Cited from the last paragraph of the "Introduction." See C. H. H. Scobie, "Three Twentieth Century Biblical Theologies," *HBT* 14 (1992) 51–52.

17 Compare R. Rendtorff, *Canon and Theology* (Minneapolis: Fortress, 1993) 38–39.

18 C. H. H. Scobie, describing works by Millar Burrows (1946), Samuel Terrien (1978), and Horst See-

The historical and relativistic concerns addressed in Hoppe's fourth and fifth points derive from a broad acceptance of critical biblical studies and a willingness to engage conclusions of avowedly non-theological scholars because the "methods of study used by biblical scholars can result directly in the discovery of truth necessary for authentic religious living."[19] These "truths," even though considered useful for Catholic self-understanding, do not define the nature of Catholic theology. They are deemed useful only for illustrating early stages in divine revelations and human comprehensions of them. As Johannes B. Bauer claimed in his preface to an earlier Catholic undertaking in 1959, contemporary doctrine reflects developments since the biblical period and is presented in terms of philosophical systems foreign to the way biblical authors presented their views. "Dogmatic theology cannot be reduced to biblical theology. It arises out of tradition, although tradition can never be considered independently of the bible, any more than the bible can be fully understood independently of tradition."[20] His statement is remarkably similar to

---

bass (1982), characterizes them as committed to the historical-critical enterprise but as using the fruits of such research to bridge between systematic theology and related disciplines. Furthermore, Scobie observes that biblical theology, a term that often refers to Old Testament theology alone, has generally been undertaken by Old Testament scholars who believe that the Old Testament is as important as the new, not by scholars focused on New Testament (Scobie, "Three Twentieth Century Biblical Theologies," 56–57, 63–65).

19 Hoppe, "Biblical Theology," p. li. In a volume of essays by evangelical scholars addressing conservative Christians concerned with how to make use of the historical tools of critical scholarship and the conclusions of critical scholars, C. C. Broyles takes the sting out of the word *critical* by pointing out that to read the Bible critically is not to read it with a "faultfinding attitude, but with the exacting tools of scholarship" (C. C. Broyles, "Interpreting the Old Testament: Principles and Steps," in C. C. Broyles, ed., *Interpreting the Old Testament: A Guide for Exegesis* [Grand Rapids, Mich.: Baker, 2001] 17–18).

20 J. B. Bauer, "Preface to the First German Edition," in J. B. Bauer, ed., *Encyclopedia of Biblical Theology* (New York: Crossroad, 1981), *Bibeltheologisches Wörterbuch* (Graz: Verlag Styria, 1959) (Ger.) xxv–xxvi. Bauer also notes that Catholic undertakings in biblical theology require collaboration with Protestants because it "is to them what dogmatic theology is to us Roman Catholics, since the bible is their only norm and they have to consult it to a correspondingly greater degree" ("Preface," xxvii). To be sure, Bauer's statement, which reflects the ecumenical settings such as the Catholic Biblical Association, SBL, IOOTS (and journals such as *CBQ*) where many sophisticated scholarly exchanges take place today, gives rise to questions concerning the Catholic nature of such undertakings.

J. J. Collins, a Catholic scholar, argues that biblical theology could be critically neutral, biased but fair and open. Historical criticism could contribute, he suggests, to an understanding of God-talk that, while not a self-sufficient discipline, "is a subdiscipline that has a contribution to make to the broader subject of theology." What Collins has in mind is "confessional theology committed to specific doctrines on the basis of faith." See his "Is a Critical Biblical Theology Possible?" in W. H. Propp, B. Halpern, D. N. Freedman, eds., *The Hebrew Bible and Its Interpreters* (Winona Lake, Ind.: Eisenbrauns, 1990) 14.

R. E. Murphy argues that despite tensions arising between Catholic traditions and doctrines

the traditional Jewish claim that the "oral Torah," that is, the rabbinic tradition, determines the meaning of the written Torah operative in the work of some Jewish scholars considered below.

Although Protestant scholars might disagree partially with the tenor of Hoppe's third and fifth points, arguing that they allow for a particular set of non-biblical considerations from Catholic traditions to inform the final product, some scholars within the Protestant evangelical tradition make similar statements. For example, aware of the limitations of the historical method for providing complete answers to pressing theological questions, E. A. Martens suggests that the job of the exegete is first to ground the text in its historical setting and then to elevate it into a contemporary theological one.[21] That is, the results of biblical studies are limited unless interpreted and applied within what is understood to be the proper theological framework that renders them meaningful. The main difference between these Catholic and Protestant approaches is that whereas the former works with a well defined tradition not based exclusively on Scripture, the latter operates with an ill-defined tradition based on an

---

and between the assumptions of Protestant scholarship, and despite an innate connection between exegesis and theology, it is the appropriation of academic research by Catholics and its application within the "living tradition" that makes it Catholic ("What is Catholic about Catholic Biblical Scholarship? – Revisited," *BTB* 28 [1998] 112–15, 118–19; "Questions Concerning Biblical Theology," *BTB* 30 [2000] 84). See also a study by P. S. Williamson that shows, on the basis of official documents, that the church's special role comes into play only at the level of interpretation and actualization after the philological, historical, and literary research, conducted according to prevailing standards, is complete ("Catholic Principles for Interpreting Scripture," *CBQ* 65 [2003] 336–40, 345–80).

A Catholic position addressing the matter of Jewish scholarship directly is found in the fourth chapter of a Vatican II document. *Nostra aetate* states that "the Church cannot forget that she received the revelation of the Old Testament by way of that people with whom God established the ancient covenant. Nor can she forget that she draws nourishment from that good olive tree onto which the wild olive branches of the gentiles have been grafted." (Note the use of present tense forms. Cited from H. Wansbrough, "The Jewish People and its Holy Scripture in the Christian Bible," *ScrB* 32:2 [2002] 50. On the validity of Jewish readings, see also p. 54.) This revolutionary document formally declared as changed views held in the church since the fourth-fifth centuries.

The positive implications of *Nostra aetate* were developed in a document prepared by the Pontifical Biblical Commission: *The Jewish People and Their Sacred Scriptures in the Christian Bible* (Rome: Libreria Editrice Vaticana, 2002). (The document is available in book form or online via the web page of the Catholic Biblical Association, http://www.vatican.va/roman_curia/congregations/cfaith/pcb_index.htm.) Four critical analyses of this document's importance and shortcomings, three by Catholics and one by a Jew, are found in *TBT*, May/June 2003 (M. C. Boys, "A Resource for a Journey of Rethinking," 141–47; M. O'Connor, "Scripture and Its Fulfillment," 154–59; J. T. Pawlikowski, "The Jews in the New Testament," 161–66; A-J Levine, "A Jewish Reading of the Document," 167–72). They point out that one major shortcoming is the document's failure to grapple with rabbinic Judaism as a vital source of legitimate interpretations.

21 E. A. Martens, "The History of Religion, Biblical Theology and Exegesis," in Broyles, *Interpreting the Old Testament*, 177–86.

understanding of the Reformation principle that the Bible is *norma normans sed non normata*, that is, the Bible self-sufficiently constitutes the norm that evaluates every other norm, but is not evaluated by any other.[22]

This principle is one that divides conservative Protestants from less conservative ones. At stake is the degree to which the qualifying phrase, *sed non normata*, is applicable nowadays in the light of informing insights from the authoritative claims made by practitioners of historical research and the social sciences or, put differently, what role such claims may play in determining the content of biblical norms. One difference between conservatives and liberals may lie in whether or not the qualifying phrase is meaningful at all or even whether or not the key statement that the Bible is *norma normans* has (or should have) epistemological status in contemporary thinking.[23]

Succinctly put, *biblical theology* is an ill-defined term used to describe a synthesis of particular categories of information imbedded in the Bible but, as the various ways that people employ it indicate, it can include extra-biblical data and historical considerations also. Originally, the object of such studies was God and related topics such as soteriology, ecclesiology, messianism and the like. Nowadays, the range of topics is broader as theologians search for new topics. Generally, a topic is selected, that is, an abstracted notion about some biblical theme such as God's relationship to people, Israel, promise, sacrifice, community, covenant, war, peace, lordship, leadership, stewardship, discipleship, kindness, charity, faith, feminism, sexism, communitarianism, and individualism, passages related to it are collected, studied, and applied.[24] That is, after the collecting and sorting, after the exegesis, after a scholar reaches a

22 See Stone, *How to Think Theologically*, 47–50.

23 Stone, *How to Think Theologically*, 44–47.

24 I ignore the stage represented by theological undertakings that sought something identified as the "theological center" of the Bible/Old Testament/New Testament such as W. Eichrodt's "covenant," E. Sellin's "holiness of God," R. Knierim's "God's universal rule in justice and righteousness," H. D. Preuss' "election and its obedient reaction," and S. Terrien's "reality of the presence of God." Their approaches are critiqued constructively by D. M. Carr who finds heuristic value in searching for many and diverse centers in "Passion for God: A Center in Biblical Theology," *HBT* 23:1 (2001) 1–5. Carr's sensibility enables scholars to view seemingly contradictory proposals as not necessarily vying against each other but as filling the center, no longer imagined as a Euclidian point, in different ways for different reasons. Carr is not the first to criticize this reductionist approach.

Already in 1899, working with S. R. Driver's breakdown of sources, dates, and authorship, C. F. Burney, a master of text, exposed how complicated and unhomogonizable were Israelite ideas about deity, sacrifice, covenant, polity, and history expressed in the Bible. His *Outlines of Old Testament Theology* (London: Rivingtons, 1899) was not concerned "with the further meaning which passages of the Old Testament may be found to bear when read in the light of New Testament Revelation" (p. 120). Consequently, he did not seek to generalize from what was found in the literature or to create comfortable symmetries.

conclusion about what the Bible (or Hebrew Bible and/or New Testament or a particular book such as Joshua or Psalms or Matthew or collection of books such as Wisdom/Prophetic/Historiographic literature or the Pastorals) says/teaches about a selected topic, the lesson is applied to some set of contemporary circumstances or settings. These studies can be characterized as "What does the Bible say (or teach) about X" types. Although the "proof-text" method is supplemented by literary, historical, form-critical, and canonical considerations, the enterprise rests – as indeed it must – on control of all relevant passages.[25]

Most such undertakings are historically light, at best. And this is not by accident since most people engaged in a biblical theology project are not working within research paradigms associated with the history of ideas or history of religions.[26] Depending on the topics or theme selected, the number of relevant verses available for study may be small, forcing the researcher to consider them *en bloc* so as to be able to say something about the theme.[27] When

25 R. C. Denton, *Preface to Old Testament Theology* (rev. ed.; New York: Seabury Press, 1963) 18–20. The period of the great thematic collections was from the late seventeenth century through the late eighteenth century. The conception that biblical theology consisted of commenting on such texts was most likely discontinued because, 1. it had been done and because, 2. new ways of viewing the Bible that began to emerge during the Enlightenment.

26 J. P. Gabler's 1787 call for a historically sensitive study of relevant verses is exemplified in G. L. Bauer's still interesting and useful, *The Theology of the Old Testament* (see n. 16 above). In the title of Bauer's late eighteenth century book, "theology" refers to religious ideas, without any suggestion that they have any normative value for his readers. The crucial sections of Gabler's address in Latin are translated by B. C. Ollenburger in Ollenburger, ed., *Old Testament Theology: Flowering and Future* (Winona Lake, Ind.: Eisenbrauns, 2004) 498–506.

W. Brueggemann's *Theology of the Old Testament: Testimony, Disputes, Advocacy* (Minneapolis: Fortress, 1997) adopts an ahistorical approach to the data that he presents under the banner of postmodernism with its particular jargon, rhetorical ploys and menagerie of bêtes-noire (pp. 66, 71, 118–19, 330, 558–64, 574, 740). Since Brueggemann's earlier works typically aim at providing useful theology for the intellectual climate prevalent at time of their writing, I assume that this work took shape during the late 1980s-early 1990s when postmodernism's advance through the humanities and social sciences seemed inevitable. Writing in the academic fashion of that time, Brueggemann chose to ignore historical considerations. With regard to this attitude, his work is not premodern, but postmodern.

A caution, however, is warranted. Brueggemann claims that the Old Testament with its web of intertextual references is a product of the resettled community during the Persian period (p. 80). For him, in this particular book, that date provides its historical and theological context. It allows him to read intertexts as if all originated or functioned within the same chronological horizon. This determination, whether correct or incorrect, is historical, not ideological.

27 It is useful to distinguish between the number of verses that actually relate to a particular topic and the number of verses designated as relevant for discussion as a percentage of the total. In addition to indicating the theological proclivities of writers, study of the discarded (or ignored) data, may reveal topics towards which they are antipathetic and reveal significant, if not purposeful, distortions of the picture presented. See Scobie, "Three Twentieth Century Biblical Theologies," 56–57; J. Barr, "The Problem of Old Testament Theology and the History of Religion," *CJT* 3 (1957) 147–49.

a sufficiently large number of verses are available, it is possible to treat them diachronically and, when the number is very large, to consider them according to genre. But, although this borders on an historical exercise in the contemporary sense, it remains an ahistoric, literary one in which the world created in the text is the only world inhabited by the text. It is literary because it restricts itself to the text of the Bible and ahistoric because it does not deal with the world of thought within which the literature was created. The limited study may be compared to a study of the theme of loyalty in Shakespeare's *Timon of Athens*; and a broader, diachronic undertaking to a study of the same theme in all of Shakespeare's writings. Both undertakings would be ahistorical because neither would engage the loyalty theme in the setting of Elizabethan England. A better parallel, however, might be a study of selected themes in any literary anthology including many compositions from miscellaneous genres by different authors over a 500 year period.

Much biblical theology is similar to the search for themes in literary compositions, but with an additional element. It inquires also after the moral of the story knowing in advance that the story exists for its moral, which must be good and relevant.[28] Consequently, there are few biblical theological studies that cannot be turned into a decent sermon by a talented preacher.[29] In the Christian tradition, the end-users of biblical theology are the people in the pews.

Seemingly, there is nothing remiss in this that should disqualify biblical theology from being considered an academic discipline. As James Barr pointed out in 1957, nobody objects when a professor of classics considers Plato's ideas living values. Barr appears to suggest that so long as the discipline remains descriptive in both intent and practice, so long as its exegesis of collected verses is sound, and so long as its inferences from the particular ideas expressed in

28 M. Tsevat, "Theology of the Old Testament – A Jewish View," *HBT* 8 (1986) 38–39. Tsevat attempts to locate theology, which begins as a literary undertaking, at the nexus of Romanticism, philology, history of ideas, and philosophy.

29 G. von Rad was long committed to the notion that there was an essential connection between preaching and scientific exegesis. He believed that biblical texts, comprehended in a sophisticated way, must be preached in an appropriate fashion for people who need them for living (and for dying) because there was a dynamic quality to the proper word delivered at the proper time. See G. von Rad, *Biblical Interpretations in Preaching* (Nashville: Abingdon, 1977) 11–18. The book contains 21 developed sermon ideas based on theologically interpreted texts. This strikes me as providing a better sense of von Rad's theology of the Old Testament than his more academic publications on the topic, in which the appropriation and application elements and overt Christian connections were played down, though not eliminated. It is likely that much in his scientific publications originated in his sermonizing.

See also the presentation of material in W. Brueggemann's pithy *Reverberations of Faith: A Theological Handbook of Old Testament Themes* (Louisville: Westminster John Knox, 2002), a book designed for pastors and thoughtful lay persons "who want to understand more fully the Bible and its faith" (p. xii). The book draws liberally from theological studies and expositions listed in its bibliographies.

individual verses or pericopes to implicit general notions remain historically based and backed by evidence, a contemporarily relevant insight or application may be considered a bonus of the research, though not actually part of biblical theology.

Intellectually committed to historical and philological analysis, Barr distinguishes between interpretations of the Hebrew Bible and their adaptation to the needs of Christian faith. He excludes the move toward the normative and dogmatic, that is, the position that what the biblical authors said was true must be considered to be true, along with the move from interpretation to adaptation from his understanding of biblical theology. He implies that although the fruits of biblical theology may inform the contents of a living faith, that faith may not inform biblical theology. Consequently, he opines that Jews and Christians can both participate in the undertaking up to the stage of appropriation and application.[30] This is because the move to application, that is, to influence and prescribe the actions and speech of a faith community, consists of a move from biblical theology to doctrinal theology, a type of theology that originates in creedal statements that are all post-biblical.[31] Barr's biblical theology is defined as "something like a comprehensive description of implied intellectual concepts, taken within the terms and boundaries of the Hebrew Bible and seen as far as possible within its own self undersanding. . . ." It is "theology as it . . . was thought or believed within the time, languages, and cultures of the Bible itself."[32] His approach, only with regard to this particular point, is not unlike the Catholic one vis-à-vis the research of non-Catholic scholars discussed above.[33]

Rolf Rendtorff's call for a "common Jewish-Christian reading of the Hebrew Bible" acknowledges the validity of historical awareness like Barr and similarly limits the theological enterprise to the stage before application or importation

30 Barr, "The Problem of Old Testament Theology," 144–46; J. Barr, *The Concept of Biblical Theology: An Old Testament Perspective* (Minneapolis: Fortress, 1999) 6, 15–17, 74–76. In his chapter on Jewish Biblical Theology, he finds most agreement with Jewish scholars whose notions of Biblical Theology are close to his but which, like his own, are atypical of the field. Contrast his sharp debate with Jon Levenson (pp. 291–302) with his evaluation of Sara Japhet whom he dragoons into the ranks of theologians on the strength of her historical study of what she terms the "ideology" of Chronicles in the context of biblical thought (pp. 306–7) and with his favorable comments about Marvin Sweeney (pp. 307–9).

31 Barr, *The Concept of Biblical Theology*, 5, 74.

32 Barr, *The Concept of Biblical Theology*, 4, 289.

33 See also Barr's clear exposition of this point in J. Barr, "Predictions and Surprises: A Response to Walter Brueggemann's Review," *HBT* 22 (2000) 118–19. R. W. Yarborough provides a learned attempt to accommodate Barr's critique to conservative theologizing by a tight parsing of what Barr has written and what he has not written. Yarborough concludes that Barr's "criticism of biblical theology, as a whole or in part, is not tantamount to rejection." See Yarborough "James Barr and the Future of Revelation in History in New Testament Theology," *BBR* 14:1 (2004) 113–21.

into the parochial tradition. His presuppositions for maintaining a common biblical theology include the following: 1. Recognizing that the Hebrew Bible acquired final form before either rabbinic Judaism or Christianity existed, he concludes that neither a rabbinic nor a Christian interpretation can be historically correct, that is, reflect the meaning of the text in its own time. 2. Since the Hebrew Bible is a foundation document for both communities, but not the only one, he recognizes that unique post-biblical traditions are of essential importance to each community.[34] 3. The particular ways each community developed for interpreting the Bible cannot claim acceptance by the other. 4. The theological interpretation of the Hebrew Bible in its own context is not dependent on the theological system of the community to which a particular scholar belongs. 5. "...Jewish and Christian biblical scholars can work together toward a theological interpretation of the Hebrew Bible."[35] For Rendtorff, the particular body of knowledge that Jewish scholars bring to the table is an authentic, ancient way of reading the Bible relevant to Christian scholars because early Christians also knew midrashic exegesis before there was a New Testament.[36] In addition, however, he senses that dialogue between Jewish and Christian scholars about contemporary issues that might be related to biblical theology can be useful.[37]

Walter Brueggemann writes in a more guarded vein from a perspective that he calls "postmodern." He believes himself living in an age after that cultural period "that was dominated by objective positivism that made a thin kind of historical scholarship possible, and that granted interpretive privilege to certain advantaged perspectives."[38] From his perspective, "...the dislocation of Christian privilege in interpretation may permit renewed participation in a shared conversation of Jewish voices in what passes for biblical theological interpretation." The implication of what he says, directing himself to Christian interpreters, is profound.

Given that an argument may be made that no hegemonic readings are possible, all must view their interpretations as one among many. Christian biblical

34 This point is made also by E. Frerichs who cites Jacob Neusner to the effect that both Judaism and Christianity inherited Hebrew Scriptures and appropriated them by rereading them respectively in light of the notion that Moses gave Israel the "whole" torah, both oral and written, or in the light that Jesus Christ is he who was resurrected (Frerichs, "The Torah Canon of Judaism," 22).

35 Rendtorff, *Canon and Theology*, 40.

36 Rendtorff, *Canon and Theology*, 13–15, 34–36.

37 Rendtorff, *Canon and Theology*, 44. A. Brawley suggests that the reasons Christian scholars are interested in a Jewish biblical theology is because Christians recognize in Judaism shared scriptures, tradition, God, law, ideas about salvation and the like, "and because they share in this rich root, they have a concern about that which the Jews are doing in their bible study." She sees no necessary mutual undertakings and no particular reason why Jews should be interested in Christian biblical theology. See Brawley, "Grafted In: Why Christians Are Thinking about a Jewish Biblical Theology," *BTB* 30 (2000) 127.

38 Brueggemann, *Theology of the Old Testament*, 61.

theologians "may be expected to be instructed by many other voices, not only Jewish, but by other Christian interpreters in other social locations."[39] In a cultural setting where everything goes anyway, where the text is considered "plurivocal" and "does not admit of settled, enforceable larger categories," Jews and Christians not part of the Western European-American intellectual tradition may participate.[40] The reason for welcoming Jewish interpretation is that the plurivocality of the text "has, of course, long been recognized in Jewish interpretation, which has proceeded since the time of the ancient rabbis by way of commentary, in contrast to the Christian propensity to systematization."[41] Citing Jon Levenson's writings for praise, Brueggemann claims that they are impressive examples of biblical theology because they permit "the categories of interpretation to arise from the text itself."[42] But although he refers to the "resiliently Jewish" nature of the Bible, by which he means that it is anchored in

39 W. Brueggemann, "Biblical Theology Appropriately Postmodern," *BTB* 27 (1997) 4. I take this as a reference to Christians in the developing world.

40 R. P. Knierim, like Brueggemann, is acutely aware that the Old Testament contains a plurality of theologies and perceives this as the problem for which a proper method of analysis must of needs be developed. Likewise, he has little use for historical analysis or consideration of the socio-historical contexts of theology-laden statements, but sees nothing postmodern about his position. See Knierim, *The Task of Old Testament Theology: Substance, Method, and Cases* (Grand Rapids, Mich.: Eerdmans, 1995) 1, 7–8. In contrast, Israel Knohl distinguishes different theological strands in the Hebrew Bible and traces some into the early rabbinic period from whence much of contemporary Jewish theology derives. Knohl does not try to harmonize the strands or normalize them or argue that the later developments are already inherent in the earlier theologies. See Knohl, *The Divine Symphony: The Bible's Many Voices* (Philadelphia: JPS, 2003).

41 Brueggemann, "Biblical Theology Appropriately Postmodern," 5. One element of Brueggemann's analysis is that not only may recorded events be considered grist for theologians, but the narratives themselves containing the description of the events, their vocabulary, and their grammar are also to be considered, in their entirety as expressions of theology (Brueggemann, *Theology of the Old Testament*, 61–73). This is similar to the approach that Martin Buber learned from Franz Rosenzweig during their joint translation undertakings and then applied in his philosophical-theological hermeneutics, all pre-postmodern. See S. Kepnes, *The Text As Thou: Martin Buber's Dialogical Hermeneutics and Narrative Theology* (Bloomington, Ind.: Indiana Univ. Press, 1992) 19–78, esp. 54–60. It also reflects elements of W. Dilthey's hermeneutics of the dynamic relationship between the *Geist*, that is, mind/intention/human creativity, of the author and the inquiring *Geist* of the person in the here and now as applied to theology by Will Herberg, *Faith Enacted as History: Essays in Biblical Theology* (Philadelphia: Westminster Press, 1976) 107.

42 Brueggemann, "Biblical Theology Appropriately Postmodern," 5. Consequently, Brueggemann argues against using conventional theological categories in sorting out passages, preferring sets of "themes," each of which might have been considered a singular candidate for "theological center," but which in fact are all present in creative interaction. (Also compare, Carr, "Passion for God," 2, 23, which arrives at a similar conclusion without appealing to postmodernism.) I find Brueggemann's precise presentation in this article easier to comprehend than in its application in his *Theology of the Old Testament*.

quotidian reality, immediacy, refusing transcendentalism – in contrast to a "Western, Christian propensity to flatten, to refuse ambiguity, to lose density and to give universalizing closure"– Jewish readings are legitimate only when integral to "lived faith" of Christians.[43]

2. TYPOLOGIES OF BIBLICAL THEOLOGIES

The approaches described and discussed above may be distinguished and classified by their relationship to the historical context of religious ideas, by their emphasis on the appropriation of ideas and their application to contemporary settings, by their degree of concern with the New Testament, by the measure of authority that they grant to extra-biblical traditions, and by the degree to which they are Christian centered.

1. The first type understands that which has been written in the Bible, understood as the combined Old and New Testaments, as existing in and addressing an eternal present. That which is in the Bible exists for the present. It is relevant always to the present but in need of theologians to clarify the relevancy. This is the most common comprehension of biblical theology among Protestants.

2. The second works with a tradition of theology – written or oral, explicit or implicit – esteemed as discovered or revealed knowledge that was present at the beginning. For this, the Bible is a source of supporting knowledge, definitely time-bound, but bearing one message for one time and simultaneously a different message for another. The tradition determines what the new message can be. This view is most common among Catholics, but is also expressed by Protestant theologians with different degrees of emphasis.

3. The third type allows for historical and religious development and distinguishes clearly between what it meant and what it can mean. It reserves the term *biblical theology* for theology *in* the Bible and is expressed most clearly by Barr and with qualifications by Rendtorff.

4. A fourth type acknowledges historical and religious development but sidesteps issues emanating from them as no more than interesting. It focuses, like the first type, on canonized scripture and engages whatever literary methodologies enable it to generate theological statements. It proceeds directly from text study to appropriation for Christian application on the assumption that there is little distinction between "what it meant" and "what it means." This is mainly a Protestant position.

43 Brueggemann, *Theology of the Old Testament*, 80–81, 93–94, 109, 735.

III. Calls for Jewish Biblical Theology and Their Typologies

Moshe H. Goshen-Gottstein. As mentioned at the beginning of this study, Goshen-Gottstein is credited with first proposing Jewish biblical theology (or Tanakh Theology) as a new sub-discipline within biblical studies. In a 1981 article in Hebrew followed six years later by a shorter, more focused (and considerably tamed down study) in English, he argued that Jewish scholars, secular and religious, informed by Jewish traditions, should undertake a theological study of the Jewish canon, that is, the Hebrew Bible, that would parallel Christian theological undertakings but be unlike them in any way that could be recognized as reflecting their presuppositions, biases, particular concerns and the like. It would not be concerned with historical or archaeological matters – to do so would disqualify the work as theology – but would focus exclusively on what the text said without querying into the accuracy and truthfulness of statements.

According to him, Jewish biblical theology should select topics or themes relevant to Judaism such as "land, Sabbath, people Israel, national (not individual) salvation, temple," collect and study everything stated about them in context, consider all references according to literary genre, and evaluate permutations of the topic/theme in relationship to other topics/themes. The point of individual monographic studies would be to respond to the question: What does the Tanakh come to teach about X throughout or in one of its sub-corpuses?

Jewish biblical theology would presuppose that the Bible doesn't have a theological center – a notion transferred from New Testament to Old Testament theology – does not represent a yet-to-be-discovered over-arching theological system, though some systemic insights might be discovered from groupings of related statements.[44] This would be akin to the discovery and mapping of a semantic field. The ahistorical program envisioned by Goshen-Gottstein is essentially descriptive and literary. It represents the purposeful adoption of a naïve reading, the only type that all Jews could share.

His programmatic articles neither addressed the theoretical problems inevitable in working out the connections and relationships between different topics and arranging them in some hierarchy nor – and this is more important in the context of contemporary hermeneutics – did they address the problems of language and meaning that investigators would encounter in analyzing biblical metaphors.[45] Consequently, his proposal appears very much like the study

44 Goshen-Gottstein, "Jewish Biblical Theology," 50–54, 56–64; "Tanakh Theology," 626–34. Most of the Hebrew article and large parts of the second comprise a severe critique of what he considered wrong in mainstream, mostly European, Christian biblical theology.

45 The importance of semantics, figurative language, and the production of meaning in any such

of literary themes in Shakespeare described above. Accordingly, as a type, it is closest to type 4 absent the Christian application.

Both of his articles leave unsettled to what end studies in Jewish biblical theology should be undertaken. Through personal meetings with him in the 1980s, I learned that he hoped such studies, engaging similar disciplined studies of rabbinic materials, could lead to serious reevaluation of many halakhic issues in traditional Judaism; in particular, he mulled over how reconceptualizing the Sabbath might affect *halakhah*.[46]

The students whom he felt best prepared in terms of their familiarity with both *halakhah* and traditional rabbinic texts and whom he hoped would write doctoral dissertations exploring theological themes were at Bar Ilan University, an Orthodox institutions, where he was a Prof. of Bible – in Jerusalem he was a Prof. of Ancient Semitic Languages – but, to his disappointment, they were uninterested in doing so.

Matitiahu Tsevat. In 1986, Tsevat distinguished between a theology of the Old Testament based on sound philological principles that considers both text and literature in their historical, cultural contexts and a Jewish theology of the same material whose analytic program derives from outside the Old Testament in sources such as the Talmud, midrash, and/or other Jewish authorities in which the biblical text is creatively read out of its historical context and into another; and sermonics, a type of theologizing that loosely hangs contemporary ideas on biblical texts to garnish a speaker's ideas with authority.[47] Acknowledging a tension between the essences of "objective" and "judaizing" theologies, Tsevat concluded that the two cannot and should not be combined, nor should they

investigation, particularly in its post-collection, analytic stage is well illustrated by the amount of space dedicated to it in a study of Ugaritic theology following a Goshen-Gottstein–like program. See M. C. A. Korpel, *A Rift in the Clouds: Ugaritic and Hebrew Descriptions of the Divine* (Münster: Ugarit-Verlag, 1990) 35–87.

46 He clearly denied that such considerations were part of what he was proposing in his pioneering articles, anticipating being attacked over this point: "… I ought to stress at present is that in the 1980s a model of biblicistic reinterpretation of *halakhah* is the last thing we would be suggesting. Such a model of biblical theology need not be contemplated, nor would be of any interest for Tanakh studies" (Goshen-Gottstein, "Tanakh Theology," 627).

This practical side of his project, that is, considering the *halakhic* implications of theological insights, although not reflected in what he wrote, but always present in our conversations, seemed to ignite the passion. Although what he described seems to fall in line with H. Wheeler Robinson's justly famous *The Religious Ideas of the Old Testament* (2nd ed.; London: Gerald Duckworth & Co., 1956) and Norman H. Snaith's, *The Distinctive Ideas of the Old Testament* (London: Epworth Press, 1944), Goshen-Gottstein's suggestion excludes working through material with insights from historical and philological scholarship as did theirs. Similar, but quite conservatively Jewish, is E. Berkovits' not well known *Man and God: Studies in Biblical Theology* (Detroit: Wayne State Univ., 1969).

47 Tsevat, "Theology of the Old Testament," 40, 42.

even be compared, only differentiated. They occupy different, unbroachable realms and to not recognize this, he cautions, is both "presumptuous" and "stupid."[48] This explicit approach situates Tsevat with scholars maintaining a type 3 position.

Isaac Kalimi. Kalimi's many contribution are characterized by three intertwined motifs: a broad comprehension of Jewish biblical theology, an understanding of what biblical theology ought to be, and an explanation of why Jewish scholars do not yet participate in biblical theology. He is a particularly important figure among advocates for the new discipline because in addition to teaching in institutions in both Israel and the United States, he has lived for extended periods in Europe where he taught in Dutch, Swiss, and German theological institutions. His variegated academic experiences and interactions with theology in general and biblical theology in particular have influenced his richly textured and complex approach. Additionally, because he publishes in German and English for both European and North American journals, his ideas have reached a wide variety of biblicists and theologians.

Kalimi, like Tsevat, believes that the history of Israelite religion is mutually exclusive of Hebrew Bible/Old Testament Theology and that the two are incompatible and incapable of being mixed: "Choosing one subject automatically rejects the other. It is misleading to assume that there is a choice." Though both are independent, legitimate branches of biblical study, he views the former as a philological historical undertaking and the latter as "a close study of the different religious messages *in their entirety*. It unfolds . . . the meaningful, social and human values of the Bible by applying the achievements of textual, linguistic, literary and exegetical methods in addition to various findings from other disciplines" (emphasis added). The former is a diachronic study while the latter "is synchronic, ahistorical and from time to time even subjective."[49]

Despite this sharp distinction, Kalimi allows that diachronic considerations can play a role since individual authors had their own theologies, as did editors of different books such as the redactor of the Pentateuch and the editor of Psalms. He notes, that the "canonists," collectors of the various books in the canon also had their own theology.[50] Consequently, he avers that there are common theological topics that Jews and Christians can address together.

48 Tsevat, "Theology of the Old Testament," 49–50.

49 I. Kalimi, *Early Jewish Exegesis and Theological Controversy: Studies in Scriptures in the Shadow of Internal and External Controversies* (Assen: Royal Van Gorcum, 2002) 107–8, 114, 130. Chapter 6 of this book, to which I refer (expanded from *JSOT* 11 [1997] 100–123) is entitled, "History of Israelite Religion or Hebrew Bible/Old Testament Theology? Jewish Interest in Biblical Theology."

50 Kalimi, *Early Jewish Exegesis*, 110–18. This proposal does not address John Barton's insight that canonical meanings "are a function of the shape of the canon and do not depend on our being able to reconstruct the mind of the canonizers." See J. Barton, *Reading the Old Testament:*

This part of Kalimi's program is sensitive to two different degrees of diachronic consideration: the history of religions approach which is absolutely diachronic and theology's approach that studies messages *in their entirety* somewhat less so. This phrase seems to allow for distinguishing between biblical and post-biblical thought and between pre- and post-Temple restoration theology in the Bible itself while allowing for the synchronic telescoping of ideas.

Kalimi discerns the importance of *biblical theology* to lie beyond its quest for the theology of biblical authors, editors and canonizers. It is significant because it reads the Bible for "its religious messages and for the moral promotion of humanity" and helps discover the "values of the Scriptures for our generation." Allowing that biblical theology can be a parochial undertaking within Judaism or Christianity, he charges that within the university it should be objective and engage "secular, academic-intellectual viewpoints" which can then be appropriated by Church and Synagogue.[51] The biblical theology in which he is interested is normative, universal and non-parochial. It is relevant and applicable to a humanity that includes both Christians and Jews but is not about Christianity or Judaism. It is a common-ground theology that neither exposes nor betrays particularistic beliefs.

In order for his program to be implemented, he argues that contemporary biblical theology must change. Kalimi considers biblical theology spoiled by those who impose the notion of a single theological center on the Bible, by those who combine "Old" and "New" Testaments, by those who read the "Old" Christologically – that is, by those writing theologies of types 1 and 4 – and by those who "introduce anti-Semitic and anti-Jewish theology," as well as by those "who define Christianity through the negation of Judaism, portraying the Jewish people in an unfavorable light to show the superiority of the Christian faith. . . ."[52] His list of offensive practices may be traced to a confused

Method in Biblical Study (Philadelphia: Westminser, 1984) 16. Kalimi's "canonizers" seem to refer to both the final redactors of various books – the subjects of redaction criticism – as well as to those that canonized the Tanakh. Knowledge of who, how, when, and where the Tanakh was canonized is vague at best. So although having some sense of their theology would be very important for either an historical or a theological project, almost nothing may be said about them. For a description of the state of contemporary discussions and a suggestion that the Tanakh was actually not canonized in some official way see Z. Zevit, "The Second-Third Century Canonization of the Hebrew Bible and Its Influence on Christian Canonizing," in A. van der Kooij and K. van der Toorn, eds., *Canonization & Decanonization* (Leiden: Brill, 1998) 139–41, 149–54, and J. P. Lewis, "Jamnia After Forty Years," *HUCA* 70–71 (1999–2000) 233–36, 251–54.

51 Kalimi, *Early Jewish Exegesis*, 113–14. Kalimi, here, approaches ideas expressed by Rendtorff, *Canon and Theology*, 34–44.

52 Kalimi, *Early Jewish Exegesis*, 113–18, 125. Kalimi's critique echoes many earlier remarks by Goshen-Gottstein (see n. 44) but, in Kalimi's hand gives rise to interesting, positive, suggestions. The theme of Jew-hatred and Israelite/Jewish reactions as a phenomena and theological problem fills his "The Place of Book Esther in Judaism and Jewish Theology," *TZ* 59 (2003) 193–294. This ar-

intermixing of *biblical theology* and *doctrinal theology* as defined by Barr.[53]

Kalimi implies that were all the negative and supercessionist traits expunged from ongoing discussions, Jewish scholars would be more involved than they are in biblical theology.[54] Kalimi's advocacy on this point attempts to clear a place for what he understand's Jewish biblical theology should be on an ideal Protestant playing field of his definition without compromising the integrity of what he feels is authentically and innately Jewish in the text.

Though I empathize with the tenor of his concerns, in the absence of evidence for anti-Semitic and anti-Jewish statements in the writings of post-Shoah Christian scholarship in the USA and England, the scholarship with which most Jews in the profession interact – I have come across none and he provides no contemporary references – this cannot be a factor for Jewish non-involvement in biblical theology.[55] More significant in explaining Jewish disinterest is the fact that Jews rarely encounter anything remotely similar to confessional or systematic or dogmatic theology in their tradition; consequently, the whole enterprise appears foreign and somewhat uninteresting.[56] No less significant in the twenty-first century is the obvious particularistic na-

ticle develops the theme in Genesis, Exodus, Psalms, the Merneptah 'Israelite' Stele, the Mesha Inscription, and, of course, Esther. A final note carries it through the Crusades, expulsion from the Iberian Penninsula, Czarist Russia and World War II (p. 294). This study is a commanding example of Jewish theologizing that also provides an innovative way of understanding the absence of God from Esther. It is not, however, an example of Jewish biblical theology as he defines it. See also his "Die Auseinandersetzung mit den internen und äusseren Opponenten in mittelalterlicher-jüdischer Schriftauslegung," *ZAW* 115 (2003) 76–83.

53 Barr, *The Concept of Biblical Theology*, 286.

54 Kalimi provides a useful list of works by Jewish scholars that either reflect theological interests as he defines them or that use the term "theology" in their title. See *Early Jewish Exegesis*, 118–24, 127–29.

55 The single post-Shoah example to which he refers is M. Noth, *A History of Israel* (London: A. & C. Black, 1959. A trans. of the 3rd Ger. ed.; Göttingen: Vanderhoeck & Ruprecht, 1956) 428–32, 454. The first page reference is to a section entitled, "The Rejection of Christ" and the second, to the last page of the book. I assume that Kalimi's attention was drawn to the closing sentences: "And so the descendants of the Israel of old had become strangers in their own former homeland just as they were in the Diaspora; and the holy city was prohibited to them. Thus ended the ghastly epilogue of Israel's history." I find the first reference innocuous and the second unfortunate and disgusting given the date of its composition, but not anti-Semitic.

56 Barr points to the presence of almost all mainstream biblical theologies in the public access Judaica reading room of the Israel National Library in Jerusalem where they all appeared well read by the scholars and graduate students using that facility. From this he concluded that there is interest in the topic by Jewish scholars. See Barr, *The Concept of Biblical Theology*, 292. As a former denizen of that room from the late 60s through the mid-70s and infrequently thereafter, I can attest that these books were once esteemed highly and recommended to graduate students as useful historical descriptions of Israelite thought, von Rad's work in particular. Professors directing students to these works were unaware of their confessional Protestant, theological subtexts reflected in what passages were examined and how they were grouped for analysis, labeled,

ture of most biblical theology undertakings: Baptist, Presbyterian, Methodist, Calvinist, Lutheran, Anglican, and so on.[57]

Although Kalimi has not defined his undertaking as a positive program, and has presented few examples of what it should look like in practice, he clearly eschews theology of type 1, acknowledges the validity of some elements in type 2, but holds some version of types 3 and 4 as academically responsible.[58]

Benjamin D. Sommer. Sommer starts an important essay inquiring about what most scholars discussed in this article take for granted: "Is there a place for the Bible and for modern biblical scholarship in contemporary Jewish theology?" His point is that if critical biblical scholarship is excluded, as it usually is across the board, Jewish theologizing, which generously claims to accommodate or, at least consider all relevant views, excludes those of ancient Israelites: tradents, authors, and redactors.[59] Sommer demonstrates how correcting for this lack by including critical biblical scholarship makes an important difference.

He studies the complicated, discontinuous revelation narratives in Exodus 19–20 as a way of responding to two historical-theological questions: What was the nature of the revelation that Israel experienced at Sinai? How much of the Ten Commandments did the nation hear? In working through the well known problems of the narrative, he employs source criticism and Hebrew philology; inner-biblical commentary (or revision) in Deuteronomy 5 and in Exodus 24 (as noted in the *Mekhilta of R. Shimon bar Yochai* and by Rashi), draws from medieval Jewish commentators along with contemporary Jewish and non-Jewish exegetes who themselves employ a variety of methodologies, medieval philosophers, comments of hasidic masters, and philosophical/theological insights by Martin Buber, Franz Rosenzweig, and Abraham Joshua Heschel. Using these resources, drawn from, what he terms in a different article, a Jewish *trans-canonical unity* – the body of uniquely Jewish, authoritative post-biblical literature that characterizes the well-appointed Jewish library[60] – Sommer concludes that there

and analyzed. It was then considered unacademic to inquire whether or not or in what way von Rad's or Eichrodt's church affiliation and personal theological commitments shaped or influenced their books.

57 Kalimi's comprehension of the problem and his solution calling on Christian theologians to change the way they do their theology is critiqued in a review of his *Early Jewish Exegesis* by Joel S. Kaminsky in *RBL* 1 (2003) http://www.bookreviews.org/bookdetail.asp?TitleId=2938&CodePage=2938 (Feb. 13, 2003).

58 The first five essays in Kalimi's *Early Jewish Exegesis*, and his "*Midrash Psalms Shocher Tov*: Some Theological and Methodological Features and a Case Study – The View of God," in J. H. Ellens, et al., eds., *God's Word for Our World: Theological and Cultural Studies in Honor of Simon John De Vries* (2 of vols.; London and New York: T & T Clark International, 2004) 2:63–76, suggest that Kalimi is interested in employing midrashic and other historical Jewish resources to work through author, redactor, canonizer theologies in order to derive something universal.

59 B. D. Sommer, "Revelation at Sinai in the Hebrew Bible and in Jewish Theology," *JR* 79 (1999) 422–23.

60 B. D. Sommer, "Unity and Plurality in Jewish Canons: The Case of the Oral and Written Torahs,"

is more than one answer to each of the questions in the Bible itself. From this conclusion – a contribution to understanding *theology in the Bible* – and following threads of discussion through Jewish sources somewhat oblique to his discussion, he extrapolates an interesting theological conclusion: the written Torah, the whole Tanakh, and all subsequent Jewish tradition is an imperfect approximation of the perfect Torah which remained with God. According to Sommer, the Bible is sacred even though its words were not dictated to Moses but reconstructed by late redactors on the basis of early traditions.[61]

Sommer is receptive to the plurivocality of the text and alert to different theologies that may emerge when texts are aligned and read off each other in various ways. Nevertheless, he works quite self-consciously with diachronically layered texts and traditions in advancing his case. Although the example cited above might appear at first blush to be a mix of types 2 and 4 sans the Christian application, it is closer to type 3. It is similar to types 2 and 4 because Sommer discovers Jewish meaning(s) for the texts of the smaller canon of Hebrew scriptures through the many resources of the large trans-canonical unity in dialogue with each other and with the biblical text; it is, however, like type 3 because it actually helps clarify an issue of theological import that can be dated to the time of the text's redaction.[62]

I question whether the far-reaching implications of his final conclusion that ultimately all of the classical Jewish texts from the Bible through the Talmud is a record of oral teachings would be considered legitimate by Christian scholars, other than the most liberal.[63] Sommer, however, unlike Kalimi, is unconcerned

---

in C. Helmer and C. Landmesser, eds., *One Scripture or Many? Canon from the Biblical, Theological, and Philosophical Perspective* (Oxford: Oxford Univ. Press, 2004) 108–11, 136–38. This concept has its parallel in a Catholic trans-canonical unity that includes the authoritative teachings of the magesterium.

61 Sommer, "Revelation at Sinai," 447–51. He describes his methodology and the reasoning behind it in n. 5, pp. 424–25. An earlier exhaustive study of the same texts reached similar text-critical and redaction critical conclusions but refrained from drawing any theological conclusions from the analysis. See A. Toeg, *Matan Torah besinai* (Lawgiving At Sinai. The course of development of the traditions bearing on the the Lawgiving at Sinai within the Pentateuch, with a special emphasis on the emergence of the literary complex in Exodus xix-xxiv) (Jerusalem: Magnes Press, 1997) 13–59, 161–62.

62 Sommer would argue that my type 3 is not a type of biblical theology but rather "intellectual history." However, insofar as type 3 is considered biblical theology by people whose published work has determined the nature of the field, I maintain its heuristic usefulness for the purposes of this study. See B. D. Sommer, "Ein neues Modell für Biblische Theologie," in B. Janowski, ed., *Theologie und Exegese des Alten testaments der Hebräischen Bible: Zwischenbilanz und Zukunftperspektiven* (SBS 200) (Stuttgart: Verlag Katholisches Bibelwerk, 2005) 198 and 206–8 where he describes his *JR* study as "dialogic theology" and deemphasizes its historical-theological aspect. I thank Dr. Sommer for drawing my attention to this article.

63 Sommer's work was uninformed by D. Weiss Halivni's innovative book addressing the theologi-

by such matters because he does not envision a future Jewish-Christian joint venture in biblical theology. He claims, echoing Tsevat somewhat, that there can be no Jewish biblical theology but only a Jewish theology that is biblically oriented. For him, *Jewish biblical theology* is a term of convenience, indicating to Christian scholars that part of Jewish theology that corresponds, at least in part, to their *biblical theology*.[64] Sommer, as did Rendtorff from a Christian perspective, suggests that what may be shared are ideas that one faith community may learn from another as each formulates and responds to theological questions involving the bible from within its own trans-canonical unity.[65]

Marc Z. Brettler. In a 1997 article intending to explore what he perceived as "some of the issues raised by the emergent venture of Jewish biblical theology," Brettler actually demonstrated that no such, well-defined venture existed.[66] Although he raised some issues – on which, see below – he did not locate them within a context of some trickle of published Jewish biblical theological studies, because none existed when he wrote. He admits as much when he does not proceed beyond noting that there is no consensus on "how Jewish biblical theology should be defined, though it clearly should be something beyond a history of religion written from a non-Christian viewpoint."[67] In the absence of serious steps in this venture, it is impossible for him to describe the outlines, concerns, objectives, or characteristic features of this theology, even though his study points to particular insights of three scholars, Stephen A. Geller, Peter Machinest, and Israel A. Knohl, that could be employed constructively in such a theological discussion.[68]

---

cal issue of imperfections and well known contradictions within the Torah –"maculations" in his terminology – long recognized in Jewish rabbinic and exegetical sources (*Revelation Restored: Divine Writ and Critical Responses* [Boulder, Colo.: Westview, 1997] 1–46, 75–85). Parts of this work may be used to provide far-reaching support for disciplined academic study and even textual emendations through its creative conjoining of textual analysis, mytho-historical reasoning, close reading, midrashic clarification, gap-filling, and historical analysis with theological boldness.

An implication of Halivni's work is that the scholarly undertaking is theologically necessary as part of the continual restoration of the original Torah. All scholars today carry through the work of the first restorer, Ezra. It is this natural extension of his views, in my opinion, that draws it into collaborative harmony with Sommer's conclusions, despite their different approaches to the same problem, their use of different methodologies, and their deployment of different texts from the corpus of rabbinic literature.

64 Sommer, "Unity and Plurality," 146–50.

65 Sommer, "Ein neues Modell für Biblische Theologie," 208–11.

66 M. Z. Brettler, "Biblical History and Jewish Biblical Theology," *JR* 77 (1997) 563–83, the quotation is from 583.

67 Brettler, "Biblical History," 566. He does not explain why it could *not* be a history of religion from a Jewish viewpoint.

68 Brettler, "Biblical History," 581–83. Elsewhere, he names Jewish scholars whose work is charac-

Brettler assumes, as did Goshen-Gottstein, that at some point, a Jewish Biblical Theology will have to gather and categorize basic data according to some literary based matrix of genres, and that one of these will include the category of history. The particular difficulty he encounters is that having eschewed strong positivistic positions, admitted that everybody works from ideologies or biases, and acknowledged that contemporary critical scholarship has raised major doubts concerning the historicity of the Exodus and Sinai, events central to Jewish self-definition, he is confronted with the problem of how to evaluate reports of these events for theological purposes. Moreover, he proposes that scholars should consider whether or not the terms "Jews" and "Judaism" are appropriately applied to the people and religion of the biblical period and questions the scholarly convention of using "Israelites" and "Israelite religion" to refer the people and religion of the biblical period. What is at stake in the different sets of terms, he suggests, is the emphases on continuities versus discontinuities, historical accuracy, and the ideological investment of contemporary Judaism and Christianity. He, as a Jew, opts for the former set of terms and the cultural and literary continuities that it implies.[69] This decision provides him a way to resolve the dilemma posed by reported events considered unhistorical by many historians and biblicists but completely accurate by many contemporary Jews and by the rabbis of Late Antiquity whose teachings comprise the foundation of all contemporary rabbinic Judaisms.

Brettler investigates the biblical sources referred to by rabbis in classical texts and determines on the basis of a citation index that they quoted all parts of the Tanakh almost equally. He then concludes that a biblical theology need not necessarily be based exclusively on Torah texts. Next, using a selec-

---

terized by a theological perspective: Moshe Greenberg, Yochanan Muffs, Jon Levenson, Michael Fishbane, and James L. Kugel (compare nn. 5, 14 on pp. 564–65). To his list, I would add Moshe Weinfeld, Jacob Milgrom, Tikvah Frymer-Kensky, Ed Greenstein, Richard E. Friedman, Athaliah Brenner, Eliezer Berkovits, Meir Gruber, as well as the scholars discussed in this article. This list can be expanded to include individuals who never considered themselves biblicists and were not considered as such by others, even though some part of their corpus of writings focused on the Bible: A. J. Heschel, Martin Buber, Will Herberg, Emile Fackenheim, Erich Fromm, and Hermann Cohen. My criterion is whether or not there is a self-conscious, Jewishly informed awareness and concern that all (or, at least, part) of a scholar's research on the Bible impinges on Jewish theological understandings of God, Torah, Israel and the like.

69 M. Z. Brettler, "Judaism in the Hebrew Bible? The Transition from Ancient Israelite Religion to Judaism," *CBQ* 61 (1999) 430, 444–46. In this study, Brettler does not consider an important 'semantic' disadvantage to his rhetorical decsion. In popular Christian parlance, Moses and David and Isaiah are described as "Jews" and their religion as "Judaism." Distinguishing between "Israelite religion" and "Judaism" eliminates confusion between religion of the Iron Age and the post-Temple religion of rabbis and diasporic Jews. This confusion, in my opinion, is infused throughout the Pontifical Biblical Commission's *The Jewish People and Their Sacred Scriptures*. See n. 20 above.

tion of illustrative rabbinic texts, he proposes that the rabbis were not overly concerned with what actually happened in the past and, after citing well known biblical doublets, he claims that neither were some biblical redactors. He proposes that these conclusions warrant contemporary theologians to view biblical historiography as reflective, mythic literature, freeing them from worrying about the lack of true history.[70]

Like Sommer, Brettler argues from rabbinic texts to the Bible, assuming that the relationship between the two is such that his conclusion about lack of concern for historical accuracy in the Bible is warranted. He does so because he works from a position developed through historical argumentation that Jewish cultural continuity bridges between the ancient Near Eastern context of ancient Israel and its literature and the Roman-Byzantine context of the rabbis and their literature. Having built the bridge, Brettler crosses it from both directions. Sommer presupposed its existence.

In a 2005 book, *How to Read the Bible*, directed to sophisticated, Jewish adults, Brettler provides a series of scholarly, "Jewishly sensitive" readings of biblical texts from a range of genres. In an Afterword, "Reading the Bible as a Committed Jew," he illustrates how the theological approach developed in his earlier studies enable him "to walk something of a tightrope between being a serious historical-critical Bible scholar, emphasizing prerabbinic norms of biblical interpretation and taking the Bible seriously as a Jew incorporating post-biblical, rabbinic norms."[71]

Brettler would construct a theology out of the biblical text analyzed critically. Since the heart of his discussion focuses on validating critical positions in the light of rabbinic traditions so as to justify their employment in Jewish theological analyses, the article may be considered an apologetic prolegomenon to the spadework. What he implies in his prospectus is clearly an undertaking of type 3 with discussion of the appropriation and application for Judaism deferred.

Marvin Sweeney. Sweeney is, perhaps, the most persistent of scholars arguing for the development of Jewish Biblical Theology in recent years and, possibly, the most eloquent.[72] Like others writing since the mid–1990s, he argues that the

70 Brettler, "Biblical History," 571–79. His conclusion that biblical redactors were not concerned goes beyond the evidence. They may not have known which of their sources was correct. Their concern for truth may have led to their decision to combine different versions into a single text or to present their in parallel.

71 M. Z. Brettler, *How to Read the Bible* (Philadelphia: Jewish Publication Society, 2005) 279–83, the citation is from 282.

72 M. A. Sweeney, "Tanak versus Old Testament: Concerning the Foundation for a Jewish Theology of the Bible" in H. T. C. Sun and K. L. Eades, eds., *Problems in Biblical Theology: Essays in Honor of Rolf Knierim* (Grand Rapids, Mich.; Eerdmans, 1997) 353–72; "Reconceiving the Paradigms of Old Testament Theology in the Post-*Shoah* Period," *BibInt* 6 (1998) 140–61 slightly revised in

postmodern intellectual climate is propitious for advancing the project, but not its justification. Recognizing that bible theology always addresses an audience and concerns contemporary with the author, he presupposes contemporary, popular perceptions of Jews, Judaism and the Bible in advancing his ideas, not academically nuanced historical descriptions. Consequently, Sweeney suggests, more forcefully than do others, that the justification for the project lies in taking full cognizance of the fact that the Old Testament is a Jewish book written by and for Jewish people, no matter that it is read and used also by Christians for their own theologizing.[73] Although he expresses the notion that the results of this undertaking might be of interest to and might even influence Christian scholars, his program is directed to serve particular Jewish interests: ". . . in an age of increasing secularization and, for Jews in the diaspora, assimilation, biblical theology serves the purposes of the larger field of Jewish theology in defining, in a positive and systematic fashion, what Jews stand for and how the Bible relates to that self-understanding."[74]

Sweeney's point of departure is the canon of scripture in the order created and used by Jews. Parts of books can be studied in relationship to other parts, books may be juxtaposed, the canon considered as a whole or in developmental units, all manner of "criticisms" engaged, that is, form, tradition, reception, and so on, and their "message or theology" considered, but, for Sweeney, the overriding question to be answered is "What is the form of the Bible, including its structure, genre, setting and intent?"[75] Sweeney's articles are not merely theoretical, pointing out what would be good; they provide examples of how insisting on his approach makes a difference. For example, he holds that the particular organization of the Hebrew Bible in the Jewish tripartite canon is of theological significance for Judaism just as the four-part division and ordering of the book in Christian canons is theologically significant for Christians.[76]

A. O. Bellis and J. S. Kaminsky, eds., *Jews, Christians, and the Theology of Hebrew Scriptures* (Atlanta: SBL, 2000) 155–72; "The Emerging Field of Jewish Biblical Theology" in Z. Garber, ed., *Academic Approaches to Teaching Jewish Studies* (Lanham: Univ. Press of America, 2000) 83–105.

73 Sweeney, "Tanak versus Old Testament," 354–55; "Reconceiving the Paradigms," 140–50. H. Wansbrough writes of a presentation at the Oxford Chaplaincy where the rabbi insisted that the priest speak first on the grounds that his was the older religion since the New Testament was written before the Talmud (compare Wansbrough "The Jewish People and its Holy Scripture," 8 n. 52).

74 Sweeney, "Tanak versus Old Testament," 355. See also "The Emerging Field," 85, where he argues that ". . . Jewish biblical theology provides a means to demonstrate that the Hebrew Bible is fundamentally a Jewish literature that must be read in relation to Jewish concerns and later Jewish tradition." His placing of "Jewish concerns" first distinguishes Sweeney from Somer and Brettler.

75 Sweeney, "Tanak versus Old Testament," 356; "Reconceiving the Paradigm," 153–54.

76 Sweeney, "Tanak versus Old Testament," 359–71; "Reconceiving the Paradigm," 154–60; "The Emerging Field," 89–99. The fact that the four-part Alexandrian canon may be of Jewish origin also or that Jewish tradition (in the Talmud) or codices sometimes arrange book in an order dif-

Although he speaks about the Bible as a "Jewish" composition, as does Brettler, his examples in different studies clarify that the adjective applies not only to post-Enlightenment, contemporary Judaism, but also to classical Rabbinic Judaism, pre-Rabbinic Judaism circa 100 C.E., and also to the biblical period itself. This is demonstrated partially by the following citation:

> Judaism shows far less concern than Christianity in exploring the nature and character of G-d; the definition or portrayal of G-d is discouraged in Judaism as it tends to compromise the sanctity of G-d and promote idolatry. Indeed, Judaism is ultimately concerned with G-d, but it focuses much more on the areas for which human beings are responsible, i.e., human action, including the care of creation and role of the Jewish people in meeting that responsibility.[77]

His statement correctly reflects most biblical literature but only when the application of metaphors to the divine is ignored. It is certainly not sufficiently nuanced to cover the types of discussions and descriptions found in rabbinic midrash on the one hand and Jewish medieval philosophy on the other. Since the theology of his project is one of the Bible, and since he applies texts directly – not necessarily through mediating rabbinic traditions – to contemporary circumstances, his "Jewish" may be characterized as reflecting a Judaism of one torah.[78]

Sweeney's work has advanced beyond Goshen-Gottstein's pioneering proposal. Sweeney works with selected critical methodologies, particularly those related to the literary and thematic elements of scripture. He is generally accepting of the historical dating of sections within books and is unabashed in demonstrating that some results from contemporary research by scholars of all faiths

---

ferent from what is considered standard – for example, Lamentations after Jeremiah or Ezra-Nehemiah after Chronicles – is not considered by him.

77 Sweeney, "The Emerging Field," 85. He does not consider the medieval, but still very relevant, Jewish philosophical tradition. For example, Maimonides (1135–204) discusses knowing God, God's uniqueness and unity, loving, fearing, and sanctifying God and the like. Throughout, he examines collections of relevant biblical verses from which he learns about the nature of God and the problem of misunderstanding biblical metaphors (*Mishneh Torah, Sefer Hamada*ʿ [Repetition of the Torah, The Book of Knowledge] [any edition], the first section, "Foundational Rules of the Torah," chaps. 1–10). I refer to Maimonides because a version of his "thirteen principles of faith" is printed in traditional prayerbooks – though they are rarely recited nowadays – while a poem restating these theological principles, "*Yigdal Elohim Hay*" (May the Living God Be Great), is sung regularly by many congregations at the conclusion of services.

78 Since Sweeney is clearly sensitive to historical issues, there is no question of him thinking that Amos was "Jewish" in the same way as Hillel or Rabbi Akiba, both of whom had the Bible available to them. Possibly he employs "Jewish" as he does for rhetorical reasons.

may be applied directly and without concerns for how the tradition handled the text. He is aware of the issues involved vis-à-vis the notion of a broad Jewish canon, but considers them irrelevant to what he advances: a Jewish equivalent to primarily Protestant Biblical Theology.[79] Sweeney's proposal embraces both theology types 3 and 4, absent Christian applications.

Jon D. Levenson. Levenson is considered by many calling for Jewish Biblical Theology one of their number. I exclude him primarily because his working assumptions differ from those in use or proposed for a theological program. Additionally, although he concedes that Jewish Biblical Theology may be significant for Jewish-Christian dialogue, he considers such dialogue as conducted in recent years a form of soft-negotiating in that it brackets core theological and doctrinal issues, sources of potential confrontation and irreconcilable contention over the interpretation of scripture, out of the conversation.[80] His work is incongruent with any of the four types described above, or any combination of them.

Levenson asserts that Rabbinic Judaism is the organic continuation of ancient Israelite religion, its evolved form. He presupposes this as a given, not as a topic that has to be negotiated, as does, for instance, Brettler. Consequently, although making no claim that rabbinic comprehensions preserve true meanings of biblical texts, he maintains that sometimes their insights inform readings of the Bible true to the texts in their own historical contexts. He considers elements from Jewish tradition, evaluated critically and historically, useful, and he factors them into the process through which he draws conclusions just as (primarily) Protestant traditions have influenced the whole historical-critical enterprise. Levenson's method does not grant classical Jewish texts any special authority, but only a vote similar to those he allows contemporary textual and ancient Near Eastern scholarship.[81] Consequently, he is sensitive to the charge that he might be backreading later views anachronistically into earlier

79 Sweeney, "The Emerging Field," 99–101.

80 J. D. Levenson, "The Agenda of *Dabru Emet*," *The Review of Rabbinic Judaism* 7 (2004) 6–10, 12, 26. Similar sentiments were expressed by William Fulco, S. J., at a plenary session of ASOR in November, 2004 during a discussion of the film, *The Passion of the Christ*, and by the Jewish New Testament scholar A-J. Levine, in a plenary presentation, "Nostra Aetate, Divino Afflante Spiritu, and Kinky Friedman," at the International Meeting of the Catholic Biblical Association of America in August, 2005.

81 Levenson, *Sinai and Zion*, p. 5; J. D. Levenson, *Creation and the Persistence of Evil: The Jewish Drama of Divine Omnipotence* (San Francisco: Harper & Row, 1988) xiv–xv. Consequently, his use of rabbinic material is very different from the way many Christian theologians doing types 1 and 2 biblical theology use the New Testament and other official traditions. Whereas the New Testament is part of the Christian biblical canon, rabbinic texts such as the Talmud and *midrash* collections are not part of the Jewish biblical canon.

texts, and so defends his interpretations regularly and details his arguments rather than making apodictic statements.[82]

Levenson's work is distinguished by his constant mining of Jewish traditional sources for relevant materials and their prominence in his analyses, his predilection for addressing theological topics considered primal by Christian theologians and essential for Christian doctrine, for example, revelation, renewal, creation, human obligations, evil, death and resurrection, his proclamation that he is a biblicist interested in broad themes, his regular abstention from particularistic theological statements in his research in favor of (often qualified) literary formulations, his regular incorporation of source critical and historical insights, his regular use of ancient Near Eastern materials, and by his refusal to be labeled (or characterized as) an Old Testament or biblical theologian. An ability to discern, analyze, and evaluate different theological motifs expressed or implied in the Bible and a talent for critiquing both liberal and traditional theologians (and insisting that they fight fairly and honestly) do not, perforce, make one a theologian, even when done well, often, and with verve.[83]

In the past, he rejected the sobriquet because his understanding of "theology" corresponds to the way the term is commonly employed by theologians. Additionally, he understands his investigation as one in the tradition of critical scholarship. For him, critical scholars are those "scholars who are prepared to interpret the text against their own preferences and traditions, in the interest of intellectual honesty."[84] The implication of what he says is that the intellectual center of the critical scholar can and should be different from his religious-theological one. Should the two coincide, fine; but when not, the difference should be acknowledged. Those who allow the latter to influence the former are not critical scholars, and their work is not critical scholarship. He distinguishes clearly between what may be "situationally appropriate" even though it violates

82 J. D. Levenson, "The Exodus and Biblical Theology: A Rejoinder to John J. Collins," *BTB* 26 (1996) 5–6. He is quick to point out these faults in his detractors.

83 J. D. Levenson, *The Hebrew Bible, the Old Testament, and Historical Criticism* (Louisville, Ky.: Westminster/John Knox Press, 1993) 117–24 in an essay entitled "Historical Criticism and the Fate of the Enlightenment Project." He points out repeatedly, referee style, that both traditionalists and liberals work from within matrixes of assumptions.

84 J. D. Levenson, *The Death and Resurrection of the Beloved Son: The Transformation of Sacrifice in Judaism and Christianity* (New Haven: Yale Univ., 1993) 3. But, protests notwithstanding, he has been anthologized as a biblical theologian, guaranteeing his enrollment in that pantheon. See Ollenburger, *Old Testament Theology*, 378, 409–23. Levenson allows that in the contemporary academic climate that allows individualistic, ethnic, and religious self-assertion within the framework of a discipline, he would apply the term "Jewish biblical theologian" to himself with the restricted understanding that his concerns might be similar to that of Christian biblical theologians engaged in enriching the encounter of bible readers with sacred texts (personal communication, August 23, 2005).

the canons of historical criticism and between scholarly work.[85]

Furthermore, in 1987 he argued that there can be no Jewish Biblical Theology that goes against the general tendencies or that isolates itself from rabbinic exegesis: "How can self-consciously Jewish biblical theologians take a personal stand on behalf of a text that they interpret against its rabbinic exegesis?"[86] Such a theology would simply be a Jewishized version of theology types 1 and 4 discussed above. (By definition, a Jewish version of type 2 could not exist other than as a form of game-playing that would involve co-opting scholarship and recasting it through dialectic in rabbinic categories.)

He does not consider theology type 3 theology, but a specialized area in the history of Israelite religion or of religious thought that does not involve any faith commitment or even any interest in how the text is to be appropriated and applied.[87] It may be considered an exercise in the history of ideas – it is certainly not theology as conventionally understood by theologians and as understood by the guild of scholars, the historians, with which Levenson associates himself.[88]

85 Levenson, "The Exodus and Biblical Theology," 6; Jon D. Levenson, "Review of J. Barr, *The Concept of Biblical Theology: An Old Testament Perspective*," *First Things* 100 (Feb. 2000) 3–4 (http://www.firstthings.com/ftissues/ft0002/reviews/levenson.html, Feb. 13, 2003).

86 J. D. Levenson, "Why Jews Are Not Interested in Biblical Theology," in Levenson, *The Hebrew Bible*, 37–39, the citation is from 38 (this essay was originally published in 1987). Although I am unable to pinpoint it, Levenson seems to refer to two types of rabbinic exegesis –"rabbinic" for him is not restricted to Tannaitic scholarship: halakhic and, to a lesser extent, aggadaic/midrashic, that is, their interpretation of great themes that inform Jewish self-awareness, the constructed myth. The latter, to be sure is always more flexible, plurivocalic, and less restrictively definitive than the latter. In his *Death and Resurrection of the Beloved Son*, an important study with profound theological implications for Jewish and Christian self-understanding, I estimate that he is far beyond accepted rabbinic exegesis – even though he used selections from their exegesis for his work.

87 Levenson, "Review of J. Barr," 2: "... it is not theology at all. The most advanced biblical theologies do not reach as far as the point at which actual theological thinking begins." He describes Barr as one who "... casts his lot not with traditional religious communities of interpretation, but that community of interpretation that is the modern pluralistic university" (p. 3). If correct, Levenson clarifies why Barr stops before the actual theologizing begins. His observation is reinforced by J. W. Groves' demonstration of how ostensibly objective, historical types of studies done with the intention that they be appropriated for theological purposes influence the research and misrepresent data because they are colored by the confessional stance of the investigator (*Actualization and Interpretation in the Old Testament*, SBLDS 86 [1987] 205–10). I am unaware of anybody who has claimed to find such hidden intents in Barr's work.

88 This is not to deny that any competent preacher could not mine Levenson's publications for topics and sermon ideas, if not almost complete sermons. From penciled notes in a library copy of his *Sinai and Zion* that I used recently, I infer that at least one previous reader did just that. There is much in *Death and Resurrection of the Beloved Son* that could be appropriated for sermonics on the second day of Rosh Hashana when the "Binding of Isaac" is read. His books, read through the eyes of one familiar with contemporary traditional Jewish sermons, combine biblical and

IV. Why Should Jewish Scholars in Secular Academic Settings Want to Undertake Projects in Jewish Theological Study?

If the analyses of sections II and III are correct, the following observations are in order: Christian interest in Jewish biblical theology extends no further than inviting Jews to engage in researching subjects that lend themselves to theologizing so as to enrich the pool of insights and information from which they may selectively draw ideas or inspiration. What catalyzes and motivates Jewish interest in such theology is uncertain. With the exception of Kalimi who envisions that the undertaking could result in a non-particularistic Judeo-Christian biblical theology that could contribute to the betterment of humanity, scholars discussed in this study do not interact in a meaningful way with *biblical theology* in their work.

Despite differences between them, all of the Jewish efforts are at least partially congruent with Barr's invitation to do what he calls *biblical theology*, but, as argued above, Barr's program, stopping before it undertakes the application and appropriation for religious thought and life, is idiosyncratic.[89] Consequently, they along with Barr are simply advancing the notion that the spadework for actual theologies may be done by both Christians and Jews. That spadework, however, is not *theology*, as the word is usually comprehended. It can be either research into certain types of literary themes when the Bible is treated almost synchronically or work in intellectual history when it is treated diachronically and in historical context.

To date, Sweeney and Kalimi alone have aggressively moved into the phase of application in their publications, promoting changes in thought and attitude that should be followed through by behavior. Their theological ideas are based on exegesis whose conclusions confront and challenge Christian theological images of the Hebrew Bible and of Jews.[90] Their remarks invite, even

---

rabbinic sources along with some materials external to the tradition in a form of mutual elucidation that leads to theological conclusions. Unlike such sermons, however, Levenson is sensitive to diachronic issues and to cross-cultural influences. Consequently, his books are not what they appear to be to some. Possibly, theology is to be found in the ear of the hearkener.

89 I find Barr's distinctions between biblical theology, doctrinal theology, non-theological study of the Bible, philosophical theology, natural theology, and history of religions approaches useful. The difficulty is that his approach and broad criticism of the field has met with broad resistance, angry rebuttal, and easy dismissal.

90 Among the themes that Sweeney treats are the structure of the Hebrew Bible as used by Jews versus the Old Testament used by Christians in their bibles in "Tanak versus Old Testament," 358–71; the nature of the presentation of God and the importance of Amos as a paradigm of the prophetic type in "Reconceiving the Paradigms," 154–58. Concerning God, the victim of much recent writing, see J. Kugel's *The God of Old: Inside the Lost World of the Bible* (New York: Free

demand, responses, setting a stage for follow-up dialogue. Sweeney's robust work, however, plays itself out on the liberal Protestant playing field as a form of both polemics and apologetics, as defined above, and is not particularly *Jewish* as I defined the adjective in section 1 above.

Why then, should Jewish scholars wish to describe the work that they do as Jewish biblical theology?

1. THEOLOGY IS A DISCIPLINE

Aside from the subject matter itself, there is the question of whether or not theology is an academic discipline within the humanities. I recognize that it is a discipline, that there are those who do it better than others and that there are standards among theologians that allow them to determine what constitute good or better or the best work, and that schools of theology and faith-based universities in this country have theologians on faculty.

Because of the particular history of European universities, faculties of Catholic and/or Protestant theology are found in many of them. That is not, however, the case in American universities that are not church-affiliated and not the case in most Jewish institutions training rabbis. With this in mind, the question remains.

2. THEOLOGY IS NOT AN ACADEMIC DISCIPLINE

R. W. L. Moberly notes that biblical theology is distinguished from other historical disciplines related to ideas about life and religion held by people in the past because of the sense that theology is beyond historical analysis and beyond considering how ancient ideas might be useful and relevant today. It is beyond being evaluated like the classic literary and philosophical texts of Western civilization. It should not only be descriptive, but prescriptive as well. The particular reason why the Bible should be privileged in the matter of prescribing rests in its key role within modern culture and this role depends on the continuing vitality of the Christian church.[91]

Press, 2003) which attempts to make biblical presentations of God both intellectually interesting and theologically relevant.

91 Moberly, *The Old Testament of the Old Testament*, 152–55, 158. This constitutes an argument against those who argue that the value of the Bible is essentially cultural and not religious. See also Levenson, *The Hebrew Bible*, 124–26. M. S. Hamilton describes a growing concern among faculties at traditional Christian colleges in the United States that increasing secularization has resulted in the inability of students to provide intellectual reasons for being Christian. One solution being attempted is to "re-Christianize" the schools by integrating "faith" into "learning" across the curriculum either by changing worldviews or by exploiting some postmodern arguments that attack the secular, Enlightenment dogma that the only true knowledge is scientific, rational, and objective. Hamilton claims that "every Christian scholar agrees that Christian truth may demand

While I have no objection to Moberly's argument, the discipline for which he advocates does not fit acceptably into the humanities at secular universities where historicism, positivism, and critical thinking still reign as methods of inquiry and problem solving in the social sciences and most of the humanities despite the postmodern critique. It is not an academic discipline in the same way that other branches of learning, even those employing intuitive, imaginative, creative and subjective analyses such as literature (which has been most receptive to the postmodern critique), are disciplines.[92] It may, perhaps, be likened to performance art. Different musicians will play the same score differently depending on their skill, formal training in different theories of interpretation, and their instrument of choice. However, unlike performers playing to an audience that enjoys idiosyncratic renderings of a score in the manner of jazz musicians, theologians play to audiences with well defined sensibilities that expect different artists to play only slight variations on a recognizable melody, like those attending a standard Bach concert.

Studying what jazz musicians do is an academic discipline in the humanities; doing what they do is not; studying what theologians do is an academic discipline in the humanities; doing what they do is not. I suspect that one of the reasons most Jewish calls stop short of the step into prescriptive theology, of addressing the question of "What does the Tanakh mean?" as Goshen-Gottstein phrased it, is that their historical and philological training warn them that they are treading into the province of rabbis.[93]

3. BIBLICAL THEOLOGY IS NOT A SUB-DISCIPLINE OF CRITICAL, ACADEMIC BIBLICAL STUDIES

John Barton fairly describes biblical criticism as neutral with respect to faith, observing that this position has marked it in the eyes of its enemies as hostile to religion. He notes that the different types of conclusions reached by the various methodologies are very confusing and that critical research is done by biblicists playing "their self-absorbed little games." Nevertheless, he notes that aside from fundamentalists, some theologians search for ways to accept the validity of critical methods and some of their conclusions as they seek to "get at

---

that we adjust our scholarly beliefs" ("A Higher Education," *Christianity Today* [June, 2005] 31–34). Ostensibly, this promotion of what some scholars have labeled "new relativism" is intended to make place for theology in the academy alongside disciplines that, at least in theory, encourage constructive skepticism that leads to innovative questions and welcomes, sometimes begrudgingly, challenges to existing authorities and paradigms. See the discussion of *theology* in section 1.3 beginning on p. 7 above.

92 See the discussion in Z. Zevit, *The Religions of Ancient Israel: A Synthesis of Parallactic Approaches* (London: Continuum, 2001) 49–68.

93 Goshen-Gottstein, "Tanakh Theology," 627.

the message the canonical text can impart as it speaks from faith to faith." That is to say, the theologian in faith can employ the results of critical scholarship, the various methodologies that it employs, the very non-theological questions that it asks and answers in order to bare authentic forms of the earlier expressions of faith.[94]

Barton's analysis indicates that although theologians may work with the results of self-correcting biblical scholarship rooted in various historical, materialistic, social-scientific, and literary disciplines, they have no particular method of their own. They have a starting position and an objective, but they do not yet know how to utilize what critical scholarship provides. I conclude from his remarks that whereas what he terms the "self-absorbed little games" that occupy biblicists are "self-critical" in a scientific sense, that which theologians do is not. He concludes his article with the following caveat: "Biblical specialists should be sensitive to calls to become more theological, but they should also know when to take them with a pinch of salt; for the church is not best served by an academic community that delivers the verdicts it wants to hear."[95]

There is no Jewish equivalent for the "church" in Barton's sentence. Certainly not the "synagogue." There is no crisis of faith in liberal Judaism of this generation caused by the conclusions of biblical scholarship (though there are plenty of other crises). Even the frightening or demonic hobgoblin, symbolic of all historical-philological analysis, the Documentary Hypothesis, taught as a matter of course in Jewish liberal seminaries, has been partially accommodated to Orthodox thinking through the theological absorption of its objective data into an understanding of revelation.[96] But this cannot be covered by the notions of faith speaking to faith or faith seeking understanding.

94 J. Barton, "Should Old Testament Study be More Theological?" *ExpTim* 100 (1988/89) 444–47.

95 Barton, "Should Old Testament Study . . . ," 448.

96 M. Breuer, "The Study of Bible and the Primacy of the Fear of Heaven: Compatibility or Contradiction?" in S. Carmy, ed., *Modern Scholarship in the Study of Torah, Contributions and Limitations* (Northvale, N.J.: Jason Aronson, 1996) 159–80. In point of fact, Breuer's position is very unpopular in Orthodox circles because it appears to grant too much to liberals. American Orthodox scholars who disagree with him, however, are unable to dismiss him. He is recognized as an individual committed to a halakhic life and acknowledged as too formidable a thinker and accomplished a scholar – having written important biblical commentaries and studies of the masorah and having been awarded the prestigious Israel Prize in 1999 for his scholarly and Torah publications – to be ignored.

Additionally, he has a significant following among Orthodox rabbis in both Israel and North America who have been well educated in some aspect of the humanities at secular universities. This acceptance of at least some of Breuer's exegetical conclusions, is made possible by a growing recognition that contemporary Orthodoxy has long operated with major misstatements by some post-Enlightenment authorities about what constituted heretical thoughts, actions, beliefs in Jewish philosophy and theological speculation. In fact, many pre-Englightenment rabbis were more open than many contemporary Orthodox rabbis acknowledge, and when guarded and conserva-

4. FACTORS THAT MAY HAVE STIMULATED THE CONTEMPORARY JEWISH INTEREST IN JEWISH BIBLICAL THEOLOGY

The recent call for a Jewish Biblical Theology is indicative that some Jewish scholars find the topic interesting. Their turn to theology occurs in particular American social, intellectual, and academic contexts. It is undoubtedly occurring in a religious context also, but not the institutional ones of seminaries or synagogues where believed Judaism, whatever its nature, finds expression in teaching and practice. In this section I propose five factors that, in combination, may have influenced this move among Jewish scholars.

Individualism. In the contemporary western world, all Jews are Jews by choice. Contemporary liberal Judaism – and to some extent, centrist Orthodoxy also – is characteristically individualistic with people determining their own patterns of public observance, private practice, and personal belief. Where individuals situate themselves in that part of the Jewish community considering itself religious is determined largely by their observance and practice.

Sophisticated historical awareness and a desire to serve. Many scholars in Jewish Studies regularly lecture before Jewish groups, often in synagogue settings, on their field of expertise and their own research, and many consider this an essential part of a personal mission to enhance the quality of Jewish culture. As professors, many share with rabbis a sense that they are the custodians of Jewish culture and have an obligation to transmit it authoritatively. Academics, however, go beyond rabbis in that the latter focus conservatively on what is known, tested, and true (and useful), while the former focus on what is not yet known or what is recently discovered but not yet tested. There is an "edge" to scholarship that does not fit easily into a mainstream of Jewish ideas, however defined, namely, the unpredictability of new insights.

Outside of the academy, Jewish academicians can be passionate and draw inferences for thought and action in the living community, be it in the areas of social action, medical research, Jewish-Christian and Jewish-Muslim dialogue, support of Israel, American politics, and even the content of Jewish belief. They can be public intellectuals. The Jewish feminist movement, for example, has drawn some of its most significant leadership and defining voices from the ranks of bonafide female and male scholars. It, of course, remains a cutting-edge, progressive movement in all branches of Judaism and in all Jewish organizations.

Jewish biblicists sensitive to currents in academic Jewish studies are aware that all forms of contemporary Judaism are derived from rabbinic Judaism. Furthermore, they are aware that in its classical Tannaitic formulation, rabbinic Judaism effectively severed direct dependence on the Bible in formulating its explicit *halakhic* system.[97] Indeed, even ethical and moral norms of Judaism that rabbis linked to biblical texts were texts sometimes misinterpreted by the rabbis, cleverly but willfully. As a consequence, the Bible as a whole is a relatively unimportant text in the traditional Jewish curriculum.

Only the Torah is taught intensively, and that primarily in elementary grades. In liturgy, however, the Torah is central to Sabbath and holiday services in that it is read then, but its sermonic interpretation or explication is usually based on the sensibilities of a rabbi working through selected classical rabbinic texts. As a result, most lay-Jews and even many in the clergy believe that everything taught by ancient and contemporary rabbis flows seamlessly and directly from the Mosaic Torah and other parts of the Bible.

Biblicists active in organized Jewish cultural and religious life who appreciate how advances in academic research might enhance or correct such ideas, or who wish to make the Bible more central to Jewish religious experience, or who wish to locate themselves within a more biblical rather than a rabbinic Judaism – whatever that might mean – may consider theologizing the Bible, returning to the core text, the way to achieve their goals.[98] In doing so, however, they confront either explicit or implicit reluctance among both rabbis and laypersons to engage with the implications of historical research bearing on the Bible and Rabbinic Literature. To do so implies taking historical conclusions seriously and deeming as credible the critical methodologies employed to obtain them. It necessitates being involved with and relating to history, being influenced by it, dissolving differences and qualifying objections rationally.[99]

It is not that the seminaries of the major Jewish groups in the United States do not have excellent historians on their faculties and that they provide some historical instruction for their students, because they do. The problem arises only when the topics investigated approach what are considered to be core notions: the historicity of God's promise to Abraham; the historicity of the Exodus event and the revelation at Sinai; the Sinaitic origin of oral halakhic (and

---

tive, were often concerned less with Jewish thought and belief than in the very practical concern about the use enemies of the Jews might make of critical observations. This is studied by M. Shapiro, *The Limits of Orthodox Theology* (Oxford and Portland Ore.: The Littman Library of Jewish Civilization, 2004). See, for example, Shapiro's useful introductory essay, 1–7 and his discussion, "Revelation of the Torah," 91–121. This book is too new for its impact to be gauged.

97 Goshen-Gottstein, "Tanakh Theology," 626–27 and 640 n. 40, but see the discussion of Brettler above.

98 I think here of people who observe "biblical kosher laws" not rabbinic ones; who celebrate holidays according to the number of days listed in the Bible, not that determined by traditional halachic authorities.

99 For part of this formulation, I thank Moshe Idel of the Hebrew University with whom I discussed this matter briefly in May, 2004.

even midrashic) traditions and Bible interpretations; the immaculate nature of the oral transmission, particularly with regard to *halakhah*; the prophets as restaters of Torah and ancient teachings (but neither as improvisers nor innovators and certainly not contradictors), and the immaculate transmission of the Torah. Although different Jewish religious groups weigh these quasi-dogmas differently, they grant some credence, either heart-felt or lip-articulated, to some of them, however interpreted. Most of these quasi-dogmatic notions, unless treated as broad poetic statements, do not withstand historical scrutiny well. Where such notions are accepted out of belief or polite convention as defining the limits of public oratory, discussion and instruction, there is no room for considering the individual theology of J, E, P or D in their Wellhausian or later articulations; or of entertaining the question of prophetic influences on Torah or the evolution of Israelite religion, and certainly not of whether or not the *Tannaim*, ca. 100 B.C.E.–200 C.E., "got it right."

Although strong *public* commitment to all of the above-mentioned quasi-dogmas is characteristic of American Orthodox, especially among young, American trained, rabbis, similar attitudes are expressed with more subtle nuances by Conservative, Reform and Reconstructionist rabbis. Thus, although the liberal movements accept critical methodologies and conclusions, aside from the seminary classes where they are taught and used in analyses, they are rarely addressed publicly in the religious life of congregations.[100] This, I suspect, is

100 D. N. Myers describes as a "firestorm" the controversy occasioned by a Passover sermon delivered by a Conservative rabbi in Los Angeles mentioning that most historians and archaeologists do not accept the historicity of the exodus as described in the bible. See his *Resisting History: Historicism and Its Discontents in German-Jewish Thought* (Princeton and Oxford: Princeton Univ. Press, 2003) 3–5. The theological implications of the rabbi's statement – regularly misquoted, slightly but significantly in the press, sermons, and debates – spilled over into the international press and was discussed online and in the Jewish press for more than a year causing consternation among Conservative congregants and glee among Orthodox opponents of Conservative and Reform for their willingness to accept the results of historical research.

What Teresa Watanabe, Religion Writer for the *Los Angeles Times*, wrote in her column of April 13, 2001 was the following:

> But did the Exodus ever actually occur? On Passover last Sunday, Rabbi David Wolpe raised that provocative question before 2,200 faithful at Sinai Temple in Westwood. He minced no words. "The Truth is that virtually every modern archaeologist who has investigated the story of the Exodus, with very few exceptions, agrees that the way the Bible describes the Exodus is not the way it happened, if it happened at all," Wolpe told his congregants.

What Rabbi David Wolpe actually said was the following:

... but what happens when modern science begins to explore an ancient story? The director of archaeology at Tel Aviv University, Professor Israel Finkelstein says, "that the exodus

because critical historical research, as all Jewish advocates for biblical theology know, involves what is described as the "disenchantment of knowledge," its demystification, rationalization and its secularization.[101]

Among liberal groups, at least at the level of clergy, no doctrinal issues are at stake. They feel, however, that the implications of historical research that unsettle traditional understandings of the biblical and (sometimes) of rabbinic periods are often of no value in enhancing the intellectual and spiritual life of their congregants. When the occasion merits and new data may be interpreted constructively, as in the case of certain archaeological discoveries such as the Tel Dan inscription mentioning the "house of David," rabbis and educators in these movements use historical-critical approaches to deal with and clarify problems unapologetically.

Orthodox rabbis are not necessarily unaware of historical critical methods and their implications, but those that do know, prefer not to discuss such matters in public, if at all. I discern a breeze of change in some Orthodox circles in the fact that a few young educators have raised publicly, but in a very small forum, the religious implications of introducing a critical historical approach into the teaching of sacred texts, particularly biblical texts when it is understood that the act of studying itself is a religiously significant one. They detect a two-fold problem: on the one hand, students will learn or read about critical historical approaches to both the Bible and rabbinic literature and on the other, these approaches will inform them about some valid (and some invalid) insights that conflict with what is usually taught.

Furthermore, young (Orthodox) Jews who spend any part of their college years at any university in Israel, even at the Orthodox Bar Ilan University, learn quickly that *some* critical ideas characterized as "gentile" or "*apikorsut*," that is, heretical, by their high-school teachers were once part of a traditional Jewish discourse in different historical periods from Late Antiquity and the Middle Ages through the Early Modern Period.[102] When the views of these educators are considered as a whole, they conclude that instruction in the results of historical inquiry is best delayed until students have matured and become socialized as (young) adults within the religious community. They disagree only whether

---

did not happen at the time described in the bible seems irrefutable." Indeed, virtually every modern archaeologist who has investigated this story of the exodus with very few exceptions agrees that the way the bible describes the Exodus is not the way it happened.

(I thank Rabbi David Wolpe of Sinai Temple in Los Angeles for providing a copy of his sermon text and tapes of his actual sermon.)

101 A. Funkenstein, "Introduction to the Disenchantment of Knowledge: Moments of Transition in the History of Western Epistemologies," *Aleph* 3 (2003) 17–18.

102 See the very sophisticated articles published online in *Jewish Studies, Internet Journal* 2 [2003]) at http://www.biu.ac.il/JS/JSIJ. See also section v beginning on p. 49 below.

or not this occurs after high school, during college or after college.[103]

Their reluctance to engage the challenging results of historical research is similar to the indifference of their more liberal counterparts and can be traced to an attitude described by David L. Myers as a resistance to history. Meyers traces it back to Jewish historians, philosophers, and theologians in the leading centers of twentieth century Jewish research, but its modern roots are to be found in the eighteenth century.[104]

The move to Jewish Biblical Theology, at least among some practitioners, may reflect a desire to overcome this resistance by filling the theological silences with the processed conclusions of critical, biblical scholarship, something only well-trained students of the text could do in Jewish religious communities.[105]

The culture of the SBL/AAR Annual Meeting. The culture of the Annual Meeting encourages tolerance on the one hand and political correctness on the other. One consequence of these attitudes is a lack of criticism and debate in many

103 All of the following are posted at the Academy for Torah Initiatives and Directions (ATID, Jerusalem) website, http://www.atid.org/journal/journal.asp. Only summaries of the articles are available online; the complete articles must be downloaded. Michael Olshin, "Textual Study as a Means of Religious Instruction," *ATID* 98 (1998) http://www.atid.org/journal/journal98/olshin_sum.asp, Dec. 16, 2003. Rachel Furst, "*Hakirah* or *Mehkar*: The Religious Implications of an Historical Approach to *Limmudei Kodesh*," *ATID* 01 (2001) http://www.atid.org/journal/journal01/furst_sum.asp, Dec. 16, 2003. Ilana Goldstein Saks, "Encounters Between *Torah Min Hashamayim* and Biblical Criticism," *ATID* 98 (1998) http://www.atid.org/journal/journal98/saks_sum.asp, Dec. 16, 2003. Layaliza Klein, "Puttering 'Round Aladdin's Cave or The Other Side of the Mushroom: The Place of Biblical Criticism in a Jewish Education," *ATID* 98 (1998) http://www.atid.org/journal/journal98/klein_sum.asp, Dec. 16, 2003. Moshe Tur-Paz, "'EMET V'EMUNA' – Bible Criticism as a Challenge to Faith: A Teacher's and Learner's Guide," *ATID* 98 (2002) http://www.atid.org/journal/journal02/tur-paz_sum.asp, Dec. 16, 2003 (Heb.). While it is difficult to determine what, if any, influence these papers will have on Orthodox education, they are a tiny challenge to the idea that parts of what defines Orthodoxy are ideas with which it will not engage and concepts that it will not discuss.

Lawrence Schiffman, a renowned scholar of the Dead Sea Scrolls, well-known as an Orthodox Jew, argues that archaeology should be introduced into Bible instruction. His article gingerly touches on the theological dangers that arise when historical conclusions create conflict, and suggests lines of approach to issues affecting divine revelation and the historicity of the Exodus. See his "Making the Bible Come to Life: Biblical Archaeology and the Teaching of Tanakh in Jewish Schools," *Tradition: A Journal of Orthodox Jewish Thought* 37:4 (2003) 39–44.

104 Myers, *Resisting History*, 13–34, 157–72 with references. Earlier roots of this resistance and willing inattention to the implications of history are analyzed by U. Simon, "*Peshat* Exegesis of Biblical Historiography: Historicism, Dogmatism, and Medievalism" in M. Cogan, B. L. Eichler, and J. H. Tigay, eds., *Tehillah le-Moshe: Biblical and Judaic Studies in Honor of Moshe Greenberg* (Winona Lake: Eisenbrauns, 1997) 171–203 (Heb.).

105 At the 2005 Annual Meeting of the SBL, a section entitled Congregation-based Biblical Scholarship was scheduled to hold a panel discussion on the theme, *What Congregations Need from Biblical Scholars*. See, 2005 Program book, p. 81 ad S21–58.

"soft sessions" where presenters sometimes display amateurism masquerading as inter-disciplinary scholarship. Literature people unfamiliar with the biblical languages discuss the literary qualities of biblical texts; theologians present on history of ideas, non-archaeologists on archaeology and the Bible, and just about anybody with the correct political orientation in units entitled "X perspectives on Problem Y," and they all get away without harsh criticism. The genteel nature of these sections contrasts sharply with what I consider "hard sessions" such as linguistics, philology, epigraphy, history, and archaeology where errors are pointed out, judgments challenged, and arguments aired, no matter the presenter. Unfortunately, the tolerance of the soft sessions promotes a sense that almost anything passes scholarly muster if the rhetoric is right.

In a popular essay circulated widely among members of the SBL and AAR in 2005, L. Orye argued that the question of whether or not scientific types of methodology should be applied to the study of religion is a false one since the Anthropology of Science describes many different types of practices and methods as scientific, challenging the whole notion of a scientific method. Orye's essay implies that since there is no singular, well-defined rigorous method operating in science, science provides nothing for religious studies to emulate. In particular, he notes that this conclusion justifies a shift away from the perspective that "science and rationality are taken as the central standard for human thought and activity. . . ." This application of the new relativism is intended to justify new, non-science types of methods to deal with claims about reality but leaves unsettled whether or not some type of methodological rigor is desiderated for research in religion.[106]

The changing face of academic publishing in the USA. One final factor is the influence of publishers on what is written by people trained to discover and create new knowledge. Representatives of many university presses along with those from denominational and more general publishers, encourage scholars to write popular trade books for the mass market, that is, non-academic books on broad topics with no complicated, overly-detailed arguments, no footnotes, and limited endnotes.

The distinction between what trade publishers want from individuals trained to work with primary sources and what they accept from "popular" writers who hang out at the fringes of the meeting and who work from secondary and tertiary sources exclusively is small. And so, individuals, particularly those who do

106 Orye, "To Be or Not To Be Scientific Is Not the Question," 14–15, 17. Orye describes and extrapolates from the studies of Bruno Latour who deconstructed the social sciences and Enlightenment scientism in a Foucauldian manner. A more learned version of this essay in which Orye refers to and cites from scholars who dismiss Latour's work as so much postmodern prattling appeared as "Reappropriating 'Religion'? Constructively Reconceptualizing (Human) Science and the Study of Religion," *Method & Theory in the Study of Religion* 17 (2005) 337–63, see 338–41.

much popular lecturing, hone an ability to communicate for the non-scholarly market by sacrificing complexity, exactitude, nuance and doubt for the lucidity of what passes for a clear, undisputable argument or interpretation of data.

In comb ination, what publishers want and what the Annual Meeting sometimes supports is work characterized by a degree of competence, not necessarily expertise, that addresses broad topics and is directed to both scholarly and sophisticated general audiences.[107] This heady mix encourages individuals to treat themselves professionally as generalists and to assume that because they possess competence in one area of biblical studies they may obtain it easily in another.[108] In such an atmosphere, biblical theology might appear particularly inviting for Jewish scholars who come from a religious tradition where the discipline doesn't exist.

Curiosity about theology. Presentations of Judaism often emphasize that Judaism is a "deedology" not a "creedology," that it is about doing, not believing. Accordingly, much time in Jewish education is dedicated to understanding the nature of divine commands and how to perform them. Jewish biblicists in the United States, however, usually study, work, teach, and communicate professionally with Christian colleagues for whom the theological comprehension of biblical topics, statements, and even lexical items is commonplace and not an esoteric matter. Perhaps, influenced by the dynamic theological exchanges and theological questioning that fill some sections at the AAR/SBL meetings, theologically challenged Jewish biblicists are stimulated to raise similar issues, if not for the purpose of formulating creedal statements, then at least for discussions.

v. Whither Jewish Biblical Theology?

Under the best of circumstances, the type of Jewish biblical theology that proceeds as type 3, actually part of the historical study of Israelite religion, will continue to find a place in academic settings and at sessions of the Annual Meeting. That which will evolve under a type 4 model may perdure

107 Information in this paragraph is drawn from two presentations before large audiences that I attended at the Annual Meeting by publishers and literary agents on how to write for the trades and from conversations with acquisition editors at different meetings of scholarly societies. See also, D. Freitas, "Publish and Perish," *Publisher's Weekly* 32 (Nov. 14, 2005) 8–9. Freitas comments on the book exhibit at the AAR/SBL meeting as reflecting the disappearing monograph and the new gods of marketability and profitability at university presses (p. 8). Her article casts the discussion of whether or not popularizing trade publications should count for tenure as a generational dispute; it does not, however, propose that trade publications increase knowledge, only that they disseminate it. Frietas' article appeared in a special issue of the magazine distributed at the 2005 AAR/SBL meeting.

108 The problem is such that some publishers' representatives conducted a workshop at the 2004 Annual Meeting on how to publish academic books.

under the guise of bad literary research and Wittgensteinian word-games and find a place at the Annual Meeting. It could be filed under Jewish hermeneutical readings or Jewish contextual readings, paralleling Africa, Afro-American, Asian, Asian-American, Feminist, and Latino/a approaches considered collectively under "Hermeneutics, Theory, and Identity."[109] Unanchored or uninformed by rabbinic Judaism, type 4 biblical theology may drift towards Neo-Karaism, rejecting or ignoring rabbinic tradition. Even so, it might produce interesting insights and prove important in the evolving intellectual topography of American Judaism.

I encourage those endeavoring to create a new, non-academic, parochial discipline to persist, but the absence of a body of explicit or implicit theory for Jewish biblical theology must be addressed. Goshen-Gottstein came close to proposing one in terms of what it should not be, while Kalimi, Brettler and, perhaps, Sommer imply one in their filtering of historical-critical conclusions through rabbinic texts and sensibilities.[110] Sweeney has avoided such theoretical issues and writes what Christian scholars recognize immediately as biblical theology.

An *ad hoc* protocol is desiderated for Jewish biblical theology, if only to precipitate discussion. Jewish theology provides no help because, although there are Jewish theologians, there is no discipline. All that exists for modeling, initially, is biblical theology as practiced.

Were I to undertake such a project, I would study Catholic biblical theology because its trans-canonical unity – to employ Sommer's term – is structurally similar to that of Judaism. It is loyal to its own traditions of learning and understanding – its own oral Torah, however comprehended and evaluated – and because it has innovatively learned to include all manner of biblical research respectfully up to a particular point and in its own way. Theologically, however, a Jewish project could approach post-biblical traditions as authoritative only in the sense that they are part of the "Mosaic discourse"– to misuse a phrase coined by Hindy Najman – the appropriation, development and ex-

109 Program Book of the AAR/SBL 2005 Annual Meeting, p. 25.

110 Brettler's work, if viewed as a "Jewish theology of *peshat*" and Sommer's as a "Jewish theology of text" can be expanded by consideration of the following studies that introduce heretofore unconsidered historical and theological concerns: Shmuel Vargon, "Samuel David Luzzatto's Critique of Rabbinic Exegesis Which Contradicts the Plain Meaning of Scripture," *Jewish Studies, an Internet Journal* (*JSIJ*) 2 (2003) 97–122 (Heb.), http://www.biu.ac.il/JS/JSIJ/2-2003/JSIJ-2-2003.pdf, Dec. 25, 2005; Richard C. Steiner, "A Jewish Theory of Biblical Redaction from Byzantium: Its Rabbinic Roots, Its Diffusion and Its Encounter with the Muslim Doctrine of Falsification," *Jewish Studies, an Internet Journal* (*JSIJ*) 2 (2003) 123–67, http://www.biu.ac.il/JS/JSIJ/2-2003/JSIJ-2-2003.pdf, Jan. 18, 2004.

tension of Moses' authority that begins in Deuteronomy and extends through the literature of the Second Temple period and beyond.[111] This allows for both continuity and historically conditioned differences.

I would also consider Protestant models because they react quickly to circumstances perceived as requiring a theological response and they provide some of the most innovative ways of wrestling with and of presenting new ideas. There is almost no social or political concern or human innovation that they cannot and do not consider theologically.

Christian biblical theology provides defined technical language from which Jewish biblical theology may borrow and conceptual systems whose elements it can remold for its own needs and against which it may polemicize and argue as it defines itself vis-à-vis a rejected other and individuates into an autonomous discipline in the service of living Judaism.

Mapping the Jewish contributions discussed in this study in terms of the proposed protocol reveals an interesting pattern. By engaging both traditional Jewish sources and historical-critical scholarship seriously, Sommer and Brettler provide theological justification for incorporating knowledge and insights from outside of Judaism into the Jewish interpretative, theological tradition. Their ideas, involving multiple literary and historical traditions encompass Levenson's unconventional work and locate it well within the tradition. They also help anchor at least part of Goshen-Gottstein's proposal within, and not at the margins of, the interpretative tradition. This in turn provides a basis not only for Kalimi's tracing of biblical theological themes through post-biblical literature and history but also for his reaching out to engage contemporary issues presented by non-Jewish theologians and the real world. Finally, the outward trajectory of Kalimi's work supports viewing the insights of Sweeney as an extension of the Mosaic discourse. Viewed as a whole, the congeries of studies can be considered a Jewish version of Catholic-Protestant biblical theology and contrasted with it. The issues on which most Jewish scholars focus seem to proceed under a motto that is a reversal of Anselm's, to wit: "(critical) understanding in search of faith."

No reason exists for Jewish scholars not to engage in this undertaking, but the odds are stacked for failure, at least in the short term. Nobody seems to want it. Nobody seems to need it. (Theologians can argue that those that do need it do not yet recognize the need.) It responds to no particular stimulus from the

111 H. Najman, *Seconding Sinai: The Development of Mosaic Discourse in Second Temple Judaism* (Leiden: Brill, 2003) 16–40. Najman's book is significant for this project because, although an historical project that addresses its topic through the lens of intellectual history, it touches on issues confronted as theological problems by Sommer and Brettler.

community and to no questions asked by pulpit rabbis. And most disconcerting, overtly parochial publications will not necessarily count for professional advancement in the academy. This last is most important, because a significant part of the authority that future Jewish biblical theologians have derives from their position in the academy.[112]

And yet, that which has been written is innovative and bold. If considered as different parts of the same religious discourse, the articles and books may stimulate changes in the ways that at least some Jewish people think about their Bible. What the undertaking requires at this point in its development, as both an individual and collective task, is definition of purpose and intent and methodological clarity.

112 These circumstances suggest that the undertaking may be pursued safely by scholars in American, secular universities only by safely tenured academics, preferably at the rank of Full Professor, and by those teaching in seminaries or any other institution whose ethos encourages such undertakings. See Freitas, "Publish and Perish," 8–9.

משכנו של האל היא „עלייה," (גם אם המתקרב נמצא בתוך גבולות הארץ המובטחת וגם אם הוא מחוצה לה) – הרי דומני שהמילים החרותות בקברו של הרב קוק בהר הזיתים משקפות נאמנה הצעה זו:

עלה לארץ ישראל כ"ח אייר התרס"ד
עלה ירושלימה ג' אלול התרע"ט
עלה השמימה ג' אלול התרצ"ה

מאמר זה הוא עיבוד של הרצאה שנתתי במסגרת הקונגרס ה-13 למדעי היהדות, אוגוסט 2001 בירושלים. ההרצאה מבוססת על עבודת הדוקטור שכתבתי בהדרכת פרופ' אד גרינשטיין.

ליצחק, „אל תרד מצרימה" [כו, ב]);[50] ואילו כניסה ארצה היא מהלך חיובי, התואמת את רצון האל – עדיף יהיה להפוך את „דגם W" על פניו, כך שיתקבל „דגם M," השומר על המבנה הסימטרי ומשמעותו, אולם, מבטא בצורה גראפית את היחס הערכי למסלול זה.

המסעות של האבות על פי „דגם M"

שימו לב: „דגם M" המוצע, מסמן בצורה גראפית את דרכם של האבות. בתרשים שלפנינו כל „עלייה" ארצה מסומנת בקו עולה, וכל „ירידה" מסומנת בקו (= חץ) יורד.

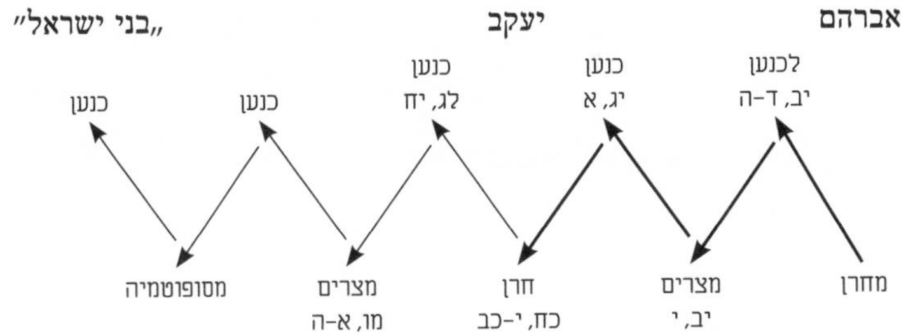

מכיוון, שדגם זה מסמל לדעתי לא רק את מסלול הליכתם של האבות, אלא גם את מסלול הליכתם של זרעם לדורותיהם, תהיה עדיפה צורה גראפית אחרת, של קוים עולים ויורדים חליפות, בצורת זיגזג.[51]

הבנת הזיקה, האנלוגיה בין „המראָה" בחלום יעקב לבין „מחזור סיפורי האבות" כ„מיזאנאבים," מנקודת המבט של כניסות לארץ ויציאות ממנה, תומכת ב„קריאה" הסימבולית של החלום ופשרו. לפנינו אנלוגיה בין עלייה ב„סולם" (שראשו מגיע השמימה וה' ניצב עליו) לבין שיבה/עלייה ב„דרך" מן הגלות אל הארץ המובטחת. המשותף לשתי הליכות/עליות אלו הוא, שבשתיהן ההליכה (הן במשמעות המילולית והן במשמעות המטאפורית) היא לקראת האל, ולכן זוכות הן להערכה חיובית.

לסיום: מאמר זה הוכתר בשם: „עלייה וירידה – מפתח לפתרון חלום יעקב." „המראָה" של עלייה וירידה בחלום, מתפרש כמסמל כניסה ויציאה מן הארץ. כשהתעורר מחלומו אמר יעקב: „אין זה כי אם בית אלהים וזה שער השמים" (פס' יז). „שער השמים," כדרכו של כל שער, מיועד לכניסה וליציאה. לימים הועתק „שער השמים,"[52] הוא „בית אלהים" מקום משכנו של האל, מ„בית אל" לכאן לירושלים. אם נכונה הצעתי – שכל התקרבות אל מקום

50 ראה בעניין זה: מאמרי, פלג, „אברם – ה,ציוני,'" 25–31.

51 אוסיף עוד כי הצגת מסלול הליכתם של האבות אל הארץ וממנה על פי דגם זה, מציבה את כנען למעלה ולפיכך, כדי להגיע לכנען יש לעלות, ואילו את מצרים, חרן, מסופוטמיה, (וכנראה, גם כל מקום אחר מחוץ לארץ כנען) מציבה למטה ולפיכך, כדי להגיע למקומות אלו יש לרדת. המבנה הצורני משקף את המשמעות הערכית של הליכה לכנען לעומת הליכה למקומות האחרים, שפירושה אינו אלא עזיבה כנען הנחשבת לפעולה שלילית.

52 ראה: דיון מפורט בנושא זה אצל יאיר זקוביץ, „המסורות במקרא על ראשית התקדשותה של ירושלים," ירושלים בימי בית ראשון (ירושלים: הוצאת עידן, תש"ן) 12–22.

המושג „יורד" נולד בסיפורו של אברהם. היהודי הראשון הוא העולה הראשון והיורד הראשון גם יחד. היהודי נושא בתוכו שתי מהויות אלו של עלייה וירידה לאורך כל ההיסטוריה.[46]

במאמרי על אברהם[47] הדגמתי את השתקפות דבריו של אברהם ב. יהושע בסיפורי בראשית. במסגרת זו, אבקש להתייחס להשתקפותו של המשפט השלישי של אברהם ב. יהושע במקרא: „היהודי נושא בתוכו שתי מהויות אלו של עלייה וירידה לאורך כל ההיסטוריה."

ואמנם, תיאור „העליות" ו„הירידות" של האבות (אברהם ויעקב) אל הארץ וממנה, זכה במחקר[48] לרישום גראפי כסכמה גיאוגרפית-היסטורית סימטרית בצורת האות W (שתזכה, להלן, לכינוי „דגם W").[49]

המסעות של האבות על פי „דגם W"

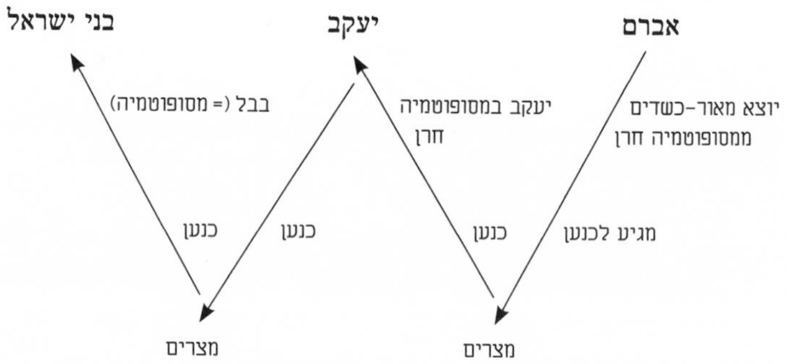

אברהם ב. יהושע, כאמור, מביט אל ההיסטוריה של העם היהודי מימי המקרא ועד היום וטוען „היהודי נושא בתוכו שתי מהויות אלו של עלייה וירידה לאורך כל ההיסטוריה." דומני כי ניתוח ההתרחשויות במקרא מנקודת תצפית זו אכן מחזק את טענתו של אברהם ב. יהושע.

דומני כי, אם ברצוננו לתאר את מסלול הליכתם של האבות מן הארץ ואליה – כך שעזיבת הארץ היא מהלך שלילי המנוגד לרצון האל (למשל, כפי שמשתקף מדבר האל

46 אברהם ב. יהושע, בזכות הנורמליות (ירושלים: הוצאת שוקן, תש"מ) 31.

47 יצחק פלג, „אברם – ה,ציוני' וה,יורד' הראשון," על הפרק 41 (תשנ"ח) 25–31 (להלן: פלג, „אברם – ה,ציוני,").

48 יאיר זקוביץ, „יציאות מצרים בספר בראשית," על הפרק 3 (תשמ"ז) 25–34, ובייחוד 28–29. וכן, Yair Zakovitch, "And You Shall Tell Your Son" *The Concept of the Exodus in the Bible* (Jerusalem: Magnes, 1991) 46–99.

49 לפי זקוביץ, „דגם W" במקרא כולל את המסלול הבא: „אברהם יצא ממסופוטמיה (חרן) ובא לכנען (יב, ד–ה), משם הוא יורד מצרימה בגלל הרעב ושב ממנה לכנען (יב, י–כ; יג, א). יעקב הולך תחילה למסופוטמיה (חרן, כח, י–כב) שב לכנען (לג, יח) וסופו שהוא יורד עם כל ביתו מצרימה, בשל הרעב, בעקבות בנו יוסף (מו) וגם זוכה לאישור אלוהי למעשה הירידה ולהבטחה כי ישובו ממצרים (מו, ג–ד). ירידת יעקב ובניו מצרימה אינה סיום הפרשה: סיפור ירידתם מניח את השיבה ארצה. ועוד, לאחר תהפוכות הישיבה בארץ נענשים בני ישראל בהליכה לגלות, למסופוטמיה ובגלות זו מסתיים הסיפור בנביאים ראשונים."

בחלום) מיוחס ל„מקור J.״[43] הנחת המוצא שלי היא, שהמספר (של בראשית כח, י–כב, על חלקיו השונים) נעזר „במסר המילולי,״ הגלוי והמפורש (המיוחס ל„מקור J״), כדי להסביר את המסר הסמוי, הנסתר והסימבולי, של ה„מראֶה בחלום״ (המיוחס ל„מקור E״).

על תופעה מבנית דומה, בה המראֶה והקול מפרשים זה את זה, כבר עמד מאיר וייס[44] בתיאור התגלות האל בישעיהו פרק ו׳. ואמנם, אם נבודד את „פעלי התנועה״ בשני המרכיבים של חלום יעקב – המראה והדיבור האלוהי – נחשוף כי המשותף לשניהם הוא שהפעלים נעים „הלוך ושוב.״ ואילו, כיוון התנועה שונה. בעוד במראֶה בחלום, התנועה היא בכיוון אנֲכי – מעלה מטה („עלים וירדים״) בין שמים וארץ, הרי „בדברי האל״ התנועה היא בכיוון מאוזן – הלוך ושוב; יציאה מן הארץ ושיבה אליה („ושמרתיך בכל אשר תלך והשבתיך אל האדמה הזאת.״) תרומתו של „המראֶה הוויזואלי״ ל„מסר המילולי״ היא בכך שהשיבה ארצה והיציאה ממנה (פס׳ טו, כ) מובנת/נתפשת כ„עלייה וירידה״ (פס׳ יב). כלומר, הליכתו של יעקב לחרן עשויה להתפרש כהתרחקות מן האל, כירידה, כלומר כפעולה שלילית ואילו שובו ארצה יתפרש כעלייה, כהתקרבות ושיבה לאל. ותרומתו של ה„מסר המילולי״ ל„מראֶה הויזואלי״ היא, שפעולת העלייה והירידה של „מלאכי אלהים״ מובנת/נתפשת כמסמלת את כניסתם של האבות אל הארץ ואת יציאתם ממנה.

הבלשן מ. ג׳וס אמר: „It takes three trees to make a row.״ מקווה שהצלחתי להציג יותר משלושה „עצים״ המציינים את ה„דרך,״[45] כלומר, את התזה המוצעת ל„פשר הסימבולי של החלום״: החל בטענה שלפנינו דגם של חלום סימבולי המצריך גם פשר סימבולי, לפיו הסולם מסמל את הדרך בין הארץ המובטחת לבין הגלות; „מלאכי אלהים,״ המופיעים במקרא רק כאשר יעקב עוזב את הארץ או שב אליה, מסמלים את האבות העולים ויורדים מן הארץ, כאשר עלייה היא פעולה חיובית היות והיא מבטאת, מילולית ומטאפורית, התקרבות לאל, ואילו ירידה נושאת משמעות הפוכה. לסיום ראינו כי „המסר המילולי״ של האל (המזכיר את הבטחת הארץ והזרע לאבות ומדבר על הליכת יעקב לחרן והבטחה להשיבו ארצה) ו„המראֶה בחלום״ מפרשים זה את זה.

סיפור חלום יעקב כ„מיזאנאבים״ של מסעות האבות אל הארץ וממנה

כזכור, פתחתי בהגדרת המונח „מיזאנאבים.״ לקראת סיום, אבקש לשוב אליו ולבחון את תרומתו לפשר הסימבולי של חלום יעקב. דומני כי התמיכה לפשר הסימבולי מתחזקת כאשר קוראים את סיפור חלום יעקב כסיפור המשובץ במסגרת סיפורי האבות – הן על פי ההקשר הסיפורי הישיר לפיו החלום מתרחש כשיעקב בדרכו לעזוב את הארץ, והן על פי ההקשר הרחב, „כשיקוף מיניאטורי״ של סיפורי האבות, הנכנסים ויוצאים מן הארץ הלוך ושוב. הסופר אברהם ב. יהושע כתב בספרו:

43 ראה: טבלה מפורטת של דה פורי (de Pury, *Genèse 28*, 43), על חלוקת פרק כח לפי חסידי השערת המקורות.

44 וייס (מקראות ככוונתם [ירושלים: הוצאת מוסד ביאליק, תשמ״ח] 99) כותב: „ואולם יש גם פרקי מראה אחדים שבהם הנודע לנביא בקול לכאורה אינו אלא המשך כרונולוגי ללא כל קשר ענייני למה שנגלה לו קודם לכן, בתמונה, כאילו אין המראה אלא תפאורה ואחר רדת המסך בא הדיבור.״

45 כדברי הנביא ירמיהו: „הציבי לך צינים שמי לך תמרורים שתי לבך למסלה דרך הלכתי \{הלכת\} שובי בתולת ישראל שבי אל עריך אלה״ (ירמיהו לא, כא).

מה ניתן ללמוד מהשוואה זו?

הפניית תשומת הלב לכך, שבשני המקומות המדובר ביעקב הנמצא לקראת יציאה או כניסה ארצה, נועדה ללמדך הקורא, שהצירוף „מלאכי אלהים" מופיע במקרא אך ורק כאשר יוצאים מן הארץ או כששבים אליה. עובדה זו אינה מקרית, והיא תומכת בהצעת ה„פשר הסימבולי" של החלום.

אם נכונה השערתי, ש„מלאכי אלהים" בחלום מסמלים את „האבות," והסולם מסמל את הדרך בין הארץ המובטחת לבין הגלות, הרי כידוע אברהם אכן קודם „עלה" ארצה ואחר כך „ירד" מצרימה. יוצא אפוא, כי מה שנראה בתחילה כבעיה שהעסיקה דורות של פרשנים – מדוע „מלאכי אלהים" בחלום קודם עולים ואחר כך יורדים[41] – דווקא מתגלה כמרמז לפתרון החלום. דומה כי, בדרך זו מפנה המספֵר את תשומת לב הקורא ומרמז לו על הפתרון. וכשנודע הפתרון לפיו, „מלאכי אלהים" מסמלים את „האבות" וזיקתם לארץ המובטחת, הרי תואם ה„תיאור בחלום" (בו הם קודם „עולים" ואחר כך „יורדים") למסופר בספר בראשית על כך שכניסתו של אברהם לארץ קדמה ליציאתו ממנה.

על תרומתו של „המסר המילולי" ל„מראֶה הסימבולי"

נשוב לסיפור חלום יעקב, אל המקום בו נפרדנו ממנו, ל„מסר המילולי" של האל (פס' יג א–טו). ובכן, לאחר תיאור המראֶה שנגלה לעיני יעקב בחלום, מתגלה האל ליעקב בחלומו. הקורא הרגיש, המכיר את סיפורי האבות אינו יכול שלא לחוש בדמיון, בלשון ובתוכן, בין „הבטחת הארץ והזרע" ליעקב כאן (פס' יגא–יד) לבין „הבטחת הארץ והזרע" לאברהם (בראשית יג, טו–יז). זיקה זו של יעקב לאברהם וליצחק נוצרת כשהאל מציג עצמו, מפורשות, בפני יעקב: „אני ה' אלהי אברהם אביך ואלהי יצחק" (פס' יג). למספֵּר חשוב היה ליצור זיקה בין יעקב לבין אבותיו (יצחק ואברהם) כדי ללמדך הקורא שהחלום ופשרו נועדו לסמל לא רק את יעקב וגורלו, כי אם גם את גורל האבות. בהמשך, בפסוק טו מתייחס המסר האלוהי למצבו של יעקב בטווח הקצר: „והנה אנכי עמך ושמרתיך בכל אשר תלך והשבתיך אל **האדמה** הזאת."

אבקש לטעון בזה, כי קיימת זיקה בין „המראֶה בחלום" (פס' יב$_א$–יג) לבין „המסר המילולי" של האל (פס' יג$_ב$–טו) זיקה זו איננה מתבטאת רק בזה שהם באים באופן ליניארי, זה אחרי זה, אלא גם בכך שהם מפרשים זה את זה.[42]

כידוע, דעה זו מנוגדת למקובל במחקר. מרבית החוקרים, ובייחוד חסידי „השערת המקורות," התמקדו והבליטו את השוני בין השניים. ה„מראֶה בחלום" מיוחס לדעתם, ל„מקור E," ואילו „המסר המילולי" של האל (המופיע, לדעתם, בהתגלות אחרת, ישירה, לא

41 אם משכנם של המלאכים הוא למעלה, יש לצפות שיהיה עליהם קודם לרדת בסולם ורק אחר כך לעלות. ראה: רש"י, תורת חיים, חמשה חומשי תורה, בראשית (ירושלים: הוצאת מוסד הרב קוק, תש"ן) מא': „עולים תחילה ואחר כך יורדים, מלאכים שליווהו בארץ אין יוצאים חוצה לארץ ועלו לרקיע, וירדו מלאכי חוצה לארץ ללוותו."

42 הרחבה בנושא זה, ראה מאמרי: יצחק פלג, „מה בין מה שראה לבין מה ששמע יעקב בחלומו?," מועד יג (תשס"ג) 55-64.

חשובה לענייננו היות וממנה משתמע כי תנועה כלפי מעלה, עלייה, פירושה התקרבות לאֵל ואילו תנועה (של „מלאכי אלהים") כלפי מטה, ירידה, מתארת התרחקות מן האל (מילולית ומטאפורית כאחד).

סביר להניח שכאן טמון ההסבר להיווצרות המשמעות המטאפורית של הפעלים המנוגדים „עלה" ו„ירד": כל התקרבות אל האל, נתפשת כפעולה חיובית וזוכה לשימוש בפועל „עלה," ואילו, התרחקות מהאל, נתפשת כפעולה שלילית וזוכה לשימוש בפועל „ירד."[37] לפיכך, אין זה מפתיע שתיאור בריחתו של יונה מלפני ה' מתוארת באמצעות „המילה המנחה" „וירד" (יונה א, ג).[38]

על הצירוף: „מַלְאֲכֵי אֱלֹהִים"

בטרם נפנה לבחינת תרומתם של דברי האל לענייננו (יגב-טו), נצא ולו לרגע קט, מסיפור חלום יעקב, ונעקוב אחר הצירוף: „מַלְאֲכֵי אֱלֹהִים" במקרא. ובכן, הצירוף: „מלאכי אלהים" מופיע רק פעמיים במקרא, האחת בסיפור חלום יעקב בבית אל והשני במחניים, שם נאמר: „ויעקב הלך לדרכו ויפגעו בו מלאכי אלהים. ויאמר יעקב כאשר ראם מחנה אלהים זה ויקרא שם המקום ההוא מחנים" (בראשית לב, ב-ג).

העובדה שהצירוף „מלאכי אלהים" מופיע רק פעמיים במקרא, מגבירה את סקרנותו של הקורא, ומפנה את תשומת לבו לכך שישנה זיקה בין שני הסיפורים. ואמנם בנוסף לצירוף „מלאכי אלהים" ישנן נקודות דמיון רבות בין השניים (כדלמשל, בשניהם – מופיע „מדרש שֵׁם" למקום; בשניהם – מדרש השם קשור להתגלות האל במקום; בשניהם – השימוש בפועל „ויפגע/ו"; בשניהם – המלאכים מתגלים אך לא אומרים דבר (אין בפיהם „מסר מילולי"); בשניהם – נודע ליעקב על נוכחות האל במקום רק לאחר/כתוצאה מן ההתגלות). ואמנם, פוקלמן העיר כי „סצנת-מחניים" מתייחסת ובנויה על „סצנת בית אל."[39] ולדעת זקוביץ סיפור מחניים הוא סיפור „בבואה"[40] לסיפור חלום יעקב בבית אל. ואמנם, כבר במבט ראשון ניתן להבחין, שמבחינת הזמן: בניגוד לסיפור הראשון המתרחש בלילה, הסיפור השני מתרחש בבוקר. בסיפור בית אל יעקב „פגע ב(מקום)" ואילו במחניים „פגעו בו." והאבחנה החשובה לענייננו היא, שמבחינת המקום והכיוון: בניגוד לסיפור הראשון, סיפור חלום יעקב, המתרחש בבית אל לקראת יציאתו של יעקב את הארץ, הרי הסיפור במחנים מתרחש לקראת שובו ארצה.

J" ואינו המשכו של פסוק יב השייך, לטעמם, ל„מקור E." חוקרים אלו, המייחסים את מילת היחס „עָלָיו" ל„יעקב," רואים בכך עדות נוספת לאבחנה בין מקורות J ו E.

37 רוזנסון, „צרעה-תמנה," 135–152.

38 ראה בעניין זה: מאמרי, פלג, „עוד ארבעים יום," 226–243.

39 כפי שניסח זאת Fokkelman, *Narrative Art*, 198: „From the beginning to the end the Mahanaim-scene refers to and builds on the Bethel-scene." ראה גם: יאיר זקוביץ, „יבוק, פנואל, מחניים, בית אל," חוברת המאה של אריאל (ירושלים: הוצאת ספרים אריאל, תשנ"ד) 191–204. בעמוד 194 טוען זקוביץ כי, „נראה שיש קשר ואף תלות בין שני הסיפורים."

40 יאיר זקוביץ, ב„פתח דבר" בספרו, מקראות בארץ המראות, 9 כותב: „ספר זה עוסק בתופעה של 'סיפורי בבואה' במקרא – סיפורים מהופכים, סיפורים בהם מצב, או דמות ומעשיה, מעוצבים על דרך הניגוד למצב או לדמות ומעשיה בסיפור קיים זה מכבר"; ראה הרחבה: זקוביץ, „סיפור הבבואה – ממד נוסף להערכת הדמויות בסיפור המקראי," תרביץ נד (תשמ"ה) 165–176.

תנועה. שימוש נוסף, המשותף לשני פעלים אלו במקרא הוא, שלהוראה הטכנית הפשוטה, נוספה גם משמעות מטאפורית. נחמה ליבוביץ העירה בצדק לדעתי כי „פעלי תנועה משמשים במקרא בהרבה הזדמנויות בהוראה מטאפורית"[35] (תשל"ג, עמוד 402). „ההוראה המטאפורית" של הפעלים „עלה" ו„ירד" מביעה עמדה ערכית, „עלה" במשמעות חיובית ואילו „ירד" במשמעות שלילית. ואמנם, בדיקת ההיקרויות של שני פעלים אלו במקרא ומשמעותן הקונטקסטואלית חושפת כי, המשמעות המטאפורית של „עלה" (המופיע 890 פעמים במקרא) במרבית המקרים היא חיובית, ואילו „ירד" (המופיע 380 פעמים במקרא) בקונטקציות שליליות. כך למשל, „ויהי רעב, בארץ **וירד** אברם מצרימה" (בראשית יב, י); סיפור יהודה ותמר פותח במילים: „ויהי בעת ההוא **וירד** יהודה מאת אחיו" (בראשית לח, א), ובהמשך מסופר: „וירבו הימים ותמת בת שוע אשת יהודה. וינחם יהודה **ויעל** על גזזי צאנו" (בראשית לח, יב); על יעקב המתאבל על יוסף מוספר: „וימאן להתנחם ויאמר כי **ארד** אל בני אבל שאלה ויבך אתו אביו" (בראשית לז, לה); יוסף כזכור, „**הורד** מצרימה" (לט, א); „הגר אשר בקרבך **יעלה** עליך מעלה מעלה ואתה תרד מטה מטה" (דברים כח, מג); „ה' ממית ומחיה מוריד שאול **ויעל**. ה' מוריש ומעשיר משפיל אף מרומם" (שמואל ב ב, ו-ז).

האבחנה בדבר היותם פעלים ניגודיים הנושאים משמעות מטאפורית מעודדת למקד את המבט והדיון אל אותן היקרויות במקרא בהם מופיעים שני פעלים אלו בסמוך זה לזה. ההנחה היא שהופעתם יחדיו אינה מקרית, וכי מופיעים הם, זה בהשוואה לזה, זה לעומת זה, לצורך הבלטת הניגוד ביניהם. דומה, שמודעות לטכניקה ספרותית זו, עשויה לחשוף משמעויות בטקסט.

לענייננו, חשוב לציין, שחשיפת השימוש של הפעלים „עלה" ו„ירד" בחלום יעקב במשמעות מטאפורית, מהווה תמיכה חשובה ל„קריאה הסימבולית" של החלום ופשרו.

כאן המקום להעיר כי, לדעתי, כינוי הגוף במילת היחס „עָלָיו" בתיאור: „והנה ה' נצב עליו" (יג א) מוסבת לסולם.[36] כלומר, האל ניצב על הסולם שראשו בשמים. הערה זו

35 נחמה ליבוביץ, עיונים חדשים בספר שמות (ירושלים: ההסתדרות הציונית, תשל"ג) 204. ראה גם: מרטין בובר, דרכו של מקרא (ירושלים: הוצאת מוסד ביאליק, תשכ"ד) 304-305; ראה: יאיר זקוביץ, חיי שמשון, (שופטים יג-טז) – ניתוח ספרותי-ביקורתי (ירושלים: הוצאת ע"ש י"ל מאגנס, תשמ"ב) 89; וכן, ישראל רוזנסון („צרעה-תמנה, עלייה – ירידה," עיון במשמעותם הפרשנית של התיאורים הגיאוגרפיים בסיפורי שמשון, בית מקרא, מא [תשנ"ו] 142) מוסיף כי, „לפעלים „עלה" „ירד" עשויה להיות הוראה טכנית פשוטה בצד משמעות מטאפורית סמויה, כפי שהראה משה גרסיאל, „דרכי תיאור מיטונימי ומטאפורי בסיפור המקראי," ביקורת ופרשנות (רמת גן: אוניברסיטת בר אילן, תשמ"ח) 15-20.

36 בין החוקרים התומכים בהצעה שהאל ניצב על הסולם: רש"י, תורת חיים, חמשה חומשי תורה, בראשית (ירושלים: הוצאת מוסד הרב קוק, תש"ן) מב; ספורנו, תורת חיים, חמשה חומשי תורה, בראשית (ירושלים: הוצאת מוסד הרב קוק, תש"ן) מב; ומן החוקרים האחרונים, ראה: Houtman, "What Did Jacob See?" 345; שמעון בר אפרת, העיצוב האמנותי של הסיפור במקרא (ישראל: הוצאת ספרית הפועלים, תשנ"ג [מהדורה רביעית]) 123, מציין ש„הסולם היה מֻצב ארצה, ועליו נִצב ה'"; וכן, יאיר זקוביץ, מקראות בארץ המראות (תל אביב: הוצאת הקיבוץ המאוחד, תשנ"ה) 115, הערה 5. יש הטוענים ש„עָלָיו" הכוונה „על יעקב": James George Frazer, *Folk-lore in the Old Testament* (London: The Macmillan Company, 1923) 225–28; Ernst Ludwig Ehrlich, *Der Traum im Alten Testament*, BZAW 73 (1953) 29; Speiser, *Genesis*, 219 וגונקל, אגדות בראשית, 218. ראה גם: Bar, *A Letter That Has Not Been Read*, 20, וביחוד הערה 56. אותם חוקרים הטוענים ש„עָלָיו" מוסב „על יעקב" מסתמכים גם על תיאור התגלות האל לאברהם, „כחם היום" ולא בחלום, שנאמר: „וירא והנה שלשה אנשים נצבים עליו" (בראשית יח, ב). המקבילה של בראשית יח, ב משרתת את החוקרים, בעיקר חסידי „השערת התעודות," הטוענים שפסוק יג שייך ל„מקור

שאלה זו זוכה למשנה תוקף כאשר עדים לכך שמלאכים, במקרא ובמזרח הקדום, מופיעים בדרך כלל כשליחים עם מסר.[29] מלאך מורכב מהשורש לא״ך ומן התחילית מ׳. רופא[30] בעבודת הדוקטור שלו מציין כי: „מלאך פירושו שליח. הדבר מתחוור הן מן האטימולוגיה – הוראת הפועל לא״ך בערבית, אתיופית ואוגריתית[31] – והן מן הסמנטיקה המקראית.״

לדעת רופא, בסיפור חלום יעקב, „מלאכי אלהים״: „אינם מביאים לו שום שליחות.״[32] אף פוקלמן[33] מניח שאין להם תפקיד מלבד היותם אחד האמצעים (כמו הסולם המגיע השמימה) המכריזים על האל העומד להופיע. כך שהופעת ה׳ עצמו אינה הפתעה. לכן, לדעתו, לאחר הופעת/התגלות האל, מסיימים הסולם והמלאכים את תפקידם, ולכן אינם מופיעים יותר. בדיוק כמו בסיפור ה„סנה הבוער״ (שמות ג), שהמַרְאֶה – „והנה הסנה בער באש והסנה איננו אכל״ (שמות ג, ב) – היה אמצעי כדי לתפוש את עיני משה, ולהפנות את תשומת לבו. והסיפור ממשיך, בשתי התגלויות אלו, להשמיע את דבר האל, והבטחתו.

כנגד טענתו, אבקש להציע כי עצם הציפייה ממלאכי אלהים להביא מסר, כדרכם של מלאכים, מובילה אותנו לחיפוש אחר מסר, אף אם אינו מילולי. לדעתי, שליחותם של „מלאכי אלהים״ משתקפת מעצם פעולתם; המסר שלהם נחשף בתנועתם, הלוך ושוב, מעלה מטה, ככתוב: „והנה מלאכי אלהים עלים וירדים בו.״ בהקשר זה מעניין לציין כי אלגביש בעבודת הדוקטור שלו מציין כי „יש סבורים, כי לא״ך מקביל בשיכול אותיות לפועל האכדי *alakum*, ללכת; לדעתם, מוטעמת בכינוי זה ההליכה, שהיא מרכיב חשוב בעבודת השליח.״[34]

על המשמעות המטאפורית של הפעלים „עלה״ ו„ירד״

טענה זו באשר למסר של „מלאכי אלהים״ הנחשף מעצם תנועתם, מקדמת אותנו בתהליך הקריאה ומובילה אותנו לבחינת הפעלים „עלה״ ו„ירד.״

הפעלים „עלה״ ו„ירד״ מציינים תנועה בכיוון מנוגד. המשותף לפעלים אלו שהם פעלי

29 דוד אלגביש, השליח והשליחות, השירות הדיפלומטי במקורות היתדיים מן המזרח הקדום ובמקרא, חיבור לשם קבלת תואר „דוקטור לפילוסופיה,״ הוגש לסינט של אוניברסיטת בר-אילן, תש״ן, 35 ואילך. אלגביש טוען כי „מלאך״ הוא המונח המקראי המקביל הקבלה מלאה למונח האכדי (= לצירוף *mar siprim*, וכן צירוף זה הנו הכינוי הרווח ביותר באכדית לשליח.

30 אלכסנדר רופא, האמונה במלאכים במקרא (ירושלים: הוצאת מקור, תשל״ט) 2.

31 ראה גם: כהן, „המוטיב הספרותי,״ 18, הערה 14) המציין, ש„פירוש המילה angel ביוונית הנו ,שליח.״ וכן, דוד אלגביש, עבודת הדוקטור יצאה לאור כספר בשם: השירות הדיפלומטי במקרא ובתעודות מן המזרח הקדום (ירושלים: הוצאת ע״ש י״ל מאגנס, תשנ״ח) 63.

32 רופא (תשל״ט, 48) מסביר עובדה זו – של היעדר שליחות מצד המלאכים – כעדות למשניות השימוש בהם. אבחנה זו אינה רלוונטית לעניינו, שהרי כל עניינו להבין את הטקסט בצורתו הנוכחית, ולא השערות על דרכי התהוותו.

33 Fokkelman, *Narrative Art*, 54; ראה גם: Sarna, *Genesis*, 198, האומר על המלאכים: „in the dream, They play no role.״

34 דוד אלגביש, השליח והשליחות, 30, הערה 20; וכן, ראה: Edward L. Greenstein, "Trans-Semitic Idiomatic Equivalency and the Derivation of Hebrew *ml'kh*," *UF* 11 (1979) 331. ראה גם: שלמה מאנדלקרן, „מלאך,״ קונקורדנציה לתנ״ך (ירושלים תל אביב: הוצאת שוקן, תשל״ה) 625. לאחרונה כתב יאיר זקוביץ, אביעה חידות מני קדם, חידות וחלומות חידה בספרות המקראית (תל אביב: הוצאת עם עובד, תשס״ו) 67: „כשם שמלאכי האלוהים יוצאים ובאים, עולים ויורדים, אף יעקב היוצא לנדודיו ישוב ארצה...״ (פס׳ טו). אולם לא קישר זיקה זו לאפשרות של הפשר הסימבולי המוצע כאן לחלום יעקב.

וההקשרים העולים מבדיקה זו – מלמדת כי השורש סל"ל מופיע 11 פעמים במקרא.[25] ראשית, חשוב לציין כי, שמות העצם הקשורים לפועל סל"ל בדוגמאות אלו הן: „נתיב," „אורח," „דרך." אבחנה זו מחזקת את ההשערה, שהציע הוטמן,[26] בדבר הוראתו של הסולם כ„דרך," כ„נתיב." שנית, שם העצם מסלה (ישעיהו סב, י)[27] נגזר מהשורש סל"ל. „מסילה" מופיעה 27 פעמים במקרא, וכן השם היחידאי מסלול: „והיה שם מסלול ודרך" (ישעיהו לה, ח). „מסילה" הנגזרת, כאמור, מהשורש סל"ל, מופיעה מספר פעמים במקרא במשמעות של „דרך סלולה" (paved way). מתוך 27 הפעמים שהמילה מופיעה במקרא, כ־50% היא מופיעה בנבואה (עשר פעמים בישעיהו, פעמיים בירמיהו, פעם אחת ביואל). נוסף לכך, מרבית המקרים (בעיקר בנבואה) השורש סל"ל מופיע בזיקה לשיבה ארצה. אבחנה זו עשויה לרמז על סימון/ציון „מסלולה" של „הדרך": „מן הגלות אל הארץ," אל מקום משכנו/ביתו של האל. כך, למשל, בדברי ישעיהו: „סלו סלו פנו דרך הרימו מכשול מדרך עמי" (ישעיהו נז, יד).

יוצא אפוא, שהבנת ה„סֻלָּם" כמזכיר ומתחבר לשורש העברי סל"ל (גם אם אינו נגזר ממנו) עשויה לעודד ולתמוך בלגיטימיות של ההצעה שמדובר ב„דרך," ואולי אף מרמזת על „דרך מסוימת," זו העוברת בין הארץ לבין הגלות.[28]

לסיכום נושא הסולם. לדעתי, מתאפשרות „שתי קריאות," המשלימות זו את זו, של המונח היחידאי „סֻלָּם":

האחת: ב„מישור הגלוי" (בכיוון מאונך), לפי פשוטו של מקרא, „הדרך," לאורך הסולם, עוברת בין הארץ לבין השמים.

והקריאה השנייה: ב„מישור הסימבולי" (בכיוון מאוזן), הסולם מסמל „דרך." דרך זו עוברת בין הארץ המובטחת לבין הגלות.

חשוב לציין כי נקודת התצפית על ה„דרך" – בשני המישורים, הגלוי והסמוי (המאונך והמאוזן) – היא ממקום משכנו של האל – אליו וממנו.

מהו תפקידם של „מלאכי אלהים"?

בחלומו רואה יעקב „מלאכי אלהים" – נשאלת השאלה, מה באים הם לסמל? מהו תפקידם, מהי שליחותם?

25 „עודך מסתולל בעמי" (שמות ט, יז); „סלו סלו פנו דרך" (ישעיהו נז, יד – פעמיים); „עברו עברו בשערים פנו דרך סלו סלו המסלה סקלו מאבן" (ישעיהו סב, י – פעמיים); „ללכת נתיבות דרך לא סלולה" (ירמיהו יח, טו); „סלוה כמו ערמים והחרימוה" (ירמיהו נ, כו); „סלו לרכב בערבות" (תהלים סח, ה); „וארח ישרים סללה" (משלי טו, יט); „יחד יבאו גדודיו ויסלו עלי דרכם" (איוב יט, יב); „ויסלו עלי ארחות אידם" (איוב ל, יב).

26 Houtman, "What Did Jacob See?" 340, כתב: „מבראשית כח, יב ומהנתונים על סל"ל והנגזרות ממנו, ניתן להסיק רק שלפנינו סוג של ramp או דרך, מעבר, שנועד לקשר שמים לארץ."

27 BDB, 700 „מְסִלָּה"; Houtman, "What Did Jacob See?" 339; על „מסילה" כתקבולת ל„דרך," ראה: במדבר כ, יט בהשוואה לבמדבר כ, יז: „דרך המלך נלך"//„במסלה נעלה." ראה גם: BDB, 202 „דֶּרֶךְ."

28 בהקשר זה ראוי לציין כי דיאנה Lipton, *Revisions of the Night*, 126, מציעה להבין את סיפור חלום יעקב על רקע „שיבת ציון." לדעתה, „נקודות המגע בין מצבו של יעקב לפני ואחרי החלום בבית אל לבין הסיטואציה של הגולים בבבל הן ברורות: הוא והם מגורשים מארץ מולדתם, שניהם נכנסו לשרת כוח זר, לשניהם אחים שנותרו בבית, שניהם שבו במעמד עליון. הקבלות אלו מהוות מקור עידוד לגולים היהודים, שמיותר להסבירו."

במילה „סֻלָּם" היא שורשית.[19] לפי ההוראה השנייה: „סֻלָּם" נגזר מהשורש העברי סל״ל,[20] שהוראתו: להרים סוללה, רמפה, דרך.[21] ראוי להדגיש, שהשורש סל״ל במובנו המקראי אינו מצוי באכדית, כך שגזרון זה אינו עולה בקנה אחד עם הדעה שהמילה שאולה מהמילה האכדית *simmiltu*. גם אם מבחינה אטימולוגית המילה „סֻלָּם" אינה נגזרת מהשורש סל״ל, נראה, להלן, שהקשר בין השניים חושף משמעות בעלת חשיבות רבה להבנת החלום ופשרו הסימבולי. ההכרעה בין שתי ההצעות אינה קלה,[22] אולם לענייננו, אינה הכרחית.

מכל מקום, הבנת המילה „סולם" כנגזרת מהמילה האכדית *simmiltu* מובילה לבחינת זיקה נוספת של הסולם המקראי לספרות המזרח הקדום. כוונתי לזיקתו של הסולם המקראי לזיגורט (Ziggurat) הבבלי, בו מצויות מדרגות *simmiltu* המובילות לפסגתו. התמיכה בזיהוי הסולם המקראי עם הזיגורט הייתה נחלתם של חוקרים רבים.[23] תיאור הזיגורט על פי תפקודו „כמגשר בין שמים וארץ" נותן יתרון ל-*simmiltu* על פני סל״ל, ומעודד את הפשר הגלוי לחלום כאיטיולוגיה פולחנית.

עידוד ל„קריאה הסימבולית" של הסולם, ניתן לקבל מהבנתו כקשור לשורש סל״ל. לפיכך, לשם הדיוק והזהירות בניסוח, עדיף, כנראה, לומר כי סולם מזכיר[24] את השורש העברי סל״ל (ולא נגזר ממנו). בחינת ההיקרויות של השורש סל״ל במקרא – על הקונוטציות

שלמת רעך עד בא השמש תשיבנו לו, כי הוא כסותה לבדה הוא שמלתו לערו" (שמות כב, כה–כו); ראה גם: Cornelis Houtman, "What Did Jacob See in His Dream at Bethel?" *VT* 27 (1977) 339 (להלן: Houtman, "What Did Jacob See?"); וכן Gnuse, *Dream Theophany*, 86.

19 כהן, „המוטיב הספרותי", 22; לדעתו, אין לגזור את המילה „סלם" מהשורש העברי סל״ל. Harold R. (Chaim) Cohen, *Biblical Hapax Legomena in the Light of Akkadian and Ugaritic* (Missoula, Mont.: Scholars Press, 1978) 34, 54–56.

20 BDB, 699; ראה גם: BDB, 336, „חנם" מלשון „חן" וסיומת ָם. בין החוקרים התומכים בהצעה ש„סלם" נגזר מהשורש סל״ל העברי: Gerhard von Rad, *Genesis, A Commentary*, OTL (1961) 279 (להלן: von Rad, *Genesis*); Ephraim Avigdor Speiser, *Genesis*, AB (1964) 218 (להלן: Speiser, *Genesis*) וכן, Houtman, "What Did Jacob See?" 338; Westermann, *Genesis*, 454.

21 Houtman, "What Did Jacob See?" 338, מציין, שהמילה סלם נגזרת מהשורש העברי סל״ל שפירושו "to pave, to heap up" רוצף, סלול (כלומר, דרך מורמת של עפר ואבנים). ראה: „וישפכו סללה אל העיר ותעמד בחל" (שמואל ב כ, טו). להלן, ארחיב בסוגיה זו.

22 על הקושי להכריע בין סל״ל לבין *simmiltu* ניתן ללמוד מתנודות שחלו בגישתו של גרינשפאן. גרינשפאן (אותו מביא כהן, „המוטיב הספרותי", 22, הערה 22) שינה את עמדתו בשאלה זו. Frederick E. Greenspahn, *Hapax Legomena in Biblical Hebrew* (Chico, Calif.: Scholars Press, 1984) 195. גרינשפאן כלל בספרו את המילה „סֻלָּם" כנגזרת מסל״ל, במסגרת רשימת מילים יחידאיות הנגזרות משורשים ידועים ממילים אחרות, ואילו במאמרו האחרון. Frederick E. Greenspahn, "A Mesopotamian Proverb and its Biblical Reverberations," *JAOS* 114 (1994) 37, n. 25. העדיף את הזיקה ל-*simmiltu*, בציינו, ש„למרות שהמילה *sullam* לעתים קשורה לשורש סל״ל – has been linked to the root *sll* – עדיף להשוות אותה למילה האכדית *simmiltu*; אף Sarna, *Genesis*, 198, מביא את האטימולוגיה מהשורש סל״ל בצד הגזרון מאכדית *simmiltu*, מבלי לנקוט כל העדפה. ראוי לשים לב לכך שסרנה כתב את דבריו לפני הוצאת ספרו של כהן וכן לפני שינוי דעתו של גרינשפאן ("Mesopotamian Proverb"), שהיה תלמידו.

23 על מקבילות מסופוטמיות ראה: von Rad, *Genesis*, 297; Speiser, *Genesis*, 218; Millard, "The Celestial Ladder". John Gwyn Griffiths, "The Celestial Ladder and the Gate of Heaven (Genesis XXVIII 12 and 17)," ExpTim 76 (1964/5) 229; Houtman, "What Did Jacob See?" 338, הערה 4, המביא את ירמיאס (1930); פידלר, חלום ההתגלות, 175; Diana Lipton, *Revisions of the Night: Politics and Promises in the Patriarchal Dreams of Genesis* (Ph.D. diss.; Cambridge Univ., 1996) 88 n. 40, 90 (להלן: Lipton, *Revisions of the Night*); E. Stone, "Ziggurat," OEANE 5 (1997) 390–91.

24 „מזכיר" ולא „נגזר מ:" גרישפאן, 1994, 37, הערה 25: „has been *linked* to the root *sll*."

הבה נתמקד בסקירת הגורמים התומכים בפשר ה„סימבולי" של „חלום יעקב"

לשם כך נכוון את הזרקורים אל המראֶה בחלום על מרכיביו – הסולם, מלאכי אלוהים והפעלים „עלה" „וירד" – לפי סדר הופעתם בסיפור. בבראשית כח, יב-יגא מסופר: „ויחלם והנה סלם מצב ארצה וראשו מגיע השמימה והנה מלאכי אלהים עלים וירדים בו. והנה ה' נצב עליו..."

נפתח בסולם: מה מסמל הסולם?[13]

הסולם מוצג כאובייקט, ענק ממדים, המשמש כ„דרך" המקשרת בין שמים וארץ. תיאור הסולם במסגרת חלום, ובייחוד חלום סימבולי, מעודד לראות בו (בסולם) לא רק אובייקט פיסי המקשר בין שמים וארץ, אלא גם אובייקט סמלי, המגשר, ויוצר זיקה בין מי שנמצא בארץ לבין השוכן בשמים, כלומר, בין האדם לבין האל, בין יעקב לבין ה' אלוהים.[14] בחיבור זה אבקש להראות שהסולם עשוי לסמל גם „דרך" נוספת. כוונתי, ל„דרך" בין הארץ המובטחת לבין הגלות. ואמנם, ה„דרך" הזו, וההליכה בה, הלוך ושוב, נזכרת שלוש פעמים במהלך הסיפור: בפעם הראשונה, בהבטחת האל: „והנה אנכי עמך ושמרתיך בכל [הדרך] אשר תלך[15] והשבתיך אל האדמה הזאת" (פס' טו). בפעם השנייה, בנדר יעקב: „אם יהיה אלהים עמדי ושמרני בדרך הזה אשר אנכי הולך" (פס' כ); ובפעם השלישית, ההליכה בדרך: „ושבתי בשלום אל בית אבי" (פס' כא).

מהי האטימולוגיה של „סֻלָּם?" ומהי זיקתו ל„זיגורט" (*Ziggurat*) הבבלי? בקרב החוקרים אין תמימות דעים בשאלה זו. סקירת הדיון במחקר[16] מעלה, שמבחינה אטימולוגית מתאפשרות, כנראה, שתי דרכים להבנת המילה „סֻלָּם." לפי ההוראה האחת: „סֻלָּם" נגזר מהמילה האכדית *simmiltu*,[17] בשׂיכול אותיות,[18] והוראתה „מערכת מדרגות" (stairway). כלומר, המ"ם

13 להרחבה, ראה מאמרי: יצחק פלג, „מהו הסולם שראה יעקב בחלומו," שנתון לחקר המקרא והמזרח הקדום יד (ירושלים: הוצאת ע"ש י"ל מאגנס, תשס"ד) 7-26.

14 ואמנם, לאחרונה, חיים כהן, „המוטיב הספרותי של סֻלם יעקב (ברא' כ"ח יב)," בתוך: יעקב בן-טולילה, עירך, שי להדסה – מחקרים בלשון העברית ובלשונות היהודים (באר שבע: הוצאת הספרים של אוניברסיטת בן גוריון בנגב, תשנ"ז) 1-45 (להלן: כהן, „המוטיב הספרותי"). כהן, האיר את פירושו של אבן עזרא, והוסיף לטיבה של זיקה זו, „בסיכומו של דבר, נראה שסמל הסולם בחלומו של יעקב מתפקד כסולם מגשר... בחלומו של יעקב, הסולם המגשר משמש לא רק כרקע למסר האלוהי שנשלח ליעקב מאלוהיו בשמים, אלא המלאכים העולים ויורדים בו באופן תמידי הופכים אותו גם לסמל של ערנותו ושליטתו המוחלטת של ה' על כל מה שמתרחש עלי אדמות," כהן, „המוטיב הספרותי," 26.

15 ראה: נוסח תרגום השבעים, המוסיף את המילה „הדרך" לאחר „בכל." *BHK* 4.

16 ראה, למשל: חיים כהן, על „הסולם," עולם התנ"ך, בראשית, בעריכת משה ויינפלד (ירושלים, רמת גן: הוצאת רביבים, תשמ"ב) 172; ראה גם: Shaul Bar, *A Letter That Has Not Been Read, Dreams in the Hebrew Bible* (Cincinnati: Hebrew Union College Press, 2001) 19, n. 49 (להלן: Bar, *A Letter That Has Not Been Read*).

17 בין החוקרים התומכים בהצעה ש„סֻלָּם" נגזר מ-*simmiltu*: *CAD*, "*simmiltu*," 15:173; Alan Ralph Millard, "The Celestial Ladder and the Gate of Heaven (Genesis XXVIII 12 and 17)," *ExpTim* 78 (1966/67) 86-87 (להלן: Millard, "The Celestial Ladder,"); וכן, Gnuse, *Dream Theophany*, 86.

18 שיכול אותיות למנ"ר היא תופעה מוכרת, ראה, למשל: חילופי „שׂלמה" ו„שׂמלה," „אם חבל תחבל

קבלת מסר מילולי מפי האל המתגלה בחלום. לדעתם, סיפור „חלום יעקב" הוא „אטיולוגיה פולחנית" המסבירה כיצד הפך המקום[9] „בית אל" למקום קדוש (*hieros logos* של בית אל).

אולם, העובדה שחלום יעקב מכיל בנוסף ל„מסר המילולי" של האל (פס' יג-טו) גם „מראֶה" (פס' יב-יגא) מחייבת לשאול, האם „למראֶה זה" ישנו מסר; ואם כן, מהו?

ואמנם, אחדים[10] ציינו את ייחודו ומורכבותו של „חלום יעקב" בזה, שכלולים בו בנוסף לסממנים של דגם „חלום התגלות" גם סממנים של דגם „חלום סימבולי"; אולם אבחנה זו לא הובילה אותם לחיפוש אחר מענה לשאלה, מה מסמל ה„מראֶה" בחלום יעקב? בדרך כלל „המראֶה" בחלום יעקב התקבל כרקע כקישוט[11] ולא כנושא מסר-בפני-עצמו.[12]

בטרם אפנה לסקירת הגורמים התומכים בטענה המוצעת, אפתח בהערה מתודית: חשוב להעיר, שהצעתי, המתמקדת, כאמור, בהיבט הסימבולי של החלום ופשרו, אינה הדרך הבלעדית לפשר החלום. הצעה זו אף אינה סותרת את הפשר המקובל במחקר, אלא מעשירה אותו, משלימה אותו וחושפת ממד נוסף, המצוי בסיפור, ובכך, כמדומני, מזכה אותו ואותנו בפשר מקיף יותר.

העובדה שב„חלום יעקב" ישנם, בו זמנית, סממנים של דגם „חלום התגלות" בצד סממנים של דגם „חלום סימבולי," מעידה, על מורכבותו של תיאור החלום. עובדה זו מאפשרת שתי „התרשמויות" במקביל – זו הגלויה (על פי דגם „חלום התגלות"), וזו הסמויה (על פי דגם „חלום סימבולי") – ומכאן מן הראוי להבין אף את פשרו על פי שתי „התרשמויות" אלו.

דומני, שגישתי הספרותית אל הטקסט – המתמקדת במגמות המשתקפות מן הטקסט כהווייתו, בצורתו הנוכחית, והמכירה באפשרות הלגיטימית של יותר מ„קריאה" אחת של טקסט – סללה את הדרך להצעת הפשר „הסימבולי" של החלום.

9 על חשיבותו של ה„מקום" כמילה מנחה בסיפור, ראה מאמרי: יצחק פלג, „„המקום' בסיפור חלום יעקב," על הפרק 18 (תשס"ב) 83-91.

10 ראה למשל: Richter, "Traum," 204-205; אלי ברוך, „תופעת החלום הנבואי ושלילתה – על ידי המחשבה הדויטרונומיסטית" (עבודת גמר המוגשת כמילוי חלק מהדרישות לקבלת תואר מוסמך; אוניברסיטת חיפה, תשמ"ז) 13; פידלר, חלום ההתגלות, 54. וכן, 29, 40; ראה גם: Murray Lichtenstein, "Dream Theophany and the E Document," *JANESCU* 1-2 (1969) 45-54. המביא דוגמאות מספרות המזרח הקדום על חלומות הבנויים במקביל על פי שני סוגי החלומות כאחד; על חלום גודאה, ראה: Oppenheim, *Interpretation of Dreams*, 245-46; ראה: פידלר, חלום ההתגלות, „נספח: תיאורי חלומות התגלות בספרות המזרח הקדום," 1. פידלר, בהמשך, אומרת, ש„חלומותיו של גודאה הם דוגמא לרבגוניותו של חלום ההתגלות מבחינת זיקתו לסוגי החלומות המקובלים" (פידלר, חלום ההתגלות, 2). וכן, על חלום גודאה (Gudea) ראה: פלג, עלייה וירידה, 139.

11 Sarna, *Genesis*, 193; וכן, Jan P. Fokkelman, *Narrative Art in Genesis* (Assen/Amsterdam: Van Gorcum, 1975) 54 (להלן: Fokkelman, *Narrative Art*). פוקלמן (54) מציע להבין את תפקיד הסולם והמלאכים, בדיוק כמו הסנה הבוער בהתגלות אל משה (שמות ג), כלומר,אמצעי להסב את תשומת לבו של יעקב, לקראת התגלות האל, ולכן, אמנם המלאכים מסיימים את תפקידם ולא מופיעים יותר. Albert de Pury, *Promesse divine et legende cultuelle dans le cycle de Jacob — Genèse 28 et les traditions patriarcales* (2 vols.; Paris: J. Gabalda, 1975) 2:378 (להלן: de Pury, *Genèse 28*). וכן, פידלר, חלום ההתגלות, 172: „כך מתרשמים אנו, ש„אירוע החלום' ועיקרו הוא הופעת האל המסר מפיו, ואילו הסולם והמלאכים אינם אלא ליווי או „תפאורה' להתגלות זו."

12 Fokkelman, *Narrative Art*, 54; Sarna, *Genesis*, 198, למשל, אומר על המלאכים: "They play no role in the dream"; ראה: פידלר, חלום ההתגלות, 155, הערה 125, המביאה רשימה של חוקרים נוספים התומכים בגישה זו.

האל ומוסר מסר מילולי, והסוג השני „חלומות סימבוליים," בו מוצגת תמונה.

המשותף לשני סוגים אלו הוא, שניתן לזהותם על פי המבנה והלשון האופייניים להם.[4] בדרך כלל ניתן לזהות „חלום התגלות"[5] בכך שהמסר שלו מועבר על ידי האל המתגלה בחלום באופן מילולי, ואילו המסר של ה"חלום הסימבולי"[6] מועבר בדרך חזותית באמצעות מראֶה, ונזקק על פי רוב לפשר.[7]

מרבית החוקרים[8] מסווגים את „חלום יעקב" כ„חלום התגלות," כלומר חלום שעיקרו הוא

Translation of an Assyrian Dream-Book (Philadelphia: American Philosophical Society, 1956) 206–17, 237–45 (להלן: Oppenheim, *The Interpretation of Dreams*); Robert Karl Gnuse, *The Dream Theophany of Samuel* (New York/London: Univ. Press of America, 1984) 16 (להלן: Gnuse, *Dream Theophany*).

4 ליאו אופנהיים, „חלום," אנציקלופדיה מקראית (9 כרכים; ירושלים: הוצאת מוסד ביאליק, תשכ"ה) ג:143 כותב: „החלומות משני הסוגים נרשמו על פי דפוס קבוע ויש בידינו לעקוב אחר הדגם ולשחזרו על סמך המקורות, שבעיקרו אחד הוא בכולם מימי שומר של האלף השלישי לפנה"ס ועד לסיפורי הומירוס ועד למצרים התלמיית...."

5 שני סוגי החלומות זכו במחקר לכינויים שונים, פרטים על כך ראה: יצחק פלג, „עלייה וירידה – מפתח לפתרון חלום יעקב" (חיבור לשם קבלת תואר דוקטור; ירושלים: מכון שכטר ללימודי היהדות, תש"ס) 9–11 (להלן: פלג, עלייה וירידה). אופנהיים, הגדיר את „חלום ההתגלות" בשם „חלום מסר" (Message dream). אולם, הגדרה זו, בייחוד כאשר נועדה היא להבדיל מ„חלום סימבולי" עלולה ליצור את הרושם כי לחלום הסימבולי אין מסר. מכיוון שלדעתי גם לחלום הסימבולי יש מסר, ובזה ארחיב בהמשך, העדפתי את הכינוי „חלום התגלות." על מאפייני חלום התגלות ראה: Oppenheim, *Interpretation of Dreams*, 186, ואילך.

מסגרת: נסיבות החלום: החולם, הזמן, המקום וכו'. הופעת האל או שליחו

גרעין: מסר מפי הישות המתגלה

מסגרת: סיום החלום, יקיצת החולם ותגובתו. התגשמות המסר (במידה והדבר רלבנטי)

נסתייעתי ברישום הגרפי של רות פידלר, „חלום ההתגלות במקרא: מקומו בתולדות הספרות המקראית ובתולדות אמונת ישראל" (חיבור לשם קבלת התואר דוקטור לפילוסופיה מוגש לסינט האוניברסיטה העברית, תשנ"ו) 16 (להלן: פידלר, חלום ההתגלות). ראה גם: Gnuse, *Dream Theophany*, 75.

6 על מאפייני חלום סימבולי ראה: Wolfgang Richter, "Traum und Traumdeutung im Alten Testament: Ihre Form und Verwendung," *BZ* (NF) 7 (1963) 203–9 (להלן: Richter, "Traum"). בדיונו על חלומות בסיפור יוסף, מכנה ריכטר דגם זה: „החלום בעל המבנה האָמנותי"; לדעתו, 204–205, חלום סימבולי בנוי על חמישה רכיבים (לעומת שלושת הרכיבים של דגם „חלום ההתגלות") והם: ציון החלום; נוסחת הפתיחה של החלום (בדרך כלל „וְהִנֵּה"); גוף החלום: תיאור המראה שראה החולם; פשר החלום; התגשמות החלום. Gnuse, *Dream Theophany*, 79–80, מזהה בדגם זה גם את החלום המדייני (שופטים ז, יג–יד) וגם את החלומות בספר דניאל. חיבור זה, בעקבות עבודת הדוקטור שלי, מוסיף את „חלום יעקב" לרשימת החלומות הסימבוליים במקרא.

7 פידלר, חלום ההתגלות, 29.

8 ראה: יצחק ליאו זליגמן, „יסודות אטיולוגיים בהיסטוריוגרפיה המקראית," ציון, כ"ו (תשכ"א) 141–169. Nahum M. Sarna, *Understanding Genesis* (New York: Schocken Books, 1966) 192 (להלן: Sarna, *Genesis*); E. Otto, "Jakob in Bet El," *ZAW* 88 (1976) 174; Rolf Rendtorff, "Jakob in Bethel," in Alexander Rofe and Yair Zakovitch, eds., *Isac Leo Seeligmann Volume: Essays on the Bible and the Ancient World* (3 vols.; Jerusalem: Elhanan Ruinstein's Publishing House, 1983) 3:120, 124; Claus Westermann, *Genesis 12–36; 37–50: A Commentary*, trans. John J. Scullion (Minneapolis: Augsburg, 1985/86) 452, 458 (להלן: Westermann, *Genesis*). פידלר, חלום ההתגלות, 153, 163–164, 188; הרמן גונקל, אגדות בראשית, מבוא לספר בראשית, ספרות המקרא (ירושלים: הוצאת מוסד ביאליק, תשנ"ח) 4, 31–37, ובייחוד 34 (להלן: גונקל, אגדות בראשית); וכן, דיון בסוגיה זו, פלג, עלייה וירידה, 65.

אם באָמנות הציור. מאטיס הרבה בציוריו להשתמש בתופעה זו. רמון-קינן[2] מציינת כי, ניתן לתאר מונח זה בסיפורת כסוג של אנלוגיה: „המקבילה למשהו בדומה לציורו המפורסם של מאטיס – ציור של חדר, שעל אחד מכתליו תלויה גרסה מיניאטורית של הציור עצמו."

המדובר בדגם ספרותי המוכר בשם: „סיפור בתוך סיפור." בדגם זה ה„סיפור בתוך סיפור" עשוי גם לתפקד כ„מיזאנאבים." כלומר, „מיזאנאבים" הוא „סיפור מיניאטורי," הדומה ל„סיפור המסגרת" בתוכו הוא משובץ. מכיוון שקיימת אנלוגיה בין השניים, „מיזאנאבים" משקף (כמראָה) את המבנה או הנושא המרכזי של „סיפור המסגרת."

אבקש להראות כי סיפור חלום יעקב, ובמיוחד המראֶה בו, מתפקד כתמצית קומפקטית המשקפת באופן סימבולי את „סיפורי האבות" בנושא: היחס לעלייתם ולירידתם של האבות מן הארץ. מוצע בזה לראות את סיפור חלום יעקב, ובייחוד את המראֶה בחלום, כמיזאנאבים, כלומר, כסיפור מיניאטורי המשובץ בתוך „סיפורי האבות" על פי הדגם הספרותי של „סיפור בתוך סיפור." וליתר דיוק, המראֶה בחלום משקף באופן קומפקטי וסימבולי את היחס ליציאתם ולכניסתם של האבות לארץ המובטחת במסגרת „סיפורי האבות."

אקדים ואציין כי אף מבחינת „ההקשר הסיפורי": „התיאור הוויזואלי" בחלום בו נראים „מלאכי אלהים עולים ויורדים" מופיע כשיעקב נמצא בדרכו לחרן, כלומר לקראת יציאתו מן הארץ והאל אומר לו במפורש: „ושמרתיך בכל אשר תלך והשבתיך אל האדמה הזאת" (כח, טו). נפתח בתיאור החלום ופשרו, ולאחר מכן, נרחיב את מעגל הפרשנות ונתבונן בשיבוצו של החלום במסגרת סיפורי האבות, ובתִפקודו כ„מיזאנאבים." אבקש להראות כי, מיקוד המבט ב„מראֶה" של חלום יעקב בבית אל, והבנתו כ„חלום סימבולי," חושפים היבט חדש, שמסייע בפיצוח החלום ופשרו.

האם חלום יעקב הוא „חלום התגלות" או „חלום סימבולי"?

חקר הדיווחים על חלומות בספרות המקרא והמזרח הקדום כאחד,[3] מלמד כי ניתן לסווג את החלומות לשני סוגים עיקריים: האחד „חלומות התגלות," או „חלומות נבואיים" בו מתגלה

recht, 1981) 317–33; Ann Jefferson, "Mise en abyme and the Prophetic in Narrative," *Style* 17 (1983) 196–208; Mieke Bal, *Narratology, Introduction to the Theory of Narrative*, trans. Christine van Boheemen (Toronto: Univ. of Toronto Press, 1985), בל (עמוד 146) מגדירה „מיזאנאבים" = "Mirror-Text„. Lucien Dallenbach, *The Mirror In The Text*, trans. Jeremy Whiteley with Emmy Hughes (Cambridge: Polity Press, 1989), "'mise en abyme' is any aspect enclosed within a work that shows a similarity with the work that contains it." Mieke Bal, "Reflections on Reflection: The Mise en Abyme," *On Meaning-Making, Essays in Semiotics* (Sonoma, Calif.: Polebridge Press, 1994) 45–58; Jean-Pierre Sonnet, "The Book Within the Book, Writing in Deuteronomy," *BibInt* 14 (1997); Edward L. Greenstein, "The Retelling of the Flood Story in the Gilgamesh Epic," in J. Magness and S. Gitin, eds., *Hesed Ve-Emet, Studies in Honor Of Ernest S. Frerichs* (Atlanta, Ga.: Scholars Press, 1998) 197–204. גרינשטיין מגדיר „מיזאנאבים": „סמל, או מבנה שבדרך כלשהי משקף בצורה מרוכזת, קומפקטית, מיניאטורית, את המבנה הגדול"; וכן, מאמרי, יצחק פלג, „עוד ארבעים יום ונינוה נהפכת," בית מקרא, קנח (תשנ"ט) 226–243 (להלן: פלג, „עוד ארבעים יום").

2 שלומית רמון-קינן, הפואטיקה של הסיפורת בימינו (תל אביב: הוצאת ספרית הפועלים, תשמ"ד). רמון-קינן (עמוד 19) מגדירה „מיזאנאבים": „שיקוף מיניאטורי." עדיף, כנראה, לתרגם „שיקוף מִזערי," הקרוב בצלילו למונח הצרפתי „מיזאנאבים."

3 על כך ראה: Leo Oppenheim, *The Interpretation of Dreams in the Ancient Near East: With a*

„עלייה וירידה"
מפתח לפתרון חלום יעקב

יצחק פלג
המכללה האקדמית בית ברל, ישראל

"Going Up and Going Down"
A Key to Interpreting Jacob's Dream

Yitzhak Peleg
Beit Berl College, Israel

A close study of Jacob's dream (Genesis 28:10–22) enables, from a literary perspective, two simultaneous readings and therefore two interpretations. Reading A: Jacob's dream is a "dream theophany." The story describes and means to explain how Beth-El became a sacred place; a story whose core is the *maqom* (place). Reading B: Jacob's dream is a "symbolic dream." The story tells about Jacob leaving Canaan (his homeland) in order to return in the future, a story whose core is the *derek* (way).

The description of the *sullam*, and especially that of the movement of the angels, is not embellishment, supplementation or scenic background, of God's message, but "the vision" symbolizes the way, the path, taken by the patriarchs to and from the Promised Land. That is to say, the *sullam* symbolizes "the way" to and from the Promised Land, and the symbolic message of the "Angels of God" in the dream is reflected in their actual movements. The vision in the dream (vv. 12–13a) functions as a *mise en abyme*. In a compact and symbolic manner, the vision in the dream reflects the attitude towards the patriarch's entering and leaving the promised land in the framework of the wider narrative.

„מיזאנאבים" מהו? – „שיקוף מזערי"

סיפור „חלום יעקב" (בראשית כח, י–כב), ובעיקר תיאור „המרְאֶה" בחלום (פס׳ יב–יג$_{א}$), מתפקד כ„מיז-אנ-אבים" (*mise en abyme*). מונח זה הוגדר לראשונה, כבר בשנות הארבעים של המאה ה-20, על ידי הסופר הצרפתי אנדרי ז׳יד (Andre' Gide). מכיוון שהשימוש במונח „מיזאנאבים" חדש הוא בחקר הסיפור המקראי, ראוי להקדיש לו כמה מילות הסבר. „מיזאנאבים"[1] הוא מונח, שמקורו אינו בתחום חקר המקרא ואף לא באָמנות הספרות, כי

1 להלן, ביבליוגרפיה מומלצת על „מזאנאבים": John Barth, "Tales Within Tales Within Tales," *Antaeus* 43 (1981) 45–63; Gregoire Rouiller, "Parabole et Mise En Abyme," in Pierre Casetti, Othmar Keel and Adrian Schenker, eds., *Melanges Dominique Barthelemy* (Gottingen: Vandenhoeck & Rup-

לאור ממצאים אלו, ניתן להציע הצעה חדשה בדרך הפרשנות המדעית לסוגיות תלמודיות, שבהן דיון בדעותיהם של רב נחמן ורב ששת. המאפיינים המתודולוגיים שבדרך לימודם של השניים, מסייעים להבהרת יסודות חשיבתם ההלכתית, ובעיקר לסוגיות המעלות קושי או דוחק בסוגיות התלמוד. להצעתנו, יש לדון כל מקרה לגופו, על פי השקפה רחבה של דרך לימודם בתלמוד, ולא רק על פי ראייה נקודתית, התולה את מקור דעתם – במקרה של קושי או דוחק – בפעולת עריכה „אינרפולטיבית" של עורך/עורכים מאוחרים.[113] שיטה כזו אף כאילו מניחה מראש, שדרכי הלימוד בקרב אמוראי בבל הם אחידים, מה שמנוגד לממצאי כמה מחקרים שנכתבו בנושא זה עד כה.[114] ושמא אין זו אלא דוגמא מייצגת לתרומה אפשרית שיש לחקר דרכי הלימוד בבבל על פרשנות מדעית של סוגיות התלמוד בכלל.

מאמר זה הינו עיבוד של פרק מעבודת דוקטור על רב ששת ודרכי לימודו.[115] תודתי לפרופ' שלמה זלמן הבלין מהמחלקה לתלמוד על הנחייתו בכתיבת העבודה. כמו-כן, תודתי למורי, פרופ' מ"ש פלדבלום (ז"ל), שקרא בזמנו כמה פרקים מן העבודה, והעיר הערות מאירות עיניים. מחקר זה נכתב בסיוע קרן הזכרון לתרבות יהודית, ותודתי נתונה בזאת להם.

העובדה שכל אמורא נוקט בדרך עקיבה בפרשנותו למקורות תנאיים, דווקא נראית כמאששת את מהימנות המקורות, ואין כאן המקום להאריך.

113 מובן, שאין אנו באים לעשות הכללה, ויש לבחון כל מקרה ומקרה לגופו. כלומר: איננו טוענים שכל „סתמא" היא בהכרח מאוחרת, שהרי יסודה – מבחינת תוכנה – יכול להיות קדום; וכן לחילופין, לא כל מימרא של אמורא, כל כולה, מקורה ממנו, ויתכן שנשתרבבו בה קטעים מן ה„סתמא." ראה בעניין זה: יעקב זוסמן, „ושוב לירושלמי נזיקין," בתוך יעקב זוסמן ודוד רוזנטל, עורכים, מחקרי תלמוד (ירושלים: הוצאת ספרים ע"ש י"ל מאגנס, האוניברסיטה העברית, תש"ן) עמ' 109, הערה 204.

114 נביא רק כמה דוגמאות מובהקות: כהן, „מר בר רב אשי," עמ' 143 ואילך; אברהם גולדברג, „שימושו של רבא ב,תוספתא' וב,תנא דבי שמואל' לפירוש המשנה," תרביץ מ (תשל"א) עמ' 144–157; אברהם גולדברג, „גישותיהם השונות של רבי יוחנן ושל ריש לקיש לשאלת יחסה של המשנה אל התוספתא ואל הברייתא," דברי הקונגרס העולמי השביעי למדעי היהדות, ג (ירושלים: הוצאת ספרים ע"ש י"ל מאגנס, האוניברסיטה העברית, תשמ"א) עמ' 109–116; דוד הנשקה, „אביי ורבא-שתי גישות למשנת התנאים," תרביץ מט (תש"מ) עמ' 187–193; כהן, „רב ששת ודרכי לימודו"; יעקב אלמן, „רבא ודרכי העיון הארץ ישראליות במדרש הלכה," בתוך ישיעה גפני, עורך, מרכז ותפוצה: ארץ ישראל והתפוצות בימי בית שני המשנה והתלמוד (ירושלים: מרכז זלמן שזר לתולדות ישראל, תשס"ד) עמ' 217–242; כהן, „אמוראי נהרדעא האחרונים."

115 ראה: כהן, „רב ששת ודרכי לימודו."

מאמוראי בבל להקל בהלכה ביחס לראשי הגולה ולאנשי ביתם (אפילו בניגוד למקורות תנאיים מפורשים!), מתוך מידת כבוד והערכה שזכו לה מתוקף מעמדם וסמכותם,[108] מה שידוע באופן ספציפי ביחס לרב נחמן.[109]

יוצא, אפוא, שגם המחלוקת שלפנינו – שאיננה ויכוח תיאורטי בלבד – מציגה עמדה „פורמלית" ו„שמרנית" של רב ששת, הנצמדת אל מובנה המילולי של הברייתא („על גביהן"), לעומת עמדת רב נחמן, המהווה פיתוח והרחבה של ההלכה התנאית.

דרך לימודו השמרנית של רב ששת מאפיינת את כלל תרומתו הספרותית לתלמודים, והיא באה לידי ביטוי גם במגוון רחב של תחומים ונושאים.[110] כמו-כן, בניגוד למה שמקובל להניח,[111] לא מצאנו בעניין זה הבדל בין הכרעה הלכתית שניתנה על ידו במסגרת דיון אקדמי בבעיה תיאורטית, לבין פסיקה שנתן במעשה בית דין, או בשאלה קונקרטית אחרת שהובאה לפניו לשם הכרעה. מתברר, שדרך לימודו של רב ששת הייתה עקבית ובלתי תלויה באופייה של השאלה שהועלתה בפניו.

רב נחמן, לעומתו, נראה כבעל גישה הלכתית „גמישה" יותר, הנוטה לפתח ולהרחיב את ההלכה התנאית באמצעות פרשנות הנראית מבוססת על הסברה. במסגרת גישה זו, הוא נוטה להעניק פרשנות דחוקה, שאיננה עולה בקנה אחד עם משמעותו הפשטנית של המקור התנאי, וע"י כך נוצרת משמעות חדשה, במטרה ליישם אותה גם בבעיה שלפניו. נטייה זו מצאנו אצלו גם בעשרות סוגיות נוספות לאורך ספרותו בבבלי, והיא משתלבת עם מחקרים נוספים שעסקו בתרומתו של רב נחמן לגיבושה ולהתפתחותה של ההלכה התנאית בבבל, בעיקר על בסיס דרכי הסברה וההיגיון. אפשר שתופעות אלו היו כרוכות גם באישיותו המיוחדת של רב נחמן בדורו.[112]

108 ראה: משה בר, „כבוד ובקורת," PAAJR 38 (1972) עמ' 47-57; בר, ראשות הגולה, עמ' 171 ואילך.

109 ראה: גייגר, „רב נחמן בר יעקב," עמ' 61.

110 ראה: כהן, „רב ששת ודרכי לימודו."

111 ראה: יחיאל גוטמן, „שאלות אקדימיות בתלמוד," דביר 1 (תרפ"ג) עמ' 43; Ben-Menahem, *Judicial Deviation*, 34.

112 יש מי שמטיל ספק בייחוס המימרות לאמוראים בתלמוד הבבלי, ראה, למשל: William Scott Green, "What's in a Name? — The Problematic of Rabbinic 'Biography,'" in Green, *Approaches to Ancient Judaism: Theory and Practice* (Missoula: Scholars Press, 1978) 77–96; Jacob Neusner, "Evaluating the Attributions of Sayings to Named Sages in the Rabbinic Literature," *JSJ* 26 (1995) 93–111.

אנו דוגלים בשיטה המסורתית, שאיננה מפקפקת באופן גורף בייחוס המימרות לאמוראים, אלא אם כן יש לכך סיבות ספציפיות בסוגיה הנידונה. המחקרים השונים של הבבלי (כרונולוגיה, טרמינולוגיה, שכבות ספרותיות, יחסי הירדכיה, ועוד) נוטים יותר ויותר לתמוך באמינות של ייחוס המימרות לאמוראים בתלמוד (אם כי יש להיזהר ולבדוק כל מקרה ומקרה לגופו). לסקירה של כמה מחקרים חשובים בנושא זה, ראה: Yaakov Elman, "How Should a Talmudic Intellectual History be Written? A Response to David Kraemer's Responses," *JQR* 89 (1999) 378. על המצויין שם, יש להוסיף גם: אבינועם כהן, „ביקורת הלכתית לעומת ביקורת ספרותית בסוגיות התלמוד," אסופות ג (תשמ"ט) עמ' שמו, הערה 75; Richard Kalmin, "Rabbinic Literature of Late Antiquity as A Source for Historical Study," in Jacob Neusner and Alan J. Avery-Peck, eds., *Judaism in Late Antiquity* (Leiden: Brill, 1999) 187–99; יונתן קלמן, „האוקימתא האמוראית ,הכא במאי עסקינן' המתייחסת למקורות התנאיים – טיבה, אופייה וצורתה" (עבודת דוקטור; רמת-גן: אוניברסיטת בר-אילן, תשס"ב) עמ' 353-354; Cohen, "Was Age the Decisive Criterion," 289, n. 35; כהן, „רב ששת ודרכי לימודו," עמ' טז-יז; דוד הלבני, „עיונים בהתהוות התלמוד," סידרא כ (תשס"ה) עמ' 69-70. ובכלל, מחקר זה פותח צוהר לשאלת המקורות האמוראיים בבבלי.

או אין צריכין ליגע? רב נחמן אמר: אין צריכין ליגע, ורב ששת אמר: צריכין ליגע. אזל רב נחמן ועבד עובדא בי ריש גלותא כשמעתיה. אמר ליה רב ששת לשמעיה, רב גדא: זיל שלוף שדינהו. אשכחוהו דבי ריש גלותא חבשוהו. אזל רב ששת קם אבבא, אמר ליה: גדא, פוק תא! נפק אתא. אשכחיה רב ששת לרבה בר שמואל,[102] אמר ליה: תני מר מידי בצורת הפתח? אמר ליה: אין, תנינא: כיפה: רבי מאיר מחייב במזוזה, וחכמים פוטרין. ושוין שאם יש ברגליה עשרה שהיא חייבת...[103] אמר ליה: אי משכחת להו, לא תימא להו לבי ריש גלותא ולא מידי מהא מתניתא דכיפה.[104]

בניגוד לרב נחמן, עמדת רב ששת היא, שעל המשקוף העליון ש„בצורת הפתח" לגעת בשתי הקורות שמתחתיה. מהמשך הסיפור עולה מידת נחישותו ותקיפותו של רב ששת, בשעה שציוה על שמשו, רב גדא, לפרק את מבנה „צורת הפתח" שבבית ראש הגולה, שנעשה על פי הוראת רב נחמן. מעשהו של רב ששת נראה כמעשה הפגנתי המופנה לא רק כלפי בית ראש הגולה, אלא אף כלפי רב נחמן, הסמכות ההלכתית שהתירה בניית סוג כזה של „צורת פתח".[105]

אם נשפוט על פי דרכו של רב ששת בפסיקת ההלכה, נראה שעמדתו נובעת מהיצמדותו למשמעותן הפשוטה של המלים שבברייתא: „...וקנה מכאן וקנה על גביהן." כלומר, קנה מכל צד, ואחד מונח על גביהן, כפי שאכן עולה ממשמעות הביטוי „על גבי" בספרות התנאית בכלל.[106] עמדת רב נחמן נראית כאן כחידוש הלכתי, שלא מצאנו לה יסוד (לפחות לא מפורש) במסורת תנאית ארצישראלית כלשהי.

לכאורה, ניתן היה להציע כאפשרות, שיסוד דעתו של רב נחמן הוא בפרשנות אמוראית לברייתת כיפה, המוצגת בדבריו של אביי בהמשך הסוגיה שם, התולה את דברי ר' מאיר וחכמים בדין „חוקקין להשלים" ומכאן למסקנה שאין חובה על המשקוף העליון לגעת בשתי הקורות שמתחתיו. ואולם, לייב מוסקוביץ הראה, שלעקרון בבלי מופשט זה („חוקקין להשלים") אין אחיזה במסורת התנאית הארצישראלית, וספק אם זה אכן מובנה המקורי של הברייתא הנידונה.[107] ייתכן שפסקו של רב נחמן הוא חלק ממגמה כללית של כמה

102 בכ"י וטיקן 127 איתא: „לרבה."

103 המקבילה לברייתא זו מצויה בשינויים במסכת מזוזה א, ז (מיכאל היגער, מסכתות קטנות [ירושלים: מקור, תשל"א] עמ' לח).

104 המשפט: „אי משכחת..." ליתא בכי"י מינכן 95, כ"י אוקספורד ודפוסים ישנים. ראה: צור, אור ישראל, עמ' 97.

105 על מעמדו של רב נחמן בבית ראש הגולה, ראה לעיל הערה 16.

106 הבדיקה נעשתה באמצעות פרויקט השו"ת של אוניברסיטת בר-אילן, והיא מתייחסת להופעת הביטוי „על גביהן" (או „על גבי") בספרות התנאית כולה. מספרם הכולל מגיע לכ-100 הופעות. בדיקתם מלמדת, שמשמעות הביטוי היא: נוגע, מונח על..., וזאת למעט המקרים המתייחסים למשמעות ספיריטואלית. בבבלי, ב"מ כה ע"ב, נמצאת ברייתא חשובה לענייננו, ושם נאמר: „...דתניא: מצא מעות מפוזרות – הרי אלו שלו, כאבני בית קוליס – חייב להכריז. ואלו הן אבני בית קוליס: אחת מכאן ואחת מכאן ואחת על גביהן." אין צריך לומר, שהכוונה – כמו במקרה שלנו – למשמעות זהה: „מונח על..." יצויין עוד, שמשמעות זו עולה אף מהופעתו של הביטוי במקור אמוראי. המקור (בבלי, עירובין ח ע"ב) מציג „איבעיא" של רמי בר חמא, אמורא בן הדור השלישי-רביעי, לרבו, רב חסדא, בן דורו של רב ששת: „בעא מיניה רמי בר חמא מרב חסדא: נעץ שתי יתידות בשני כותלי מבוי מבחוץ, והניח קורה על גביהן מהו?" ראה פירוש המיוחס לר"ח ורש"י על אתר. וראה גם: שמואל קרויס, קדמוניות התלמוד (ב' כרכים; ברלין-וינה: הוצאת בנימין הרץ, תרפ"ד) ב:346.

107 ראה: Moscovitz, *Talmudic Reasoning*, 192, n. 116.

היצמדותו של רב ששת אל ההלכה התנאית, מומחשת גם בביקורת שמתח על אמוראים שונים וכלפי בית ראש הגולה. ביקורותיו על בית ראש הגולה (שבע פעמים) – למעט מקרה יחיד – מושתתות על מקורות תנאיים.[94] בכל פעם שנראה היה לרב ששת שקיימת סתירה בין הנוהג המצוי בבית ראש הגולה לבין הלכה תנאית הנקוטה בידו, הוא ביקר את הנוהג, ולעתים אפילו בצורה בוטה. בשני מקרים בלטה התנהגותו בצורה הפגנתית בבית ראש הגולה, שכוונה גם כלפי רב נחמן. באירוע אחד, הוא ציווה על שמשו לפרק מבנה של „צורת הפתח" שנעשה בבית ראש הגולה על פי הוראתו של רב נחמן.[95] במקרה אחר, הוא סירב לאכול על שולחנו של ראש הגולה מבשר שהובא לפניו ביו"ט שני של גליות.[96] עם זאת, אין לשלול את האפשרות, שנוסף על גורם זה, היתה תגובתו החריפה במקרים אלו כרוכה גם באישיותו הביקורתית והתקיפה של רב ששת.[97] ועוד זאת מצאנו, שביקורותיו אינן מופנות כלפי אישיות ספציפית אחת, ואף לא רק כלפי אנשי ביתו של ראש הגולה, אלא אף כלפי חכמים ששהו במחיצתו בעת היותו שם.[98]

נתונים אלו ממעיטים מתוקפה של הטענה, שהביקורת נובעת ממניע אישי או פוליטי כלשהו, כפי שהציע יעקב ניוזנר.[99] אדרבה, היא יכולה להצטרף לטיעונים דלעיל, שהביקורת עניינית, והיא תוצאה ישירה מדרך לימודו של רב ששת – המשקל הדומיננטי שהוא נתן למקורות התנאיים – שלא ראה לאפשר התנהגות הסותרת את המסורות הללו. כלומר, את התנהגותו ההפגנתית של רב ששת בבית ראש הגולה, שכוונו גם אל רב נחמן, יש לראות על רקע ענייני, הנובע מדרך לימודו. נביא כאן דוגמא אחת:

בבלי, עירובין יא ע"ב

תנא:[100] צורת הפתח שאמרו – קנה מכאן וקנה מכאן וקנה על גביהן.[101] צריכין ליגע

הביע עמדות שונות ומגוונות באשר ליחסם של הסיפורים זה לזה ולמעמדם ההיסטורי. להרחבת הדיון בנושא זה, ראה: ווייס, לחקר התלמוד, עמ' 273; Neusner, *A History of the Jews in Babylonia*, 3:311; יהונתן עץ-חיים, סוגיות מוחלפות במסכת נזיקין: שלש הבבות (לוד: מכון הברמן למחקרי ספרות, תש"ס) עמ' 224–220; ולר, נשים בחברה היהודית, עמ' 64. יודגש, שאף לגירסא זו, פסקו של רב ששת מבוסס על דברי משנה מפורשת, כפירוש הגאונים. ראה: בנימין מנשה לוין, אוצר הגאונים, מסכת כתובות (ירושלים: מוסד הרב קוק, תרצ"ט) עמ' 328.

94 לניתוח ביקורותיו בבית ראש הגולה, ראה: כהן, „רב ששת ודרכי לימודו," עמ' 207–233.

95 בבלי, עירובין יא ע"ב.

96 בבלי, שם לט ע"ב.

97 על אישיותו של רב ששת, ראה: כהן, „רב ששת ודרכי לימודו," עמ' 29–30.

98 כהן, „רב ששת ודרכי לימודו," עמ' 230.

99 Neusner, *A History of the Jews in Babylonia*, 3:69–73; 4:79–80.

100 בדפוסים שאלוניקי וויניציאה ובכמה גרסאות ראשונים נוספו המלים: „אמר להו." לגירסא זו, הברייתא היא חלק ממו"מ קודם בין רב אחא בריה דרב אויא לבין תלמידי רב אשי, כשהראשון מציג ראיה מן הברייתא לרב אשי לפיו, אין צורת הפתח מחייבת „היכר ציר." ראה: אורי צור, אור ישראל: שיקול הדעת בעריכת סוגיות במסכת עירובין בתלמוד הבבלי, פרקים א–ג (לוד: מכון הברמן למחקרי ספרות, תש"ס) עמ' 101–102 (לנוסחאות הראשונים, ראה צור, שם, עמ' 95, הערה 94).

101 מסורת זו היא מקבילה של הלכה ארצישראלית משמם של כמה אמוראים בירושלמי, עירובין א, א (יח ע"ד), ושם איתא: „...צורת הפתח שאמרו קנה מכאן וקנה מכאן וגמייא על גביהן." גירסת הרשב"א למסורת ארצישראלית זו היא כבבבלי: „...וקנה על גביהן." ראה: שאול ליברמן, הירושלמי כפשוטו: שבת עירובין פסחים (ירושלים: דרום, תרצ"ה) עמ' 227.

על פי הלכה זו, שכיב מרע ש„כתב כל נכסיו לאחרים" רשאי לחזור בו ממתנתו רק אם הבריא ממחלתו. מכאן טענתו של רב ששת כלפי רב נחמן: „אי משום דהדרא בה – והא שכיבא!" על פי המשנה קיימת רק אפשרות אחת שבה רשאי שכיב מרע לחזור בו ממתנתו – במקרה שהבריא,[87] אבל הרי אימו של רמי בר חמא נפטרה ולא הבריאה, ומדוע לקיים את צוואתה השנייה?[88]

המחקר שעסק בסוגיה זו, ראה את דברי רב נחמן בשם שמואל כמייצגים התפתחות הלכתית מאוחרת ביחס להלכה התנאית, המכירה באפשרותו של שכיב מרע לחזור בו ממתנתו הראשונה עוד בשעת חוליו.[89] יעקב אלמן אף הצביע על המקבילה לדעתו של רב נחמן בדין הססאני, שאומצה על ידו במקרה זה.[90] מכל מקום, לעניינו חשובה העובדה, שרב נחמן (כמו רב ששת), אינו מכיר מסורת תנאית כלשהי בעניין זה, ומצטט את דברי שמואל, כנדבך משלים לדברי המשנה.[91] על הסברה העומדת בבסיס הלכה זו בשם שמואל, כותב שלום אלבק:

> ...שכיב מרע יכול לחזור בו ממתנתו, לא רק כשעמד מחליו אלא אף בשעת חליו בהיותו שכיב מרע כל זמן שלא מת... טעמו של דבר מפני מה אומדים את דעתו, שמן הסתם נתכוון לתנאי שלעולם יוכל לחזור בו אפילו לא עמד מחליו, שכן על דעת כן נתן, שאם יצטרך לנכסים לעצמו יוכל לחזור בו, ואם הוא חוזר בו מן הסתם הוא סבור שיחיה, אף על פי שלא עמד והבריא, ויצטרך לנכסים. לפיכך יכול לחזור בו.[92]

לסיכום, במקרה זה, כבמקרים הקודמים, רב ששת מציג עמדה הלכתית מחמירה, שאינה מאפשרת לשכיב מרע לבטל – עוד בשעת חוליו – את מתנתו הראשונה. היא נראית מבוססת על גישה פורמלית, הנצמדת אל לשון ההלכה התנאית שבמשנה. רב נחמן, לעומתו, מייצג הלכה גמישה יותר ומתפתחת (באמצעות שמואל), המאפשרת – על יסוד אומדן דעתו של השכיב מרע בשעת חוליו – לחזור בו ממתנתו הראשונה, ולהעניקה מחדש „בין לעצמו בין לאחר".[93]

87 כפי שהבינוה גם בירושלמי, פאה ג, ט (יז ע"ד). אריה אדרעי, „'מצווה לקיים דברי המת': על תוקפה של הצוואה בספרות חז"ל," HUCA 69 (1998) עמ' קיא, מפרש משנה זו באופן שונה, אבל הוא מודע לעובדה, שלא כך נתפרשה משנה זו בתלמודים (שם, הערה 31).

88 ראה גם את דברי הרשב"ם, שם, ד"ה: „והא מתה" (ע"פ דפוס ראשון [ונציה ר"פ]), שכתב: „דבשלמא אם לא מתה – תנן: לא שייר קרקע כל שהוא – אין מתנתו מתנה, וכמו שחזרה מן הראשון כשנתנה לשיני, תחזור בה מן השני נמי אם תרצה. אבל עתה שמתה – תתקיים מתנה ראשונה, ויקנה ראשון, שהרי היא נותנת במתנת בריא ודבריה ככתובין וכמסורין, וכשמתה לא אמרינן דייתיקי מבטלת דייתיקי. הכי סבירא ליה."

89 ראה, למשל, את דברי Yaron, *Gifts in Contemplation of Death*, 61. עוד למשמעויות העולות מהתפתחות הלכתית מאוחרת זו, המיוצגת כאן בדברי שמואל, ראה: ריבלין, הירושה, עמ' 146–147. והשווה: אשר גולאק, השטרות בתלמוד: לאור הפפירוסים היווניים ממצרים ולאור המשפט היווני והרומי, עורך: רנון קצוף (ירושלים: מאגנס, תשנ"ד) עמ' 157 ואילך. לניתוח המסורת התנאית שבתוספתא, ב"ב ח, י–יא (מהדורת שאול ליברמן, עמ' 157–158), ראה: Yaron, *Gifts in Contemplation of Death*, 25, 65.

90 ראה: יעקב אלמן, „ישיבות בבבל ובתי דין פרסיים בתקופה האמוראית והבתר-אמוראית," בתוך: עמנואל אטקס, עורך, ישיבות ובתי מדרשות (ירושלים: מרכז זלמן שזר לתולדות ישראל, מרכז דינור לחקר תולדות ישראל והאוניברסיטה העברית, תשס"ו) עמ' 49–50.

91 כמודגש גם בדבריו של Yaron, *Gifts in Contemplation of Death*, 73.

92 שלום אלבק, יסודות בדיני הממונות בתלמוד (רמת-גן: אוניברסיטת בר-אילן, תשנ"ד) עמ' 328.

93 בבבלי, כתובות צד ע"ב, מופיע נוסח שונה לסיפור זה, והשינויים נוגעים בעיקר לחלקו האחרון. המחקר

רב ששת הוא היחיד מבין האמוראים בסוגיה, המציג ראיה ממקור תנאי. הנחתו היא, שחובת התופש (או התופשים) בנכסי הגר היא, להחזיר את הנכסים מיד לאחר שנודע שיש לגר בן או שאשתו מעוברת, כיון שהעובר כבר זכה בהם, וכלשונו של הרשב״ם, שם, ד״ה „חייב להחזיר״: „כיון דאשתו מעוברת – עובר יורש הוי. אלמא, המזכה לעובר – קנה.״ בהתאם לכך מוסברת הסיפא של הברייתא לפיה, אם החזירו את כל הנכסים, ואחר כך שמעו שוב שמת בנו או שהפילה אשתו – המחזיק בשניה זכה, ולא זה שבראשונה, כיון „דאיגלאי מילתא שהיה לו בן או עובר. ואף על גב דסוף מת העובר בבטן... כיורש גמור חשיב ליה, ומרע לחזקת מחזיקי ראשונה. אלמא, עובר יורש, כרב ששת״ (שם, ד״ה: „בראשונה״).[83] אכן, גם הירושלמי ראה בהלכה שבברייתא סתירה לעמדתו של ר׳ אלעזר הסבור ש„אין זכין בעוברין.״ תירוץ הסתירה המובא שם – „שנייה היא הכא שהוא בנו״ – נדחה, ולמסקנה שם, עומדים בעינם דבריו של שמואל, הסבור – כרב ששת – ש„זכין בעוברין.״

נסיים את הדיון בסעיף הנוכחי בדוגמא נוספת, מן המישור הקונקרטי, שבו הכריעו השניים במעשה בית דין שהובא לפניהם. בניגוד למקרים הקודמים, רב נחמן הציג כבסיס לעמדתו מקור רישומי – מסורת הלכה בשם שמואל, אלא שאף היא מהווה התפתחות הלכתית מאוחרת להלכה התנאית.

בבלי, שם קנא ע״א

אימיה[84] דרמי בר חמא באורתא כתבתינהו לנכסה לרמי בר חמא, בצפרא כתבתינהו לרב עוקבא בר חמא.

אתא רמי בר חמא לקמיה דרב ששת, אוקמיה בנכסי.

אזל רב עוקבא בר חמא קמיה דרב נחמן, אוקמיה בנכסי.

אתא רב ששת לקמיה דרב נחמן, אמר ליה: מאי טעמא אוקמיה מר לרב עוקבא בר חמא? אי משום דהדרא בה – והא שכיבא![85]

אמר ליה: הכי אמר שמואל: כל שאילו עמד חוזר – חוזר במתנתו.

אימור דאמר שמואל – לעצמו, לאחר מי אמר?

אמר ליה: בפירוש אמר שמואל: בין לעצמו בין לאחר.

הסוגיה שלפנינו מתארת הכרעה הלכתית הפוכה של שני בני הפלוגתא – רב נחמן ורב ששת. כיצד ניתן לפרש את פסיקותיהם השונות של כל אחד מן החולקים בסוגיה? רב ששת הכריע לטובת רמי בר חמא, דהיינו, על פי צוואתה הראשונה של האם. אם לשפוט על פי דרך לימודו, נראה, שהאחרון היה צמוד אל ההלכה במשנה, שעליה מוסב הדיון התלמודי:

> שכיב מרע שכתב נכסיו לאחרים, שייר קרקע כל שהוא – מתנתו קיימת. לא שייר קרקע כל שהוא – אין מתנתו קיימת.[86]

של העובר בהלכה היהודית ובמשפט הישראלי,״ סיני קטו (תשנ״ה) עמ׳ ריט-רכ.

83 ראה גם: ריבלין, הירושה, עמ׳ 104.

84 בשאילתות דרב אחאי גאון, בראשית, ויחי, לו (מהדורת מירסקי, עמ׳ 254) איתא: „כי הא דאימיה דרמי בר חמא.״ על תפקודם של מעשי בית דין בתלמוד הבבלי, המובאים באמצעות המונח „כי הא ד...,״ ראה: Eliezer Segal, "The Use of the Formula *Ki ha de* in the Citation of Cases in the Babylonian Talmud," *HUCA* 50 (1979) 199–218.

85 המשפט „אי משום... והא שכיבא״ נעדר בכ״י מינכן 95, פירנצה 7, אסקוריאל G-I-3 ווטיקן 115.

86 משנה, בבא בתרא ט, ו. ראה גם: משנה, פאה ג, ז.

כך עשה תשובה –„אין קרבנו ריח ניחוח, נעשה משרת לעבודת כוכבים," כלשון הגמרא.[75]

בבלי, ב"ב קמא ע"ב

משנה: אם תלד אשתי זכר יטל מנה, ילדה זכר – נוטל מנה; נקבה מאתים, ילדה נקבה – נוטלת מאתים.

גמרא: ... דאמר רב נחמן: המזכה לעובר – לא קנה, „לכשתלד" – קנה, ורב הונא אמר: אף „לכשתלד" – לא קנה, ורב ששת אמר: אחד זה ואחד זה – קנה.[76]

אמר רב ששת: מנא אמינא לה – דתניא: גר שמת ובזבזו ישראל נכסיו, ושמעו שיש לו בן או שהיתה אשתו מעוברת – חייבין להחזיר. החזירו הכל, ואחר כך שמעו שמת בנו או שהפילה אשתו, החזיק בשניה – קנה, ובראשונה – לא קנה.[77] [ואי סלקא דעתך עובר לא קני, למה להו אחזוקי בשניה, הא אחזיקו להו חדא זימנא!][78]

אמר אביי: ירושה הבאה מאיליה שאני. רבא אמר: שאני התם, דרפויי מרפיאן בידייהו מעיקרא.

סוגיה זו נידונה רבות במחקר, ולפיכך נמקד את הדיון בעמדתו ההלכתית של רב ששת, הרלוונטית לדיון כאן. התלמוד מעלה כאן שאלה משפטית, שלא נידונה במפורש בספרות התנאית:[79] „המזכה לעובר" – האם קנה אם לאו. בניגוד לדעותיהם של רב הונא, רב נחמן, ר' יוחנן (ובירושלמי: ר' אלעזר),[80] נצמד רב ששת – בעל הגישה ה„פורמליסטית" – אל ההלכה שבמשנה. הוא אינו עורך הבחנה משפטית בין המזכה לעובר סתם, כבעיה תיאורטית כללית, לבין המזכה לבנו או לבתו שבמשנה, ולדעתו, כשם שעובר שהוא בנו – קונה, אותו הדין תקף גם על עובר בכלל.[81] בהתאם לתפישה זו, מובן מדוע הראיה מן הברייתא שרב ששת הציג לעמדתו, מבוססת גם היא על עובר שהוא בנו.

עמדותיהם של רב הונא ורב נחמן – מקורם בסברה, ומכאן ניסיונותיהם של החוקרים להתחקות אחר הבסיס המשפטי של עמדותיהם. רב הונא סבור, ש„המזכה לעובר" – לא קנה, „דכיון דבשעת הקנאה עובר הוא ואינו יכול לזכות – לא יקנה לכשיולד" (רשב"ם, שם, ד"ה: „ולימא"). רב נחמן גם הוא סבור, שחלות קניינית איננה קיימת ביחס לעובר, למעט מקרה שבו התנה ואמר „לכשתלד."[82]

ביחזקאל מד 9–14. להרחבת הדברים ראה: כהן, „רב ששת ודרכי לימודו," עמ' 184, הערה 224.

75 לשון הגמ'; שם קט ע"ב. ראה גם: משניות זכר חנוך: קדשים א (ירושלים: וגשל, תשנ"ט) ליקוטים, ד"ה: „לדבר אחר": „לא תנא ע"ז בהדיא לומר דאפילו בשוגג דלא היתה מחשבתו לחטוא לעבוד ע"ז אלא לד"א כלומר כמתעסק דהיינו שוגג, ודייקא מתניתין כרב ששת."

76 בעיה משפטית זו נידונה גם בירושלמי, ב"ב ט, א (טז ע"ד), ובמקבילה שם, יבמות ד, א (ה ע"ג). לדיון משווה בין דיעות האמוראים בסוגיות הנ"ל, ראה: יואל פלורסהיים, „סוגיות בבליות בירושלמי נזיקין," סיני קכ (תשנ"ז) עמ' פא.

77 ברייתא זו מובאת בשינויים גם בתוספתא, כתובות ד, טז (מהדורת ליברמן, עמ' 69–70) ובירושלמי, כתובות ד, א (ה ע"ג), ושם, ב"ב ט, א (טז ע"ד).

78 משפט זה חסר בכי"י מינכן 95, פירנציה 7, המבורג 165 ווטיקן 115.

79 ראה: יוסף ריבלין, הירושה והצוואה במשפט העברי (רמת-גן: אוניברסיטת בר-אילן, תשנ"ט) עמ' 130.

80 ראה לעיל הערה 77.

81 על היחס שבין בעיה עיונית-משפטית זו לבין המקרה הקונקרטי שהובא לפני רב הונא בעמוד הקודם (קמא ע"ב), ראה: Eliezer Segal, *Case Citation in the Babylonian Talmud* (Atlanta: Scholars Press, 1990) 150.

82 לפרשנות המתמקדת בהסבר עמדותיהם של רב הונא ורב נחמן בסוגיה כאן, ראה למשל: אליקים אלינסון, „העובר בהלכה," סיני סו (תש"ל) עמ' כב-כד; אלבק, דיני הממונות, עמ' 306; יעקב בזק, „מעמדו המשפטי

2. **דאתמר:** הזיד בשחיטה: **רב נחמן אמר:** קרבנו ריח ניחוח, **ורב ששת אמר: אין קרבנו ריח ניחוח...**[70]
3. השתחוה לעבודת כוכבים:[71] **רב נחמן אמר: קרבנו ריח ניחוח, ורב ששת אמר: אין קרבנו ריח ניחוח.**
4. הודה לעבודת כוכבים:[72] **רב נחמן אמר: קרבנו ריח ניחוח, ורב ששת אמר: אין קרבנו ריח ניחוח.**

בסוגיה שלפנינו מועלים ארבעה מקרים, בהם ביצע הכהן פעולות שונות לעבודה זרה: בראשונה, זריקת דם בהמה לעבודת כוכבים – בשוגג; בשניה, שחיטה במזיד לעבודת כוכבים; בשלישית, השתחויה לעבודת כוכבים; וברביעית, הודאה לעבודת כוכבים („אמר לה ,אלי אתה"" – רש"י, שם, ד"ה: „הודה").

דעתו של רב ששת היא מחמירה בכל המקרים, ובניגוד לעמדת רב נחמן, היא איננה מכירה בהבחנה הלכתית בין: 1. שימוש לעבודת כוכבים במזיד, למרות שאחר כך עשה תשובה. 2. עבודה שנעשתה בשוגג, וללא כוונת שימוש לעבודת כוכבים. 3. שירות ממשי לעבודת כוכבים, לעומת „דיבורא בעלמא" (שני המקרים האחרונים).

גישת רב ששת נראית צמודה להלכה התנאית שבמשנה, במלים: „כהן ששימש..." – פסול מלהקריב. לפי רב ששת, כל סוג של הקרבה, בלי קשר הכרחי לכוונתו של המשמש או למטרותיו בשעת העבודה, פוסלת אותו מלהמשיך ולהקריב בבית המקדש.[73] ואכן, שיטה זו הוצעה כאן כבר על ידי בעל ה„סתמא" ביחס לשני המקרים הראשונים, ומאוחר יותר היא הורחבה על ידי הפרשנים המסורתיים לסוגיה, גם בשני המקרים האחרונים. ונפרט: בראשון, אף על פי שהזריקה נעשתה בשוגג („זרק דם לעבודת כוכבים בשוגג, דהשתא עבד ליה שירות אלא ששוגג היה"–רש"י, שם, ד"ה: „שגג בזריקה") – „אין קורבנו ריח ניחוח, דנעשה כומר לעבודת כוכבים..."[74] גם במקרה השני, אף על פי שהזיד בשחיטה, ואחר

70 בכ"י מינכן 95 נשמטה מחלוקת רב נחמן ורב ששת, אבל, היא עולה מהמשך הסוגיה, המציגה את ראיית רב נחמן ואת דחיית הגמ'.

71 בכ"י וטיקן 120, פריז (H147A) ודפוס ויניציאה איתא: „השתחוה לע"ז."

72 בכ"י וטיקן 120, פריז (H147A) ודפוס ויניציאה איתא: „הודה לע"ז."

73 שיטה הלכתית דומה לזו המיוצגת כאן על ידי רב ששת, מצאנו גם בברייתא נוספת בבבלי, זבחים כב ע"ב, ושם איתא: „תנו רבנן: בן נכר – יכול בן נכר ממש? תלמוד לומר: ערל לב. אם כן מה תלמוד לומר: בן נכר – שנתנכרו מעשיו לאביו שבשמים. ואין לי אלא ערל לב, ערל בשר מנין? תלמוד לומר: וערל בשר."

מכאן עולה, שכהן, „שנתנכרו מעשיו לאביו שבשמים," נפסל מלעבוד ולהקריב בביהמ"ק. פסול זה נובע מעצם פעולת ההקרבה בשעה שנעשה ל„מנוכר," ללא הבחנה הלכתית כלשהי הנוגעת לכוונת המקריב או לסוג העבודה. לכן, „אפילו שב בשעת עבודה אמרינן בסוף מנחות (קט ע"א) דאין קרבנו ריח ניחוח, ואע"ג דהשתא לבו לשמים, מתחילה לא היה לבו לשמים" („בעלי התוספות," שם, ד"ה: „משום דאין ליבר"). ומכאן, כאמור, שיטה תנאית דומה, המקבילה לזו של רב ששת, כלשון ר"ש שציגר (ר' שמואל אריה שציגר, מנחת אריאל: מסכת מנחות [קרית ספר: מ"ז שצ'יגל, תשנ"ו] עמ' תקד, ד"ה: „הודה לעבודת כוכבים"): „וא"כ מבואר בהאי ברייתא דבן נכר שנתנכרו מעשיו לאביו שבשמים, הרי הוא מחלל עבודה. וא"כ צריך עיון שיטת רב נחמן שסובר דהודה לעבודת כוכבים קרבנו ריח ניחוח, הא הודה זה ממש נתנכרו מעשיו לאביו שבשמיים"!

74 לשון המיוחס לרבינו גרשלם מאור הגולה על פי דברי הגמ'; שם, ד"ה: „לעולם" (ההדגשות שלי). יצויין, שבדרך מיתודית דומה פירשו כמה פרשנים את עמדת רב ששת גם ביחס לפסוקים הרלונטיים

יוצא, שדעתו של רב ששת צמודה להלכה שבמשנה וקובעת, שבכל מקרה חלות ההגבלות על „הממלא" פשט המשנה נוטה לדעת רב ששת, כדברי בעל ה„מלאכת שלמה" בפירושו למשנתנו (ביצה, פ"ה מ"ה, ד"ה: „ושל עולי בבל"), והוא כותב: „ואם מילא מתחלה לצורך חברו פלוגתא דאמוראי בגמ' איכא מ"ד כרגלי הממלא ואיכא מ"ד כרגלי מי שנתמלאו לו, ופשטה דמתני' משתמעא כמ"ד כרגלי הממלא."

רב נחמן, לעומת זאת, נראה כמשנה את ההלכה התנאית על ידי החלת אותן מגבלות דווקא על „מי שנתמלאו לו," ולא על ה„ממלא." נקודה זו בולטת בין אם הדבר נובע, כטענת ה„סתמא דגמרא" כאן, מראיית הבור של „עולי בבל" כשיתופית לכלל (שאיננה פשט המשנה), או על פי מגמה גמישה יותר הסוברת, שבדבר שאין בעלות גמורה עליו עם כניסת יו"ט, נקבעות ההגבלות על כל אדם שבבעלותו העכשווית אותו הדבר המסוים. היטיב לסכם את הדברים בעל „חידושי הריצ"ד":

> לכי תידוק במשנתנו ובמשניות שלאחריה תשכח שתוכן כוונת חכז"ל בתקנתם לענין הולכת בהמה וכלים ביו"ט כך היא: לא תלו היתר ההולכה בחזקת מרייהו אלא ברשות מי הם נמצאים בכניסת יו"ט. ופשוט הוא דהיכא דנמצאים בחזקה וברשות אחת דכרגלי הבעלים הם... והיכא שאין לשום אחד זכות בדבר בכניסת יו"ט והיינו בדבר הפקר וזכו בו ביו"ט הרי הוא כרגלי מי שזכה בו והיינו הא דתנן: ושל עולי בבל כרגלי הממלא ואם הזוכה בו מזכה דבר זה לאחר פליגי רב נחמן ורב ששת דרב נחמן סובר דכרגלי השני ורב ששת סובר דכרגלי הזוכה בו תחלה הן.[67]

בבלי, מנחות קט ע"א-ע"ב

משנה: הכהנים ששימשו בבית נחוניון, לא ישמשו במקדש בירושלים, ואין צורך לומר לדבר אחר... הרי הם כבעלי מומים: חולקים ואוכלים, אבל לא מקריבים.[68]

גמרא:

1. איתמר: שגג בזריקה: רב נחמן אמר: קרבנו ריח ניחוח, רב ששת אמר: אין קרבנו ריח ניחוח...[69]

67 ר' יוסף צבי דינר, חידושי הריצ"ד: הגהות, פירושים, ביאורים על הבבלי והירושלמי (ירושלים: מוסד הרב קוק, תשמ"א) עמ' שטו (ד"ה: „הבהמה והכלים"). ה„סתמא דגמרא" בהמשך הסוגיה שם (לט ע"ב), מעלה אפשרות נוספת לפרש את מחלוקת רב נחמן ורב ששת ביחס לשאלה: האם המגביה מציאה לחבירו – קנה חבירו או לא. אפשרות זו נראית פחות סבירה, בעיקר משום שהיא סותרת את דעתו המפורשת של רב נחמן במקום אחר (בבלי, בבא מציעא י ע"א), ראה: ישראל פרנצוס, „מחקרים במסכת ביצה שבתלמוד הבבלי ובדרכי עריכתה," עבודת דוקטור, האוניברסיטה העברית בירושלים, ירושלים, תשכ"ח, עמ' 280-283; ד' הלבני, מקורות ומסורות, סדר מועד: יומא-חגיגה, עמ' שנה. ובכלל, ספק אם המושג „ברירה" (במסגרת השקלא וטריא שהביאה למסקנה זו), במשמעות זו של „מבורר למפרע," היתה ידועה לאמוראים מן הדור השלישי, ראה: עמינח, עריכת מסכתות, עמ' 95, ואת המצוין שם בהערה 5; אריאל גילת, „תוקפו של המושג ברירה במשנת התנאים" (עבודת מוסמך; רמת-גן: אוניברסיטת בר-אילן, תשס"א) עמ' 11, הערה 13.

68 בדומה להלכה זו, ראה גם את דברי המשנה, זבחים יב, א. למקבילה בתוספתא, ראה: תוספתא, מנחות יג, יד (מהדורת משה שמואל צוקרמנדל [פסוואלק: נדפס על פי המחבר, תר"מ; ירושלים: ווארמן, תרצ"ז] עמ' 533).

69 בכ"י מינכן 95 נשמטה דעתו של רב ששת, אבל היא עולה שם מהמשך הדברים: „אמר רב ששת: מנא אמינא לה?..."

הלכתיות בין המקרה שבמשנה לבין הבעיה שהועלתה בפניו, ובדרך זו מצטמצם מאוד השימוש בסברה כמקור הלכתי.[60]

תופעה זו של מגמה „שמרנית" אצל רב ששת, לעומת גישה „מתפתחת" אצל רב נחמן, מצויה בחמשה עשר מקרים מבין כלל המחלוקות בין השניים.[61] נסתפק כאן בשלוש דוגמאות:

בבלי, ביצה לט ע"א

משנה: באר שליחיד – כרגלי היחיד, ושלאנשי העיר – כרגלי אנשי אותה העיר, ושלעולי בבל כרגלי הממלא.

גמרא: אתמר: מילא ונתן לחבירו: רב נחמן אמר: כרגלי מי שנתמלאו לו, רב ששת[62] אמר: כרגלי הממלא.

במאי קא מיפלגי? מר סבר: בירא דהפקרא הוא, ומר סבר: בירא דשותפי הוא.

במשנה מדובר באדם ששאב לעצמו, ואילו במחלוקת רב ששת ורב נחמן, מדובר באדם ששאב (ונתן) לחבירו.[63] כבר ממבט ראשון נראה, שלמרות הבדל זה לא חל שינוי בעמדתו ההלכתית של רב ששת ביחס להלכה שבמשנה („רב ששת אמר: כרגלי הממלא"). מהי הסברה האפשרית שעמדה בבסיס דעתו על פי דברי המשנה?

מן המשנה עולה, שקיימת הבחנה משפטית בין בור של אנשי העיר (או של אדם פרטי), לבין בור של „עולי בבל" בעוד שהראשון נחשב לרכושם של כלל אנשי העיר, ולהם בעלות משותפת על רכוש זה, הרי שבאחרון, אין דין של שותפות,[64] ודינו כהפקר.[65] השואב את מי הבאר, קובע, למעשה, את בעלותו עליהם, ועליו חלה אותה מגבלה (לעניין יציאה מתחום שבת), בהתאם לכוונת המשנה במלים: „כרגלי הממלא".[66] נראה, שבהתאם להלכה זו סבור רב ששת, שהחלת מגבלה זו, תיקבע לפי הקונה את מי הבור, אף על פי שמסרו אחר כך לאדם אחר. כלומר, אין לערוך הבחנה הלכתית לעניין זה בין הקונה לעצמו לבין הקונה לאחר.

60 תופעה זו מאפיינת את הגישה הפורמליסטית של המשפט, וראה את דבריו של מאוטנר, ירידת הפורמליזם, עמ' 15.

61 בבלי, ברכות מב ע"ב (ראה גם: ירושלמי, ברכות ו, ה [י ע"ג]); בבלי, שבת צד ע"ב; בבלי, עירובין לא ע"ב–לב ע"א; בבלי, יומא ו ע"ב–ז ע"א; בבלי, פסחים צב ע"ב; בבלי, ביצה לג ע"א; בבלי, ב"ק סח ע"א; בבלי, ב"ב קמב ע"א; שם קמג ע"א; שם קנא ע"א; בבלי, מנחות קט ע"א–ע"ב (ארבעה מקרים); בבלי, בכורות כג ע"ב.

62 בכ"י וטיקן 134 איתא: „ורב שמואל" ותוקן שם ל„רב ששת."

63 הדמיון בין המקרים עולה גם מדברי רש"י על אתר (ד"ה: „מילא ונתן לחבירו") שפירש, „שמילא לצורך חבירו" ולא לעצמו, אחרת „הא תנן בהדיא: כרגלי הממלא."

64 ראה: שמואל ספראי, בימי הבית ובימי המשנה: מחקרים בתולדות ישראל (ב כרכים; ירושלים: הוצאת ספרים ע"ש י"ל מאגנס, האוניברסיטה העברית, תשנ"ד) א:471–472. ראה גם: זאב ספראי, הקהילה היהודית בארץ ישראל בתקופת המשנה והתלמוד (ירושלים: מרכז זלמן שזר לתולדות ישראל, תשנ"ה) עמ' 204–205; 210–212; 231–232.

65 כפירוש ה„סתמא דגמרא" כאן. ראה גם: חנוך אלבק, ששה סדרי משנה: סדר מועד (ירושלים – תל אביב: דביר ומוסד ביאליק, תשי"ד) עמ' 301; שאול ליברמן, תוספתא כפשוטה, מסכת יו"ט (ניו יורק: בית המדרש לרבנים באמריקה, תשכ"ב) עמ' 1011; שלום אלבק, דיני הממונות בתלמוד (תל אביב: דביר, תשל"ו) עמ' 510–511. והשווה: ספראי, הקהילה היהודית, עמ' 204, ושם בעמ' 211, הערה 100.

66 אלבק, ששה סדרי משנה: סדר מועד, עמ' 103. ראה גם את דברי הריצ"ד המצוטטים להלן בפנים.

שרב נחמן אף מציג ראיה ממשנה זו לעמדתו, בשעה שמובנה הפשטני מהווה דווקא ראיה לסתור ותמיכה בדעת רב ששת, וכלשונם של „בעלי התוספות": „תי[מא] הוא: מאי מייתי רב נחמן מהכא? כיון דרב ששת מצי דחי לה. ואדרבה, טפי יש ראי[ה] לרב ששת מכאן, כדק[אמר]: הכי נמי מסתברא, ורב נחמן איצטרי[ך] לשנויי בדוחק."[57]

כבמקרה הקודם, הפתרון שהוצע לבעיה זו במחקר, תולה את הפתרון בשיטת עריכה אינטרפולטיבית של ה„סתמאים," וכלשונו של דוד הלבני:

> התוס׳ [התוספות] ד"ה מאי שואלים וכי לא ידע רב נחמן שאפשר בנקל לדחות את המנא אמינא שלו מן המשנה מסרון לחזנים וכו׳ ולהפוך אותה, על ידי הכי נמי מסתברא וכו׳, כראיה לרב ששת. הם גם שואלים למה אמר רב ששת מנא אמינא לה מן הברייתא ולא מן המשנה „דקאמר איהי גופיה ה"נ מסתברא." אין הכרח שרב ששת עצמו אמר הכי נמי מסתברא וכו׳ וגם י"ל שהמנא אמינא לה של רב נחמן ורב ששת אינו מהם...הכל הוא מסתמא דגמרא...היא [הסתמא דגמרא], אמנם בחרה במנא אמינא לה בצורה תקבולית, ששניהם רב נחמן ורב ששת אמרו מנא אמינא לה, והצטרכה משום כך לומר שרב נחמן ולא רב ששת הביא ראיה מן המשנה ולא הספיקה לסיים עד שדחתה ועוד הוסיפה הכי נמי מסתברא וכו׳.[58]

דברי הלבני ממחישים, שוב, את הבעייתיות המצויה בפרשנותו של רב נחמן למקורות תנאיים, ואת הפתרון המוצע לה במחקר. מכל מקום, מה שנראה בולט גם מן המקרה שלפנינו הוא, שרב נחמן אינו נמנע מלפסוק ומלפרש נגד פשט המשנה, ולעומתו רב ששת – לא זו בלבד שהוא מקבל את המשנה כפשוטה, אלא שטורח – ברוב בקיאותו – להצטייד בברייתא נוספת, התומכת בדעתו.[59] לפנינו, שוב, שתי גישות: גישת רב ששת, הצמודה אל מובנה המילולי של המשנה, לעומת זו של רב נחמן, המציגה פרשנות המרחיבה את משמעותה המילולית, ובדומה לתפיסתו לעיל, מכירה במושג „בית דין" אפילו בהרכב של שני דיינים.

השאלה העומדת כאן לדיון היא, באיזו דרך ימצא רב ששת – בעל ה„גישה הפורמליסטית" – פתרון לבעיות שאין להם פתרון במקור תנאי מפורש?

במקרים כאלו מצאנו את רב ששת, כדרכו, נצמד אל ההלכה שבמשנה, ומחיל אותה על הבעיה שלפניו, באמצעות היסקים לוגיים. בהכרעותיו, אין רב ששת עורך הבחנות

חגיגה, יומא מגילה (בני ברק: הוצאת המחבר, תשל"ו) עמ׳ י.

57 „בעלי התוספות," שם, ד"ה: „מאי לאו" (הציטוט הוא על פי דפוס ראשון [ונציה ר"פ], וההשלמות בסוגריים מרובעים הם שלי).

58 הלבני, מקורות ומסורות, סדר מועד: יומא-חגיגה, עמ׳ מז-מח.

59 דברינו מתייחסים למחלוקת ההלכתית של רב נחמן ורב ששת ופירושם למקורות התנאיים, במסגרת המונח „מנא אמינא לה." הקטעים שב„הכי נמי מסתברא" והניסיון לפרש את הברייתא אליבא דרב נחמן („אין, כדתני רב יהודה...") נראים מן ה„סתמא דגמרא," ובעניין זה דעתנו זהה לשיטת הלבני דלעיל. אכן, המונח „הכי נמי מסתברא" רגיל בדברי „הסתמא," ומתוך כמאה מהיקרויותיו בבבלי, רק שלושה מיוחסים לאמוראים מאוחרים, בני הדור החמישי-שביעי (רב הונא בריה דרב יהושע [בבלי, הוריות ג ע"ב]; רב אשי [שם, פסחים עא ע"א]; מר זוטרא בריה דרב מרי [שם, תמורה יט ע"א]). כאמור, באופן דומה ניתן לומר גם ביחס למשפט „אין, כדתני רב יהודה..." המהווה דחיה לפירושו של רב ששת, ויעידו על כך השינויים הרבים של כתבי היד למשפט זה (ראה לעיל, הערה 53).

בבלי, יומא כד ע"ב–כה ע"א

במה מפיסין? רב נחמן אמר: בבגדי חול, ורב ששת אמר:[50] בבגדי קדש...

אמר רב נחמן: מנא אמינא לה – דתנן: **„מסרון לחזנין, והיו מפשיטין אותן את בגדיהן ולא היו מניחין עליהן אלא מכנסים בלבד." מאי לאו באותן שזכו לפייס?**

אמר רב הונא בר יהודה אמר רב ששת:[51] לא, באותן שלא זכו פייס.

הכי נמי מסתברא, דאי סלקא דעתך באותן שזכו לפיס – לא היו מניחין עליהן אלא מכנסים בלבד, והתניא: „מנין שלא יהא דבר קודם למכנסים? תלמוד לומר: ומכנסי בד יהיו על בשרו..."[52]

אמר רב ששת: מנא אמינא לה? **דתניא: „לשכת הגזית כמין בסילקי גדולה היתה, פייס במזרחה... והממונה בא ונוטל מצנפת מראשו של אחד מהן, ויודעין שממנו פייס מתחיל." ואי סלקא דעתך בבגדי חול – מצנפת בבגדי חול מי איכא?**

אין, כדתני רב יהודה ואיתימא רב שמואל בר יהודה[53] [כהן שעשתה לו אמו כתונת – עובד בה עבודת יחיד].[54]

הנחת רב נחמן, שהמשנה בתמיד ה, ג דנה דווקא באותם הכהנים שזכו לפייס תמוהה. מן העיון במשנה זו ובהקשרה, מסתברת יותר ההנחה, שהמדובר דוקא בכהנים שלא זכו בפייס, שכן המשנה מתארת שם את מסירתם של כהנים אלו לשמשים, הפשטת בגדיהם, בגדי הקדש, והלבשתם בבגדי החול.[55] וכבר חשו בבעיה זו הפרשנים המסורתיים, תוך העלאת הצעות לפירוש אוקימתת רב נחמן למשנה זו.[56] בעיה זו בולטת בחריפותה לנוכח העובדה,

ומסורות, סדר מועד: יומא–חגיגה, עמ' רמו, הערה 5) מסייג קביעה גורפת זו, ומעמיד את המונח על „חזקתו," דהיינו, על מקורו האמוראי. ראה גם את דבריו של ל' מוסקוביץ, שהתייחס לבעיה זו באופן כללי Leib Moscovitz, *Talmudic Reasoning: From Casuistics to Conceptualization* (Tübingen: Mohr Siebeck, 2002) 247, n. 65 וכותב: „However, the evidence offered to support this position is not wholly convincing, even if it is impossible to dismiss this suggestion out of hand."

50 בכ"י וטיקן 134 איתא: „ורב אשי אמר." אך שם בהמשך איתא: „רב ששת אמר בבגדי קודש...."

51 בכ"י מינכן 95 ליתא „אמר רב ששת," ובכ"י לונדון (Harl. 5508) ליתא המשפט כולו („א"ר הונא בר יהודה א"ר ששת"). בכ"י הסמינר התיאולוגי 270 איתא: „אמ' רב חונא בר יהודה מנא אמינא לה אמ' רב ששת," ונראה שלפנינו שיבוש. בכ"י וטיקן 134 נשמטה התשובה כולה (מהמלים „אמר רב הונא" עד „שלא זכו לפייס"), ונמצא שם „הכי נמי מסתברא דאי ס"ד באותן שזכו לפייס...."

52 בתורת כהנים, צו, פרק ב, ג איתא: „כשהוא אומר להלן מכנסי בד יהיו על בשרו שלא יהיה דבר קודם למכנסים."

53 רבים הם השינויים המצויים בכתבי היד למשפט זה. השינויים מתייחסים בעיקר לתחילתו (כי"י הסמינר התיאולוגי 270, הסמינר התיאולוגי 271 ומינכן 6: „דילמא כדתני..."), ולשמו של החכם שבשמו מצוטטת הברייתא (בכ"י וטיקן 134 איתא: „ר' חייא בר יהודה ואמרי לה רב שמואל בר יהודה"; בכי"י הסמינר התיאולוגי 270, הסמינר התיאולוגי 271, מינכן 6 ולונדון [Harl. 5508] איתא: „רב חונא [מינכן 95: ‚שימי'] בר יהודה ואמרי לה רב שמואל בר יהודה").

54 בכי"י מינכן 95, מינכן 6, הסמינר התיאולוגי 218 ו–1623 וגירסאות רש"י ריטב"א ועוד ליתא, והוסיפוה בגיליון על פי המופיע להלן בבבלי, יומא לה ע"ב. מדברי הגמ' כאן לכאורה משמע, שעבודת יחיד נעשית בבגדי חול. על הבעייתיות הכרוכה במתן פירוש כזה לברייתא, תוך ניסיון לתרץ את דברי רב נחמן, ראה: שאול ליברמן, תוספתא כפשוטה, תענית (ניו יורק: בית המדרש לרבנים באמריקה, תשכ"ב) עמ' 751–750.

55 ראה, למשל: חנוך אלבק, ששה סדרי משנה: סדר קודשים (ירושלים – תל אביב: מוסד ביאליק ודביר, תשי"ב–תשי"ט) עמ' 305.

56 ראה, למשל, את ניסיונו (הדחוק) של ר' חיים שאול גריינימן לפרש את שיטת רב נחמן – חדושים ובאורים:

עדים.״[44] דיעה נוספת סבורה, שלפי רב נחמן הביטול הוא עניין של הצהרה ומודעה ודי בשניים בלבד (״אודועי בעלמא הוא, ובתרי סגי״ – רש״י, שם, ד״ה: ״בפני שנים״).[45]

לאור הדברים דלעיל נראה, שדעתו של רב נחמן, בניגוד לשיטת רב ששת, היא רחוקה ממובנה הפשטני של המשנה. זאת ועוד, שתי הראיות שמציג כאן רב נחמן לביסוס דעתו מן המשנה בשביעית י, ד נראות תמוהות. במשנה זו נאמר:

> זה הוא גופו שלפרוזבול: ״מוסר אני לכם איש פל׳ ופל׳ והדיינים שבמקום פל׳, שכל חוב שיש לי, שאגבנו כל זמן שארצה,״ והדיינים חותמין מלמטן או העדים.

ראייתו הראשונה של רב נחמן מבוססת על ההנחה – שקשה לפרנסה במובנה הפשטני של המשנה – שכוונת המשנה במלים ״פלוני ופלוני הדיינים,״ היא למנות את מספרם של הדיינים הנחוצים לשם ביטול הגט. ואכן, הנחה זו של רב נחמן נדחתה כבר על ידי הגמרא עצמה: ״אטו תנא כי רוכלא ליחשיב וליזיל?!״[46] כמו-כן, תמוהה גם ראייתו השניה של רב נחמן מסופה של משנה זו: ״והדיינים חותמין מלמטן או העדים.״ ההיקש שהוא עורך בין דינם של העדים (שניים) לדינם של הדיינים, נדחה גם הוא כבר על ידי הגמרא עצמה, בטענה שחתימות הדיינים או העדים, נקבעות על פי הרכבם הנחוץ באותו העניין: הדיינים בשלושה, והעדים בשניים.

שני טיעוניו הדחוקים של רב נחמן בסוגיה שלפנינו, הובילו את אברהם ווייס למסקנה, ששתי הראיות שמציג רב נחמן מן המשנה בשביעית, הן מן ״הסתמא״ ולא מרב נחמן.[47] הצעתו של ווייס ממחישה לא רק את הקושי המצוי בהסבר אוקימתות רב נחמן למשנה בשביעית, אלא גם את הדרך בה נוהג המחקר להציע פתרון לקושי או לדוחק המצוי בפרשנותו של רב נחמן למקורות תנאיים.[48] ואולם, נראה שאין צורך בפתרון זה. לאור מאפייני דרך לימודו של רב נחמן בתלמוד ניתן להציע, ששתי הראיות של רב נחמן – כפי שהן לפנינו בסוגיה – אכן משקפות את הדברים במקורם. הקושי שבפירושו למשנה בשביעית, מאפיין את דרך לימודו של רב נחמן גם במקומות רבים, ומכאן שדווקא אופיין הדחוק של הראיות נראות כמשקפות את הדברים במקורם הראשוני.[49]

44 פלדבלום, פירושים ומחקרים בתלמוד, עמ׳ 147.

45 ווייס, ״יסוד מחלוקת רב נחמן ורב ששת,״ עמ׳ 357; ווייס, מחקרים בתלמוד, עמ׳ 126–127; זפרני, ״שרשור הלכות,״ עמ׳ 158, הערה 6.

46 ונתקשו בה גם רבים מן הפרשנים המסורתיים, אפילו אותם שפסקו כרב נחמן. ראה למשל: ר׳ יהודה בר ברזילי הברצלוני, ספר השטרות, מהדורת שלמה זלמן חיים הלברשטם (ברלין: חברת מקיצי נרדמים, תרנ״ט) עמ׳ 71; ר׳ מנחם המאירי, בית הבחירה, מסכת גיטין, מהדורת קלמן שלזינגר (ירושלים: מוסד הרב קוק, תש״ג) עמ׳ 139. לקושי נוסף העולה מפירוש זה של רב נחמן, ראה: ר׳ יוסף דוד זינצהיים, יד דוד (ירושלים: מכון ירושלים, תשל״ו) ד״ה: ״פלוני ופלוני הדיינין.״

47 ווייס, ״יסוד מחלוקת,״ עמ׳ 357–358; ווייס, מחקרים, עמ׳ 126–127.

48 והדוגמאות לכך הן למכביר. לכמה מן הדוגמאות, ראה את המובא לעיל הערה 29.

49 היו חוקרים שזיהו כמה מן הראיות המוצגות בבבלי באמצעות המונח ״מנא אמינא לה-דתניא״ כמאוחרות, וזאת בעיקר על סמך מגמה אפשרית של עורכי הסוגיה לפסוק הלכה (מנחם כהנא, ״גילוי דעת ואונס בגיטין: לחקר השתלשלות המסורות המוחלפות בעריכתן המגמתית של סוגיות מאוחרות,״ תרביץ כב [תשנ״ג] עמ׳ 229, הערה 16), או בשל קושי מהותי אחר. ראה, למשל: זכריה פרנקל, מבוא הירושלמי [ירושלים: דפוס אמנים, תשכ״ז] עמ׳ לה; Julius Kaplan, *The Redaction of the Babylonian Talmud* [New York: Bloch, 1933] 155; ד׳ הלבני, מקורות ומסורות, סדר מועד: עירובין-פסחים, עמ׳ 345. והשווה: אברהם ווייס, לחקר התלמוד (ניו יורק: פלדהיים, תשט״ו) עמ׳ 25. עם זאת יודגש, שהלבני עצמו (מקורות

יותר, המבוססת על הסברה, ומבחינה זו, פרשנותו של רב נחמן למשנה משקפת התפתחות מאוחרת שלה.

בבלי, גיטין לב ע"ב–לג ע"א

משנה: **השולח גט לאשתו והיגיע בשליח, או ששילח אחריו שליח, אמר לו: גט שנתתי לך בטל הוא – הרי זה בטל. קידם אצל אשתו, או ששילח אצלה שליח, אמר לה: גט ששלחתי ליך בטל הוא – הרי זה בטל. אם משהגיע גט על ידה – אינו יכול לבטלו. בראשונה היה עושה בית דין במקום אחר ומבטלו. היתקין רבן גמליאל הזקן שלא יהו עושין כן, מפני תקון העולם.**

גמרא: **איתמר: בפני כמה הוא מבטלו? רב נחמן אמר: בפני ב', רב ששת אמר: בפני ג'.**

רב ששת אמר: בפני ג',[41] **ב"ד קתני, ורב נחמן אמר: בפני ב', לבי תרי נמי ב"ד קרי להו.**

אמר רב נחמן: מנא אמינא לה – **דתנן: מוסרני לפניכם פלוני ופלוני הדיינין שבמקום פלוני.**

ורב ששת: אטו תנא כי רוכלא ליחשיב וליזיל?!

אמר רב נחמן: מנא אמינא לה – **דתנן: הדיינים חותמין למטה או העדים. מאי לאו דיינים דומיא דעדים, מה עדים שנים אף דיינים נמי שנים?**

ורב ששת: מידי איריא?! הא כדאיתא והא כדאיתא.

רב ששת, כדרכו, דוגל במשמעות הפשוטה של המלים „בית דין" ביחס להרכב של שלושה דיינים, ובדבר זה חש כבר בעל ה„סתמא" כאן. אכן, בשיטה זו נקט גם המחקר.[42]

רב נחמן סבור, לעומתו, שפעולה זו איננה זוקקת הרכב מלא של שלושה דיינים, ודי בשניים בלבד. יסוד שיטת רב נחמן איננה ברורה, ורבים נתלבטו בה. ה„סתמא" כאן – ובעקבותיה גם הגאונים – רואים ביסוד שיטת רב נחמן את הדיעה ש„לבי תרי נמי בית דין קרי להו" המתקשרת עם דברי שמואל במקום אחר.[43] דיעה אחרת במחקר גורסת, ש„לרב נחמן שמבטלו בפני שנים, פירושו, שכמו שמינוי שליחות צריך עדים, כך ביטולו צריך

והגליל ליום תשעה באב והשתקפותם בדיני היום," *HUCA* 73 (2002) עמ' י–יד.

41 בכ"י וטיקן 130 ליתא המשפט כולו („רב ששת אמר: בפני ג"). בכ"י וטיקן 140 סומן משפט זה למחיקה. ראה דקדוקי סופרים השלם על אתר.

42 ראה בעיקר: אברהם ווייס, „יסוד מחלוקת רב נחמן ורב ששת בביטול גט בפני שנים או שלושה," הגות עברית באמריקה, עורכים: מנחם זהרי, אריה טרטקובר, חיים אורמיאן (ג' כרכים; תל אביב: ברית עברית עולמית ע"י יבנה, תשל"ב–תשל"ד) א:357; אברהם ווייס, מחקרים בתלמוד (ירושלים: מוסד הרב קוק בשיתוף עם אוניברסיטת בר-אילן, תשל"ה) עמ' 126–127; מאיר שמחה פלדבלום, פירושים ומחקרים בתלמוד: מסכת גיטין, עם מבוא כללי על המשנה, התוספתא, ושני התלמודים (ניו יורק: ישיבה אוניברסיטה, תשכ"ט) עמ' 147; דוד זפרני, „שרשור הלכות בתלמוד הבבלי: לביאור ,והלכתא כנחמן והלכתא כנחמן והלכתא כנחמני,'" תלפיות יב (תשס"ב) עמ' 158, הערה 6. למושג „בית דין" בהרכב של שלושה דיינים, ראה: חנוך אלבק, ששה סדרי משנה: סדר נשים (ירושלים-תל אביב: מוסד ביאליק ודביר, תשי"ב–תשי"ט) עמ' 281; שלום אלבק, בתי הדין בימי התלמוד (רמת-גן: אוניברסיטת בר-אילן, תשמ"ז) עמ' 17–18; זפרני, „שרשור הלכות," עמ' 158, הערה 6.

43 בבלי, סנהדרין ה ע"ב (ירושלמי, סנהדרין א, א [יא ע"א]). ראה, למשל: שאילתות דרב אחאי גאון, שמות, משפטים סה (מהדורת שמואל קלמן מירסקי [ירושלם: המכון למחקר ולהוצאת ספרים סורא וישיבה אוניברסיטה, ובהשתתפות מוסד הרב קוק, תש"ך] עמ' קעד). רב נחמן אף ראה את עצמו בגדר „מומחה לרבים," המוסמך לדון דיני ממונות כיחידי, ראה לעיל, ליד הערה 16.

לעולם לכבס וללבוש, וכשאין לו אלא חלוק אחד...
מיתיבי: אסור לכבס לפני תשעה באב אפילו להניח לאחר תשעה באב...[37] תיובתא.[38]

בעוד שרב ששת רואה את איסור הכיבוס בשבוע שחל בו תשעה באב כאיסור אבסולוטי, הנובע מעצם פעולת הכיבוס, תולה רב נחמן את האיסור בזיקה אל כוונת המכבס ללובשו לפני תשעה באב או לאחריו. דבריו של רב ששת („אפילו לכבס ולהניח אסור"), לא זו בלבד שהם מופיעים בצורה מפורשת בברייתא, אלא הם אף מסתברים מלשון המשנה, כפי שנימק זאת הרא"ש על אתר (ד"ה: „משנכנס אב"): „...ורב ששת אמר אפי' לכבס ולהניח אסור... דלישנא דמתניתין דקתני ומלכבס מוכח כן, דלר"נ (דלרב נחמן) הוה ליה למימר אסור ללבוש כלים מכובסין... ועוד דתניא כוותיה אסור לכבס לפני ט' באב אפי' לכבס ולהניח אחר תשעה באב'.

הדברים מתאשרים גם מנוסח המשנה בתענית ב, ז: „אנשי משמר ואנשי מעמד אסורין מלספר ומלכבס, ובחמישי מתרין מפני כבוד השבת," מה שמקשה עוד יותר על הבנת אוקימתת רב נחמן למשנה זו:

> יש לדעת מה דחקו לר"נ לאפוקה למתני' מפשטה דכיבוס אסור, **דומיא דאנשי משמר ואנשי מעמד דקתני בהו נמי לעיל ט"ו ב' דאסורין לספר ולכבס והיינו רק כיבוס דללבוש מכובסין שרי, ונהי דהכא אף ללבוש יש לאסור, אבל מנ"ל להתיר כיבוס, וגם לפ"ז צריך לדחוק דבחמשי מותרין היינו באין לו אלא חלוק אחד.** [ההדגשות שלי][39]

כמו-כן, אף נסיונה של הגמרא לתרץ את תיובתת רב המנונא על רב נחמן ולהעמיד את המשנה „בחלוק אחד," אינו הולם את פשט הדברים שם, וכלשונו של דוד הלבני:

> מלבד הדוחק להעמיד את המשנה בשאין לו רק חלוק אחד – ועוד יותר דוחק לומר כן בברייתא להלן ששם נאמר „מותר לכבס בחמישי" אחרי „חל להיות באחד בשבת מותר לכבס כל השבת כולה" ודוחק לפרש מלים דומות באותה הברייתא בהוראות משתנות – גם יש לשאול, אם אין לו אלא חלוק אחד למה לא יהא מותר לו לכבס בשבוע שחל בו ת"ב [תשעה באב] גם בשאר הימים ולא רק בחמישי, כשם שמותר לו לכבס במועד.[40]

יוצא, אפוא, שעמדתו ההלכתית המחמירה של רב ששת תואמת את דרך לימודו, הצמודה אל ההלכה התנאית ומשקפת אותה. לעומתו, עמדת רב נחמן נראית מקילה ו„גמישה"

37 בכ"י מינכן 95 נשמט המשפט כולו מהמלים „תשעה באב" ועד „תשעה באב," כנראה, מפני הדומות, ראה: צבי מלטר, מסכת תענית מן תלמוד בבלי (ניו יורק: האקדמיה האמריקנית למדעי היהדות, תר"ץ) עמ' 139.

38 לניתוח מבני וספרותי המתרכז בהשוואה בין סוגיה זו למקבילתה בירושלמי, תענית ד, ט (סט ע"ב), ראה: נח עמינח, עריכת מסכתות ביצה, ראש השנה ותענית (תל אביב: ביה"ס למדעי היהדות ע"ש חיים רוזנברג, אוניברסיטת תל אביב מפעלים אוניברסיטאיים, תשמ"ו) עמ' 335-336.

39 ר' חיים שאול גריינימן, ספר חדושים ובאורים: ביצה, ראש השנה, תענית, מועד קטן (בני ברק: הוצאת המחבר, תשנ"ט) ע ע"ב, ד"ה: „אר"נ ל"ש אלא." ראה גם מה שכתב שם, עא ע"א: „ועו"ק (ועוד קשה) דהא כי האי לישנא תנן נמי לעיל טו ב' גבי אנשי משמר ואנשי מעמד, והתם ודאי מותרין ללבוש מכובסין ואינם אסורים אלא מלכבס!"

40 הלבני, מקורות ומסורות, סדר מועד: יומא-חגיגה, עמ' תס. לדיון נרחב העוסק באיסור הכיבוס והתספורת בשבוע שחל בו תשעה באב בספרות התנאית, ראה: דב הרמן, „הבדלי הגישות בין חכמי יבנה לוד

ושמונה סוגיות מכלל מחלוקותיו עם רב ששת (כ-75%).[30] רק בששה מקרים מצאנו תיאום בין עמדת רב נחמן לבין ההלכה התנאית.[31] במלים אחרות, רובן המכריע של עמדותיו במחלוקות עם רב ששת, נוטות להתבסס על הסברה, והן נראות בלתי תלויות במקורות התנאיים.

בסוגיות שלהלן תומחש גישתם השונה של רב ששת ורב נחמן, כשהראשון נצמד אל מובנה המילולי או המשמעות ההקשרית של הטכסט התנאי. רב נחמן, לעומת זאת, מתבסס יותר על הסברה וההיגיון, או, לחילופין, על הלכה אמוראית, שהיא עצמה כבר התפתחות הלכתית מאוחרת ביחס להלכה התנאית. תופעה זו מצויה באחד עשר מקרים במסגרת מחלוקותיהם ההלכתיות של השניים.[32]

בבלי, תענית כט ע"ב

משנה:[33] משניכנס אב ממעטים בשמחה. שבת שחל תשעה באב להיות בתוכה – אסורים מלספר ומלכבס. ובחמישי – מותרים מפני כבוד השבת.

גמרא: אמר רב נחמן:[34] לא שנו אלא לכבס וללבוש, אבל לכבס ולהניח – מותר.

ורב ששת אמר: אפילו לכבס ולהניח אסור.

אמר רב ששת:[35] תדע דבטלי קצרי דבי רב.[36]

מתיב רב המנונא: בחמישי מותרים מפני כבוד השבת. למאי, אילימא לכבס וללבוש – מאי כבוד שבת איכא, אלא להניח. ובחמישי הוא דשרי, אבל השבת כולה – אסור.

באמריקה, תשנ"א] עמ' 125–126); שם, קיח ע"א; בבלי, סנהדרין ה ע"ב (שני מקרים); שם לא ע"ב; בבלי, שבועות טז ע"א; בבלי, חולין לא ע"ב (שני מקרים); בבלי, תמורה ז ע"ב (שני מקרים); בבלי, כריתות יח ע"א.

לשם ההשוואה אל רב ששת יאמר, שכלל ה„תיובתות" המועלות על דיעותיו בבבלי, מגיע לכדי שלושה מקרים בלבד (בבלי, קידושין כא ע"א; בבלי, ב"ב ע ע"א; בבלי, סנהדרין לג ע"א). דומה, שלממצא זה, כשלעצמו, יש משמעות על רקע ההבדל המתואר לעיל ביחס לדרך לימודם של השניים: רב ששת הסומך את עיקר תורתו על המקורות התנאיים, לעומת רב נחמן, הבונה את עיקר תורתו על הסברה וההיגיון.

30 בבלי, ברכות מא ע"ב; שם מב ע"ב; שם מו ע"א; שם מט ע"א; בבלי, שבת צד ע"ב; בבלי, עירובין יא ע"ב; שם לב ע"א; בבלי, פסחים צב ע"ב–צג ע"א; בבלי, יומא ו ע"ב–ז ע"א; שם כד ע"ב–כה ע"א; בבלי, סוכה מד ע"ב (ירושלמי, סוכה ד, ג [נד ע"ג]); שם לט ע"א; בבלי, תענית כט ע"ב; בבלי, גיטין לב ע"ב–לג ע"א (שני מקרים); בבלי, ב"ק סח ע"א; בבלי, ב"מ מז ע"א; בבלי, ב"ב קמב ע"א; שם קמג ע"א; שם קנא ע"א; בבלי, מנחות קט ע"א–ע"ב (ארבעה מקרים); בבלי, בכורות כג ע"ב.

31 בבלי, שבת קכג ע"א–ע"ב; בבלי, ביצה לג ע"א; בבלי, תענית יד ע"ב; בבלי, סוכה מז ע"ב; כתובות קי ע"א (ירושלמי, כתובות יג, ט [לו ע"ב]); בבלי, ב"ב קא ע"א.

32 בבלי, ברכות מו ע"א (ראה ניתוחו של שמש, „ברכת המזון," עמ' 153–166); בבלי, עירובין יא ע"ב; שם לט ע"ב; בבלי, יומא כד ע"ב–כה ע"א; בבלי, תענית יד ע"ב; שם כט ע"ב; בבלי, סוכה מד ע"ב; בבלי, גיטין לב ע"ב–לג ע"א (שני מקרים); בבלי, ב"מ מז ע"א; שם קא ע"א.

33 המשניות מכאן ולהלן מובאות על פי כ"י קויפמן.

34 בכ"י לונדון (Harl. 5508) ובאוצר הגאונים (מהדורת בנימין מנשה לוין, כרך ה [ירושלים: ח' וגשל, תשמ"ד] עמ' 64) [להלן: אוצה"ג] איתא „רב הונא."

35 „אמר רב ששת' ליתא בכי"י גטינגן 3, יד הרב הרצוג, וטיקן 134 ובאוצה"ג, שם.

36 באוצה"ג, שם, איתא: „תדע דבטלי כובסין של ראש גלות." עוד על גרסא זו, ראה: כהן, „רב ששת ודרכי לימודו," עמ' 229.

זאת ועוד, תופעות אלו ניכרות גם באופי פרשנותו של רב נחמן למקורות תנאיים, והדבר בולט בעיקר בהשוואה אל רב ששת. כך למשל: כמחצית מכלל הכרעותיו ההלכתיות של רב נחמן בבבלי, מן הסוג המוצע על ידו באמצעות המונח „תניתוה," וכן מחצית מכלל הראיות שהוא מציג לתמיכה בדעתו בבבלי ממקורות תנאיים, באמצעות המונח „מנא אמינא לה-דתניא," מבוססות על פרשנות דחוקה – ולעתים אפילו דחוקה ביותר – למקורות התנאיים.[25] על תופעה זו מעידה אף כמותם של קושיותיהם של רבא וחכמים נוספים על רב נחמן ממקורות תנאיים, ותשובותיו – באמצעות פרשנות דחוקה.[26] במקום אחד, מצאנו אפילו את תלמידו, רמי בר חמא – מי שתורתו בנויה ברובה על הסברה וההיגיון – מעיר לו על כך.[27]

תופעה זו היא כה בולטת לעין אחר עיון בספרותו של רב נחמן, עד שבחלק ניכר מן המקרים ייחס המחקר את פרשנותו ל„סתמאים,"[28] אף על פי שברובם הניסוח מובע בדיבור ישיר של רב נחמן עצמו („אמר ליה..."; „אמר רב נחמן: מנא אמינא לה"; „א"ל תניתוה," ועוד). נראה, שמספר ההיקרויות הגדול של התופעה דווקא אצל רב נחמן, מלמד משהו על דרך לימודו הייחודי.[29]

מגמה זו של שימוש בסברה – כמקור הלכתי או כבסיס לפירוש (דחוק) – נמצאה בעשרים

25 „תניתוה": בבלי, שבת צא ע"א; בבלי, נדרים לה ע"א; שם פא ע"ב; בבלי, גיטין פה ע"א (ארבע פעמים); בבלי, ב"מ כג ע"ב; בבלי, סנהדרין ח ע"א. „מנא אמינא לה": בבלי, פסחים צב ע"ב; בבלי, יומא כד ע"ב; בבלי, גיטין לב ע"ב; שם, לג ע"א; בבלי, מנחות קט ע"א.

26 ראה להלן, הערה 29.

27 בבלי, ב"ק קו ע"א. לדרך לימודו של רמי בר חמא, ראה: כהן, „רמי בר חמא."

28 על סימן זה כגורם מחשיד להיותו של קטע נידון פרי עריכה מאוחרת, ראה, למשל: דוד הלבני, מקורות ומסורות, סדר נשים (תל אביב: דביר, תשכ"ט) עמ' 8 („פירושים דחוקים סימנים מובהקים הם... שאין לפנינו המקורות בצורתם הראשונה"). ראה גם: מאיר שמחה פלדבלום, „,משנה יתירא': סידור המשנה באספקלריה של החומר הסתמי שבתלמוד," בתוך ליאו לנדמן, עורך, ספר זכרון להרב יוסף חיים לוקשטין (ניו יורק: כתב, תש"מ) עמ' יד („דרך כלל אפשר לומר שהסימן להכיר סוגיא מאוחרת או חומר מאוחר הוא שהקושיות הן קלושות והתרוצים דחוקים...").

29 לדוגמאות ראה להלן בפנים. דוגמאות רבות מצויות גם בניסיונותיהם של החוקרים להתמודד עם פרשנותו של רב נחמן למקורות תנאיים, לאור ה„תיובתות" של רבא וחכמים נוספים. מספר ה„תיובתות" בתלמוד הבבלי המועלות בפני רב נחמן, מגיע לכדי חמישים ושלושה מקרים. מתוכם, ביותר ממחצית מכלל המקרים (עשרים ושמונה מקרים) מציג רב נחמן (או בכמה מקרים – ה„סתמא") פרשנות דחוקה למקור התנאי, מה שגרר חוקרים שונים באופן עקבי לייחס את מקור הפרשנות לעורך מאוחר. להלן פרשנותו הדחוקה של רב נחמן בכלל המקרים: בבלי, עירובין עו ע"ב (ראה: דוד הלבני, מקורות ומסורות, עירובין-פסחים [ירושלים: בית המדרש לרבנים באמריקה, תשמ"ב] עמ' קצח); בבלי, פסחים טו ע"א (ראה: הלבני, שם, עמ' שיח); בבלי, ביצה לט ע"ב; בבלי, מגילה יד ע"ב; בבלי, חגיגה יט ע"א (ראה: דוד הלבני, מקורות ומסורות, סדר מועד: יומא-חגיגה [ירושלים: בית המדרש לרבנים באמריקה, תשל"ה] עמ' תקצה ואילך); בבלי, גיטין כ ע"ב; שם כג ע"א (שני מקרים); בבלי, קידושין ח ע"ב; בבלי, ב"ק נ ע"ב [שלושה מקרים] (ראה: דוד הלבני, מקורות ומסורות, בבא קמא [ירושלים: הוצאת ספרים ע"ש י"ל מאגנס, האוניברסיטה העברית, תשנ"ג] עמ' רו); שם סח ע"א; שם עח ע"ב; שם צז ע"ב; שם קו ע"א; בבלי, בבא מציעא סו ע"א (ראה: ברכיהו ליפשיץ, אסמכתא: חיוב וקנין במשפט העברי [ירושלים: הוצאת ספרים ע"ש י"ל מאגנס, האוניברסיטה העברית, תשמ"ח] עמ' 5); שם ע ע"ב (ראה: A. Cohen, *The Development of the Prohibition Against Usury in Jewish Law During the Mishnaic and Talmudic Periods* [Master's Thesis; Montreal: Concordia Univ., 1974] 117); שם עח ע"א (ראה: שמא יהודה פרידמן, תלמוד ערוך: פרק השוכר את האומנין, הפירושים [ירושלים: בית המדרש לרבנים

במסורת הלכה בשם רבי יוחנן.[17] במקרה קונקרטי אחר, נמצא רב נחמן פוסק בניגוד להכרעתו של ראש הגולה עצמו.[18]

רב נחמן מוצג גם כאישיות סמכותית ותקיפה בדורו. מצאנו דיין „שהמציא" מסורת הלכה בשם רב הונא, או חכם אחר שהעלים מסורת הלכה ארצישראלית בשם ר' אלעזר, רק בשל חששם להתעמת עימו פנים אל פנים.[19] הוא איים על דיינים לחזור בהם מפסק דינם ולקבל את דעתו, את עמדותיו ההלכתיות הוא כפה – לעתים באיומים – על בעלי דין סרבנים, הלקה עבריינים, היה ידוע בהתבטאויותיו הבוטות כלפי בני דורו והדור הקודם, ועוד.[20] אפילו חכמים הנראים קשישים ממנו, מבני הדור השני, באים להתדיין לפניו.[21] תופעות אלו ואחרות – כך נראה – נבעו מאופיו הדומיננטי, ממומחיותו בדיני ממונות, וממידת קרבתו אל בית ראש הגולה.[22]

חוקרים רבים עמדו בעבר על המקום הבולט שיש לסברה וההיגיון כמקור ליצירת הלכות חדשות אצל רב נחמן, לעתים אפילו במחיר של סטייה מן ההלכה המקובלת. מחקרים אלו – שעסקו הן בתחומי ההלכה והמשפט העברי בכלל[23] והן בדרך לימודו של רב נחמן בפרט[24] – הצביעו על מידת השפעתו ותרומתו של רב נחמן על התפתחותה של ההלכה התנאית בבבל.

17 בבלי, חולין קכד ע"א.

18 בבלי, ב"ק נח ע"ב. להרחבת הדברים, ראה: בר, ראשות הגולה, עמ' 88–89.

19 בבלי, ב"ק יב ע"א; שם, ב"ב קיא ע"א.

20 ראה, למשל: בבלי, כתובות נ ע"ב (שני מקרים); שם, ב"ב קיא ע"א; שם, ב"ב קנא ע"ב; שם, ב"ק כא ע"א; שם, ב"מ לה ע"א; שם, כתובות י ע"ב. על התבטאויותיו של רב נחמן כלפי חכמים מבני דורו והדור הקודם, כבר העיר פלורסהיים, „היחסים," עמ' 285–286: „אין ספק שרב נחמן הוא אישיות מיוחדת. ייחודיות זו נתנה מקום לחוקרי חכמת ישראל להתגדר בו, שכן אין כמוהו לריבוי הסגנונות והלשונות, שלא מצינו כיוצא בהם אצל חכמים אחרים." ראה גם: רדזינר „יסודות ,דיני קנסות,'" עמ' 233–236. למערכת יחסיו עם חכמי הדור השני, ראה: פלורסהיים, „היחסים," עמ' 285 ואילך; Kalmin, *Sages, Stories*, 81–85.

21 ראה, למשל, בבלי, קידושין ע ע"א–ע"ב. לממצאים נוספים הקשורים באישיותו התקיפה של רב נחמן, ראה: יצחק גייגר, „רב נחמן בר יעקב – האיש ופועלו הציבורי" (עבודת מוסמך; רמת-גן: אוניברסיטת בר-אילן, תשמ"ח) עמ' 16 ואילך.

22 ראה: אבינועם כהן, רבינא וחכמי דורו: עיונים בסדר הזמנים של אמוראים אחרונים בבבל (רמת-גן: אוניברסיטת בר-אילן, תשס"א) עמ' 103; Avinoam Cohen, "Was Age the Decisive Criterion of Subordination Among the Amoraim?" *JQR* 92 (2002) 310–313.

23 ראה: Reuven Yaron, *Gifts in Contemplation of Death in Jewish and Roman Law* (Oxford: Clarendon Press, 1960) 73–74, 92–94, 161–62, 218–20 (בעקבות מחקרו הנ"ל של ירון, יעקב ניוזנר כינה את רב נחמן כאחד ה„חדשנים הגדולים" בדיני ירושות וצוואות, ראה: Jacob Neusner, *A History of the Jews in Babylonia* [3 vols.; Leiden: Brill, 1965–70] 3:288–89; Hanina Ben-Menahem, *Judicial Deviation in Talmudic Law* [Boston: Harwood Academic Publishers, 1991] 112–17; שולמית ולר, נשים בחברה היהודית בתקופת המשנה והתלמוד (תל אביב: הקיבוץ המאוחד, תשס"א) עמ' 124–140; Shulamit Valler, "Women in Rav Nahman's Court," *Nashim* 4 (2001) 35–55.

24 על תקנותיו של רב נחמן, המיוסדות על הסברה וההיגיון, ראה למשל: Salomon Funk, *Die Juden in Babylonien 200–500* (Berlin: Poppelauer, 1902–8) 130–31; גרץ, דברי ימי ישראל, ב:392; Wilhelm Bacher, "Nahman Bar Jacob," *JE* (1901–6) 4:143–44; יעבץ, תולדות ישראל, ז:126; ווייס, דור דור ודורשיו, ג:159. ראה גם את יחסו של רב נחמן לתפילה בציבור (בבלי, ברכות ז ע"ב), כפועל יוצא של אישיותו: Stefan Reif, *Judaism and Hebrew Prayer: New Perspectives on Jewish Liturgical History* (Cambridge: Cambridge Univ. Press, 1993) 117.

מערכת יחסיו עם בית ראש הגולה בבבל; ביקורותיו על רב באמצעות הביטוי: „אמינא, כי ניים ושכיב רב אמר להא שמעתא"; מחלוקותיו ההלכתיות עם חכמים מבני דורו והדור הקודם; ביקורתו על תלמידו, רב עמרם, באמצעות תגובתו המפורסמת: „דלמא מפומבדיתא את, דמעיילין פילא בקופא דמחטא" ועל חכמים מבני דורו; ועוד.[11] תופעה זו, כאמור, מצויה גם במחלוקותיו עם רב נחמן, והיא באה לידי ביטוי בעשרים ושש סוגיות מכלל מחלוקותיהם ההלכתיות (מעל 70%).[12]

דמותו של רב נחמן, לעומת זאת, שונה מזו שמצאנו אצל רב ששת, ודומה שקיים קשר בין מעמדו ואישיותו הנועזת לבין אופי תרומתו הספרותית לתלמודים.[13] רב נחמן הינו אחד מן האמוראים הבולטים בדור השלישי בבבל, ואף מי שהוכר – כבר בדורו – כאישיות דומיננטית וכמומחה בדיני ממונות.[14] הוא מוצג בתלמוד כ„חתנא דבי נשיאה," כבעל מעמד וסמכות בבית ראש הגולה בבבל (בעיקר כדיין וכמורה הוראה), וכמי ששימש גם בראשות ישיבה מקומית בנהרדעא או במחוזא.[15] כמו-כן, הוא מופיע כחכם בעל הכרה עצמית גבוהה, ומיוחסים לו התבטאויות כגון: „אנא ושבור מלכא אחי בדינא," „כגון אנא דן דיני ממונות ביחידי," או „דכולי עלמא לגבי דידי בדינא דרדקי נינהו," ועוד.[16] הוא אף הואשם על ידי חכם ארצישראלי – רבי אמי – כאילו בשל קירבתו לראש הגולה, התיר לעצמו „לזלזל"

11 ראה: כהן, „רב ששת ודרכי לימודו," עמ' 59-63; 117-133; 148-195; 207-233.

12 בבלי, ברכות מב ע"ב (ראה גם: ירושלמי, ברכות ו, ה [י ע"ג]); שם מו ע"א (לניתוח מקור זה, ראה: אהרן שמש, „ברכת המזון: שלוש או ארבע?," סידרא יא [תשנ"ה] עמ' 153-166); שם צד ע"ב; שם קכג ע"א-ע"ב; בבלי, עירובין יא ע"ב; שם לב ע"א; שם לט ע"ב; בבלי, פסחים צב ע"ב; בבלי, יומא ו ע"ב-ז ע"א; שם כד ע"ב-כה ע"א; בבלי, סוכה מד ע"א; שם מז ע"ב; בבלי, ביצה לג ע"א; שם לט ע"א; בבלי, תענית יד ע"ב; שם כט ע"ב; בבלי, גיטין לב ע"ב-לג ע"א (שני מקרים); בבלי, ב"ק סח ע"א; בבלי, ב"מ מז ע"א; שם קא ע"א; בבלי, ב"ב קמב ע"א; שם קכג ע"א; שם קנא ע"א; בבלי, מנחות קט ע"א-ע"ב (ארבעה מקרים); בבלי, בכורות כג ע"ב. בכל עשרת המקרים הנותרים, לא מצאנו מקור תנאי כלשהו – ישיר או עקיף – התומך בדעתו של רב ששת.

13 לדוגמא נוספת לקשר בין דמותו הנועזת של חכם לבין אופי תרומתו הספרותית לתלמודים, ראה: אבינועם כהן, „מר בר רב אשי: האיש במסגרת תקופתו, ותרומתו הספרותית" (עבודת דוקטור; ניו יורק: ישיבה אוניברסיטה, תש"מ) עמ' 22-27.

14 ראה: אפרים בצלאל הלבני, כללי פסק ההלכה בתלמוד (לוד: מכון הברמן למחקרי ספרות, תשנ"ט) עמ' 108-112.

15 על מעמדו של רב נחמן בבית ראש הגולה בבבל, ראה בעיקר: משה בר, ראשות הגולה בבבל בימי המשנה והתלמוד (תל אביב: דביר, תשל"ו) עמ' 75-79, 88-90. לשימושו של רב נחמן בראשות ישיבה מקומית בנהרדעא, ראה: יואל פלורסהיים, „ייסודן וראשית התפתחותן של ישיבות בבל-סורא ופומבדיתא," ציון לט (תשל"ד) עמ' 183-197; פלורסהיים, „היחסים בין חכמי הדור השני של אמוראי בבל," ציון נא (תשמ"ו) עמ' 282-283; אלבק, מבוא לתלמודים, עמ' 299-300. על כך יש, כמובן, להוסיף את עובדת הימצאותו של רב נחמן ברשימת ראשי הישיבות שבסדר תנאים ואמוראים, מהדורת כהנא, עמ' 5. והשווה: היימאן, תולדות תנאים ואמוראים, ב:939. מסקנת היימאן היא, שרב נחמן לא עמד בראשות ישיבה כלשהי, וזאת על בסיס ההנחה שלפיה חכם שלא נזכר ברשימת ראשי הישיבות באיגרת רב שרירא גאון לא שימש בראשות ישיבה כלל. לבחינתה של הנחה זו, המיוצגת כאן בדבריו של היימאן (וחוקרים נוספים), ראה: ברק שלמה כהן, „ישיבות מקומיות בבבל בתקופת התלמוד (רב אדא בר אהבה, רב ששת ורב המנונא)," ציון ע (תשס"ה) עמ' 470-471, ושם הערה 168.

16 בבלי, ב"ק צו ע"ב; שם, סנהדרין ה ע"א; שם, ב"מ סו ע"א. ראה גם את שהעיד על עצמו ביחס למידת מומחיותו בהתרת בכורות – שם, בכורות לז ע"א. לעדויות נוספות בעניין זה, ראה: עמיחי רדזינר, „יסודות ,דיני קנסות' במשפט התלמוד" (עבודת דוקטור; רמת-גן: אוניברסיטת בר-אילן, תשס"א) עמ' 233-236.

המקורות התנאיים, תואמת את מה שמוכר כ„גישה הפורמליסטית" של המשפט.[7] גישה זו מתאפיינת בעיקר בהתבססות שיטתית על מקורות תנאיים מפורשים או, לחילופין, על היסקים לוגיים. ניתוח כלל ספרותו בשני התלמודים, מבליט את התופעה בשני מישורים מרכזיים:

א. רב ששת מגלה נטייה להכריע, להקשות, לבקר ולפרש על פי מובן מילולי (מלה, משפט, מקטע), או קונטכסטואלי של המקורות התנאיים.[8]

ב. בהיעדר קיומו של מקור תנאי מפורש כבסיס להכרעה בבעיה הלכתית המועלית בפניו, עדיין נשמרת אצלו הנטייה להיצמד אל הנאמר במקור התנאי, באמצעות היסקים לוגיים. עמדותיו ההלכתיות הן בעלות קשר צמוד והדוק עם הטכסט התנאי.[9]

לעומת דרכו של רב ששת, אצל רב נחמן בולט השימוש בסברה, הן כמקור הלכתי, והן כמקור פרשני, מה שגורר אחריו, בדרך כלל, גם שינוי הלכתי (ראה להלן). שתי התופעות יוצרות רושם של „שמרן" או „פורמליסט" ובעל עמדה הלכתית מחמירה הנעדרת סממנים התפתחותיים. מסקנה זו נסמכת על שורה של ממצאים שנדלו במהלך ניתוח ספרותו בתלמודים, תוך השוואה אל ממצאי ספרותם המקבילה של חכמי דורו הבולטים: רב נחמן, רב חסדא, רבה ורב יוסף (ובמקרים מסוימים גם רמי בר חמא), ואפילו ביחס לאמוראי נהרדעא האחרונים, בני הדור הרביעי, החמישי והשישי („אמרי נהרדע[א]י," רב חמא ואמימר).[10]

התופעה הנ"ל היא גם הרקע להבנת מספר אירועים הקשורים ברב ששת, ובכלל זה:

העמוקה והסברא השכלית, השאלות השנונות היא תעופת הרעיון מענין לענין, ממחשבה למחשבה עד בא אל המסקנה... קם ויהי בדור ההוא, דור שלישי לאמוראי בבל." קביעה כללית זו של גרץ זכתה ברבות הימים לחיזוקם של מחקרים ספרותיים. ראה, למשל: D. C. Kraemer, *Stylistic Characteristics of Amoraic Literature* (Ph.D diss., Jewish Theological Seminary of America, New York, 1984) 94; Kraemer, *The Mind of the Talmud: An Intellectual History of the Bavli* (New York: Oxford Univ. Press, 1990) 26–39. בדומה לכך עמד י"נ אפשטיין, מבוא לנוסח המשנה[3], א:353 על שלבי התמורה וההתפתחות בשימוש בסברה וההיגיון כבסיס להגהות שבתוכן ובלשון, במשנה. מסקנתו העיקרית היתה, שתהליך התגבשותן של דרכי הסברה וההיגיון בלטו ביותר למן הדור השלישי, והדבר בא לידי ביטוי בתיקונים ובהגהות שנעשו באופן תדיר במשנה, עד שהוציאוה מידי פשוטה.

7 להגדרת הגישה ה„פורמליסטית" של המשפט, ראה: מנחם מאוטנר, ירידת הפורמליזם ועליית הערכים במשפט הישראלי (תל אביב: במעגלי דעת, תשנ"ג) עמ' 13; David Lyons, "Legal Formalism and Instrumentalism — A Pathological Study," *Cornell Law Review* 66 (1981) 649, 950; אהרן ברק, פרשנות במשפט, כרך ראשון: תורת הפרשנות הכללית (ירושלים: נבו, תשנ"ב) עמ' 246, ושם בציונים הביבליוגרפיים המצויים בהערה 126. ראה גם: משה הלברטל, מהפכות פרשניות בהתהוותן: ערכים כשיקולים פרשניים במדרשי ההלכה (ירושלים: הוצאת ספרים ע"ש י"ל מאגנס, האוניברסיטה העברית, תשנ"ז) עמ' 38, ובספרות המצוינת שם בהערה 48.

8 ראה: ברק שלמה כהן, „רב ששת ודרכי לימודו במסגרת תקופתו," (עבודת דוקטור; אוניברסיטת בר-אילן, רמת-גן, תשס"ג) עמ' 38–82; 83–116; 117–133; 148–195.

9 ראה: כהן, „רב ששת ודרכי לימודו," עמ' 148–195.

10 דרך לימודם של אמוראי נהרדעא האחרונים ובראשם רב חמא ואמימר (שפעלו בנהרדעא במחצית השנייה של המאה השלישית ותחילת המאה הרביעית לסה"נ), משקפת מגמה הפוכה מזו השמרנית המיוצגת על ידי רב ששת, ראה: ברק שלמה כהן, „ניגודים בדרכי הלימוד של אמוראי נהרדעא האחרונים," *HUCA* 77 (2008) (בדפוס).

הממצאים אל יתר ספרותם בתלמוד, מעלה ניגוד בולט בדרך לימודם, ניגוד המתבטא באופי פרשנותם ובדרך הסקת מסקנות לוגיות מן המקורות התנאיים. באמצעות ניתוח ההבדל שבדרכי לימודם, ניתן להציע הסבר שיטתי ועקבי ליסוד עמדותיהם המנוגדות של שני החכמים בסוגיות התלמוד. הוא גם מציע פתרון חלופי – על זו המוצעת במחקר השכבתי – להבהרת פרשנותו הדחוקה של רב נחמן למקורות התנאיים. לעניין זה השלכה גם על דרך הפרשנות המדעית המקובלת של סוגיות תלמודיות בכלל.

חוקרים שעסקו בדרכי הלימוד בישיבות בבל בדורות הראשונים של תקופת התלמוד, נתעוררו – בעקבות התלמוד בהוריות, יד ע"א ומקבילתה – לאפיין את החכמים על פי אמת המידה של בקיאות („סיני") לעומת חריפות („עוקר הרים").[3] במסגרת זו, נתפש גם רב ששת כחכם הבולט במידת בקיאותו במקורות התנאיים. טענה זו מושתתת בעיקר על ביטויים שכיחים, המיוחסים לרב ששת: „תניתוה"; „מנא אמינא לה-דתניא"; „אנא מתניתא ידענא" ועוד, או המסופרים עליו: „אנא [רב נחמן] ורב ששת דתנינא הלכתא וספרא וספרי ותוספתא וכולי תלמודא"; „אמר רב עמרם: הא מילתא אמר לן רב ששת ואנהרינהו לעיינין ממתניתין/ממתניתא," ועוד.[4] בהתאם לכך, הוצג רב ששת לא רק כניגוד לרב חסדא, „השנון," „החריף," אלא גם כניגוד לרמי בר חמא, הידוע אף הוא ב„חריפותו."[5]

ואולם, מן המחקר על רב ששת עולה, שאין הוא חכם המציג רק ידע ובקיאות טכנית בספרות התנאית, אלא גם חכם ששימר – ואפילו בקנאות – את ההלכה התנאית בבבל, וזאת בדור שכבר מצויה בו תופעת הפלפול והלימוד מן הסברא, ונתלבטו בו אם „סיני" עדיף או „עוקר הרים."[6] אנו מציעים, שהתבססותו העקבית והשיטתית של רב ששת על

3 ראה, למשל, את סקירת דרכי הלימוד של אמוראי בבל בדור השני והשלישי על ידי: צבי גרץ, דברי ימי ישראל, מהדיר: שאול פנחם רבינוביץ (ח' חלקים; ירושלים: מקור, תשל"ב) ב:382 ואילך; אייזיק הירש ווייס, דור דור ודורשיו (ה' כרכים; ווין: הרצפלד ובאור, תרל"א-תרנ"א. ירושלים: זיו, תשכ"ד) ג:156 ואילך; זאב יעבץ, תולדות ישראל (י"ד חלקים; ווארשא: האחים שולדברג, תרנ"ד-ת"ש; תל אביב: עם עולם, תשט"ו-תשכ"ג) ז:122 ואילך; יהודה ליב מימון, אביי ורבא (ירושלים: מוסד הרב קוק, תשכ"ה) עמ' יא-יד. והשווה: יצחק אייזיק הלוי, דורות הראשונים (ו' חלקים; פרנקפורט: הוצאת המחבר, תרס"א) ב:422.

4 ראה: גרץ, דברי ימי ישראל, ב:390–391; ווייס, דור דור ודורשיו, ג:160–161; יעבץ, תולדות ישראל, ג:139–141; אהרן היימאן, תולדות תנאים ואמוראים (ג' כרכים; ירושלים: קריה נאמנה, תשכ"ד) ג:1232; יעקב שמואל צורי, שלטון ראשות הגולה והישיבות (תל אביב: מצפה, תרצ"ט) עמ' 151; מרדכי דב יודילוביץ, חיי היהודים בזמן התלמוד: ספר נהרדעא (ירושלים: מקור, תשל"א) עמ' 71–73; יעקב נחום אפשטיין, מבוא לנוסח המשנה[3] (ב' כרכים; ירושלים: הוצאת ספרים ע"ש י"ל מאגנס, האוניברסיטה העברית, תש"ס) א:360; חנוך אלבק, מבוא לתלמודים (תל אביב: דביר, תשכ"ט) עמ' 212–213; עזרא ציון מלמד, מדרשי הלכה של התנאים בתלמוד בבלי (ירושלים: הוצאת ספרים ע"ש י"ל מאגנס, האוניברסיטה העברית, תשמ"ח) עמ' 19–23; David Goodblatt, *Rabbinic Instruction in Sasanian Babylonia* (Leiden: Brill, 1975) 269; Richard Kalmin, *Sages, Stories, Authors and Editors in Rabbinic Babylonia* (Atlanta: Scholars Press, 1994) 8, n. 23.

5 ראה, למשל: יעבץ, תולדות ישראל, ג:139; גרץ, דברי ימי ישראל, ב:390; Goodblatt, *Rabbinic Instruction*, 269; אפרים אלימלך אורבך, חז"ל: פרקי אמונות ודעות[2] (ירושלים: הוצאת ספרים ע"ש י"ל מאגנס, האוניברסיטה העברית, תשנ"ח) עמ' 562. לניתוח דרך לימודו של רמי בר חמא, ראה: ברק שלמה כהן, „רמי בר חמא: דרכי לימודו וביקורתו של רבא," (עבודת מוסמך; אוניברסיטת בר-אילן, רמת-גן, תש"ס).

6 צויין במחקר, שבדור השלישי לאמוראי בבל החלה מגמה של שימוש בדרכי הסברה וההיגיון, והדבר בא לידי ביטוי בתרומתם הספרותית בתלמוד. גרץ, דברי ימי ישראל, ב:420, למשל, כותב: „עבודת המחשבה

רב ששת לעומת רב נחמן
שתי שיטות פרשניות למקורות תנאיים

ברק שלמה כהן
אוניברסיטת בר-אילן

Rav Nahman and Rav Sheshet
Conflicting Methods of Exegesis of Tannaitic Sources

Barak S. Cohen
Bar-Ilan University

Rav Nahman and Rav Sheshet, who lived in the early fourth century C.E., are two of the most prominent Babylonian *amoraim*. They are known for their numerous disagreements, having conflicting opinions on halakhic issues in over thirty five instances in both Talmuds. The present study presents a systematic analysis of the entire corpus of their disagreements revealing significant differences in their system of study and exegesis, primarily with regard to the use and interpretation of tannaitic sources. Their diverse approaches originate from differing methods of study: Rav Sheshet had a conservative approach, employing formalistic exegesis of tannaitic sources, while Rav Nahman employed an innovative technique, tending to expand tannaitic sources through creative interpretation. Moreover, there is a clear relationship between the data derived from an analysis of their respective methodologies and the rest of their literary legacy in talmudic literature. Indeed, the examination of the methodologies of Rav Nahman and Rav Sheshet demonstrates the importance of the careful examination of the *collective corpus* of amoraic literature. Ultimately this is the key to building a coherent intellectual history of the *amoraim*.

בשלושים ושש סוגיות בתלמודים,[1] מוצגות מחלוקות הלכתיות בין רב ששת ורב נחמן, מהבולטים שבין בני הפלוגתא של הדור השלישי בבבל.[2] ניתוח המחלוקות, והשוואת

1 תלמוד בבלי: ברכות מא ע״ב; שם מב ע״ב; שם מו ע״א; שם מט ע״א; שבת צד ע״ב; שם קכג ע״א; עירובין יא ע״ב; שם לב ע״ב; שם לט ע״ב; פסחים צב ע״ב; יומא ו ע״ב; שם כד ע״ב; סוכה מד ע״ב (ירושלמי, סוכה ד, ג [נד ע״ג]); שם מז ע״ב; ביצה לג ע״א; שם לט ע״א; תענית יד ע״ב; שם כט ע״ב; כתובות קי ע״א (ירושלמי, כתובות יג, ט [לו ע״ב]); גיטין לב ע״ב; שם סז ע״א; ב״ק סח ע״א; ב״מ מז ע״א; שם קא ע״א; ב״ב נב ע״ב; שם קמב ע״א; שם קמג ע״א; שם קנא ע״א; סנהדרין כו ע״ב; שם לג ע״א; מנחות קט ע״א-ע״ב (ארבעה מקרים); בכורות כג ע״ב. תלמוד ירושלמי: ברכות ד, ד (ח ע״ב). לא נכללים כאן שני מקרים הנוגעים לתחום האגדה (בבלי, נדרים מא ע״א; שם, ב״ב צא ע״ב), ומקרה נוסף (ירושלמי, שביעית י, א [לט ע״ג] והמקבילה במכות א, ב [לא ע״ב]), שבו פרשנותם נובעת ממגמה לתרץ מקורות תנאיים סותרים, והוא אינו מעניינו כאן.

2 לגישתנו בשאלת מהימנות ייחוס המימרות לאמוראים בבבלי, ראה להלן, הערה 112.

דוִד, מלך ישראל, מצליח המספר לחשוף את דמותו השלילית של דוִד אל מול דמותו ההרואית של אוריה.

כך גם בסיפור במלכים ב ט. אומנם איזבל אינה דמות חיובית, להפך, היא דמות שלילית מאוד, אך העמדת איזבל, שאינה מעם ישראל אלא מצידון, ברגעים האחרונים לחייה לבושה בבגדי מלכות, מכובדת, אמיצה ונלחמת על חייה אל מול דמותו השלילית כל כך של יהוא,[43] מלך ישראל, מבליטה את הפער בין שתי הדמויות הללו ברגע השיא של הסיפור.

בשני הסיפורים ניתן לראות את הקשר ההדוק בין פעולות הגיבורים ובין הדברים שבפיהם. על הקשר בין הפעולה ובין דברי הגיבור לא נכתב עדיין כל מחקר, ומוזר הדבר בעיני.[44] תיאור מעשי הגיבור והבאת דבריו משלימים זה את זה, ומגישים לקורא תמונה שלמה באשר לרגשות הגיבור.

בסיפור דוִד ובת שבע אוריה אינו יורד לביתו, וכל מאמצי דוִד לפתותו להיכנס לביתו עולים בתוהו.[45] עקביותו של אוריה מתבטאת גם בעת שכרותו, ואף במצב זה הוא נשאר ללון בפתח הארמון. פעולתו זו של אוריה מקבלת משנה תוקף כאשר הוא מדבר. רק אז הקורא משוכנע מה מתחולל בנפש אוריה פנימה.

כך גם איזבל: היא מתייפה, ועדיין הקורא אינו משוכנע מה היו מניעיה. רק כאשר היא אומרת: „השלום זמרי הרג אדוניו" אנחנו מבינים מה מתחולל בנפשה. שני הסיפורים דומים זה לזה בסיטואציה שהם מציגים: אוריה ואיזבל מעיזים פנים כלפי אנשים חזקים מהם, למרות שהם יודעים שדבר זה יכול לעלות להם בחייהם. המספרים העמידו את שתי הדמויות כדמויות הרואיות רגע לפני מותן, ולעומתם העמידו את דוִד ואת יהוא (מלכי ישראל) כאנשים שפלים, שאינם בוחלים בכל אמצעי. דוִד רוצח את אוריה, ויהוא רוצח את איזבל, שניהם עשו זאת ללא כל רחמים. רק דברי שני הנרצחים לפני מותם מהדהדים באזני הקורא, ומציגים את הרוצחים במלוא שפלותם.

דוד ראה במאמרם של מנחם פרי ומאיר שטרנברג, „המלך במבט אירוני – על תחבולותיו של המספר בסיפור דוד ובת שבע ושתי הפלגות לתיאוריה של הפרוזה," הספרות א (תשכ"ה) עמ' 263–293.

43 ראה בנימין אופנהיימר, „משמעותו של סיפור יהוא," ספר בן גוריון (ירושלים: עז לדוד, תשכ"ד) עמ' 302–304. תדמור לעומת זאת טוען שהמספר מתכוון לשבח את יהוא: חיים תדמור, אנציקלופדיה מקראית ג, ערך „יהוא," עמ' 473–478.

44 כפי שציינתי, החוקרים התמקדו באפיון הגיבור באמצעות פעולותיו או באמצעות דבריו, אך לא עמדו על הקשר בין שניהם.

45 על השאלה מדוע אין אוריה יורד אל ביתו, ראה בהרחבה: בעז ערפלי, „זהירות, סיפור מקראי – הערות לסיפור דוד ובת שבע ולשאלות הפואטיקה של הסיפור המקראי," הספרות ב, מספר 3 (תש"מ) עמ' 591–592.

לעיתים שיהוא הוא האיש הנבחר על ידי האל, ושהוא האדם העומד לרשת את כס המלוכה בישראל. מעשיו של יהוא מתאפיינים בפרק ט בזלזול בסובבים אותו, בהפחדות חוזרות ונשנות, בניבול פה ובהתנהגות ברוטלית קיצונית. התכונות המאפיינות את יהוא בפרק זה הן: אכזריות, קור רוח, מהירות פעולה, ערמומיות וארוגנטיות. תכונות אלה הן תכונות מובהקות של שר צבא, ותכונות אלה הכשירו אותו, כנראה, להגיע למלוכה.

מיד וללא שהיות, עם הכרזת המלוכה, יהוא קושר על יהורם: „...ויאמרו מלך יהוא; ויתקשר יהוא בן יהושפט..." (פסוקים 13–14). המרד מתרחש כאשר יורם, שנפצע במלחמה נגד ארם שוכב ביזרעאל כדי להתרפא (פסוקים 15–16). הניגוד בין מטרת ביקורו של אחזיה, מלך יהודה, ובין מטרת בואו של יהוא בולט לעין. בעוד אחזיה עושה דבר אנושי במצב זה: מצוות ביקור חולים, הרי יהוא מנצל את חולשתו של יורם כדי להורגו. לפני בוא יהוא ליזרעאל הוא מזהיר את מחנהו בלשון הפחדה מאיימת: „אם יש נפשכם אל יצא פליט מן העיר ללכת להגיד ביזרעאל" (פסוק 15). תשובותיו הלועגות לרוכבי הסוס, המבקשים את שלומו „מה לך ולשלום" (פסוקים 18–19) מתאימות לרוח מילות האיום הקודמות. המספר מוסיף הערת שוליים אחת המתארת את אופיו של יהוא לאורך כל הסיפור: „והמנהג כמנהג יהוא בן נמשי כי בשגעון ינהג" (פסוק 20). תשובתו ליורם השואל בשלומו „מה השלום עד זנוני איזבל אמך וכשפיה הרבים" (פסוק 22) אינה מותירה בלב הקורא ספק בדבר אופיו הגס של יהוא. תפקידו של יהוא היה להכרית את בית אחאב, אך תאוות הרצח מעבירה אותו על דעתו, והוא ממשיך במסע זה עד שהוא מחסל גם את אחזיה, מלך יהודה (פסוק 27). שיא הברוטליות של יהוא מתגלה, כאמור, לאחר הרצח המחריד של איזבל: „ויבא ויאכל וישת" (פסוק 34).[40]

נראה לי, כי ניתן להשוות את הדמויות בסיפור יהוא – איזבל לדמויות בסיפור דוִד – אוריה החיתי (שמואל ב יא). דוִד, מלך ישראל, מוצג באור שלילי ביותר במעשיו עם בת שבע ועם אוריה, אך המספר ממעט לשפוט את דוִד. המספר מעמיד את דמות אוריה כנגד דמותו של דוִד,[41] ודבריו היחידים של אוריה בפרק יא הם דברי הביקורת החריפים ביותר כלפי דוִד.[42] בהעמדת המספר את אוריה, שאינו מעם ישראל אלא מבני חת, כנגד

40 על ההשוואה בין יהוא ובין דוִד, ראה אצל ישראל רוזנסון, „קושר או מלך עם ה' – יהוא מול דוד," מגדים לב (תש"ס) עמ' 69–81. במאמר מובלטת דמותו החיובית של דוִד בהשוואה לדמותו השלילית של יהוא הן מבחינת הדרך לביסוס הממלכה, הן מבחינת שיגעונם וכיוצא בזה, אך אין המאמר עוסק בהשוואה בין הצמדים דוִד – אוריה ויהוא – איזבל, כפי שאני מראה בפסקה הבאה.

41 על דרכו זו של המספר המקראי ראה: סימון, קריאה ספרותית במקרא, עמ' 323: „הנגדה כזאת עם דמות משנית חיובית, שערכיה והתנהגותה משקפות את הגישה הרווחת והמקובלת, מאפשרת למספר להורות על מעלתו היתירה של גיבורו מבלי לפארו בלשון המדברת גבוהה...לעומת זאת משמש העימות עם אוריה החיתי, המסרב לרדת אל ביתו שלו, כדי להוקיע את חטאו של דוד באשת קצינו...."

42 המספר מציג את דברי אוריה בפרק זה פעם אחת בלבד (פסוק 11): „ויאמר אוריה אל דוד הארון וישראל ויהודה ישבים בסכות ואדני יואב ועבדי אדני על פני השדה חנים ואני אבוא אל ביתי לאכל ולשתות ולשכב עם אשתי חיך וחי נפשך אם אעשה את הדבר הזה." בדברי אוריה טבועה ביקורת נוקבת כלפי דוִד, ביקורת שהמספר נמנע מלהציגה במילים מפורשות. אוריה טוען כלפי דוִד שהוא שלח את כל העם למלחמה, ואילו הוא עצמו נשאר בביתו ונהנה ממנעמי החיים הטובים. הוא, אוריה, אינו מסוגל לנהוג כדוִד, כי הוא מרגיש אחריות כלפי חבריו. אוריה בדבריו מוצג כאדם לויאלי, ואילו דוִד מוצג כדמות אגוצנטרית, הדואג לצרכיו האישיים בלבד. אינני נכנס לשאלה האם בדברים אלה אוריה מביע את הרגשתו האישית, או האם המספר בוחר באוריה כדי לבקר את דוִד ושם בפיו את הדברים. על דברי אוריה והקשר שלהם למשל כבשת הרש ראה: אוריאל סימון, „סיפור מקראי בתפיסה אירונית – על האינטרפרטאציה של סיפור דוד ובת שבע," הספרות ב, מספר 3 (תש"מ) עמ' 598–607. על הביקורת הסמויה של המחבר כלפי

מה ביקש המספר לומר על הדמות המרכזית בסיפור של פרק ט – יהוא?[36] יהוא נבחר על ידי האל להוציא לפועל את הכרתת בית אחאב. יהוא מופיע בסיפור כאדם החלטי הפועל ללא מורא, אך יחד עם זאת הוא מתגלה כאדם רע מעללים, שאינו יודע כל מעצורים. כך גם איזבל. איזבל היא דמות שלילית ביותר בסיפור, כפי שכבר הראיתי. בהשוואה בין שתי הדמויות נראה לי, שהמספר הציג את איזבל ברגע מותה כדמות חיובית אמיצה ובעלת כבוד. לעומתה, מוצג יהוא ברגע מותה באור שלילי מאוד. המספר מתאר את פעולותיו של יהוא ברציפות וללא הפסקות להרהר בהן. פעולות יהוא מצביעות על אדם קשוח, רע לב, שאין לו כל מחשבות חרטה על מעשיו. רגע השיא של אטימות לב מצוי בפעולתו של יהוא מיד לאחר הריגת איזבל. מצד אחד מצוי התיאור המצמרר: „וישמטוה ויז מדמה אל הקיר ואל הסוסים וירמסנה," וללא שהיות מצד שני: „ויבא ויאכל וישת"[37] (פסוקים 33–34). איזבל, שאין לנו לומר אף לא מילה אחת לזכותה, זכתה לרגע של חסד מצד המספר בשעת מותה. הסיפור המקראי מעצב את דמויותיו בדרך זו לעיתים קרובות: דמויות חיוביות ביותר זוכות מנגד גם לביקורת וליחס פחות אוהד מצד המספר. כך גם דמויות שליליות זוכות ליחס אוהד, ולעיתים אף אוהב, מצד המספר.[38] בכך מצליחים מספרי המקרא להציג דמויות מורכבות, הרחוקות מאוד מסטריאוטיפ קבוע של שחור ולבן.[39] אפילו איזבל זכתה עם מותה להיות דמות מורכבת ולא דמות חד-ממדית, שכל פעולותיה צפויות מראש.

דווקא דמותו של יהוא מפתיעה אותנו. היינו מצפים, שבחירת האלוהים באדם שיוציא לפועל את תכניתו, תהיה בחירה של אדם חיובי, אך לעינינו נגלה אדם שלילי ביותר. המספר מציג אדם כוחני ללא כל גבולות, שאינו בוחל בשום אמצעי, והקורא אינו מאמין

36 על אופיו של יהוא בסיפור ראה: ישראל רוזנסון, „סיפור יהוא ושאלת המסר הכפול," מגדים כה (תשנ"ו) עמ' 111–124; עדין שטיינזלץ, „יהוא – מלך ישראל," דמויות מן המקרא (תל אביב: אוניברסיטה משודרת, תשמ"א) עמ' 88–95.

37 על הפער בין המעשים האכזריים של יהוא לבין המעשים היום-יומיים שעשה מיד לאחר מכן, ראה: בר אפרת, העיצוב האמנותי, עמ' 101; רוזנסון, „סיפור יהוא," עמ' 114: „העובדה שיהוא אוכל ושותה בין רמיסתה של איזבל לקבורתה מעוררת תחושה של אטימות ואכזריות מיותרות." המספר המקראי מצליח להמחיש את רגש השנאה בדרך דומה בסיפור יוסף ואחיו (בראשית לז). לאחר השלכת יוסף אל הבור מתאר המספר את הבור „והבור רק אין בו מים" (פסוק 24), ומיד לאחר מכן „וישבו לאכל לחם" (פסוק 25). הפער העצום בין השלכת יוסף אל הבור, שאפילו מים אין בו, לבין הישיבה בניחותא לאכול לחם כמעשה יום-יום מצביע על רגשות השנאה של האחים כלפי יוסף. כך גם תיאור רציחתה הנורא של איזבל בהשוואה לפעולות יום-יומיות כמו שתייה ואכילה מיד לאחר מכן מראה על רגשותיו השליליים של יהוא כלפי איזבל. וראה על סיפור יוסף ואחיו בעמודים 2–3 של מאמר זה.

38 אביא שתי דוגמאות לכך, דוגמה לכל צד: דוִד המלך, שזכה לשבחים רבים מצד מספרי המקרא, מוצג באור לא סימפתי ביותר בסיפור בת שבע (שמואל ב יא), והמספר אינו חושש להציגו כדמות אנושית בעלת יצרים אפלים. כך גם מצטיירות דמויותיהם של משה, של אברהם, של יעקב ושל דמויות אחרות. לעומת זאת, שאול, המלך הראשון בישראל, מוצג בסיפורים בספר שמואל כדמות שלילית, לעיתים על גבול שיגעון, הפועל בניגוד לדברי ה', מתעמת עם הנביא שמואל, מאשים את העם במעשיו הוא (סיפור עמלק – שמואל א טו 15), מנסה לחסל את דוִד, ובכל אופן מציג אותו המספר בסופרלטיבים, שלא היו מביישים איש: „... בחור וטוב ואין איש מבני ישראל טוב ממנו משכמו ומעלה גבה מכל העם" (שמואל א ט 2).

39 ראה על הדמויות המורכבות בסיפורי המקרא אצל פולק, הסיפור במקרא, עמ' 261–262; בר אפרת, העיצוב האמנותי, עמ' 73–112; יאירה אמית, לקרוא סיפור מקראי (בלי מקום: משרד הביטחון, תש"ס) עמ' 76–87; גויטיין, „אומנות הסיפור במקרא," עמ' 36. גויטיין כותב כך: „כפי שהודגש לעיל, אין בדרך כלל בסיפור התנכי רשע גמור או צדיק גמור. אפילו באחאב המתמכר לעשות רעה יש כמה צדדים טובים, גם עשו אינו כלל טיפוס של רשע, אלא תופעה מובנה ומוצדקה מתוך עצמה."

מפני איזבל באופן גלוי לעין. למזלו, שניים שלושה סריסים האמינו בכוחו ועזרו לו לשים קץ לחיי איזבל. הן בגמגום של יהוא והן בביטוי „שנים שלשה" מוביל אותנו המספר אל שיאו של הסיפור.[32] בחירתה של איזבל במילים „השלום זמרי הרג אדניו" היא מחושבת מאוד, בדיוק כמו בחירתה בפעולות שקדמו למילים אלה. זמרי שמרד במלך והרגו, מלך רק שבעה ימים, „וזכה" גם הוא להיות מודח מכס המלוכה בשל מרד נגדו. בהשוואה שעושה איזבל בין יהוא ובין זמרי, היא לא רק אומרת ליהוא שהיא יודעת שהוא רצח את בנה, אלא גם רומזת לכך שימיו ספורים.

כדי להבין את התמונה המדויקת המתוארת בפסוקים אלה, אנסה להציג את הסיפור כמחזה חי לפני קהל על במה: לאחר הרצח של מלך ישראל ומלך יהודה בידי יהוא, יהוא מגיע ליזרעאל כדי להשלים את המרד ולהרוג את איזבל, היורשת הרשמית של בנה. כניסתו וודאי מלווה במוסיקה מסתורית המשרה מתח באולם. איזבל שמעה על בואו ועל מות בנה, ובמקום ללבוש בגדי אבלות ולמרר בבכי, כפי שעשתה אם סיסרא[33] בספר שופטים פרק ה 28 „בעד החלון נשקפה ותיבב אם סיסרא בעד האשנב," היא לובשת בגדי מלכות ומשדרת עוצמה וביטחון.[34] יהוא נכנס עם פמלייתו בשער הארמון, וברגע זה מופיעה איזבל ממרומי הארמון. יהוא אינו יודע אם היא שמעה מה קרה עד כה, והוא שואב עידוד רב מהמילה הראשונה שהיא אומרת „השלום." את המילה הזו הוא כבר שמע מספר פעמים בעבר, ובכל המקרים ידו הייתה על העליונה. הפעם הזו מצליחה איזבל להפתיע אותו כל כך שלשונו נאלמת. המילים „זמרי הורג אדוניו" אינן משאירות ספק בלב יהוא שהוא מצוי בסכנה מוחשית לחייו. הוא נושא את עיניו לעבר החלון ומבין שלאיזבל יש יתרון גובה, ואין לו ברירה אלא לנסות את מזלו בחיפוש עזרה, שם במרומי הארמון.[35] גם השאלה המגומגמת שהוא מצליח לפלוט מראה את המתחולל בנפשו. רק מזל (שניים שלושה סריסים) מציל את חייו וחורץ את גורל איזבל. המספר הצליח בדרך זו לבנות תמונה דרמתית מעולה המתקדמת לשיאה, והקורא סקרן לדעת כיצד תסתיים הדרמה הזו.

על שניים שלושה סריסים להשליך את איזבל מן החלון, בדיוק כפי שעשה לאורך כל הפרק. הפעם הוא אינו בטוח ביכולתו לגרום לסובבים אותו למלא את בקשתו בציווי חד משמעי, וזאת בשל ההלם שהוא שרוי בו בעקבות שאלתה המפתיעה של איזבל. נראה לי, שניתן להשוות את הלך רוחו של יהוא, המתבטא בחזרה על המילה „מי" להלך רוחו של עשו, המתבטא בחזרה על המילה „אדום," וראה על כך את דבריו של הרשב"ם לבראשית כה 30: „דרך אדם הממהר לשאול מחברו כופל את דבריו וזה שהיה רעב הרי הוא כאומר תן לי מהרה אוכל."

32 שיאו של הסיפור מצוי בנקודה שבה הקורא אינו יודע מי יגבר על מי. במילים ,שניים שלושה' מדגיש המספר את גורם המקריות, שהוא קבע את גורלה של איזבל.

33 כמה חוקרים ראו את הקשר בין אם סיסרא ובין איזבל בשל השתקפותן בעד החלון. ראה על כך למשל: קיל, „ספר מלכים"; בוסתנאי, עולם התנ"ך. השוני בין שתי ההופעות בחלון מתבטא בעיקר במטרת ההופעה של שתי הנשים. בעוד אם סיסרא משקיפה בעד החלון כשהיא ממררת בבכי, הרי איזבל מופיעה בחלון כמלכה לכל דבר, ומבליטה את בטחונה בשלטונה, וראה על כך אצל קוגן ותדמור (Cogan, *2 Kings*). על המשמעות המיוחדת של הפועל „יבבה" ראה אצל יהודה רצהבי, „פסוק ותרגומו," בית מקרא, תש"ס ב (קס"א), עמ' 170.

34 וראה על הקשר בין הדברים בהערה 28.

35 לחיזוק דברים אלה ראה את תרגום השבעים: „ויאמר: מי את, רדי אלי!" חיים שלי, מתרגם, תרגום לעברית של נוסח השבעים לנביאים ראשונים (תל אביב: הוצאת שלי, תשמ"ג) עמ' 130. לפי השבעים, יהוא אכן חושש מיתרון הגובה שיש לאיזבל, ומבקש ממנה לרדת אליו. מובן מאליו גם שיהוא משים עצמו כאדם שאינו מכיר את איזבל, וזאת כדי להרוויח זמן.

מונטגומרי, הובס ובוסתנאי.[25] לעומתם טוען פרקר, שמטרת איזבל לפי פעולותיה ודבריה הייתה לפתות את יהוא.[26] מהי אם כך מטרתו של המספר בתארו את פעולותיה האחרונות של איזבל? נדמה לי שאי אפשר להפריד בין פעולותיה של איזבל לבין דבריה. מיד לאחר הפעולות מופיעות מילים שאין לפרשן בשתי דרכים: „השלום זמרי הרג אדניו" (פסוק 31). לפי מלכים א טז 8–20 זמרי מרד באלה בן בעשא, מלך שבעה ימים, והתאבד בביתו בשל מרד עמרי. המילים „השלום זמרי הרג אדניו" נאמרות בסרקזם.[27] הניגוד בין המילה הראשונה „השלום" ובין המשך דבריה של איזבל בולט מאוד. אין קשר בין זמרי הקשור למרד ולרצח מלך ישראל ובין עשיית שלום. מי שמנסה להשוות בין מעשה יעל בספר שופטים לבין כוונת איזבל בסיפור שלנו טועה, לדעתי, בהבנת כוונתה של איזבל. בעוד יעל עושה הכל כדי לפתות את סיסרא להיכנס לאוהלה כדי להורגו, הרי איזבל אינה עושה דבר כדי למצוא חן בעיני יהוא. ראשית, יעל יוצאת לקראת סיסרא כדי לקבל את פניו. לעומת זאת איזבל נשארת בתוך הארמון משקיפה בעד החלון.[28] יעל פונה אל סיסרא בלשון מתרפסת „סורה אדני סורה" (שופטים ד 18).[29] תחינתה של יעל מתבטאת בהכפלת השורש סו"ר, בכינוי „אדני" אל סיסרא, ובשימוש הקוהורטאטיב הכפול הבא לציין דרך של בקשה. איזבל לעומת זאת אינה אומרת דבר הרומז על התרפסות. לו איזבל הייתה מעונינת לפתות את יהוא, אין ספק שהזכרת זמרי אינה משרתת כוונה זו. מתגובת יהוא ניתן לראות שהוא הבין היטב את כוונתה של איזבל. לאורך כל הסיפור היו ליהוא מעני לשון חדים וברוטליים.[30] זו הפעם היחידה שהוא אינו מוצא מילים מתאימות, והאלם מתבטא גם בפנייתו אל החלון שממנו נשקפת איזבל. דבריו המגומגמים: „מי אתי מי" (פסוק 32),[31] מביעים את חששו

---

on a sarcastic nuance.... There is no sense of false hope in her question. She taunts Jehu openly. To label him 'Zimri' is the ultimate insult."

25 J.A. Montgomery, *The Books of Kings*, ICC (1960) 403; Trevor R. Hobbs, *2 Kings*, WBC (1985) 118; עודד בוסתנאי, עולם התנ"ך: ספר מלכים ב (תל אביב: דודזון-עתי, 1994) עמ' 78–80.

26 ראה Parker, "Jezebel's Reception of Jehu." התנגדות נחרצת לדעה זו של פרקר ראה בביקורתו של Olyan, "Hashalom," 668.

27 ראה Olyan, "Hashalom," 668. כבר רלב"ג (אברבנאל, פירוש על נביאים ראשונים) הבין כך את המילים: „...ולזה אמרה בגאווה ליהוא השלום זמרי הורג אדוניו."

28 המוטיב של „האישה בחלון" ידוע לנו מפיניקיה, ממצרים, ומבבל. מלוחית שנהב מהמאה השמינית לפני הספירה ניתן לראות ראש אישה המביטה נכחה, מחייכת קלות, שערותיה מסורקות בתסרוקת מצרית, והיא נשקפת בעד החלון. ראה: J. B. Pritchard, *The Ancient Near East in Pictures* (2nd ed.; Princeton, N.J.: Princeton Univ. Press, 1969) 131; בוסתנאי, עולם התנ"ך, עמ' 78–79. לפי בוסתנאי, איזבל מבליטה את מעמדה כגבירה, מתפנה להתאפר ולהתקשט ומשקיפה בעד החלון, וכל זה מעיד על אופיה החזק של איזבל ועל בטחונה. ראה על כך גם: Cogan, *2 Kings*, 111. מוטיב „האישה בחלון" נפוץ באומנות הפניקית ומופיע על שנהבים רבים. החוקרים נוטים לזהות את האישה שבחלון עם עשתורת. התפתחותו של נושא „האישה בחלון" נעוצה באגדה קיפרית של נערה בשם עשתורת, המשיבה את פני אהובה, אדוניס, ריקם. משהתאבד אדוניס, וגופתו נשרפת, מחייכת עשתורת ללא רחם. חיוך זה מעורר את חמתה של האלה אפרודיטי, והיא מקפיאה אותה באבן. נראה לי (כמו לקוגן ולתדמור, Cogan, *2 Kings*), שאין קשר לסיפור איזבל עם אגדה זו, אך יש קשר הדוק בין הופעת איזבל בחלון ובין הופעתה המלכותית כפי שרואים בלוחיות המלכותיות בכל האזור.

29 ראה יוסי לשם, „אמה ושפחה בסיפורי המקרא של תקופת המלוכה," בית מקרא קנא (תשנ"ז) עמ' 330.

30 ראה על מעני הלשון ועל פעולותיו של יהוא בהמשך המאמר.

31 המילים „מי אתי מי" נאמרות בהיסוס, שהוא על גבול הגמגום. זאת ניתן לראות משתי בחינות: א) החזרה על המילה „מי" מדגישה את היסוסו של יהוא. מילת השאלה הראשונה די בה להראות את תחינת יהוא למתן עזרה. החזרה עליה נוטעת בלב הקורא הרגשה של חוסר ביטחון והיסוס. ב) יהוא יכול היה לצוות

בהבנת פעולותיה של איזבל. רש"י[17] מבין שפעולותיה של איזבל נעשו כדי שתמצא חן בעיני יהוא והוא ישא אותה לאישה. רד"ק[18] מסכים עם רש"י, אך מציאת החן היא לשם הצלת חייה שלא יהרגה. רלב"ג[19] לעומת זאת טוען שהיא קישטה את עצמה כדי שיהוא יחמול עליה, אך ממשיך ואומר „או עשתה זה להחזיק המלוכה עדיין והוא יותר נכון...." אברבנאל רואה את פעולותיה של איזבל כמצביעות על כך שהיא מתנהגת כדרך הזונות.[20] אורי אלטר בספרו אמנות הסיפור במקרא מקדיש פרק לדרכי אפיון ואמנות השתיקה במקרא. בראשית פרק זה הוא כותב: „כל הרמזים הניתנים לנו על רגש, על גישה, או על כוונה הם מזעריים. מעניקים לנו רק את הרמזים הפשוטים ביותר על הופעה חיצונית, על תנועות ועל הבעות פנים, על לבוש הדמויות ועל כליהן, או על הסביבה החומרית שבה הן פועלות."[21] כך גם כותב ש"ד גוטיין במאמרו „אמנות הסיפור במקרא": „לא ניתן תיאור הגוף או הלבוש של האישים או תיאור של הנוף אלא עד כמה שהוא צריך לקידום עצם המעשה."[22]

נראה שתיאור פעולותיה של איזבל משרת את קידום העלילה, ויותר מכך הוא מציג את איזבל באור מיוחד במינו. האור השלילי, שבו מוצגת איזבל לאורך כל הסיפור, מתעמעם במעט כבר לאור פירושיהם של פרשני ימי הביניים, שאינם תמימי דעות לגבי הבנת מעשיה של איזבל. רוב הפרשנים המודרניים אינם רואים בפעולותיה של איזבל גורם שלילי אלא להפך. כך למשל, י. קיל הטוען שאיזבל החליטה ללבוש בגדי מלכות ולהפגין בכך את זכותה למלוך במקום בנה שנהרג בידי מורדים.[23] או ש. אוליין, שאינו רואה כל משמעות של התרפסות מצד איזבל במעשיה אלא רק הפגנת כוח כנגד רוצח בנה.[24] וכך גם רואים זאת

17 מקראות גדולות הכתר, מלכים א–ב (מהדורת מנחם כהן; רמת גן: הוצאת אוניברסיטת בר-אילן, תשנ"ה) עמ' 201.

18 מקראות גדולות הכתר, מלכים א–ב, עמ' 201.

19 מקראות גדולות הכתר, מלכים א–ב, עמ' 201.

20 דון יצחק אברבנאל, פירוש על נביאים ראשונים (ירושלים: תורה ודעת, תשט"ו) עמ' תרל"א.

21 אלטר, אומנות הסיפור במקרא, עמ' 133. בעמוד 135 כותב אלטר:

> בסיפורים... קיים מערך שלם של אמצעים, בעלי דרגות שונות של בהירות וודאות, למסירת מידע על המניעים, על העמדות ועל טבען המוסרי של הדמויות. ניתן לחשוב על מערך זה של אמצעים כעל סולם דרגות המסודר לפי מידת הוודאות והמפורשות שבה האמצעים הללו מציגים את אופי הדמויות. האופי יכול להתגלות באמצעות דיווח על מעשים; באמצעות ההופעה, התנועות, צורת העמידה, הלבוש... הקצה הנמוך ביותר של סולם זה – כאשר האופי מתגלה באמצעות המעשים והפעולות או באמצעות ההופעה החיצונית של הדמות – מותיר אותנו בעצם בתחום ההיקש.

ראה גם אצל Parker, "Jezebel's Reception of Jehu," 67: "Nevertheless, motives are conveyed to the listener or reader, especially through what a character does and says. If the motives are not apparent to us, that may be because we do not understand the implications or connections of the character's words and acts."

22 שלמה דוב גויטיין, „אומנות הסיפור במקרא," עיונים במקרא (תל אביב: יבנה, תשי"ח) עמ' 11–40, בעיקר ראה עמ' 24–25.

23 ראה קיל, „ספר מלכים," עמ' תקע: „בימי יהורם בנה היה לה מעמד של גבירה (י 13). עם מות בנה ראתה את עצמה למלוך תחתיו... היא החליטה ללבוש בגדי מלכות... ולהפגין בכך את זכותה למלוך במקום בנה שנהרג בקשר של מורדים וחומסי שלטון."

24 ראה Olyan, "Hashalom," 668: "For the first time in the story, the question 'hashalom' has taken

במלכים ב פרק ט.[13] הסיפור עצמו מגנה את איזבל מספר פעמים: בפסוק 7 איזבל נושאת באחריות לאחריתו של בית אחאב „ונקמתי... מיד איזבל." נבואת מותה של איזבל גם היא מתוארת במילים קשות מאוד: „ואת איזבל יאכלו הכלבים בחלק יזרעאל ואין קבר..." (פסוק 10). מותה של איזבל מתואר בצבעים קודרים עוד יותר: „... וישמטוה ויז מדמה אל הקיר ואל הסוסים וירמסנה" (פסוק 33). כך גם קללתו של יהוא את יהורם, בנה, „עד זנוני איזבל אמך וכשפיה הרבים" (פסוק 22). נדמה שאין עוד אישה במקרא ש„זכתה" לכינויים כה בוטים. לאור דברים אלה אין תמה, אפוא, שקורא נוטה לפרש את כל מעשיה של איזבל כמעשים שפלים, שכל תכליתם היא לזרוע הרס, לכשף, ולזנות.

בדיקה מדוקדקת של הכתובים מעלה תמונה שונה ומורכבת יותר. אחת המילים המנחות בפרק ט היא המילה „השלום."[14] מילה זו מופיעה חמש פעמים בפרקנו: לראשונה שואלים עבדי המלך את יהוא אם הנער הנביא בא בשלום (פסוק 11). לאחר מכן שני רוכבי הסוס ששלח יהורם שואלים את יהוא שאלה זו (פסוקים 18–19),[15] ויהורם הנאיבי אינו מבין עדיין שיהוא בא לרוצחו. יהורם עצמו שואל שוב את יהוא „השלום," ורק לאחר הקללה הנמרצת של יהוא הוא מבין את כוונתו הזדונית, ומספיק לקרוא לעבר אחזיה מילה אחת בלבד: „מרמה" (פסוק 23). הפעם החמישית מופיעה בדברי איזבל בפסוק 31. לכאורה, גם איזבל עדיין לא הפנימה את כוונתו של יהוא, וגם היא נוקטת אותה לשון „השלום," אך התבוננות נוספת בדבריה ובמעשיה של איזבל תראה לנו שעתה למילה „השלום" יש משמעות שונה לחלוטין.

עם בוא יהוא בשער הארמון ביזרעאל, נאמר „ואיזבל שמעה." מה שמעה איזבל? האם היא שמעה שיהוא הגיע? האם היא שמעה שבנה נרצח על ידי יהוא, או שמא היא שמעה את שני הדברים גם יחד? מן הפסוק הזה אין לקורא תשובה חד-משמעית, כי המספר כדרכו אינו מציין זאת במפורש. לעומת זאת, המספר מתאר שתי פעולות שאיזבל עושה לאחר ששמעה מה ששמעה: היא צובעת את עיניה[16] ואחר סורקת שערה. הפרשנים נחלקים

13 על מורכבות הסיפור ראה: בנימין אופנהיימר, הנבואה הקדומה בישראל (ירושלים: מאגנס, תשל"ג) עמ' 209–211; אברהם רופא, סיפורי הנביאים: הסיפורת הנבואית במקרא, סוגיה ותולדותיה (ירושלים: מאגנס, תשמ"ג) עמ' 72–78.

14 על המילה המנחה ראה אצל מרטין מרדכי בובר, „סגנון המילה המנחה בסיפורי התורה," דרכו של מקרא (ירושלים: מוסד ביאליק, תשל"ח) עמ' 284, 286–307; פולק, הסיפור במקרא, עמ' 91–93, ושם ביבליוגרפיה רחבה; פרנץ רוזנצוויג, בסוד הצורה של סיפורי המקרא (ירושלים: נהריים, תשל"ח) עמ' 12–16; בר אפרת, העיצוב האמנותי של הסיפור במקרא, עמ' 22–25, 147; אלטר, אומנות הסיפור במקרא, עמ' 110–114. דוגמאות מהשירה ראה: Wilfred G.E. Watson, *Classical Hebrew Poetry*, JSOT Suppl. 26 (Sheffield: Sheffield Univ. Press, 1984) 287–95; על המילה המנחה „שלום" ועל משמעות השורש של"מ, ראה: Saul Olyan, "Hashalom: Some Literary Considerations of 2 Kings 9," *CBQ* 46 (1984) 652–68.

15 במקרה השני כתוב „שלום" ולא „השלום." נראה לי, שהמספר בפעם השניה שם בפי רוכב הסוס שאלה מהוססת יותר. לאחר שרוכב הסוס הראשון לא חזר, רוכב הסוס השני מבין, שמשהו אינו כשורה. הרגשה זו מתבטאת בהיסוס שבו מנוסחת השאלה.

16 על משמעותו המדויקת של ה„פוך," ראה: חיים רבין, אנציקלופדיה מקראית (ט' כרכים; ירושלים: מוסד ביאליק, תש"י–תשי"ט) ו, ערך „פוך," עמ' 442; W. Sommer, "The Meaning of 'puch' in the Old Testament," *JBL* 62 (1943) 33–35; יהודה קיל, „ספר מלכים," דעת מקרא (ירושלים: מוסד הרב קוק, תשמ"ט) עמ' תקע"א; ולאחרונה ראה: M. Cogan and H. Tadmor, *2 Kings*, AB (New York: Doubleday, 1988) 111–12. בהוראה זו של אבן בעלת גוון כחול היא מופיעה גם בירמיהו ד 30, וההקשר הוא זנותי: „מאסו בך עגבים."

הסיפור המקראי ממחיש לקורא את רגשות הגיבור דרך פעולותיו, כי מאז ומתמיד בספרות העולמית הפעולה נחשבה כמראה לנפש הגיבור. אם ניקח למשל את ספרו של תומאס מאן, יוסף ואחיו,[8] שאין ספק שהוא רומן ולא סיפור דרמתי, כי הרי הוא מכיל תיאורים ארוכים ומפורטים שאינם מצויים במקרא, הרי גם הוא משתמש בפעולת הגיבור כדי לשפוך אור על רגשותיו. תומאס מאן מתאר באריכות את התלבטויותיהם הקשות של האחים לפני שהם משליכים את יוסף אל הבור. בניגוד לתיאורים המפורטים האלה כותב תומאס מאן מיד לאחר מכן: „ועתה, כתום מלאכתם, ישבו אפוא האחים על מעלות מבוא הבאר כדי לנוח שם ואחדים מהם הוציאו לחם וגבינה מחפת חגורתם לערוך את סעודת היום."[9] הדמיון בין התיאור המקראי ובין תיאורו של תומאס מאן בולט לעין. בסיפור יוסף ואחיו המקראי מתאר הספר את השלכת יוסף אל הבור: „ויקחהו וישלכו אתו הברה והבור רק אין בו מים" (בראשית לז 24), וללא שהיות: „וישבו לאכל לחם" (שם 25). תומאס מאן מתאר בהרחבה רבה את התלבטויותיהם של האחים לפני השלכתו של יוסף אל הבור. עם זאת הוא בחר לתאר את פעולת האכילה מיד לאחר השלכת יוסף אל הבור, כמו שעשה המספר המקראי, כדי להמחיש בדרך הטובה ביותר את שנאת האחים ליוסף. מספרי סיפורי המקרא בחרו בדרך כלל בדרך זו: כך למשל, בראשית חייו של משה (שמות ב 11–17) מתאר המספר שלוש פעולות של משה מצד אחד, אך מצד שני אין הוא מתאר את רגשותיו של משה בעת מעשיו.[10] לא תמיד תיאור פעולות הגיבור מלמד על הלך רוחה של הנפש הפועלת, אך בדרך כלל ניתן ללמוד ממעשי הגיבור על המתחולל בנפשו.[11]

בסיפור מותה של איזבל נוקט המספר לשון דומה לזו שראינו בסיפור משה, בשמות פרק ב. מצד אחד, המספר מתאר את פעולות איזבל ברגעים האחרונים לפני מותה, ומצד שני לא מתואר בפסוקים דרמתיים אלה כל רגש: בשל כך הקורא שואל עצמו מה משמעות הפעולות של איזבל: האם איזבל חוששת? האם היא בטוחה בעליונותה על יהוא? האם איזבל מעונינת להישאר בארמון המלך? האם היא מתכננת כיצד לפתות את יהוא כדי להורגו, בדיוק כפי שעשתה יעל לסיסרא? תשובות לשאלות אלה הן המפתח להבנת מעשיה ודבריה של איזבל טרם מותה. מאיר שטרנברג[12] הצביע על ההבדל בין האמת ובין כל האמת מבחינת אומנות המסירה של המספר המקראי. מצד אחד המספר הוא יודע כל ואוטוריטטיבי, החושף את האמת של גיבוריו, כפי שהיא מצטיירת בעיניו, ומצד שני, כמספר שתקן הוא נמנע מלפרש את כל האמת, ומשאיר לקורא להשלים את הפער. כך עשה המספר גם בסיפור איזבל.

לא קשה להבחין בדמותה השלילית של איזבל, כפי שהיא מוצגת בפנינו בסיפור מותה

8 תומאס מאן, יוסף ואחיו, תרגם מגרמנית: מרדכי אבי-שאול (תל-אביב: הוצאת הקיבוץ הארצי השומר הצעיר, 1988).

9 מאן, יוסף ואחיו, כרך א, עמ' 367.

10 שלוש הפעולות של משה מתוארות ברצף. בפעולה הראשונה (11–12) משה הורג איש מצרי כדי להציל איש עברי. בפעולה השנייה (13–14) הוא מנסה לתווך בין שני עברים מתקוטטים, ובפעולה השלישית (16–17) הוא מציל את בנות מדין מידי הרועים. פעולות אלה מצריכות מחשבה, התלבטות, רגשות וכו', אך המספר אינו מערב את הקורא בכך, אלא מתאר הוא רק את רצף הפעולות של משה, ומשאיר לכל קורא להשלים את הרגשות או את המחשבות של משה בפסוקים אלה. על הפעולה הראשונה של משה, ראה: מאיר שטרנברג, „בין האמת לכל האמת בסיפור המקראי," הספרות ט, מספר 2 (תשמ"ט) עמ' 117.

11 ראה פולק, הסיפור במקרא, עמ' 270–271.

12 שטרנברג, „בין האמת לכל האמת," עמ' 129–130.

יותר ממאה שנה בספרו מבוא לספר בראשית[2] קנתה לה אוהדים רבים מצד אחד, אך גם מתנגדים חריפים מצד שני. לדעת גונקל, חיי הנפש של הגיבורים במקרא הם פשוטים משום שהאדם בתקופה העתיקה היה פחות מורכב מן האדם המודרני, והם מבטאים דרגת התפתחות חברתית קמאית, אשר בה לא מובחן היחיד כראוי מן הכלל. הסיפור המקראי הוא פועל יוצא של קוצר ידם של המספרים הקדמונים בהבחנתם ובעיצובם של קווי ההיכר האישיים ובהעמדתן של סצינות רבות משתתפים.

חיזוק לגונקל ניתן על ידי סקולס וקלוג:[3] „הספרות הסיפורית הפרימיטיבית, בין אם עברית או הלנית, מניחה שהחיים הפנימיים קיימים אך אינה מציגה אותם. חוסר האפשרות לרדת לעומקן של הדמויות, האטימות שלהן, אינה מגרעת ואף אינה מגבלה. זהו פשוט מאפיין.״ מצד שני, אריך אאורבך[4] טוען שהמקרא נבדל מן האפוס ההומרי באינדיבידואליות ובמורכבות של הדמויות: „אפילו בני אדם בסיפורי המקרא בעלי ,רקע אחורי׳ הם יותר מאשר אנשי הומרוס, יש להם יותר עומק זמן, גורל ותודעה. מחשבותיהם והרגשותיהם הן רב שכבתיות ומורכבות יותר... הסיפור העברי מצליח להביא לידי ביטוי את רובדי ההכרה, המונחים כאחת זה על גבי זה, ואת הסכסוך ביניהם.״[5] לעומת זאת מסתמנת תמימות דעים כמעט לאורך כל הקו בדרך המקרא לתאר את המתחולל בנפש גיבוריו: במידה שחיי הנפש מופיעים במקרא, הם אינם נמסרים מבפנים, בדרך של תיאורים נפשיים מפורטים, היינו „תיאורים פסיכולוגיים,״ אלא מומחזים חיצונית, בעיקר בצורת פעולה. הרגשות והמחשבות אינם „מובעים״ אלא „נרמזים״ כמו שגונקל למשל אומר: „במקרים רבים מאוד, שהמספר בן ימינו היה נותן בהם ניתוח פסיכולוגי, נותן המספר העתיק עלילה.״[6] ובעקבותיו הולך גם שמריהו טלמון: „תהליכי הגייה ומצבי רוח משתקפים מבעד מעשיהם של הנפשות הפועלות ואינם מובאים בפנינו בהרצאת המחבר. אין המספר מרבה לומר לנו שפלוני עצב או שמח או שאלמוני חושב או מתחרט, אינו נוהג לפרט תהליכים נפשיים של שיקול ואיזון, של תכנון ובדיקה. במעשיו מגלה האדם את צפונות ליבו.״[7] אין ספק שמאז הופעתו של הרומן המודרני נוטה הסיפור להתעסק ישירות בהיבטים הפסיכולוגיים של הגיבורים.

הפעולה היא אחת מדרכי האפיון העיקריות של הגיבורים בסיפור המקראי, אך לא רק

„כאמצעים עקיפים לעיצוב הדמויות משמשים כל אותם גילויים חיצוניים, שניתן ללמוד מהם על פנימיותם, כמו דיבור או מעשים״; מאיר שטרנברג, „בין האמת לכל האמת בסיפור המקראי – נקודת התצפית ועיצוב חיי הנפש בחדירה הסיכומית ובמונולוג הפנימי,״ הספרות 29 (תשל״ט) עמ׳ 110–146; Mayer I. Gruber, *Aspects of Non-verbal Communication in the Ancient Near East*, Studia Pohl 12 (Rome: Biblical Institute Press, 1980); אוריאל סימון, קריאה ספרותית במקרא: סיפורי נביאים (ירושלים: מוסד ביאליק, תשנ״ז). לגבי הפער בין תיאור מעשי איזבל לבין שתיקתו של הסיפור הדרמתי באשר לתיאור רגשות או מחשבות, ראה: Samuel B. Parker, "Jezebel's Reception of Jehu," *Maarav* 1 (1978) 67–68.

2 Hermann Gunkel, *Genesis* (Göttingen: Vandenhöck & Ruprecht, 1902).

3 Robert Scholes and Robert Kellogg, *The Nature of Narrative* (New York: Oxford Univ. Press, 1966).

4 אריך אאורבך, מימזיס: התגלמות המציאות בספרות המערב, תרגם: ברוך קרוא (ירושלים: מוסד ביאליק, תשי״ח). כן מתנגד לדברי גונקל סימון, קריאה ספרותית במקרא, בעיקר עמ׳ 317.

5 אאורבך, מימזיס, עמ׳ 10.

6 Gunkel, *Genesis*, 91.

7 שמריהו טלמון, מלאכת הסיפור במקרא, ערך לפי הרצאות גיל גבריאל (ירושלים: האוניברסיטה העברית בירושלים, 1985) עמ׳ 32.

„ותשם בפוך עיניה ותיטב את ראשה"
מלכים ב ט 30

יוסי לשם

היברו יוניון קולג' – מכון למדעי היהדות

"She Painted Her Eyes with Kohl and Dressed Her Hair"

2 Kings 9:30

Yossi Leshem

Hebrew Union College-Jewish Institute of Religion

Dramatic narrative in the Bible offers few descriptions. The biblical narrator tends to characterize his heroes by means of their actions and words, rather than proffering any direct judgement of his own. There is no denying the negative portrayal of Jezebel and Jehu in 2 Kings 9. However, verse 30 can be interpreted in two ways: either Jezebel is interested in seducing Jehu, or perhaps she is at pains to appear presentable, as behooves a woman about to inherit the throne. The puzzle is solved by her words in the following verse: "Do you come in peace, Zimri, murderer of your master"?

The biblical narrator deals kindly with Jezebel in her last moments, portraying her as an honorable, brave woman fighting for her life. Jehu, on the other hand, is revealed at the height of his cruelty, as the narrator describes Jezebel's most brutal death: ". . . her blood spattered on the wall and on the horses, and they trampled her" (v. 33). Jehu, meanwhile, "went inside and ate and drank" (v. 34) – engaging in normal quotidian activities.

The character of Jezebel is portrayed like such other complex biblical characters as David, Saul, Moses, and Abraham – decidedly human characters who have both positive and negative aspects. Jezebel is a most human negative character, who does have her positive qualities. In this she is similar to Ahab.

הסיפור המקראי הדרמתי ממעט בפרטים תיאוריים של רגשות, מחשבות, תיאורי טבע וכדומה, אך מרבה לעומת זאת לתאר את פעולותיהם של גיבוריו.[1] נשאלת השאלה האם המקרא מתעניין בחיי הנפש של דמויותיו? הדעה המקובלת של הרמן גונקל כבר לפני

1 על תפקידה של הפעולה בעיצוב האופי של הגיבור בספרות ראה אצל: Uri Margolin, "The Doer and the Deed: Action as a Base for Characterization in Narrative," *Poetics Today* 7 (1986) 205–25. על הפער בין מיעוט תיאורים רגשיים לבין ריבוי תיאורי פעולות בסיפור המקראי וכן על תפקיד הפעולה במקרא, ראה: פרנק פולק, הסיפור במקרא (ירושלים: מוסד ביאליק, תשנ"ט) עמ' 263–269, ושם ביבליוגרפיה רחבה; אורי אלטר, אומנות הסיפור במקרא (תל אביב: אדם, תשמ"ח) עמ' 133–149; בספרו של שמעון בר אפרת, העיצוב האמנותי של הסיפור במקרא (תל אביב: ספריית הפועלים, תש"ם) עמ' 89, הוא כותב: